ECONOMICS
TODAY & TOMORROW

Roger LeRoy Miller
The University of Texas at Arlington

GLENCOE
McGraw-Hill

New York, New York   Columbus, Ohio   Mission Hills, California   Peoria, Illinois

ABOUT THE AUTHOR

Roger LeRoy Miller graduated Phi Beta Kappa from the University of California at Berkeley, where he also won the Department Prize in Economics. He was a Woodrow Wilson Honor Fellow, National Science Foundation Fellow, and Lilly Honor Fellow at the University of Chicago, where he received his Ph.D. in economics in 1968. Now at the University of Texas, Arlington, Dr. Miller has taught at the University of Washington, the University of Miami, and Clemson University. He has also taught methodology to teachers of high school economics for the National Council on Economic Education. Among the more than 100 books he has written or co-authored are works on economics, statistics, law, consumer finance, and government. Dr. Miller also has operated several businesses and served as a consultant to government agencies, private corporations, and law firms.

Send all inquiries to:
Glencoe/McGraw-Hill, 936 Eastwind Drive, Westerville, Ohio 43081

ISBN 0-02-823102-3 (Student Edition) ISBN 0-02-823104-X (Teacher's Wraparound Edition)
Printed in the United States of America

3 4 5 6 7 8 9 10 QPK/LP 00 99 98 97 96 95

iii

CONTENTS

UNIT

3 MICROECONOMICS: MARKETS, PRICES, AND BUSINESS COMPETITION

A Typical Product Life Cycle

Manual Typewriters

Introduction   Growth   Maturity   Declining
Time

Before Devaluation

Japanese VCR
costs 20,000 yen

Exchange Rate:
100 yen = $1 U.S.

$VCR = \dfrac{20,000\ yen}{100\ yen\ per\ \$} = \$200.00$

An American would have to pay
$200 for the Japanese VCR

After Devaluation

Japanese VCR
costs 20,000 yen

Exchange Rate:
200 yen = $1 U.S.

$VCR = \dfrac{20,000\ yen}{200\ yen\ per\ \$} = \$100.00$

An American would have to pay
$100 for the Japanese VCR

UNIT

5 THE INTERNATIONAL SCENE

SKILLS

Personal Perspective

News Clip

Point ◄► Counterpoint

CASE STUDY Focus on Free Enterprise

ECONOMICS LAB

Home Equity Loan
40% Interest

CHECKLISTS

TABLES AND CHARTS

Beef Price (per pound)	Quantity Supplied (thousands of pounds)
$1.89	1,000
$1.99	2,500
$2.09	3,500
$2.39	4,000
$2.69	6,000

GRAPHS

MAPS

Basic Economic Concepts

Economics: Today and Tomorrow incorporates the 22 Basic Concepts established in "A Framework for Teaching the Basic Concepts," published by the National Council on Economic Education.

1 Scarcity

Scarcity is the condition that results from the imbalance between relatively unlimited wants and the relatively limited resources available for satisfying those wants.

2 Opportunity Costs and Trade-Offs

Opportunity cost is the foregone benefit of the next best alternative when scarce resources are used for one purpose rather than another. **Trade-offs** involve accepting or choosing less of one thing to get more of something else.

3 Productivity

Productivity is the amount of output (goods and services) produced per unit of input (productive resources) used.

4 Economic Systems

Economic Systems are the ways in which people organize economic life to deal with the basic economics problems of scarcity and opportunity cost.

5 Economic Institutions and Incentives

Economic institutions include households and families and formal organizations such as corporations, government agencies, banks, labor unions, and cooperatives. **Incentives** are factors that motivate and influence human behavior.

6 Exchange, Money, and Interdependence

Exchange indicates the transactions in which producers trade their surpluses. **Money** serves as a medium of exchange. **Interdependence** means that decisions or events in one part of the world or in one sector of the economy affect decisions and events in other parts of the world or sector of the economy.

7 Markets and Prices

Markets are institutional arrangements that enable buyers and sellers to exchange goods and services. **Prices** are the amounts of money that people pay in exchange for a unit of a particular good or service.

8 Supply and Demand

Supply is defined as the different quantities of a resource, good, or service that will be offered for sale at various possible prices during a specific time period. **Demand** is defined as the different quantities of a resource, good, or service that will be purchased at various possible prices during a specific time period.

9 Competition and Market Structure

Competition is determined by the number of buyers and sellers in particular markets. **Market structures** refer to the extent to which competition prevails in particular markets.

10 Income Distribution

Income distribution may be classified into functional distribution— the division of an economy's total income into wages and salaries, rent, interest, and profit; or income distribution may be classified into personal distribution of income, classifying the different population groups by the number of them receiving different amounts of income.

11 Market Failures

Market failures occur when there is inadequate competition, lack of access to reliable information, resource immobility, externalities, and the need for public goods.

12 The Role of Government

The **role of government** includes establishing a framework of law and order in which a market economy functions.

MACROECONOMIC CONCEPTS

13 Gross Domestic Product*

Gross Domestic Product (GDP) is defined as the market value of the total output of all final goods and services produced within a country's boundaries during one year.

14 Aggregate Supply

Aggregate supply is the total amount of goods and services produced by the economy in a period of time.

15 Aggregate Demand

Aggregate demand is the total amount of spending on goods and services in the economy during a period of time.

16 Unemployment

Unemployment is defined in United States statistics as the number of people without jobs who are actively seeking work.

17 Inflation and Deflation

Inflation is a sustained increase in the average price level of the entire economy. **Deflation** is a sustained decrease in the average price level of an entire economy.

18 Monetary Policy

Monetary policy seeks to affect the amount of money available in the economy and its costs.

19 Fiscal Policy

Fiscal policy consists of changes in taxes, in government expenditures on goods and services, and in transfer payments that are designed to affect the level of aggregate demand in the economy.

INTERNATIONAL ECONOMIC CONCEPTS

20 Absolute and Comparative Advantage and Barriers to Trade

Absolute advantage and **comparative advantage** are concepts that are used to explain why trade takes place. **Barriers to trade** include tariffs, quotas, import licenses, and cartels.

21 Exchange Rate and Balance of Payments

An **exchange rate** is the price of one nation's currency in terms of another nation's currency. The **balance of payments** of a country is a statistical accounting that records, for a given period, all payments one country makes to the rest of the world and all the receipts that they receive from the rest of the world.

22 International Aspects of Growth and Stability

Growth and **stability** are more important today than in the past because all nations are much more interdependent.

*In the fall of 1991, the United States Department of Commerce replaced GNP with GDP as the nation's most inclusive measure of output.

U N I T

AN INTRODUCTION TO ECONOMICS

Did You Know

- Your choice of jeans as a consumer determines how many will be produced.
- Most new jobs in the 1990s are in the services and professional specialties.
- Taxes account for about 60 percent of the price of fuel in the United States.
- Experts predict that the amount of travel will double in the next 25 years.
- Russia plans to turn over most state factories to private individuals.

In this unit you will learn what economics is, and how different societies have chosen what goods and services should be produced and how they should be distributed.

WHAT IS ECONOMICS?

What benefit are these students receiving from this activity?

What would be the benefit of studying instead of watching television?

What are these students doing?

Your Economics Journal

During a one-week period, keep track of how you spend your time. At the end of the week, list the most frequent activities in which you engage and how many hours you spent on each.

SECTION 1 FOCUS

Terms to Know economics, resource, scarcity, wants, land, labor, capital, productivity, entrepreneurship, factors of production, goods and services, technology

Objectives *After reading this section, you should be able to:*
① Explain why scarcity faces all people at all times.
② Distinguish between wants and needs.
③ List and summarize the four types of resources.

Economics—The Study of Choices

Economics is the study of how individuals and nations make choices about how to use scarce resources to fulfill their wants. A **resource** is anything that people can use to make or obtain what they want.

As a student, you probably have a small amount of money—from an allowance or a part-time job—to spend. As a result, you have to make choices about its use. Whenever you make such a spending decision, each available choice competes with every other available choice. Suppose you have $20 to spend. You could use it to buy lunch for four days or two budget compact discs or a sweatshirt and so on as shown in **Figure 1.1**.

The Problem of Scarcity

The need to make choices arises because everything that exists is limited, even though some items may appear to be in overabundant supply. At any one moment in the United States, or anywhere, a fixed, or set, amount of resources is available. At the same time, people may have competing uses

◄ **Figure 1.1 Economic Choices**
When you decide whether to spend your money on clothes or a new CD, you are making an economic choice. The basic economic problem of scarcity makes the choice necessary.

for these resources. This situation results in the problem of scarcity—the basic problem of economics.

Scarcity means that people do not and cannot have enough income, time, or other resources to satisfy their every desire. What you can buy with your income as a student is limited by the amount of income you have. In this case, your income is the scarce resource. Scarcity is not the same as *shortage*, as **Figure 1.2** shows.

Choices The problem of scarcity faces businesses as well as individuals. Businesspeople make decisions daily about what to produce now, what to produce later, and what to stop producing. These decisions in turn affect people's income and their ability to buy. Nations, too, face the problem of choosing how to spend their scarce resources. The United States, for example, must decide how much to spend on Social Security benefits and aid to higher education. How people make these choices is the subject of economics.

Wants versus Needs

How many times have you said that you "need" something? How often do you think about what you "want"? When you say, "I need some new clothes," are you stating a want, or a real need? Typically the term *need* is used very casually. When most people use the word *need*, they really mean that they want something they do not have.

The difference between wants and needs is not a clear one. Everyone needs certain basic things—enough food, clothing, and shelter to survive. Americans also consider a good education and adequate health care as needs.

Economists call everything other than these basic needs **wants.** People want such items as new cars and personal computers. Although more and more people have these items, this does not mean that anyone actually needs them.

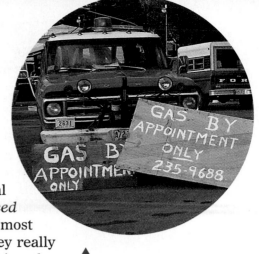

▲

B Temporary shortages of products such as gasoline may be caused when imports are dramatically decreased for any reason.

Figure 1.2
Shortage vs Scarcity

It is important not to confuse shortage and scarcity. Scarcity always exists, whereas shortages are always temporary.

A Shortages often exist after major hurricanes or floods that destroy goods ▼ and property.

For example, people entertained themselves and informed themselves of news long before the invention of the radio. As the wonders of radio were advertised, more people began to believe they needed one. What began as a luxury, or want, became to many people a necessity. This cycle of wants and perceived needs is repeated over and over. In economics, however, only a few true needs, such as minimal food and shelter, exist.

Types of Resources

Besides the question of whether you need or want a VCR, there is the issue of whether there will be enough VCRs to allow every person to own one. Also, not everyone would have enough money to buy one. Only a certain amount of resources exist, regardless of wants and needs. Traditionally, economists have classified resources as land, labor, capital, or entrepreneurship.

Land As an economic term, **land** refers to natural resources, as shown in Figure 1.3, not just to surface land. Among the most important natural resources in economic terms are land and mineral deposits such as iron ore. In economics, the location of land is also important in establishing its value as a resource.

Labor The work people do is **labor**—often called a human resource. The labor resource includes anyone who works.

Capital All the property people use to make other goods and services is **capital**. For example, the machines used to make automobiles are capital. The cars are not considered capital unless they are used, for example, as taxicabs, to produce services. Combining capital with land and labor increases the value of all resources by increasing their productivity. **Productivity** is the ability to produce greater quantities of goods and services in better and faster ways.

When you read references to "capital" in newspapers, they generally mean *financial capital*, such as the funds made available in the stock market for starting a new business. In this book, if we mean such funds, we will always say *financial* or *money* capital.

**Figure 1.3
Natural Resources**
Natural resources are all the things found in nature—on or in water and the earth—such as fish, animals, forests, and minerals as well as land and water.

Entrepreneurship The fourth type of resource is **entrepreneurship** (AHN-truh-pruh-NUHR-ship), which refers to the ability of individuals to start new businesses, to introduce new products and techniques, and to improve management techniques.

All changes in business organization are part of entrepreneurship. It involves initiative and individual willingness to take risks to make profit. Entrepreneurs succeed when they produce new products, improve an existing product or produce it more efficiently, or reorganize a business to run more smoothly.

Together, the resources of land, labor, capital, and entrepreneurship are called the **factors of production.** They are used to produce **goods and services.** Goods are the items that people buy. Services are the activities done for others for a fee.

Technology Some economists add technology to the list of resources. Any use of land, labor, and capital that produces goods and services more efficiently is technology. For example, a computer keyboard is a technological advance over the typewriter.

Today, however, **technology** usually describes the use of science to develop new products and new methods for producing and distributing goods and services. **Figure 1.4** illustrates a modern application of technology.

Figure 1.4 ▲
Technology in Action
Advanced machinery and new production and distribution methods increase the productivity of the other resources. For example, without modern drilling machinery, it would be impossible to tap the oil resources of the ocean.

Look

SECTION 1 REVIEW

Understanding Vocabulary
Define economics, resource, scarcity, wants, land, labor, capital, productivity, entrepreneurship, factors of production, goods and services, technology.

Reviewing Objectives
1. Why does scarcity always exist?
2. What is the difference between wants and needs?
3. What are the four types of resources? Give an example of each.

Reading Tables and Graphs

Tables and graphs are easy to read and show much information in a small space. Do you know how to interpret them?

Tables

Tables, such as **Figure A** below, represent data in rows and columns according to topics.

Figure A. Understanding How Americans Traveled in a Recent Year

Forms of Transportation	Miles in Billions	Percent Distribution
Automobiles	1,287	83.4
Airlines	213	13.8
Other	43	2.8

Graphs

Graphs are a visual representation of statistical data and are often easier to read than tables. The three types of graphs include circle ("pie") graphs, bar graphs, and line graphs.

Circle Graph Circle graphs show the proportions of the elements of a whole. **Figure B** shows the percentage distribution of forms of transportation from **Figure A** in a circle graph.

Bar Graph The bar graph in **Figure C** shows teenage unemployment over four years.

Line Graph Line graphs are often used to show the same information as a bar graph. **Figure D**, for example, is a line graph representation of the information in **Figure C**.

Figure B. Understanding How Americans Traveled in a Recent Year

- 83.4% Automobiles
- 13.8% Airlines
- 2.8% Other

Figure C. Teenage Unemployment Rates (1990-1993)

Percentage of teen unemployment: 20%, 15%, 10%, 5%, 0 — 1990 '91 '92 '93

Figure D. Teenage Unemployment Rates (1990-1993)

Percentage of teen unemployment: 20%, 15%, 10%, 5%, 0 — 1990 '91 '92 '93

Practicing the Skill

❶ What information does **Figure A** provide that **Figure B** does not?

❷ According to **Figure C**, when was teenage unemployment highest?

Choices Involve Opportunity Costs

Scarcity forces people to make choices about how they will use their resources. Those choices affect not only how people live today, but how people will live in the future. It is important to realize that the economic choices people make involve exchanging one good or service for another. If you choose to buy a video for your VCR, you are exchanging your money for the right to own the video. Exchanging one thing for the use of another is called a **trade-off.**

Figure 1.5
Trade-Offs
Trade-offs involve making choices that are unavoidable because of the problem of scarcity. Having high levels of automobile pollution or higher car manufacturing costs (to reduce pollution) is an example.

▼

Opportunity Costs

As **Figure 1.5** shows, individuals, businesses, and nations are forced to make trade-offs every time they use their resources in one way and not another. For example, as a student you may be faced with a decision about going to college or vocational school to increase future earnings, or going to work right after high school.

The Cost of Choices Another way to describe a trade-off is in terms of the cost of something a person gives up in order to get something else. When you decide to study economics for one hour, you are making a choice. You are giving up any other activities you could choose to do. Because time is a scarce resource—there are only so many hours in a day—you must decide how to use it.

In other words, there is a cost involved in time spent studying this book. Economists call it an **opportunity cost**—the value of the next best alternative that had to be given up for the alternative that was chosen. Whatever you consider as the value of the next best alternative to studying—watch

ing television, for example—is the opportunity cost of your studying for one hour.

The opportunity cost of any action is the value of what is given up because the choice was made. What is important is the choice that you would have made if you had not studied one hour. Your opportunity cost is generated from the next-highest-ranked alternative, not all alternatives. Therefore, in economics, cost is always a foregone opportunity.

A good way to think about opportunity cost is to realize that when you choose to do something, you lose. What do you lose? You lose the ability to engage in your next-highest-valued alternative.

A Practical Example Consider an example at the national level. Suppose Congress votes $2 billion for projects to clean up polluted rivers. The opportunity cost of its vote is the next best alternative use of those same tax dollars. For example, Congress could have voted for increased spending on space research. Then the opportunity cost of clean rivers would be fewer space flights.

Considering Opportunity Costs

Being aware of opportunity costs and trade-offs is important in making economic decisions of all kinds. For example, you will be able to make wiser use of your own resources if you know the opportunity costs and trade-offs involved. You will be able to vote more intelligently if you are aware of the choices your elected officials face. Businesspeople, too, must consider opportunity costs and trade-offs.

Production Possibilities

The term *mix* brings up another fact about resources. How do people determine how much of each item to produce? What are the trade-offs and opportunity costs involved in each decision? The concept of production possibilities is useful in examining this problem.

Production possibilities are all the combinations of goods and services that can be produced from a fixed amount of resources in a given period of time. For each situation, only a limited number of factors are considered. A fixed amount of resources and a given period of time exist.

The Classic Example The classic example for explaining production possibilities in economics is the trade-off between military defense and civilian goods, sometimes referred to as *guns* versus *butter*. The extremes for a nation would be using all its resources to produce only one or the other. **Figure 1.6** shows the two extremes.

The federal government determines where on the production-possibilities curve the nation will be. The government takes income from citizens through taxes. It uses this revenue, which could have been used for butter, to produce guns. "The nation" on the curve is Congress and the

▼ **Figure 1.6**
Guns or Butter?

Point A on the graph represents all resources being used to produce only guns (military defense). Point E represents the other extreme—all resources being used to produce only butter (civilian goods).

Countries produce combinations, or mixes, of goods. That is shown by the curve between points A and E. The curve represents the production possibilities between guns and butter in a nation during one year.

The maximum quantity of guns made per year is shown by the vertical distance from point 0 to point A. What is shown by the horizontal distance from point 0 to point E?

Production Possibilities Curve

Figure 1.7 ▲
From Military to Civilian Goods
A small defense contractor, Harris, was able to outbid AT&T to obtain a $1.66 billion contract to manufacture a new civilian air-traffic control system such as the one shown.

President, who make decisions for the American public.

Production-possibilities curves are a good way to show trade-offs and opportunity costs visually. As you can see from **Figure 1.6** (page 15), a nation or a business cannot produce more of one thing without giving up something. For example, if a nation starts with all civilian goods production and no military production—point E—it can only get to point D—some weapons production—by giving up some butter production. In other words, the price of having some weapons production (represented by the vertical distance from 0 to point X) is giving up some butter

production (represented by the horizontal distance from point E to point Y). The amount of civilian goods production given up in the year is the opportunity cost for increasing military production.

By using a production-possibilities curve, a nation or a business can decide how best to use its resources. By "best" is meant using resources most efficiently for economic growth. Such a curve is useful in locating the opportunity costs if a particular course of action is followed.

A Real-World Example: Military Downsizing in the 1990s From the 1950s until the early 1990s, the United States was engaged in a so-called cold war with the Soviet Union, and we produced more and more military goods. When that country split up into 15 separate republics, our major military adversary seemingly disappeared. Consequently, we needed to move from, say, point C to point D in **Figure 1.6**.

The real world and our graphs are not always quite the same, however. In the real world, it takes time to move from point C to point D. For example, our military had been purchasing guns, bombs, and planes from such major contractors as McDonnell-Douglas and Rockwell. In the 1990s, much of their military business evaporated. Some former military-hardware companies started making civilian goods as **Figure 1.7** shows.

SECTION 2 REVIEW

Understanding Vocabulary
Define trade-off, opportunity cost, production possibilities.

Reviewing Objectives
1. How are trade-offs and opportunity cost related?
2. Explain how a production possibilities curve can show society's trade-offs.

Personal Perspective

Robert L. Heilbroner on the Great Economists

Profile

- 1919–
- attended Harvard University and the New School for Social Research in New York City
- has taught at the New School for Social Research since 1972
- published works include *The Worldly Philosophers* (1953), *The Future as History* (1960), *The Great Ascent* (1963), *Between Capitalism and Socialism* (1970), and *The Nature and Logic of Capitalism* (1985)

Robert L. Heilbroner's book *The Worldly Philosophers* gives a unique and insightful look into the lives and works of the great economists of the past. In his introduction, Heilbroner explains the importance of these great economists to history.

By all the rules of schoolboy history books, they were nonentities: they commanded no armies, sent no men to their deaths, ruled no empires, took little part in history-making decisions. . . . Yet what they did was more decisive for history than many acts of statesmen who basked in brighter glory, often more profoundly disturbing than the shuttling of armies back and forth across frontiers, more powerful for good and bad than the edicts of kings and legislatures. It was this: they shaped and swayed men's minds.

Heilbroner expresses his belief that economists have a major impact on the world:

And because he who enlists a man's mind wields a power even greater than the sword or the scepter, these men shaped and swayed the world. Few of them ever lifted a finger in action; . . . But they left in their train shattered empires and exploded continents, they buttressed and undermined regimes, they set class against class and even nation against nation— not because they plotted mischief, but because of the extraordinary power of their ideas.

He disagrees with the perception that the work of economists is dull and boring:

. . . A man who thinks that economics is only a matter for professors forgets that this is the science that has sent men to the barricades. . . . No, the great economists pursued an inquiry as exciting—and as dangerous—as any the world has ever known. . . . The notions of the great economists were world-shaking, and their mistakes nothing short of calamitous.

Checking for Understanding

1. Why is it important to study the great economists of the past?
2. Have economists made a real difference in the world?
3. What does Heilbroner believe about the power of economists' ideas?

SECTION **3** *What Do Economists Do?*

S E C T I O N 3 F O C U S

Terms to Know economy, economic model, hypotheses, values, generalization

Objectives *After reading this section, you should be able to:*

❶ Describe and give examples of economic models.

❷ Explain the purpose of economic models.

❸ Explain why there are different schools of economic thought.

❹ Tell why economists do not normally work with values.

Economists Use Models to Study the Real World

Economics is concerned with the ways individuals and nations choose to use their scarce resources. For example, economists might analyze teenagers' spending and its effect on the economy. See **Figure 1.8.** To economists, **economy** means all the activity in a nation that together affects the production, distribution, and use of goods and services.

To carry out their investigations, economists often gather information from the real world. These data then become the basis for testing theories that explain an event, such as rising unemployment. The theories or solutions then become the basis for actual decisions by private business or government agencies.

Figure 1.8
Teen Buying Power
United States teenagers spend billions of dollars each year on clothing and other items. Their buying patterns definitely affect the types of goods that are produced.

Economic Models

In their work, economists use economic models, or theories. An **economic model** is a simplified representation of the real world. Physicists, chemists, biologists, and other scientists also use models to explain in simple terms the complex workings of the world.

What Models Show Economic models show the way people react to changes in the economy. The most frequently used model explains how people react to changes in the prices of goods and services they want to purchase. An economist has three ways of presenting such a model: through an explanation in words, in a graph, or with a mathematical equation. Whichever method is chosen, the information in the model is the same, as shown in **Figure 1.9**.

Limits of Models No economic model records every detail and relationship that exists about a problem to be studied. A model will show only the basic factors needed to analyze the problem. For example, economists have found that they need to analyze only three basic factors to determine buyer reaction to price changes. These factors are the price of the item, the income of the average buyer, and the price of alternative items.

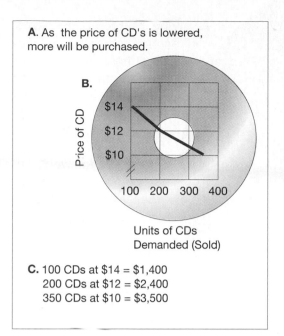

A. As the price of CD's is lowered, more will be purchased.

B.

Price of CD

$14
$12
$10

100 200 300 400

Units of CDs
Demanded (Sold)

C. 100 CDs at $14 = $1,400
200 CDs at $12 = $2,400
350 CDs at $10 = $3,500

◀

Figure 1.9
Economic Models of CD Prices
In the case of prices, these three ways of presenting the model all show that consumers respond to lower prices by purchasing more of less expensive items.

The Purpose of Models

As you study economics, it is important to keep in mind the purpose of economic models. They are not supposed to account for all the possible factors that might influence a problem. They take into account only the most important ones.

Creating An economist considers a model *good* if it provides useful material for analyzing the way the real world works. As in forming a hypothesis, an economist begins with some idea about the way things work, then collects facts and discards those that are not relevant. Once a conclusion is reached, the only way an economist can find out whether a model works is to test it.

Testing Suppose an economist has developed the model shown in **Figure 1.10** (page 20). The economist tests the model in the same way that other scientists test **hypotheses,** educated guesses, or predictions, used as the starting points for investigations, as shown in **Figure 1.11** (page 21).

For the model in **Figure 1.10** (page 20), an economist would collect data on the amount of teenage unemployment every year for the last 30 years.

He or she also would gather information on the frequency of federal legislation increasing the legal minimum wage paid to teenagers.

Suppose the economist finds that every time the minimum wage rate increased, teenage unemployment increased. The economist can be fairly satisfied with the model. See **Figure 1.10**, graph A.

Suppose that the data does not seem to show a relationship between teenage unemployment and increases in the legal minimum wage. See **Figure 1.10**, graph B. The economist then will have to develop another model to explain changes in teenage unemployment.

Applying Much of the work of economists involves predicting how people will react in a particular situation. Individual human behavior is not always predictable, however. As a result, an economist's answer to a specific problem may turn out not to work for everyone.

For example, to stimulate the economy, some economists believe that taxes should be cut and government spending increased. These economists believe that cutting taxes will raise personal spending, which, in turn, will increase total production.

However, some people's fears concerning possible higher taxes in the future might cause them to save the extra money rather than spend it. As this illustrates, economists cannot predict all the factors that may influence people's behavior.

Schools of Economic Thought

Economists deal with facts. Their personal opinions and beliefs may nonetheless influence how they view those facts and fit them to theories. The government under which an economist lives also shapes how he or she views the world. As a result, all economists will not agree that a partic-

ular theory offers the best solution to a problem. Often, economists from competing schools of thought claim that their theories alone will predict a certain result.

At a particular time, a nation's political leaders may agree with one school of economic thought and develop policies based on it. Later, leaders may agree with another group of economists. For example, during the 1980s, many economists stressed the role of businesses and consumers rather than of the government in preventing increased unemployment and inflation. In the 1990s, however, many influential national leaders proposed that the federal government should intervene in the economy to reduce unemployment.

Values and Economics

Economics will help you to predict what may happen if certain events occur or certain policies are followed. Economics will not, however, tell you whether the result will be good or bad. That judgment will depend on your values.

Values are the beliefs or characteristics that a person or group considers important, such as religious freedom,

**Figure 1.10 ▲
Testing an Economic Model**
Economists, like scientists, must collect data to prove or disprove their theories. Graph A supports the direct relationship between increases in the legal minimum wage rate and increases in teenage unemployment. Graph B does not support that relationship.

Figure 1.11 Using a Hypothesis

The list below reviews the steps involved in making and testing hypotheses. In working with models, economists use these same steps.

1. Define the problem.
2. From the possible alternatives, state a hypothesis that appears to offer the best solution to a problem or explanation of an event.
3. Gather data to test the hypothesis. Besides using facts from the real world, an economist must identify economic principles involved.
4. Evaluate the data and discard any that are not relevant, or related to the immediate situation, or that are not objective (those that are based on fact).
5. Make sure there are enough data to test the hypothesis thoroughly.
6. Develop a conclusion based on the data. To do this, an economist evaluates whether the alternative is the best, in view of its consequences and trade-offs.
7. If the hypothesis appears to be proved, retest it with new data to see if the same results can be obtained again.
8. If the hypothesis appears to be proved, form a generalization that can be applied to other cases. A **generalization** pulls together common ideas among facts and is true in most cases. For an economist, this step involves developing an economic policy based on the best alternative.

equal opportunity, individual initiative, freedom from want, and so on. Suppose, for example, that you believe the nation should do something to lower unemployment among teenagers. This belief is a value judgment on your part.

If you were a legislator, you might show your commitment to this value by introducing a bill to decrease teenage unemployment. The

economists who help you research the causes of teenage unemployment may not tell you whether your bill is good or bad. They will tell you whether the proposed solution may be workable or not.

Having the same values does not mean that people will agree about solutions, strategies, or interpretation of data. For example, those in favor of decreasing teenage unemployment may disagree about the best way to solve this problem.

Look ↓

S E C T I O N 3 R E V I E W

Understanding Vocabulary
Define economy, economic model, hypotheses, values, generalization.

Reviewing Objectives
1. What are three ways of presenting an economic model?

2. What is the purpose of economic models?
3. Why do not all economists agree on the same solutions to problems?
4. Briefly explain why economists do not deal with values.

Readings in Economics

THE BOSTON GLOBE   **JUNE 8, 1993**

RUNNER'S HIGH
by Aaron Zitner

A few well chosen complimentary words in a consumer magazine have meant more than a few dollars to Hyde Athletic Industries Inc. Sales of Hyde's Saucony running shoes soared after both men's and women's models received "No. 1" performance ratings from *Consumer Reports* in May 1992. Shares in the Peabody footwear company raced ahead 275 percent for the 12 months ended on May 14, the biggest gain by a Massachusetts stock.

Saucony shoes were selling well before the rating appeared, said Lisa Costa, a company spokeswoman. But they were little known outside the small world of high-performance athletes.

"The article got our name out there to the masses," Costa said. "We had some momentum going, and when the article hit, it took the momentum and really carried it."

Hyde also makes roller skates, ice skates and skateboards under the Brookfield name and shoes for coaches and officials under the Spotbilt name.

Saucony produces walking, tennis, and hiking shoes.

But the Saucony running shoes are Hyde's chief product. The company employs about 120 people at its corporate office in Peabody and about 300 at its running shoe factory in Bangor, Maine.

In 1992, Hyde's earnings rose 230 percent to $3.4 million. Revenue rose 40 percent to $81.3 million. Hyde shares went for 22½ in mid-May, up from 6 a year earlier.

The company is redoubling its efforts to make its name known overseas. It recently opened an office in Britain and enhanced its relationships with distributors in the Netherlands and Canada.

• THINK ABOUT IT •

1. *How did* Consumer Reports' *rating of Saucony shoes affect sales?*

2. *How is Hyde Athletic Industries trying to broaden its markets?*

Highlights

The Basic Problem in Economics

Key Terms

economics (p. 8)
resource (p. 8)
scarcity (p. 9)
wants (p. 9)
land (p. 10)
labor (p. 10)

capital (p. 10)
productivity (p. 10)
entrepreneurship (p. 11)
factors of production (p. 11)
goods and services (p. 11)
technology (p. 11)

Summary

Scarcity is the basic problem in economics. Economics is the study of how individuals and nations make choices about how to use scarce resources to fulfill their wants. Production involves the factors of land, labor, capital, and entrepreneurship. Some economists also include technology.

Trade-Offs

Key Terms

trade-off (p. 13)
opportunity cost (p. 14)
production
   possibilities (p. 15)

Summary

Whenever one thing or activity must be given up in order to have another thing or activity, a trade-off has occurred. Whatever has to be given up is called the opportunity cost of an action. A production-possibilities curve shows the maximum amount of goods that can be produced with the nation's resources during any given time period. When a nation operates on the production-possibilities curve, it is producing in an efficient manner.

What Do Economists Do?

Key Terms

economy (p. 18)
economic model (p. 18)
hypotheses (p. 19)
values (p. 20)
generalization (p. 21)

Summary

Economists look at economic data from the real world to test economic models that they formulate about the behavior of people and businesses. Economic models are representative of reality that take into account only the most important factors that might influence a problem. Economic models and economists do not tell whether certain policies are good or bad, because such judgments depend on a person's values.

Review

Identifying Key Terms

Use the correct terms to fill in the blanks in the paragraph below:

scarcity (p. 9)
wants (p. 9)
factors of production (p. 11)
goods and services (p. 11)
technology (p. 11)
trade-off (p. 13)

opportunity cost (p. 14)
production possibilities (p. 15)
economic models (p. 18)
hypotheses (p. 19)
values (p. 20)
generalization (p. 21)

Human __(1)__ are unlimited. Consequently, the problem of __(2)__ faces even the richest person on earth, particularly because that person has a limited amount of time on earth. When __(3)__ are used together to produce __(4)__, human wants can be satisfied. The use of __(5)__ can help us increase the amount of production we get from the resources in our economy. No matter how many resources we have, though, we always face a __(6)__. The production of one good always involves giving up the production of some other good or goods. This is called a(n) __(7)__. The graphic representation of this trade-off is called a __(8)__ curve. Economists use __(9)__ to represent how the economy works. They set up a __(10)__ that they test with real-world information. If their tests work well, they come up with a __(11)__, but economists never can tell us about __(12)__.

Write a short paragraph about the factors of production in the United States using the following terms:

land (p. 10)
labor (p. 10)
capital (p. 10)
entrepreneurship (p. 11)

Recalling Facts and Ideas

Section 1

1. What is the condition that results because wants are unlimited, yet people cannot satisfy every desire?
2. What is the difference between scarcity and shortages?
3. Your friend says, "I need some new clothes." Under what conditions would this be expressing a need? A want?
4. List the four factors of production.

Section 2

5. What does making a trade-off require you to do?
6. What do economists call the next best alternative that had to be given up for the one chosen?
7. In economics, what is cost?
8. What do economists call a graph showing the combination of goods and services that can be produced from a fixed amount of resources in a given time period?

Section 3

9. For what purposes do economists use real-world data in building models?
10. An economic theory is another name for what?
11. When will an economist consider an economic model useful?

Critical Thinking

Section 1

Identifying Central Issues Tell why entrepreneurship is considered a factor of production.

Section 2

Synthesizing Information Look again at the Production Possibilities Curve in **Figure 1.6** (page 15). What is the balance between military and civilian production that is represented by point C on the graph?

Section 3

Analyzing Information What is the reason that economists will not tell you whether a possible solution to a problem will be good or bad?

Applying Economic Concepts

Trade-Offs and Opportunity Costs Because your time is scarce, you are constantly facing trade-offs. Make a list of the trade-offs you have made in choosing how you used your time during a one-week period. What activities did you choose to do? What were the opportunity costs involved in your choices?

Chapter Projects

1. **Individual Project** Watch the TV news and read newspapers for one week. Make a list of proposed actions on the part of federal, state, or local governments that may involve opportunity costs.
2. **Cooperative Learning Project** Working in groups of four, choose a consumer product such as a VCR, pencil, or automobile. Try to determine the elements of each of the four factors of production that went into making that consumer product. Consider, for example, that in making a VCR, there has to be land on which to put a factory. Consider also that in making a VCR, somebody has to take the risk of putting together the other three factors of production to form a company that will produce the VCR, and so on.

Reviewing Skills

Reading Tables and Graphs

1. The following graph shows the number of men and women in the U.S. labor force from 1980 to 2005. Approximately how many men were in the labor force in 1990? How many women? What is the estimated total number of people in the labor force in 2000?

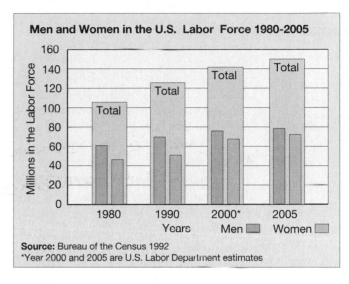

Men and Women in the U.S. Labor Force 1980-2005

Millions in the Labor Force

Years — Men ▮ Women ▯

Source: Bureau of the Census 1992
*Year 2000 and 2005 are U.S. Labor Department estimates

2. Make a bar graph of the following information.

Age of School Teachers in a Recent Year

Under 30 years old	66,000
30 to 39 years old	104,000
40 to 49 years old	83,000
over 50 years old	49,000

Writing About Economics

Descriptive Writing Refer to the activities you listed in Your Economics Journal. Write one or more paragraphs describing how you spent your time during that week. Be sure to consider the following question when you write: Why did you choose to spend more time on certain activities than on others?

Point

ISSUE: Should the Government Require Domestic National Service?

During times of war, many Americans have been required to join the military. Until 1973, males over the age of 18 could be drafted into the military for a two-year period, even in peacetime. Never, however, has this nation required its young people to perform any other type of public service. Nonetheless, the idea of national service has been around for at least 100 years.

PRO One proposal by the Democratic Leadership Council in the late 1980s suggested that the government should form a "citizens' corps" of up to a million "volunteers" who would be paid $100 per week plus room and board. They would then be rewarded with government vouchers worth about $10,000 for each year of service. These vouchers could be used only for education or for buying a home.

Sociologist Charles C. Moskos claims that we need more national service programs because of the nation's unmet needs. Moskos contends that 3.5 million tasks that should be done are presently left undone in our society. These include many environmental and health-related tasks.

Nicola Clark, an editorial writer for the *Wall Street Journal*, believes strongly in the use of a national service corps. She argues that many countries use such a method:

The Danes, for example, dispatch their national servants as civilian public works laborers and foresters. French and Portuguese [national servants] are funneled to various humanitarian organizations or are sent to do development work in their former colonies. And in 1992 . . . doctors in Switzerland actually proposed supplementing the newly introduced Swiss national service with a corps devoted to providing low-cost ambulatory care for the elderly.

[President] Clinton has inundated Americans with proposals for expanded government programs in public works, environmental conservation, child care, health care, community policing—many of which are the kinds of things that are done by extremely low-paid conscripted national servants in other advanced industrialized countries. Why? Because it's the only way these governments can afford to make good on the generous welfare promises they have made to voters without burying their nations in debt. . . .

CON Opponents of domestic national service stress that except in times of war, no one should be required to participate in any work that that person does not wish to do. They also contend that there is no way to define or quantify a nation's "unmet" needs because they are in fact infinite—there is no limit.

Opponents of domestic national service also use the opportunity cost concept. If a skilled individual holds a job for which he or she has no particular expertise, the opportunity cost is the lost production for the nation. We would be operating inside the production possibilities curve in **Figure 1.6** (page 15) and would, therefore, be using resources inefficiently. Critics contend that requiring people to work in jobs that pay less than the market wage rate they could obtain elsewhere involves tremendous opportunity costs.

Another issue is the impact on private charities that would not receive funds. Bruce Chapman, president of Discovery Institution (a public policy center in Seattle, Washington), says:

Congressional hearings on President Clinton's national service plan and the public relations campaign advancing it almost always bring forward as spokesmen young, ingenuous participants in private charities. . . . But these admirable youngsters are not the organizers of the scheme, and they are not likely to understand its long-term implications for the voluntary sector as a whole. Nei-

ther, apparently, does much of the disorganized opposition.

One sees this especially in respect to religious organizations, now the source of roughly half of all charitable activities. Because of understandable concerns over separation of church and state, national service will not support any programs that provide "religious instruction, conduct worship services or proselytize." But, effectively, that means that a church or synagogue running a youth leadership program or day-care center will be at a disadvantage against comparable national service programs.

Exploring the Issue

Reviewing Facts

1. What types of jobs would be done by people in a domestic national service program?

2. Explain the opportunity cost argument against having a domestic national service.

Critical Thinking

3. Who would most benefit from a mandatory domestic national service program? Who would lose the most?

2 ECONOMIC SYSTEMS AND THE AMERICAN ECONOMY

Who produced these jeans?

How were they produced?

How did they know how many to make?

Does the producer or the government guarantee the quality of these jeans?

What factors determined the price of these jeans?

How much do these jeans cost?

Who will buy this product?

Your Economics Journal

Keep track of the consumer goods and services you purchase in a week. List these items and their prices in your journal. Next to each item explain why you made the purchase.

SECTION **1** *Economic Systems*

SECTION 1 FOCUS

Terms to Know economic system, distribution of income, traditional economic system, command economic system, market economic system, market, mixed economy

Objectives *After reading this section, you should be able to:*

❶ List the **four questions** that all economic systems must answer.

❷ List and summarize the **major types of economic systems** and their differences.

Economic Systems Determine Use of Resources

As a young adult, you probably have set some goals for your life, even if they are short-term. They might be no more distant than finishing this year in school or getting a part-time job. You may have long-term goals such as going to vocational school or to college, learning a trade or profession, or opening a business.

If you were to make a list of your personal goals and compare it with a list a person of your age made in another part of the world, the lists would be very different. One of the reasons the lists would be very different is that each nation has a different **economic system,** or way in which it uses its resources to satisfy its people's needs and wants.

Four Basic Questions

Every nation's economic system is faced with answering the same four basic questions: What goods and services and how much of each should be produced? Who should produce them? How should they be produced? Who should share in their use? **Figure 2.1** examines these questions.

Businesses must determine the most efficient mix of the factors of production. Prices affect decisions about what and how much to produce. The type of economic system determines who should produce what.

Figure 2.1 The Four Basic Economic Questions

The way each economic system answers these questions affects how every person within that system uses goods and services.

A How Should Goods and Services Be Produced? ▶

For each good and service produced, there is always a trade-off possible among the available factors of production. For example, a farmer could use 10 laborers with horse-drawn plows to plow a field or 1 tractor and driver. Owners and/or managers of businesses must decide what combination of available resources will get the job done for the least cost.

B What and How Much Should Be Produced? ◀

We live in a world of scarcity and trade-offs. If more of one item is produced, then less of something else will be produced. For example, an automobile manufacturer must decide how to use its limited supply of labor, steel, rubber, and so on. Should it produce pickup trucks or full-sized automobiles? How much of each?

C Who Should Produce What?

Within each economic system, different people do different jobs. Who decides which people will produce which goods and services? This question relates directly to choice of career—auto mechanic, teacher, musician, and so forth. ▼

D Who Should Share in What is Produced?

Money payment for work, the amount of health care, education, food, and so on, that each person receives are all part of the **distribution of income.** This last question relates to how goods and services are distributed among all members of an economic system. ◀

Types of Economic Systems

Each society answers the four basic questions according to its view of how best to satisfy the needs and wants of its people. The values and goals that a society sets for itself determine the kind of economic system it will have. Economists have identified four types of economic systems: traditional; command, or controlled; market, or capitalist; and mixed. Remember as you read this section that the economic systems described are pure, or ideal, types. They are economic models, not examples of the real world.

Traditional System A pure **traditional economic system** answers the four basic questions according to tradition. **Figure 2.2** illustrates one such system in which tradition dictates the role each individual plays. In such a system, things are done "the way they have always been done." Economic decisions are based on customs, beliefs—often religious—and ways of doing things that have been handed down from generation to generation. Traditional economic systems exist today in very limited parts of Asia, the Middle East, Africa, and Latin America.

Figure 2.2
Traditional Economy

The San people of the Kalahari (kal-uh-HAHR-ee) Desert of southern Africa lived in a traditional economy for many years. They were nomadic, or roving, hunters and plant gatherers. When the food in an area was used up, the group moved on in search of new food supplies. ▶

Command, or Controlled, System

The traditional economic system is in some ways similar to a pure command economic system. In a pure **command economic system**, the individual has little, if any, influence over how the basic economic questions are answered. See **Figure 2.3**. Government controls the factors of production and, therefore, makes all decisions about their use. This is why this form of economic system is also called a controlled economy.

The government may be one person, a small group of leaders, or a group of central planners in a government agency. These people choose how resources are to be used at each stage in production and decide the distribution of goods and services. They even decide who will do what. The government, through a series of regulations about the kinds and amount of education available to different groups, guides people into certain jobs.

Market, or Capitalist, System The opposite of a pure command economic system is a pure **market economic system**—or capitalism. In a pure market economic system, government does not intervene. Individuals own the factors of production, and they decide for themselves the answers to the four basic economic questions.

Economic decisions are made through the free interaction of individuals looking out for their own best interests in the market. **Market** in this sense is not a place. Rather, it is the freely chosen activity between buyers and sellers of goods and services.

Buyers and sellers freely choose to do business with those who best satisfy their needs and wants. The exchange of goods and services may take place in a worldwide market for a good such as crude oil. It may also take place in a neighborhood market for the services of someone to mow lawns, deliver papers, or shovel the snow.

In a pure market economic system, producers of goods and services decide how to use their resources based solely on signals from the market. Government planning has no part in the decisions. Whether people buy a certain good or service or not indicates to producers the various ways to use or not use their resources, as shown in **Figure 2.4** (page 34).

People are also free in a pure market economic system to sell their

Figure 2.3 ▲ Command Economy
Only a couple of countries in the entire world still have much of a command economy—North Korea and parts of the People's Republic of China are the two main examples because so much economic activity there is government-planned.

labor as they wish. They may take, refuse, or change jobs whenever they choose. This assumes, of course, that there is a demand for their labor. **Figure 2.5** illustrates the flow of economic activity through the market in the capitalist system.

Mixed Economic System With the exception of the traditional economic system, it is doubtful whether these pure or ideal systems ever existed. They are useful models for analyzing existing systems, however. Today, almost all economic systems are what economists call mixed

economies. A **mixed economy** contains characteristics of a command economy and a pure market economy. **Figure 2.6** shows the two most prominent examples of mixed economies—one leans heavily toward the market model, the other toward the command model.

Figure 2.4
Demand Affects Production

Suppose that in a specific market economy more people begin buying the compact discs (CDs) of a particular rap group. This increase in demand signals the record company to invest more resources—time, money, effort—into producing CDs by that group. If, however, few people are buying CDs by another rap group, the CD company will not sign that group again. Buyers have signaled that they do not want more CDs by that group. ▼

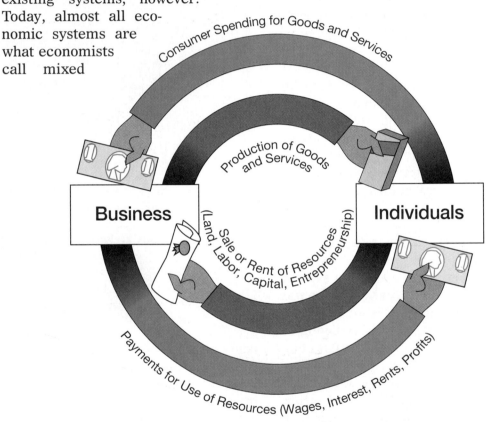

Figure 2.5 ▲
Circular Flow of Economic Activity in a Market Economy

The inside arrows on the graph show individuals selling the factors of production to businesses, who use them to produce goods and services. The flow of money from businesses to individuals in the form of rent, wages, interest, and profits and its return to business as consumer spending, is illustrated on the outside of the graph.

Figure 2.6
Two Mixed Economies

In mixed economies, the mix will vary so that any one economic system leans more toward one pure type than another.

A The United States tends much more toward the market system than toward the command system. Not all decisions, however, are made by individuals reacting to the market. Federal, state, and local governments make laws regulating some areas of business. Among these, for instance, are the rates that electric companies may charge.

B Although the People's Republic of China still tends much more toward the command than toward the pure market system, the economy is changing. Many factories in China are owned by the government. Government officials tell the managers of those factories what to produce and how much. They also tell the factory managers at what price they should sell their output. There is a growing unrestricted market sector within that country, however. In some "special economic zones," citizens in the People's Republic of China make economic decisions without interference by the government.

SECTION 1 REVIEW

Understanding Vocabulary

Define economic system, distribution of income, traditional economic system, command economic system, market economic system, market, mixed economy.

Reviewing Objectives

❶ What four questions must all economic systems answer?

❷ What are the major types of economic systems, and what are their differences?

Understanding Percentages and Discounts

Economists use statistics to describe different population characteristics—occupations, income, and so on. Percentages are a useful form of statistics. Do you know how to use them?

Percentages

Percent means "parts per hundred." Sales taxes are figured in percents. Suppose a skirt costs $24 and the sales tax is 6 percent. As **Figure A** shows, the tax adds $.06 for every dollar of the price.

Figuring Percentages

Suppose a pair of shoes is 30 percent off the regular price. If the regular price was $57, what will the new price be? You can find the price by multiplying percent off by the original price and subtracting the discount. Or, as **Figure B** shows, you can multiply the original price by the percent you will pay (70 percent).

If the $57 shoes are on sale for $39.90, you can find the percent you are paying by dividing the amount you pay by the original price. See **Figure C**.

Percent and Actual Number

Is it a better discount if the store says you can buy the first pair for $57 and get the second pair for half price? You would pay 100 percent for the first pair of shoes and 50 percent (half) of the second. Total these percentages and divide by the number of pairs of shoes. You would pay 75 percent. **Figure D** shows that the discount is only 25 percent.

Figure A
6% = .06
$24.00
X   .06
$ 1.44 sales tax

Figure B

$57.00	$57.00
X .30	−17.10
$17.10	$39.90

or

$57.00
X .70
$39.90

Figure C
$39.90 ÷ $57 = .70 X 100 = 70%

Figure D
100% + 50% = 150%
150% ÷ 2 = 75%
100% − 75% = 25%

Practicing the Skill

❶ A store advertises jeans at 33 percent off the original price of $37. What is the new price?

2 Characteristics of the American Economy

Terms to Know invisible hand, capitalism, free enterprise system, private property, profit, profit incentive, competition

Objectives *After reading this section, you should be able to:*

1. Describe the **role of government** in the free enterprise system.
2. Explain the importance of **freedom of enterprise** in the American economy.
3. Define **freedom of choice** as it applies to the American free enterprise system.
4. List the advantages of **private property**.
5. Identify the role of the **profit incentive**.
6. Evaluate **competition** in the American free enterprise system.

Free Enterprise with Some Regulations

A pure market economic system has six major characteristics: (1) little or no government control, (2) freedom of enterprise, (3) freedom of choice, (4) private property, (5) profit incentive, and (6) competition. These characteristics are interrelated, and to varying degrees all are present in the American economy.

In his book, *The Wealth of Nations,* Adam Smith in 1776 described a system in which government has little to do with a nation's economic activity. He said that individuals left on their own would work for their own self-interests. In doing this, they would be guided as if by an **invisible hand** of competition to achieve the maximum good for society.

The Role of Government

Smith's idea of the ideal economic system is called capitalism, another name for the market system. Economists argue whether capitalism in its pure form, as Smith described it, has ever existed. **Capitalism** as practiced in the United States today would be best defined as an economic system in which private individuals own the factors of production and decide how to use them within the limits of the law.

Smith's ideas influenced the Founders of the United States, who limited the role of government mainly to national defense and keeping peace. Also, the Constitution as originally written and interpreted, limits the national government's control over economic activities.

Since the 1880s, the role of government—federal, state, and local—has increased significantly in the United States. This is especially true in the areas of regulating business and providing public services, as shown in **Figure 2.7**.

Freedom of Enterprise

The American economy is also called the **free enterprise system.** This term emphasizes that individuals are free to own and control the factors of production. For example, if you decide to go into business for yourself, your abilities and resources will help you decide the good or service to produce, the quantity, and the methods of production. Of course, you may lose your money. You, or any entrepreneur, have no guarantee of success. In addition, as **Figure 2.8** shows, certain legal limits restrict freedom of enterprise.

Freedom of Choice

Freedom of choice is the other side of freedom of enterprise. Freedom of choice means that buyers make the decisions about what should be produced. The success or failure of a good or service in the marketplace depends on individuals freely choosing what they want. The earlier example of people buying or not buying a particular group's CDs and the effects on the CD company illustrates this idea. The music company, in reality, may choose to continue making CDs with the group anyway, even though it knows it will not make much profit.

Although buyers are free to exercise their choice, the marketplace has become increasingly complex in this century. As a result, the government has intervened in various areas of the economy to protect buyers. Laws set safety standards for such things as toys, appliances, and automobiles. In industries in which only a few companies provide services, government regulates the price they may charge. This has happened with public utilities.

Private Property

Private property is simply what is owned by individuals or groups rather than by the federal, state, or local government. The Constitution guarantees an owner's rights to private property and its use. You as an individual are free to buy whatever you can afford whether it is land, a business, a home, an automobile, and so on. You can also control how, when, and by whom your property is used. If you own a business, you can keep any profit you make.

**Figure 2.7
U.S.
Government
Regulation**
Today the work of federal agencies includes regulating the quality of various foods and drugs, watching over the nation's money and banking system, inspecting workplaces for hazardous conditions, and guarding against damage to the environment. The federal government also uses tax money to provide social programs such as Medicare. State and local governments have also expanded their role in recent years in such areas as education, job training, recreation, support for the arts, and care for the elderly. ▶

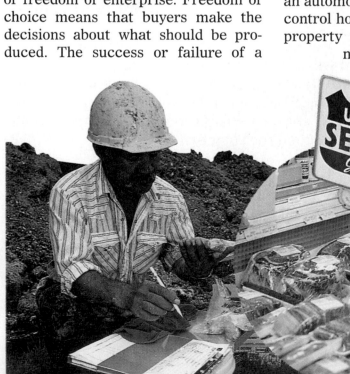

38

Profit is the money left after all the costs of production have been paid. These costs include wages, rent, interest, and taxes.

Within the United States, government at all levels owns some property. Parks, fire-fighting and police equipment, military bases, municipal buildings, and post offices are some examples of government-owned property. Under no circumstances, though, can any level of government in the United States expand its economic role by simply taking private property. This provision is one of the underlying principles of the Bill of Rights. Part of the Fifth Amendment reads:

Nor shall private property be taken for public use, without just compensation.

That clause simply means that if the federal, state, or local government believes it has to use private property, it must pay the private owners. Also, the government cannot make citizens use their private property to house soldiers.

Profit Incentive

Whenever a person invests time, know-how, money, and other capital resources in a business, that investment is made with the idea of making a profit. The desire to make a profit is called the **profit incentive** (in-SENT-iv), and it is mainly this hope that moves people to produce things that others want to buy. After all, if no one buys what a seller produces, there will be no profit, only losses. See **Figure 2.9**.

The risk of failing is part of the free enterprise system. Some industries, however, are so large that their failure would seriously damage the economy and throw thousands of people out of work. In the past several decades, the federal government has passed laws providing special private loan guarantees to big corporations such as Lockheed and Chrysler, and even to the city of New York. The federal government has also aided farmers by providing them with loans.

Competition

Competition is the rivalry among producers or sellers of similar goods to win more business by offering the lowest prices or better quality.

Number of Competitors In many industries, effective competition requires a large number of independent buyers and sellers. This large number of competitors means that no one company can noticeably affect the price of a particular product.

Figure 2.9 ▲
Making a Profit
If you went into business decorating and selling T-shirts, you would expect to make enough money to cover your expenses and make some profit. What would some of this seller's expenses be?

Figure 2.8 ▲
Limits on Free Enterprise
In most states, teenagers must be 16 before they can work, and then laws set limits on how many hours they can work.

Figure 2.10 Competition and Price

Suppose that only one business makes a particular product such as a personal computer. It could charge as much as people who really want a personal computer are willing to pay. They have no alternative seller to turn to. Suppose a second company enters the market with a similar computer at a lower price. Then competition for buyers between the two businesses would force the price down. ▼

If one company attempts to raise its prices, potential customers can simply go to one of the many other sellers. In the ideal world, this is how competition would work. In practice, however, the federal government over the past 100 years has regulated some business practices in an attempt to make sure that competition exists. The opportunity to make a profit encourages competition, as **Figure 2.10** shows.

Businesses have to keep prices low enough to attract buyers yet high enough to make a profit. This forces businesses to keep the costs of production as low as possible. Competitors who succeed do so because they are able to produce those goods that people want most at a price that makes people want to buy.

Easy Entry and Exit Competition also requires that companies can enter or exit any industry they choose. Those who feel that they could make more profit in another industry are free to get out of the industry they are in. Some companies expand into new industries while staying in their old one. A company currently producing and selling VCRs may determine that people prefer the added convenience and higher quality of videodiscs. The company may decide to move out of its old business and begin making videodisc players.

Economists say that such an economy has weak barriers to entry and exit from industries. For the most part, the United States has such weak barriers. Some industries, however, have tougher barriers to entry. For example, a person cannot become a doctor until he or she has passed through an approved medical school and received a license from a state government to practice medicine in that state. Government approval is needed to start a public utility or set up a television or radio station.

LOWEST PRICE $1099!

HURRY! LIMITED STOCK

NOW $629

NEW LOWER PRICE

SECTION 2 REVIEW

Understanding Vocabulary
Define invisible hand, capitalism, free enterprise system, private property, profit, profit incentive, competition.

Reviewing Objectives
1. What role does government play in the free enterprise system?
2. Why is freedom of enterprise one of the cornerstones of the American economy?
3. How does freedom of choice apply to the American free enterprise system?
4. What are the advantages of private property?
5. How does the profit incentive encourage business in the American economy?
6. Why is competition important in the American free enterprise system?

Personal Perspective

Adam Smith on Free Enterprise

Profile

- 1723-1790
- born Kirkaldy, County Fife, Scotland
- teacher at University of Glasgow
- lectured and wrote on moral philosophy
- published *An Inquiry into the Nature and Causes of the Wealth of Nations,* 1776
- called by many the founder of modern economics

In Adam Smith's *An Inquiry into the Nature and Causes of the Wealth of Nations,* he explains why government should not regulate business. He believed that individuals, seeking profit, direct their resources more efficiently than governments.

*... **N**o regulation of commerce can increase the quantity of industry in any society beyond what its capital [resources] can maintain. It can only divert a part of it into a direction into which it might not otherwise have gone. ... It is only for the sake of profit that any man employs a capital in support of industry; and he will always, therefore, endeavor to employ it in the support of that industry of which the produce is likely to be of the greatest value.*

Smith then describes how the sum of all individual decisions will benefit society as a whole.

*... **A**s every individual, therefore, endeavors ... to employ his capital in the support of domestic industry, and so to direct that industry that its produce may be of the greatest value, every individual necessarily labours to render [direct] that annual revenue of the society as great as he can. He ... neither intends to promote the public interest, nor knows how much he is promoting it. By preferring the support of domestic to that of foreign industry, he intends only his own security; ... he intends only his own gain. ...*

Smith concludes that government officials who would try to regulate business are overstepping their authority or lack good sense.

***T**he statesman, who would attempt to direct private people in what manner they ought to employ their capitals, would ... assume an authority which could safely be trusted, not only to no single person, but to no council or senate whatever, and which would nowhere be so dangerous as in the hands of a man who had folly and presumption [reckless disregard] enough to fancy himself fit to exercise it.*

Checking for Understanding

1. Why do individuals invest their capital?
2. How will the economic choices of the individual benefit society as a whole?
3. According to Smith, which government officials are presumptuous?

Blue Bell Creameries, Inc.

 The Main Ingredient In 1907 the Brenham Creamery Company of Texas found a good use for the excess cream in the milk from area farms. They started making butter. Four years later the creamery found another, more delightful use for the cream. They made their first ice cream in a wooden tub filled with ice. Maximum production was two gallons per day. By 1919 Brenham Creamery was still small and struggling. E. F. Kruse, the new plant manager, knew that it was close to going out of business. He kept the company from going under by not cashing his paychecks until the creamery became profitable several months later.

Rising to the Top In 1930 the Brenham Creamery Company changed its name to Blue Bell Creameries, after a Texas wildflower. Like cream, Blue Bell began to rise to the top of the frozen dessert business. One factor that helped the company was the invention of home freezers.

Having freezers in the home created demand for a packaged take-home product. During World War II, E. F. Kruse's sons Ed and Howard, at ages 13 and 11, came to work, hand-wrapping ice cream sandwiches. Today they are respectively chairman of the board and chief executive officer of Blue Bell. One key move in Blue Bell's history was its decision to replace butter with ice cream as the featured product in 1958. Blue Bell began to branch out, opening facilities in Houston, Austin, Beaumont, and Dallas in the next 20 years.

 Advertising and Growth Opening new branches in major Texas cities nearly every year, Blue Bell decided to build its own advertising agency. Blue Bell Advertising Associates was launched in 1987. A new corporate headquarters and visitor center in Brenham opened the following year.

Diversifying Like other businesses, Blue Bell learned to pay attention to its customers' wants. As a result, the company added many new products. In 1989 Diet Blue Bell, the nation's first frozen dairy dessert made with NutraSweet and marketed in a half-gallon container, was introduced. Blue Bell Nonfat Frozen Yogurt and Blue Bell Free, a no-fat, no-sugar frozen dietary dessert, followed in 1991. In addition, the dairy now offers ice cream and yogurt in containers of many shapes and sizes: mini sandwiches, creme pops, fudge bars, drumsticks, cups, and tubs.

Crossing the State Line Distribution of Blue Bell products to Louisiana, Kansas, and Mexico began in the 1990s. Strict quality control measures and fresh ingredients have enhanced the company's reputation. *TIME, Sports Illustrated,* and *Forbes* have each touted Blue Bell's products. Perhaps that's because one key ingredient has not changed over the years—care.

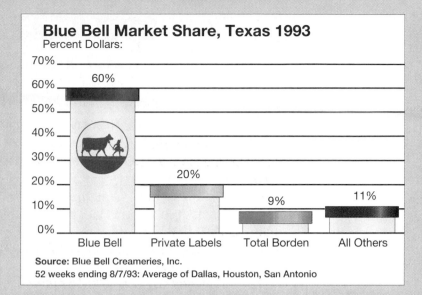

Blue Bell Market Share, Texas 1993
Percent Dollars:

Blue Bell	Private Labels	Total Borden	All Others
60%	20%	9%	11%

Source: Blue Bell Creameries, Inc.
52 weeks ending 8/7/93: Average of Dallas, Houston, San Antonio

Serving the Community Today Blue Bell Creameries, Inc., employs more than 600 Brenham-area workers. In addition, the company has about 900 workers distributing its ice cream in its distribution areas. In a recent year more than 100,000 people toured the facilities in Brenham.

Free Enterprise in Action

1 What was Brenham Creamery's first product?

2 What invention in the 1930s allowed the creamery to expand its take-home business?

3 Why do you think Blue Bell diversified its product line?

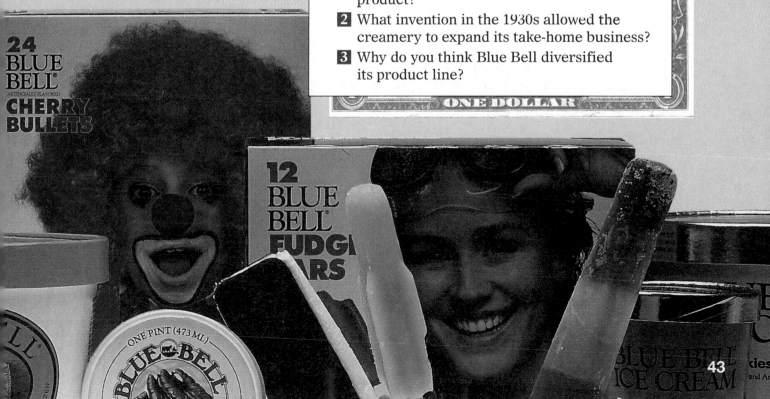

43

SECTION 3 The Goals of the Nation

SECTION 3 FOCUS

Terms to Know economic efficiency, economic growth, equity, standard of living

Objectives *After reading this section, you should be able to:*
1. Describe the major **aims of a market economy.**
2. List ways in which people can **balance economic rights with economic responsibilities.**

Policies and Goals in a Free Market Economy

Nations—and the United States is no exception—have national values and set goals for themselves based on these values. These goals are evident in government policies and in the actions of people like yourself and those around you. The values and goals of a nation determine which of the several kinds of economic systems that nation will have.

Aims of a Market Economy

The United States tends toward a market, or capitalist, system. Therefore, the major characteristics of a market economy should be evident in its goals. Among the national goals of Americans are efficiency, growth, security, equity, stability, and individual freedom. **Figure 2.11** describes these goals in economic terms because this is an economics text. These goals however, have ethical, social, and religious elements as well.

Turning National Goals into Reality
A plan of action must be developed in order to accomplish the nation's goals. Such a plan often involves economic policy-making by elected or appointed officials who must also deal with the reality of scarcity. Because all resources are scarce, when one person gets something, that something will not be available for anyone else.

Consider the goal of economic (income) security. Many individuals can afford to buy private insurance policies and retirement plans. The government, however, has public policies such as Social Security, Medicare, and Medicaid that offer income security and health care.

Figure 2.11 Our National Goals

There are many national goals. Differences on how these goals should be accomplished are reasons for the existence of political parties.

A Economic Efficiency ▶
Economic efficiency means using resources wisely so that people will be as well off as possible given our available resources.

B Economic Growth ▲
Economic growth means an expansion of the economy to produce more goods, jobs, and wealth. Some disagreement exists about whether or not economic growth too often causes problems such as environmental pollution.

C Security and Equity ▶
Security means protecting people against poverty and supplying them with the means to provide for a medical emergency through an increasing number of government social programs directed, among others, to the elderly. The related goal of **equity** means that which is fair and just.

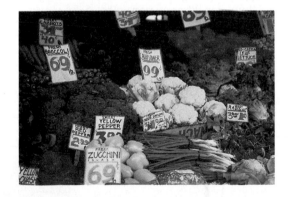

D Individual Freedom
The goal of individual freedom allows each member of society to enjoy the freedoms of enterprise, choice, and private property and to make his or her own decisions ◀ in the marketplace.

E Stability
The goal of stability seeks to reduce extreme ups and downs in the standard of living. **Standard of living** is the material well-being of an individual, group, or nation measured by the average value of goods and services used by the average citizen during a given period of time, usually a year.

Figure 2.12
Advantages of Free Enterprise
The American economic system offers many benefits.

▲ **A A High Level of Economic and Personal Freedom**
Proponents of the free enterprise system point out that of all nationalities, Americans enjoy perhaps the highest degree of freedom in the world to start their own businesses and to pursue their own economic choices. This freedom extends to all aspects of life. With this extreme amount of economic and personal freedom, though, come certain costs. In particular, in our free enterprise system individuals must normally accept the consequences of their decisions.

▲ **B A High Standard of Living**
Supporters of the American economy explain that the nation has more individuals enjoying a high standard of living than almost anywhere else in the world. They believe that the ability of Americans to enjoy such high standards of living is directly tied to the ability of individuals to work where they want, how they want, and with whom, and to invest in whichever businesses they think will make profits.

C Diverse Lifestyles ▶
The great variety of economic opportunities in the United States allows for a wide range of lifestyles. People may choose to work nights, part-time, at two jobs in different parts of the country for different seasons of the year, and so on. In contrast, command economies result in much less diversity in styles of living.

When the government provides for plans such as Medicare, some people must agree to give up some of their income in order to transfer it to people in need. These people may be in need because they are too poor, too disabled, or too ill to care for themselves, or because they have not saved enough for emergencies or retirement.

In a world of scarcity, achieving national goals requires sacrifices by certain members of society. Any program to provide more economic security, more justice, or more equitable treatment of people involves a trade-off. Once you understand this, you will be well on your way to understanding not only the nation's economic system but also its political system. It is this economic and political system that makes many of the decisions about how resources are used in the nation. Such an understanding will help you realize that not all political desires can be turned into economic reality.

Benefits of the Free Enterprise System Those who support the American free enterprise system emphasize the many benefits that it provides for its citizens. **Figure 2.12** illustrates some of these benefits.

Balancing Economic Rights and Responsibilities

The American free enterprise system bestows numerous economic rights and protections on individuals like you, your teachers, your relatives, and your friends. You have the right to enter into just about any profession or business you want. You have the right to work very little or to become a "workaholic." You have the right to buy those products and brands that you like and to reject all others. In short, you have the right to do just about anything that is legal.

A well-functioning free enterprise system will not continue if individuals do not take on certain economic responsibilities. The first, of course, is to be able to support yourself. Additionally, just because education may be offered to you free of charge, it is not free to society. An opportunity cost goes along with it. Consequently, you have a responsibility to use that education in a reasonable manner that helps you become a productive member of the free enterprise system.

Finally, because government has become such an important part of our economy, individuals in our system have the responsibility of electing responsible government officials. This responsibility requires both the knowledge of possible government policies and the ability to analyze the consequences of different government policies.

SECTION 3 REVIEW

Understanding Vocabulary
Define economic efficiency, economic growth, equity, standard of living.

Reviewing Objectives
1. What are the major aims of a market economy?
2. How can you balance your economic rights with your economic responsibilities?

Readings in Economics

TIME	JANUARY 25, 1993

PRINCE OF MIDAIR
by Richard Woodbury

Imagine a major airline that seems to go out of its way to put its passengers in a blind rage: it routinely denies them assigned seats, refuses to transfer their baggage or arrange connections, and crams them three abreast into planes with only crackers and cookies to nibble. It sells no tickets through the industry's computerized reservations system and avoids flying to many large-city airports. As though to compensate for all this, its chief executive dresses in clown suits and Elvis costumes and paints his planes to resemble whales.

Yet Southwest Airlines has used just such perverse tactics to accomplish what no other big carrier has during the current aviation

downturn, the industry's worst: make consistent operating profits. . . .

When it was a Texas puddle jumper, Southwest and its fun-loving chairman were dismissed as an oddity. But now that the Dallas-based airline has made money for 20 straight years and spread to 34 cities in 15 states, the industry is paying it sober respect. . . .

None of this would have happened without [Chief Executive Officer Herb] Kelleher, 61, a folksy ex-San Antonio, Texas, lawyer who runs the company like a carnival sideshow. He schmoozes with employees, who know him as "Uncle Herb"; stages weekly parties at corporate headquarters; and encourages such zany antics by his flight attendants as organizing trivia contests, delivering instructions in rap and awarding prizes for the passengers with the largest holes in their socks. The wackiness has a calculated purpose—to generate a gung-ho spirit that will boost productivity, the key to Southwest's goal of carefully scripted growth.

• THINK ABOUT IT •

1. How does Southwest's service differ from that of other airlines?

2. Why does Kelleher try to instill a "gung-ho" spirit among his employees?

2 *Highlights*

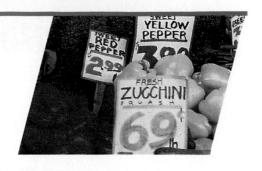

Economic Systems

Key Terms

economic system (p. 30)
distribution of income (p. 31)
traditional economic system (p. 32)
command economic system (p. 33)

market economic system (p. 33)
market (p. 33)
mixed economy (p. 34)

Summary

Every economic system answers four basic questions that determine the use of resources. In a traditional system economic decisions are dictated by what was done in the past. The government controls the factors of production in a command system. In a market system individuals serving their own interests decide the answers to the four basic questions. A mixed system contains elements of command and market systems.

Characteristics of the American Economy

Key Terms

invisible hand (p. 37)
capitalism (p. 37)
free enterprise system (p. 38)

private property (p. 38)
profit (p. 39)
profit incentive (p. 39)
competition (p. 39)

Summary

Consumer choice is the key to the use of resources in a free enterprise system. Free enterprise means that private individuals own property, compete in free markets, and earn profits. The government's role in a market economy is a subject of public debate.

The Goals of the Nation

Key Terms

economic efficiency (p. 45)
economic growth (p. 45)
equity (p. 45)
standard of living (p. 45)

Summary

A nation sets economic goals based on its values. Some goals of the American economic system are efficiency, growth, security, equity, stability, and individual freedom. Personal freedom, lifestyle diversity, and a high standard of living are benefits of the free enterprise system.

Review

Identifying Key Terms

Use terms from the following list to fill in the blanks in the paragraph below.

traditional economic
   system (p. 32)
command economic
   system (p. 33)
mixed economy
   (p. 34)
capitalism (p. 37)
free enterprise
   system (p. 38)
private property
   (p. 38)

profit (p. 39)
competition
   (p. 39)
economic growth
   (p. 45)
equity (p. 45)
standard of living
   (p. 45)

Another term for the market economic system is the _(1)_, or _(2)_. Many Americans believe that this system helps to account for the high _(3)_ in the United States. This system is based on concepts such as _(4)_ that allows people to buy and own land, a home, or their own business. A person may keep the _(5)_ earned from selling in _(6)_ with other businesses. Most people, including Americans, actually live in a _(7)_ economic system that contains some characteristics of a _(8)_. The government promotes both _(9)_ and _(10)_, or fair and just policies.

Write a short paragraph about the American economy using all of the following terms.

economic system (p. 30)
market (p. 33)
mixed economy (p. 34)
invisible hand (p. 37)
profit incentive (p. 39)
competition (p. 39)

Recalling Facts and Ideas

Section 1
1. "The more of one item that is produced, the less of something else will be produced." What term describes this economic condition?
2. What basic economic question helps determine the career path of individuals?
3. What economic question is being answered if an industry decides to replace some workers with machines?
4. Why do economic systems differ in the way they answer the question "Who should share in what is produced?"
5. How does a traditional economic system answer the question "Who should produce what?"
6. Who answers the basic economic questions in a command system?
7. Who owns the factors of production in a market economic system?
8. Why should the United States economic system be called a mixed system?

Section 2
9. What are six important characteristics of free enterprise?
10. Who wrote *The Wealth of Nations*?
11. What is government's limited role in pure capitalism?
12. Why is private property important in the American economic system?

Section 3
13. What are three benefits of the free enterprise system?
14. What does the United States do to promote economic security for individuals?

Critical Thinking

Section 1
Determining Cause and Effect How might the answers to each of the four basic economic questions affect your personal decisions?

Section 2
Making Comparisons Are recent economic trends in Russia and the United States similar or different? Explain your answer.

Section 3
Identifying Alternatives What are two ways that each of the following services may be provided: health care, mass transit, energy?

Applying Economic Concepts

Economic Systems An economic system within your school determines the answer to the basic question *who should share in what is produced.* Make a list of the goods and services available to students within the school. After each, write whether the distribution of this good or service is determined according to market, command, or traditional economic system principles.

Chapter Projects

1. **Individual Project** Review economic news from national magazines. List the economic decisions of several nations and make a table that classifies them as supporting free markets or command systems.
2. **Cooperative Learning Project** In small groups that will serve as committees, submit proposals for planning a national education system in a command economy. The system should provide answers to such questions as:
   - What level of education should be available without cost to everyone?
   - Should academic achievement or testing be used to qualify students for higher levels of education or specialized fields?

Compare the different answers to each of the issues. What other issues have surfaced during student discussions within each group? What are the major hurdles to building a national education system?

Reviewing Skills

Understanding Percentages and Discounts
1. **Figuring Percentages** A local insurance company increased the number of its employees from 550 to 667 over a five-year period. What was the percentage increase in employees?
2. **Using Percentages** Study the table below, then apply your skills to determine the numbers that fit the four blank spaces.

original price	percent off	discount	new price
$100.00	30%	$30.00	$70.00
$80.00	15%		
$56.00		$3.92	$52.08
	20%	$12.00	$48.00

Writing About Economics

Descriptive Writing Imagine you are a young person writing to a group of students who live in a society that has a traditional economic system. Social customs determine the economic decisions they make. Write a letter describing how the economic decisions you make are a part of your daily life. Refer to the list of goods and services in Your Economics Journal as you write.

Using Economic Models

From the classroom of Michelle Farthing, Alvin High School, Alvin, Texas

In Unit 1 you read about using models, a basic tool of the economist. In this experiment, you will use models to study competition. (You may want to reread the material on pages 18–21 of the text.)

Competition among producers forces businesses to keep prices low enough to attract customers. Some businesses emphasize price when marketing their products. This is called **price competition.** Some businesses choose to emphasize service, product quality, packaging, or factors other than price to distinguish their products. In this lab study, you will try to determine whether certain businesses are using price competition and, if so, how they are using it.

Tools

1. Copies of a local newspaper over a 4-week period
2. Pencils, writing paper, graph paper

Procedures

Step A Depending on the size of your class, choose 5 to 10 products or services from the following list:

1. gasoline
2. hair cuts
3. jeans
4. face soap
5. hamburgers
6. dishwashers
7. motorcycles
8. pizza
9. tennis shoes
10. oranges
11. golf fees
12. motel rooms

Step B Write the names of the brands, stores, distributors, etc., for one product or service that you plan to study in the left column of a table such as the one below.

Example
Gasoline
(87 octane)

Sunoco (Oak St.)			
Ray's Texaco			
Shell (downtown)			
Certified			

Step C Keep a record of the price changes by the supplier of the service or product you are studying over time.

Example

Gasoline (87 octane)	March 5	12	19	26
Sunoco (Oak St.)	$1.09	$1.14	$1.19	$1.13
Ray's Texaco	1.09	1.12	1.15	1.12
Shell (downtown)	1.04	1.10	1.13	1.15
Certified	.99	1.05	1.06	1.04

Step D Make a list of the different kinds of advertising messages used for the competing products or services during this period.

Example

Sunoco	better mileage	more selection	quality
Ray's Texaco	lower price	friendly	contest, prizes

Step E Build a graph similar to the one below that shows the price changes of the products or services you studied.

Example

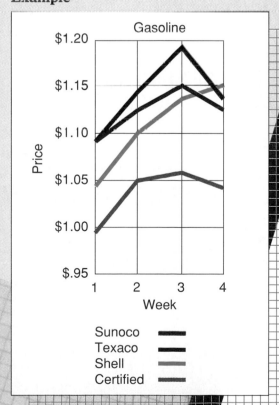

Gasoline

Price

$1.20
$1.15
$1.10
$1.05
$1.00
$.95

1   2   3   4
Week

Sunoco ▬
Texaco ▬
Shell ▬
Certified ▬

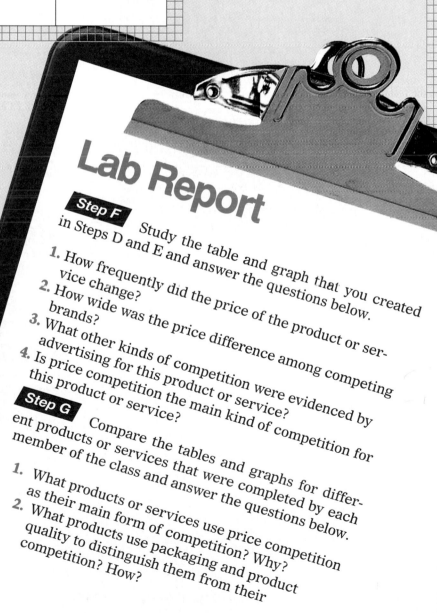

Lab Report

Step F Study the table and graph that you created in Steps D and E and answer the questions below.

1. How frequently did the price of the product or service change?
2. How wide was the price difference among competing brands?
3. What other kinds of competition were evidenced by advertising for this product or service?
4. Is price competition the main kind of competition for this product or service?

Step G Compare the tables and graphs for different products or services that were completed by each member of the class and answer the questions below.

1. What products or services use price competition as their main form of competition? Why?
2. What products use packaging and product quality to distinguish them from their competition? How?

U N I T

2

PRACTICAL ECONOMICS: HOW THEORY WORKS FOR YOU

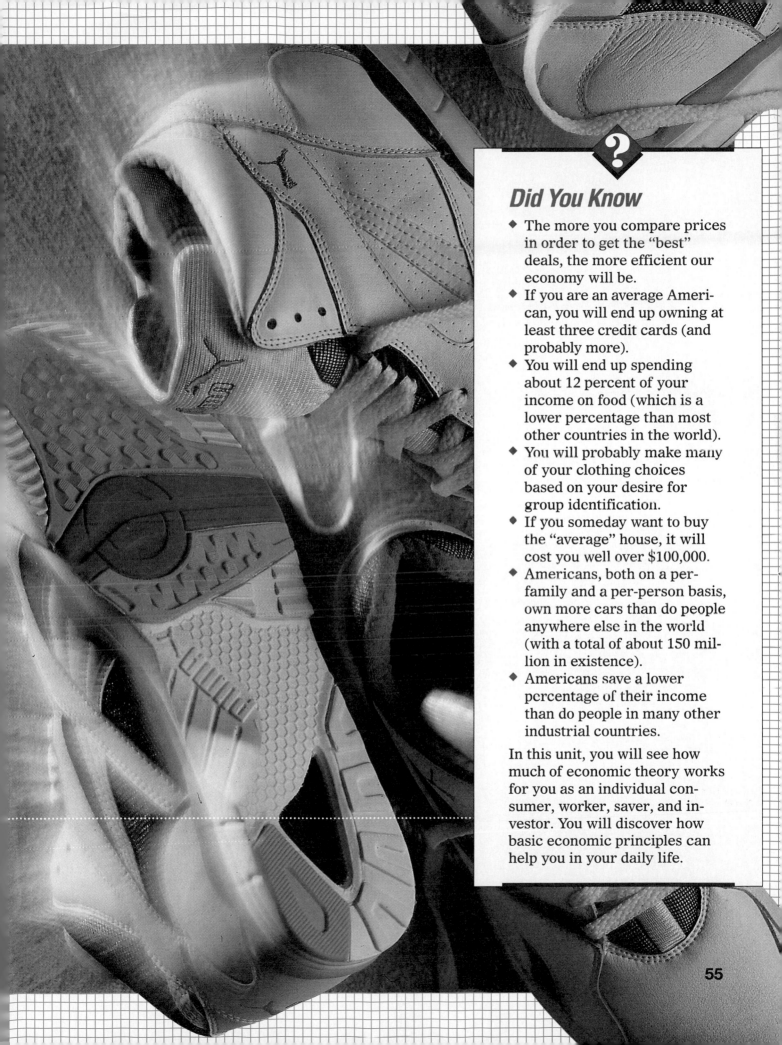

? Did You Know

- The more you compare prices in order to get the "best" deals, the more efficient our economy will be.
- If you are an average American, you will end up owning at least three credit cards (and probably more).
- You will end up spending about 12 percent of your income on food (which is a lower percentage than most other countries in the world).
- You will probably make many of your clothing choices based on your desire for group identification.
- If you someday want to buy the "average" house, it will cost you well over $100,000.
- Americans, both on a per-family and a per-person basis, own more cars than do people anywhere else in the world (with a total of about 150 million in existence).
- Americans save a lower percentage of their income than do people in many other industrial countries.

In this unit, you will see how much of economic theory works for you as an individual consumer, worker, saver, and investor. You will discover how basic economic principles can help you in your daily life.

55

CHAPTER 3

YOUR ROLE AS A CONSUMER

Do you know what is required to make rational decisions when you shop for a computer?

Do you think that when you are shopping for a computer you should visit every store carrying that product in your community?

Do you have alternative sources from which you can buy a computer in addition to stores in your community?

If you and a friend visit the same stores and hear the same sales pitch in each one, will you necessarily decide on the same brand and model computer?

Your Economics Journal

Keep track of the steps used by you, a friend, or one of your parents in buying a small appliance or electronic item. List the number of alternative sources that were considered. Next to each source, write why that store or catalog source was or was not chosen.

SECTION 1 Consumption, Income, and Decision Making

SECTION 1 FOCUS

Terms to Know consumer, disposable income, discretionary income, warranty, rational choice

Objectives *After reading this section, you should be able to:*
1. Explain the difference between **disposable and discretionary income.**
2. List three considerations in **decision making as a consumer.**

Consumers Can Learn to Make Rational Choices

You and everyone around you are consumers and, as such, play important roles in the economic system. A **consumer** is any person or group that buys or uses goods and services to satisfy personal wants. As consumers, people buy a wide variety of things—food, clothing, dental and medical care, automobiles, computers, and so on. To see how typical American consumers spend their money, study the circle graph in Figure 3.1.

Disposable and Discretionary Income

A person's role as a consumer depends on his or her ability to consume. This ability to consume, in turn, depends on the income available and how much of it a person chooses to spend now or save for the future.

Income can be both disposable and discretionary (dis-KRESH-uh-ner-ee). **Disposable income** is the money income a person has left after all taxes have been paid. People spend their disposable income on many kinds of goods and services. First, they buy the necessities: food, clothing, and housing. Once these needs have been met, there may be some income left. This income, which can be spent on extras such as entertainment and luxury items, is called **discretionary income.** See **Figure 3.2.**

Education, occupation, age, gender, and health can all make differences in a person's earning power and

Figure 3.1 Consumer Spending
The circle graph shows how Americans spend their income. What are the top three categories of consumer spending?

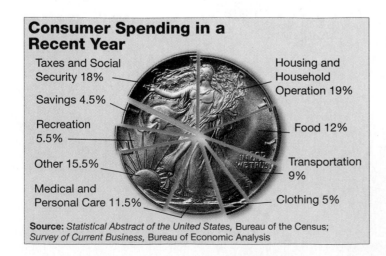

Consumer Spending in a Recent Year

Taxes and Social Security 18%
Savings 4.5%
Recreation 5.5%
Other 15.5%
Medical and Personal Care 11.5%
Housing and Household Operation 19%
Food 12%
Transportation 9%
Clothing 5%

Source: *Statistical Abstract of the United States,* Bureau of the Census; *Survey of Current Business,* Bureau of Economic Analysis thus in his or her ability to consume. Where a person lives can also influence how much he or she earns. City dwellers tend to earn more than those who live in rural areas. Wages in some regions of the country tend to be higher than those in other regions. How much a person has to spend can also be influenced by inheriting money or property.

Regardless of the size of a person's income, spending that income requires constant decision making. As a consumer, each person has a series of choices to make.

Decision Making as a Consumer

The first decision a consumer must make is whether to buy an item or not. This may sound so basic as to be unnecessary to mention, but how many times do you actually think about the reasons for the purchase you are about to make? Do you think about whether you really need the item? Do you consider the trade-offs involved? Part I of **Figure 3.3**—Checklist for Consumer Decision Making—on page 60 will help you analyze this first consumer decision.

Scarce Resources Once you have decided to make a purchase, at least two scarce resources are involved—income and time. Once you have decided to spend your money income, you need to invest time in obtaining information about the product you wish to buy. The time you spend making a decision to buy something cannot be used for anything else. Suppose you decide to buy a mountain bike. The time spent visiting stores checking models and prices is a cost to you.

Making consumer decisions involves three parts, each including several steps. The Checklist for

Consumer Decision Making in **Figure 3.3** can help to guide you through the entire process.

Opportunity Cost Virtually all of the steps in consumer decision making shown in **Figure 3.3** involve an opportunity cost. Opportunity cost is the value of your highest alternative choice that you did not make. In step 1 of Part II of the checklist, for example, your choice between a low-, medium-, or high-quality product involves an opportunity cost.

In general, a high-quality product costs more than a low-quality product. Here is an example: You are trying to decide between new cross-training shoes. One model has a pump system that allows you to get a closer fit on your foot. The other model does not. The pump system model costs $80 more than the other model. If you choose the superior-quality, higher-priced pump system shoe, you will

Figure 3.2 ▲
Using Discretionary Income
The consumer's wants are his or her guide in spending income. Some people have more disposable and discretionary income and can therefore spend more than others on entertainment.

✓ Checklist

Figure 3.3
Consumer Decision Making

Part I. Deciding to Spend Your Money

Before you buy anything, you should ask yourself:

1 Do I really need this item? Why? Remember the discussion about wants and needs in Chapter 1. Real needs are few, but wants are unlimited. Unless you answer this question honestly, you may find your wants are always greater than your ability to satisfy them.

2 Is this good or service worth the time I spent earning the income to pay for it?

3 Is there any better use for my income now? Should I save instead for future needs?

Part II. Deciding on the Right Purchase

Once you have made up your mind to buy a certain good or service, you are faced with more questions:

1 Do I want high, medium, or low quality? Quality refers to appearance, materials used, and the length of time a product will last. Most goods are of medium or average quality. For a higher price, you can usually get higher quality. For a lower price, you can usually expect a product that may not be as attractive or as long lasting. At times such a purchase may suit your needs very well, however.

2 If I am buying an appliance or car, do I want one that will be the most efficient—least costly—to operate each year? The answer will probably involve a trade-off. A small automobile, for example, may use less gasoline than a larger one, but it provides less protection in an accident.·

3 Does this particular item—a Brand Y stereo, for example—require more service than Brands A, B, and C? If so, do I want this additional problem and expense?

4 Should I wait until there is a sale on the item I want? Sales of certain items are seasonal. For example, winter clothes are on sale after Christmas and summer clothes in August.

5 If I am looking for an expensive item, such as an entertainment center, should I buy it new or used? What things are better to buy new than used? How can I protect myself if I buy a used item?

6 Should I choose a product with a well-known brand name even though it costs more than a similar product without a brand name? Are there any benefits to buying a brand-name product? What are they?

7 Does anyone I know own this product so that I can get a firsthand opinion?

8 Is the warranty on this particular product comparable to warranties on similar items? A **warranty** is a promise made by a manufacturer or a seller to repair or replace a product if it is found to be faulty within a certain period of time.

9 Is the return or exchange policy where I am thinking of buying a product comparable to the policies of other stores selling similar items?

10 What do consumer magazines say about it?

Part III. Deciding How to Use Your Purchase

Decision making for you, the consumer, does not stop after you have bought an item. It continues for as long as you have a choice about using it. Once you own something—whether it is clothing, a VCR, or an automobile—you must decide:

1 How much time and effort should I spend on repairs and maintenance?

2 How much money should I spend on repairs and maintenance?

3 At what point should I replace this item? Why? (This brings you back to number 1 under Deciding to Spend Your Money.)

Figure 3.4 Buying Decisions

If you choose the higher-priced product, you must believe that the opportunity cost for the higher quality is worth $80—nothing else at that instant will give you as much value. ▼

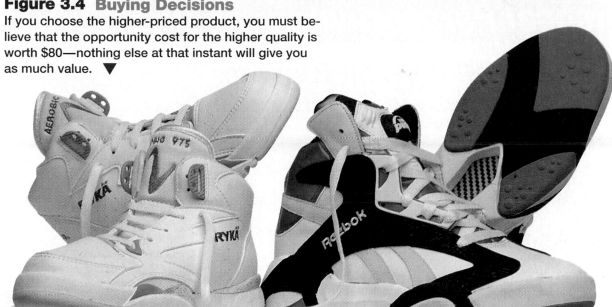

sacrifice $80. The opportunity cost of the pump model over the lesser-quality model shoe is therefore $80, or what you could have bought with that $80. See **Figure 3.4**.

Rational Choice When you make consumer decisions based on opportunity cost, you are engaging in **rational choice.** Economists define rational choice as the alternative that has the greatest value.

Rational choice involves choosing the item that is the least expensive from among comparable quality products. As a consumer, you will make rational choices when you purchase the goods and services you believe can best satisfy your wants.

Do not get the impression that rational consumers will all make the same choices. Remember the definition: A rational choice is one that generates the greatest value for any given expenditure. Rational choices that are based on careful consumer decision making will still lead to billions of different consumer choices yearly.

Value is very subjective. You may choose to buy the higher-priced, superior-quality pump cross-training shoes, and your best friend may think you are crazy. If he or she tells you, "That's a rip-off; you shouldn't pay that kind of money for those shoes," your friend is expressing a value judgment about how you are choosing to spend your limited income.

SECTION 1 REVIEW

Understanding Vocabulary

Define consumer, disposable income, discretionary income, warranty, rational choice.

Reviewing Objectives

1. What kinds of products are purchased with discretionary income?
2. What three things should a consumer consider when making a purchase?

Susan Bowen on Running a Business in Tough Times

- 1941–
- founder and president of Memphis-based Champion Awards, Inc.
- started Champion Awards in a friend's barn in 1970
- originally sold trophies to saddle clubs and expanded into T-shirt printing
- over $10 million in sales by early 1990s

Susan Bowen runs a retail business that sells trophies and T-shirts and is very sensitive to economic downturns. In 1990 her company, Champion Awards, Inc., had to cut a number of employees in order to survive during the worst financial situation in its history. By the end of 1991, however, it was well on the road to recovery and had hired back most of its employees. In the *Memphis Business Journal*, January 28, 1991, Bowen shares some insights on how her company coped in a tough retail environment.

... *In good times, our sales people are more like order-takers. In harder times, they've got to be more aggressive.*
... *We're taking some orders we wouldn't have taken before. We haven't lowered prices, but we've lowered the volume we do. We have a distribution business where we sell blank goods to other printers—that business has really slowed.*

Bowen explains how hard times forced her company to make wise economic choices.

... *When you see your equipment just sitting there, that's really going to cost you.*
... *It's probably the best thing that we have had happen to us. It's made us more aware of the* expense side of the business, instead of sales.
... *When you're growing and the money's coming in, you don't pay attention to that. We still want to grow—you're going to have to grow in our industry to stay even. But we're not going to grow at the expense of the bottom line.*

I don't want any inventory in this building until the day we need it. We should cut inventory. We're just going to get lean and mean, and get aggressive with our sales.

In *Commercial Appeal*, October 30, 1991, Bowen explains why Champion raised salaries in spite of tough times.

It's these people out here that work their rears off that need the money, not somebody sitting up there at a computer. These are the people we want to keep.... We're getting the best employees we've ever had.

Checking for Understanding

1. What kind of adjustments did Champion Awards have to make?
2. How did hard times make Champion Awards more efficient?
3. Why did Champion raise salaries at the same time they cut costs in other areas?

SECTION 2 Buying Principles, or Strategies

SECTION 2 FOCUS

Terms to Know competitive advertising, informative advertising, bait and switch, generic brands, brand name, comparison shopping

Objectives *After reading this section, you should be able to:*
1. Evaluate the trade-offs when **gathering information**.
2. Analyze various **forms of advertising** wisely.
3. Practice **comparison shopping**.

The Three Basic Buying Principles

Assume that you have decided to make a purchase. Because of the problems of scarce income and time, your goal should be to obtain the most satisfaction from your limited income and time. Three basic buying principles can help you and all consumers achieve this goal. They are: (1) gathering information; (2) using advertising wisely; and (3) comparison shopping.

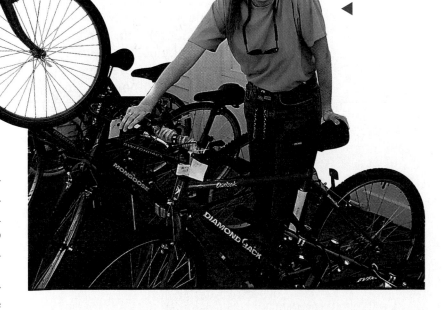

Figure 3.5 How Much Time and Effort? You can spend time testing out friends' mountain bikes. You could also go to different stores and discuss the good and bad points of various makes and models with salespeople. Actually, as a wise consumer, you would do both.

Gathering Information

Suppose that you are going to buy a mountain bike. Once you have decided that, you have to decide on a brand and a model. How? You first have to obtain information about mountain bikes. See **Figure 3.5**.

Information is costly because obtaining it involves your time. You are

Checklist

Figure 3.6
Analyzing Advertisements

Ask yourself these questions as you read advertisements:

1. Does the ad only appeal to my emotions or does it provide facts?

2. What are the special features of the product? Do these special features make any sense in terms of my needs?

3. If I am interested in an automobile or appliance, does the ad tell me anything about operating costs?

4. Does the ad tell me anything about a product's durability, or ability to last?

5. Does the advertised price compare favorably with the price of similar products?

6. Is the advertised price the entire price, or are there extra costs in small print for installation or for separate parts, such as batteries?

faced with the problem of deciding how much information to obtain.

In the case of the mountain bike, the buying principle to follow is: Obtain only as much information as is worthwhile. What does *worthwhile* mean? The value of your time and effort spent gathering information should not be greater than the value you receive from making the best choice of product for yourself.

You would not, for example, want to go to every bike store in your town or city and spend two hours with every salesperson discussing every model. In contrast, you would probably want to spend more than two minutes reading one advertisement about one model. The less valuable a person considers his or her time, the more comparison shopping he or she should do. A nonworking college student generally should spend more time in comparison shopping than a business executive.

As you shop for different products, you will begin to develop a consumer-knowledge base. Information you obtain looking for a mountain bike might help you someday to make decisions about choosing a car or a computer.

Simply getting salespeople to give you accurate information is a skill that you can acquire and hone, or sharpen, over time while you shop for other products.

Using Advertising Wisely

Advertising is all around you. Whenever you turn on the radio or television, you will more than likely hear or see a commercial. Wherever you go, you read advertising on billboards, on posters on buses, and so on. The Checklist for Analyzing Advertisements in **Figure 3.6** gives you some tips for reading these ads, which can generally be classified as competitive or informative.

Competitive Advertising Advertising that attempts to persuade consumers that a product is different from and superior to any other is **competitive advertising.** Its purpose may be to take customers away from competitors or to keep competitors from taking away customers. Ads for well-established brand names and products, such as Apple computers and L.A. Gear, are often of this type. The ads are meant to keep the public aware of a company's name and its specific products.

Informative Advertising Informa**tive advertising** benefits consumers by giving information about a product. From such ads, you can learn about the existence, price, quality, and special features of products without spending much time or effort.

Informative advertising may also be competitive in nature.

Bait and Switch Unfortunately, advertising can be misleading. Although most advertisers try to present their products accurately, some use deceptive, or false, advertising. Sellers may misrepresent the quality, features, or the true (full) price of goods.

One of the most widely used methods of deceptive advertising is **bait and switch.** The bait is an advertised item at an unrealistically low price. When the consumer gets to the store, the item is no longer available, or the salesperson points out all the bad features of the advertised item and how dissatisfied the customer will be with it.

The salesperson then shows higher-priced models and points out all their good features. This is the switch. Instead of being able to buy a $249

videodisc player, for example, the customer finds all the available ones are $400 or more. This practice is both deceptive and illegal.

Comparison Shopping

Once you have gathered the information and made a decision about a product you want, you must decide where to buy it. The price you will have to pay will affect your decision. Because you have limited income, a lower price will mean that you will have more income to spend on other purchases. You will be best off as a consumer when you are able to pay the lowest price for what you want. See **Figure 3.7**.

Figure 3.7
Efficient Comparison Shopping
To efficiently comparison shop for bikes, read newspaper advertisements, make telephone calls, and visit different stores. Remember, however, that finding out price information requires time. ▶

A Some companies produce and sell **generic brands.** The word *generic* means "pertaining to a general class." A generic brand of cereal means there is no brand name at all. It is difficult to know who produced the product.

▼

B A **brand name** is a word, picture, or logo on a product that helps consumers distinguish it from similar products. Brand names are usually sold nationwide and are backed by major companies.

▼

Figure 3.8
Generic versus Brand Name
Your selection of generic or brand–name products makes a difference in price and sometimes in quality. Wise shoppers can often find non-brand names of equally high quality and reliability.

Shopping around suggests a third buying principle. Whenever you decide to make a purchase, it is generally worthwhile to get information on the types and prices of products available from different stores or companies. This process is known as **comparison shopping.**

Even when you apply rational buying principles to consumer decision making, you may still find that being a wise consumer is not always easy. The marketplace is a complex world with many sellers. Some sellers do not always include complete or reliable information about their products. Others may not readily repair or replace faulty products.

Brand-Name or Generic Products
Another consumer choice is between buying generic and brand-name products. Some consumers find that national brand-name products are worth the higher prices they often command. **Figure 3.8** explains more about choosing between brand-name and other products.

SECTION 2 REVIEW

Understanding Vocabulary
Define competitive advertising, informative advertising, bait and switch, generic brands, brand name, comparison shopping.

Reviewing Objectives
❶ What trade-offs should a consumer consider when gathering information?

❷ How does informative advertising differ from competitive advertising?

❸ What is comparison shopping?

LEARNING ECONOMIC SKILLS

Handling a Consumer Problem

Dealing with a faulty product or with a repair that was done incorrectly are two common consumer problems. Getting the results you want requires special communications skills.

Problem-Solving Steps

The Office of Consumer Affairs suggests that you:

1. Report the problem immediately. Do not try to fix a product yourself, because doing so may cancel the warranty.

2. State the problem and suggest a fair and just solution—replacement, refund, etc.

3. Include important details and copies of receipts, guarantees, and contracts to support your case.

4. Describe any action you have taken to try to correct the problem.

5. Keep an accurate record of your efforts to get the problem solved. Include names of people you speak or write to and dates.

6. Allow each person reasonable time, such as three weeks, to solve the problem before contacting another source.

7. Keep cool. The person who will help you solve your problem is probably not responsible for the problem.

If you need to write to the manufacturer, be sure your writing is neat and easy to read. Type your letter, if possible. Keep a copy of the letter for your records and future reference.

Practicing the Skill

1. Using the sample, write a letter to the company that shipped you a computer game diskette that will not operate in your home computer.

2. If you do not receive satisfaction on a complaint in a reasonable time, what might you do next?

Your Address
City, State, Zip Code
Date

Customer Service Department
Company Name
Street Address
City, State, Zip Code

Dear Customer Service
Representative:

I bought a (product name, serial no., model no.) at (location and date of purchase). Unfortunately, (state problem, history of problem, and efforts to solve it).

I would appreciate your (state specific actions to be taken). Enclosed are copies of the following records: (list and enclose all documents connected with the problem).

I am looking forward to your reply and resolution of my problem and will wait (state resonable time period) before seeking third party assistance. Please contact me at the above address or by phone (work and home numbers).

Sincerely,

Your Name

SECTION 3 Consumerism

SECTION 3 FOCUS

Terms to Know consumerism, ethical behavior

Objectives *After reading this section, you should be able to:*

1. List five **consumer rights.**
2. List sources of **private and federal help for consumers.**
3. Define **consumer responsibilities.**
4. Describe **ethical consumer behavior.**

Consumers Have Rights and Responsibilities

Today the decisions Americans face as consumers are increasingly complex. Many Americans are greatly concerned with the safety and reliability of the products and services they use. **Consumerism** is a movement to educate buyers about the purchases they make and to demand better and safer products from manufacturers. Many government agencies and private groups work to ensure the well-being of consumers. Since the early 1960s, consumerism has grown steadily. Business can no longer assume it is the buyer's responsibility to know whether a product is safe, food is healthful, or advertising is accurate. See **Figure 3.9.**

Figure 3.9
Consumer Protection
Government inspection of many products protects consumers' health and safety and raises quality standards.

▼

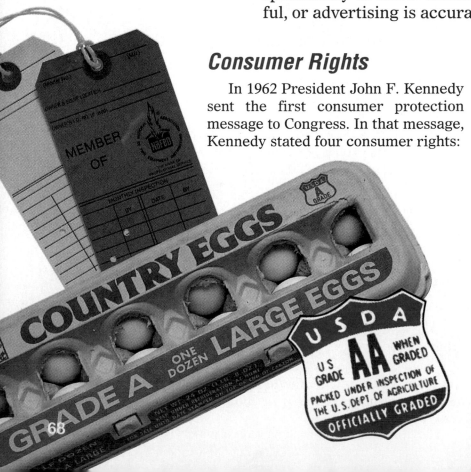

Consumer Rights

In 1962 President John F. Kennedy sent the first consumer protection message to Congress. In that message, Kennedy stated four consumer rights:

- the right to safety—protection against goods that are dangerous to life or health;
- the right to be informed—information for use not only as protection against fraud but also as the basis for reasoned choices;
- the right to choose—the need for markets to be competitive (have many firms) and for protection by government in those other markets, such as electric service, where competition does not exist;
- the right to be heard—the guarantee that consumer interests will be listened to when laws are being written.

Figure 3.10
Informing Yourself

A good consumer reads all contracts and warranties and asks about return and refund policies. After the purchase, he or she reads any instruction booklet and follows the directions for proper use of the product. ▶

To the four listed by President Kennedy, most consumer advocates would add a fifth:

- the right to redress—the ability to obtain from the manufacturers adequate payment in money or goods for financial or physical damages caused by their products.

Following the concepts that President Kennedy listed, Congress passed consumer-protection legislation. Today, consumers dissatisfied with a specific product can complain to the store manager or write to the manufacturer. They can also hire a lawyer or take the case to small claims court. Many private and public agencies can also help consumers.

Consumer Help: Private and Federal

Among the private groups that aid consumers are local citizens' action groups and local chapters of the Better Business Bureau. Many major cities and some smaller ones have better business bureaus. The bureaus provide information on products as well as selling practices to consumers and help settle disagreements between consumers and sellers. Before using these agencies, however, consumers need to learn about the products they wish to purchase as **Figure 3.10** shows.

A trade association is a group of companies in the same business that work together to promote that specific industry. Trade associations in some industries also provide consumers with information.

Two national organizations provide excellent sources of consumer information. The Consumers Union of the United States, Inc., publishes a monthly magazine called *Consumer Reports*. An informational magazine, *Consumer Reports* accepts no advertising. A competing publication is *Consumers' Research Magazine*, published by Consumers' Research, Inc.

Numerous federal agencies also have programs to aid consumers. **Figure 3.11** (pages 70–71) lists these agencies and what they do. Much of the information that now appears on product labels and in warranties is a result of federal regulations to protect consumers. States also have consumer affairs councils or agencies.

Consumer Responsibilities

Consumers have responsibilities as well as rights. Learning as much as possible about the product or service he or she wishes to buy will enable the consumer to purchase the best product at the best price.

Figure 3.11 Federal Agencies and Consumerism

Agency	How It Helps the Consumer	For More Information
Consumer Information Center Program	Provides free catalog of government publications on consumer topics	*Consumer's Resource Handbook* Consumer Information Center Pueblo, Colorado 81009
Federal Trade Commission	Promotes free and fair competition by enforcing laws against monopolies, price fixing, false advertising, and other illegal business practices; regulates packaging and labeling of products and protects the public against violations of consumer credit laws	Federal Trade Commission 6th St. and Pennsylvania Avenue, N.W. Office of Public Information Washington, D.C. 20580
Consumer Product Safety Commission	Protects the public against unreasonable risk of injury from consumer products; sets product safety requirements, forbids the production and sale of dangerous consumer products, and conducts research and education programs on safety concerns for industry and the public	Office of the Secretary, Consumer Product Safety Commission 5401 Westbard Avenue Bethesda, MD 20207
Government Printing Office	Sells more than 15,000 government publications on a wide variety of topics; lists those of interest to consumers in free booklet: *Consumer Information Subject Bibliography*	Superintendent of Documents Government Printing Office North Capitol and H Streets NW Washington, D.C. 20401
U.S. Postal Service	Through its Inspection Services protects public from mail fraud and other violations of postal laws; through Consumer Advocate's office acts on complaints and suggestions from individual consumers and provides information on past and present schemes used to cheat the public	Consumer Advocate U.S. Postal Service 474 L'Enfant Plaza SW Washington, D.C. 20260
U.S. Department of Agriculture	Inspects and grades meat, fish, poultry, dairy products, and fruits and vegetables through the department's Food Safety and Quality Service; ensures that food production is sanitary and that products are labeled truthfully	Office of the Consumer Adviser Administration Building U.S. Department of Agriculture Washington, D.C. 20250

Figure 3.11 Federal Agencies and Consumerism

Agency	How It Helps the Consumer	For More Information
U.S. Office of Consumer Affairs (Department of Health and Human Services)	Coordinates all federal activities on behalf of consumers, advises President on consumer affairs, and works for and testifies on behalf of consumer legislation; the Complaint Coordination Center helps solve consumer problems	U.S. Office of Consumer Affairs Humphrey Building 200 Independence Avenue Washington, D.C. 20201
Food and Drug Administration (Department of Health and Human Services)	Protects the public against impure and unsafe foods, drugs, and cosmetics; researches and tests new products in these areas and ensures accurate labeling; publishes *FDA Consumer* magazine and maintains regional consumer affairs offices	Food and Drug Administration 5600 Fishers Lane Rockville, Maryland 20857
National Highway Traffic Safety Administration (Department of Transportation)	Sets requirements for automobile safety, maintenance, and fuel economy and tests products for compliance; researches ways to save fuel and make highways safer and investigates complaints from consumers about vehicle safety	National Highway Traffic Safety Administration Department of Transportation Washington, D.C. 20590

Ethical Behavior

Consumers should respect the rights of producers and sellers of goods and services. **Ethical behavior** involves acting in accordance with one's moral and ethical convictions about right and wrong. For example, a responsible consumer will not try to return a used item because it has been advertised elsewhere for a lower price. Nor will a consumer misuse an item and then attempt to return it, saying it was defective—faulty or broken—when bought.

SECTION 3 REVIEW

Understanding Vocabulary

Define consumerism, ethical behavior.

Reviewing Objectives

1. What are the five important rights that consumers have?

2. What private and federal groups aid consumers?

3. Why should consumers learn about products they wish to buy?

4. What role does ethical behavior play in consumers' actions?

Readings in Economics

THE NEW YORK TIMES   **JUNE 6, 1993**

BEHIND THE 'CLEAR' TREND

by Barnaby J. Feder

From drinks to deodorants to dishwashing liquid, not to mention gasoline and mouthwash, the hot color for new products is no color at all.

Marketers like to have something novel to sell, but the driving force in the trend is an effort to tap into consumers' associations of clarity with health, purity, freshness and no-frills functionality. And if consumers see ... transparent antiperspirant as more "natural" than colored competitors, so much the better.

But clear products are usually as thoroughly processed as any tinted cousins, if not more so. In creating Crystal Pepsi, for example, Pepsi needed 14 months to iron out the formula and production process. Pepsi takes longer and spends more to produce the clear cola, which requires greater quality controls than the brown stuff. . . .

"This isn't rocket science," said Thomas Pirko, president of Bevmark, food and beverage consul-tants based in Los Angeles. "The technology is clearly subservient to the marketing consideration."

. . . Perhaps the clearest case of technology being subservient to marketing in the trend toward clear products is that of Crystal Clear Amoco Ultimate gasoline. The colorless premium gasoline has been on the market since 1915 in the eastern United States, originally under the White Crown name.

Only in the last five years, though, has the petroleum industry had the tools to analyze auto emissions in great detail. One result was that the Amoco Oil Company discovered that its clear gas—renamed as Crystal Clear last year—has an environmental advantage over its competitors. . . . [it] cut emissions of hydrocarbons by 13 percent.

• THINK ABOUT IT •

1. Why are "clear" products gaining popularity?

2. What is the environmental advantage of Crystal Clear Amoco?

3 *Highlights*

Consumption, Income, and Decision Making

Key Terms
consumer (p. 58)
disposable income (p. 58)
discretionary income
  (p. 58)
warranty (p. 60)
rational choice (p. 61)

Summary
  Some disposable income is discretionary and does not have to be spent on necessities. A wise consumer considers many factors before making a purchase.

Buying Principles, or Strategies

Key Terms
competitive advertising
  (p. 64)
informative advertising
  (p. 64)
bait and switch (p. 65)

generic brands (p. 66)
brand name (p. 66)
comparison shopping
  (p. 66)

Summary
  The value of a consumer's time and effort in obtaining information should not be greater than the value received from making the best choice of a product. Some advertising is informative, other advertising is mainly competitive. Before buying, consumers should practice comparison shopping.

Consumerism

Key Terms
consumerism (p. 68)
ethical behavior (p. 71)

Summary
  Consumers have important rights as well as sources of help. Private agencies and government agencies offer consumer information and assistance. Consumers also have several responsibilities, including the responsibility to behave ethically.

Identifying Key Terms

Write the letter of the definition in Column B that correctly defines each term in Column A.

Column A
1. disposable income (p. 58)
2. warranty (p. 60)
3. bait and switch (p. 65)
4. comparison shopping (p. 66)
5. competitive advertising (p. 64)

Column B
a. deceptive advertising intended to defraud the consumer
b. getting information about similar types of products and prices
c. money income left after taxes have been paid
d. attempts to persuade consumers that certain products are different and superior to others
e. written guarantee of a product for a certain period of time

Use terms from the following list to fill in the blanks in the paragraph below.

ethical behavior (p. 71)
informative advertising (p. 64)
generic brand (p. 66)
consumer (p. 58)
discretionary income (p. 58)
brand name (p. 66)

Every one of us is at one time or another a (6) . Sometimes we have (7) to spend on "fun" things. In order to make our purchases, we may use (8) , which tells us about the product. We often have the choice between a (9) and a (10) , which is usually cheaper. In any event, as a consumer, you should always be responsible and be concerned about your (11) .

Recalling Facts and Ideas

Section 1
1. After people have bought necessities, they are left with what type of income?
2. Income is one scarce resource that you use when you are a consumer. What is the other scarce resource?
3. Before you buy anything, what three questions should you ask yourself?
4. Do all rational consumers think alike? Why or why not?

Section 2
5. What are three important buying principles?
6. What are the two major types of commercial advertising?
7. How much information should you obtain before you make a purchase?
8. What type of shopping allows you to be a rational consumer?

Section 3
9. What are the major purposes of consumerism today?
10. What three types of help do federal agencies give to consumers?
11. What are the four consumer rights that President John F. Kennedy stated?
12. What are two consumer responsibilities?

Critical Thinking

Section 1
Determining Cause and Effect How might education, occupation, and health make a difference in a person's earning power (income) and therefore in his or her ability to consume?

Section 2

Analyzing Information Why do some people buy brand–name products and other people buy generic products? What are the trade-offs involved in this decision?

Section 3

Making Comparisons How do consumer rights compare with consumer responsibilities?

Applying Economic Concepts

Competition and Market Structure Choose an advertisement from a newspaper or a magazine, and use the checklist on page 64 to analyze it. Write a sentence to answer each of the questions on the checklist. Do you think it is a competitive ad, an informative ad, or both? Explain the reasons for your choice.

Reviewing Skills

Handling a Consumer Problem

1. List 10 items of information that a person should include in a letter of complaint to a product manufacturer.
2. What should consumers keep in their records when dealing with the problem of a faulty product?
3. What impact do you think your consumer complaint will have on the product manufacturer? Do you think your complaint will result in an improved product?

Chapter Projects

1. **Individual Project** Imagine that you have decided to buy a car, but you still have to decide on the size (not the make and model, but only the size). Go through the steps you would use to research your decision. Keep a record of the information you find.
2. **Cooperative Learning Project** Working in groups of four, take the Checklist for Consumer Decision Making on page 60 and the

three buying principles listed in the text and shop for one of the following: VCR, portable compact disc player, or personal computer. Each of you should keep a record of the steps you take and the information you gather using a table like the one shown. Compare your information with what others in the class found.

Checklist Number	Step	Information
1.		
2.		
3.		
4.		
5.		
6.		
7.		
8.		
9.		
10.		

Writing About Economics

Persuasive Writing Choose one of the items you purchased and recorded in Your Economics Journal. Write a persuasive letter trying to convince a friend to purchase a similar item from the same store.

Point

ISSUE: Should "Pollution Taxes" Be Used to Help the Environment and Lower the Deficit?

In 1970 the Environmental Protection Agency (EPA) was set up to combat the growing problem of pollution. After President Clinton took office in 1993, the idea of pollution taxes to help the environment and reduce the federal budget deficit gained popularity and became the subject of debate.

PRO Some of the groups in favor of pollution taxes seem to think that these taxes will not only help the environment, but will increase productivity and raise individual welfare as well.

According to the World Resources Institute, shifting 10 to 15 percent of the nation's tax burden from "goods" to "bads" could yield an annual economic "dividend" that is greater than 1 percent of annual national output. The National Commission of the Environment argues that such a tax would send the "right economic signals." The Progressive Policy Institute asserts that government regulations to help the environment end up hampering innovation in pollution control methods, while pollution taxes can promote energy efficiency and put the U.S. "on an energy path consistent with sustainable development."

Jonathan Marshall, the economics editor of the *San Francisco Chronicle*, writes in *Reason* that pollution taxes have too much potential *not* to give them a try. He feels that the benefits of such taxes are too great to ignore:

And yet, for all these objections, pollution taxes deserve a hearing among free-market advocates as a viable "second-best" strategy in the absence of some libertarians' utopia. You don't have to be a green zealot to concede that heavy smog impairs lungs and toxic compounds can kill people.... Barring an intellectual or institutional breakthrough, some form of collective action is needed to control pollution. Once that premise is accepted, pollution taxes in principle are cheaper and more effective in most instances than command-and-control regulations.

... Like any social policy, pollution taxes must be done right. Given the political system's overwhelming predisposition toward "government failure," that may be wishful thinking. But killing the idea is hardly a superior alternative if it just means accepting the status quo *by default.*

Counterpoint

CON Those against pollution taxes tend to be political conservatives, who are worried that the costs of such taxes will outweigh their benefits. Unfortunately, both costs and benefits are hard to measure; the benefits even more so than the costs. Fred Smith, president of the Competitive Enterprise Institute, expresses the concern that pollution tax schemes "look a lot better than they may turn out to be in practice."

With one particular type of pollution tax, the carbon tax (a tax based on the carbon content of fossil fuels such as gasoline), Lawrence Goulder of Stanford University questions whether the uncertain benefits will really be greater than the costs. He had been a supporter of carbon taxes, but in his study of the potential effects of the tax, he came up with higher costs and greater economic distortions than expected.

Critics also argue that carbon or energy taxes will hurt U.S. competitiveness in foreign markets, and lead to higher prices for consumers. Economist Anthony Riccardi asserts that taxes on energy are essentially regressive taxes. The working poor would be the group most severely hurt by this type of tax, as a large percentage of their income goes to costs such as gasoline and heating oil.

Writing for the *Asbury Park* (New Jersey) *Press*, Larry McDonnell points out some local criticisms of a carbon tax:

Who could argue with a tax on pollutants threatening the planet? Especially a tax that would take a big bite out of the deficit. As it turns out, many people will argue, particularly the chemical and petroleum industries, two of New Jersey's larger employers.

"Attempting to impose yesterday's costs on today's U.S.-based production undermines our international competitiveness," said Sean T. Crimmins, vice president and general tax counsel for Ashland Oil Inc., testifying before Congress this spring. "To do so at this time—in the face of already large U.S. trade deficits—is the economic equivalent of shooting oneself in the foot."

Exploring the Issue

Reviewing Facts

1. What would be the benefits of pollution taxes? What would be the costs?

2. What individuals and groups support pollution taxes? What individuals and groups oppose pollution taxes?

Critical Thinking

3. **Identifying Alternatives** What methods, other than pollution taxes, might the government use to encourage the wise use of natural resources?

What are the costs of using credit cards?

What is this card?

How does having this kind of card make shopping more convenient?

When do you think you might be offered a credit card?

What types of companies issue this kind of card?

Your Economics Journal

Keep track of the ads that you see or hear about that relate to credit and debt. List the different types of companies that advertise to offer you credit. Next to each name, indicate which companies offer credit for large purchases and which offer credit for small purchases.

SECTION 1 FOCUS

Terms to Know credit, principal, interest, installment debt, consumer durables, mortgage

Objectives *After reading this section, you should be able to:*

❶ List the advantages of repaying **installment debt** over a long period.

❷ Explain **why people use credit.**

❸ Describe how consumers **decide to use credit.**

Americans Use Credit to Make Many Purchases

For the nation as a whole, the total amount of money borrowed and lent each year is enormous. Federal, state, and local governments all borrow each year. The nation's economy depends on individuals and groups being able to buy and borrow on credit. **Credit** is the receiving of money either directly or indirectly to buy goods and services today with the promise to pay for them in the future. The amount owed—the debt—is equal to the principal plus interest. The **principal** is the amount originally borrowed. The **interest** is the amount the borrower must pay for the use of someone else's money. That someone else may be a bank, a credit card company, or a store.

Any time you receive credit, you are borrowing money and going into debt. Taking out a loan is the same as buying an item on credit. In both cases, you must pay interest for the use of someone else's purchasing power.

Figure 4.1
How Much Debt?
By how much did consumer debt increase between 1982 and 1992?

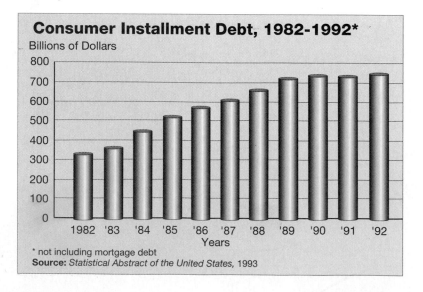

Consumer Installment Debt, 1982-1992*

Billions of Dollars

* not including mortgage debt
Source: *Statistical Abstract of the United States,* 1993

Installment Debt

One of the most common types of debt is **installment debt.** Figure 4.1 shows the change in installment debt owed each year in the United States from 1982 to 1992. Consumers repay this type of loan with equal payments, or installments, over a period of time, for example, 36 months. Many people buy such consumer durables as automobiles, refrigerators, washers, and other appliances on an installment plan. **Consumer durables** are manufactured items that people use for long periods of time before replacing them. People can also borrow cash and pay it back in installments.

The length of the installment period is important in determining the size of the borrower's monthly payments and the total amount of interest he or she must pay. A longer repayment period results in a smaller monthly payment. For example, **Figure 4.2** shows that if the repayment of a loan is spread over three years, the monthly payments will be smaller than if the loan were repaid in two years. There is a trade-off, however. The longer it takes to repay an installment loan, the greater the total interest the lender charges.

The largest form of installment debt in this country is the money people owe on mortgages. A **mortgage** is an installment debt owed on real property—houses, buildings, or land. See **Figure 4.3**.

Figure 4.2
Loan Payments
How much more interest will a borrower pay who spreads loan payments over 36 rather than 24 months? ▼

$1,000 Installment Loan at 9% Interest		
Term of Loan	24 months	36 months
Monthly Payments	$45.69	$31.80
Total Interest	$96.56	$114.80
Total Payments	$1,096.56	$1,144.80

▼ **Figure 4.3 Mortgages as Debts**
Most people who owe only a mortgage on their home or farm do not consider themselves deeply in debt. They do not think of a mortgage as being similar to other kinds of debt. A mortgage is a debt, however, because somebody has provided the owner with money to purchase property. In return, the owner must repay the loan with interest in installments over a number of years.

Why People Use Credit

Most Americans are accustomed to borrowing and buying on credit. At times, especially when buying such expensive consumer durables as automobiles and fine furniture, they consider borrowing to be necessary.

Immediate Need In a sense, people feel forced to buy items on credit because they believe they need them immediately. They do not want to wait. Of course, consumers are not really "forced" to buy most goods and services on credit. They could decide instead to save the money needed to make their purchases.

To illustrate this point, a savings bank once ran a clever advertisement on buying a truck. See **Figure 4.4**. Obviously, there is a big difference between $13,500 and $18,500. As these figures show, it is better to save now and buy later than to buy now and go into debt. The ad, however, omitted an important point. During the three-year saving period, the person would not be able to enjoy the use of the truck. Many people would not wait that long for an important durable good they want. They would rather buy on credit and enjoy the use of the item now rather than later.

Spread Payments Another reason for going into debt is to spread the payments over the life of the item being purchased. For example, people do not buy a truck or car to have it sit in the garage. What they buy is the availability of the vehicle each day, week, month, and year that they own it.

Suppose you buy a car that costs $15,000 and plan to keep it for five years. At the end of that time, it will be worth only $5,000. Over that five-year period, you will get approximately $2,000 worth of use per year, or $166 per month. By buying on the installment plan, a person makes monthly payments that more or less correspond to the value of the use he or she receives.

Figure 4.4

If a person saved for 36 months to buy a $15,000 truck, the truck would cost only $13,500. The remaining $1,500 would be made up by the interest paid on the savings over the three years. According to the ad, however, if the person bought the $15,000 truck immediately on a 36-month installment plan, the actual cost would be $18,500. The $3,500 difference would be the interest the person would have to pay on the borrowed money. In addition, the person would not receive any interest on savings.

▼

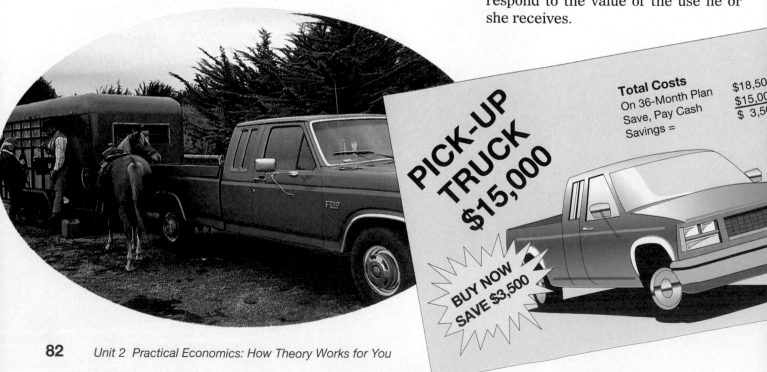

Deciding To Use Credit

Borrowing or using credit is a question of whether the satisfaction the borrower gets from the purchases is greater than the interest payments. It is basically a question of comparing costs and benefits. The benefit of borrowing is being able to buy and enjoy the good or service now rather than later. The cost is whatever the borrower must pay in interest or lost opportunities to buy other items. The benefit of borrowing is something only you can decide for yourself. You and every other borrower, however, should be aware of the costs involved.

The Checklist for Buying on Credit, **Figure 4.5** above, can help you decide when to use credit. It can also help you avoid the improper use of credit by overspending. Every day in the United States, thousands of families get into financial trouble because they have ignored the total costs of all their borrowing. They have too many credit cards and too many charge accounts and own a home that is too expensive with too large a mortgage. Just because someone offers you credit or allows you to borrow does not mean that you must accept. Buying on credit is a serious consumer activity. You should keep the information in the checklist in mind before you take the credit plunge.

Ronald Homer on Running a Bank

Profile

- 1947–
- born and raised in Brooklyn, New York
- graduated from Notre Dame with a degree in psychology
- MBA (Masters in Business Administration) from University of Rochester
- Chair and CEO of Boston Bank of Commerce, a minority-owned-and-operated bank

Ronald Homer described his efforts to make the Boston Bank of Commerce successful in *New England Business,* April 1, 1989.

The bank was an embarrassment to the community. It really wasn't serving much of a purpose, other than as a place that didn't charge you if you bounced checks. It was a bank of last resort for people who had difficulty getting checking accounts other places. . . .

At the start, we had to figure out quickly how we would stop the bleeding and make money. But more important, we had to make ourselves relevant to the community. There was an innate sense that there should be a minority-owned bank in town, and everybody wanted it. But for what purpose? Was it there to cash welfare checks, so that the large banks won't have to deal with those people? Or was it supposed to be doing something more?

Homer decided to serve the needs of the local community.

We approached all the major businesses and institutions in Roxbury and said, "We want to be your bank: what will it take?". . . Gradually, we showed them we could help in a way the other banks weren't equipped or able to do.

. . . We've grown the maximum we can grow with our capital, without raising additional capital. . . .

On the other hand, [the capital situation] has turned out to be a blessing in disguise, because had we raised capital two years ago—a public offering, for example, to raise $5 million—we would probably have been tempted like a lot of these other banks to start doing condo loans and other things. But because we were growing in a controlled area, we found enough business among our core constituency to satisfy us. . . . If we had gotten capital outside of that, we would probably have been lending money outside of our community rather than inside.

Checking for Understanding

1. What problems did the Boston Bank of Commerce face?
2. What important questions did Ronald Homer believe his bank had to answer?
3. How did the bank's financial (capital) situation help it to respond to local needs?

S E C T I O N 2 F O C U S

Terms to Know commercial bank, savings and loan association, savings banks, credit union, finance company, consumer finance company, charge account, regular charge account, credit limit, revolving charge account, installment charge account, credit card, debit card, finance charge, annual percentage rate

Objectives *After reading this section, you should be able to:*

❶ List the six **types of financial institutions**.

❷ Explain the three types of **charge accounts**.

❸ Describe how **credit and debit cards** are used.

❹ Contrast a **finance charge and the annual percentage rate**.

Lending Institutions Differ

Borrowing money directly by taking out a loan is one of the two major types of credit. Many financial institutions, including commercial banks, savings and loan associations, savings banks, credit unions, and finance and consumer finance companies grant loans. Each of these sources, however, works in the same way, by charging interest on the money it lends. The amount of interest charged can vary widely as **Figure 4.6** shows.

Types of Financial Institutions

As with other items you buy, you should comparison shop when you have decided to apply for a loan. You should check various lending agencies by visiting or phoning them to gather information, because financial institutions differ in several ways as **Figure 4.7** (pages 86–87) shows.

Figure 4.6
Interest Rates Vary
On a typical day interest rates may be higher or lower at any given lending institution.

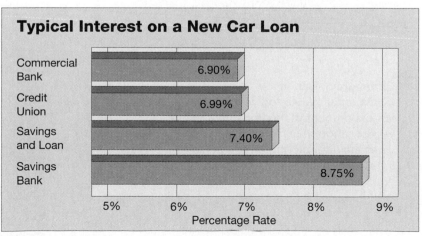

Typical Interest on a New Car Loan

Institution	Percentage Rate
Commercial Bank	6.90%
Credit Union	6.99%
Savings and Loan	7.40%
Savings Bank	8.75%

Percentage Rate (5% 6% 7% 8% 9%)

Commercial Banks The first place you might think to go for a loan is a **commercial bank.** Their main functions are to accept deposits; to lend money; and to transfer funds among banks, individuals, and businesses.

Savings and Loan Associations A **savings and loan association** (S&L), like a commercial bank, accepts deposits and lends money. When S&Ls were first established in the United States in the mid-nineteenth century, they were called "building societies." Members of a society would combine their money over a period of time and take turns borrowing until each member was able to build a home. Today, most savings deposits still come from individuals and families.

Savings Banks **Savings banks** are similar to S&Ls in that most of their business comes from savings accounts and home loans. Since 1980, savings banks, like commercial banks, have been able to offer services similar to checking accounts. Savings banks were first set up in the United States in the early nineteenth century. They were meant to serve the small savers who were overlooked by the large commercial banks.

Figure 4.7 Comparing Financial Institutions
The financial institution you choose will depend on several factors, including differences in interest rates and loan repayment terms.

A Commercial Banks ▲
Commercial banks today control the largest amount of money and offer the widest range of services. These services include offering checking, savings, and loan services to individual consumers.

B Savings and Loan Associations
Savings and loan associations make many single-family and multi-family mortgage loans. They also finance commercial mortgages and auto loans. In the 1980s federal laws permitted savings and loans to provide some of the same services as banks. ▼

Credit Unions Union members and employees of many companies often have a credit union. A **credit union** is owned and operated by its members to provide savings accounts and low-interest loans only to its members. In general, credit unions offer higher interest rates on savings and charge lower interest rates on loans than other financial institutions.

Finance Companies and Consumer Finance Companies A **finance company** takes over contracts for installment debts from stores and adds a fee for collecting the debt. The consumer pays the fee in the form of slightly higher interest than he or she would pay to the retailer. Retailers use this method to avoid the risks involved in lending money to consumers. Finance companies also make loans directly to consumers.

D Credit Unions
Credit unions primarily make personal, auto, and home improvement loans, though some larger credit unions offer home mortgages as well. They also offer share drafts, which are similar to checking accounts at commercial banks.
▼

▲
C Consumer Finance Companies
People who use consumer finance companies are usually unable to borrow from commercial banks or other sources with lower rates because of nonpayment of loans in the past or an uneven employment record. Consumer finance companies are the largest supplier of installment cash loans for purposes other than buying consumer durables.

▼ E Savings Banks
Names of savings banks often include such words as *farmers'* or *seamen's* to indicate the group for whom the bank was originally intended. The majority of savings banks are located in New England and the Mid-Atlantic states. Most of their loans are for home mortgages, although they do make personal and auto loans. Because of their small number, savings banks account for only a small percentage of the country's home mortgages and other consumer installment debt. Their interest rates for loans, like those of S&Ls, are often slightly less than those for commercial banks.

A **consumer finance company** makes loans directly to consumers at high rates of interest. These rates are often more than 20 percent a year. Some states allow consumer finance companies to charge as much as 36 percent a year on small amounts of money.

Crisis and Changes In the 1980s changes in federal laws expanded the activities of S&Ls, permitting them to offer checking-type accounts and business and consumer loans. While most loans were still used to buy homes, many S&Ls made risky commercial investments. By 1988 many S&Ls were in financial trouble. Congress set up the Resolution Trust Corporation to manage the crisis and save the S&L industry. Experts predicted that the bailout would cost the federal government and taxpayers hundreds of billions of dollars. See **Figure 4.8**.

The Resolution Trust Corporation sold off assets of failed savings and loans, bailed out other S&Ls with federal money, and stabilized the weaker institutions. The so-called bailout was the way the government began to meet its obligation to insure depositors' accounts.

When it became evident that the Federal Deposit Insurance Corporation had nearly depleted its funds, the agency voted to increase its insurance premiums. This meant that lending institutions would have to pay more for FDIC coverage.

▼ **Figure 4.8**
The Bailout
The Resolution Trust Corporation continued to ask Congress for more and more money to bail out S&Ls. Taxpayers began to wonder whether the bailout would ever end.

Charge Accounts

A major type of credit is extended directly to an individual, without that person's having to borrow money first. This credit may be in the form of a charge account or a credit card. A **charge account** allows a customer to buy goods or services from a particular company and pay for them later. Department stores, for example, offer their customers three basic types of charge accounts: regular, revolving, or installment.

Regular Charge Accounts A **regular charge account,** also known as a 30-day charge, has a credit limit such as $500 or $1,000. A **credit limit** is the maximum amount of goods or services a person or business can buy on the promise to pay in the future. The cardholder and usually any member of his or her family can charge items up to this limit. At the end of every 30-day period, the store sends a bill for the entire amount. No interest is charged, but the entire bill must be paid at that time. If it is not, interest is charged on that part of the account.

Revolving Charge Accounts A **revolving charge account** allows you to make additional purchases from the same store even if you have not paid the previous month's bill in full. See **Figure 4.9**. Usually you must pay a certain portion of your balance each month, for instance one-fifth of the amount due. Interest is charged on the

◄ **Figure 4.9**
Store Charge Cards
Stores allow their customers to choose regular, revolving, or installment accounts. They all allow consumers to purchase more now, but with the latter two customers must normally pay interest.

amount you do not pay. Of course, if you pay everything you owe each month, no interest is charged. This type of account also has a credit limit.

Installment Charge Accounts Major items such as couches, televisions, and refrigerators are often purchased through an **installment charge account.** The items are purchased and paid for through equal payments spread over a period of time. Part of the amount paid each month is applied to the interest, and part is applied to the principal. At the end of the payment period, the borrower owns whatever he or she has made payments on.

Credit and Debit Cards

A **credit card**, like a charge account, allows a person to make purchases without paying cash. The difference is that credit cards can be used at many kinds of stores, restaurants, hotels, and other businesses throughout the United States and even foreign countries. Visa, MasterCard, and others issue cards through banks. These cards can be used to purchase items in stores that accept them, or they may be used to borrow money, up to a certain limit. This gives consumers access to loans at all times without having to apply for them. So many cards have been marketed that it is not unusual for a person to have several different kinds. **Figure 4.10** illustrates sample credit and charge cards.

Credit cards usually charge high interest. In the early 1990s, banks

Figure 4.10
The Credit Card Trade-Off

Individual stores, such as Pier I and Home Depot, issue their own charge cards, which consumers may use to purchase goods. Consumers may also use credit cards, such as MasterCard and Optima. Although using credit cards is convenient, it is also costly. Stores must pay a certain percentage of credit purchases to the credit card company or bank that issued the card. The stores include this cost in the price they charge customers, making prices higher for everyone.

▼

charged an average of 18 percent on MasterCard and Visa. The high interest rates eventually brought additional issuers into the market. Sears, Roebuck & Co. issued its Discover Card. General Electric Co. and General Motors joined American Telephone & Telegraph in issuing cards with more attractive interest rates and other benefits.

Gradually the competition brought credit card interest rates down, but one factor kept rates from dropping very low—bad loans. Visa and MasterCard issuers charge off almost 25 percent of the revenues collected in bad loans. Because of this some issuers began to offer lower rates to special categories of customers who they believed were more reliable.

A **debit card** does not provide a loan. Instead it makes cashless purchases easier by enabling the customer to transfer funds electronically. Debit cards were first available in the 1970s, but they did not catch on with the public. Popular use of automated

teller machines (ATMs) has paved the way for acceptance of debit cards. In 1992 Visa and MasterCard launched a campaign to sign up banks combining their credit cards with debit cards.

Finance Charges and Annual Percentage Rates

The terms *finance charge* and *annual percentage rate* tell the consumer the same thing—the cost of credit—but each is expressed in a different way.

Finance Charges The **finance charge** is the cost of credit expressed in dollars and cents. It must take into account interest costs plus any other charges connected with credit. For example, yearly membership fees for the use of a credit card are included in the finance charge.

Computing Finance Charges The way finance charges are computed is an important factor in determining the cost of credit. The method can vary from creditor to creditor. Store charge accounts and credit cards use one of four methods to determine how much people will pay for credit: previous balance, average daily balance,

Figure 4.11 Different Methods for Computing Finance Charges

Type of Method	How Finance Charge Is Computed	Example (Based on opening balance of $300, $150 paid halfway through month, monthly interest rate=1.5%)		
Previous Balance	Charge is computed on the month's opening balance, even if the bill has been paid in full by the time the finance charge is figured. There is no benefit in paying off a debt early with this method.	Amount on which interest is due:	$300, despite payment	
		Calculation:	$300 x .015 = $4.50	
		Finance charge:	$4.50	
		Balance due:	$154.50	
Adjusted Balance	Payments made during the month are deducted from the opening balance. Charge is then computed on the balance due the last day of the month. With this method you are best off paying your bill as soon as possible.	Amount on which interest is due:	$150, balance on last day of billing period	
		Calculation:	$150 x .015 = $2.25	
		Finance charge:	$2.25	
		Balance due:	$152.25	
Average Daily Balance	Charge is applied to the sum of the actual amounts owed each day during the billing period, divided by the number of days in that period. Payments and credits–return of goods–are subtracted on the exact date of payment. With this method you are best off paying your bill as soon as possible.	Amount on which interest is due:	$225	
		Calculation:	15 days x $300 = $4,500	
			15 days x $150 = $2,250	
			30 days total = $6,750	
			$6,750÷30 = $225	
			$225 x .015 = $3.38	
		Finance charge:	$3.38	
		Balance due:	$153.38	
Past Due Balance	No finance charge is applied if full payment is received within a certain period, usually within 25 days after the date of the last billing statement. If full payment is not received, then a finance charge for the unpaid amount is added to the next month's bill.	Amount on which interest is due:	$0	
		Calculation:	$150 x 0 = 0	
		Finance charge:	$0	
		Balance due:	$150.00	
		Finance charge of $2.25 (.015 x $150) will be added to next month's bill		

adjusted balance, or past due balance. Each method applies the interest rate to an account's balance at a different point during the month. The different methods can result in widely varying finance charges. **Figure 4.11** describes these four methods for computing and shows the difference in finance charges that can result. Creditors must inform their customers in writing of which method they use for computing finance charges.

Annual Percentage Rates The **annual percentage rate** (APR) is the cost of credit expressed as a yearly percentage. Like the finance charge, the APR must take into account any non-interest costs of credit such as a membership fee. **Figure 4.12** shows how a sample APR affects the cost of credit.

Understanding and using APRs makes it easier to shop around for the best deal on credit. For example, if you are looking for a car, creditor A might ask for a large down payment and offer in return small monthly payments. Creditor B might not require a down payment at all, but charge large monthly payments instead. Creditor C might ask for small payments over a much longer period of time.

Knowing which creditor is charging the most for credit would be very difficult without some guide for comparison. The APR provides that guide by allowing consumers to compare costs regardless of the dollar amount of those costs or the length of the credit agreement. Suppose creditor A is charging an APR of 16 percent, while creditor B is charging 17 percent, and creditor C is charging 18½ percent. On a yearly basis, creditor C is charging the most for credit and creditor A the least.

Figure 4.12 ▶
Annual Percentage Rates
Say you charge $200 worth of clothes. The interest rate charged to you, let's say, is 10 percent, but the annual fee for the credit card is $5. Your APR will be $20 of interest plus the $5 fee, or 12½ percent. The APR is normally larger than the interest because it includes the noninterest cost of extending credit.

Credit Card Charge of $200 at 10% Interest		
Amount Charged	$200.00	$200.00
Interest at 10%	$20.00	$20.00
Annual Membership Fee	none	$5.00
APR	10%	12.5%

SECTION 2 REVIEW

Understanding Vocabulary
Define commercial bank, savings and loan association, savings banks, credit union, finance company, consumer finance company, charge account, regular charge account, credit limit, revolving charge account, installment charge account, credit card, debit card, finance charge, annual percentage rate.

Reviewing Objectives
1. What are the six types of financial institutions?
2. How do regular, revolving, and installment charge accounts differ?
3. How are credit and debit cards used?
4. How is a finance charge different from an annual percentage rate?

SECTION **3** *Applying for Credit*

SECTION 3 FOCUS

Terms to Know credit bureau, credit check, credit rating, collateral, secured loan, unsecured loan, cosigner, past-due notices

Objectives *After reading this section, you should be able to:*
1. Explain the four factors that determine a person's **credit rating.**
2. List your **responsibilities as a borrower.**

Several Factors Determine a Person's Credit Worthiness

When you apply for credit, you usually will be asked to fill out a credit application. Once you have filled out the application, the store, bank, or other lending agency will hire a **credit bureau,** a private business, to do a **credit check.** This investigation will reveal your income, any current debts, details about your personal life, and how well you have repaid debts in the past.

The Credit Rating

The information supplied by the credit bureau provides the creditor with a **credit rating** for you. This is a rating of the risk—good, average, or poor—involved in lending money to a specific person or business. If a person has a history of poor credit

Figure 4.13
Three Credit Check Factors

A Capacity to Pay
Capacity to pay is related to income and debt. If your employment has been spotty, your capacity to pay will be considered questionable. The amount of debt that you are already carrying is also a factor. If your debts are large, creditors will be reluctant to loan you more. ◀

use—usually late in paying debts—he or she will receive a poor credit rating. As a result, the creditor reviewing the credit check will be less willing to lend that person money.

Though past history of credit use is important in deciding a person's creditworthiness, the creditor also looks at three other factors that a credit check reveals. These are: capacity to pay, character, and collateral (kuh-LAT-uh-ruhl). **Figure 4.13** examines these three factors.

Secured Loans Usually when a bank, S&L, or other financial institution makes a loan, it will ask for collateral from the borrower. The **collateral** may be the item purchased with the loan money, such as a house or car. It may be something of value the borrower already owns. For example, a borrower might offer his or her car as collateral to obtain cash for home im-

provements. The borrower then signs a legal agreement allowing the lender to claim the collateral if the loan is not repaid. A loan that is backed up with collateral in this way is called a **secured loan.**

Unsecured Loans Usually a young person will have little to offer as collateral. When dealing with a trusted customer, financial institutions will sometimes lend money on the person's reputation alone. Such a loan is called an **unsecured loan.** It is not guaranteed by anything other than a promise to repay it. Most young people have not had enough experience

B Character ▶
Character refers to a person's reputation as a reliable and trustworthy person—educational background, whether or not he or she has had any problems with the law, and any other factors that might indicate something questionable.

◀ **C Collateral**
Lenders also consider collateral. The size of your capital, or personal wealth, is important because it indicates your past ability to save and accumulate. It also indicates your present ability to pay off a loan, even if you lose your job, because you could sell some of your belongings in order to make the payments.

◀ **Figure 4.14**
Cosigning a Loan
A bank will sometimes lend money to a person without a financial reputation if he or she has a cosigner. A **cosigner** is a person who signs a loan contract along with the borrower and promises to repay the loan if the borrower does not.

with borrowing and repaying money to have established this type of trust. See **Figure 4.14**.

Your Responsibilities as a Borrower

Once you have applied for credit and obtained it, you have also taken on responsibilities. After all, the businesses that gave you credit expect to earn a profit, although in earning that profit they are helping you satisfy your consumer needs by allowing you to buy goods and services on credit.

Paying on Time If you do not pay your debts on time, the costs to businesses are higher. At the very least, there will be extra mailing costs to send **past-due notices.** The business that lends you money may have to hire a collection agency to help get back the money loaned to you. If you never pay off your debt, the lending institution has to write it off and take a loss.

When lending institutions end up paying higher costs, they have to pass these costs on to all consumers in the form of higher prices—higher interest rates charged. Ethical consumers pay their debts on time except under extraordinary circumstances.

Another thing happens when you do not pay your debts. You get a bad credit history. You may then have a difficult or impossible time when you really need credit for something else, say, to purchase a house. Consumers who cannot obtain credit sometimes find it difficult to achieve their personal goals.

Keeping Records If you applied for a credit card and got one, you have additional responsibilities. You need to keep a complete record of all the charges you made. This way you will not go over your credit limit in any one month. You also have the responsibility of notifying the credit-card issuer immediately if your card is lost or stolen.

SECTION 3 REVIEW

Understanding Vocabulary
Define credit bureau, credit check, credit rating, collateral, secured loan, unsecured loan, cosigner, past-due notices.

Reviewing Objectives
1. What four factors determine a person's credit rating?
2. What are your responsibilities as a borrower?

Determining a Safe Debt Load

At some time in your life, you will most likely use credit. Everyone does. Do you know how to determine your *safe debt load*--the amount of debt you can safely afford after paying for necessities?

Determining Your Safe Debt Load

To figure out the amount of credit debt that is safe for you to carry, follow these steps, as shown in **Figure A**, Smith Family Safe Debt Load:

1. List your total annual income after taxes. Include any gifts from parents and friends.
2. Estimate your total annual expenses for the necessities of housing, food, clothing, and transportation.
3. Subtract the total from your after-tax income.
4. Divide the difference by three. This is your "safe debt load." (By dividing by three, this calculation takes unforeseen expenses into consideration.

This safe debt load is the amount of credit debt you can safely afford. Look at **Figure B**. It shows the amount of credit carried by the Smith family. Note that their present credit debt is more than their safe debt load. It would not be wise for the Smiths to assume additional credit at this time.

Practicing the Skill

1. Charlene's after-tax income is $24,250. Her annual expenses for necessities are $6,500 for housing, $4,250 for food, $1,100 for clothing, and $750 for transportation. What is her safe debt load?
2. She currently has no credit debt. Can she safely afford to buy a new car with monthly loan payments of $250? Why or why not?

Figure A

Smith Family Safe Debt Load

Total annual after-tax income	$ 21,750
Annual expenses for:	
housing	$ 5,000
food	$ 3,750
clothing	$ 1,250
transportation	$ 500
TOTAL ANNUAL EXPENSES	$ 10,500
Subtract expenses from income	$ 11,250
Divide difference by 3 to determine safe debt load	$ 3,750

Figure B

Smith Family Credit Debt (per month)

Car payments	$ 225
Payment on store revolving charge account	$ 46
Payment on credit cards	$ 52
Payment on loan for last year's vacation	$ 41
MONTHLY TOTAL	$ 364

Total for year $364 x 12 = $4,368

SECTION 4 Government Regulation of Credit

SECTION 4 FOCUS

Terms to Know usury law, bankruptcy

Objectives *After reading this section, you should be able to:*

1. State how the **Equal Credit Opportunity Act** affected consumer credit.
2. Describe **state usury laws**.
3. Explain why a person might declare **personal bankruptcy**.

The Government Regulates Credit to Protect Consumers

Both the federal and state governments regulate the credit industry. Most states, for example, have set a maximum on the interest rates charged for certain types of credit. The federal government has also passed laws designed to increase the flow of credit information to consumers and to protect consumers from unfair credit practices.

The Truth in Lending Act of 1968 was the first of a series of major federal laws that greatly expanded the government's role in protecting users of consumer credit. An important aspect of the government regulation of credit is to make sure that everyone has equal access.

The Equal Credit Opportunity Act

In 1974 Congress enacted the Equal Credit Opportunity Act (ECOA) as an addition to the Truth in Lending Act of 1968. Among other things, those who provide credit cannot deny you such credit solely on the basis of your race, religion, national origin, gender, marital status, or age. In addition, no one is allowed to discriminate against you in offering you credit simply because your income might come from public assistance benefits.

Because there had been so much credit discrimination against married women, the 1974 Credit Act made it illegal for a creditor to require an applicant's spouse to sign unless an application for credit was made jointly by husband and wife. See **Figure 4.15**. If a woman on her own qualifies for the amount and terms of credit requested, she does not have to get her husband to sign the credit application. **Figure 4.16** (pages 100–101) presents the important points about five major federal government laws that regulate credit.

State Usury Laws

A law restricting the amount of interest that can be charged for credit is called a **usury** (YOOZH-uh-ree) **law.** Often states set up different maximum rates for different types of consumer credit. Maximum rates on charge accounts and credit cards, for example, are often about 18 percent a year, or 1½ percent per month. Consumer finance agencies, in contrast, are often allowed to charge higher rates because their loans involve higher risks.

Interest Ceilings The ceilings for usury laws were controversial in past years when interest ceilings in many states were as low as 6 or 10 percent. When interest rates in general began to rise in the early 1970s, many lenders complained that they could not keep within such ceilings and still make a profit. In states that were slow to raise interest ceilings, some lenders cut back on the amount of credit they offered. Others stopped lending money completely. Many consumers, particularly those who were poor credit risks, found it hard to obtain credit. People opposed to raising interest ceilings claimed people with lower incomes would not be able to afford credit. Supporters of higher ceilings claimed that low rates made credit less available because it was less profitable for lenders. Low rates actually hurt those they were supposed to help.

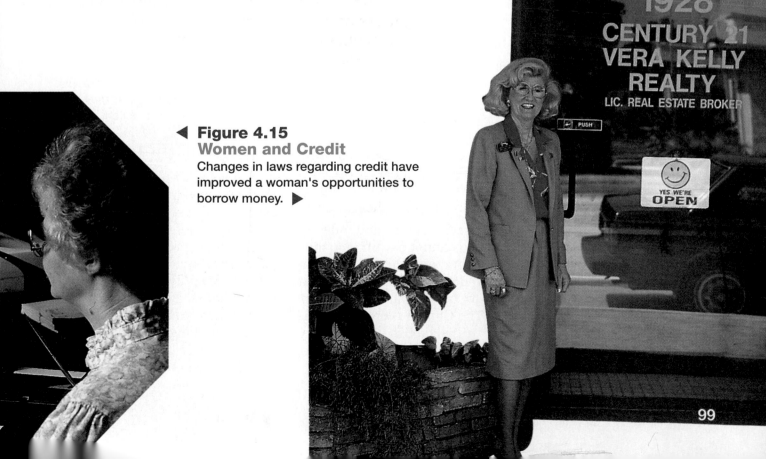

◀ **Figure 4.15**
Women and Credit
Changes in laws regarding credit have improved a woman's opportunities to borrow money. ▶

99

Figure 4.16 Major Federal Laws Regulating Consumer Credit

Name of Law	Main Purpose	Major Provisions
Truth in Lending Act (1968)	Ensures that consumers are fully informed about the costs and conditions of borrowing	<ul><li>Creditors must keep borrowers informed in writing of a credit agreement's annual percentage rate, the way charges and fees are calculated, and the payment schedule.</li><li>Borrowers must be told 15 days in advance of any changes in the items listed above.</li><li>Consumers have a 3-day cooling-off period in which to cancel certain contracts.</li><li>Consumers are liable for only the first $50 in unauthorized purchases made on a credit card before it is reported lost or stolen.</li></ul>
Fair Credit Reporting Act (1970)	Protects the privacy and accuracy of information in a credit check	<ul><li>If refused credit, a consumer can request from the lender the name and address of the credit bureau issuing the report.</li><li>The credit bureau, if requested, must provide at least a summary of a consumer's credit file.</li><li>If the consumer claims part of the file is in error, the bureau must correct the record or explain why it thinks the information is correct.</li><li>A consumer can have a statement of disagreement placed in his or her file about the item.</li><li>Outdated information must be removed from a consumer's file.</li><li>Credit records can be shown only to those with a true business need.</li></ul>
Equal Credit Opportunity Act (1974)	Prohibits discrimination in giving credit on the basis of sex, race, color, religion, national	<ul><li>The same guidelines for credit worthiness must be applied to all borrowers.</li><li>Lenders cannot extend credit to an individual on terms different from those given another individual in a similar economic situation.</li></ul>

Personal Bankruptcy

If you take out too many loans, use too many credit cards, and pile up debts that you cannot pay off, you may have to file personal **bankruptcy.** In bankruptcy, debtors give most of what they own to be distributed to their creditors. The Constitution authorizes Congress to establish bankruptcy laws. Certain debts, such as taxes, cannot be discharged.

If you declare personal bankruptcy, you may have a fresh start. Be aware, however, that it is very difficult to reestablish credit as long as the bankruptcy proceedings remain on your credit record. That is why choosing bankruptcy to get out of your credit "mess" should be a last resort. Also, when you declare bankruptcy, you are making sure that your creditors will never be paid off (at least not in full) for what they loaned you.

Figure 4.16 Major Federal Laws Regulating Consumer Credit

Name of Law	Main Purpose	Major Provisions
Equal Credit Opportunity Act (1974) (cont.)	origin, marital status, age, or receipt of public assistance	■ Questions about age, sex, and marital status can be asked only if those questions relate directly to a person's ability to repay a loan. ■ Loan applicants must receive notice of a decision within 30 days. If the loan is denied, the lender must give the reasons or inform the applicant of the right to request the information.
Fair Credit Billing Act (1974)	Sets up a procedure for the quick correction of mistakes that appear on consumer credit accounts	■ Consumers may challenge a billing statement for errors. ■ Consumers have 60 days to notify a creditor of a disputed item. The creditor must investigate and either correct the mistake or explain why the charge is not an error. ■ While the mistake is checked, the consumer can withhold payment of the disputed sum but must pay for other items on the account. ■ Under certain circumstances, a consumer can withhold payment for merchandise that has been purchased and found defective. ■ Creditors must supply consumers with a statement of their rights under the act.
Fair Debt Collection Practices Act (1977)	Prevents abuse by professional debt collectors; applies to anyone employed to collect debts owed to others; does not apply to banks or other businesses that collect their own accounts	■ Collectors can contact a person other than the debtor only to discover the debtor's location. ■ The debtor cannot be contacted at an inconvenient time or place. ■ All harassing behavior is prohibited. This includes the use or threat of violence, the use of annoying or repetitive phone calls, etc.

SECTION 4 REVIEW

Understanding Vocabulary
Define usury law, bankruptcy.

Reviewing Objectives
❶ What are the major provisions of the Equal Credit Opportunity Act?

❷ Why do many states have usury laws?

❸ Why might a person declare personal bankruptcy?

Readings in Economics

DATELINE: CHANGING TIMES   **MARCH 1991**

DIGGING OUT OF THE DEBT TRAP

— *by Kristin Davis and Rebecca Little* —

It's no surprise that consumer credit counselors say they're getting busier. Here's what they advise for consumers overwhelmed with debt.

Don't avoid creditors. Instead of skipping a payment, contact creditors to explain why you can't pay. "Creditors will fall off their chairs if you contact them first," says Tom Hufford, executive director of the Consumer Credit Counseling Service (CCCS) of Northeastern Indiana. They have a lot of latitude early on, he says, to temporarily waive or reduce payments.

Beware of consolidation loans. Many people hope to stretch out payments over a

longer period with a consolidation loan. But the finance companies that offer those loans typically charge high interest rates. Using a home-equity loan for this purpose may seem an ideal solution—interest rates are relatively low and inter-

est on up to $100,000 is tax-deductible. But your home is collateral and you risk losing it if you fall behind. Warns Hufford: "You start again with zero balances on your credit cards, and old habits die hard."

Work out your own plan. Although secured creditors may not be as flexible, unsecured creditors may be receptive to a revised payment plan. William Kent Brunette, author of *Conquer Your Debt*, suggests figuring out how much you can afford to pay toward all debts monthly and prorating payments based on how much you owe each creditor. Assure creditors that they're all being treated equally and that you won't take on new debt until the accounts are paid, he advises. . . .

Seek credit counseling. If bill collectors' calls get unpleasant, contact a CCCS. These nonprofit agencies can serve as a buffer between you and anxious creditors.

• THINK ABOUT IT •

1. What four major things do the authors urge indebted consumers to do?

2. What is the drawback of a consolidation loan?

Highlights

Americans and Credit

Key Terms

credit (p. 80)
principal (p. 80)
interest (p. 80)

installment debt (p. 80)
consumer durables (p. 80)
mortgage (p. 81)

Summary

Repaying an installment debt over a long period provides some advantages to the borrower. People use credit for a variety of reasons. In all cases, however, consumers must carefully decide whether to use credit as well as how much to use.

Sources of Loans and Credit

Key Terms

commercial bank (p. 86)
savings and loan
    association (p. 86)
savings banks (p. 86)
credit union (p. 87)
finance company (p. 87)
consumer finance
    company (p. 88)

charge account (p. 89)
regular charge account
    (p. 89)
credit limit (p. 89)
revolving charge account
    (p. 89)
installment charge
    account (p. 90)
credit card (p. 90)
debit card (p. 91)
finance charge (p. 91)
annual percentage rate
    (p. 93)

Summary

Consumers who wish to borrow money may choose from among six types of financial institutions. Consumers who wish to open a charge account may choose between a regular, a revolving, or an installment account. In all cases, consumers should realize that the annual percentage rate is not the same as the stated finance charge.

Applying for Credit

Key Terms

credit bureau (p. 94)
credit check (p. 94)
credit rating (p. 94)
collateral (p. 95)

secured loan (p. 95)
unsecured loan (p. 95)
cosigner (p. 96)
past-due notices (p. 96)

Summary

Several factors are considered when financial institutions determine a person's credit rating. Once a person is granted credit, he or she has a responsibility to use it wisely.

Government Regulation of Credit

Key Terms

usury law (p. 99)
bankruptcy (p. 100)

Summary

The Equal Credit Opportunity Act prohibits discrimination in lending based upon several factors. Many states have usury laws that also protect borrowers. Borrowers who overextend their credit may choose to declare personal bankruptcy.

Review

Identifying Key Terms

Write a short paragraph about the different types of lending institutions and their differences using all of the following terms.

commercial bank (p. 86)   credit union (p. 87)
savings banks (p. 86)   consumer finance
                           company (p. 88)

Write the letter of the definition in Column B below that correctly defines each term in Column A.

Column A
1. principal (p. 80)
2. usury law (p. 99)
3. collateral (p. 95)
4. annual percentage rate (p. 93)
5. unsecured loan (p. 95)

Column B
a. restricts the amount of interest that can be charged for credit
b. requires only a promise to repay
c. amount of money borrowed in a loan
d. something of value that a borrower uses as a promise of loan repayment
e. cost of credit expressed as a yearly percentage

Recalling Facts and Ideas

Section 1
1. What do you have to pay when you borrow?
2. How is taking out a loan similar to buying an item on credit?
3. People typically use installment debt to buy what type of goods?
4. Why do people use credit?

Section 2
5. What are the six types of basic lending insti-

tutions in our economy?
6. What are some of the most common types of credit cards used today?
7. When you take out a loan, what do you call the total cost of credit expressed in dollars and cents?

Section 3
8. When you make an application for a loan, what are four factors that a creditor looks at to determine whether you are creditworthy?
9. What is the difference between a secured and unsecured loan?
10. What are your responsibilities as a borrower?

Section 4
11. What does the Equal Credit Opportunity Act of 1974 prohibit?
12. States often restrict the maximum amount of interest that can be charged on loans. What are such laws called?
13. What are the three important federal laws regulating consumer credit?

Critical Thinking

Section 1
Evaluating Information In deciding whether to pay cash or use credit for a personal purchase, what are the costs involved and the benefits of each choice?

Section 2
Identifying Alternatives How would you decide which of the six types of lending institutions discussed in this section would be most appropriate for a particular loan?

Section 3

Making Comparisons What are the differences between a secured and an unsecured loan?

Section 4

Demonstrating Reasoned Judgment If you declare personal bankruptcy, your creditors clearly lose. What ethical concerns should you have before ever taking this action?

Applying Economic Concepts

The Role of Government Sometimes credit cards are lost or stolen. The owner must take steps to keep his or her card from being used by an unauthorized person. Find out by researching the Truth in Lending Act what a credit card holder must do when his or her card is lost or stolen.

Chapter Projects

1. **Individual Project** Call various retail stores in your area as well as some gas stations and ask them to send you a credit card application. Write a list of the questions asked that are virtually the same on each application.
2. **Cooperative Learning Project** Work in small groups to create a loan application that is appropriate for high school students and circulate it in class. Based on the application, discuss why it is or is not difficult to decide who should receive loans. Is it difficult to decide who should *not* receive loans?

Reviewing Skills

Determining a Safe Debt Load

1. Look at the table below. What is this family's safe debt load?
2. How much more can this family safely take on in debt?

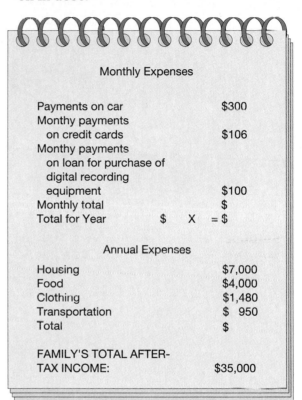

Monthly Expenses			
Payments on car			$300
Monthy payments on credit cards			$106
Monthy payments on loan for purchase of digital recording equipment			$100
Monthly total			$
Total for Year	$	X	= $

Annual Expenses	
Housing	$7,000
Food	$4,000
Clothing	$1,480
Transportation	$ 950
Total	$

FAMILY'S TOTAL AFTER-TAX INCOME:	$35,000

Writing About Economics

Persuasive Writing Write a letter to the editor about the positive or negative effects of credit on the American economy and on consumers. Refer to Your Economics Journal to mention the kinds of advertising on TV and radio that relate to credit and debt.

BUYING THE NECESSITIES: FOOD AND CLOTHING

How often do you buy a jacket?

How long will the jacket last?

Does each jacket's price have anything to do with how long it will last?

Why does the style of jackets change?

What happens to the value of a jacket when it is out of style?

Your Economics Journal

Keep track of where your parents purchase food over a period of one week. List the types of food stores and the items purchased for each type. Next to each type of food store indicate why your parents went there.

1 Shopping for Food

SECTION 1 FOCUS

Terms to Know warehouse food store, convenience stores, private-labeled products

Objectives *After reading this section, you should be able to:*
1. Describe the advantages of **comparison food shopping.**
2. List the three major types of **food stores.**

Grocery Shopping Is a Skill You Can Learn

Because of our diverse ethnic groups, Americans consume a great variety of foods. They can choose from thousands of different food products and buy them at thousands of stores. Hundreds of brands offer numerous choices: sliced carrots, whole carrots, carrots with peas—canned or frozen. In all, American consumers spend hundreds of billions of dollars a year on food.

Comparison Shopping

Because American families spend so much for food, comparison shopping is important. A consumer should, however, do only as much comparison shopping as is worthwhile to that person. It does not pay a shopper to go far out of his or her way to shop at a store that has only a few needed items at low prices. Such savings would be outweighed by the additional costs of time and transportation.

Reading advertisements is a good, inexpensive way to comparison shop. Food store ads describe sales and often contain cents-off coupons.

Comparison shopping involves making comparisons among brands and sizes as well as stores. You need to decide not only where to shop but what to shop for. **Figure 5.1** will also be a useful guide.

Food Stores

Figure 5.2 shows the three major types of stores. Each has its own characteristics.

Checklist

Figure 5.1
Food Shopping

The following are some helpful tips for getting the most from your money when you food shop.

1. Read the newspapers ahead of time for sales and cents-off coupons.

2. Go with a shopping list and your coupons. If possible, plan your week's meals before you shop so that you will buy only what you need. A list will also help you avoid additional trips to the store for items that you forgot.

3. Avoid impulsive buying, or buying without thinking about the purchase beforehand. Be especially careful in the checkout line because stores often place special offers for nonessential items such as cookies and gum by the cash register.

4. Check labels on canned and frozen goods for nutritional value.

5. Check freshness dates on dairy and bakery items.

6. Compare prices on private, generic, and national brands.

7. Check unit prices. Buy large sizes only if you will be able to use the items immediately or can store them.

8. Do not shop when you are hungry. You will be tempted to buy snack foods.

Figure 5.2
Major Types of Food Stores
Where you choose to shop for food regularly can have a major impact on your budget.

B Warehouse Food Store
The **warehouse food store** has only a *limited number of brands and items*. They are less expensive than in supermarkets, however. In many warehouse stores, goods are *sold only by the case*. Therefore, warehouse food stores are best for consumers who can buy in large quantities. ▼

C Convenience Stores
Convenience stores seem to be everywhere. They are usually open 16 to 24 hours a day and carry a limited selection of items. The price per unit of almost anything is higher than in a supermarket or warehouse store because consumers are paying for the cost of convenience. ▼

A Supermarkets
Just about anything in the way of meats, fresh vegetables, paper products, canned goods, and so on, can be bought in a supermarket. Prices may be relatively high, however, so it is important to be aware of supermarket sales.

Brand-Name Products Versus Private-Labeled Products When you go shopping in virtually any food store, many of the food items have well-known brand names. Some food stores also carry regional brands that are found only in certain areas of the country.

As an alternative to expensive national brands, some big supermarket chains as well as club wholesale chains carry their own store-brand products. These are also called **private-labeled products.** According to some consumer surveys, it is possible to save as much as 40 percent by buying store-brand (private-labeled) products. As **Figure 5.3** shows, you can save even more when you buy generic or bulk items.

The Trade-Off Between Price, Quantity, and Quality There is often a trade-off between quality and price in the products you buy. A lower-priced generic dishwasher soap might leave a slight film on your drinking glasses compared to a more expensive national-brand alternative.

Often you will find that the larger the quantity of any item you buy in a supermarket, the lower the per-unit price. Most states require stores to provide unit pricing for food and other products. That makes it easy to compare prices not only for different brands, but for different sizes of the same brand. For example, the price of milk might be expressed in terms of cents per ounce. You can then tell how much you save per ounce if you buy milk in larger containers.

Cents-Off Coupons Many manufacturers give cents-off coupons as shown in **Figure 5.4.** To take advantage of them, a consumer has to buy the brand, size, and quantity named on the coupon. The store then reduces the price paid by the amount printed on the coupon. The manufacturer, in turn, pays the store.

Convenience Foods In most food stores, you can buy either foods that require preparation, such as fresh meat and vegetables, or foods that require little or no preparation, such as complete frozen dinners. The latter are called convenience foods and usually require no work other than heating. Some nutritionists (noo-TRISH-uh-nists)—experts on food and health—believe that convenience foods are

Figure 5.3
Generic and Bulk Foods
Some food products are available in brand-name, store-label, generic, or bulk form. Generally, price decreases in that order. ▼

BRAND NAME
Rice
$2.59
32 OZ.

STORE BRAND
Rice
$1.29
32 OZ.

GENERIC
Rice
$1.09
32 OZ.

BULK
Rice
$ .89
32 o

unhealthful. They believe they contain too many added chemicals, too much sugar, and too many preservatives. The economic issue involved is time.

The purchase of a convenience food involves a trade-off. Convenience foods are more expensive than foods that you must prepare. Because of the higher price you pay when you buy convenience foods, you sacrifice the purchase of other goods and services. You are gaining more time for leisure or making extra money, however, because convenience foods require less work. Convenience foods illustrate one of the situations in which the consumer must choose between having more free time or having more money to spend on other items.

◀ **Figure 5.4**
Coupon Trade-Off
If you make a habit of using coupons, you can reduce your food bill by more than 10 percent over a one-year period. The use of such coupons, however, requires time—the time to collect and match them to items when shopping. Because time is a scarce resource, you have to decide if the money you save using coupons is worth the time you spend.

SECTION 1 REVIEW

Understanding Vocabulary
Define warehouse food store, convenience stores, private-labeled products.

Reviewing Objectives
❶ What are the advantages of comparison food shopping?

❷ How do the three kinds of food stores differ?

Personal Perspective

Barbara Ward on Saving Our Resources for the Future

Profile

- 1914-1981
- born in England
- educated in France, Germany, and England
- lectured on the growing gap between the rich nations and the poor nations
- authored many books, including *The West at Bay* (1948), *Nationalism and Ideology* (1967), *The Rich Nations and the Poor Nations* (1962), *Spaceship Earth* (1966), and *Only One Earth* (1972) with René Dubos

Ward's earlier works, such as *The Rich Nations and the Poor Nations*, emphasized the growing gap between the wealth of different countries. Her later works, including *Only One Earth* excerpted below, extended her ideas to look at the availability of resources such as energy for the future.

... But the really new risk, foreseen in the past by only a few of the world's economists, is that such a pressure of rising demand may begin to put intolerable strains on what had appeared to be the planet's limitless resources. This risk had been masked in the thrusting nineteenth century by the opening up of all the planet's temperate lands to European settlement and later by the extraordinary productivity of new forms of energy and chemical transformations.

Ward offers ideas for planning for the future.

... The first step toward devising a strategy for planet Earth is for the nations to accept a collective responsibility for discovering more— much more—about the natural system and how it is affected by man's activities and vice versa. This implies cooperative monitoring, research, and study on an unprecedented scale. It implies an intensive world-wide network for the systematic exchange of knowledge and experience.

... Here again, no one nation, not even groups of nations, can, acting separately, avoid the tragedy of increasing divisions between wealthy north and poverty-stricken south in our planet. No nations, on their own, can offset the risk of deepening disorder.... Either they will move on to a community based upon a more systematic sharing of wealth—through progressive income tax, through general policies for education, shelter, health, and housing—or they will break down in revolt and anarchy.

Checking for Understanding

1. Why does Ward believe that resources once regarded as unlimited are proving to be limited?
2. What does she believe should be done now to prepare for the future?
3. According to Ward's view of the world, what should happen to the availability of such necessary items as food and clothing in the future? Do you agree or disagree?

SECTION 2 Clothing Choices

SECTION 2 FOCUS

Terms to Know durability, service flow

Objectives *After reading this section, you should be able to:*

1. Explain how **personal values affect clothing choices.**
2. List three factors that determine **clothing value.**
3. Decide when to take advantage of **clothing sales.**

Factors to Consider When Buying Clothing

Americans spend about $300 billion annually on clothing and other personal products, as **Figure 5.5** shows. Most people could buy a few very durable, sturdy, and even good-looking pieces of clothing that would last much longer than their owners might want to keep them. By purchasing such clothing, consumers could reduce their clothing budget considerably. These clothes would protect them from the cold, sun, wind, and so on. The clothes, however, would not serve another purpose—variety. Variety is just one factor involved in clothing choice. Custom, attitude about one's self, and values are other factors that cannot be judged statistically.

Figure 5.5 Sales of Clothing and Personal Products

Personal care and clothing are huge industries. How many dollars does each category on this graph represent? ▼

Clothing and Personal Values

Historically, people's dress reflected their social position, or status. When the American colonies were founded, the influence of social class on clothing began to break down. In this country today, clothing is more a reflection of personal values than of position. In this sense, the clothing that a person buys makes a statement about his or her values. For example, it may not be important to you to have special clothes to wear for a date, while it may be important to someone else. An individual's values are linked to the larger value system—family, friends, and culture. See **Figure 5.6** (pages 114–115).

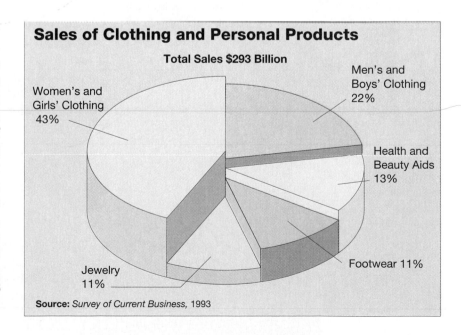

Sales of Clothing and Personal Products

Total Sales $293 Billion

- Women's and Girls' Clothing 43%
- Men's and Boys' Clothing 22%
- Health and Beauty Aids 13%
- Footwear 11%
- Jewelry 11%

Source: *Survey of Current Business,* 1993

Comparing Clothing Value

Comparison shopping is an important part of buying wisely. Comparing value in clothing means more than simply purchasing an item from the store that offers the best price. Clothing value depends on at least three other factors: style, durability, and cost of care.

Figure 5.6
Why So Many Clothes?
Several major factors combine to influence the types and styles of clothing we choose to wear.

Style You may be able to buy the minimum amount of clothing you need at a very low cost. You will, however, generally give up style to do it. Wearing clothes that are stylish—up-to-date—is usually expensive because you need to buy new clothes each year.

Wearing current styles costs more than wearing what are called classic styles, which are the more basic clothing designs and colors that do not change much through the years. Again, you are faced with a trade-off. Should you buy stylish clothes each year to keep up with fashion and have

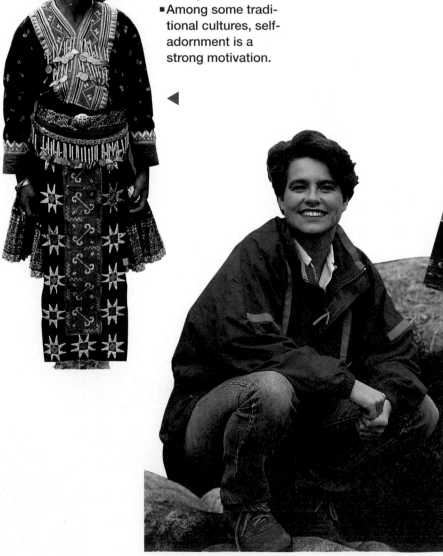

A Customs
- Customs sometimes determine styles of clothing.
- Customs change slowly.
- Among some traditional cultures, self-adornment is a strong motivation.

◀

B Self-Image ▲
- Clothing conveys a message to others about what you do, what you believe, and what you are.
- We dress to preserve our self-image. This is aesthetic; it has to do solely with our ideas of beauty.

◀

less money to spend on other items? Or should you buy less stylish clothes that you can wear from year to year and have more money?

Durability The ability of an item to last is known as **durability.** The longer a piece of clothing—or any item— lasts, the more durable it is. When you purchase an item of clothing, you are purchasing it for the service flow that it yields per time period. This **service flow** is how much you get to use it over time and the value you place on this use. If you buy a jacket that will last three years and costs $300, the cost per service flow per year is $100.

A consumer would not really be comparing similar value if he or she automatically bought the less expensive coat, dress, or shirt. In the long run, it might be more expensive. An inexpensive but poorly made pair of pants, for example, might have to be replaced after one season. A slightly more expensive but more durable pair might last for several seasons.

In comparison shopping for clothing, you should try to determine how long an item will last and how long you will need it. Then you should compare prices. Suppose you think Coat A will last twice as long as Coat B, and Coat A costs only 20 percent more. Then Coat A is a better buy. You should also try to decide, however, if the coat will still be in style in a year.

D Variety
- Many people want to have different "looks" for different occasions.
- People in different climates need different wardrobes for summer and winter. ▶

C Values
- Values determine choice of clothes because such choice is a statement of what we consider important.
- Clothing reflects values instilled in us by society as well as our own individual attitudes and values.
- Values inherent in clothes are self-expression, esteem, and comfort.
- Unconventional dress often identifies a person as part of a small group. ▼

Checklist

Figure 5.7
Determining Clothing Needs

In deciding on clothing purchases, ask yourself the following questions:

1 What do I already have? Check the condition of the clothes you have, and see what you need to replace.

2 What clothes do I need for:
- school?
- job?
- social life?
- recreational activities?

3 How many changes of clothes do I need to meet my minimum requirements for:
- cleanliness?
- variety?
- social status, or standing in society?

4 How do my answers to questions 1 through 3 compare with the amount of money I have to spend?

5 Should I pay cash or charge my purchases? Consider the trade-offs involved in paying cash or using credit.

Cost of Care Finally, the cost of care is another important factor in deciding value. Two shirts or blouses may cost the same, but one may need dry cleaning, an expensive alternative to hand or machine washing. When deciding on the best choice in a clothing purchase you must consider maintenance costs.

Figure 5.8 ▶
Seasonal Sales
In many cases when you buy clothes on sale, you will not be able to wear them until the following year. For example, you might be buying winter clothes at the end of the winter or summer clothes in late August.

Clothing Sales

Clothing sales are numerous throughout the year, and it is easy to become a bargain fanatic, buying sale items just because they are on sale. Before going shopping, wise consumers make a list of the clothing they have and decide what they need. **Figure 5.7** can help you evaluate your needs. Take your list with you when you go shopping. It will help you keep your spending within limits. Remember, too, that finding the best deal involves using time.

You should be aware of the timing factor in clothing sales. Generally, a clothing sale occurs when a store owner is trying to get rid of goods that he or she could not sell during the regular selling season. See **Figure 5.8**.

SECTION 2 REVIEW

Understanding Vocabulary
Define durability, service flow.

Reviewing Objectives
1 How do personal values affect clothing choices?

2 What three factors determine clothing value?

3 When should you buy clothing that is on sale?

Learning About Percentage Changes

Many important economic statistics change every year. Economists use *percentages* to describe such changes. Can you express a change in percentage terms?

Calculating Arithmetic Changes

The calculation of an arithmetic change is a simple task of subtraction. This year Americans consumed 1.6 billion pounds of butter. Last year they consumed 1.5 billion pounds. As **Figure A** shows, the difference is 0.1 billion pounds. This seems large. Is it?

Computing Percentage Change

It is often more meaningful to compare the arithmetic change in a statistic with what that statistic was before it changed. In this example, how does the arithmetic change in pounds of butter consumed from last year to this year (0.1 billion) compare to the total amount consumed last year (1.5 billion pounds)? After all, 0.1 billion pounds of butter sounds like a tremendous amount. Expressed as a percentage of last year, however, it is not so much.

Figure B shows how to determine the percentage change in the amount of butter consumed. First calculate the arithmetic difference, which in this case is 0.1 billion pounds of butter. Then divide the difference by the original quantity (1.5) and multiply by 100.

Figure A

$$1.6 \text{ billion pounds} \\ -1.5 \text{ billion pounds} \\ \hline 0.1 \text{ billion pounds}$$

Figure B

Increase in butter =
  0.1 billion pounds
Original quantity =
  1.5 billion pounds
Percentage change =

$$\frac{0.1}{1.5} = .067 \times 100 = 6.7 \text{ percent}$$

Figure C
(expressed in thousands)

Year	Men's Suits	Men's Shirts
1991	9,559	90,439
1992	10,062	106,855

Practicing the Skill

❶ Last month 3,300,000 women's coats were sold. This month 3,450,000 women's coats were sold. What was the percentage increase in coat sales?

❷ Look at **Figure C**. It shows annual sales of men's suits and shirts in 1991 and 1992. Which had a greater percentage increase?

DON'T GET CHEATED BY SUPERMARKET SCANNERS

by Vanessa O'Connell

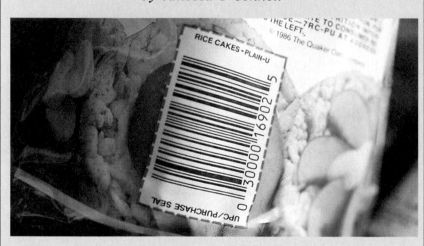

Like most smart shoppers, you probably scout supermarket specials and compare prices. Yet you have a one-in-10 chance of losing some savings when you hit the checkout counter. Consumer rights attorney Eugene DeSantis, 39 . . . noticed mistakes in his grocery bills so often he decided to fight back. Last December, a small-claims court judge ruled DeSantis had been overcharged five times in three months. . . . "I'm incensed," says DeSantis. "The same errors happen over and over. It's worth my time to take a stand." . . .

Money's reporting, plus an exclusive, two-month survey, has discovered:
- Scanners may overcharge at 30% of stores. . . .
- While scanner abuse may represent only nickels and dimes for any one customer, those errors add up. Based on *Money*'s sample, we estimate annual losses to consumers of $1 billion owing to scanner overcharges.

Information Week, a trade publication for computer system managers, estimates those losses at $2.5 billion.
- Scanner errors

account for more than half of supermarket profits.

How do scanners cheat? When a cashier whisks your groceries over the glass-enclosed electronic eye, the scanner reads the bar code, called the Universal Product Code (UPC), on each item and calls up the price from the store's computer. Many supermarket chains, especially the larger ones, have a central data base that electronically sends as many as 1,000 to 3,000 weekly price changes to each store. But store personnel may neglect to correctly or immediately update either the shelf tags or the store's own computer listings.

• THINK ABOUT IT •

1. **How much of a supermarket's profits come from scanner errors?**

2. **How do scanners cheat?**

Shopping for Food

Key Terms
warehouse food store
  (p. 109)
convenience stores (p. 109)
private-labeled products
  (p. 110)

Summary
Consumers should be aware of many helpful suggestions in comparison shopping for food. There are three major types of food stores, each offering certain advantages.

Clothing Choices

Key Terms
durability (p. 115)
service flow (p. 115)

Summary
Each person's own values affect his or her choices of clothing. Clothing value is determined by style, durability, and cost of care. Timing is an important factor in clothing sales.

5 Review

Identifying Key Terms

Use terms from the following list to fill in the blanks in the sentences below.

service flow (p. 115)   durability (p. 115)
private-labeled   warehouse food
  products (p. 110)   store (p. 109)
convenience stores (p. 109)

When you are shopping for food, the most expensive place to buy is in __(1)__ . The cheapest place to buy is usually in a __(2)__ . When you are in a store, you will see national brands, generic brands, and __(3)__ . This last kind of food products usually carries the name of the store.

You can buy clothes that are attractive, but fall apart after a while. They lack the quality of __(4)__ . If you buy a coat that you think will last five years, it will give you a __(5)__ per year.

Recalling Facts and Ideas

Section 1

1. What is one of the best ways to engage in comparison shopping for food products?
2. What are the most expensive and the least expensive places to buy food?
3. What is the trade-off involved when you buy a generic brand rather than a brand-name product?
4. What trade-off does buying convenience food involve?

Section 2

5. What four factors influence the kind of clothing choices people make?
6. What is the normal relationship between how long an article of clothing will last and its price?

7. State two things consumers should remember about clothing sales.

Critical Thinking

Section 1
Identifying Alternatives Warehouse food stores almost always sell food at a lower price than any other place from which you can buy food. Why do some consumers, nonetheless, shop at supermarkets instead of at warehouse stores?

Section 2
Recognizing Bias "I went clothes shopping with Ingrid last weekend. You won't believe what she bought. She went to one of the most expensive stores in the neighborhood and paid way too much for the blouses that she got. I don't know what's wrong with her." Could the opinion this person is expressing ever be valid? Why or why not?

Applying Economic Concepts

Competition and Market Structure Examine the food ads in your local newspaper for one week. Write down those food items that are common to each ad. For example, milk is usually advertised by all supermarkets on a specific day of the week. Compare the prices from the different food stores for the common items advertised. What is the largest percentage difference between the highest and lowest price for an advertised common food item? Are any of the food items advertised at exactly the same price for the same brand and the same size?

Chapter Projects

1. **Individual Project** Go to your favorite clothing store or department store. Look at all of the suits, coats, or dresses. Write down the prices for one type of clothing item, such as a raincoat. With your list in hand, ask a salesperson to show you the most durable and least durable brand. Is there a relationship between the price and what the salesperson believes is the most durable brand? What is that relationship?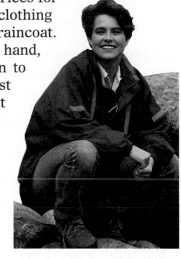

2. **Cooperative Learning Project** You now know that the type of clothes that we choose to buy and wear depends on many things such as customs, aesthetic considerations, values, and group identification. Work in small groups to analyze what is most important in determining the clothes that you buy and wear.

   Write down the list of determinants in order of importance. In a class discussion, see if there is a consensus—a meeting of the minds—about which determinant is most important for the class. During the discussion, make sure that you distinguish between what is truly an aesthetic consideration that you, as an individual, and your classmates, as individuals, really believe and what is the result of "peer pressure."

   At the end of this exercise, you might want to discuss the importance of clothing you have seen on television in terms of what you and your friends think is "in style." Are you influenced by clothing styles seen on television? If so, why?

Reviewing Skills

Learning About Percentage Changes

1. **Figuring Percentage Changes** Last year stores in your city sold 26,450 T-shirts. This year those same stores sold 23,160. Describe what happened in terms of percentage of T-shirts sold.

2. **Using Percentages** Study the table below and then apply your skills to determine the numbers that fit in the blank spaces and complete the table.

Price Last Year	Price This Year	Percentage Change in Price
$1.00		53.7%
	$2,000	100%
$5,721.00	$6,821.00	
$2.00	$1.00	

Writing About Economics

Persuasive Writing Use the entries in Your Economics Journal about your parents' food purchases as the basis for a persuasive essay. Your essay should persuade consumers to shop at a specific kind of food store.

CHAPTER 6
BUYING THE NECESSITIES: HOUSING AND TRANSPORTATION

Why are Americans so fascinated with cars?

What are the costs of owning a car?

Do you automatically think that you "need" a car?

How much insurance does a car owner need?

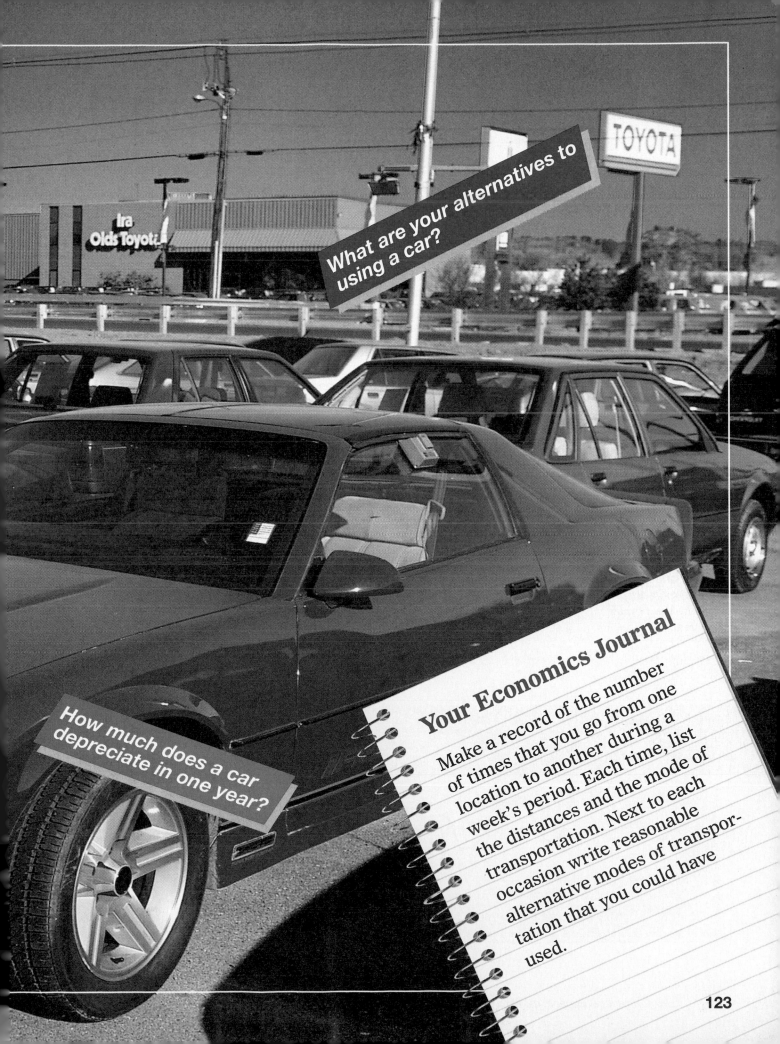

What are your alternatives to using a car?

How much does a car depreciate in one year?

Your Economics Journal

Make a record of the number of times that you go from one location to another during a week's period. Each time, list the distances and the mode of transportation. Next to each occasion write reasonable alternative modes of transportation that you could have used.

SECTION **1** *Housing Needs and Wants*

SECTION 1 FOCUS

Terms to Know real estate taxes, condominium, cooperative, lease, depreciate

Objectives *After reading this section, you should be able to:*

1. List five **types of housing** available.
2. Explain **the pros and cons of sharing an apartment or house.**

American Consumers Have Many Housing Alternatives

Besides food and clothing, housing and transportation are the two important necessities in virtually everybody's budget. If you are living at home with your parents, you are probably not too concerned with housing. Some day, however, you are going to have to make the decision about renting an apartment or a house. At some time you may have to make the decision about buying a house. As **Figure 6.1** shows, construction begins on an average of 1 to 2 million new houses each year. Americans also spend billions of dollars remodeling existing houses.

Figure 6.1
Housing Construction

New housing starts peaked in the early 1970s. Although they have decreased since then, Americans still demand more than 1 million new homes each year.

Types of Housing

The average American family spends about one-fourth of its annual income on housing. The United States has more than 100 million housing units, of which about 60 percent are owned by the people living in them. The rest are rented. Families or individuals are not just buying or renting a place to live. They are also paying for the satisfaction gained by living in a place called "home." The amount of satisfaction depends on many things. Among them are the size of the dwelling, the neighborhood, the quality of construction and furnishings, and how well the house suits the family's or individual's needs. **Figure 6.2** explains some types of housing.

New Housing Starts, 1965-1992

Millions of Housing Starts

2.5
2.0
1.5
1.0
.5
0

1965   '70   '75   '80   '85   '90 1992

Source: *Statistical Abstract of the U.S.*, Bureau of the Census.

Figure 6.2 Housing Choices
Several types of housing are available in the United States for single people, families, and different age groups. Besides renting apartments, Americans may choose to buy, rent, or lease housing. This housing includes single-family homes, town houses, condominiums, cooperatives, and mobile homes.

A Single-Family Houses
The single-family house is one that is separate from neighboring homes and has some land around it. This type of housing usually is the most expensive type to buy and maintain. Owners are responsible for insurance and real estate taxes. **Real estate taxes** are taxes paid on land and buildings. The single-family house perhaps is also the type of housing that most Americans hope to own. It is part of the American dream and here, more than in any other country, it is a symbol of success and happiness.

◀

B Town Houses ▶
A town house is a house of two or more floors with a front yard and backyard but with common sidewalls. The advantage of a town house is its economy of construction. Its style saves on the amount of land, insulation, windows, foundation, roof, and walls needed, which makes it less expensive to buy and maintain. Unfortunately, noise often carries through the common walls.

125

Figure 6.2 Housing Choices (cont.)

C Condominiums ▶

Some town houses are condominiums. A **condominium** (KAHN-duh-MIN-ee-uhm) is a single unit in an apartment building or in a series of town houses that is owned separately. Common areas such as hallways and the land on which the building is built are owned in common by the owners of the single units. Owners pay a monthly maintenance fee for upkeep of these common areas. Ownership rights in a condominium are similar to those in a single-family house, with some exceptions. Owners are free to make any changes they wish within their own units. However, the need for repairs to common areas is usually determined by a majority vote of the owners of all the units.

D Cooperatives ▶

Owners of **cooperative** apartments, in contrast, own equal shares in the company that owns the apartment building and the land on which the building stands. They do not own their apartments but rather hold leases on them. A **lease** is a long-term agreement describing the terms under which the property is being rented. All operating costs such as real estate taxes and maintenance are divided among the owners according to the number of shares each owns. A major problem with cooperative apartments is that individual members usually must obtain approval from the co-op before remodeling, renting, or selling their units.

E Mobile Homes

Mobile homes are a popular form of low-cost housing in the United States. One reason is that mobile homes are often taxed as motor vehicles rather than as real estate. Another reason is that they often are the least expensive form of housing to buy and maintain. However, owners of mobile homes face unique problems. The purchase of a mobile home does not always guarantee a space in a mobile home park. Mobile homes are also more likely to suffer damage during storms than are other types of housing. Third, mobile homes, like automobiles and boats, **depreciate** (di-PREE-shee-AYT)—decline in value over time—as the mobile homes or the fixtures that are part of them wear out or become ◀ outdated in style.

The Pros and Cons of Sharing an Apartment or House

If you go on to college or start working right out of high school, you may find that sharing a rented house or apartment with one or more friends makes sense. Sharing involves a number of human problems and a number of economic problems as shown in **Figure 6.3**.

▲ **Figure 6.3 Sharing Housing**
Answering these questions before you begin to share housing will avoid problems and conflict.
- How will responsibilities be shared? Are you splitting the rent in exactly the same amounts? If something needs to be repaired, will you share in the expenses?
- Will one person be responsible to the landlord, or will each of you put money in a special bank account from which the rent can be paid?
- How will you share the payment of telephone and utility bills?
- Who is going to be responsible for household expenses such as cleaning supplies and light bulbs?
- What about furniture? What if a nice sofa that your parents gave you gets stained by someone else? Who is responsible?
- Who is responsible for cleaning up what and when?

SECTION 1 REVIEW

Understanding Vocabulary
Define real estate taxes, condominium, cooperative, lease, depreciate.

Reviewing Objectives
1. What are the five types of housing available to consumers?
2. What pros and cons should persons consider if they plan to share an apartment or house?

Thorstein Veblen on Conspicuous Consumption

Profile

- 1857-1929
- lectured at University of Chicago
- harsh critic of American capitalism
- major published work: *The Theory of the Leisure Class,* 1899

In *The Theory of the Leisure Class*, Veblen criticized the rich, or leisure, class and its spending habits. He talked about conspicuous consumption, which is buying goods and services to impress others.

The quasi-peaceable gentleman of leisure, then, not only consumes of the staff of life beyond the minimum required for subsistence and physical efficiency, but his consumption also undergoes a specialization as regards the quality of good consumed.... Since the consumption of these more excellent goods is an evidence of wealth, it becomes honorific [conferring honor]; and conversely, the failure to consume in due quantity and quality becomes a mark of inferiority and demerit.

Veblen adds that conspicuous consumption is more common in an urban population than in a rural one.

... Conspicuous consumption claims a relatively larger portion of the income of the urban than of the rural population, and the claim is also more imperative.... In the struggle to outdo one another the city population push their normal standard of conspicuous consumption to a higher point.

Veblen calls conspicuous consumption waste because it does not serve human life well. He concludes that it does not have the approval of the conscience—it is not ethical.

In the view of economic theory the expenditure ... is here called "waste" because this expenditure does not serve human life or human well-being on the whole.

... The popular reprobation [disapproval] of waste goes to say that in order to be at peace with himself the common man must be able to see in any and all human effort and human enjoyment an enhancement of life and well-being on the whole.... Relative or competitive advantage of one individual in comparison with another does not satisfy the economic conscience, and therefore competitive expenditure has not the approval of this conscience.

Checking for Understanding

1. What is conspicuous consumption?
2. What groups tend to engage more in conspicuous consumption?
3. According to Veblen, what is wrong with conspicuous consumption or with competitive expenditures?

SECTION 2 To Rent or to Buy

SECTION 2 FOCUS

Terms to Know closing costs, points, equity, security deposit

Objectives *After reading this section, you should be able to:*
1. List three rules that determine **how much you should spend** for a house.
2. Explain the **rights and responsibilities** of renters.

Deciding to Buy Housing Is a Big Step, But Renters Also Have Responsibilities

Some people will save for years and scrimp on food and clothing their whole lives in order to buy a nice house. Others simply rent most of their lives.

No matter what type of housing you decide to live in, you have to make the decision whether to rent or buy. **Figure 6.5** (page 130) compares the advantages and disadvantages—both economic and psychological—of owning and renting. Wise consumers should consider both when deciding whether to buy or to rent housing.

If You Buy, How Much Should You Spend?

When you decide to buy housing, it is important that you do not take on financial obligations that are beyond your budget. As **Figure 6.4** shows, lenders use certain rules to help buyers determine how much housing they can afford.

In addition to the cash down payment, you will need money for **closing costs.** These are costs involved in arranging for a mortgage or in transferring ownership of the property. Closing costs can include fees for such items as the title search, legal costs, loan application, credit report,

house inspections, and taxes. Although the person buying the house usually pays these fees, the seller may agree to pay part or all of them if this will make it easier to sell the house.

In arranging for a mortgage, it is important to know about **points,** which are included in closing costs. Points are the fee paid to the lender and computed as percentage points of the

**Figure 6.4
What Can You Borrow?**
Why would it be unwise for both you and the lender if you spent more than a third of your income on the mortgage?

▼

Lenders' Rules		
RULE 1		Purchase Price ÷ Annual Income = 2.0 or less
RULE 2		Mortgage Payment ÷ Monthly Take-Home Income = less than 33.3 percent
RULE 3		Loan Amount ÷ Value of the Housing = 95 percent or less (often 80 percent)

Chapter 6 Buying the Necessities: Housing and Transportation **129**

Figure 6.5 Advantages and Disadvantages of Owning and Renting

Advantages	Disadvantages

Ownership provides the following for a family or individual:

- freedom of use; owners can remodel whenever or however they choose
- the pride of ownership; people tend to take better care of things they own
- greater privacy
- a good investment that in the past has risen in value as much as, or more than, the general rise in prices
- significant income tax benefits
- creation of **equity** (EK-wuht-ee), the amount of money invested in the property minus the debt—mortgage payments—still owed
- a good credit rating if mortgage payments are made on time
- property to use as collateral for other loans

Ownership has the following drawbacks:

- less mobility, especially in years when interest rates on mortgages are high and housing is difficult to sell
- less feeling of being able to move to another property because the present one is too small, too big, and so on
- necessity of a large outlay of money for a down payment
- maintenance costs, real estate taxes, and possible depreciation
- less money for other purchases because of high monthly mortgage payments
- possibility of overextending a family's debt load to make home improvements or repairs

Renting provides an individual or family:

- greater mobility; a renter does not have to worry about trying to sell property quickly if he or she must move
- a feeling of freedom to choose another place to live if dissatisfied with current rental unit
- having to pay only a small security deposit rather than a large outlay of money for a down payment. A **security deposit** is money the renter gives to the owner to hold in case the rent is not paid or the apartment is damaged.
- no direct maintenance costs, real estate taxes, or depreciation
- a good credit rating if rent is paid on time
- more money for other purchases because monthly rental payments are often less than monthly mortgage payments
- no temptation to overspend on home improvements

Renting has the following drawbacks:

- no freedom of use; renters may not remodel or even paint without the owner's permission
- no return on rental money; a renter will never own the property regardless of how much rent he or she pays, regardless of the length of this period of time
- little or no tax benefits
- often less privacy
- little feeling of responsibility for seeing that the property is well taken care of
- no property for use as collateral
- need to wait for maintenance work at the convenience of the owner

loan. Each point the lender charges equals 1 percent of the amount borrowed. Lenders charge points—usually one to four—when they believe that the current interest rate is not high enough to pay the expenses involved in handling the mortgage and still make a profit.

Financing a Housing Purchase

One of the major problems facing today's home buyer is that of financing. Almost every home buyer has a mortgage. **Figure 6.6** shows several kinds of mortgages that are available. Mortgages are available from savings and loan associations, savings and

Figure 6.6 Types of Mortgages

Type of Mortgage	Interest Rate Changes	Monthly Payment Changes	Term Changes	Description
Standard Fixed-Rate Mortgage	No	No	No	Interest rate and monthly payments remain the same over the term of the mortgage. Term is fixed, usually at 15 to 30 years.
Flexible Rate Mortgage	Yes	Yes	Yes	The interest rate and monthly payments float up or down along with interest rates in general. Rates can increase by no more than a few percentage points over the life of a mortgage, while there is often no limit on the amount of decrease. Three such plans are variable rate mortgage (VRM), adjustable rate mortgage (ARM), and renegotiable rate mortgage (RRM).
Federal Housing Administration (FHA) Mortgage	No	No	No	The FHA will insure the entire amount of its mortgages. This added security makes it possible for borrowers to obtain a larger loan than they could with an uninsured mortgage.
Graduated Payment Mortgage (GPM)	No	Yes	No	Interest rate and term are usually fixed for the life of the mortgage. Monthly payments are small at the beginning and increase gradually over the years. GPMs are used by people who expect their incomes to increase steadily from year to year.
Veteran's Administration (VA) Mortgage	No	No	No	These loans can be obtained only by qualified veterans or their widows. The interest rate is generally lower than for other mortgages. The VA guarantees a large percentage of the loan. Loans with no down payment are possible under the VA program.

commercial banks, and sometimes from the seller of the house, co-op, or condominium.

A mortgage usually involves a down payment and interest. If you buy a house for $100,000 and make a $20,000 down payment, you will need to obtain a mortgage for the remaining $80,000. The mortgage will then be repaid in monthly installments that include interest on the loan.

If You Rent: Rights and Responsibilities

Most renters sign a lease that contains several clauses. A prospective tenant should read the lease carefully. See **Figure 6.7**. Most leases are for one to three years.

Checklist
Figure 6.7
Clauses in Housing Leases

You should be aware of several types of clauses to avoid in leases.

1 According to a confession-of-judgment clause, the lawyer for the owner of the rental unit has the right to plead guilty for you in court in the event the owner thinks his or her rights have been violated. If you sign a lease with a confession-of-judgment clause, you are admitting guilt before committing any act. Such a clause is, in fact, illegal in some states.

2 According to the inability-to-sue clause, you give up your right to sue the owner if you suffer injury or damage through some fault of the owner, such as neglected repair work.

3 Leases may include arbitrary clauses, or those based on one's wishes rather than a rule or law. These give the owner the right to cancel the lease because he or she is dissatisfied with your behavior. Some leases include clauses that:
- forbid hanging pictures.
- forbid overnight guests. This is usually done to make sure the apartment is occupied only by the renter and members of the renter's immediate family.
- forbid subleasing, or the leasing of the apartment by the tenant to someone else.
- allow the owner to cancel the lease if you are only one day late in paying the rent but hold you legally responsible to pay the rent for the rest of the lease.
- allow the owner or a representative, such as a plumber, to enter your apartment when you are not home.
- make you legally responsible for all repairs.
- make you obey rules that have not yet been written.

If you have the opportunity, these are some clauses that you should have added to your lease.

1 If the person renting the unit to you says that it comes with dishwasher, garbage disposal, and air conditioner, make sure the lease lists them.

2 If you have been promised the use of a recreation room, a parking lot, or a swimming pool, make sure that the lease states this. Also have it indicate whether or not you must pay extra for their use.

3 If the owner has promised to have the apartment painted, have this stated in the lease. If you wish to be able to choose the color, also have this stated in the lease.

4 In certain cases, you may be able to cancel your lease if you are transferred to a job in another city or state. Usually, however, you must agree to pay a certain amount to do this. The amount should be stated in the lease.

5 If you plan to put in lighting fixtures, shelves, and so on, and wish them to remain your property when you move, have this stated in the lease. Otherwise they become part of the apartment and you may not take them with you.

Tenant Rights Among the rights of tenants is the use of the property for the purpose stated in the lease. Tenants also have the right to a certain amount of privacy. A landlord usually cannot enter an apartment any time he or she chooses. A landlord may enter only to make necessary repairs or to show the apartment to a potential renter.

Tenant Responsibilities In turn, the tenant must pay the rent on time and take reasonable care of the property. If major repairs such as replacing a leaky roof are needed, the tenant is responsible for notifying the landlord. Often a lease will limit how an apartment can be used. The lease may forbid pets, for example, or forbid anyone other than the person named on the lease from living there. In signing a lease, the tenant is usually required to give a security deposit equal to one month's rent. The deposit is returned after the tenant has moved. The purpose of the security deposit is to pay for repairing any damages that the tenant caused, such as cracked plaster from hanging pictures. The amount returned depends on the condition of the apartment, as determined by the landlord. **Figure 6.8** offers tips on ensuring that your deposit is returned.

The tenant is also required to give notice, or a formal warning, if he or she plans to move before the term of

the lease is up. In this event, the landlord may ask for several month's rent to pay for any time the apartment is empty before a new tenant moves in.

Landlord Responsibilities In many states, landlords must make sure apartments have certain minimum services, such as heat, and that their apartments are fit to live in. Landlords may also have to obey building safety laws. For example, fire escapes and smoke detectors may be required. Leases usually call for the landlord to make repairs within a reasonable amount of time. In many states, a tenant has the right to pay for the repairs and withhold that amount of rent if the landlord does not make the repairs.

Figure 6.8 ▲
Making Sure You Get Your Security Deposit Returned

1. Do a "walk through" with the manager or owner to record any damage that already exists.
2. Take photos of the apartment when you move in and when you leave.
3. Keep copies of all the bills that you paid for repairs, improvements, or cleaning.
4. Find out what the local regulations are. They might require that an apartment be "broom cleaned" before you move out.

SECTION 2 REVIEW

Understanding Vocabulary

Define closing costs, points, equity, security deposit.

Reviewing Objectives

❶ How much should a consumer spend on a house?
❷ What are the rights and responsibilities of renters?

LEARNING ECONOMIC SKILLS
Comparing Insurance

When you are purchasing automobile insurance there are many options available to you. Do you know how to compare auto insurance coverages?

The Basic Policy

Insurance companies sell individual insurance agreements—called policies—to cover almost any type of risk. In general, the higher the risk, the more the insurance premium will cost.

Liability Insurance

This type of insurance covers you, or anyone you allow to drive your car, against financial obligation for injury or death to others and for property damage caused by your car. Liability insurance is usually described by the amount of coverage. Look at the set of numbers in **Figure A**. **Figure B** lists other types of coverage that you can and usually should buy.

The Deductible

The deductible is the portion of the cost of repairs that you must pay before the insurance company pays anything. For example, if your policy has a $500 deductible and repairs cost $1,000, you would pay $500 and the insurance company would pay the remaining $500.

Practicing the Skill

❶ Look at **Figure C**. Describe the limits of the liability coverage shown.

❷ You have an insurance policy that provides for collision coverage. To make it cheap, you took out a $750 deductible. You are involved in an auto accident in which the total repairs cost $2,167.47. How much does your insurance company have to pay?

Figure A

10/50/10
This set of numbers means that the insurance company would pay up to $10,000 for any one person injured in an accident, up to a total of $50,000 for all personal injuries, and up to $10,000 for damages to private or public property.

Figure B

Medical	Covers the cost of health care and hospitalization resulting from an accident for you, your family, and any passengers.
Collision	Covers the cost of repairs to your car resulting from an accident.
Comprehensive physical damage	Protects against damage to, or loss of, your car due to fire, flood, theft, vandalism, and so on.

Figure C

100/300/50

134

SECTION 3 Buying and Operating an Automobile

SECTION 3 FOCUS

Terms to Know excise tax, registration fee, liability insurance

Objectives *After reading this section, you should be able to:*
1. List the costs of **buying an automobile.**
2. Identify four costs of **operating an automobile.**

Automobiles Cost More Than a Monthly Loan Payment

In many places in the United States, an automobile is a necessity. Some Americans rent or lease cars because they do not have the down payment or because they wish to gain a tax advantage by leasing or renting for business purposes. Nevertheless, most people prefer to own their own automobiles. Therefore, it is probable that at some point in your life you will buy a car. You should be aware of certain factors as you shop for a car. Your choice of an automobile, like all other decisions, involves trade-offs. See **Figure 6.9** for some of the major trade-offs you should consider.

The Costs of Buying an Automobile

Buying a car involves opportunity costs. One is the amount of money and time spent shopping for the car. Another is the amount of money and time spent in actually purchasing the car. Because people have limited resources, most people have to borrow to buy a car. The costs of the loan are the interest, the down payment, and the monthly payments on the principal. Interest is an important cost of buying an automobile on credit, but buying a car with cash has a cost, too. By paying cash, a person loses the ability to purchase other goods and services. See **Figure 6.10** (page 136) for tips on choosing a new or used car.

**Figure 6.9
Car Buying Trade-Offs**

- Usually, the smaller the engine, the less gas an automobile burns. This makes a car with a smaller engine less costly to operate, but the car will accelerate less quickly.
- Newer automobiles cost more, but they require fewer repairs than older ones.
- The smaller the automobile, the more energy efficient it is and the easier it is to park and turn. In an accident, however, larger automobiles usually protect passengers better than smaller automobiles.

Checklist
Figure 6.10
Buying an Automobile

These tips will help you in making a good choice of a new car or used car:

1 Ask friends and relatives about their satisfaction or dissatisfaction with their cars.

2 Read articles about different makes and models in car magazines such as *Car and Driver* and *Road and Track.*

3 Read *Consumer Reports* and *Consumers' Research Magazine* for reviews of new automobiles. Read their reports on repair records of different models carefully.

4 Visit various dealers and read the material they hand out about their automobiles. Remember that these pamphlets are advertisements that promote the best features.

5 Personally inspect various makes and models. Automobile showrooms are open to provide you the chance to complete your inspection.

6 Check what is covered by the service warranty for each make and model as you compare automobiles. Warranties may vary from manufacturer to manufacturer. If you are buying a used car that is only a year or two old, check to see if it is still covered under the original manufacturer's warranty. Also, some dealers offer their own limited warranties for used cars.

7 Once you decide on the particular make and model that you want, compare the prices offered by several dealers.

8 If you are buying an automobile off the lot rather than ordering one, check the options on the car and their prices. Options are the extra features and equipment on a car—such as air conditioning, a compact disc player, special paint, and so on—that you must pay for in addition to the basic price. If you do not want any of the options, such as white sidewall tires, you may be able to get the dealer to take some additional money off the price.

9 If you are buying a used car, have an automobile diagnostic (DY-ig-NAHS-tik) center or a mechanic not connected with the dealer check it. Add to the dealer's price the cost of any repairs the mechanic thinks the car will need. This is the real cost of the automobile to you.

10 Make sure the price given includes federal excise tax and dealer preparation charges. An **excise** (EK-syz) **tax** is a tax on the manufacture, sale, or use within the country of specific products, such as liquor, gasoline, and automobiles. Dealer preparation charges cover the costs of taking a car as it arrives from the factory and preparing it to be driven away. This can include the costs of cleaning, installing certain options, and checking the car's engine. The price given by the dealer will not include state and local sales taxes. These will be added later.

11 Check various dealers for the reputation of their service departments. Your warranty usually allows you to take your car to any dealer selling that make of car. However, it may be most convenient to return to the service department of the dealer who sold you the car for maintenance and repair work.

12 Do not put a deposit on a car unless you are sure you are going to buy it. You may have a problem getting your deposit back if you change your mind.

The Costs of Operating an Automobile

As with other purchases, a consumer's responsibilities do not end with the purchase of the automobile; nor do the costs. Ongoing costs include a registration fee, normal maintenance, major repairs, depreciation, and insurance.

Registration Fee The owner of an automobile must pay a state licensing fee, or a **registration fee,** to use the car. Usually the fee must be paid annually. In many states, the amount of the fee varies depending on the car's age, weight, type, and value.

Normal Maintenance and Major Repairs The amount of normal maintenance—oil and filter changes and minor tune-ups—that an owner gives a car depends on the amount the car is driven and how carefully the owner maintains the car. The more maintenance an owner gives a car, the better service it will give and the longer it will last. The trade-off is that the owner will have less money available for other things.

Major repairs are those that are normally unexpected and expensive. They include rebuilding the transmission and replacing the exhaust system. No one can guarantee that an automobile will not require major repairs while you own it, but you can follow certain steps to reduce the probability.

As you read in **Figure 6.10**, you should check the repair records of different cars before deciding on a particular make and model. If you are considering a used car, you should also take it to a diagnostic center, or have a mechanic check it. Sometimes dealers offer warranties for used cars for a limited time period, such as 30 days, or you can purchase a warranty covering a longer period for a used car. See **Figure 6.11**.

Extended Warranty One way to guard against having to pay for major repairs is to buy extended warranty coverage. New-car warranties generally protect owners for all major repairs except tune-ups and damage resulting from improper use of the automobile. New-car warranties usually last only a few years, or up to a certain limit of miles or kilometers. These warranties, however, can often

Figure 6.11 Used Car Warranties
Used car dealers' warranties often provide for the buyer and the dealer to share the cost of repairs. The warranty coverage may be an indication of the used car's quality.

▶

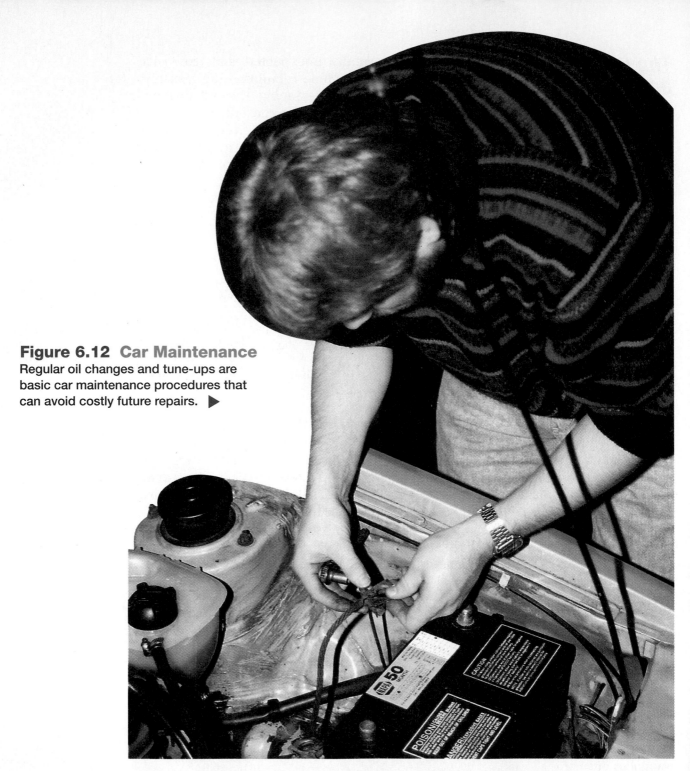

Figure 6.12 Car Maintenance
Regular oil changes and tune-ups are basic car maintenance procedures that can avoid costly future repairs. ▶

be extended for another one, two, or three years by paying additional money when the car is purchased.

Depreciation Depreciation—a decline in value over time—takes place as an item wears out or becomes outdated. Age, obsolescence, and wear and tear cause a car to depreciate. Age is the major factor. A car loses value every year even if it is not driven because an automobile is a consumer durable. All consumer durables deteriorate, or become worse. Second, new makes and models include current technology and new features. These changes make older models obsolete—out of date and out of style.

Physical wear and tear depends on how hard a car is driven, how many miles or kilometers it is driven, and how well it is maintained. See **Figure 6.12**. Generally, cars depreciate about 20 percent each year.

Figure 6.13 Factors Affecting Automobile Insurance Rates

When you buy automobile insurance, the rate you are charged is determined, in addition to your age and sex, by the following:

1. **The type of car you drive.** Insurance companies consider the safety record of a car and the costs to repair it if it is involved in an accident.

2. **Where you drive.** If the rate of thefts and accidents is high in an area, the risk to the insurance company is greater. A city, for example, would have more thefts and accidents than would a rural area. Therefore, the rate the insurance company charges in a city will be higher.

3. **What you use the car for.** If you drive your car for business on a daily basis, the rate will be higher than if you use it only for errands and occasional trips.

4. **Marital status.** In general, married men and women have lower accident rates than single men and women and, therefore, pay lower insurance rates.

5. **Safety record.** If you have a history of accidents and traffic tickets, then you will be charged a high rate. Whether a new driver has had driver education is often considered in determining a rate.

6. **Number of drivers.** The number of drivers using a car increases the insurance rate.

Insurance A major cost of owning an automobile, especially for someone under age 25, is insurance. Many states require that **liability insurance** be purchased before an automobile can be licensed. Insurance companies classify drivers in various ways, usually according to age, gender, and marital status. Rates depend on the category into which a person fits. These amounts are based on statistics that show that different types of drivers have different accident rates.

Young people almost always have to pay higher insurance rates. For example, single males in the 16–25 age group have the highest accident rate of all drivers. Not surprisingly, most insurance companies charge these drivers the highest insurance rates. Married women 25–45 have the fewest accidents and the lowest rates. **Figure 6.13** shows factors in addition to age and sex that affect insurance rates. Rates cannot vary widely because states set limits on the rates companies can charge within their borders.

SECTION 3 REVIEW

Understanding Vocabulary

Define excise tax, registration fee, liability insurance.

Reviewing Objectives

1. What are the costs of buying an automobile?
2. What are the costs of operating an automobile?

Readings in Economics

KIPLINGER'S PERSONAL FINANCE MAGAZINE   **FEBRUARY, 1993**

FIGHTING RACIAL DISCRIMINATION IN HOME LENDING

by Elizabeth Razzi

Despite years of open-housing laws, African-American and Hispanic mortgage applicants are still much more likely to be turned down than whites, regardless of income, reports the Federal Reserve Board. Nationwide last year, the mortgage applications of 38% of African Americans, 27% of Hispanics, 17% of whites and 15% of Asians were rejected by lenders.

. . . Two years ago, Orlando and Gail Walton applied for a low-interest loan through an Ohio program for first-time buyers. . . . Gail's calls to the lender went unreturned.

Finally Gail arranged a meeting. She was told by the loan officer that there was "no way" she could get the loan because of her credit record. . . . Embarrassed and upset, she assumed that she and her husband didn't have a chance of getting the home they wanted.

"My husband got so discouraged," she says, "but I was determined that something was not right here." . . . The Waltons applied to another lender for the same loan in the same program. They got it, based on the same underwriting standards. Then, Gail's mother pointed her toward a Toledo fair-housing group.

The Waltons and the Toledo Fair Housing Center filed suit, charging that the first mortgage company had handled the Waltons' loan application differently from other borrowers' because of race. They settled with the mortgage company last fall for $20,000.

. . . If you are a member of a minority group and are turned down for a mortgage, describe your experience to a local fair-housing group. They can help confirm whether a denial was legitimate. Know your rights; if a lender denies you credit, the institution has 30 days from the day you applied to tell you why.

. . . If you believe you've been treated unfairly, . . . call the HUD Housing Discrimination Hotline . . . to file a complaint.

• THINK ABOUT IT •

1. **How do the figures for African Americans turned down for mortgages compare to the number of whites that are turned down?**

2. **What should you do if you suspect that a lender has discriminated against you?**

Highlights

Section 1

Housing Needs and Wants

Key Terms

real estate taxes
(p. 125)
condominium (p. 126)
cooperative (p. 126)
lease (p. 126)
depreciate (p. 126)

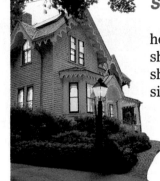

Summary

There are five different types of housing available to consumers. Renters should consider the pros and cons of sharing an apartment or house before signing a lease.

Section 2

To Rent or to Buy

Key Terms

closing costs (p. 129)
points (p. 129)
equity (p. 130)
security deposit
(p. 130)

Summary

Several advantages and disadvantages of renting and buying should be considered when deciding about housing. There are rules that determine how much you should spend on a house. Both renters and landlords have rights and responsibilities.

Section 3

Buying and Operating an Automobile

Key Terms

excise tax (p. 136)
registration fee
(p. 137)
liability insurance
(p. 139)

Summary

There are several costs of buying an automobile. The auto owner also must pay for operating and maintaining an automobile.

6 Review

Identifying Key Terms

Write the letter of the definition in Column B below that correctly defines each term in Column A.

Column A
1. equity (p. 130)
2. depreciate (p. 126)
3. excise tax (p. 136)
4. liability insurance (p. 139)
5. closing costs (p. 129)
6. security deposit (p. 130)

Column B
a. pays for bodily injury or property damage
b. a tax on the manufacture, sale, or use within a country of specific products
c. to decline in value over time
d. usually one month's rent left on deposit with the landlord
e. fee charged by lender for paperwork, taxes, and other activities
f. market value of property minus debt owed on it

Use terms from the following list to fill in the blanks in the paragraph below.

lease (p. 126)
cooperative (p. 126)
depreciate (p. 126)

real estate taxes (p. 125)
condominium (p. 126)

Owners of __(7)__ apartments do not own their apartments, but rather hold a __(8)__ on their apartments so that they have a long-term agreement describing the terms under which the property is being rented. One of the things that such owners have to pay are __(9)__, which are paid on the value of the land and buildings. The owner of a __(10)__, in contrast, owns his or her unit separately. All types of housing tend to __(11)__ and therefore must be maintained.

Recalling Facts and Ideas

Section 1
1. What is the type of ownership called if a person owns part of an apartment building and also owns in common the lobbies, recreational facilities, and so on?
2. What is one advantage and one disadvantage of living in each of the five types of housing?
3. What potential human and economic problems should friends seriously consider before sharing a rented house or apartment?

Section 2
4. What are some of the disadvantages of owning a house?
5. What are some of the disadvantages of renting a house or apartment?
6. What are some responsibilities of landlords?
7. How can you help make sure that you get your security deposit back if you rent?

Section 3
8. If you do not pay cash for a car, what expense must be included in the cost of buying the car?
9. What is included in the cost of operating an automobile?
10. A car's value tends to decrease over time. What do we call this process?
11. Virtually every state requires what type of insurance for owners of automobiles?

Critical Thinking

Section 1
Making Inferences Why do you think that in recent years condominiums have become increasingly popular among Americans?

Section 2

Making Comparisons The two basic types of mortgages used today are flexible rate and fixed rate. What are the advantages and disadvantages of each?

Section 3

Demonstrating Reasoned Judgment Why do you think that automobile insurance companies charge more for unmarried males between the ages of 16 and 25 than they do for married males between the ages of 16 and 25?

Applying Economic Concepts

Competition and Market Structure Examine your local newspaper carefully for at least one week. Cut out all of the ads that banks and mortgage companies present for mortgages. Write out a comparison table that shows the different mortgage rates.

Chapter Projects

1. **Individual Project** In the library, look up the section of the most recent Census of Housing entitled *Selected Housing Characteristics by States and Counties*. Make a table listing the following statistics for your county: (1) number of total housing units; (2) number of year-round housing units (those used throughout the year); (3) number of units occupied by owners; and (4) number occupied by renters.

2. **Cooperative Learning Project** Working in six groups, call separate automobile insurance agents and ask for a rate quote by giving the following facts:
   - Age: 21
   - Gender: Male or female (depending on who is calling)
   - Automobile type: 1994 Chevy Caprice
   - Use: Drive to college and part-time job—80 miles a week
   - Coverage desired: 100/300/50, which means up to $100,000 for one person injured in an accident, up to a total of

$300,000 for all personal injuries suffered in the accident, and up to $50,000 for damages to private or public property
   - Collision and comprehensive deductible: $500; no medical or towing

After you receive the quotes, compare them.
a. Which agent/insurance company gave the highest quote? The lowest?
b. Was there a substantial difference between the rates for females and males?
c. What was the average percentage difference between the rates quoted for females and males?

Reviewing Skills

Comparing Insurance

1. **Figuring Liability** The following policies are presented to you:
   a. 10/500/200 policy
   b. 100/300/1,000 policy
   Which policy pays the most to any one person injured? Which policy pays the most for damage to private or public property?

2. **Understanding Deductibles** You have an insurance policy with an $800 deductible. If you have an accident that causes $6,123.43 in damages, how much will the insurance company pay?

Writing About Economics

Persuasive Writing Write a paragraph in which you try to persuade someone to use public transportation rather than private automobiles. You may wish to emphasize the advantages of one type of transportation over another type. Use the facts you recorded in Your Economics Journal as you write.

7 SAVING AND INVESTING

Where can a person save besides banks and savings and loan associations?

Why are some investments risky?

How much should a person save?

What is the difference between savings and investments?

What are some reasons you might want to save?

What are some of the reasons people save money?

Who insures bank savings deposits?

Your Economics Journal

Keep a record of the names and types of the various institutions that offer to pay you interest for your savings. Next to each entry list the interest rate offered for different kinds of accounts.

SECTION 1 FOCUS

Terms to Know saving, interest, passbook savings account, statement savings account, money market deposit account, time deposits, maturity, certificates of deposit

Objectives *After reading this section, you should be able to:*
1. Decide when to **save and invest**.
2. Compare passbook, statement, and money market **savings accounts**.
3. Explain the advantages of **time deposits**.

When You Save, You Have Several Investment Choices

Suppose you have a part-time job that pays $60 a week and you want to buy a stereo that costs $240. Because your monthly income equals the price of the stereo, you cannot collect enough money to buy the stereo and pay your other monthly expenses. An adult could charge the stereo, but as a dependent you probably have no credit rating. You will have to save the money. Economists define **saving** as the nonuse of income for a period of time so that it can be used later. You may already be setting aside some of your income for some future use such as continuing your education.

Deciding to Save and Invest

Any saving that you do now may be only for purchases that require more money than you usually have at one time. When you are self-supporting and have more responsibilities, you will probably save for other reasons. For example, you may save to have money in case of emergencies, such as losing your job, and for your retirement. Most Americans who save do so for these reasons. Saving evens out a person's ability to spend throughout his or her lifetime. **Figure 7.1** shows the rate of personal saving of Americans in recent years.

The saving of any individual benefits the economy as a whole. Saving provides money for others to invest or spend. Additional savings also allow businesses to expand, which provides increased income for consumers and raises the standard of living.

Generally, when people think of saving, they think of putting their money in a savings bank or a similar institution where it will earn interest. **Interest** is the payment people receive when they lend money—allow someone else to use their money. A person receives interest on his or her savings account or similar savings plan for as long as money is in the account.

You have many options of places and ways to invest your savings. The most common places are commercial banks, savings and loan associations, savings banks, and credit unions. Before depositing money, investigate the different types of financial institutions in your area and the services they offer. Each institution usually has several types of savings plans, each paying a different interest rate. In comparison shopping for the best savings plan for you, you need to consider the trade-offs. Some savings plans allow immediate access to your money but pay a low rate of interest. Others pay higher interest and allow immediate use of your money, but require a large minimum balance.

Savings Accounts

Passbook savings accounts are also called regular savings accounts. With a **passbook savings account,** the depositor receives a booklet in which deposits, withdrawals, and interest are recorded. A customer must present the passbook each time one of these transactions, or business operations, takes place. A **statement savings account** is basically the same type of account. Instead of a passbook that must be presented for each transaction, however, the depositor receives a monthly statement showing all transactions. The chief appeal of these accounts is that they offer easy availability of funds. The depositor can usually withdraw money at any

Figure 7.1
Personal Saving

Compare the percentage of personal saving in 1992 with that in 1982. ▼

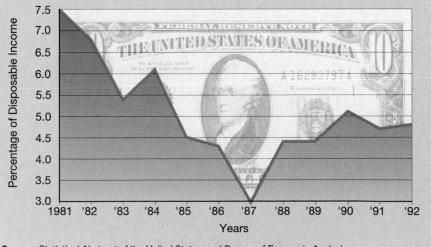

Personal Saving Expressed as a Percentage of Disposable Income, 1981-1992

Percentage of Disposable Income (y-axis: 3.0 to 7.5)
Years (x-axis: 1981 to '92)

Source: *Statistical Abstract of the United States,* and Bureau of Economic Analysis.

time without paying a penalty—forfeiting any money—but there is a trade-off, as **Figure 7.2** shows.

A **money market deposit account** (MMDA) is another type of account that pays relatively high rates of interest and allows immediate access to money. The trade-off is that these accounts also have a $1,000 to $2,500 minimum balance requirement. Customers can usually make withdrawals from a money market account in person at any time, but they are allowed to write only a few checks a month against the account.

Time Deposits

The term *time deposits* refers to a wide variety of savings plans that require a saver to leave his or her money on deposit for a certain period of time. The period of time is called the **maturity**, and may vary from seven days to eight years or more. Time deposits are often called **certificates of deposit** (CDs), or savings certificates as shown in **Figure 7.3**. They state the amount of the deposit, the maturity, and the rate of interest being paid. The amount of deposit and interest rates vary widely. Some CDs, particularly those paying higher interest, require a minimum deposit. The minimum may be as small as $250 or as large as $100,000. CDs at credit unions are called share certificates.

◀ **Figure 7.2 Savings Trade-Off**
The interest paid on passbook and statement accounts is low compared to the interest on other savings plans. Savings accounts are called share accounts at credit unions.

148

Insuring Deposits Before the 1930s, people who deposited money in banks risked losing their entire deposits if the bank failed. When the stock market collapsed in 1929, it caused a panic in the banking industry. The resulting crisis wiped out people's entire savings and destroyed investors' confidence in banks. Congress passed, and President Franklin Roosevelt signed, legislation to restore confidence in banks and to protect deposits. This legislation created the Federal Deposit Insurance Corporation (FDIC).

Today there are several federal agencies that insure most savings institutions in the United States. Each depositor's money is insured up to $100,000. If an insured institution fails, each depositor will be paid the full amount of his or her savings up to $100,000. **Figure 7.4** (page 150) lists the federal agencies that insure each type of institution and shows comparisons of the various places where you

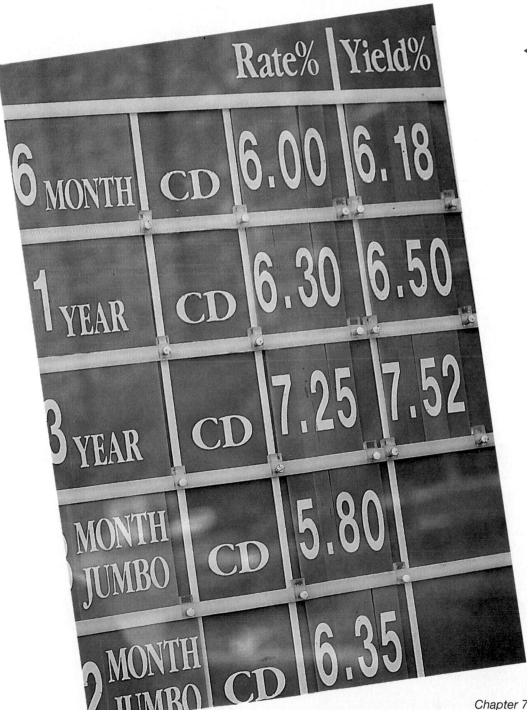

◀ **Figure 7.3**
Time Deposits
Time deposits offer higher interest rates than passbook or statement savings accounts. The longer it is to the maturity date, the higher the interest rate that is paid. For example, a certificate of deposit (CD) with a short-term maturity of 90 days pays less interest than a CD with a two-year maturity. Savers who decide to cash a time deposit before maturity pay a penalty.

Financial institutions also offer a number of special CDs. One example is the small saver's certificates. Their rates are tied to the current interest rates the federal government pays on certain types of borrowing that it does.

Figure 7.4 Savings Institutions' Services and Insurers

Institution	Savings Services Offered	Insured by	Number of Institutions***
Commercial banks	Passbook and statement savings accounts, Certificates of deposit, Money market accounts	Federal Deposit Insurance Corporation (FDIC)	12,000
Savings and loan associations	Passbook and statement savings accounts, Certificates of deposit, Money market accounts	Savings Association Insurance Fund (SAIF)	1,900
Savings banks	Passbook and statement savings accounts, Certificates of deposit, Money market accounts	Federal Deposit Insurance Corporation* (FDIC)	1,500
Credit unions	Share drafts,** Share accounts, Share certificates	National Credit Union Share Insurance Fund	13,000

*Some insured by SAIF.
**Interest-earning account similar to checking account
***Number of saving institutions changes often.

can save your money. Keep in mind that different institutions may offer different rates on the same type of accounts. Different institutions may also use different methods for figuring interest. Some savings institutions are not insured, or they carry private insurance. Those who put their money in these institutions run a higher risk of losing funds if the institution fails.

SECTION 1 REVIEW

Understanding Vocabulary

Define saving, interest, passbook savings account, statement savings account, money market deposit account, time deposits, maturity, certificates of deposit.

Reviewing Objectives

1 What are three reasons that people save and invest?

2 Why is it more difficult for the beginning saver to open a money market deposit account than a passbook savings account?

3 What determines the rate of interest on a time deposit?

H. Ross Perot on Saving and Investing

- born June 27, 1930, in Texarkana, Texas
- graduate of the U.S. Naval Academy at Annapolis, Maryland
- started out as a sales representative for IBM
- incorporated EDS (Electronic Data Systems) in 1962
- unsuccessful bid for President as an independent candidate in 1992
- authored *United We Stand* in 1992

H. Ross Perot has many ideas on how to improve this country and the American standard of living. These ideas were well publicized during his 1992 presidential bid. Among other things, he believes that Americans must increase their levels of saving and investment. Many of his ideas are stated in some detail in his book *United We Stand*.

*N*obody believes any longer that their home equity values will rise indefinitely, giving them a tidy nest egg for retirement. In fact, in this recession many home values have declined.... Nobody believes that their paychecks will increase ahead of inflation every year. Most feel fortunate to have a paycheck at all. Everyone knows someone who is unemployed. Nobody in the baby boom generation that I've met believes any longer that he or she will be able to count on Social Security being solvent twenty-five or thirty years from now when it's time for their retirement. Many believe they will have to provide for themselves.

... Our economic engine needs capital, and it needs it now.

We need it for two good reasons.

First, our companies now pay a higher cost for money than companies in Japan and Ger-many. It's tough to compete when your interest payments are higher than your competitors'.

Second, we are borrowing foreign money. Foreign money kept us afloat during the 1980s. That money can leave just as easily as it came.

... We need to take steps to reinstill the ethic of saving among the American people.

... We need to press immediately for pro-savings incentives on all fronts.

... Our children today need to know how important savings are. Our goal should be to ingrain in the next generation the lesson that was temporarily lost in the present one.

... We're not investing in our future. From 1980 to 1989 Japan had an investment rate of 16 percent of gross domestic product. Ours was 4.5 percent. Who is going to win the race?

Checking for Understanding

❶ What are two reasons Americans who do not save may face difficult retirement years?

❷ What goal that was temporarily lost does Perot believe America should teach their children?

❸ What was the savings rate in the United States from 1980 to 1989?

Motown Records

From Failure to Success In Detroit during the 1950s, Berry Gordy was a lover of music (especially jazz) and an aspiring songwriter. When he came out of the Army in 1953, he purchased the 3-D Record Mart, a store specializing in jazz records. In 1955, 3-D went under and Gordy went to work for Ford Motor Company. Working for Ford, however, did not satisfy Gordy. In 1957 he quit to concentrate on songwriting. He and Tyran Carlo co-wrote "Reet Petite," the song that launched pop singer Jackie Wilson's career. Gordy's own career, though, did not take off until 1959, when he borrowed $800 to found his first record label, Tamla Records. The first release on Tamla records was Marvin Gaye's "Come to Me."

From Tamla to Motown Gordy expanded his fledgling empire by establishing a second record label, Motown Records, in 1960. The first release under the Motown label was the Satintones' "My Beloved." Gordy established two separate record labels for a variety of reasons. At that time, his record labels were actually released by different record distributors. Gordy felt he could market the different labels to different distributors, thus getting more individual attention. The second label would also allow for more airplay, because many program directors would agree to play only one record per label at any given time. Finally, Gordy felt that having his employees compete against each other for competing labels would lead to greater productivity and creativity.

The Tamla and Motown record labels became successful very quickly. Tamla Records had its first million seller in 1961 (the Miracles' "Shop Around"). In 1962, yet a third record label, Gordy Records (originally Miracle Records) was established. Motown expanded still further when it went into the record pressing and distribution business. By the early 1960s, Gordy was running out of record companies to distribute his records, so he decided to press "Way Over There" by the Miracles himself, and ended up selling 60,000 copies.

Hitsville, U.S.A. From this beginning, Motown Records went on to be one of the most successful record labels of the 1960s and 1970s. Between 1960 and 1970, Motown released 535 singles, of which 357 were chart hits. In 1966 alone, 75 percent of the company's releases made the charts, in an industry where the average is about 10 percent. Part of the reason for this success came from Gordy's philosophy in choosing which songs to release. Unlike other record labels, Gordy did not release songs he did not believe were hit material. Overall, Gordy released less than 10 percent of the material that Motown recorded.

The $61 Million Sale By 1972 Gordy moved his company to Los Angeles and turned to film, producing such movies as "Lady Sings the Blues" and "The Wiz." During the 1980s, Motown's popularity declined. In 1984 Motown lost its ranking as the largest African American-owned company. In 1988 Gordy sold Motown Records to MCA and a private investment firm (Boston Ventures) for $61 million, but retained Motown's publishing division and film and television production company. It continues to publish sheet music and produce television shows today.

Free Enterprise in Action

1 What was Gordy's first record label called?

2 Why did Gordy choose to establish more than one record label?

3 Why do you think Motown was so successful in the 1960s and 1970s?

153

SECTION 2 Investing: Taking Risks With Your Savings

Stocks and Bonds Offer Investors Better Returns, But With More Risk

People usually distinguish between saving and investing. People have savings plans because they want a sure, fixed rate of interest. If people are willing to take a chance on earning a higher rate of return, however, they can invest their money in other ways, such as stocks and bonds. Nevertheless, it is usually impossible to get a higher rate of return without taking some risk. Of course, the very nature of risk implies that such investment may yield a lower rate of interest, too.

Stocks and Bonds

Stock, or shares of stock, entitles the buyer to a certain part of the future profits and assets of the corporation selling the stock. The person buying stock, therefore, becomes a part owner of a corporation. As proof of ownership, the corporation issues stock certificates similar to the ones in **Figure 7.5**. By issuing stock for sale, a company obtains funds for use in expanding its business and, it hopes, in making a large profit.

Stockholders—owners of stock—make money from stock in two ways. One is through **dividends,** the money return a stockholder receives on the amount he or she originally invested in the company.

The corporation may declare a dividend at one or more times during a year. Dividends, however, are paid only when the company makes a profit. The other way people make money on stock is by selling it for more than they paid for it. Some people buy stock just to speculate. They buy stock hoping that the price will increase greatly so they can sell at a profit. They do not buy it for the dividends.

Instead of buying stock, people with money to invest can buy bonds. A **bond** is a certificate a company or the government issues in exchange for borrowed money. It promises to pay a stated rate of interest over a stated period of time, and then to repay the borrowed amount in full at the end of that time. A bondholder lends money for a period of time to a company or government and is paid interest on that money. At the end of the period, the full amount of borrowed money is repaid. The period of time is called the bond's maturity.

Unlike buying stock, buying a bond does not make a bondholder part owner of the company or government that issued the bond. The bond be-comes part of the debt of the corporation or government, and the bondholder becomes a creditor. **Figure 7.6** (page 156) lists some of the other differences between stocks and bonds.

Tax-Exempt Bonds Local and state governments also sell **tax-exempt bonds.** The interest on this type of bond, unlike bonds issued by companies, is not taxed by the federal government. Interest that you earn on bonds your own city or state issues is also exempt from city and state income taxes. Tax-exempt bonds are good investments for wealthier people who would otherwise pay high taxes on interest earned from investments.

Savings Bonds The United States government issues **savings bonds** as one of its ways of borrowing money. They range in face value from $50 up to $10,000. The purchase of a U.S. savings bond is similar to buying a bank's certificate of deposit. A very safe form of investment, savings bonds are attractive to people with limited money to invest. A person buying a savings bond pays half the bond's face value. Then the bond increases in

◀ **Figure 7.5**
Stock Certificates ▶
Stock certificates like these are issued to people who have invested in a corporation. How is owning stock a form of saving?

Figure 7.6 Difference Between Stocks and Bonds

Stocks	Bonds
1. All corporations issue or offer to sell stock. That act is what makes them corporations.	1. Corporations are not required to issue bonds.
2. Stocks represent ownership.	2. Bonds represent debt.
3. Stocks do not have a fixed dividend rate (except preferred stocks).	3. Bonds pay a fixed rate of interest.
4. Dividends on stock are paid only if the corporation makes a profit.	4. Interest on bonds normally must always be paid, whether or not the corporation earns a profit.
5. Stocks do not have a maturity date. The corporation issuing the stock does not repay the stockholder.	5. Bonds have a maturity date. The bondholder is to be repaid the value of the bond, although if the corporation goes out of business it does not normally repay the bondholders.
6. Stockholders (except those with preferred stock) can elect a board of directors who control the corporation.	6. Bondholders usually have no voice in or control over how the corporation is run.
7. Stockholders have a claim against the property and income of a corporation only after the claims of all creditors (including bondholders and holders of preferred stock) have been met.	7. Bondholders have a claim against the property and income of a corporation that must be met before the claims of any stockholders, including those holding preferred stock.

value every six months until its full face value is reached—usually within 10 years. If you choose to turn in a U.S. savings bond before it matures, you are guaranteed a certain rate of interest, which changes depending on rates of interest in the economy. Many savers purchase these bonds because of the tax advantages they offer. The interest on U.S. savings bonds is not taxed by the federal government until the bond is turned in for cash. These bonds are also exempt from state and local taxes.

The Treasury Department also sells several types of larger investments. **Treasury bills** mature in anywhere from 3 months to 1 year. The minimum amount of investment for Treasury bills is $10,000. **Treasury notes** have maturity dates of 2 to 10 years, and **Treasury bonds** mature in 10 or more years. Notes and bonds are sold in minimums of $1,000 or $5,000. The interest on all three of these government securities is exempt from state and local income taxes, but not from federal income tax.

Stock and Bond Markets

Stocks are bought and sold through brokers. See **Figure 7.7**. The largest stock market is the New York Stock Exchange (NYSE) in New York City. The second largest is the American Stock Exchange (AMEX), also in New York. The stocks listed on these 2 exchanges account for more than 70 percent of the market value of all stocks listed on all of the exchanges in the United States.

In addition to the New York and American exchanges, there are supplemental stock exchanges and regional exchanges. One is the Midwest

Stock Exchange in Chicago. Stocks must be listed to be sold on all of these exchanges. A corporation offering stocks for sale must prove to the exchange that it is in good financial condition and engages in legal business. Most of the companies traded on stock exchanges are among the larger corporations.

Over-the-Counter Markets Stocks can also be sold on the **over-the-counter market.** Most of them are quoted on the National Association of Securities Dealers Automated Quotations (NASDAQ) national market system. Unlike stock exchanges, over-the-counter stocks are not traded in any specific place. Brokerage firms hold quantities of shares of stock that they buy and sell for investors. The stocks of smaller, lesser-known companies are often traded in this way. For example, assume that XYZ Corporation is a small company that sells computers. If an investor wanted to buy stock in it, he or she would check the stock market listings in the local newspaper. The table of over-the-counter stocks would list XYZ Corporation, the number of shares of stock sold the day before, and the price at which shares were bought and sold that

day. The investor would then call a broker and tell him or her to buy a certain number of shares. Usually stocks are sold in amounts of 100 shares, but some brokers will handle smaller amounts. The largest volume of over-the-counter transactions occurs through the NASDAQ.

Bond Markets The New York Stock Exchange Bond Market and the American Exchange Bond Market are the two largest bond exchanges. Bonds, including U.S. government bonds, are also sold over-the-counter.

Capital Gains and Losses Suppose a person buys stock at $20 a share and sells it for $30. The profit of $10 per share is called a **capital gain.** The person has had an increase in his or her capital, or wealth, of $10 a share. Of course, the value of stock may also

**Figure 7.7 ▲
Buying Stocks
or Bonds**
If you decide to buy stocks or bonds, you will have to use a broker. A **broker** is a person who acts as a go-between for buyers and sellers. Thousands of brokerage firms throughout the country buy and sell daily for ordinary investors. Brokerage houses communicate directly with the busy floors of the stock exchanges.

▼

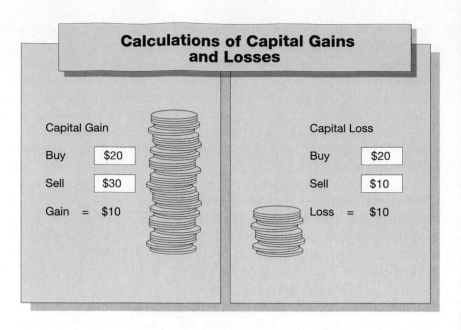

Figure 7.8 ▶
Capital Gains and Losses
Potential gains or losses may be calculated "on paper" before a person makes a decision to sell securities. No taxable gain or loss takes place, however, until the sale is completed.

Calculations of Capital Gains and Losses

Capital Gain	
Buy	$20
Sell	$30
Gain =	$10

Capital Loss	
Buy	$20
Sell	$10
Loss =	$10

fall. If a person decides to sell stock at a lower price than he or she paid for it, that person suffers a **capital loss.** Money may be made or lost on bonds in much the same way. See **Figure 7.8**.

Mutual Funds: An Easy Way to Invest One of the easiest ways to invest in stocks and bonds is to participate in a mutual fund. A **mutual fund** is an investment company that pools the money of many individuals to buy stocks, bonds, or other investments. By putting savings into a mutual fund, an individual usually is able to purchase a little bit of a large number of stocks or bonds.

Mutual funds have several other important advantages for small investors. One is that the risk of losing money from a poor investment is decreased. Professionals with experience in the stock or bond market make decisions about how to invest the fund's money. Most mutual funds hold a variety of stocks or bonds. Losses in one area are likely to be made up by gains in another. Some funds invest in stocks that are likely to increase rapidly in value, some in stocks and bonds that pay high dividends and interest, and some in tax-exempt bonds. As **Figure 7.9** shows, a

bewildering array of mutual funds is available to investors.

One type of mutual fund, called a **money market fund,** normally uses investors' money to buy the short-term debt of businesses and banks. Most money market funds allow investors to write checks against their money in the fund. Any check, however, must be above some minimum amount, usually $500. The investor then earns money only on the amount left in the account. Banks, savings and loan associations, and savings banks now offer a similar service, called money market deposit accounts (MMDA). A major advantage of MMDA accounts is that the federal government insures them against loss. Mutual funds and money market funds are not insured by the federal government.

Regulating Securities and Exchanges The securities market is heavily regulated today, both at the state and federal levels. The Securities and Exchange Commission (SEC), created by the Securities Exchange Act of 1934, is responsible for administering all federal securities laws. It has regulatory authority over brokerage firms, stock exchanges, and most businesses that issue stock. It also investigates any dealings between or among corporations, such as mergers, that affect the value of stocks.

Congress passed the Securities Act of 1933 to avoid another stock market crash like that of 1929. The act requires that all essential information concerning the issuing of stocks or bonds be made available to investors. This requirement is fulfilled with a registration statement filed with the federal government. A briefer description, called a prospectus, must be given to each potential buyer. It lists the amount offered, the price, and the use that the company plans to make of the money raised by the stock or bonds. Mutual funds must also distribute a prospectus describing the fund and the way in which the money will be invested.

Today states also have securities laws. These are designed mostly to prevent schemes that would take advantage of small investors.

Can You Get Rich Quick in the Stock Market?

You may have heard about some persons becoming millionaires overnight by making smart investments in the stock market. A stockbroker may give you advice about which stocks to buy; he or she may even have a "hot" tip. If that broker truly has information that no one else has, he or she is in possession of **inside information.** It is illegal for a broker to give out this information and also illegal for a client to profit from it.

Figure 7.9
Many Mutual Funds
The small investor should find out how the mutual fund he or she may choose has performed compared to other funds over a period of several years. Investors' magazines track the performance of well-known funds.

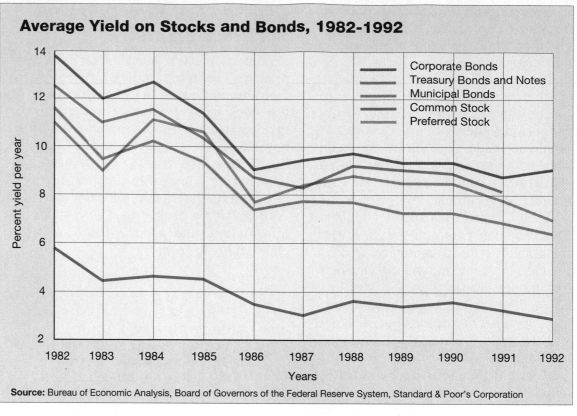

Average Yield on Stocks and Bonds, 1982-1992

Percent yield per year

Legend:
— Corporate Bonds
— Treasury Bonds and Notes
— Municipal Bonds
— Common Stock
— Preferred Stock

Years: 1982 1983 1984 1985 1986 1987 1988 1989 1990 1991 1992

Source: Bureau of Economic Analysis, Board of Governors of the Federal Reserve System, Standard & Poor's Corporation

**Figure 7.10 ▲
Yield on Stocks and Bonds**

The term *yield* means actual return on investment. Which type of investment has had the highest average yield from 1982 to 1992? Which type of investment has the lowest percentage yield?

If the broker's information came from his or her company's research department, then that information is available to a large number of people. The value of public investment research information to you as an investor is essentially zero.

You will do no better by following the advice of researchers from a stock brokerage company than you would by randomly selecting stocks. **Figure 7.10** gives a more realistic reflection of what an investor in stocks and bonds should expect to earn.

Public Information Information flows rapidly in the stock market. The value of public information for an investor is basically what that investor paid for it—zero. According to Nobel prize-winning economist Paul Samuelson:

Even the best investors seem to find it hard to do better than comprehensive common stock averages, or better on the average than random selection among stocks of comparable variability.

SECTION 2 REVIEW

Understanding Vocabulary

Define stock, stockholders, dividends, bond, tax-exempt bonds, savings bonds, Treasury bills, Treasury notes, Treasury bonds, over-the-counter market, capital gain, broker, capital loss, mutual fund, money market fund, inside information.

Reviewing Objectives

1. How do stocks differ from bonds?
2. What are the benefits of mutual funds and money market funds?
3. Why are "hot" tips of no value to investors?

SECTION **3** *Special Savings Plans and Goals*

SECTION 3 FOCUS

Terms to Know pension plans, Keogh Plan, Individual Retirement Account, diversification

Objectives *After reading this section, you should be able to:*
1. Describe three kinds of **retirement investments**.
2. Decide **how much to save and invest**.

Special Savings Plans Protect Your Future

One of the reasons that people save is to have income to spend when they retire. In addition to their savings, most Americans have additional sources of income for the years after they stop work.

Investing for Retirement

Many individuals have company retirement plans called **pension plans** that provide retirement income. Also, most people are eligible for, or able to receive, Social Security payments when they reach retirement. Nevertheless, many people choose to save and invest in private retirement plans. See **Figure 7.11**.

A major benefit of a private or personal pension plan is the tax savings. You do not have to pay federal income tax *immediately* on the earned income that you invest in one of these retirement plans, or on the interest that the plan earns if it does not exceed a certain amount. Should you need to take money out of the plan early, however, you have to pay a tax penalty. Otherwise, you pay income tax only as you withdraw money from the plan at retirement. Because your yearly income will in all probability be less then, your tax rate will be lower.

Individual Pension Plans The Keogh (KEE-oh) Act of 1972 was passed to help self-employed people set up their own pension plans. The **Keogh Plan** allows those people who are

Figure 7.11 Comfortable Retirement Americans are living longer so there are more years of retirement for many. How do their earlier investing and saving decisions affect their lives? ▼

self-employed to set aside a maximum of 15 percent of their income up to a specified amount each year and deduct that amount from their yearly taxable income.

Another form of retirement plan is the **Individual Retirement Account** (IRA). As of 1986, a person who earns less than $25,000 can contribute up to $2,000 per year and deduct it from taxable income. For married couples who both work outside the home and have a combined income of less than $40,000, the allowable deduction is $4,000. If only one spouse works, the amount allowed is $2,250. For people covered by an employer pension plan, only a partial deduction is allowed for single people who earn between $25,000 and $35,000 and married couples who earn between $40,000 and $50,000. For people whose incomes exceed those limits, the law allows yearly nondeductible contributions of up to $2,000 or $2,250, with tax deferred on the interest.

Real Estate as an Investment Buying real estate, such as land and buildings, is another form of investing. For the past 50 years or so, an investment in one's own home, condominium, or co-op has often proven to be wise in many parts of the country. Resale values have soared at times, especially during the late 1970s. See **Figure 7.12**. In the early 1980s and again in the early 1990s, however, the growth in the price of housing slowed in some areas. In some places real estate values fell for a few years. Buying raw, or undeveloped, land is a much riskier investment. No one can guarantee that there will be a demand in the future for a particular piece of land. The same is true for housing, too, but most people do not buy housing for the purpose of selling it.

Figure 7.12 ▶
Home Prices

Variations in supply and demand produce different prices in different parts of the country. Which two regions of the country have had the highest housing price increases since 1975?

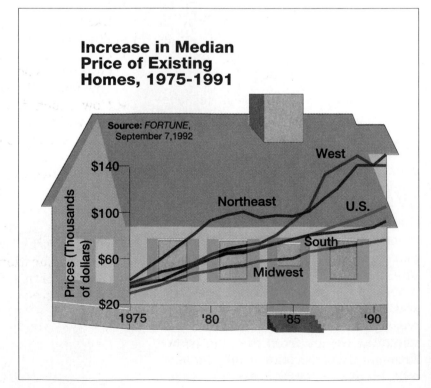

Increase in Median Price of Existing Homes, 1975-1991

Source: FORTUNE, September 7, 1992

Selected Investments Ranked by Risk and Potential Return

High

Risk

Low

Stocks

Bonds

Stock-Based Mutual Funds

Bond-Based Mutual Funds

Certificates of Deposit

Passbook Savings Accounts

Low   Rate of Return   High

◀ **Figure 7.13 Risk and Returns**

Perhaps the most risk-free investment is an insured passbook savings account. Certainly, a CD is relatively risk-free. A slightly riskier investment is a mutual fund that invests in bonds issued by businesses. Why is this riskier? The market value of those bonds could fall. Some of the companies might go out of business and not be able to repay the bonds at maturity. In both cases, the value of your shares in the mutual fund would fall. You could also invest your savings in the stock or bond market directly. Here, you are taking the most risk. The market value of stocks can rise and fall dramatically and so, too, can the value of your investment.

Real estate, either as raw land or developed land, is not very easy to turn into cash on short notice. Sometimes real property stays on the market for long periods of time. This difficulty in getting cash for your investment is one of the trade-offs involved in investing in real estate. You cannot get your money as quickly as you could if you had invested in stocks, bonds, a CD, or some other savings plan.

Deciding How Much to Save and Invest

Saving involves a trade-off like every other activity. The more you save today, the more you can buy and consume a year from now, 10 years from now, or 30 years from now. You will, however, have less to spend today. Deciding what percentage of income to save depends on the following factors:

- How much do you spend on your fixed expenses?
- What are your reasons for saving?
- How much interest can you earn on your savings and, therefore, how fast will they grow?
- How much income do you think you will be earning in the future?

If you expect to make a much higher income tomorrow, you have less reason to save a large percentage of today's income. In this case, it would be better to wait to start a large savings plan. It is a good idea, however, to have some sort of savings plan. There are several questions to answer before you decide on this plan:

- What degree of risk are you willing to take? **Figure 7.13** ranks various investments according to risk.
- How important is it that your savings be readily available in case you need immediate cash?
- Will your standard of living at retirement depend largely on your accumulated savings?

Figure 7.14
Lowering Risk
"Don't put all your eggs in one basket" is a phrase you have certainly heard before. The theory behind it can be applied to how a person chooses to invest.

Spreading Out Your Investments

Investing money in several different types of accounts lowers the overall risk, as **Figure 7.14** shows. If one investment turns sour, the others may do better. Financial planners and economists call spreading out your investments **diversification.**

When you have very little income and cannot afford any investment losses, you should probably put your savings in insured accounts in a local bank or savings and loan, or you should buy U.S. government savings bonds. The greater your income and the more savings you have, the more you can diversify into stocks, bonds, and so on.

Amount of Risk Such questions are difficult to answer because there are so many ways to save and invest. Perhaps the most important factor to consider is the amount of risk that you are willing to take with your savings.

If you put a lesser amount in the more risky types of investments, you would have some security with your savings and have some money available should you need cash in a hurry. You would also have a chance of making high returns.

Your Values Are Important, Too

Your values may also determine where you invest your money. If you believe that your community needs more development, you might choose to put your savings in a savings and loan there that guarantees that a large percentage of its investments are made in community loans. You may also choose to invest in stocks issued by environmentally responsible companies or companies that have aggressive equal opportunity programs.

SECTION 3 REVIEW

Understanding Vocabulary
Define pension plans, Keogh Plan, Individual Retirement Account, diversification.

Reviewing Objectives
1. What are three ways of investing for retirement?
2. How should a person determine the amount to save and invest?

Understanding Interest

Two types of interest exist: simple and compound. Do you know what the difference is?

Simple Interest

Simple interest is figured only on the original amount deposited, not on any interest earned. Figuring interest is similar to figuring percents. **Figure A** shows that a $100 savings account that pays 6 percent simple interest will earn $6 the first year. Therefore the account balance at the end of the year will be $106—the original amount plus the first year's interest. The second year the interest will also be $6, even though the account has grown, and the balance will be $112.

Compound Interest

Compound interest is paid on the original amount deposited plus any interest that has been earned. As **Figure B** shows, if you deposit $100 in an account earning 6 percent interest compounded annually, it will earn $6 the first year and $6.36 the second year. With compound interest, your savings the second year will amount to $112.36.

Figure A

6% = .06

```
$  100
x   .06
$ 6.00  interest earned each year

$  100  Original amount saved
     6  First year's interest
+    6  Second year's interest
$  112  Total after two years
```

Figure B

```
$  100
x   .06
$ 6.00  interest earned first year

$  106
x   .06
$ 6.36  interest earned second year
```

Total after two years
$100 + $6 + $6.36 = $112.36

Practicing the Skill

❶ Assume that your bank pays 5.5 percent on savings deposits. What is the simple interest paid in the third year on an initial $50 deposit? How much is the total savings at the end of the third year?

❷ Assume that on $100 the interest paid is 5.5 percent compounded annually. How much interest is earned in the first, second, and third year? What is the total amount in the savings account after three years?

Readings in Economics

THE CASE FOR U.S. SAVINGS BONDS

by Michael Sivy

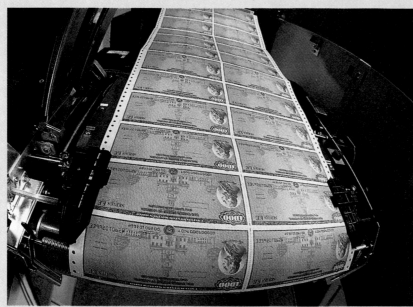

How can you beat the pitiful yields on today's CDs [certificates of deposit] without taking crazy risks? . . .

If you think you might need your money [soon], go with U.S. Savings Bonds. That's right: Series EE savings bonds. . . .

■ Fully backed by the U.S. Government, the bonds can be bought at most banks and may be available through payroll-deduction plans.

■ You can invest as much as $15,000 each year.

■ The bonds come in denominations as small as . . . a $50 face value. (The face value, which is double the purchase price, shows the minimum that a bond would grow to in 12 years.)

■ EE bonds don't pay cash interest; instead, the interest accrues and the bonds rise in value until you cash them in.

■ You can redeem the bonds after six months or hold them for as long as 30 years.

■ If you cash them in after six months, you collect an annualized rate that starts at 4.16% and rises to a minimum of 6% for bonds held five years or longer. . . .

■ In addition to being exempt from state and local taxes, your interest is not subject to federal income tax until you redeem the EEs.

■ After six months, you have the option of swapping $500 or more of Series EE bonds for Series HH issues, which pay 6% cash interest. If you swap, you don't have to pay taxes on the accumulated EE interest until you redeem the HHs. . . .

If all those terms sound complicated, just keep your eye on the bottom line: You get more than the average 3.2% a money fund pays if you cash in after six months. . . . So don't buy savings bonds only for patriotic reasons—buy them for profit, too.

• THINK ABOUT IT •

1. How does Michael Sivy think consumers can beat the low CD interest rates?

2. When will a savings bond be worth its face value?

7 *Highlights*

Why Save?

Key Terms

saving (p. 146)
interest (p. 146)
passbook savings account
   (p. 147)
statement savings
   account (p. 147)

money market deposit
   account (p. 148)
time deposits (p. 148)
maturity (p. 148)
certificates of deposit
   (p. 148)

Summary

   Every person must decide when it is best to save and invest. Beginning investors should compare passbook, statement, and money market savings accounts. There are also advantages to saving in time deposit accounts.

Investing: Taking Risks With Your Savings

Key Terms

stock (p. 154)
stockholders (p. 155)
dividends (p. 155)
bond (p. 155)
tax-exempt bonds (p. 155)
savings bonds (p. 155)
Treasury bills (p. 156)
Treasury notes (p. 156)
Treasury bonds (p. 156)

over-the-counter market
   (p. 157)
capital gain (p. 157)
broker (p. 157)
capital loss (p. 158)
mutual fund (p. 158)
money market fund
   (p. 158)
inside information
   (p. 159)

Summary

   Stocks and bonds offer an investor choices with distinct advantages. There are investment funds available in stock and bond markets that have less risk than individual stocks and bonds. "Hot" tips will not help an investor get rich quick in the stock market.

Special Savings Plans and Goals

Key Terms

pension plans (p. 161)
Keogh Plan (p. 161)
Individual Retirement
   Account, or IRA (p. 162)
diversification (p. 164)

Summary

   Individual and company-sponsored pensions plans help people save for retirement. A person should consider interest and risk in deciding how much to save and invest.

Identifying Key Terms

Write the letter of the definition in Column B below that correctly defines each term in Column A.

Column A
1. mutual fund (p. 158)
2. savings bond (p. 155)
3. stock (p. 154)
4. dividend (p. 155)
5. capital gain (p. 157)

Column B
a. represents part ownership in a corporation
b. an increase in wealth realized when a person sells an asset
c. the money return a stockholder receives from a corporation on an investment
d. a less risky way to invest in stocks and bonds
e. a government security attractive to small investors

Write a paragraph describing the different types of accounts that are available in banks, savings and loan associations, and credit unions. Make sure you include the following:

passbook savings account (p. 147)
statement savings account (p. 147)
money market deposit account (p. 148)
time deposit (p. 148)
certificate of deposit (CD) (p. 148)

Recalling Facts and Ideas

Section 1
1. What is the main advantage of passbook and statement savings accounts?
2. Why is a certificate of deposit (CD) called a time deposit?
3. Why are deposits of up to $100,000 in savings institutions often considered very safe?

Section 2
4. What is the basic difference between a stock and a bond?
5. What are two advantages of United States savings bonds?
6. What term describes the difference between the purchase price of a stock and the sale price of a stock?
7. What kind of investment company hires professionals to manage the investments of a pool of investors?
8. What government agency regulates stock and bond markets?

Section 3
9. What are the two most common types of pension plans for individuals?
10. What are some of the ways you can decide how much you should save?
11. "Don't put all your eggs in one basket." This quotation is an example of what principle of investing?

Critical Thinking

Section 1
Understanding Cause and Effect How does buying a U.S. savings bond increase the United States government's debt?

Section 2
Drawing Conclusions Bonds yield a more certain return than stocks. Why do individuals, nonetheless, invest in stocks?

Section 3

Identifying Alternatives Assume that you have $100,000 in savings. Write a list of the potential investments you might make and what percentage of the $100,000 you would invest in each. Would your plan be diversified?

Applying Economic Concepts

Scarcity Write down a list of short-term saving goals, such as saving to buy a new portable CD player. Make a list of the typical ways in which you can save for such a purchase. Then make a list of long-term saving goals, such as saving for a house or retirement. Make a separate list of the ways you could achieve your goals. What is the major difference between the two ways of saving?

Chapter Projects

1. **Individual Project** Choose two stocks on the New York or American stock exchange, and follow their prices for two weeks in the financial pages of a newspaper. You will need to read only the last column of figures. Note the daily closing prices for each stock, and then make a line graph showing the stocks' performance over the two-week period.
2. **Cooperative Learning Project** Work in groups of four. Each group will study the results of an investment of $100,000 in one of the following (choose from the list depending on the number of groups you have):

   - One particular stock
   - One particular bond
   - A mutual fund
   - U.S. Treasury bonds
   - Residential real estate
   - Commercial real estate (office buildings, for example)
   - Old masters paintings (such as those by Renoir and Rembrandt)
   - Gold
   - Diamonds

Each group should research either in the library or through a securities brokerage firm in your area to determine what $100,000 placed in each one of those investments 10 years ago would be worth today. Rank and compare those rates of return.

Reviewing Skills

Understanding Interest

1. **Figuring Simple Interest** A local bank is offering simple interest on savings accounts at 6.6 percent per year. If you deposit $1,000, how much will you have in the account at the end of four years?
2. **Understanding Compound Interest** Another bank in the same area is offering the same interest rate but indicates that it is compounding interest annually. If you deposit your $1,000 there, how much more will you have in your savings account at the end of three years in the second bank than in the first bank?

Writing About Economics

Descriptive Writing Reexamine the list of interest rates paid by various institutions that you compiled for Your Economics Journal. Write a descriptive paragraph explaining in which institution you will deposit your savings. Explain why.

Planning a Trip

From the classroom of Art Benfield, South High School, Pueblo, Colorado

In Unit 2 you studied practical economics for the consumer. In this experiment, you will apply consumer decisions in planning a vacation trip. (You may want to reread the material on pages 58–61 of the text.)

One important means of making wise consumer choices is planning those choices. For example, planning a vacation trip is a challenge because of the many trade-offs and opportunity costs involved in your decisions. Also, you should determine before taking a vacation what the total costs in time and money are going to be.

Libraries and media centers contain many materials that will help you plan the trip. Many have newspapers from several cities that carry local advertising for food, lodging, and entertainment. In addition, travel agents, family, and friends may suggest places to visit and may be able to estimate costs for lodging or entertainment in these locations.

Tools

1. A travel atlas
2. Motel guidebooks
3. Chamber of Commerce guide books
4. Government guides

Procedures

Step A Using a travel atlas and other guidebooks and resources, plan a trip from your home to anywhere in North America that can be reached by car. The round-trip must be at least 2,000 miles in length, but not more than 350 miles in one day. You should include the names or number of people who will be going along. At some point along the way, you must do all of the following at least once:

1. Visit a geographic point of interest: high mountain, body of water, desert, national forest, etc.
2. Visit a scientific point of interest: aquarium, natural history museum, museum of science and industry, NASA, etc.
3. Stay overnight in one large city and eat in a fancy restaurant.
4. Attend one cultural event such as a play, symphony, or ethnic festival.
5. Attend one sports event or entertainment point of interest such as a theme park or dude ranch.

Step B Research the costs and complete a daily journal, like the one on this page, for each day of the trip. Include the following:
1. route and miles traveled
2. fuel and food costs
3. lodging (name of motel or other lodging and location) and cost
4. itemized list of entertainment and costs

Step C Complete a map highlighting the route of your trip.

Example

Sample Daily Journal
DAY 1
Route and miles traveled: _____
Places of interest visited: _____

Item	Cost		
Entertainment			
Fuel			
Food	breakfast	lunch	dinner
Shopping/other costs			
Lodging	room	phone	other

Lab Report

Step D Use your journal and planning experience to answer the questions below.
1. What were the total costs of food, lodging, entertainment, and fuel on your trip?
2. Which of the above categories of costs could have been reduced by the greatest amount by trade-offs such as choosing different restaurants, motels, etc?
3. How much did you spend each day?
4. What was the average total expenditure per person?

Step E Write a two-page report that explains the economic choices of the trip in terms of trade-offs and opportunity costs.

U N I T

3

MICROECONOMICS: MARKETS, PRICES, AND BUSINESS COMPETITION

173

8 SUPPLY AND DEMAND

What are these people doing?

Does anyone tell them how many CDs to purchase?

What determines how many CDs they want to purchase?

Will the price of CDs go up or down in the future?

Why are there sales for specific CDs at certain stores?

Does the government ever regulate the price of CDs?

Your Economics Journal

Keep a record of the things that you thought about buying, but did not buy during one week. After you list these items, indicate next to each one why you decided *not* to buy that item.

SECTION **1** Demand

SECTION 1 FOCUS

Terms to Know voluntary exchange, law of demand, utility, law of diminishing marginal utility, real income effect, substitution effect

Objectives *After reading this section, you should be able to:*

① Describe how the principle of **voluntary exchange** operates in a market economy.

② Explain how diminishing marginal utility, the real income effect, and the substitution effect relate to the **law of demand**.

Demand Plays a Major Role in a Market Economy

When you buy something, do you ever wonder why it sells at that particular price? Few individual consumers feel they have any influence over the price of an item. In a market economy, however, all consumers collectively, or as a group, have a great influence on the price of all goods and services. Perhaps the best way to understand this is to look first at how people in the marketplace decide what to buy and at what price. This is demand. Then examine how the people who want to sell those things decide how much to sell and at what price. This is supply.

What is the marketplace? A market represents the freely chosen action between buyers and sellers of goods and services. A market for a particular item can be local, national, and international. In a market economy, individuals looking out for their own best interests decide for themselves the answers to the four basic economic questions you studied in Chapter 2.

The Market and Voluntary Exchange

The basis of activity in a market economy is the principle of **voluntary exchange.** A buyer and a seller exercise their economic freedoms by working out on their own the terms of an exchange. For example in **Figure 8.1**, the seller of an automobile sets a price based on the market, and the buyer,

Figure 8.1 Voluntary Exchange

By definition, the two parties to a voluntary exchange are freely choosing to engage in that transaction, or business deal. In order to make the exchange, both must believe they will be better off—happier and richer.

▼

through the act of buying, agrees to the product and the price.

Through the principle of voluntary exchange, supply and demand enter into the activity of a market economy. Remember, supply and demand analysis is a model of how buyers and sellers operate in the marketplace. Such analysis is a way of explaining cause and effect in relation to price.

The Law of Demand

The **law of demand** explains how people react to changing prices in terms of the quantities of a good or service that they purchase. Look at **Figure 8.2** to see this relationship. The word *demand* has a special meaning in economics. It represents all of the different quantities of a good or service that consumers will purchase at various prices. It includes both the willingness and the ability to pay. A person may say he or she wants a new compact disc. Until that person is both willing and able to buy it, no demand for compact discs has been created by that individual.

Several factors affect how much people will buy of any item at a particular price. These factors include diminishing marginal utility, real income, and possible substitutes.

Diminishing Marginal Utility Almost everything that people like, desire, use, think they would like to use, and so on, gives satisfaction. The term economists use for satisfaction is *utility*. **Utility** is defined as the power that a good or service has to satisfy a want. People decide what to buy and how much they are willing and able to pay based on utility. In deciding to make a purchase, they decide the amount of satisfaction, or use, they think they will get from a good or service. Consider the utility that can be derived from a compact disc.

At $8.00 per compact disc, how many will you buy? Assuming that you have money, you will buy at least one. Will you buy a second? A third? A

fourth? That decision depends on the additional utility, or satisfaction, you expect to receive from buying and listening to another compact disc. You will have a higher level of total, or overall, satisfaction from owning more compact discs. Most likely, the satisfaction you receive from each additional one, however, will be less than for each previous one. This example explains the **law of diminishing marginal utility**. See **Figure 8.3**.

Your *total* satisfaction will rise with each unit bought. But the amount of *additional* satisfaction, or marginal

Law of Demand

Price Goes Down — Quantity Demanded Goes Up

Price Goes Up — Quantity Demanded Goes Down

▲ **Figure 8.2 The Law of Demand**
According to the law of demand, quantity demanded and price move in opposite directions.

As price goes up, quantity demanded goes down. As price goes down, quantity demanded goes up. There is an inverse, or opposite, relationship between demand and price.

Figure 8.3 Diminishing Satisfaction ▼
Regardless of how satisfying the first taste of an item is, satisfaction declines with additional consumption. Even at a zero price, eventually the consumer receives no additional satisfaction and stops eating.

177

utility, will diminish, or lessen, with each additional unit.

At some point, you will stop buying additional compact discs. At that point, the satisfaction that you receive from owning more compact discs is less than the value you place on the $8.00 that you must pay for the item. People stop buying an item when one event occurs—when the value that they place on additional satisfaction from the next unit of the same item becomes less than the price they must pay for it. Assume that at a price of $8.00 per disc, you have enough after buying three. Thus, the value you place on additional satisfaction from a fourth one would be less than $8.00. According to what will give you the most satisfaction, you will save or spend the $8.00 on something else.

What if the price drops? Suppose the owner of the music store decided to have a special and sell compact discs at $7.00 each. You might buy at least one additional one.

If you look at the law of diminishing marginal utility again, the reason becomes clear. People will buy an item to the point at which the value they place on the satisfaction from the last unit bought is equal to the price. At that point, people will stop buying. If the price falls again, the lower price will attract people to buy more. This principle is true even though the satisfaction from each additional unit is less. People will continue to buy to the point again at which the satisfaction they receive falls below the price they must pay. This concept explains part of the law of demand. As the price of an item that people want decreases, they will generally buy more.

Real Income Effect The basis for the law of demand, however, does not rest only on diminishing marginal utility. No one—not even the wealthiest person in the world—will ever be able to buy everything he or she wants to buy. People's incomes limit the amount of

Real Income Effects

More Real Income	CD Price	Pizza Price	More Real Income
	$8x2=$16 spent	$1 per slice x 6 slices= $ 6 spent	
	$10x2=$20 spent		
Less Real Income	$12x2=$24 spent	$2 per slice x 6 slices= $12 spent	Less Real Income

▲ **Figure 8.4**
Income Limits Spending

A Suppose that you normally buy two new compact discs (CDs) per month at $8 per disc. That means that you spend $16. If the price goes up to $10 per CD, you would have to spend $20 per month to buy two. If the price of CDs continues to rise while your income does not, eventually you would not be able to buy two CDs per month because your real income, or purchasing power, has been reduced.

money they are able to spend as shown in **Figure 8.4**.

Individuals cannot keep buying the same quantity of a good if its price rises while their income stays the same. This concept is known as the **real income effect** on demand. In order to keep buying the same number of compact discs per month, you would need to cut back on buying other things. The real income effect forces you to make a trade-off. The same is true for every item you buy, particularly those you buy on a regular basis.

The real income effect works in the opposite direction, too. If you are already buying two compact discs a month and the price drops in half, your real income increases. You will have more purchasing power and will probably increase the number of compact discs that you buy each month.

Substitution Effect Suppose two items that are not exactly the same satisfy basically the same need. Their cost is about the same. If the price of one falls, people will most likely substitute it in favor of the now higher-priced good. If the price of one of the items rises in relation to the price of the other, people will substitute the now lower-priced good. This principle is called the **substitution effect.** Suppose, for example, that you listen to both compact discs and audiocassettes. If the price of audiocassettes drops dramatically, you will probably buy more cassettes and fewer compact discs. In effect, you are substituting the lower-priced cassettes for the now relatively higher-priced compact discs. Alternatively, if the price of audiocassettes doubles, you probably will increase the number of compact discs you buy.

B Suppose you normally buy one medium cheese pizza every Saturday night. If the price of cheese pizzas doubles, you obviously cannot continue buying one every Saturday night and purchase everything else that you normally buy (with the same income, of course).

SECTION 1 REVIEW

Understanding Vocabulary
Define voluntary exchange, law of demand, utility, law of diminishing marginal utility, real income effect, substitution effect.

Reviewing Objectives
1. How does the principle of voluntary exchange operate in a market economy?

2. How do diminishing marginal utility, the real income effect, and the substitution effect influence the quantity demanded for a given product or service?

The Body Shop

Starting Out The Body Shop was founded by Anita Roddick, a 33-year-old English woman with two young daughters and a husband—Gordon. The original idea was to open a store that would feature lotions and cosmetics made from all-natural ingredients. Shortly after the first store was established, Gordon left on an extended trip to South America (a lifelong dream to ride from Buenos Aires to New York on horseback). Anita proceeded and opened her second store (in Chichester, U.K.) using a small loan from a local gas station owner. By the time Gordon returned, the second store was successful. The Roddicks were ready to expand The Body Shop throughout England.

The company grew quickly, raising capital by a public stock offering in 1984. On the first day of its trading, the price of a share of The Body Shop stock rose dramatically. By 1988, Anita Roddick decided to expand to the United States. Originally, she planned to start slowly and forego franchising, but the slow expansion left The Body Shop lagging in the United States natural cosmetics market. Vigorous expansion in the United States began when Roddick started franchising The Body Shop in 1990.

Anita's Causes The success of The Body Shop is driven not only by its products, but by its "causes." Anita Roddick may be as well known for her environmentalism as for her business sense. From the beginning, The Body Shop has been environmentally conscious, using, for example, biodegradable products and refillable containers. Roddick also uses her stores to promote such causes as saving the whales and saving rain forests. In 1992 she used her United States shops as voter registration centers, signing up 50,000 new voters. In late 1993, she planned to open a store in Harlem, and invest the store's profits in the surrounding community.

Information Please Part of The Body Shop's success stems from its unique marketing plan. The Body Shop has no official marketing department and does not advertise, but instead makes plenty of information available to clients inside the stores. Store shelves are packed with all sorts of information (labels, pamphlets, etc.) about its products. While most of the cosmetics industry promotes fantasy and glamour, The Body Shop promotes well-being. To reach the more socially conscious customer of the '90s, The Body Shop presents information that shows it really cares about its clients, as well as about environmental and social issues.

Free Enterprise in Action

1 What type of products does The Body Shop sell?

2 How does The Body Shop show concern for environmental and social issues?

3 Why would information replace advertising as a marketing tool?

SECTION **2** The Demand Curve and the Elasticity of Demand

SECTION 2 FOCUS

Terms to Know demand curve, elasticity, price elasticity of demand, elastic demand, inelastic demand, complementary good

Objectives *After reading this section, you should be able to:*

❶ Explain what you can learn by **graphing the demand curve.**

❷ Describe how the **price elasticity of demand** affects how much the price for a given product can vary.

❸ Discuss the **determinants of demand.**

Price and Quantity Demanded Are Directly Related

Figure 8.5
Height and Weight
The graph shows a composite of heights and weights of men and women in the United States.

They say that a picture is worth a thousand words. For much of economic analysis the "picture" is a graph. The graph shows a picture of the relationship between two statistics or concepts that are related. Think about the relationship between height and weight. On average, people who are six feet tall weigh more than people who are five and one-half feet tall. If we wanted to graph this relationship it would look something like **Figure 8.5**.

Graphing the Demand Curve

The law of demand can also be graphed. The relationship between the quantity demanded and price is one in which as the price goes up, the quantity demanded goes down. As the price goes down, the quantity demanded goes up. We should therefore be able to graph this relationship the same way we did the relationship between height and weight. We do so in **Figure 8.6**.

Let us use compact discs as an example. **Figure 8.6A** shows various prices and the quantity of compact discs demanded in a table. **Figure 8.6B**

Typical Relationship Between Height and Weight

Height (inches) vs *Weight (lbs.)*

and **Figure 8.6C** show this same information as graphs.

Time and Quality Are Important Notice that on the bottom of the graphs in **Figures 8.6B** and **8.6C** we refer to the quantity of compact discs demanded per year. The time period is one year. We could have said one day, one week, one month, or two years. Typically, economists talk about quantity demanded per year. It is important to know the

Plotting the Price-Quantity Pairs for Compact Discs (CDs)

▲ **B Plotting the Price-Quantity Pairs**
The bottom axis shows the quantity demanded. The side axis shows the price per compact disc.
Each pair of price and quantity demanded represents a point on the graph. We label these points A, B, C, D, E, F, G, H, I, J, K.

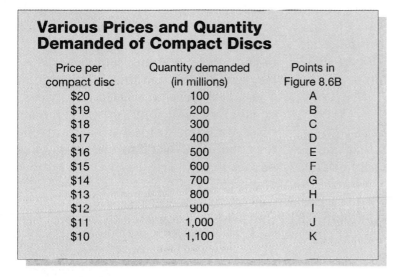

Various Prices and Quantity Demanded of Compact Discs

Price per compact disc	Quantity demanded (in millions)	Points in Figure 8.6B
$20	100	A
$19	200	B
$18	300	C
$17	400	D
$16	500	E
$15	600	F
$14	700	G
$13	800	H
$12	900	I
$11	1,000	J
$10	1,100	K

Figure 8.6
Relationship of Demand to Price
The series of three graphs shows how the price of goods and services affects the quantity demanded.

A Table of Prices and Quantity ▲
Demanded
The numbers in Figure 8.6A show that as the prices per CD decrease, the quantity of CDs demanded increases.

The Demand Curve for Compact Discs (CDs)

Demand Curve

C Demand Curve
When we connect the points from Figure 8.6B with a line, we end up with the **demand curve.**
A demand curve shows the quantity demanded of a good or service at each possible price. It slopes downward (falls from left to right). You can see the *inverse* relationship between price and quantity demanded here.

◀

time period during which you are measuring the quantity demanded. The longer the time period, the more the quantity demanded will be for any given price. Therefore, do not forget to indicate the time period in any discussion of the quantity demanded of anything.

Compact discs are not all of the same quality. Often in the "budget-lines" of CDs the sound quality is sort of tinny. When you talk about the demand curve for different items, you have to assume a *constant-quality unit*. You do not have to actually figure out what that standard quality unit is. Just be aware that when you draw a demand curve such as in **Figure 8.6C** (page 183) you are holding quality constant.

What if Demand Increases? Sometimes something happens that causes demand to increase for certain items. As **Figure 8.7** shows, demand increases can occur for many varied reasons. Using CDs as an example, **Figure 8.8**

shows what happens when demand increases.

Actually, the shift in the demand curve in **Figure 8.8** happens all the time to many goods and services simply because population increases. Even at the same price, more compact discs will be demanded 5 years from now because there will be more consumers.

The Price Elasticity of Demand

The law of demand is straightforward: The higher the price charged, the lower the quantity demanded, and vice versa. If you were the owner of a music store selling compact discs, how could you use this information? You know that if you lower prices, consumers will buy more compact discs. Imagine you have extra inventory, and you want to sell it quickly because you are expecting a new shipment of compact discs. You know that if you have a big sale and lower the price of compact discs, you are

Figure 8.7 Increases in Demand

If suddenly fashion trends make everybody want to wear high-top tennis shoes, we say that the demand for high-top tennis shoes has increased. If latest medical research proves that taking vitamin E pills reduces the chance of heart attacks, the demand for vitamin E pills will increase. If scientists were to prove that listening to more music increases life span, then the demand for compact discs would increase.

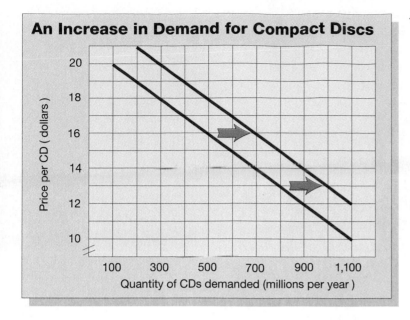

An Increase in Demand for Compact Discs

Price per CD (dollars)

20

18

16

14

12

10

100   300   500   700   900   1,100

Quantity of CDs demanded (millions per year)

◀ **Figure 8.8**
An Increase in Demand for Compact Discs
An increase in demand for compact discs means that people will want, and be willing to buy, more compact discs per year at all prices. How do we show this with our demand curve? Here you see two demand curves. The first one is exactly the same as the one in Figure 8.6C. The second one has moved to the right. It has moved because of the increase in the demand for compact discs. Just take one price, for example, $15. Before the scientists proved that listening to more music increases life span, the quantity demanded was 600 million compact discs per year. Now that number has increased to 800 million compact discs per year. The quantity demanded at any price has gone up.

going to sell more. That is the law of demand. Should you lower your prices by 1 percent, 2 percent, or 30 percent in order to sell your excess stock? You cannot really answer this question unless you know how *responsive* consumers will be to a decrease in the price of compact discs. Economists call this price responsiveness **elasticity**. The measure of the **price elasticity of demand** is how much consumers respond to a given change in price.

A good way to think about elasticity is to use the example of two rubber dollar bills: one you can stretch very easily and the other you can hardly stretch at all, as **Figure 8.9** (page 186) shows.

Elastic Demand For some goods a rise or fall in price greatly affects the amount people are willing to buy. The demand for these goods is considered elastic, as is the demand for the highly specific food products on the left side of **Figure 8.10** (page 186). For example, one particular brand of coffee probably has a very **elastic demand**. Consumers consider the many competing brands to be almost the same. A small rise in the price of one brand will probably cause many consumers to purchase the cheaper substitute brands.

Inelastic Demand If a price change does not result in a substantial change in the quantity demanded, that demand is considered inelastic, as the general food categories on the right side of **Figure 8.10** show. Electricity, salt, pepper, sugar, and certain types

Figure 8.9 ▲
Elasticity
The economic concept of price elasticity deals with how much quantity demanded changes in reaction to a change in price.

of medicine normally have **inelastic demand.** We can compare a relatively inelastic demand with a relatively elastic demand at a particular price using two demand curves in one diagram. See **Figure 8.11**.

What Determines Price Elasticity of Demand? Why do some goods have elastic demand and others have inelastic demand? At least three factors determine the price elasticity of demand of a particular item: (1) the existence and similarity of substitutes, (2) the percentage of a person's total budget devoted to the purchases

of that good, and (3) how much time we allow for the consumer to adjust to the change in price.

Clearly, the more substitutes that exist for a good, the more responsive consumers will be to a change in the price of that good. A diabetic needs insulin, which has virtually no substitutes. The price elasticity of demand

Figure 8.10
Elastic versus Inelastic Demand
If the prices of certain goods rise, consumers will buy more of other goods—an example of elastic demand. Inelastic demand means that price changes have little impact on quantity demanded.

▼

elastic demand

inelastic demand

for insulin, therefore, is very low—it is inelastic. The opposite is true for Diet Coke. If the price of Diet Coke goes up by very much, many consumers may switch to Diet Pepsi. Because of the many substitutes available, its demand is relatively elastic.

If you do not spend much of your total budget on a particular good, you probably will not often notice increases in the price of that good. The percentage of a family's budget devoted to pepper is very small. If the price of pepper goes up, most people will keep buying about the same amount. Their demand for pepper is relatively inelastic. People spend much of their budget, however, on housing. If the price of new housing increases rapidly, fewer new homes will be sold. Housing demand is relatively elastic because it represents such a large proportion of a household's total yearly budget.

Finally, people take time to adjust and adapt to all changes, even changes in prices. If the price of electricity goes up by 100 percent tomorrow, you will have a hard time adjusting your behavior immediately in the face of this higher price. The longer the time allowed for adjustment, however, the more you can figure out ways to reduce the amount of electricity you use—by putting in lower wattage light bulbs, learning to live with a warmer house in the summer and a colder house in the winter, adding insulation to your attic, and so on. Therefore, the longer the time allowed for adjustment to the changes, the greater the price elasticity of demand.

Determinants of Demand

Many factors help determine demand for a specific product. Among these factors are changes in population and income, and in people's tastes

Figure 8.11
▼ **Graphing Elasticity of Demand**
The green line shows that with a very slight decrease in price, the quantity demanded increases dramatically (elastic demand). The purple line shows that the quantity demanded is not as responsive to price (inelastic demand).

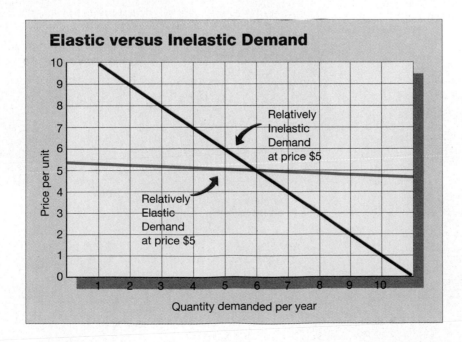

Elastic versus Inelastic Demand

Relatively Inelastic Demand at price $5

Relatively Elastic Demand at price $5

Price per unit

Quantity demanded per year

and preferences. **Figure 8.13** shows some of the determinants of demand and the reasons for demand changes.

Substitutes The existence of substitutes also affects demand. People often think of butter and margarine as substitutes. Suppose that the price of butter remains the same and the price of margarine falls. People will buy more margarine and less butter at all prices. The demand curve for butter will shift to the left. As the price of the substitute (margarine) decreases, the demand for the item under study (butter) also decreases. If the price of margarine rises, however, people will buy less margarine and more butter at all prices. The demand curve for butter will shift to the right. As the price of the substitute (margarine) increases, the demand for the item under study (butter) also increases. **Figure**

8.12 shows that not all substitutes are equal, however.

Complementary   Goods Although bread and butter can be used separately, they are often used together. Suppose the price of butter remains the same. If the price of bread drops, people will probably buy more bread. They will also probably buy more butter to use on the bread. Therefore, a decrease in the price of bread leads to an increase in the demand for its **complementary good**, butter. As a result, the demand curve for butter will shift to the right. If the price of bread increases, however, consumers will buy less bread and, as a result, will need less butter. An increase in the price of bread leads to a decrease in the demand for butter. Consequently, the demand curve for butter will shift to the left.

Figure 8.12
Substitutes

Margarine is an obvious substitute for butter. The price of one directly affects the price of the other. If, in contrast, the price of carrots increased, it would not affect the price of broccoli as directly. People might substitute one of several other vegetables.

What Determines Demand?

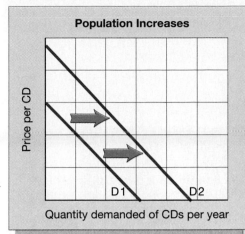

Population Increases

Price per CD

D1   D2

Quantity demanded of CDs per year

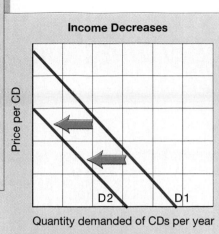

Income Decreases

Price per CD

D2   D1

Quantity demanded of CDs per year

Tastes and Preferences Change

Price per pair of bleached jeans

D1   D2

Quantity demanded of bleached jeans per year

Figure 8.13
What Determines Demand?

A Population ▲
When population increases, the market increases. Naturally, the demand for most products increases. This means that the demand curve for, say, CDs, shifts to the right. At each price, more CDs will be demanded as population increases. D1 represents CD demand before the population increased. D2 represents demand after the population increased.

B Income ▲
The demand for most goods and services depends on income. Your demand for compact discs would certainly decrease if your income dropped in half and you expected it to stay there. The demand curve for CDs for you would shift to the left as shown above. D1 represents CD demand before income decreased. D2 represents CD demand after income decreased.

C Tastes and Preferences ▲
One of the key factors that determines demand is people's tastes and preferences. If there were a sudden new fad at schools around the country in which everyone wants to wear bleached jeans, then the demand curve for bleached jeans will shift to the right as shown here. D1 represents demand for bleached jeans before they became a fad. D2 represents demand after they became a fad.

SECTION 2 REVIEW

Understanding Vocabulary
Define demand curve, elasticity, price elasticity of demand, elastic demand, inelastic demand, complementary good.

Reviewing Objectives
1. What does graphing the demand curve show you about the relationship between price and quantity demanded?
2. What is the difference between a good that has elastic demand and one that has inelastic demand?
3. What are the determinants of demand?

Alfred Marshall on Supply and Demand

- 1842–1924
- started career as a mathematician
- chair of political economy at Cambridge University, England
- developed supply and demand analysis as centerpiece of his work
- published his *Principles of Economics* in 1890 and *Elements of Economics* in 1892

Alfred Marshall is known for introducing the concept of supply and demand analysis to economics. The following excerpt from *Elements of Economics* explains the equilibrium of supply and demand.

The simplest case of balance, or equilibrium, between desire and effort is found when a person satisfies one of his wants by his own direct work. When a boy picks blackberries for his own eating, the action of picking may itself be pleasurable for a while. . . .

Equilibrium is reached, when at last his eagerness to play and his disinclination for the work of picking counterbalance the desire for eating. The satisfaction which he can get from picking fruit has arrived at its maximum. . . .

Marshall explains how equilibrium is established in a local market. Buyers and sellers, having perfect knowledge of the market, freely negotiate for their own best interest. In so doing they arrive at a price that exactly equates supply and demand.

. . . [A price may be] called the true equilibrium price: because if it were fixed on at the beginning, and adhered to throughout, it would exactly equate demand and supply. (i.e. the amount which buyers were willing to purchase at that price would be just equal to that for which sellers were willing to take that price). . . .

In our typical market then we assume that the forces of demand and supply have free play; that there is no combination among dealers on either side; but each acts for himself, and there is much free competition; that is, buyers generally compete freely with buyers, and sellers compete freely with sellers. But though everyone acts for himself, his knowledge of what others are doing is supposed to be generally sufficient to prevent him from taking a lower or paying a higher price than others are doing.

Checking for Understanding

❶ What does Marshall mean by "equilibrium between desire and effort"?

❷ What is an equilibrium price?

❸ What market conditions are necessary to establish an equilibrium price?

3 The Law of Supply and the Supply Curve

Terms to Know law of supply, law of diminishing returns, supply curve

Objectives *After reading this section, you should be able to:*

1 Explain how the **incentive of greater profit** affects supply.

2 Describe the relationships that the **supply curve** shows.

In Addition to Demand, Supply is a Factor in Determining Price

The law of demand alone is not enough to explain what determines price. To understand how prices are set, you also have to look at supply—the willingness and ability of producers to provide goods and services at different prices in the marketplace. The **law of supply** states:

As the price rises for a good, the quantity supplied rises. As the price falls, the quantity supplied also falls.

Figure 8.14 shows this law. Unlike demand, a direct relationship between the price and quantity supplied exists. With demand, price and quantity demanded move in opposite directions.

Although producers may be willing, they may not be able. Increased costs and possibly a time lag affect a company's ability to respond to changes in price.

Figure 8.14
The Law of Supply
A larger quantity will generally be supplied at higher prices than at lower prices. A smaller quantity will generally be supplied at lower prices than at higher prices.

▼

The Incentive of Greater Profit

The higher the price of a good, the greater the incentive is for a producer to produce more. The producer will expect to make a higher profit because of the higher price. The profit incentive is one of the factors that motivates people in a market economy. Suppose you own a music company that produces and sells compact discs. **Figure 8.15** (page 192) shows some of the costs involved in producing compact discs.

Figure 8.15 ▲
Some Costs of Producing CDs

The costs of producing CDs include: the price of the machines to make them; the price of the materials used in the compact disc itself; the price of the plastic "jewel box" in which they are sold; and even the price of paper and printing used to make the cover and booklet insert. You also have buildings in which to produce the compact discs, and you may have mortgage payments on those buildings and the land. You have employees to whom you must pay wages. You have taxes and insurance. These are all considered costs of production.

Suppose, for the moment, that the price you charge for your compact discs covers all of your costs and gives you a small profit. Under what circumstances would you be willing to produce more compact discs? Remember that increasing output means expanding production. Expanding production usually means higher costs because of the law of diminishing returns.

The Law of Diminishing Returns Normally after some point, if you are expanding production, the additional workers that you hire do not add as much to total output as the previous workers that you hired. Assume you employ 10 workers. You hire an eleventh worker. Compact disc production increases by 1,000 per week. When you hire the twelfth worker, compact disc production might increase by only 900 per week. This example illustrates the **law of diminishing returns.** According to this law, after some point, adding units of a factor of production—such as labor—to all the other factors of production—such as equipment—increases total output for a time. After a certain point, however, the extra output for each additional unit hired will begin to decrease.

You Must Charge a Higher Price To take on the expense of expanding production, you would have to be able to charge a higher price for your compact discs. If the price at which you could sell compact discs went up enough, you would probably be willing to hire more workers, buy more machines, and even build more factories.

At a higher price per compact disc, you would be willing to supply—

produce and sell—more than you would at the current lower price. Even though each compact disc might cost more to produce—because of overtime payments to workers, more repairs on machines, and so on—you could afford to pay the additional cost of increasing the quantity sold. This fact is the basis of the law of supply.

Many businesses produce compact discs in the United States. The law of supply works not only for each individual producer, but also for the industry as a whole. At a higher selling price of compact discs, it is even possible that new producers will enter the industry. They could be computer businesses that decide to branch out into the compact disc business because the profits seem so high. At a higher price, these potential compact disc producers see a possibility for a larger profit in that business than before the price of compact discs went up. This example, of course, assumes that no other prices in the economy increase.

An interesting question arises when new producers enter the industry simply because the price of the product went up. Why were they not producing before? The answer is that they were not as efficient as the other producers already in the industry. Their costs were too high. They had to wait until the price of the product went up in order to cover their higher costs. See **Figure 8.16**.

In any event, at higher prices, present suppliers will increase what they make or sell. And at higher prices *potential* suppliers will become *actual* suppliers because of the attraction of profits. Both add to the total output.

The Supply Curve

As with the law of demand, special tables and graphs can show the law of supply. Using the example of compact disc producers, how could we show a visual relationship between the price and the quantity supplied? **Figure 8.17** (page 194) shows this process.

Figure 8.17
Relationship of Supply to Price

The series of three graphs shows how the price of goods and services affects the quantity supplied.

A Table of Prices and Quantity Supplied ▶
The numbers here show that as the price per CD increases, the quantity supplied increases.

Various Prices and Quantities Supplied Of Compact Discs

Price per compact disc	Quantity supplied (in millions)	Points in Figure 8.17B
$10	100	L
$11	200	M
$12	300	N
$13	400	O
$14	500	P
$15	600	Q
$16	700	R
$17	800	S
$18	900	T
$19	1,000	U
$20	1,100	V

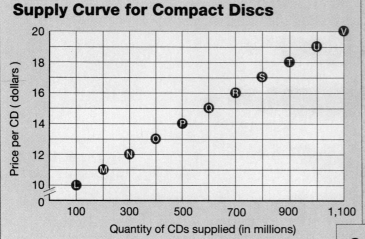

Supply Curve for Compact Discs

◀ **B** Plotting the Price-Quantity Pairs
The bottom axis shows the quantity supplied. The side axis shows the price per compact disc.

Each pair of price and quantity supplied represents a point on the graph. We label these points L, M, N, O, P, Q, R, S, T, U, V.

C Supply Curve ▶
When we connect the points from Figure 8.17B with a line, we end up with the **supply curve**.

A supply curve shows the quantities supplied at each possible price. It slopes upward from left to right. You can see that the relationship between price and quantity supplied is direct.

Supply Curve for Compact Discs

SECTION 3 REVIEW

Understanding Vocabulary

Define law of supply, law of diminishing returns, supply curve.

Reviewing Objectives

❶ How does the incentive of greater profit affect the supply of a given good or service?

❷ What does the supply curve show?

Critical Thinking Skills

Determining Cause and Effect

In order to understand economics, you have to know about cause and effect. Can you determine what is a cause and what is an effect?

Defining Cause and Effect

A cause is the action or situation that produces an event. An effect is the result or consequence of an action or situation. Often, the effect of one action or event causes yet another action or event. See **Figure A**.

Price and Quantity Demanded

The classic cause-and-effect relationship in economics is between price and quantity demanded. The law of demand is simply that: at higher prices, consumers purchase lower quantities. Look at the demand curve for home interactive entertainment systems in **Figure B**. If the price of interactive entertainment systems is $5,000, only 1 million will be demanded per year. If the price drops to $1,000, 5 million will be demanded per year. This cause-effect relationship is valid if other determinants of demand, such as population and income, do not change.

Figure A

CAUSE

EFFECT
(CAUSE)

EFFECT

Figure B

Price (in $1,000) vs. Quantity demanded (in millions)

Practicing the Skill

❶ Every time the moon is full, the price of a particular stock seems to go up. Can you therefore infer that the moon causes stock prices to change? Why or why not?

❷ Every President from William Henry Harrison to John F. Kennedy who was elected on the first year of a new decade died in office. What cause-and-effect conclusion, if any, can you draw from these data?

S E C T I O N 4 F O C U S

Terms to Know equilibrium price, technology, shortages, surplus

Objectives *After reading this section, you should be able to:*

❶ List the four **determinants of supply** and describe how they change supply.

❷ Explain how the **equilibrium price** is determined.

❸ Explain how **shortages and surpluses** affect price.

❹ Describe how **shifts in equilibrium price** occur.

❺ Discuss how the **forces underlying supply and demand** affect prices.

The Interaction of Supply and Demand Determines Price

As with demand, several factors help determine supply. We know that when the price changes, the quantity supplied changes. What if factors other than price change? What would happen to the supply of compact discs if the cost of the machines used to produce them decreased? Producers would be able to supply more CDs at the same market price. See **Figure 8.18**. The price of inputs used to produce the product is, therefore, another factor that determines its supply.

◀ **Figure 8.18**
Technology
As the cost of technology decreases, the supply of CDs increases.

The Determinants of Supply

Look at **Figure 8.19** and you will see an explanation of the price of inputs and some of the other determinants of supply. You see in **Figure 8.19** that we show supply curves that shift in each of the explanations. A change in supply causes the entire supply curve to shift. See **Figure 8.20** on page 198.

Equilibrium Price

In the real world, demand and supply operate together. As the price of a good goes down, the quantity demanded rises, and the quantity supplied falls. As the price goes up, the quantity demanded falls, and the quantity supplied rises.

Is there a price at which the quantity demanded and the quantity supplied meet? Yes. This level is called the **equilibrium price.** It means that the price of any good or service will find the level at which the quantity demanded and the quantity supplied are balanced. At this point, there is

Figure 8.19 The Determinants of Supply

Four of the major determinants of supply are explained here. These include the price of inputs, taxes, and the number of firms in the industry. They also include **technology**— the use of science to develop new products and new methods for producing and distributing goods and services.

The Determinants of Supply

A The Price of Inputs ▲
If the price of inputs drops dramatically, the supply curve will shift to the right. This occurred, for example, when the price of computer processing and memory chips fell during the 1980s and 1990s. More computers were supplied at any given price than before. On the graph S1 equals the supply of computers before the price of memory chips fell. S2 equals the supply of computers after the price of memory chips fell.

B Technology ▲
Any improvement in technology will increase the supply curve to the right. The technology for making compact discs improved during the 1980s. The supply curve shifted to the right so that at each price a larger quantity was supplied. On the graph S1 equals the supply of CDs before the improvement in technology. S2 equals supply after the improvement.

C Number of Firms in the Industry
When more firms enter the industry, the supply curve shifts outward to the right. For example, if more firms entered the videodisc player industry, the supply curve would shift to the right as in **A** and **B** above.

D Taxes ▲
If the government imposes more taxes on businesses, they will not be willing to supply as much as before. The supply curve for products will shift to the left. For example, if taxes increased on businesses supplying silk blouses, the supply curve would shift to the left. On the graph S1 equals the supply of silk blouses before the government raised taxes on this business. S2 equals the supply after the government raised taxes.

Increase in Supply of Compact Discs

Price per CD (dollars)

Quantity of CDs supplied (millions per year)

Supply Curve

New Supply Curve

**Figure 8.20 ▲
Increase in
Supply of
Compact Discs**

You see what happens when there is a breakthrough in compact disc production technology. Now producers can produce compact discs at one-half the cost they used to pay. The supply curve shifts outward to the right. That means that at all prices, producers will be willing to produce and sell more compact discs. Before the new technology, at a price of $15, suppliers would be willing to supply 600 million compact discs per year. After the breakthrough in technology they would be willing to supply 800 million compact discs per year.

enough of the good to satisfy consumers. Suppliers provide the amount that is demanded by consumers. One way to visualize equilibrium price is to put supply and demand curves on one graph as in **Figure 8.21**. Where the two curves intersect is the equilibrium price.

Shortages and Surpluses

Shortages occur when, at the going price, the quantity demanded is greater than the quantity supplied. If the market is unrestricted, without government regulations or other restrictions, shortages put pressure on prices to rise. Consumers reduce their purchases while suppliers increase the quantity they supply.

At prices above the equilibrium price, suppliers produce more than consumers want to purchase in the marketplace. Suppliers end up with large inventories of goods, and this and other forces put pressure on the price to drop to the equilibrium price. When the price drops, suppliers have less incentive to supply as much as before, while consumers begin to purchase a greater quantity. The drop in

price toward the equilibrium price, therefore, eliminates the **surplus**.

One of the benefits of the market economy is that when it operates without restriction, it eliminates shortages and surpluses. See **Figure 8.22**. Whenever shortages occur, the market ends up taking care of itself—the price goes up to eliminate the shortage. Whenever surpluses occur, the market again ends up taking care of itself—the price falls to eliminate the surplus. In command, or controlled, economies, such automatic market forces usually are not allowed to operate. In the United States and other countries with mainly free enterprise systems, prices serve as signals to producers and consumers. Rising prices signal producers to produce more and consumers to purchase less. Falling prices signal producers to produce less and consumers to purchase more. This free changing of the price of goods and services is a major strength of free enterprise.

Shifts in Equilibrium Price

Now we can show what happens when there is an increase in the demand for compact discs. Assume that scientists prove that listening to more

Figure 8.21
Reaching Equilibrium Price ▶
We have taken the demand curve for compact discs from Figure 8.6C and the supply curve for compact discs from Figure 8.17C and put them into one diagram. The demand and the supply curves for compact discs intersect at a special place. It is called the equilibrium price. In our particular example it is $15 per compact disc. At that price, the quantity of compact discs that consumers are willing and able to purchase is 600 million per year. At the same time, suppliers are willing to supply exactly that same amount. If the price were to go above $15, the quantity demanded would be less than the quantity supplied. There would be a surplus as is indicated in the diagram. If the price fell below $15 per compact disc, the quantity demanded would exceed the quantity supplied. There would be a shortage.

Putting Demand and Supply Together: The Case of Compact Discs

Figure 8.22
Construction
Changing prices effectively help to eliminate shortages and surpluses in the construction industry.

◀

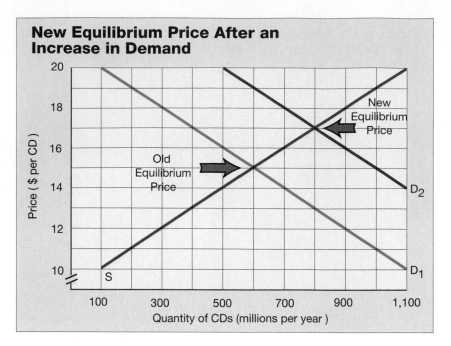

New Equilibrium Price After an Increase in Demand

Price ($ per CD)

20

18

16 — Old Equilibrium Price

14 — D₂

12

10 — S — D₁

New Equilibrium Price

100   300   500   700   900   1,100

Quantity of CDs (millions per year)

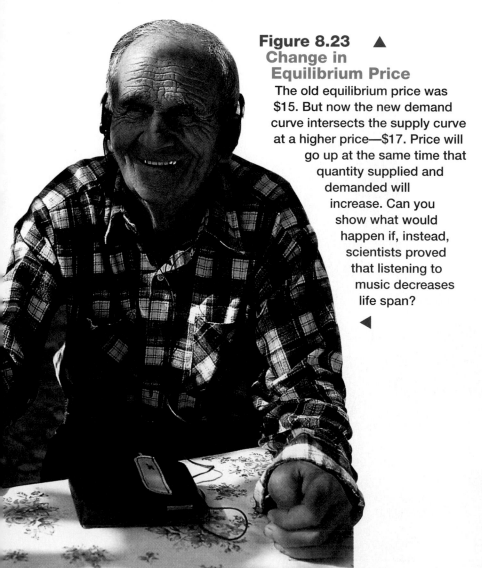

Figure 8.23 ▲
Change in Equilibrium Price

The old equilibrium price was $15. But now the new demand curve intersects the supply curve at a higher price—$17. Price will go up at the same time that quantity supplied and demanded will increase. Can you show what would happen if, instead, scientists proved that listening to music decreases life span?

◀

music increases life span. This discovery will cause the demand curve to shift outward to the right, as shown in **Figure 8.23**.

What about changes in supply? You can show these in a similar fashion. Assume that there is a major breakthrough in the technology of producing compact discs. The supply curve shifts outward to the right. The new equilibrium price will fall, and the quantity both supplied and demanded will increase.

Forces Underlying Supply and Demand

Do supply and demand determine all prices? Yes and no. Supply and demand are important aspects of the economy, and they do affect prices. The *forces* that determine supply and demand, however, really determine prices. Many such forces operate in the economy. On the demand side are people's income and their tastes and preferences. On the supply side, among determining factors are the ability of suppliers to produce, the profit incentive, and costs of production. The forces underlying supply and demand really determine price. *Underlying* is the important word.

Difficult to Measure The forces underlying demand and supply are sometimes obscure and often hard to measure. This makes the task of determining the effect of demand and supply on price a difficult one. For example, in the 1950s and early 1960s, the supply of doctors in the United States grew at an annual rate of less than 2%. Medical costs meanwhile increased at about 8% per year. At this point it seemed easy to show that the forces of demand and supply were affecting health-care costs (prices). Demand for medical services was rising faster than the supply of doctors and accounted for much of the increase in prices. Doctors' incomes rose rapidly, attracting more people into the medical profession. By the 1980s there were many more doctors per capita than there were in the 1960s. One would have expected rising medical costs to slow down. They did not. Other underlying factors affected price. Increasing per capita use of medical services, rising costs of technology, the growth of the medical insurance industry, and aging of the population, among other things, affected medical care costs. See **Figure 8.24.**

Then, too, even these forces do not always determine price. Legislation or government regulations, for example, fix many prices in the United States. Many states set the rates public utilities may charge for natural gas and electricity. The forces of supply and demand set prices only in a market system. In a command economy, such as that of North Korea or parts of the People's Republic of China, government planners set most prices.

Figure 8.24
Rising Medical Costs
The difficulty in determining the causes of rising medical costs was reflected in the great debate that followed President Clinton's announced plan to create a national health-care program.

◀

SECTION 4 REVIEW

Understanding Vocabulary
Define equilibrium price, technology, shortages, surplus.

Reviewing Objectives
❶ What are some of the determinants of supply?

❷ When one of these determinants changes, what happens to the supply curve?

❸ How do shortages and surpluses affect price?

❹ In what ways do shifts in equilibrium price occur?

❺ How do the forces underlying supply and demand affect prices?

Readings in Economics

FORBES   **APRIL 26, 1993**

BLUE JEANS AS TUNA FISH

by Amy Feldman

"**D**enim works for us like tuna fish works for a grocery store," says Harry Call, executive vice president of Goody's Family Clothing, of Knoxville, Tenn. He means that Goody's customers come in for discounted blue jeans, and leave with armloads of higher-margin Alfred Dunner dresses, Bugle Boy kiddie clothes, and other name-brand apparel goods. There's nothing accidental about this. The jeans shelves are in the back of Goody's stores, meaning customers must walk as much as 35 yards past racks of merchandise on which Goody's makes its real money.

Jeans are great bait. In the past five years Goody's sales and earnings have tripled, and the number of stores it leases and operates in small towns throughout the Southeast has almost doubled to 127. In its latest fiscal year (ended last Jan. 30) sales were up 26% to $455 million; profits climbed 49% to $16 million ($1.50 per share). Goody's comparable store sales rose 9% last year.... Bobby Goodfriend [the founder's son] joined the company in 1972, after graduating from Babson College. When his father turned the company over to him in 1977, the young man changed the company name to Goody's, his college nickname, and began focusing his buying on brand-name merchandise. If bought right, Goodfriend understood, brand-name merchandise could yield big markups from Goody's cost, yet still be sold at big markdowns relative to department store prices.

The business evolved.... By taking a $5 markup on a pair of jeans that cost Goody's $15, the company gave up over half its percentage markup. But it was able to undercut the going price of $30 and sell out quickly—and send the customers home with other items that more than made up for the margins given up on the jeans....

• THINK ABOUT IT •

1. *What product do most Goody's customers come to buy?*

2. *How does Goody's make up for the low profit margins on blue jeans?*

Summary

In a market economy, the principle of voluntary exchange helps determine the price that people are willing to pay for a given good or service. The law of demand, as generated by diminishing marginal utility, the real income effect, and the substitution effect, explains how people react to changing prices.

Summary

Economists often graph the demand curve in order to understand more about price determination. The price elasticity of demand has an impact on how much the price for a given product can vary. In addition to this elasticity, several factors determine demand in a market economy.

Summary

In the free enterprise system, the incentive of greater profit affects the quantity of goods that producers are willing and able to supply. As with the demand curve, the supply curve shows the relationship between quantity supplied and price.

Summary

Four factors determine supply in a market economy. A change in supply can often result in tremendous changes in price. Both shortages and surpluses also affect price in a market economy. Sometimes this change takes the form of a change in equilibrium price. Although supply and demand interact to determine price, the forces underlying supply and demand also can actually alter the price of a good or service.

8 Review

Identifying Key Terms

Write a short paragraph about demand using all of the following terms.

law of demand (p. 177)
law of diminishing
   marginal utility
   (p. 177)
real income effect
   (p. 179)

substitution effect
   (p. 179)
demand curve (p. 183)
price elasticity of
   demand (p. 185)

Use terms from the following list to fill in the blanks in the paragraph below.

law of supply (p. 191)
law of diminishing
   returns (p. 192)
supply curve (p. 194)

shortage (p. 198)
equilibrium price
   (p. 197)
surplus (p. 198)

The __(1)__ indicates that at higher prices a larger quantity will generally be supplied than at lower prices. Therefore, the __(2)__ slopes upward (rises from left to right). Suppliers face the __(3)__; therefore when they add more workers, each worker contributes less and less to the increase in total output. When we put a supply curve and demand curve on the same graph, we come up with the __(4)__. Any price that is above the equilibrium price will create a __(5)__. Any price that is below the equilibrium price will create a __(6)__.

Recalling Facts and Ideas

Section 1

1. What is the basis of most activity in a market economy?

2. What generally happens to quantity demanded when the price of a good goes up (and other prices stay the same)?
3. Generally, the more you have of something, the less satisfaction you get from an additional unit. This principle is called what?
4. When the price of a good changes, what two effects tend to create the law of demand?

Section 2

5. What term identifies the graphic representation of the law of demand?
6. How do we show in a graph an increase in the demand for a good?
7. What is the distinction between elastic and inelastic demand?
8. How do the existence and similarity of substitutes affect the price elasticity of demand for a good?
9. If income and population increase, what tends to happen to demand curves?

Section 3

10. Do suppliers tend to produce more or less when the price goes up? Why?
11. What term identifies the graphic representation of the law of supply?

Section 4

12. What would an increase in taxes do to the position of the supply curve?
13. How do you find the equilibrium price on a graph of demand and supply?
14. If the price of a product is above its equilibrium price, what is the result?
15. If the price of a product is below its equilibrium price, what is the result?

Critical Thinking

Section 1
Making Generalizations To what extent do you think the law of demand is applicable in the world around you? Are there any goods or services that you think do not follow the law of demand?

Section 2
Making Comparisons If you had to guess the relative price elasticities of demand for compact discs compared to that of insulin needed by diabetics, what would you say?

Section 3
Making Predictions The price of computing power continues to fall, but some scientists believe that it cannot continue to fall as rapidly as it has in the last decade. What do you predict will happen to the change in the price of computers over the next 20 years?

Section 4
Drawing Conclusions You have been told that telecommunications depends on computers. Computers are getting cheaper. What conclusion can you draw about how much interchange will occur between nations in the future?

Applying Economic Concepts

The Interaction of Supply and Demand Some prices change in our economy very seldom and others change all the time, even daily. Make a list of products whose prices change slowly, if at all. Make another list of products whose prices you think change quickly. For example, the price of houses changes slowly. In contrast, the prices of other countries' currencies change every day and, in fact, change every second.

Chapter Projects

1. **Individual Project** Clip articles from newspapers or magazines that show the laws of supply and/or demand operating in the real-world. Possibilities would be weather damages to crops and economic conditions affecting housing starts, and so on.

2. **Cooperative Learning Project** Working in groups of four, each group will interview a local merchant. During the interview, ask the merchant at least the following questions:
   - What determines the prices that you charge?
   - What determines when you change prices?
   - Are there any costs to you of changing prices (such as reprinting price lists)?

   One person in each group should write a summary of the interview. Now compare these summaries.

Reviewing Skills

Determining Cause and Effect
The Supply of Beef Look at the table below. What do you infer as the cause-and-effect relationship here?

Beef Price (per pound)	Quantity Supplied (thousands of pounds)
$1.89	1,000
$1.99	2,500
$2.09	3,500
$2.39	4,000
$2.69	6,000

Writing About Economics

Narrative Writing Choose one of the items listed in Your Economics Journal and explain why you decided not to buy it.

BUSINESS ORGANIZATIONS

BONANZA®
Steak · Chicken · Seafood · Salad

Who owns these businesses?

What are the costs of operating this kind of business?

FIVE LUNCH SPECIALS
WITH DRINK FOR 2.99
MON THRU FRI 11 TILL 4

TACO MAYO

Why have they been successful?

Could you ever own a business such as this yourself?

What kinds of businesses are these?

Your Economics Journal

Keep track of all the goods that you and your family buy and the services that you purchase during one week. List these items with the name of the business that provided them. Indicate whether you think each business is small, medium, or large and whether it has one owner or several owners.

SECTION 1 Starting a Business

Starting a Business Involves Risks and Expectations

Suppose that you have been tinkering with electronic equipment since you were a child. By now you can take apart and reassemble cassette and CD players, VCRs, and televisions without difficulty. You are so good at repairing this kind of equipment that you have been doing it for your friends and relatives for some time. Then an idea occurs to you: Why not charge people for your services? Why not go into business for yourself? By starting your own business, you will become an entrepreneur.

The Steps in Starting a Business

Nearly every person who makes the decision to start a business is an **entrepreneur** because he or she is willing to take a risk. Usually people decide to start a business to gain profits and to "do something on their own" or to be their own boss.

Entrepreneurs then gather the factors of production and decide on the form of business organization that best suits their purposes. Anyone hoping to become an entrepreneur must also learn as much as possible about the business he or she plans to start. This process includes learning about the laws, regulations, and tax codes that will apply to the business.

Elements of Business Operation

Figure 9.1 shows four elements every business must consider.

To start a business, you must make potential customers aware that your services are available for a price. You could have one-page fliers printed to advertise your business and pass them out. You could also buy advertising space in the local newspaper.

Figure 9.1
Four Elements of Business

Every business, regardless of size, involves four elements: expenses, advertising, receipts and record keeping, and risk.

C Receipts and Record Keeping

No matter how small your business is, having a system to track your expenses and income is key to your success. All receipts should be safely filed and saved.

▼

B Advertising ▲

You will quickly find out that letting potential customers know that you are in business is costly. Once you have customers, however, information about your business will spread by word of mouth.

◄ **A Expenses**

If you own a painting business, you will need to purchase brushes and paint. As your business grows, you might invest in paint sprayers or electric sanders so that you can complete jobs faster. This new equipment would add to your income, but will probably take more money capital than you have on hand.

D Risk

Every business involves risks. You must balance the risks against the advantages of being in business for yourself—including profit versus loss.

◄

Calculating Your Profit

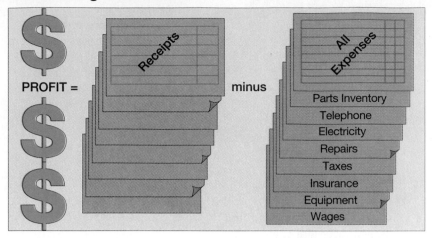

PROFIT = [Receipts] minus [All Expenses: Parts Inventory, Telephone, Electricity, Repairs, Taxes, Insurance, Equipment, Wages]

◄ **Figure 9.2**
Calculating Your Profit
By adding your wages to your other expenses, including taxes, and then subtracting the total from your receipts, you will have your profit. Keep records of how much you owe and to whom, and of how much your business is taking in. You will need this information to do your taxes.

Depending on the kinds of jobs you do, you will need equipment and replacement parts. At first, you might buy parts as you need them for a particular job. In time, you will find it easier to have an **inventory**. An inventory is a supply of whatever items are used in a business.

Will your business make a profit? **Figure 9.2** shows how to determine your profit. Because you could be working for someone else and earning an income, you should pay yourself a wage equal to what you could earn elsewhere. It's important not to forget this opportunity cost when you figure out the profits and losses your new business is making.

Computers Probably one of the first things you want to do, if you have not already done so, is buy a computer. With the computer, you also should purchase the programs that will allow you to keep track of all your expenses and all your receipts. Many such programs exist and are relatively inexpensive. Programs write checks for you, calculate your monthly profit and loss, tell you the difference between

what you own and what you owe (called net worth), and so on. As an entrepreneur, you are taking many risks, but the profit you expect to make is your incentive for taking those risks. For example, if you spend part of your savings to pay for advertising and equipment, you are taking a risk. You may not get enough business to cover these costs. Whenever you buy a special part for a job, you are taking a risk. Suppose you do the work and your customer never pays you. The owner who started the small business shown in **Figure 9.3** had to consider the risks.

The Time Factor You are even taking a risk with the time you spend. You are using time to think about what you will do, to write ads, to set up the bookkeeping, and so on. This time is an opportunity cost. You could have used it to do something else, including work for someone for a wage. If you work for someone else, you take only the risk of not being paid, which is usually small. As an entrepreneur your risks are great, but so are the potential rewards.

Figure 9.3
Owning a Business
What factors do you think the owner considered before he started his own business? What rewards do you think he might expect? ▼

SECTION 1 REVIEW

Understanding Vocabulary
Define entrepreneur, inventory.

Reviewing Objectives
① What are two steps you must take to start a business?

② What are the four elements common to all businesses?

Personal Perspective

William Gates on Running a Business

Profile

- 1955–
- founder and chief executive officer of Microsoft, probably the most successful corporation of the 1980s
- "the richest man in America," according to *Forbes* annual survey

The following excerpts are taken from an interview with William Gates by *Forbes* (December 7, 1992). Gates answers questions about Microsoft's success and the company's future.

Somebody reports down profits and they say, This industry is in trouble! No, this industry has become more competitive.... Is the structure of the industry changing? Units of PCs [computer sales] have gone up very healthily, more than the industry followers suggest that they have. We've been very open about that.

... I never think we are unassailable. We are in a bizarre position where there is this wild mixture of people who overestimate us and people who underestimate us. They cook up wild scenarios. They certainly tend to overestimate us when they go back and look at why we did various things and come up with how certain events are all part of some master plan. They wildly overestimate us in terms of thinking that we couldn't be in a lot of trouble very quickly if we didn't keep in touch with customers....

Gates talked about the intense competition in the computer software industry. He said his focus is not on short-term profits, but rather on long-term leadership.

... We try to get expectations to be realistic, both about growth and about profitability, because we aren't a company that's really thinking of this in short-term ways. You know, you're dealing with a company where, despite all of its profitability, all the decisions have been based toward being a force and doing good things in five years. I may be making mistakes, but ... I think I have smarter guys just in my research group alone than any other software company has in their entire company. Can I translate that into good products that people care about? That's up to me. It's a bet. It's a risk. I think we'll be around for quite some time doing good things.

Checking for Understanding

1. How does Gates respond to people who think the computer business is in trouble?
2. Why does Microsoft try to develop realistic expectations?
3. What is the risk that Gates talks about?

2 Sole Proprietorships and Partnerships

Sole Proprietorships and Partnerships Are Common in the United States Today

B usiness can be organized in the United States in a number of ways. The two most common are a sole proprietorship and a partnership.

Sole Proprietorship

The most basic type of business organization is the **sole proprietorship,** a business owned by one person. It is the oldest form of business organization and also the most common. The colonies of Maryland and Pennsylvania were founded as sole proprietorships. When we speak of a **proprietor,** we are always referring to the owner of a business as **Figure 9.4** shows. The word *proprietor* comes from the Latin word *proprietas,* meaning "property." A business is a kind of property.

Today, the United States has about 14 million such businesses, and many of them are small. For that reason,

Figure 9.4
One Owner
This business has one owner as a sole proprietor who enjoys all the profits, but also must bear all the risks and losses.
▼

Figure 9.5 Advantages and Disadvantages of Sole Proprietorships

	Advantages	Disadvantages
Profits and losses	As sole owner, the proprietor receives all the profits because he or she takes all the risks.	Losses are not shared.
Liability		The proprietor has complete legal responsibility for all debts and damages brought upon oneself in doing business. This is known as **unlimited liability**. If the firm is unable to pay its bills or if someone is injured as a result of the business, the proprietor can be forced to sell his or her personal assets as well as the business to pay these debts. **Assets** are items of value such as houses, cars, jewelry, and so on.
Management	Decisions on starting and running the business can be made quickly because the owner does not have to consult with other people. Because a proprietorship is usually small, the operation of the business is less complicated than other types of business. There are generally fewer government regulations than with corporations.	A proprietor must handle all decision making, even for unfamiliar areas of the business. For example, the owner of a manufacturing firm may know a great deal about product design, but very little about selling. This is a severe problem for many sole proprietorships.

they usually are easier and less expensive to start and run. You probably have contact with many sole proprietorships every day without realizing it—owners of corner grocery stores, repair shops, dry cleaners, and so on. Many doctors, dentists, lawyers, and accountants are sole proprietors. In farming, construction, and contracting, sole proprietorships are the most numerous types of business organization. **Figure 9.5** lists the advantages and disadvantages of operating a sole proprietorship.

Help in Starting a Small Business

For a person who wants to start a sole proprietorship, help is available. The federal government's Small Business Administration often helps finance **startups**, which are new small businesses. State departments of commerce and community affairs also offer assistance. Many community college and university campuses have federally funded small business development centers that will help a small business get started.

Figure 9.5 Advantages and Disadvantages of Sole Proprietorships

	Advantages	Disadvantages
Taxes	A proprietor must pay personal income taxes on profits, but these taxes may be lower than taxes for a corporation.	
Personal satisfaction	The proprietor has full pride in owning the business. The person is his or her own boss and makes the business whatever it is.	Running a sole proprietorship is demanding and time-consuming. If the proprietor does not enjoy such responsibility, he or she will find ownership a burden.
Financing growth	Because the proprietor has liability for all debts, it is occasionally easier for a proprietorship to obtain credit than for a corporation of the same size. Lenders are more willing to extend credit knowing that they can take over not only the assets of the business, but also the assets of the proprietor if the loan is not paid back.	A sole proprietor must rely on his or her own funds plus money that can be borrowed from others. Borrowing small amounts may be easier for a sole proprietorship than for a corporation of similar size, but borrowing large amounts can be difficult.
Life of the business		A sole proprietorship depends on one individual. If that person dies, goes bankrupt, or is unwilling or unable to work, the business will probably close. This uncertainty about the future increases the risk to both employees and creditors.

A **small business incubator** might also aid businesses. Just as incubators help hatch chickens, there are business incubators that help "hatch" small businesses. They are often operated with state and federal funds. A small business incubator might provide a low-rent building, management advice, and computers. The incubator's goal is to generate job creation and economic growth, particularly in depressed states.

Partnerships

To take the example of your repair business a little further, suppose that your business is doing so well that your workload has increased to the point at which you have little time for anything else. You could expand your business by hiring an employee. You also need financial capital, but would rather not take out a loan. You may look into taking on a partner.

Figure 9.6 Advantages and Disadvantages of Partnerships

	Advantages	Disadvantages
Profits and losses	Losses are shared. Several individuals can sometimes survive a loss that might bankrupt a sole proprietor.	Because partners share the risks of the business, they also share the profits.
Liability		Partners as a group have unlimited liability for all debts and damages incurred in business. If a partner is unable to pay his or her share of a debt, the others must make up for the difference.
Management	Partnerships are usually more efficient than proprietorships. They allow each partner to work in areas of the business that he or she knows most about or is best at doing.	Decision making is often slow because of the need to reach agreement among several people. Disagreements can lead to problems in running the business.
Taxes	Partners must pay personal income taxes on their share of profits. These taxes are sometimes lower than those for a corporation.	
Personal satisfaction	Partners, like sole proprietors, often feel pride in owning and operating their own company.	If partners do not get along with each other, trying to work together can result in constant arguments.
Financing growth	A partnership combines the capital of two or more people. It makes more money available to operate a larger and perhaps more profitable business. Because the risk is shared, creditors are often willing to lend more money to a partnership than to a sole proprietorship.	Like sole proprietorships, partnerships can have trouble obtaining large amounts of capital. The amount that partnerships can borrow is usually limited by the combined value of the assets of the business and of the partners.
Life of the business		If one partner dies or leaves, the partnership must be ended and reorganized. The others may be unable or unwilling to continue operating, and the business may close. This uncertainty is a risk to employees and creditors.

You decide that the best solution is to look for someone who can keep books, handle customers, and invest in the business. You offer to form a partnership. A **partnership** is a business that two or more individuals own and operate. You may sign a partnership agreement that is legally binding. It describes the duties of each partner, the division of profits, and the distribution of assets should the partners end the agreement.

Many doctors, dentists, architects, and lawyers work in partnerships. Two or more people often own small stores. **Figure 9.6** lists some of the major advantages and disadvantages of partnerships.

Limited Partnerships

A **limited partnership** is a special form of partnership in which the partners are not equal. One partner is called the general partner. This person (or persons) assumes all of the management duties and has full responsibilities for the debts of the limited partnership. The other partners are "limited" because all they do is contribute money or property. They have no voice in the partnership's management.

The advantage to the limited partners is that they have no liability for the losses beyond what they initially invest. The disadvantage, of course, is that they have no say in how the business is run. Limited partnerships must follow specific guidelines when they are formed. Two or more partners must sign a certificate of limited partnership in which they present, at a minimum, the following information:

- The company name
- The nature of the business
- The principal place of business
- The name and place of residence of each partner
- How long the partnership will last
- The amount of cash or other property contributed by each partner

Joint Ventures

Sometimes individuals or companies want to do a special project together. They do not have any desire to work together after the project is done. What they might do is form a **joint venture.** A joint venture is a temporary partnership set up for a specific purpose and for a short period of time. **Figure 9.7** shows one example.

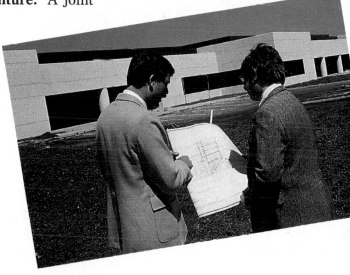

Figure 9.7
A Typical Joint Venture
Suppose investors want to purchase real estate as a short-term investment. They may later plan to resell the property for profit. At that point, the joint venture ends—unlike a general partnership that is set up to be a continuing business.

▼

SECTION 2 REVIEW

Understanding Vocabulary

Define sole proprietorship, proprietor, unlimited liability, assets, startups, small business incubator, partnership, limited partnership, joint venture.

Reviewing Objectives

❶ What are two advantages and two disadvantages of a sole proprietorship?

❷ How can people starting a small business get help?

❸ What are two advantages and two disadvantages of a partnership?

Reading the Financial Page

You can buy and sell shares of stock in corporations. The financial pages of newspapers provide information about the stocks.

Reading Stock Market Quotations

At the beginning of each trading day, stocks open at the same prices they closed at the day before. Prices will move up or down as shares are bought and sold. At the end of the day, each stock has a closing price. This and other information is provided in tables such as the one in **Figure A**.

Figure A Sample Stock Quotations

52-Week			Sales				
High	Low	Stock	100s	High	Low	Last	Change
$25\frac{1}{4}$	$20\frac{3}{4}$	TxEt pf	13	$24\frac{3}{4}$	$24\frac{1}{4}$	$24\frac{1}{4}$	$-\frac{3}{4}$
$37\frac{1}{4}$	$22\frac{1}{4}$	TexGT	77	$31\frac{5}{8}$	31	$31\frac{5}{8}$	$+\frac{5}{8}$
$32\frac{1}{8}$	18	TexInd	180	$31\frac{5}{8}$	$30\frac{5}{8}$	$31\frac{1}{2}$	$+1$
$111\frac{1}{2}$	$70\frac{1}{2}$	TexInst	1738	110	$105\frac{5}{8}$	110	$+4\frac{1}{8}$

Prices are listed in dollars and fractions of a dollar. $24\frac{1}{4}$, for example, means $24.25.

The name of each company is printed in an abbreviated form. In this listing, TexInst refers to Texas Instruments. The 52-Week High/Low columns show the highest and lowest price of the stock during the previous 52 weeks.

The number of shares bought and sold (in hundreds) is reported in the Sales column. The High column reports the highest price for that day, and the Low column reports the lowest. The closing price is shown in the Last column. The Change column shows the change in closing price from the previous day.

Figure B Stock Quotations

Stock	Sales 100s	High	Low	Last	Change
GlbPrt	347	$14\frac{7}{8}$	$14\frac{3}{4}$	$14\frac{3}{4}$	---
GlobYld	2175	$7\frac{7}{8}$	$7\frac{3}{4}$	$7\frac{3}{4}$	$-\frac{1}{8}$
GldWF	1278	$39\frac{5}{8}$	$39\frac{1}{4}$	$39\frac{1}{2}$	$+1$
Gdrich	621	$41\frac{7}{8}$	$41\frac{1}{2}$	$41\frac{5}{8}$	$-\frac{1}{2}$
Goodyr	4361	$44\frac{7}{8}$	44	44	$+\frac{5}{8}$
Grace	1513	$40\frac{3}{8}$	40	$40\frac{1}{8}$	$-\frac{1}{4}$
Graco	244	$34\frac{1}{2}$	33	$34\frac{1}{2}$	$+2$
GrhmFl	1242	$4\frac{7}{8}$	$4\frac{1}{4}$	$4\frac{1}{4}$	$+\frac{1}{2}$
Graingr	551	$58\frac{3}{8}$	$57\frac{1}{4}$	$57\frac{5}{8}$	---
Grndmet	2424	$27\frac{1}{4}$	$26\frac{3}{4}$	$27\frac{1}{4}$	$+\frac{3}{4}$

Practicing the Skill

❶ Find the listing for Goodyear Tire and Rubber Company (Goodyr) in **Figure B**. What was the closing price for this stock?

❷ How much of a change was this from the previous day?

SECTION 3 The Corporate World and Franchises

SECTION 3 FOCUS

Terms to Know corporation, limited liability, articles of incorporation, corporate charter, franchise

Objectives *After reading this section, you should be able to:*

1. Summarize the advantages and disadvantages of **corporations**.
2. Explain what types of businesses are involved in **franchises**.

Many People Share in the Ownership of a Corporation

Suppose your electronic repair business has grown. You now have several partners and have turned your garage into a shop. You would like to expand and rent a store so that your business would be more visible. See **Figure 9.8**. You would like to buy the latest equipment, charge a little less than your competitors, and capture a larger share of the market for electronic repair work. You need money capital, however.

You have decided that you do not want any more partners. You would have to consult with them about every detail of the business as you do now with your present partners. What you want is financial backers who will let you use their money while letting you run the business. What you are proposing is a corporation. **Figure 9.9** (page 220) shows the advantages and disadvantages of corporations.

Figure 9.8 Business Location
When you select a location for your business, you must consider many factors including cost and parking areas for your customers.

Corporations

A **corporation** is an organization owned by many people but treated by the law as though it were a person. It can own property, pay taxes, make contracts, sue and be sued, and so on. It has a separate and distinct existence from the stockholders who own

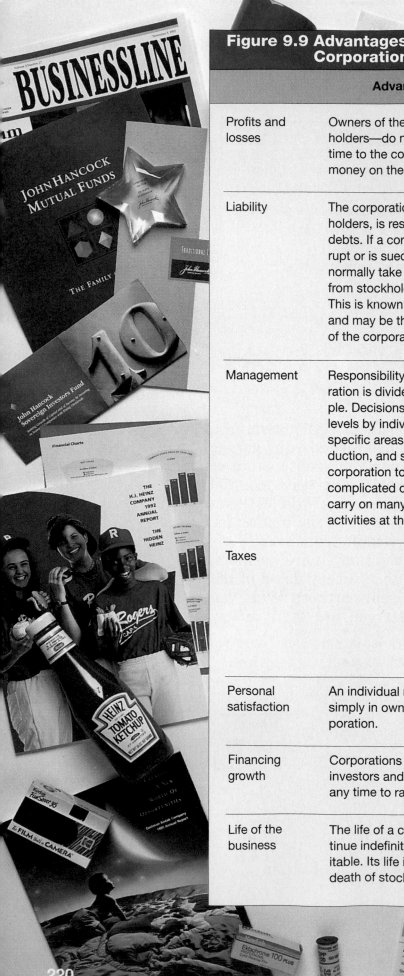

Figure 9.9 Advantages and Disadvantages of Corporations

	Advantages	Disadvantages
Profits and losses	Owners of the corporation—stockholders—do not have to devote time to the company to make money on their investment.	
Liability	The corporation, and not its stockholders, is responsible for its debts. If a corporation goes bankrupt or is sued, creditors cannot normally take personal property from stockholders to pay debts. This is known as **limited liability**, and may be the major advantage of the corporate form of business.	
Management	Responsibility for running a corporation is divided among many people. Decisions are made at many levels by individuals trained in specific areas, such as sales, production, and so on. This allows a corporation to handle large and complicated operations and to carry on many types of business activities at the same time.	Decision making can be slow and complicated because so many levels of management are involved. Also, the interests of those running the corporation, who may not be stockholders, are not always the same as those of the stockholders, who often seek an immediate return on investment.
Taxes		The federal government and some state and local governments tax corporate profits. The profits that are paid to stockholders as dividends are again taxed as income to those individuals. Some states also tax corporate property.
Personal satisfaction	An individual may feel satisfaction simply in owning a part of a corporation.	Individual stockholders have little or no say in how a corporation is run.
Financing growth	Corporations draw on resources of investors and may issue stock at any time to raise capital.	
Life of the business	The life of a corporation can continue indefinitely if it remains profitable. Its life is not affected by the death of stockholders.	

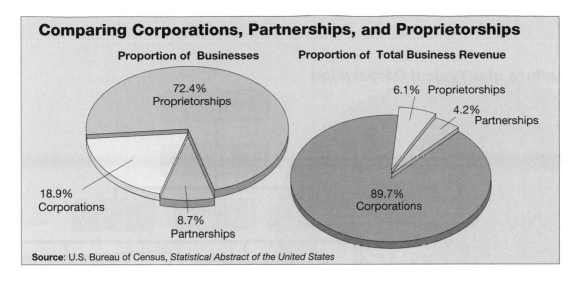

Comparing Corporations, Partnerships, and Proprietorships

Proportion of Businesses

72.4%
Proprietorships

18.9%
Corporations

8.7%
Partnerships

Proportion of Total Business Revenue

6.1% Proprietorships

4.2%
Partnerships

89.7%
Corporations

Source: U.S. Bureau of Census, *Statistical Abstract of the United States*

Figure 9.10
Comparing Types of Business
Although only about 19 percent of American businesses are organized as corporations, they generate almost 90 percent of total business revenue.

◀

the corporation's stock. Stock represents ownership rights to a certain portion of the profits and assets of the company that issues the stock.

In terms of the amount of business done (measured in dollars), the corporation is the most important type of business organization in the United States today. **Figure 9.10** compares corporations to other forms of business in terms of numbers and revenue.

In order to form a corporation, its founders must do three things. First, they must register their company with the government of the state in which it will be headquartered. Second, they must sell stock. Third, along with the other shareholders, they must elect a board of directors.

Registering the Corporation Every state has laws governing the formation of corporations, but most state laws are similar. Suppose that you and your partners decide to form a corporation. You will have to file an **articles of incorporation** application with the state in which you will run your corporation. In general, these articles include four items:

1. Name, address, and purpose of the corporation;
2. Names and addresses of the initial board of directors (these men and women will serve until the first stockholders' meeting, when a new board may be elected);
3. Number of shares of stock to be issued;
4. Amount of money capital to be raised through issuing stock.

If the articles are in agreement with state law, the state will grant you a **corporate charter**—a license to operate from that state.

Selling Stock To continue the example of your electronic repair business, you could sell shares of either common or preferred stock in your new corporation. Common stock gives the holder part ownership in the corporation and voting rights at the annual stockholders' meeting. It does not guarantee a dividend—money return on the money invested in a company's stock. Preferred stock does guarantee a certain amount of dividend each year. Preferred stock also guarantees to the stockholder first claim, after creditors have been paid, on whatever value is left in the corporation if it goes out of business. Holders of preferred stock usually do not have voting rights in the corporation, although they are part owners.

If your corporation were to become large, you might find its stock

Readings in Economics

THE BOSTON GLOBE   JUNE 8, 1993

THE NORDIC WAY

by Frederic M. Biddle

From the Nor- dicTrack store, it's a brisk mall lap to Scientific Revolution. Then, around the corner to another store, NordicSport by NordicTrack. Finally, down the corridor to The Nature Co. and Britches Great Outdoors.

Schlepping around the Mall of America with Charles M. Leighton, chairman of CML Group Inc., doesn't match the aerobic benefits of the company's Nordic-Track fitness machines. But there's probably no better place to see what CML has become—and how the company has tapped a 1990s consumer philosophy as few other retailers have—than here in the country's biggest shopping mall, where most of CML's retail businesses can be found under one roof. . . .

Leighton, 58, can feel good about his Acton [Massachusetts]-based holding company. CML pumped up sales 45 per-cent to a record $582 million in the four quarters ended Jan. 30, while profits rose 38 percent to $47.4 million. Those results, plus a 35 percent return on equity, won it the title of The Globe 100 Company of the Year. . . .

Just four years ago, however, CML was targeted by corporate raider Irwin Jacobs after it loaded up on debt to make several acquisitions. Leighton fought off Jacobs but was forced to restructure. When the dust settled three main units were left; NordicTrack; The Nature Co., a retailer of products considered environmentally responsible; and Britches of Georgetowne, a men's apparel retailer. . . .

But . . . NordicTrack is the star of Leighton's miniconglomerate. It generates just over half of CML's sales and more than 80 percent of earnings.

Section 1

Starting a Business

Key Terms
entrepreneur (p. 208)
inventory (p. 210)

Summary
Two steps are involved in starting a business. Once these steps have been taken, entrepreneurs must carefully consider the four key elements that every business involves.

Section 2

Sole Proprietorships and Partnerships

Key Terms
sole proprietorship (p. 213)
proprietor (p. 213)
unlimited liability (p. 214)
assets (p. 214)
startups (p. 214)
small business incubator
  (p. 215)
partnership (p. 217)
limited partnership (p. 217)
joint venture (p. 217)

Summary
The most common form of business organization in the United States is a sole proprietorship, which has advantages and disadvantages. Partnerships, owned by two or more people, involve their own set of advantages and disadvantages. Limited partnerships must follow specific guidelines.

Section 3

The Corporate World and Franchises

Key Terms
corporation (p. 219)
limited liability (p. 220)
articles of incorporation
  (p. 221)
corporate charter
  (p. 221)
franchise (p. 222)

Summary
Many people share in the ownership of corporations, which have advantages and disadvantages different from those of other forms of business organization. Franchises, in which a franchisor sells to another business the right to use its name and sell its products, are common in some industries.

Review

Identifying Key Terms

Write the letter of the definition in Column B below that correctly defines each term in Column A.

Column A
1. inventory (p. 210)
2. corporate charter (p. 221)
3. assets (p. 214)
4. franchise (p. 222)
5. unlimited liability (p. 214)

Column B
a. items of value
b. supply of items that are used in a business
c. sale by a business of the right to use its name to another business or individual
d. right to operate
e. legal responsibility for all debts and damages incurred when doing business

Write a paragraph about the advantages and disadvantages of different types of business organizations using the following terms.

sole proprietorship (p. 213)
partnership (p. 217)
limited partnership (p. 217)
joint venture (p. 217)
corporation (p. 219)
franchise (p. 222)

Recalling Facts and Ideas

Section 1

1. Every business involves expenses and receipts and record keeping. What are two other elements?
2. When you calculate your profits, it is especially important for you to include the value of your time. What is this called?

Section 2
3. What is the most common form of business organization?
4. What are the advantages and disadvantages of a sole proprietorship?
5. If you need help in starting a small business, where can you look?
6. Often two or more individuals want to start a business. What is one form of business organization they can use?
7. What is the difference between a limited partnership and a joint venture?

Section 3
8. What are the elements of every corporation?
9. Who grants corporate charters?
10. Which group within a corporation chooses the board of directors?
11. How does a franchise operate?

Critical Thinking

Section 1
Demonstrating Reasoned Judgment Why do you have to include the opportunity cost of your time when you calculate your profits in your own business?

Section 2
Drawing Conclusions Why would a person decide in favor of a partnership rather than a sole proprietorship?

Section 3
Analyzing Information What kind of problems in a corporation might be due to its complex organizational structure?

Applying Economic Concepts

Comparing Business Organizations In this chapter you have seen numerous advantages and disadvantages of different types of business organizations. Make a list of the following: sole proprietorship, partnership, limited partnership, joint venture, corporation, and franchise. After each type, indicate the single most important advantage that you believe this form of business organization has.

Chapter Projects

1. **Individual Project** Three major business news magazines report the top several hundred corporations in America every year, usually in May or June. They are *Forbes*, *Fortune*, and *Business Week*. Find one or more of these magazines in a library. Make a list of the latest information on the top five industrial corporations, such as General Motors and Microsoft. Indicate for each the following information: (1) number of employees, (2) total sales in billions of dollars, (3) total market value as given by the stock market (if available), and (4) change in ranking from the previous year.

2. **Cooperative Learning Project** Work in groups of four. Each group should select a corporation listed in the financial pages of a newspaper. Then use business magazines and financial and annual reports, if possible, to determine the annual earnings, dividends, and stock prices of that corporation over the last year. Compare the corporation with those selected by other groups and discuss which stocks would have been the best investments during the past year.

Reviewing Skills

Reading the Financial Page

1. How many shares of Apple Computer (AppleCptr) were traded?
2. What was the net change in the price of the stock of Apple Computer on this day?
3. Compare this day's closing price for Apple Computer with its 52-week high. How much less is this day's closing price?

52 Weeks High	52 Weeks Low	Stock	Sales 100s	High	Low	Last	Change
19¼	14½	AMTROL	45	19½	18½	18½	-¾
16⅞	5¹⁵⁄₁₆	AmvstrFnl	314	10⅜	10	10⅛	-¼
15½	5¾	AmylinPharm	96	9	8¾	8¾	-¼
16¾	10¼	Analogic	489	15½	15	15⅛	-⅜
14½	9¾	Anly&Tech	532	14½	13⅝	13⅝	-⅜
35¾	16¼	Anlyint	72	29	28	29	…
18	10⅞	Anangel	2	17⅛	17⅛	17⅛	…
15	5⅝	AnchrBcp	560	14¼	14	14¼	…
24¾	11⅞	AnchrBcpWis	117	22½	22	22½	+¼
14¾	5¾	AndovrBcp	193	14¼	13⅞	14⅛	…
4¾	2¼	AndovrTog	67	2½	2¼	2½	…
30¼	16	AndrewCp	1055	28¼	27¼	28	+¼
19¼	10⅞	Andros	44	14½	14	14⅜	-⅛
13½	5½	Anergen	8	7	6½	6½	-½
5⅝	1⁷⁄₁₆	ApertusTech	341	3¼	3	3	-⅛
12½	8⅝	ApogeeEnt	82	12	11¾	12	+¼
65¼	26½	AppleCptr	72258	28¾	25½	25⅝	-1⅞
24¾	5⅝	AppleSouth	402	23	22¼	23	…
22¼	8¼	Applebee	323	20¼	19¼	19¾	-¼
20	8¾	ApplncRecyc	136	9¾	9	9¼	-¼
15¼	4½	AppldBiosci	254	6	5⅞	5⅛	…
2¼	⅞	AppliedCrbn	39	1½	1⅜	1⅜	-⅛
25¼	11	AppldImuSci	393	20¼	19½	19½	…
62½	18	AppldMati	2338	59¼	56½	58¼	+1

Writing About Economics

Persuasive Writing Review the information that you recorded in Your Economics Journal for this chapter. Then write a persuasive paragraph explaining why someone should patronize locally owned businesses.

Point

ISSUE: Role of the Government in the Economy: Should Industry be Deregulated?

Deregulation of industries gained popularity in the 1980s, especially during the Reagan years (1981-89). Airlines, banking, and trucking were three of the most important industries deregulated. Cable TV had also been deregulated, so consumers blamed rising cable charges on this action. In 1992 Congress reregulated the cable TV industry in the hope of promoting competition and lowering prices. Many now believe that the government should reregulate other industries.

PRO

Deregulation brought many changes to the airline industry. Economist Alfred E. Kahn, a former chairman of the Civil Aeronautics Board (disbanded with deregulation), writes that the two most important consequences of airline deregulation have been lower fares and higher productivity. He also asserts that safety has increased since deregulation. Accident rates dropped 20-45 percent from the regulated years.

Economist Thomas Gale Moore also argues that deregulation works. He writes that previous regulation of the trucking industry increased costs and rates significantly, as well as lowered quality of service. Rates for the industry fell after deregulation, and competition increased as well. Moore writes on this success of deregulation in stimulating competition:

The number of new firms has increased dramatically. By 1990 the total number of licensed carriers exceeded forty thousand, considerably more than double the number authorized in 1980. The ICC [Interstate Commerce Commission] had also awarded nationwide authority to about five thousand freight carriers. The value of operating rights granted by the ICC, once worth hundreds of thousands of dollars when such authority was almost impossible to secure from the commission, has plummeted to close to zero now that operating rights are easy to obtain.

Finally, Alfred Kahn warns against the recent reregulation trend:

Airline deregulation has worked. It would be ironic if, by misdiagnosing our present discontents, we were to return to policies of protectionism and centralized planning at the very time when countries as dissimilar as China, the Soviet Union, Chile, Australia, France, Spain, and Poland are all discovering the superiority of the free market.

Counterpoint

CON Those who oppose deregulation argue that it has a tendency to make markets less competitive. Since deregulation in 1986, monthly basic cable rates have increased sharply. Gene Kimmelman, legislative director of the Consumer Federation of America, states that the reregulating of the cable TV industry is "a first step in the right direction. It's the first real cost savings to consumers that's come out of the (FCC) in a decade."

Others worry that deregulating the airlines also may not have been such a good idea. Airline fares are lower, but those against deregulation see the price cutting as fare wars designed to drive weaker competitors out of business, thus leading to less competition and higher fares in the long run. John Greenwald explains this position in *TIME* :

> But there is a darker side to the fare war: many experts see it as a thinly veiled declaration of war against low-cost rivals like TWA and Continental, which currently fly under the protective wing of the bankruptcy courts and thus pay no interest on part of their debt. Life will get rougher for them once they emerge from Chapter 11 protection and are forced to survive on their own resources—something many analysts fear these weaker carriers may be unable to do for long. Once rid of such pesky competitors and their cutthroat tactics, the major airlines *could regain full control of airfares— and might then be free to raise them.*

Exploring the Issue

Reviewing Facts

1. What kind of changes did deregulation bring to the airline industry?

2. What is one argument for deregulation? One against?

Critical Thinking

3. Why do you think deregulation brought higher cable rates but lower airline fares?

10 COMPETITION AND MONOPOLIES

Where can you obtain information on air fares?

How do airlines determine air fares?

How many airline companies can you name?

How do these companies compete for business?

CONTINENTAL

←RY

Do you think all airline companies make profits?

Your Economics Journal

Keep track for one week of your use of the following items: soft drinks, breakfast cereals, toothpaste, and soap. List these items and the brand that you chose to use. Next to each item explain why you chose that brand over the many others that exist.

SECTION 1 FOCUS

Terms to Know perfect competition

Objectives *After reading this section, you should be able to:*
1 List the five **conditions of perfect competition.**
2 Explain why **agriculture is sometimes considered an example of perfect competition.**
3 Assess the **desirability of perfect competition.**

Perfect Competition—An Ideal Rarely Realized

Competition is one of the basic characteristics of our market economic system. Regardless of its legal form of organization, each business attempts to capture as large a share of its market as possible. **Figure 10.1** shows the four basic market structures in the American economy.

Conditions of Perfect Competition

All businesses must engage in some form of competition as long as other businesses produce similar goods or services. When a market includes so many sellers of a particular good or service that each seller accounts for a small part of the total market, a special situation exists. Economists term it **perfect competition.** Perfect competition has five conditions as shown in **Figure 10.2**.

On the supply side, perfect competition requires a large number of suppliers of a similar product. On the demand side, perfect competition requires a large number of informed buyers who know exactly what the market price is for the good or service. The market price is the equilibrium price. In a perfectly competitive market, total supply and total demand are allowed to interact to reach the equilibrium price. That is the only

Comparing Four Market Structures

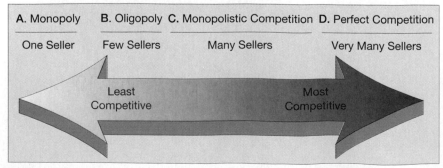

A. Monopoly	B. Oligopoly	C. Monopolistic Competition	D. Perfect Competition
One Seller	Few Sellers	Many Sellers	Very Many Sellers

Least Competitive   Most Competitive

Figure 10.1
Comparing Market Structures
Markets that are either perfectly competitive or pure monopolies are rare. Most industries in the United States fit one of the two other forms.

price at which quantity demanded equals quantity supplied. In a world of perfect competition, each individual seller would accept that price. Because so many buyers and sellers exist, one person charging a higher or lower price would not affect the market price.

Perfect competition is rarely seen in the real world. For one thing, information is not often easily obtainable. In order for the price of a good or service to be the same for all sellers at every moment, all buyers and sellers would have to know what is happening to prices for that good or service everywhere at every moment. Obviously, business information is never that complete.

Agriculture as an Example

Few perfectly competitive industries exist in the United States. The one that perhaps comes closest is agriculture before the 1930s, when the federal government started to protect and regulate it. Since that time the government has sought to protect farmers by keeping the prices of some

▼ **Figure 10.2**
The Five Conditions of Perfect Competition
Perfect competition is rare, as these five conditions are difficult to attain.

1 **A Large Market**   Numerous sellers and buyers.
2 **Similar Product**   A nearly identical good or service is sold.
3 **Easy Entry and Exit**   Sellers already in the market cannot prevent competition, or entrance into the market. In addition, the initial costs of investment are small, and the good or service is easy to learn to produce.
4 **Easily Obtainable Information**
Information about prices, quality, and sources of supply is easy for both buyers and sellers to obtain.
As a result, there is:
5 **No Control Over Price**
The workings of supply and demand control the market, not a single seller or buyer.

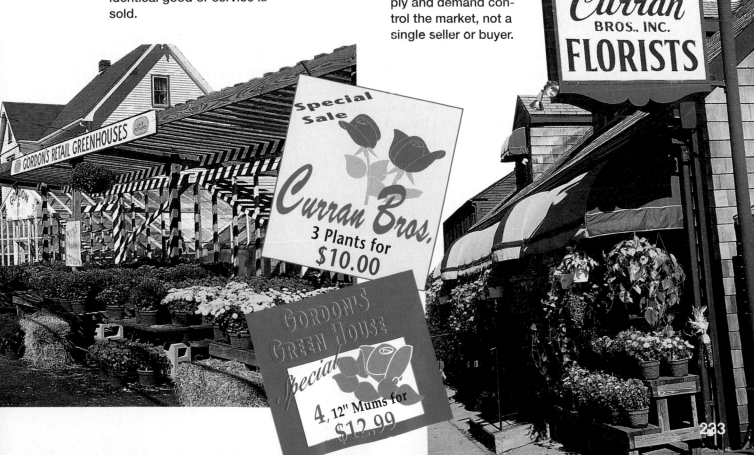

Figure 10.3 ▶
Five Factors that Make Wheat Farming Competitive

Consider the wheat market.

1 Thousands of wheat farmers and thousands of wholesalers buy wheat.
2 All wheat is fairly similar.
3 The costs of buying or renting farmland are low compared to starting a corporation, and farming methods can be learned.
4 Because wheat is sold to wholesalers, information about prices is fairly easy to obtain.
5 No one farmer has any great influence on price.

agricultural products high and by restricting the production of some products. Nonetheless, the agricultural market is often used as an example of perfect competition, because individual farmers have almost no control over the market price of their goods. The wheat farm illustrated in **Figure 10.3** provides one example.

The interaction of supply and demand determines the price of wheat. The supply is the total supply all wheat farmers produce. The demand is the total demand for all uses of wheat. The equilibrium price is the price where supply and demand meet.

Individual wheat farmers have to accept the market price. If the price is $5 per bushel, that is the price every farmer must accept. Farmers who attempt to raise their price above $5 will find that no one will buy their wheat. Neither will a farmer sell his or her crop for less than $5 per bushel. The market price is the only price that both buyers and sellers will accept.

The demand for wheat—and food in general—is somewhat different from the demand for many other products. People's demand for food is, for the most part, inelastic. People can use wheat in only so many ways, and people can eat only so many wheat products. The supply side of most agricultural markets is also unique. It is highly dependent on conditions over which farmers have little control such as those shown in **Figure 10.4**.

The Desirability of Perfect Competition

While we know that perfect competition is possible only in theory, any industry that tends toward it does have special characteristics. The intense competition in a perfectly competitive industry forces the price down to one that just covers the costs of production plus a normal profit. This price is beneficial to society because it means that consumers of products from perfectly competitive industries are paying only what society has to put in to make those products—the opportunity cost of the use of land, labor, capital, and entrepreneurship. The price that consumers pay for such products is a correct signal about the value of that product in society. Perfectly competitive industries yield economic efficiency. No rearrangement of the land, labor, capital, and entrepreneurship would generate a higher valued output. In an efficient situation such as this, it is impossible to make one person better off without making some other individual worse off. All inputs are used in the most advantageous way possible, and society therefore enjoys an efficient allocation of productive resources. All goods and services are sold at their opportunity cost.

Figure 10.4 ▲
Disasters for Farmers
Variations in weather, a crop disease, or a crop-destroying insect can wipe out entire harvests. This means that farmers may have a good harvest one year and a poor one the next. As a result, there are widely fluctuating, or changing, supplies of goods in the agricultural market.

SECTION 1 REVIEW

Understanding Vocabulary
Define perfect competition.

Reviewing Objectives
1. What five requirements are needed to have perfect competition?

2. What elements of agriculture make it almost perfectly competitive?

3. Why is perfect competition good for consumers?

Analyzing Economic Cartoons

Editorial cartoonists often make economic news the subject of their cartoons. Being able to analyze these cartoons helps you understand the news.

Steps to Analyze Economic Cartoons

Editorial/economic cartoons are usually based on current economic events. To understand the cartoon it is important to know about the events or the economic issue behind the cartoon. Follow these steps:

❶ Read the economic news in a newspaper or magazine.
❷ Check the opinion page for related editorials.
❸ Study the labels and symbols in the cartoon to identify people or issues.
❹ Ask what the cartoonist is trying to say about the economic event or issue.

Example

Look at **Figure A.** To interpret the cartoon, apply the last two directions under "Steps to Analyze Economic Cartoons." The automobile labeled "Total Deficit" has crashed; the vehicle is totaled. At the wheel is President Ronald Reagan with a Democrat sitting in the back seat. Looking to deflect the blame for the mishap, Reagan immediately remarks that the car—the deficit—was not in perfect shape when he inherited it from the Democrats. The cartoonist thinks Reagan's explanation is unsatisfactory.

Practicing the Skill

Look at **Figure B.** Apply the last two directions under "Steps to Analyze Economic Cartoons." How does this cartoonist feel about the economic recovery?

Figure A

"WELL, WHEN YOU WERE DRIVING YOU DENTED THE FENDERS"

May 31, 1984   ©1984 HERBLOCK

Figure B

2 Monopoly, Oligopoly, and Monopolistic Competition

SECTION 2 FOCUS

Terms to Know imperfect competition, pure monopoly, barriers to entry, cartel, natural monopolies, geographic monopolies, technological monopoly, patent, government monopolies, product differentiation, oligopoly, monopolistic competition

Objectives *After reading this section, you should be able to:*
① List the four characteristics of a pure **monopoly**.
② Describe the five characteristics of an **oligopoly**.
③ Explain the five characteristics of **monopolistic competition**.

From One Seller to Many Sellers— Different Market Structures

Most industries in the American economy are not perfectly competitive. Most represent some form of imperfect competition. **Imperfect competition** exists when any individual or group buys or sells a good or service in amounts large enough to affect price. Many market structures are imperfectly competitive, including monopoly, oligopoly, and monopolistic competition.

Monopoly

The most extreme form of imperfect competition is a **pure monopoly** whereby a single seller controls the supply of the good or service and thus determines the price. A few such markets do exist in the real world. Local electric utilities like the one in **Figure 10.5** are monopolies. The United States Postal Service's delivery of first-class mail is another example of a pure monopoly. **Figure 10.6** (page 238) shows four characteristics of a pure monopoly.

Figure 10.5
Local Electric Companies
Because local electric utilities are the sole providers and the consumer has no other option, they are monopolies.

▼

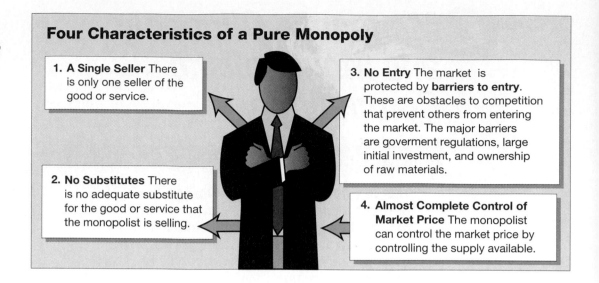

Figure 10.6 ▶
What Makes a Pure Monopoly?
Four specific characteristics must exist:

1 A Single Seller
2 No Substitutes
3 No Entry
4 Almost Complete Control of Market Price

Four Characteristics of a Pure Monopoly

1. A Single Seller There is only one seller of the good or service.

2. No Substitutes There is no adequate substitute for the good or service that the monopolist is selling.

3. No Entry The market is protected by **barriers to entry**. These are obstacles to competition that prevent others from entering the market. The major barriers are goverment regulations, large initial investment, and ownership of raw materials.

4. Almost Complete Control of Market Price The monopolist can control the market price by controlling the supply available.

In a pure monopoly, the supplier can raise prices without fear of losing business to competitors. Unless buyers choose to pay the new price, they have nowhere else to buy the good or service. A monopolist, however, cannot charge outrageous prices. In a monopoly market, the law of demand is still operating. As the price of a good or service rises, consumers buy less. Profits, as a result, may decrease. In other cases buyers may turn to an alternative good or service.

For example, some people believe that for years the United States Postal Service has provided poor service for the delivery of first-class mail, at steadily rising prices. Customers have increasingly turned to alternatives, such as telephone calls, fax transmissions, and overnight delivery service provided by such competitors as Federal Express, Airborne, United Parcel Service, and DHL. Also, it is now possible to easily send documents around the world through computers via modems and phone lines. Hence, the United States Postal Service's monopoly on first-class mail has not meant that it can charge any price and provide any level of service and still keep customers using it at the same level as before.

Barriers to Entry The most obvious barriers to entry into a monopolistic market are legal ones. For example, state laws prevent a competing electric, gas, or water company from operating in an area where there already is a public utility company. The reasoning against competition in public utility industries is that too much competition may lead to wasteful duplication. For example, if your town had two electric companies, they might both have electric lines strung around the city. They might be duplicating efforts, which might result in a wasteful use of resources. It might also result in higher rates to customers because of the lack of efficiency in operation.

Another barrier to entry is the cost of getting started. This barrier to entry is called excessive money capital costs. It is found in industries, such as cars and steel, in which initial investment is high because of the amount and cost of the equipment. The first company to make the investment will clearly have an advantage over later companies that want to enter the market.

Ownership of essential raw materials can also provide a barrier to entry. A good example is the diamond industry. The DeBeers Company of the Republic of South Africa controls the marketing of nearly all the world's diamonds. An example from American history is the Aluminum Company of America (ALCOA). At the turn of the twentieth century, it controlled almost all sources of bauxite (BAHK-syt), the major ore used in aluminum. For many years, ALCOA was able to keep its near-monopoly in aluminum because it would not sell bauxite to potential competitors.

Types of Monopolies Pure monopolies can be separated into four categories depending on why the mono-

poly exists. **Figure 10.7** explains these categories.

An international form of monopoly is the cartel. A **cartel** is an arrangement among groups of industrial businesses, often in different countries, to reduce international competition by controlling price, production, and the distribution of goods. Among the best-known cartels is the Organization of Petroleum Exporting Countries (OPEC), which was formed in 1960. Today OPEC includes several nations in the Middle East and North Africa,

Figure 10.7
Types of Monopolies

Monopolies can be separated into four categories:

A Natural Monopolies
- Produce products for lowest cost and force competitors out of business
- Need large investment
- More efficient to have one company

Example: An electric company
▼

B Geographic Monopolies
- Best location
- But less important now; customers can buy from catalogs, etc.

Example: A small-town auto repair shop
▼

C Technological Monopoly
- Seller has a government **patent,** the right to exclusively manufacture an invention for a specified number of years

Example: Polaroid film
▼

D Government ▶ Monopolies
- Created by legal barriers to entry

Example: Tennessee Valley Authority (TVA)

Figure 10.8
Characteristics of an Oligopoly

The domestic airline industry illustrates the characteristics of an oligopoly.

1 **Domination by a Few Sellers**
Several large firms dominate the entire industry.

2 **Barriers to Entry**
Capital costs of airlines are high, and it is difficult for new companies to enter major markets.

3 **Identical or Slightly Different Products**
Most airlines offer essentially the same service.

4 **Nonprice Competition**
While most airline services are about the same, some competition takes the form of **product differentiation.** Advertising emphasizes minor differences and attempts to build customer loyalty.

5 **Limited Control Over Price**
The airline industry has frequent price wars. If one airline lowers its fares, other airlines lower theirs even more.

▼

as well as Nigeria, Gabon, Venezuela, Ecuador, and Indonesia.

How Important Are Monopolies?

Monopolies today are far less important than they once were. Geographic monopolies probably have little effect because of potential competition from mail-order businesses. You can also be fairly certain that a technological monopoly will not last much longer than the life of a patent. Because of modern technology, competitors can make and patent slight variations in new products quickly. The microcomputer revolution in the early 1980s followed such a pattern. One company copied another's product, making changes and adding features to obtain a patent of its own.

International Business Machines (IBM) had at one time controlled a "lock" on the computer business. It sold mainframes—the biggest kind of computer—and made huge profits. In the 1990s, IBM faced decline because of the technological revolution in microcomputers. IBM failed to adapt quickly enough to the changing market and lost its near monopoly.

Oligopoly

An **oligopoly** (AHL-uh-GAHP-uh-lee) is an industry in which a few suppliers that exercise some control over price dominate. Some economists argue that the airline industry, as **Figure 10.8** suggests, is an example of an

oligopoly. They point out that until very recently, it was almost impossible for foreign airlines to compete in domestic markets.

Figure 10.9 shows a number of industries in which the four largest firms produce more than 80 percent of the total industry output. All these industries are oligopolies. Saying that an industry is an oligopoly does not necessarily mean that the situation should be changed.

Stable Prices A surprising feature of the general criticism of oligopolies is that little proof exists that they are harmful. It is true that consumers may be paying more than if they were buying in a perfectly competitive market in which supply and demand would set the price. Oligopolistic markets, however, tend to have generally stable prices. They also offer consumers a wider variety of different products than would a perfectly competitive industry.

Monopolistic Competition

In **monopolistic competition,** a large number of sellers offer similar but slightly different products. Obvious examples are such brand-name items as toothpaste, cosmetics, and designer clothes.

Monopolistic competition characterizes many industries in the United States. Qualities of this type of industry are shown in **Figure 10.10** (page 242).

Comparisons of Oligopolies and Pure Monopolies

Many of the characteristics of monopolistic competition are the same as those of an oligopoly. The major differences, however, are in the number of sellers of a product and in the product. In an oligopoly, a few companies dominate an industry, and control over price is interdependent. The products may or may not be similar. Monopolistic competition has

many firms, no real interdependence, and some slight difference among products.

Perfect competition has so many buyers and sellers that no one has any control over price. Everyone must take the price the interaction of total demand and total supply determines. In monopolistic competition each competitor has some control over the price of its product. A monopolistic competitor, however, does not have as much control over price as a pure

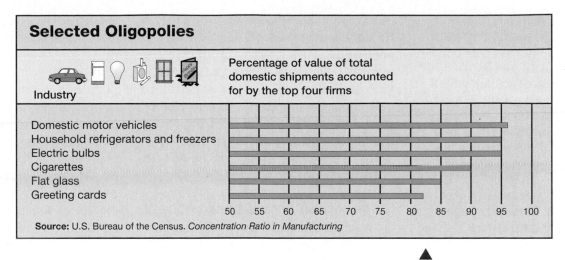

Selected Oligopolies

Industry	Percentage of value of total domestic shipments accounted for by the top four firms

	50	55	60	65	70	75	80	85	90	95	100
Domestic motor vehicles										■	
Household refrigerators and freezers										■	
Electric bulbs										■	
Cigarettes									■		
Flat glass									■		
Greeting cards							■				

Source: U.S. Bureau of the Census. *Concentration Ratio in Manufacturing*

▲
Figure 10.9
Oligopolies
Oligopolies exist in a number of industries throughout the United States. Here, a wide range of industries are highlighted.

Figure 10.10
Characteristics of Monopolistic Competition

The characteristics of monopolistic competition within an industry are:

1 **Numerous Sellers** No one seller or small group dominates the market.

2 **Relatively Easy Entry** Entry is easier than in other types of imperfectly competitive markets. One drawback is the high cost of advertising.

3 **Differentiated Products** Each seller sells a slightly different product to attract customers.

4 **Nonprice Competition** Businesses compete by product differentiation and by advertising. These result in:

5 **Some Control Over Price** Each firm has some control over the price it charges due to customer loyalty and product differentiation. ▶

monopolist because other monopolistic competitors are selling almost, but not quite, the same product. The quantity demanded of a good or service will drop if the price is raised and cheaper substitutes are available. If one monopolistic competitor raises the price too much, most customers will buy another brand, or substitute, of the same good.

Neighborhood Businesses Neighborhood businesses such as cleaners and drugstores are involved in monopolistic competition. Each business within the neighborhood has an identity of its own even though the differences between its good or service and those of its competitors may be small.

Competitive Advertising Competitive advertising is especially important in monopolistic competition. Competitive advertising attempts to persuade consumers that the product being advertised is different from, and superior to, any other. Businesses also compete for shelf space—space on store shelves for displaying their products and attracting buyers. A cosmetics company, for example, may produce several lines of cosmetics. Each is aimed at a different market segment, or section. By having three lines, the company competes in three areas with competitors. The differences in products attract different customers and add to the profits of the company.

SECTION 2 REVIEW

Understanding Vocabulary
Define imperfect competition, pure monopoly, barriers to entry, cartel, natural monopolies, geographic monopolies, technological monopoly, patent, government monopolies, product differentiation, oligopoly, monopolistic competition.

Reviewing Objectives
1 What are the four characteristics of a pure monopoly?
2 What characteristics of an oligopoly allow it to have a limited control over price?
3 What are the five characteristics of monopolistic competition?

Joan Robinson on Imperfect Competition

Profile

- 1903–1983
- was Professor of Economics at Cambridge University in England
- best known for developing theory of monopolistic competition
- authored many books, including *The Economics of Imperfect Competition* (1933) and *Economic Heresies: Some Old-Fashioned Questions in Economic Theory* (1971)

Joan Robinson, who produced her first major work in economics during the Great Depression, believed that there was something wrong with the theory of competition. Adam Smith had said competition would benefit society as individuals maximized their own best interests. Robinson disagreed. She criticized economists who ignored social and moral issues. In *The Economics of Imperfect Competition*, Robinson said the model of competition Smith used does not exist in the real world.

The traditional assumption of perfect competition is an exceedingly convenient one for simplifying the analysis of price, but there is no reason to expect it to be fulfilled in the real world. It depends, in the first place, upon the existence of such a large number of producers that a change in the output of any one of them has a negligible effect upon the output of the commodity as a whole, and it depends, in the second place, upon the existence of a perfect market. The first condition may often be approximately fulfilled, but the existence of a perfect market is likely to be extremely rare in the real world.

Robinson believed that price is only one of the factors that consumers consider. Convenience, quality, speed of service, or even the manners of salespeople influence consumers.

. . . Rival producers compete against each other in quality, in facilities, and in advertisement, as well as in price, and the very intensity of competition, by forcing them to attract customers in every possible way, itself breaks up the market and ensures that not all the customers, who are attached in varying degrees to a particular firm by the advantages which it offers them, will immediately forsake it for a rival who offers similar goods at an infinitesimally smaller price.

Checking for Understanding

1. What two conditions are necessary to have perfect competition?
2. Which condition of perfect competition is extremely rare?
3. Besides price, what do producers use to attract customers?

SECTION **3** Government Policies Toward Competition

SECTION 3 FOCUS

Terms to Know antitrust legislation, interlocking directorate, merger, horizontal merger, vertical merger, conglomerates, conglomerate merger, deregulation, reregulation

Objectives *After reading this section, you should be able to:*

1. Explain the difference between **interlocking directorates and mergers.**
2. List at least four major federal **regulatory agencies.**
3. Explain the movement toward **reregulation.**

The Government Regulates Business in an Attempt to Protect Consumers

Historically, one of the goals of government in the United States has been to encourage competition in the economy. Through the years, federal and state governments have passed laws and established regulatory agencies in an attempt to force monopolies to act more competitively. Known as **antitrust legislation,** these laws act to prevent new monopolies, or trusts, from forming and to break up those that already exist. See **Figures 10.11 and 10.12.**

Figure 10.11
Antitrust History
President Theodore Roosevelt, portrayed here breaking up trusts in the early 1900s, believed monopolies were "the tyranny of mere wealth."

NO MOLLY-CODDLING HERE

Interlocking Directorates and Mergers

You should be familiar with two terms from the table: *interlocking directorate* and *merger.* An **interlocking directorate** occurs when some members of the boards of directors of competing corporations are the same. In effect, only one group of people manages both companies. Because the same people control both companies, it is easy for them to make sure that the two companies do not compete with one another.

The last point in the table under the Clayton Act refers to corporate mergers. A **merger** occurs when one

Figure 10.12 Antitrust Legislation

Federal Law	Function
Sherman Act (1890)	Outlawed agreements and conspiracies that restrain interstate trade. Made it illegal to monopolize or even attempt to monopolize any part of interstate commerce.
Clayton Act (1914)	Restricted the practice of selling the same good to different buyers at different prices. Prohibited seller from requiring that a buyer not deal with a competitor. Outlawed interlocking directorates between competitors. Outlawed mergers that substantially lessen competition.
Federal Trade Commission Act (1914)	Established the Federal Trade Commission (FTC) as an independent antitrust agency. Gave the FTC power to bring court cases against private businesses engaging in unfair trade practices.
Robinson-Patman Act (1936)	Strengthened the law against charging different prices for the same product to different buyers. An amendment to the Clayton Act of 1914.
Celler-Kefauver Antimerger Act (1950)	Strengthened the law against firms joining together to control too large a part of the market. An amendment to the Clayton Act of 1914.
Hart-Scott-Rodino Antitrust Improvements Act (1976)	Restricted mergers that would lessen competition. It required big corporations planning to merge to notify the Federal Trade Commission (FTC) and the Department of Justice. They would then decide whether to challenge the merger under the terms of the Clayton Act of 1914.

corporation joins with another corporation.

Three kinds of mergers exist. When the two corporations are in the same business, it is called a **horizontal merger.** When a business that is buying from or selling to another business merges with that business, a **vertical merger** takes place. Some corporations have become big by buying out other corporations dealing in totally unrelated activities. These expanded corporations are called **conglomerates.** The buying out of an unrelated business is termed **conglomerate merger.**

The Clayton Act forbids mergers when they tend to lessen competition substantially. The Clayton Act, however, does not state what the term *substantially* means. As a result, it is up to the federal government to make a subjective decision as to whether the merging of two corporations would substantially lessen competition.

Regulatory Agencies

Besides using antitrust laws to foster a competitive atmosphere, the government uses direct regulation of business pricing and product quality.

Government regulatory agencies oversee these regulations. See **Figure 10.14**. These agencies exist not only at the federal level, but at the state level and even at local levels.

Although the aim of most government regulations is to promote efficiency and competition, recent evidence indicates something quite different. Many regulations, as a by-product of their goals to protect consumers and companies within industries from unfair practices, have actually decreased the amount of competition in the economy.

The Interstate Commerce Commission (ICC) raised the prices that consumers paid to ship goods by preventing entry into the trucking industry and restricting price competition.

For many years the Federal Communications Commission (FCC), in an effort to help UHF stations, in effect prevented the entry of competitive pay-TV, cable, and satellite systems into the television market.

While the Civil Aeronautics Board (CAB) regulated air fares, these fares were 20 to 30 percent higher than they were after deregulation when competition was allowed to set prices.

Because of findings such as these, the 1980s were called the years of **deregulation** as government gradually reduced regulations and control over business activity. For example, the

CAB no longer controlled air fares or route selection by the nation's airlines. The cable television industry provides another example, as **Figure 10.13** shows. The many regulations in the banking industry were slowly decreased, allowing consumers to obtain competitive interest rates on savings for the first time in years.

Should There Be Reregulation?

Congress has considered **reregulation** of a number of formerly heavily regulated industries. Many heads of airlines have asked for reregulation of the airline industry. Many people criticized the deregulation of the cable TV industry. Consequently, Congress began reregulation with the 1992 Cable Reregulation Act. Since then, rates that cable operators can charge per month have been regulated.

Figure 10.13 ▶
Cable Deregulation
The Federal Communications Commission (FCC), which had prevented the entry of pay-TV, cable, and satellite systems into the TV market, now allows almost open competition in the direct-satellite television transmission fields.

Figure 10.14 Federal Regulatory Agencies

Agency	Function
Interstate Commerce Commision (ICC) (1887)	Regulates interstate commerce, primarily railroads and trucking.
Federal Trade Commission (FTC) (1914)	Regulates product warranties, unfair methods of competition in interstate commerce, and fraud in advertising.
Food and Drug Administration (FDA) (1927)	Regulates purity and safety of foods, drugs, and cosmetics.
Federal Communications Commission (FCC) (1934)	Regulates television, radio, telegraph, and telephone; grants licenses, creates and enforces rules of behavior for broadcasting; most recently, regulates satellite transmissions and cable TV.
Securities and Exchange Commission (SEC) (1934)	Regulates the sale of stocks, bonds, and other investments.
Equal Employment Opportunity Commission (EEOC) (1964)	Responsible for working to reduce discrimination based on religion, gender, race, national origin, or age.
Occupational Safety and Health Administration (OSHA) (1970)	Regulates the workplace environment; makes sure that businesses provide workers with safe and healthful working conditions.
Nuclear Regulatory Commission (NRC) (1975)	Regulates the nuclear power industry; licenses and oversees the design, construction, and operation of nuclear power plants.

SECTION 3 REVIEW

Understanding Vocabulary

Define antitrust legislation, interlocking directorate, merger, horizontal merger, vertical merger, conglomerates, conglomerate merger, deregulation, reregulation.

Reviewing Objectives

1. How do interlocking directorates differ from mergers?
2. What are some major federal regulatory agencies in the United States?
3. Why do some Americans favor reregulation?

Readings in Economics

| TIME | APRIL 26, 1993 |

IS NIKE GETTING TOO BIG?

by David E. Thigpen

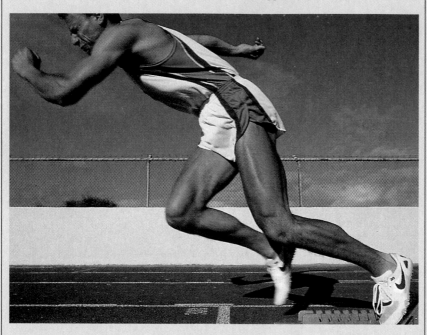

Every sports fan has seen the flashy TV commercials: Michael Jordan, leaping for the basket, seems to break free of gravity as he goes up, up, and still higher up. The trajectory has been the same for the company whose shoes the commercial touts. Since its founding 21 years ago, Nike, the Beaverton, Oregon, sportswear conglomerate, has soared to greater and greater heights, becoming the $3.7 billion-a-year titan of the industry. The key has been Nike's endorsement contracts with such top professional athletes as Jordan, baseball's Bo Jackson ("Bo knows . . . "), football's Jerry Rice and, to a lesser extent, several hundred others. But as it has lavished ever more millions of dollars on such tie-ins, Nike has seen something else rise along with its profile and its profits: concern in the sports world about whether it exerts too much control over its player-pitchmen and wields too much influence over the sports in which they compete.

Nike's increasing clout has long troubled the National Football League, and even the mighty National Basketball Association. Two years ago, Nike ordered 90 of the athletes it has under contract to withdraw from part of the rich apparel-licensing deal by which the N.B.A. sells the players' likenesses on shirts and hats—depriving the league of $1.5 million a year in revenue. In February Nike, along with Michael Jordan, wrestled from the N.B.A. the rights to the multimillion-dollar market for T shirts bearing Jordan's image. "In marketing, Nike is far more powerful than the league," says N.B.A. deputy commissioner Russ Granik. . . .

• THINK ABOUT IT •

1. What about the Nike contracts concerns many in the sports world?

2. Why does Nike wield so much power in professional sports?

10 *Highlights*

Summary

Perfect competition has five conditions that include businesses having no control over price. In the United States, agriculture comes closest to meeting these conditions. Although ideal, perfect competition almost never exists in the real world.

Summary

Pure monopoly has four conditions that include one business having almost complete control over the market price. The five characteristics of an oligopoly include limited control over price. Monopolistic competition is the most common type of market structure in the United States.

Summary

Federal laws prohibit interlocking directorates, yet allow mergers as long as they do not create monopolies. To foster competition and protect consumers, the government has created numerous federal regulatory agencies. Some of this regulation has been eliminated, though certain people favor reregulation.

10 Review

Identifying Key Terms

Write the letter of the definition in Column B below that correctly defines each term in Column A.

Column A
1. barriers to entry (p. 238)
2. deregulation (p. 246)
3. conglomerate (p. 245)
4. interlocking directorate (p. 244)
5. natural monopoly (p. 239)
6. merger (p. 244)

Column B
a. large corporation made up of smaller companies dealing in unrelated activities
b. the joining together of two corporations
c. obstacles to competition that prevent new companies from being formed
d. process of removing goverment restrictions of business
e. production by one company rather than several, due to efficient operation
f. situation in which some of the board of directors for competing companies are the same

Use terms from the list below to fill in the blanks in the paragraph that follows.

monopolistic competition (p. 240)
oligopoly (p. 240)
government monopoly (p. 239)
geographic monopoly (p. 239)
antitrust legislation (p. 244)

One form of imperfect competition in which a few firms compete is __(7)__. Another form of imperfect competition in which many firms compete, but each has a differentiated product is __(8)__. Monopolies have great control over price. Even a small mom and pop store in an isolated town has a __(9)__. Many times the federal government creates legal barriers to entry and thereby forms a __(10)__, such as the United States Postal Service. In order to prevent monopolies, there are federal laws called __(11)__.

Recalling Facts and Ideas

Section 1
1. In a perfectly competitive market structure, how much control does a single seller have over market price?
2. What is the relationship between the types of products that sellers sell in a perfectly competitive market?
3. What is one example of an almost perfectly competitive market?

Section 2
4. What are the three types of imperfectly competitive market structures?
5. What is the difference between a geographic monopoly and a technological monopoly?
6. How much control does an oligopoly have over price?
7. In monopolistic competition, how many sellers are there?

Section 3
8. What is the difference between a horizontal merger and a vertical merger?
9. What two methods does the federal government use to keep business competitive?

Critical Thinking

Section 1
Identifying Central Issues Explain in a paragraph how supply and demand work in the agricultural market when government controls are not operating.

Section 2
Making Generalizations Explain how the free enterprise system works to break the power of monopolies.

Section 3
Making Comparisons What are the fundamental differences between the goals of antitrust legislation and the goals of federal government regulations enforced through regulatory agencies?

Applying Economic Concepts

Competition and Market Structure Make a list of the different types of monopolies that can exist. Under each type, make a list of examples. Under government monopolies, for example, you have already learned about the United States Postal Service and the Tennessee Valley Authority. Others exist at the state and local levels.

Chapter Projects

1. **Individual Project** Choose one of the regulatory agencies mentioned in this chapter and write to the agency for information about its functions. Use the information you receive to write a report summarizing the main functions of that agency.
2. **Cooperative Learning Project** Numerous firms operate in imperfectly competitive market structures. Work in three groups—one representing monopolies, one oligopolies, and one monopolistic competition. Each member of each group should clip out ads and articles that give examples of firms that have the characteristics of the type of mar-

ket structure her or his group represents.

Compare the sets of ads for each of the three groups. There undoubtedly will be some overlap. One group might claim that a particular company is an oligopoly, whereas another group might claim that it is a monopoly. Your group should be able to defend the reason it places a particular company in its particular grouping.

Reviewing Skills

Analyzing Economic Cartoons
Defense Spending After the cold war ended in the early 1990s, the United States began to scale back its defense spending. What is this cartoonist's opinion of this cut in spending? What hidden costs does this cartoonist think the cuts have had?

NOT SO GOOD.... HOW'S *YOUR* DEFENSE CONVERSION ?

Writing About Economics

Persuasive Writing Write copy for an advertisement for the toothpaste, soft drink, soap, or breakfast cereal that you chose in Your Economics Journal.

Running a Business

From the classroom of Judy B. Smitherman, Thompson High School, Alabaster, Alabama

In Unit 3 you read about markets, prices, and business competition. In this lab, you will make decisions as the sole proprietor of a business called Sidewalk Tees that sells screen printed T-shirts. (You may want to reread the material on pages 208–211 of the text.)

Tools

1. Ruler, pencils, writing paper, graph paper
2. Calculator

Procedures

Step A Read the following description of your production requirements and costs:

The screen printing equipment and display hangers cost $4,800. For this you need a bank loan. The monthly payment on this loan is $220. One month's supply of ink and screens costs $240. The best wholesale price for good T-shirts is $3.25. You should order an equal number of large and extra-large shirts in assorted colors. Gas for your car for business purposes costs $15 each week. Utilities and miscellaneous costs will be an additional $40 per month. Bank checking charges total $8 monthly. A yearly business license costs $52, and you can rent a booth from the Beachfront Flea

Market for $26 per day. You plan to rent a booth Friday, Saturday, and Sunday each week. Operating alone, you can produce 80 shirts in a 20-hour week (4 per hour). By adding a part-time worker for 20 hours, you can produce 200 shirts (10 per hour). Expenses for a part-time worker total $7 per hour.

Step B Using a table like the one below, draw up a weekly financial plan for Sidewalk Tees.

Example

TOTAL WEEKLY COSTS

Item	Cost per week
Booth rental	
Utilities, gasoline, and miscellaneous costs	
Bank loan	
Bank checking	
Ink and screens	
T-shirts	
License	
Wages	
Total weekly costs	

Step C Pricing your product is important because your prices will help determine how well the product sells and how much profit you make. After studying the market for T-shirts, you project the effect of price changes on quantities demanded in a table like this one:

Price per shirt	Quantity demanded per week
$ 8.00	200
$ 9.00	170
$10.00	140
$11.00	110
$12.00	90

Determine your costs for each shirt, and find your profits. Remember that labor and other variable costs will change depending on the quantity of goods you produce. Copy the following table and complete different pricing plans:

Example

PRODUCT PRICING AND PROFIT

Item	Amount	
	Plan A	Plan B
Price per unit		
Estimated units sold per weekend		
Net revenues per weekend		
Less expenses per week		
Weekly gross profits		
Less 8% taxes		
Weekly net profits		

Step D Review your decisions. What are your variable costs? Could you have earned more profit by increasing or reducing your part-time worker's hours? What would result if you increased or reduced prices for the T-shirts?

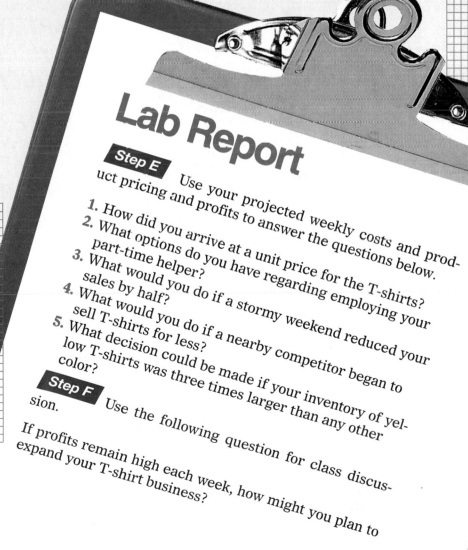

Lab Report

Step E Use your projected weekly costs and product pricing and profits to answer the questions below.

1. How did you arrive at a unit price for the T-shirts?
2. What options do you have regarding employing your part-time helper?
3. What would you do if a stormy weekend reduced your sales by half?
4. What would you do if a nearby competitor began to sell T-shirts for less?
5. What decision could be made if your inventory of yellow T-shirts was three times larger than any other color?

Step F Use the following question for class discussion.

If profits remain high each week, how might you plan to expand your T-shirt business?

U N I T 4

MICROECONOMICS: AMERICAN BUSINESS IN ACTION

11 FINANCING AND PRODUCING GOODS

How much do you think it cost to build and equip this plant?

What is being produced here?

Would the product being produced cost more or less if everything were done by hand?

Do you think this physical work would be interesting or boring?

Why is the production process set up in this way?

Your Economics Journal

Keep track of the consumer products that you use in your house during a one-week period, excluding food, cosmetics, and the like. List these items as simple or complex and explain whether you think the production process used for each was highly automated.

SECTION 1 FOCUS

Terms to Know cost-benefit analysis

Objectives *After reading this section, you should be able to:*

1. List the different institutions through which people can **turn savings into investments.**
2. Explain **why people are willing to finance investment.**
3. Describe how **bidding for investment financing allocates resources in a market economy.**

Investment is the Backbone of the Free Enterprise System

If you were an entrepreneur who started a small electronics repair company, you would face many hurdles on your road to success. One hurdle would be finding sufficient financing to pay for your company's current needs—parts and so on—and its long-term needs—growth. Both the short-term and long-term needs of business can be financed in a variety of ways. Financing business operations and growth is an integral part of our free enterprise system.

Turning Savings into Investments

People who save money often deposit their funds in one of several types of financial institutions in exchange for interest on their accounts. The financial institutions, in turn, make these deposits available to businesses to finance growth and expansion as **Figure 11.1** shows.

Making Financing Decisions Let's assume that you own an electronics repair company that you have incorporated. You now have the opportunity to open additional repair shops in other locations, but you do not have enough extra cash to invest in the expansion. Fortunately, you can obtain this financing in one of many ways, including borrowing from a financial institution, digging into your own personal savings, asking your friends and parents to loan the company money, or selling more shares of stock. Even if you are able to finance the expansion, one important question remains. Should you expand?

Businesses usually answer this question by making a standard **cost-benefit analysis.** This analysis requires that you estimate the cost of an action and compare it with the benefits of that action.

Financing Business Expansion

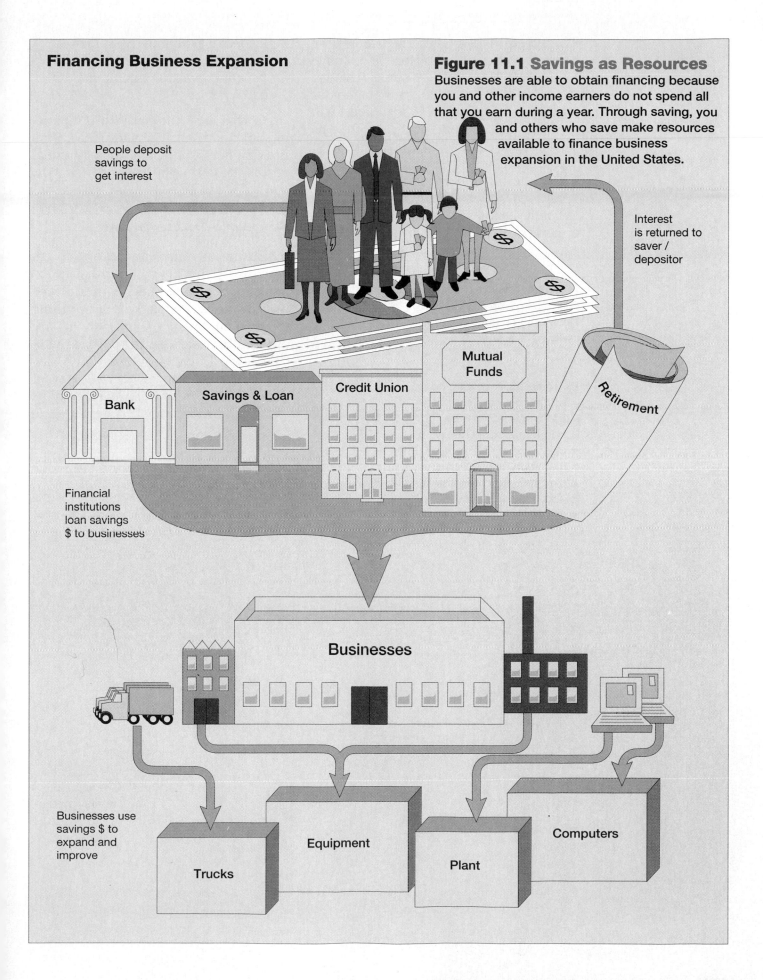

Figure 11.1 Savings as Resources

Businesses are able to obtain financing because you and other income earners do not spend all that you earn during a year. Through saving, you and others who save make resources available to finance business expansion in the United States.

People deposit savings to get interest

Interest is returned to saver / depositor

Bank

Savings & Loan

Credit Union

Mutual Funds

Retirement

Financial institutions loan savings $ to businesses

Businesses

Businesses use savings $ to expand and improve

Trucks

Equipment

Plant

Computers

Figure 11.2 shows the steps of a cost-benefit analysis. Here is a simple numerical example. Assume that you can borrow $1 million to finance your business expansion. Your bank will charge 10 percent per year for the loan. That equals $100,000 per year. If you could generate additional profits because of the expansion of $200,000 per year, then borrowing $1 million would certainly be worthwhile. Remember the rule that always applies:

Undertake an activity up to the point at which the additional benefit equals the additional cost.

In this case the activity is financing an expansion. The additional benefit is higher profits, and the additional cost is the cost of borrowing.

Why People Are Willing to Finance Investment

Businesses are interested in financing so that they can invest in expansion, hoping to make higher profits in the future. People who are willing to finance such an investment are seeking a reward from their activity. The reward may be interest on a savings account or a certificate of deposit. The reward, however, may be

Figure 11.2
A Cost-Benefit Analysis
Developing a cost-benefit analysis involves five steps.

Step 1:
Estimate the following costs:
- renting new stores
- training new workers
- additional bookkeeping
- opportunity cost of your time to check on new shops
- electricity and other utilities
- additional insurance
- any other expenses that apply

▼

Step 2: Calculate expected revenues. ▼

Step 3:
Calculate expected profits: revenues minus costs listed in Step 1.

◀

interest on a corporate bond that they purchase, or dividends (or an increase in value) from the stock that they buy in an expanding company.

Sometimes the same individual is both a lender and a borrower. As the owner of an electronics repair corporation, you could be going to a bank to ask for a loan to finance expansion, while personally having money on deposit in the same bank in the form of savings accounts or certificates of deposit. Even corporations themselves may be financing the expansion of an unrelated company while asking their bank for financing for their own expansion. Most of us are both creditors and debtors. The same is true for businesses and governments. Some day you may be paying interest on a mortgage while earning interest on a savings account.

Bidding for Investment Financing

In a free enterprise system, resources normally go where they generate the highest value. Financing investment often directs the allocation of these resources. If you are certain that expanding your business into other locations will yield high profits, then you will be aggressive in finding financing for that expansion. If one bank turns down your loan, you may decide to borrow elsewhere, even at a higher interest rate. Another way to finance expansion would be to sell corporate bonds at relatively high interest rates. You might also offer stock to new and old shareholders at an attractive price per share. The point is that the more convinced you are that you will make high profits by expanding, the more you will be willing to finance this investment.

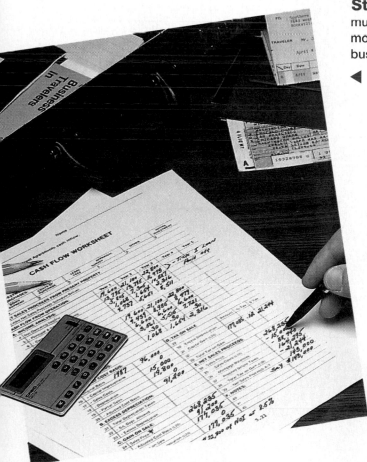

Step 4: Now calculate how much it will cost you to borrow the money to finance your proposed business expansion.

◀

Step 5: If expected profits more than cover the cost of financing the expansion, then the expansion is probably warranted. ▼

When one business succeeds at obtaining financing, it uses funds that might have helped another business. In a market economy each business competes for scarce financial resources. If the cost to finance business expansion is relatively high, only those businesses that believe they have the most profitable expansion projects will be willing to pay the high cost of financing. **Figure 11.3** shows one example of such a business expansion. If the cost of financing is relatively low, more companies will decide that they, too, can profitably engage in additional business investment.

Figure 11.3
Typical Business Expansion

Many American hotels have expanded by building in other countries after calculating that their profits will outweigh the costs of financing the expansion. ▼

Financing is simply an intermediate step between the desire to use additional resources and the actual use of those resources. The financing of investment itself does not create the investment and use the resources. It is when the financing funds are spent that the resources become used. Financing is, in effect, the "grease" that makes America's free enterprise system work.

Remember, there are several methods of financing business expansion, including borrowing, selling bonds, and offering stock. You can borrow money from banks or other institutions. **Figure 11.4** discusses alternative financing.

Figure 11.4
Alternate Financing
You must be sure to recalculate the total cost of your loan if it is offered at a higher interest rate than a bank would charge you. Many loan shops and "money stores" offer financing that may not be worth the price.

▼

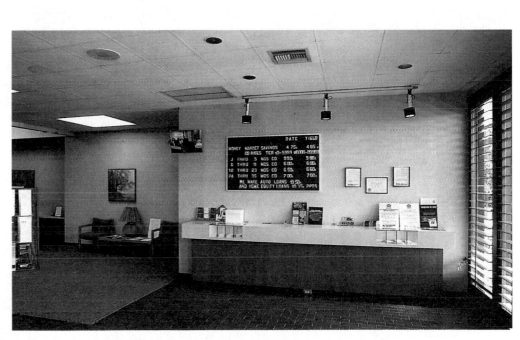

SECTION 1 REVIEW

Understanding Vocabulary
Define cost-benefit analysis.

Reviewing Objectives
① Where can people deposit their savings so that businesses can obtain investment funds for expansion?

② What do people who finance investments hope to gain?

③ How does bidding for investment financing affect resources in a market economy?

Building Graphs

It is important that you know how to present statistical material graphically in your presentations, reports, and research projects.

Developing a Bar Graph

To create a bar graph, put the correct measurements on the two axes of your graph and enter the data in the form of horizontal or vertical bars. The following 1992 changes in selected consumer price index categories are shown in the bar graph in Figure A: food, 1.5%; shelter, 2.9%; medical care, 6.6%.

Data Over Time—the Line Graph

The following actual and predicted percentages of total population 75 years or older are plotted on **Figure B**: 1950 = 2.5%, 1970 = 3.7%, 1980 = 4.4%, 1990 = 5.2%, 2000 = 6.2%, 2010 = 6.5%.

Developing Circle Graphs

If your information totals 100 percent, you can present it in a circle graph. The following imaginary data for a family are used to create **Figure C**: Total income, $200; amount spent on food, $32; on housing, $48; on transportation, $36; all other expenditures, $84. To build the graph, convert the figures to percentages, then enter them in the circle.

Figure A

Figure B

Figure C

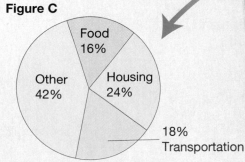

Practicing the Skill

❶ Convert the information in **Figure C** to a bar graph.

❷ Make a line graph using these statistics about crude oil production: 1988, 693 million barrels; 1989, 646 million; 1990, 640 million; 1991, 638 million; 1992, 605 million.

2 Types of Financing for Business Operations

Businesses Choose from Among Several Financing Options

Business borrowing is similar in many ways to borrowing by individuals. A business that wants to borrow must show credit worthiness by undergoing a credit check. A credit rating of good, average, or poor is then assigned to the business. Like an individual who borrows money, a business must pay interest on its loan. It must also repay the loan within a stated period of time.

Three Kinds of Financing

Raising money for a business through borrowing, or **debt financing**, can be divided into three categories— short-term, intermediate-term, and long-term financing. **Short-term financing** involves borrowing money for any period of time less than a year. Borrowing money for 1 to 10 years is considered **intermediate-term financing**. Borrowing for any longer period is called **long-term financing**. As **Figure 11.5** (pages 266–267) shows, the types and sources of financing differ depending upon the types of debt.

Short-Term Financing A business may seek short-term financing for many reasons. Because most billing is done monthly, a company may have excellent business during the month but not be paid until the beginning of the following month. In the meantime, the company needs money to pay salaries and its bills. During a growing season, a farmer may have to borrow to buy seed, repair equipment, and pay workers. In both cases, it would be unwise for the business to take out a long-term loan for a short-term need.

Figure 11.5 Types of Financing

Short-Term Financing

Trade credit

Trade credit is extended by a seller to a business buying goods. It allows a buyer to take possession of goods immediately and pay for them at some future date–usually 30 to 90 days later. Trade credit accounts for more than half of all transactions involving goods. By using trade credit, a business does not have to tie up its money capital in inventory. At the same time, trade credit benefits the seller by increasing its sales.

Trade credit involves a cost to the user. Often a buyer receives a discount, for example 2 percent, if a bill is paid within 10 days. If the buyer does not receive the discount, he or she is, in effect, paying 2 percent interest for the use of the trade credit.

Unsecured loans

Most short-term bank credit for businesses is in the form of unsecured bank loans. These are loans not guaranteed by anything other than the promise to repay them. The borrower must sign a **promissory** (PRAHM-uh-SOHR-ee) **note** to repay the money in full by a specified time and with a specified rate of interest. The usual repayment period is one year.

Secured loans

Secured loans are backed by collateral—something of value that a borrower uses as a promise to repay a loan. Businesses offer as collateral property such as machinery, inventories, or **accounts receivable**—money owed to a business by its customers.

Line of credit

A **line of credit** is the maximum amount of money a company can borrow from a bank during a period of time, usually one year. Rather than apply each time for a loan, a company may automatically borrow up to the amount of the line of credit, for example, $100,000. Banks establish lines of credit for larger businesses with good credit ratings.

Intermediate-Term Financing

Loans

Intermediate-term loans have repayment periods of from 1 to 10 years and generally require collateral such as stocks, bonds, equipment, or machinery. The loan is considered a mortgage if it is secured by property, such as the building in which the business is located. Sometimes large, financially sound companies may be able to get unsecured intermediate-term loans.

Leasing

Leasing means renting rather than buying equipment. One advantage of leasing is that the leasing company will often service the equipment at low cost. Another advantage is that the company may deduct a part of the money spent on a lease before figuring its income taxes. One disadvantage is that taking out a long-term lease often costs more than borrowing the money to buy the same equipment.

Figure 11.5 Types of Financing

Long-Term Financing

Bonds	Bonds promise to pay a stated	rate of interest over a stated period of time and to repay the full amount bor-	rowed at the end of that time.
Stock	Selling stock is called **equity** (EK-wuht-ee) **financing**	because part of the ownership, or equity, of the company is being sold. Corporations may sell	either preferred or common stock. The differences are described below.

Common Stock	Preferred Stock
1. Common stock is issued by all corporations; it is the stock most often bought and sold. A corporation is an organization owned by many people but treated by the law as though it were a person; it can own property, pay taxes, make contracts, sue and be sued, and so on.	1. Many corporations do not issue preferred stock.
2. Holders of common stock have voting rights in a corporation. As a group, they elect the board of directors.	2. Holders of preferred stock have no voting rights.
3. Common stock pays dividends based on a corporation's performance. If the company does well, dividends may be high; if it does poorly, the dividends may be low or zero.	3. Preferred stock pays a fixed dividend. This amount must be paid before holders of common stock receive any dividends. If a company is unable to pay a fixed dividend on time, it must usually make up the missed payment at a later date.
4. Value of common stock rises and falls in relation to the corporation's performance and what investors expect it to do in the future.	4. The value of preferred stock changes in relation to how well the company is doing.
5. If a corporation fails, holders of common stock are the last to be paid with whatever money is left after paying all creditors.	5. If a corporation fails, holders of preferred stock must be paid before any holders of common stock are paid.

Intermediate-Term Financing When a company wants to expand its business by buying more land, buildings, or equipment, short-term financing generally is not adequate. For example, if you decided to expand your electronics repair business by opening another shop, you would not apply for a 90-day loan. In 90 days, you would not be able to do enough repair jobs to earn the additional revenue to repay the loan. Instead, you would look for intermediate-term financing.

Long-Term Financing For financing debts lasting 10 to 15 years or more, corporations either sell bonds or issue stock. Long-term financing is used for major expansion, such as building a new plant or buying new machines to replace outdated ones. See **Figure 11.6**. Usually only large corporations finance long-term debt by selling bonds. Unlike smaller companies, large corporations with huge assets appear to be better risks to investors who are interested in buying bonds.

Figure 11.6
Major Equipment Purchases
Long-term financing is used to match the length of the borrowing with the useful life of the building or the equipment being purchased.

▼

Choosing the Right Financing

Financial managers try to obtain capital at a minimum cost to the company. To do so, they try to choose the best mix of financing. The length of a loan that a company takes out or a corporation's decision regarding whether to sell bonds or issue stock depends on several factors as shown in **Figure 11.7**. These factors include interest costs, market climate, control of the company, and the financial condition of the company itself.

Figure 11.7 ▲
Four Factors Affecting Loan Choices

1 **Interest Costs**
   When interest rates in general are high, a business may be reluctant to take out a loan. For example, a company may delay its expansion until it can borrow at better interest rates or take out a series of short-term loans at high rates, hoping that interest rates will drop. When that happens, the company will then take out a long-term loan. Interest rates also affect the decision to issue bonds. When rates are high, corporations must offer high rates of interest on their bonds to attract investors. When interest rates in general drop, corporations can offer lower rates of return on their bonds.

2 **Market Climate**
   If economic growth appears to be slow, investors may prefer the fixed rate of return of bonds or preferred stock to the unknown return on common stock.

3 **Control of the Company**
   Bonds do not have voting rights attached to them. Most preferred stocks do not give voting rights to shareholders either. The owners of common stocks, however, do have the right to vote in company elections.

4 **Financial Condition of the Company**
   If a company's or corporation's sales and profits are stable or are expected to increase, taking on more debt would probably be safe—if its current debt load is not too large.

SECTION 2 REVIEW

Understanding Vocabulary

Define debt financing, short-term financing, intermediate-term financing, long-term financing, trade credit, promissory note, accounts receivable, line of credit, leasing, equity financing.

Reviewing Objectives

1 What three kinds of debt financing are available according to the repayment period?

2 What four factors affect a company's financing plans?

Judith Resnick on Starting Up a Financial Business

- 1941–
- chair and CEO of Dabney/Resnick & Wagner, Inc., a California investment banking, brokerage, and money management firm
- entered brokerage business at age 41 in 1983 with no professional experience
- started as a broker with Drexel Burnham Lambert
- founded Dabney/Resnick in 1989

Judith Resnick, a divorced, single mother, had been supported by her father until he died in 1977. Without job skills, without an income, she says, "All of a sudden, I had nowhere to turn." She looked to the stock market because it interested her, even though her broker had lost what little investment she had.

... Although I was losing money, I noticed that he [the broker] was making it. I said to myself, "Even I could do that."

When the larger firms would not hire her, a friend introduced Resnick to a broker at Drexel Burnham Lambert in downtown Los Angeles, and the broker's office manager hired her as a trainee. How did she get started selling?

I made a list of everyone I knew on the earth and called them. I just didn't have time to make excuses for myself. I guess I didn't know that I was oppressed.

By her third year, Resnick was one of the top producers at the brokerage house. A colleague urged her to sell some Eastern Air Lines bonds to her clients. They were trading at 75 cents on the dollar, but Resnick refused. The bonds fell to only 4 cents on the dollar by 1993.

I didn't think they were appropriate for my customers, so I said 'no.' That was the day I figured it was time to go out on my own.

In 1989 Judith Resnick and another salesperson at Drexel, Neil Dabney, launched out to start their own firm. At first they faced an uphill battle because Drexel's reputation for selling junk [high risk] bonds preceded them.

We went to the NASD [National Association of Securities Dealers] and told them we were from Drexel and wanted to start our own firm. They looked at us like we had three heads.

The firm of Dabney/Resnick secured a local bank loan and opened for business in July 1989. After only four months in business, the firm paid off its bank debt.

Checking for Understanding

1. How did Judith Resnick get her first job in the brokerage business?
2. What obstacle did Dabney/Resnick have to overcome to obtain financing?
3. What was the new firm's early evidence of successful management?

Perfecting the Production Process is Key to a Business's Success

Once businesses have the necessary financing, they can begin production. **Production** is the process of changing resources into goods that satisfy the needs and wants of individuals and other businesses. Businesses may produce one of two kinds of goods. Goods that are produced for individuals are called **consumer goods.** They are sold directly to the public to be used as they are. Goods produced for businesses to use in making other goods are called **producer goods.** The machines used in an auto assembly line are examples of producer goods.

Steps in Production Operations

Besides the actual manufacturing of a good, the production process for both types of goods involves several operations. **Figure 11.8** provides an example of one of these operations, which include planning, purchasing, quality control, and inventory control. Each becomes a cost of production. You will read more about product design in Chapter 12.

Planning Planning includes choosing a location for the business and scheduling production. Where a business is located is directly related to how successful the business will be. This fact is as true for a company that is opening its first factory or store as it is for

Figure 11.8 Production Costs
Designing, engineering, and planning all add substantially to the total cost of producing goods such as automobiles.
▼

an older business that is expanding into a new area. Among the factors to consider are nearness to markets, raw materials, labor supply, and transportation facilities. In the past, most cities grew up near waterways. Today, with railroads, airlines, and pipelines, it is not so important to be located near waterways.

Scheduling production operations involves setting beginning and ending times for each step in the production process. It includes planning and checking the use of labor, machinery, and materials so that production moves smoothly. Scheduling ensures that work will be finished on time whether it is manufacturing automobiles or books or dry cleaning a blouse or shirt.

Purchasing In order to do business, a company needs the raw materials to produce its goods or offer its services. It also must have machinery, office supplies, and any other supplies it uses. Obtaining raw materials, machines, and supplies is the purchasing function of the production process and involves getting the best deal for the company. The people who buy goods for a business have to decide what to buy, from whom, and at what price. **Figure 11.9** outlines the major factors to consider in making purchasing decisions.

D Services
Does this supplier offer such services as equipment repair?
▼

Figure 11.9
Purchasing Decisions
A company must include all of these factors before purchasing.

A Price
Is this the best price?

B Quality
Are these goods made well? Will they last?

C Number of Suppliers
Should the company buy from several suppliers to encourage competition?
▼

Quality Control Quality control is checking the quality of the goods produced. It involves overseeing the grade or freshness of goods, their strength or workability, the workmanship or design, harmlessness, adherence to federal or industry standards, and many other factors. Quality control systems can be as simple as testing the thousandth item produced or testing each product as it is finished. As **Figure 11.10** (page 274) shows, every production manager faces a trade-off in quality control.

Inventory Control Almost all manufacturers and many service businesses, such as dry cleaners, need inventories, or stockpiles, of the materials they use in making their products or offering their services.

Manufacturers and businesses, such as supermarkets, also keep inventories of finished goods on hand for sale, but inventories are costly. The more inventory a business has, the less capital it has for other activities. For example, it costs money to warehouse and insure goods against fire and theft. Some goods such as film and medicines spoil if kept beyond a certain period of time. Other goods such as cars and stylish clothes become obsolete, or out of date, in time.

E Shipping
Who pays shipping costs and how will goods be shipped?
▼

F Delivery
How much time is there between ordering and receiving goods?

Figure 11.10 ▲
The Quality Control Trade-Off
The more time spent on quality control, the higher the production costs. This extra cost raises the price to consumers. Less quality control, however, may result in items of poor quality and unhappy customers.

Figure 11.11
Technology and Production
From the time of the Industrial Revolution, methods of production have been changing. Five major advances in technology have most affected this process. These are mechanization, the assembly line, division of labor, automation, and robotics.

In deciding how much inventory to keep on hand, those in charge of inventory control also have other costs to consider. If the price of a raw material is expected to rise, a business may stockpile it to keep future costs down. Often a supplier will discount large orders. Some businesses may decide that the discounts outweigh the other costs of maintaining a large inventory.

Technology and Methods of Production

Technology is the use of science to develop new products and new methods for producing and distributing goods and services. Technology influences businesses in many ways.

The use of technology on a large scale began in the textile industry in England in the late 1700s. From there the machine-powered textile industry spread to the United States. **Figure 11.11** shows five advances that have since changed the way goods are produced.

A Mechanization
The Industrial Revolution, as the beginning of the factory system is called, came about through **mechanization,** which combines the labor of people and large power-driven machines. For example, with the introduction of spinning and weaving machines in factories, entrepreneurs replaced skilled handwork with machines run by unskilled workers. The rate of output per labor hour increased greatly as a result.

▼

B **The Assembly Line**
An outgrowth of mechanization is the assembly line. An **assembly line** is a production system in which the good being produced moves on a conveyor belt past workers who perform individual tasks in assembling it. The Ford Motor Company developed the modern assembly-line process at the beginning of the twentieth century. Because the assembly line results in more efficient use of machines and labor, the costs of production drop. ▼

C **Division of Labor** ▲
Assembly-line production is only possible with interchangeable parts made in standard sizes and with **division of labor,** the breaking down of a job into small tasks. A different worker performs each task.

D **Automation** ▲
Mechanization combines the labor of people and machines. In **automation,** machines do the work and people oversee them.

E **Robotics**
Robotics refers to sophisticated computer-controlled machinery that operates the assembly line. ▼

SECTION 3 REVIEW

Understanding Vocabulary
Define production, consumer goods, producer goods, mechanization, assembly line, division of labor, automation, robotics.

Reviewing Objectives
1 What are the most important steps in the production process?
2 How has technology changed production methods since the early 1800s?

Readings in Economics

FORBES **APRIL 12, 1993**

WHISTLE BLOWER
by Fleming Meeks

When Howard Wright was a teenager ... his two preoccupations were skin diving and inventing. After reading a *Scientific American* story about the physics of whistles, young Wright set out to design a whistle he and his buddies could use while diving.

After six months of trial and error, ... he attached two hollowed-out flash-cubes to a plastic whistle. It worked. But after making up three or four for his friends, he lost interest. ... So the idea sat on the shelf through college [and dental school] ... Finally, in January 1989, it was time for a break. He took his wife, Victoria ... and their three kids on a Caribbean cruise.

When the passengers lined up for the mandatory life vest drill, Vicki turned to her husband with an excited grin and said, "Look Howard, we even have whistles." Wright shook his head. "If that whistle gets wet, it's not gonna work," he said. "But don't worry." Then he told her about his old invention. ...

Once back home, Wright began spending every night in his basement, often past midnight, experimenting with different whistles. ...

Thus in early 1992 was born the All-Weather Safety Whistle Co. In their first 12 months of selling, ... the Wrights sold 40,000 whistles for $107,000. Ranked loudest by *Boating* magazine, their $5.95 (retail price) Storm Safety whistle is today used by the Army Special Forces as well as by the Los Angeles County Department of Beaches and Harbors. ...

Which leaves Wright with a problem. "I love dentistry," he says, ... But with cash flow increasing and with capacity up to 10,000 whistles a day, he and his spouse are trying to talk their way into Wal-Mart. Howard Wright concedes he may soon have to cut his dentistry back to three days a week.

• THINK ABOUT IT •

1. What prompted Wright to start working on a new whistle design?

2. What problem has Wright's success caused?

Section 1

Investing in the Free Enterprise System

Key Terms
cost-benefit analysis
(p. 258)

Summary
People and businesses invest their savings in many places including various banks, mutual funds, and pension plans. By financing investment, people hope to earn interest. Businesses draw upon these investments in order to finance expansion. This financing of expansion is one way that the allocation of resources is eventually determined in a free market system.

Section 2

Types of Financing for Business Operations

Key Terms
debt financing (p. 265)
short-term financing
(p. 265)
intermediate-term
financing (p. 265)
long-term financing
(p. 265)

trade credit (p. 266)
promissory note (p. 266)
accounts receivable
(p. 266)
line of credit (p. 266)
leasing (p. 266)
equity financing (p. 267)

Summary
When businesses borrow, the length of the repayment term is an important consideration. Businesses that borrow also consider the rate of interest, the climate of the market, and their ability to handle the debt load. Sometimes businesses raise financial capital by selling stocks or bonds.

Section 3

The Production Process

Key Terms
production (p. 271)
consumer goods (p. 271)
producer goods (p. 271)
mechanization (p. 274)

assembly line (p. 275)
division of labor (p. 275)
automation (p. 275)
robotics (p. 275)

Summary
The production process involves product design, planning, purchasing, quality control, and inventory control. Technology has increased productivity. Mechanization, the assembly line, division of labor, automation, and robotics have combined to make production more efficient.

11 Review

Identifying Key Terms

Write a short paragraph about alternative types of short-term and intermediate-term financing using all of the following terms.

trade credit (p. 266)   line of credit (p. 266)
promissory note (p. 266)   leasing (p. 266)
accounts receivable (p. 266)

Use terms from the following list to fill in the blanks in the paragraph below.

trade credit (p. 266)   producer goods
consumer goods (p. 271)   (p. 271)
long-term   cost-benefit analysis
   financing (p. 265)   (p. 258)
assembly line (p. 275)   division of labor
                               (p. 275)

  As with any activity, the decision to obtain financing for an investment expansion requires using a __(1)__ . Besides short-term and intermediate-term financing, there is __(2)__ . Sometimes businesses finance purchases by taking posession now but paying for them in the future. This is called __(3)__ . The goods that businesses make are either __(4)__ or __(5)__ . Sometimes they are produced on a highly automated __(6)__ . This leads to an extreme form of __(7)__ .

Recalling Facts and Ideas

Section 1
1. How do individuals turn savings into investments?
2. Outline the steps you would use in reaching a necessary financial decision.
3. Which types of businesses will most often pursue financing?

Section 2
4. What are two reasons a business may need short-term financing?
5. Leasing is a form of what type of financing?
6. Do holders of common stock have any rights in a corporation? Explain.

Section 3
7. Besides quality and inventory control, what other steps are involved in the production process?
8. When did assembly-line production first develop in the United States?
9. What does assembly-line production require?

Critical Thinking

Section 1
Understanding Cause and Effect How does the free enterprise system cause financing to be used for projects that have the most profit potential?

Section 2
Identifying Alternatives Assume that you have to buy new inventory that you sell off completely by the end of each month. Determine the most appropriate type of financing to use when you buy this inventory.

Section 3
Evaluating Information "Because full automation eliminates workers from the assembly line, soon there will be no need for any workers." What is wrong with the line of reasoning in this statement?

Applying Economic Concepts

Making Financing Decisions In your lifetime, you will make a large number of financing decisions to purchase things that will last, such as expensive stereos, major appliances, cars, and houses. Imagine you are a businessperson who has to make decisions about financing. Make a list of the kind of business expansions that might require financing. Note after each type of business expansion, such as buying a low-powered desk computer, what the appropriate type of business financing might be.

Chapter Projects

1. **Individual Project** The federal government's Small Business Administration (SBA) was designed to help small businesses with short-term financing. You can obtain information about this federal government agency by calling or writing the SBA in Washington, D.C. You can also obtain information about the SBA from your local library. Research and write a three-paragraph report describing the functions of the SBA.
2. **Cooperative Learning Project** Work in three groups. As a group, work on one of the following topics:

   A. Division of Labor The most famous example of the division of labor focuses on a pin factory. Adam Smith discussed it in his book *The Wealth of Nations*. The group studying this example should do the following:
   - find the passage in the book about the pin factory
   - develop a chart showing the elements of Adam Smith's arithmetic example
   - calculate the percentage increase in productivity due to the division of labor

   B. Assembly-Line Techniques This group can divide into two smaller groups. One will develop a short report on how Henry Ford first developed the assembly-line process. The second group will look at what Eli Whitney developed with the use of interchangeable parts. This second group will write a short report explaining the importance of interchangeable parts in the manufacturing process.

   C. Robotics This group will research how robotics developed and how much of American manufacturing is controlled by robotics. One part of this group can look at the future of robotics.

Reviewing Skills

Building Graphs

Making a Circle Graph Here is some sample information about the ownership of Texas farms. Make a circle graph showing this information.

sole proprietorships = 167,602
partnerships = 15,947
family held corporations = 3,414
other = 1,826

Writing About Economics

Classificatory Writing Classify the items you listed in Your Economics Journal for this chapter as the results of highly automated production or labor-intensive production. Give reasons to justify your classifications.

12 MARKETING AND DISTRIBUTION

Is listening to music a need or a want?

What influenced the type of portable cassette player each person decided to buy?

Where can you buy these products?

Could these students have bought such small cassette players 20 years ago?

Are there alternatives to portable cassette players today?

Your Economics Journal

During a one-week period, keep track of the products that you see offered for sale directly to consumers, either through the mail or over the phone, whether they are advertised on TV, in magazines, or in the newspaper. Make a list, noting after each item how it was advertised and why you think it was advertised for sale directly to you.

SECTION 1 The Changing Role of Marketing

SECTION 1 FOCUS

Terms to Know marketing, utility, form utility, place utility, time utility, ownership utility, market research, market survey, test marketing

Objectives *After reading this section, you should be able to:*
1. List the four stages of the **development of marketing** in the United States.
2. Describe the elements of **market research**.

Marketing Helps Determine the Economic Value of Goods and Services

In addition to financing and producing a product, businesses must promote and eventually sell the products and services they produce. **Marketing** involves all of the activities needed to move goods and services from the producer to the consumer. These activities include market research, advertising and promotion, and the actual distribution of goods and services from the producer to the consumer. Some economists estimate that about 50 percent of the price people pay for an item is for the cost of marketing.

The Development of Marketing

The idea and importance of marketing in the United States has changed considerably since 1900. Historically, marketing has developed through four stages: production, sales, marketing, and consumer sovereignty. **Figure 12.1** shows this development.

The 1950s saw the rise of marketing as a combining of the production and sales functions. At the same time, a greater variety of goods became available to satisfy consumer needs.

By the late 1950s and early 1960s, marketing had changed. Instead of just creating demand, businesses found they could take a larger share of the consumer dollar by designing products that matched what consumers wanted.

Today, marketing involves many activities, all of which add to the utility that marketing creates. **Utility** is the ability of any good or service to satisfy consumer wants. Utility can be divided into four major types: form utility, place utility, time utility, and ownership utility. **Figure 12.2** (page 284) illustrates the differences among these types of utility.

Figure 12.1 Four Stages of Marketing

A The Early 1900s
Marketing at this time dealt with getting goods to the consumers who wanted them. Supply was often unable to satisfy demand. Companies emphasized the production of goods.

B The 1920s and 1930s
Many consumers had most of the necessities and some of the luxuries of American life by this time. Technology was increasing productivity. Companies found that to increase sales they had to stimulate demand by actively selling their products. They began to use advertising to promote their goods.

C The 1950s
Businesses were able to produce more than consumers normally would use, actively created demand for the goods and services that they sold, and faced increased competition.

D The Late 1950s and Early 1960s
Producers began researching and meeting consumer tastes and preferences. The consumer became the most important element in product development. Consumer sovereignty had arrived.

Figure 12.2
Types of Utility

Utility can be divided into four major types.

A **Form utility,** created by production, is the conversion of raw materials to finished goods. An example is refining crude oil into gasoline. ◀

B **Place utility** is created ▼ by having a good available where a consumer wants to buy it. Locating a gas station on a busy corner is an example.

▲

C **Time utility** is created by having a good available when a consumer wants to buy it. This 24-hour coffee shop is one example.

D **Ownership utility** is created by assuring orderly transfer of ownership of desired goods. Catalog selling is one example. ◀

Market Research

Finding out what consumers want can be difficult. It is crucial, however, because so many markets are nationwide. An increase in sales of a few percentage points can result in millions of dollars in profits. Therefore, before a product is produced or a service is offered, businesses research their market. Market in this sense means the people who are potential buyers of the good or service. Through **market research** a company gathers, records, and analyzes data about the types of goods and services that people want. From cosmetics companies to automakers to frozen food processors, all major companies and many smaller ones do market research.

During the **market survey,** researchers gather information about who might be possible users of the product. Such characteristics as age, sex, income, education, and location—urban, suburban, rural—are important to a producer in deciding the market at which to aim a product. For example, in the 1980s and 1990s the concern of Americans with physical fitness and good health led many cereal companies to test and then market bran, oat, and granola cereals. Though there had been some "adult" cereals before this, most cereals had been presweetened and aimed at children.

A market survey typically involves a series of carefully worded questions. The questions may be administered in the form of a written questionnaire, which is mailed to consumers. Market researchers might also conduct personal interviews. Manufacturers of such small appliances as hair dryers and microwave ovens often put a questionnaire on the back of the warranty card that purchasers are to return.

When Should Market Research Be Done?
Market research may be done at several stages of product development. It can be done at the very beginning when the first ideas about a new product are being developed. It can be conducted again to test sample products and alternative packaging designs.

Early market research has several purposes. It helps producers determine whether there is a market for their good or service and what that market is. It can also indicate any changes in quality, features, or design that should be made before a product is offered for sale.

To investigate initial consumer response, market research is often done immediately after a product is released for sale. Some companies even test their advertising to make sure it is attracting the market for which the product was designed. Information can also be gathered about a product

that has been on the market for a while. Market researchers then attempt to discover what should be done to maintain or increase sales.

Testing New Products
As a final step before offering a product for national distribution, market researchers will often test market a product such as a detergent or a toothpaste. **Test marketing** means offering a product for sale in a small area, perhaps several cities, for two months to two years to see how well it sells before offering it nationally. For example, before attempting to market a new granola cereal, a company might sell it in several selected areas where the product is most likely to attract the market that the company is seeking.

Researchers keep track of the units sold and test different prices and ad campaigns within the test markets. If the cereal is successful, the company will offer it nationally. If sales are disappointing, the company has two choices. It can make changes based on the data collected in the test market. Or, rather than spend more money redesigning the product, the company can abandon the idea.

Most new products introduced every year in the United States are not profitable and do not survive in the marketplace. It is the constant lure of developing a high-profit item, however, that motivates companies to continue developing new products.

SECTION 1 REVIEW

Understanding Vocabulary
Define marketing, utility, form utility, place utility, time utility, ownership utility, market research, market survey, test marketing.

Reviewing Objectives
1 What are the four stages of the development of marketing in the United States?

2 If you want to do market research, what do you have to do?

Harley-Davidson

The Early Years When you think about motorcycles, there is a very good chance you will think of Harley-Davidsons. In 1901, William S. Harley and Arthur Davidson of Milwaukee strapped a gasoline engine to a bicycle, and started production shortly thereafter. Harley-Davidson has been building motorcycles since 1903. For years motorcycles were a small but profitable segment of the motor vehicle industry. Harley-Davidson motorcycles became a symbol of defiance and the "age-old hobo-rebel."

Bad Times In 1969 Harley-Davidson was bought by sporting goods manufacturer AMF. AMF immediately modernized production facilities and increased production from 15,000 units annually to more than 50,000 units. Most business analysts agreed that the heavy investment in equipment was necessary for the firm, but it was also accompanied by a decline in quality. The quick rise in production led to lower-quality motorcycles. Harley-Davidsons slowly lost their image.

In the 1970s the public perception of motorcycles changed. The oil crisis and resulting high gasoline prices left the average driver searching for alternatives. Experts predicted that gasoline prices would continue to rise to astronomical levels. Motorcycles suddenly seemed to be a fuel-saving alternative to traditional automobiles. People started buying more motorcycles, and forecasters predicted that demand would continue to increase. What happened, instead, was that the experts significantly overestimated demand. Japanese manufacturers flooded the American market with motorcycles and then were left with large inventories. Motorcycle prices collapsed.

Emphasis on Quality Against this backdrop, a group of AMF executives led a management buyout and took Harley-Davidson private. Since that time, this group has worked to upgrade its motorcycles. The owners revived the company by completely changing the way it did business. They changed the production process, management philosophy, and marketing strategy.

Harley-Davidson started to use some Japanese production techniques, reducing inventory and freeing up capital and labor. By reducing inventory, any defects and quality problems became easier to spot, while at the same time inventory costs were reduced. Workers were encouraged to make suggestions and were given more authority to make quality checks.

Harley-Davidson devised a new marketing technique, encouraging the formation of the Harley Owners Group (HOG), a social club for Harley owners operating out of local dealerships. These clubs became a means of getting Harley owners together. This made Harley-Davidsons more visible to the general public.

Since the buyout in 1981, Harley-Davidson's success has been steady and impressive. Harley is now a major exporter of motorcycles, shipping 25 percent of its production abroad—much of it to Germany. Harley-David-son once again is a symbol for quality.

Free Enterprise in Action

1. Who bought Harley-Davidson in 1969?
2. Why did the oil crisis of the 1970s stimulate demand for Harley-Davidsons?
3. How did the new management and production techniques employed by Harley-Davidson after its buyout in 1981 lead to a higher-quality product?

Personal Perspective

Charles Wang on Challenges in the Computer Industry

Profile

■ 1944–

■ born in Shanghai, China

■ immigrated to the United States at age 8

■ graduated from Queen's College in New York

■ started Computer Associates International, Inc., a computer software company, in 1976

■ Computer Associates became the first computer software company to bring in $1 billion in revenue

Charles Wang built a successful software firm through technological innovation and acquisition. Wang, a college math and physics major, is not a typical business manager. His unconventional style is evident in the following excerpts from interviews in the *New York Post*, February 17, 1992; *Newsday*, April 16, 1989; and *Mass High Tech*, July 13, 1992.

... We developed more products than we acquired. People don't realize this.... You've got to make sure what comes in exceeds what goes out. If you can count, you can do that. It's not that complicated. That's it! And the difference is called profit.

Charles Wang trains his own executives, moves managers often, and reorganizes the entire company every April based on what he calls zero-based thinking.

You ever hear of the government saying we need less people anywhere? No. That's incremental thinking. So what I try to do is force my people to look at it fresh. Justify it to me again. [For example, suppose] we went and bought a new computer. It's supposed to save something, so why are you asking for more people again?

Another unique approach Wang takes is that he does not adopt every new system that comes along, just because it is new.

... The common characteristic of the mythmakers is that they must destroy the old in order for the new to succeed. Old technologies must be proven to be useless to create a market for the new....

Wang explains his evolutionary approach.

... One, you do not throw your legacy systems away. Imagine leveling a building every time you wanted to add a new door or central air-conditioning. It's the same thing with implementing new technology.

Checking for Understanding

❶ What is Wang's definition of "profit"?

❷ What does Wang mean by zero-based thinking?

❸ According to Wang, how should old technology be treated when new technology is developed?

SECTION 3 FOCUS

Terms to Know channels of distribution, wholesalers, retailers

Objectives *After reading this section, you should be able to:*
❶ Explain the difference between **wholesale and retail distribution**.
❷ List two new **types of distribution channels**.

Moving Goods to Market

Distribution, moving goods from where they are produced to the people who will buy them, is another function of marketing. The routes by which goods are moved are called **channels of distribution. Figure 12.8** (page 294) Shows the various distribution channels for different kinds of goods.

Wholesalers and Retailers

Some consumer goods, such as clothing and farm products, are usually sold by a producer to a wholesaler and then to a retailer, who sells them to consumers. See **Figure 12.7**. Other consumer goods, such as automobiles, are normally sold by the producer directly to a retailer and then to consumers. With each transaction, or business deal, the price increases. Some goods, such as vegetables sold at a farmer's roadside stand, go directly from producer to consumer.

Wholesalers Wholesalers are businesses that purchase large quantities of goods from producers for resale to other businesses. They may buy goods from manufacturers and sell them to retail stores that then deal directly with consumers. They may also buy and sell raw materials or producer goods to manufacturers. Various types of wholesalers exist.

Full-service wholesalers warehouse goods and deliver them once retailers buy them. They may also extend trade

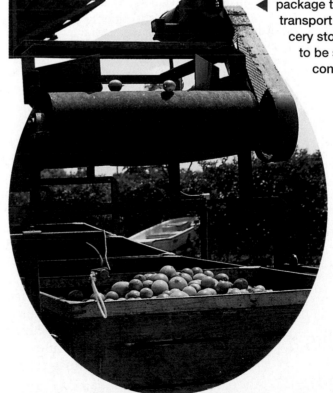

**Figure 12.7
Distributing Goods**
Orchard owners have sold these limes to wholesalers who will package them and transport them to grocery stores to be sold to consumers.

293

Channels of Distribution

Consumer Goods

Manufacturer → Consumer

Manufacturer → Retailer → Consumer

Manufacturer → Wholesaler → Retailer → Consumer

Raw Materials and Producer Goods

Producer (Manufacturer or Producer of raw material) → Business

Producer (Manufacturer or Producer of raw material) → Wholesaler → Business

credit. Wholesalers known as drop shippers, in contrast, never take possession of goods. They buy merchandise with the agreement that the producer will store it. After the drop shipper sells the goods, the producer must deliver them. A cash-and-carry wholesaler has inventory and sells merchandise, but the buyer must ship it. A truck wholesaler sells and delivers at the same time.

Retailers Retailers sell consumer goods directly to the public. Hundreds of thousands of retailers sell all types of goods. You are probably familiar with many of them: department stores, specialty stores such as bookshops, discount stores, supermarkets, mail-order houses, and so on.

Storage and Transportation Part of the distribution process is warehousing goods for future sales. The producer, wholesaler, or retailer may perform this function. Most retailers

keep some inventory on hand for immediate sale. Many have a two- to three-month supply, depending on the type of merchandise.

Transportation involves the physical movement of goods from producers and/or sellers to buyers. Various means of transportation, such as airlines, railroads, trucks, and automobiles, can be used. Pipelines transport some goods such as petroleum and natural gas. In deciding the method of transportation, businesspeople must consider the type of good, such as perishable food. The size and weight of the good are also important. Airfreighting tons of wheat is impractical, but airfreighting small machine parts is not. Speed may be necessary to fulfill a sale or to get fresh fruit to a food plant. The cost of the different types of transportation is a factor.

Expanding Types of Distribution Channels

In the last 10 to 15 years, distribution channels have expanded rapidly due to the growth of club warehouses and direct marketing. Some of the biggest club warehouses are Price/Costco and Sam's (a division of Wal-Mart). **Figure 12.9** shows some of the characteristics of warehouse club shopping.

Direct marketing is done mainly through catalogs as illustrated in **Figure 12.10** (page 296). Advertising called space ads in newspapers and magazines is also direct marketing.

One reason that catalog shopping has become a popular distribution channel is to avoid state sales taxes. As state sales taxes have increased in most states, consumers have purchased more goods through catalogs from out-of-state companies. The purchaser of catalog goods normally does not pay sales tax if the catalog company is located in another state.

Figure 12.9
Differences in Warehouse Club Shopping

A typical club warehouse requires membership. Memberships usually cost $25 a year for individuals and more for businesses. Individual club members usually have to be part of a larger group such as a teacher's union or a credit union. A typical club warehouse, unlike other stores, is an extremely large building, where the choices of merchandise and food are often limited, but the prices are usually lower than most others available in the immediate geographical area. The club warehouse formula is to buy a limited number of models and brands of each product in such huge quantities that the club warehouse gets very favorable prices from the manufacturers. Typically, the listed price in the club warehouse is what the individual member pays. Businesses get a 5 percent discount off that price.

▼

Figure 12.10
Catalog Boom
Catalog shopping has increased dramatically in the United States in the last 20 years. Virtually everything is available by catalog overnight. As an expanding distribution channel, this form of direct marketing has yet to reach its full potential. ▼

SECTION 3 REVIEW

Understanding Vocabulary
Define channels of distribution, wholesalers, retailers.

Reviewing Objectives
❶ How would you describe the difference between a whole-saler and a retailer?

❷ What are two relatively new distribution channels for goods?

Distinguishing Fact From Opinion

Whenever you are listening to someone talk, reading a newspaper, or watching a news program on TV, you are bombarded with facts. Many times, however, you are being given personal opinions. Do you know how to distinguish between fact and opinion?

What is a Fact?

A *fact* is a statement that can be proven by such evidence as records, documents, government statistics, and unbiased historical sources. **Figure A** lists some facts that few people would dispute.

Discovering Opinions

An *opinion* is a statement that may contain some truth, but it also contains a personal view or judgment, sometimes called a value-based statement. Consider the following statement: "The state fund for the arts does not have enough money." Whether this agency has enough money is a matter of opinion, based on personal values. Consider the statements of opinion in **Figure B**.

Use the following guidelines when distinguishing between fact and opinion.

❶ For each statement ask yourself what idea the writer or speaker wants you to accept.

❷ Ask yourself if and how these statements can be verified or proven.

Figure A
Facts

- The population of the United States exceeds 250 million people.
- There is normally less sun on rainy days than on other days.
- President Bill Clinton took office in 1993.
- During the majority of years since World War II, average prices have increased in the United States.

Figure B
Opinions

- The crime rate is too high.
- We should eliminate poverty in the United States.
- We are not spending enough money on public education.
- Young people today do not take school seriously enough.

Practicing the Skill

Read several paragraphs of a politician's speech from a newspaper or magazine. Make a list of statements of fact and statements of opinion. Tell why you classify each statement as you do.

297

Readings in Economics

TIME	APRIL 26, 1993

TESTING THE WATERS
by Thomas McCarroll

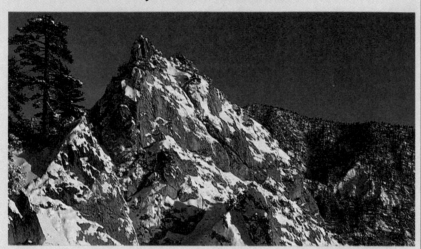

The label on Crystal Geyser Natural Alpine spring water boasts that it is nothing less than "nature's perfect beverage." The drink, reads the label, "begins as the pure snow and rain that falls on 12,000-ft. Olancha peak in the towering Sierra. This pristine water is naturally filtered through the mountain's bedrock."

The language is evocative and the imagery idyllic. Unfortunately Crystal Geyser's claims are something of an exaggeration. Or so says the North Carolina agriculture department, which recently ordered Crystal Geyser and seven other bottled waters, including the popular Naya and Poland Spring brands, removed from store shelves in that state because of "false and deceptive labeling."

... That is bad news for producers of the nation's 700 brands of bottled water, many of which convey the impression in their advertising that they have tapped an unspoiled river.... Regulators an consumer groups are starting to question whether bottled waters are worth the $2.7 billion a year that customers spend on them....

In an effort to clean up the industry, the FDA is proposing the most sweeping new regulations in two decades. The most controversial would set uniform definitions for types of bottled waters, such as "artesian," "mineral," "distilled," and "natural spring." These terms are now generally ill-defined. Some names, such as Grayson's "mountain water" and Music's "glacier water," defy definition since no such categories exist.

• THINK ABOUT IT •

1. Why did the North Carolina agriculture department pull certain brands of water from store shelves?

2. What is the FDA currently proposing?

12 *Highlights*

The Changing Role of Marketing

Key Terms
marketing (p. 282)
utility (p. 282)
form utility (p. 284)
place utility (p. 284)
time utility (p. 284)

ownership utility (p. 284)
market research (p. 284)
market survey (p. 284)
test marketing (p. 285)

Summary
Marketing in the United States has developed through four stages ending with consumer sovereignty. Through a series of predesigned questions, market research attempts to discover the quality, features, and style that consumers find desirable in a product, the type of packaging that will attract consumers, and the price that will get them to buy.

The Marketing Mix

Key Terms
price leadership (p. 289)
penetration pricing
 (p. 290)
promotion (p. 290)

direct-mail advertising
 (p. 291)
product life cycle (p. 291)

Summary
The "four *P*s" of the marketing mix arc product, price, place, and promotion. In setting price, a company has to consider the costs of producing, advertising, selling, and distributing the product, as well as the profit it wishes to make and the price its competitors are charging for the same product. Price is also used in marketing strategies. The place to sell a product and the kinds of promotion used help to determine the success of a product.

Distribution Channels

Key Terms
channels of distribution
 (p. 293)
wholesalers (p. 293)
retailers (p. 294)

Summary
Wholesalers purchase large quantities of goods from producers for resale to other businesses. Retailers sell consumer goods directly to the public. As part of the distribution process, goods may be warehoused by the producer, wholesaler, or retailer for future sales. The largest growth in distribution of goods is through club warehouses and direct-mail marketing.

12 *Review*

Identifying Key Terms

Write the letter of the definition in Column B below that correctly defines each term in Column A.

Column A
1. test marketing (p. 285)
2. penetration pricing (p. 290)
3. price leadership (p. 289)
4. retailer (p. 294)
5. promotion (p. 290)

Column B
a. use of advertising to inform consumers about a product and to persuade them to purchase it
b. business that sells goods directly to the consumer
c. selling a new product at a low price to attract new customers away from an established product
d. offering a product in a small area for a limited time to see how well it sells
e. setting prices close to those of competing companies

Recalling Facts and Ideas

Section 1
1. What is the relationship between marketing and utility?
2. How is market research conducted?
3. What are the historic stages of development of marketing in the United States?

Section 2
4. What are the "four *P*s" of planning a marketing strategy?

5. How are goods and services promoted?
6. In the marketing mix, to what does *place* refer?
7. What are the last two stages of a typical product life cycle?

Section 3
8. What are distribution channels?
9. How does a club warehouse differ from a standard retail outlet?
10. Who may perform the storage function of distribution?
11. What are the factors that a business must consider in choosing a method of transporting goods?

Critical Thinking

Section 1
Formulating Questions Suppose you were put in charge of doing a market survey for a new type of running shoe. What questions should you ask? Where would you conduct the survey?

Section 2
Identifying Alternatives What are alternative ways to extend the life of an old product that is in its declining stage?

Section 3
Making Generalizations Write a summary of the information on channels of distribution found in **Figure 12.8**.

Applying Economic Concepts

The Rising Opportunity Cost of Time When individuals earn higher incomes, by definition the opportunity cost of their time increases. Economic theory says that they will react in a predictable way—reducing the amount of time they spend shopping. Make a list of the various methods that people can use to reduce the time they spend when they shop for (1) presents for various holidays, Mother's Day, birthdays, etc., (2) food, and (3) photographic and stereo equipment.

Chapter Projects

1. **Individual Project** Suppose you are about to try a new product on the market such as cereal or soap. **(a)** In making your decision to try the new product, how important is each of the "four Ps"? **(b)** Rank them in their order of importance to you, and write a paragraph explaining why you chose this ranking related to trying the new product.

2. **Cooperative Learning Project** Work in three or more groups. Each group will choose a particular product from the following categories of consumer goods:
   - Home electronics
   - Food
   - Clothing
   - Electric steam generators
   - Automobiles
   - Computers

   After each group has chosen one product or brand within one of the above categories, research, as a team or alone, depending on the number in your group, the following:
   - Product packaging
   - Pricing strategies
   - The place where the product is sold
   - How the product is promoted
   - The product life cycle

   Each person or team within each group should write a summary of the research results, preferably in graphic form. When the results of each group are finished, contrast and compare the differences in the five categories across the various products.

Reviewing Skills

Distinguishing Fact From Opinion

1. **When the Distinction is Clear** Which of the following statements are fact and which are opinion?
   a. Unemployment in the early 1990s exceeded 6 percent.
   b. Millions of Americans did not have jobs.
   c. During the early 1990s, the inflation rate was less than 6 percent per year.
   d. This was a good rate of inflation.

2. **When the Distinction is Not Clear** Try to pick out the statements in the following paragraph that are not necessarily facts or at least that you would want to confirm.

   The club warehouse phenomenon has been around the United States since the 1970s. The people who shop at club warehouses swear by them. They know that they are a good deal for everybody because prices are so low. Because club warehouses price their products so low, though, they force many small retailers out of business. This is bad. Nonetheless, club warehouses are here to stay because they offer such a great deal.

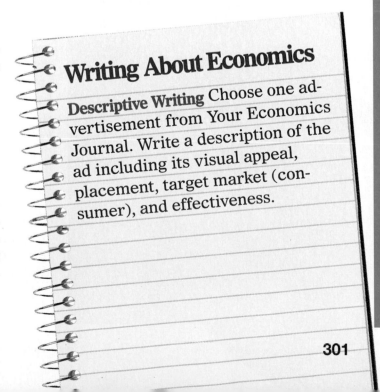

Writing About Economics

Descriptive Writing Choose one advertisement from Your Economics Journal. Write a description of the ad including its visual appeal, placement, target market (consumer), and effectiveness.

Point

ISSUE: Is Affirmative Action Necessary to End Discriminatory Hiring Practices?

Affirmative action means that employers and other institutions must take steps to remedy the effects of past discrimination against women and minorities. Does it work? Or does it harm the economy by giving special status to certain groups? Affirmative action began in 1965 with the monitoring of the hiring and promotion practices of federal contractors. In the 1970s, a series of executive orders required businesses and universities that received federal moneys to set affirmative action goals.

PRO > Those who favor government-sponsored affirmative action programs feel that, even though affirmative action has not worked perfectly, things are better today than they would have been without it. David J. Shaffer, staff writer for the *Indianapolis Star*, tells about some of the positive aspects of affirmative action. He presents the following view:

"While it has helped, it hasn't been completely successful," said Suzanne Steinmetz, sociology department chairwoman of the IU School of Liberal Arts at Indiana University-Purdue University at Indianapolis.

"It's going to take many generations until our visions of what kinds of people are appropriate for certain jobs are no longer tied to race and gender," Steinmetz said. "However," she added, "as bad as things are, we don't know what things would have been like without affirmative action."

Many executives feel that affirmative action is still needed to correct past hiring injustices. There are a number of women and minority executives who are upset because affirmative action stirs up such negative connotations to many people in recent years. Some individuals, especially white males, talk about "reverse discrimination." In a *Washington Post* article, staff writer Lynne Duke quotes investment banker Crystal Jones on the way some people have misinterpreted the goals and effects of affirmative action:

While I believe that the concept of affirmative action needs to stay in place in order to preserve access, people twist it around to make us feel we don't deserve to be where we are.

Counterpoint

CON Those who argue against affirmative action say that it is nothing but a system of quotas that has devastating effects on the American economy. According to Peter Brimelaw and Leslie Spencer, writing for *Forbes* magazine, the two major arguments—that quotas are necessary to force companies to tap new labor pools and that companies need a diverse work force to service a diverse population—are simply wrong. The markets should take care of these things.

Economist and Nobel Laureate Gary Becker also argues that free markets and competition should eventually tend to eliminate discrimination. The process is hampered by government intervention and monopoly; in competitive situations, discrimination should decline itself with no need for quotas.

Finally, those against affirmative action claim it is very expensive. Economist Peter Griffin estimates that affirmative action programs have increased federal contractors' labor and capital costs by about 6.5 percent. Brimelaw and Spencer write in *Forbes* about these costs:

What does the replacement of merit with quotas cost the American people? The answer is: plenty. The impact may easily have already depressed GNP [now GDP] by a staggering four percentage points—about as much as we spend on the entire public school system. . . .

Corporate America seems to have resigned itself to quotas as yet another tax. But they are a peculiarly debilitating sort of tax, levied not on the bottom line but on every phase of the corporation's activities, increasing inefficiency throughout. . . .

That affirmative action quotas lead to lowered standards is all but guaranteed by the fact that all standards are suspect to Equal Employment enforcers. "Many of these people believe there really is no such thing as job performance or productivity objectively defined . . . ," says Frank Schmidt, a University of Iowa industrial psychologist.

Exploring the Issue

Reviewing Facts

① What is affirmative action?

② Who benefits from affirmative action? Who loses?

Critical Thinking

③ Do you think the benefits of affirmative action outweigh the costs? Why or why not?

What skills are required for
this job?

Who is likely to seek this kind
of employment?

For how many years will
these individuals probably
do this activity?

Do any government regulations restrict how little these individuals can be paid?

Do any government regulations restrict how long they can work each day or each week?

Who determines how much they are paid?

Your Economics Journal

Keep track of the employed individuals with whom you come in contact over a one-week period. Write down the types of jobs that they do. Next to each type, indicate whether you think their work would be considered low skilled, semiskilled, or highly skilled.

Factors That Affect Wages Three major factors affect how supply and demand determine prices or, in this case, wages in the labor market. These factors include: skill, type of job, and location.

The first factor, skill, is the ability a person brings to a job. It may come from talent, initiative, education and/or training, or experience. A brain surgeon and a major-league home-run hitter, for example, may be paid large sums of money, even though their educational backgrounds are quite different. Employers wishing to hire skilled workers must usually pay high wages to bid them away from other potential employers. Another factor in measuring a worker's value is his or her attitude toward work. Some individuals take their jobs seriously and work very hard; others do not. Generally, those who are serious about their work have the "right" attitude—that is, the attitude that will help them succeed in the workplace.

The type of job also affects the amount an employer is willing to pay and a potential employee is willing to accept. Jobs that are unpleasant or dangerous, such as coal mining, often pay high wages compared to other jobs requiring equal levels of skill. In contrast, some jobs are enjoyable or prestigious or desired enough that people are willing to take them even at low wages. Many young people take lower-paying jobs in industries such as filmmaking and publishing for these reasons.

The location of both jobs and workers is the third factor in determining wages. **Figure 13.3** shows the differences in wages for three occupations depending on location. If workers are relatively scarce in an area, companies may have to pay high wages to attract workers to move. Alaska, for example, has the highest wages per person in the country. If many unemployed people live in an area and a company needs only a few workers, however, it often can hire enough people even at relatively low wages.

Hourly Wage Difference by Location

Industrial Machinery Repairers	Midwest	$16.17
	West	$14.96
	Northeast	$13.86
	South	$13.22
Insulation Workers	New York City	$39.00
	New Orleans	$18.00
Roustabouts in Oil and Gas	Offshore	$14.00
	Onshore	$12.20

Source: *Occupational Outlook Handbook, 1992-93*

Figure 13.3
Geography and Wages
A skilled machinery repairer will earn much more in the Midwest where blue-collar wages are higher than in the South, which has traditionally had lower wages.

 ◄

Restrictions on Wages Demand for a product also affects wages. If demand is low, even highly skilled workers may not receive high wages as **Figure 13.4** shows.

If the labor market were perfectly competitive, the changing supply and demand for labor would result in constantly shifting wage rates. The labor market, however, is not perfectly competitive. For one thing, the flow of information about jobs is imperfect. Workers cannot know exactly what all other employers will pay for their services. Employers, for their part, do not know what all workers are willing to accept.

In the real world, two other factors affect wages. One is the federal—and sometimes state or city—**minimum wage law**, which sets the lowest legal hourly wage rate that may be paid to certain types of workers. The other is the process of wage negotiations between organized labor and management. Supply and demand have less influence on negotiations than do such things as seniority, or length of time on the job, the company's ability to pay higher wages, and the length of the contract.

Figure 13.4
Demand and Wages
A person may be a highly-skilled electronics worker. His or her wages, however, will probably not be very high if the demand for electronics suddenly drops. ▼

SECTION 1 REVIEW

Understanding Vocabulary
Define civilian labor force, blue-collar, professionals, white-collar, service workers, unskilled workers, semiskilled workers, skilled worker, minimum wage law.

Reviewing Objectives
1. What are four categories of workers as determined by skill level and education?
2. How do skill, type of job, and location affect supply and demand in the labor market?

The most commonly used summary statistic is the average. There are two ways to compute the average: by using the mean or the median. Do you know how to distinguish between these two measures?

Computing the Mean

The *mean* is the average of a series of items. It is found by adding the items and dividing the sum by the number of items in the series. You can find the mean salary of students with part-time jobs by adding the weekly wages and then dividing by the number of students (seven) as shown in **Figure A**.

Computing the Median

Sometimes using the mean to interpret statistics is misleading. This is especially true if one or two numbers in the series are much larger than the others. A median can be more accurate.

The *median* is the midpoint in any series of numbers arranged in order. For example, in **Figure A**, $41 is the median weekly wage. In this case, the mean of the series, $60, is much larger than the median, $41. This is because one student earns $175 a week—more than twice as much as any other student.

If an even number of figures are in a series, the median is the mean of the two middle numbers. If you wanted to find the median weekly income of the four students with the highest salaries, you would arrange the incomes in order, add the second and third numbers, and then divide by two as shown in **Figure B**.

Figure A

$ 20
32
34
41
53
65
175
$420 ÷ 7 = $60.

The mean weekly salary for these students is $60.

Figure B

$ 41
53      $ 53
65   + 65 $118 ÷ 2 = $59
175    $118

The median weekly income of the four highest paid students is $59.

Figure C

Number of Farm Employees for a 5–year period

3,774,000
3,383,000
3,321,000
3,179,000
3,241,000

Practicing the Skill

❶ Use **Figure C** to find the mean number of farm workers employed.

❷ Using **Figure C**, determine the median number of farm workers employed.

SECTION 2 *Organized Labor*

SECTION 2 FOCUS

Terms to Know labor union, strike, craft union, industrial union, local union, closed shop, union shop, agency shop, right-to-work laws

Objectives *After reading this section, you should be able to:*

1. Describe the difficulties that **labor unions** faced when they began to organize in the 1800s.

2. Explain the difference between closed, union, and agency shops as forms of **labor organization**.

Labor Unions Give Workers Some Control Over Wages and Working Conditions

To have some control over the wages they receive as well as over other working conditions, American workers have formed labor unions. A **labor union** is an association of workers organized to improve wages and working conditions for its members. Unions are based on the idea that workers as a group will have more influence on management than will individual workers acting alone. In discussing labor-management relations, the term *management* refers to those in charge of a company—the executives and managers.

Development of Labor Unions

Working conditions in the 1800s were very different from those of today as **Figure 13.5** shows. The buildings were sometimes poorly lighted and ventilated, and the machinery was sometimes dangerous to operate. When business slumped, factory owners fired employees. When business improved, new employees were hired. No unemployment insurance helped those who were out of work until they found new jobs. Health-care benefits, sick leave, and paid vacations and holidays did not exist. Workers began to form unions to force employers to improve working conditions, shorten the workday, and end child labor.

Unionism met strong resistance. In the 1800s, state legislatures, influenced by business interests, passed

**Figure 13.5
Poor Working Conditions**
In the 1800s men, women, and children as young as 5 years old labored from 12 to 14 hours a day, sometimes 6 days a week, often in unsanitary and unsafe factories.

▼

laws against unions, and courts upheld them. Many businesses refused to hire union members or deal with unions. Workers who were found trying to organize unions were fired and blacklisted—kept from being employed. As shown in **Figure 13.6**, strikes during the late 1800s and early 1900s often resulted in violence between strikers and police. A **strike** is a deliberate work stoppage by workers to force an employer to give in to their demands.

The American Labor Movement The time line in **Figure 13.8** (pages 314–315) shows the major dates in the development of the American labor movement. For much of its history, organized labor in the United States has been split into two groups: craft unions and industrial unions. A **craft union** is made up of skilled workers in a specific trade or industry, such as carpentry or printing. For many years, craft unions dominated the labor movement. The first permanent federation, or organization of national labor unions, was the American Federation of Labor (AFL), composed of craft unions.

An **industrial union** is made up of all the workers in an industry regardless of job or level of skill. Attempts to organize industrial unions date back to the late 1800s. The major effort to unionize unskilled and semiskilled workers did not begin until the formation of the Congress of Industrial Organizations (CIO) in 1938. Because they employ large numbers of unskilled and semiskilled work-

ers, the automobile and steel industries were among the first to be organized.

The AFL-CIO During the late 1930s and early 1940s, both the AFL and the CIO launched organizing campaigns that made the lines between industrial and craft unions less clear. AFL unions began recruiting semiskilled and unskilled workers, while the CIO began organizing workers in the skilled trades. The resulting rivalry cost both union federations time and effort. By the mid-1950s, union leaders realized that the labor movement would make greater gains if craft and industrial unions worked together. As a result, the two federations merged in 1955 to form the present AFL-CIO. Today, many unions are affiliated, or joined, with the AFL-CIO. Several independent unions, however, including the National Education Association (NEA), also exist.

Figure 13.6
Violent Strikes ▶
Not until the mid-1930s did Congress begin to pass laws to regulate labor-management relations. Before that time, many strikes resulted in violence and injuries.

Figure 13.7 ▶
Local Union Members

Not all local unions are alike. Membership requirements and the ways in which management relates to union members vary from one kind of shop to another.

Union Membership Policies

Closed Shop	In a **closed shop**, companies had to hire only union members. The Taft-Hartley Act of 1947 outlawed closed shops.
UNION SHOP	In a **union shop**, a new employee must join the union after a specific period of time, usually three months.
Agency Shop	In an **agency shop**, employees are not required to join the union, but they must pay union dues.

Labor Organization

Today, organized labor operates at three levels: the local union, the national or international union, and the federation. A **local union** consists of the members of a union in a particular factory, company, or geographic area. The local deals with a company by negotiating a contract and making sure the terms of the contract are kept.

The influence that a local has often depends on the type of membership policy it negotiated with management. See **Figure 13.7.**

Supporters of union and agency shops argue that employees in companies that are unionized should be required to pay union dues because they benefit from contracts the union negotiates. Opponents believe that a person should not be required to join a union. Since 1947 a number of states have passed **right-to-work laws** that forbid union shops and closed shops. These laws allow workers to continue working in a particular job without joining a union. The employee benefits negotiated by the union must be made available to workers who do not join the union. The power of unions in states with right-to-work laws is less than in other states.

Above the locals are the national unions. These organizations are the individual craft or industrial unions that represent locals nationwide.

Figure 13.8 Time Line of American Unionism

1790s	Skilled workers in a particular craft join to fight division of labor and unfair hiring practices. To save money, employers are organizing workers into teams to do only parts of jobs and hiring women and children at low wages for some jobs. Most associations disband after demands are met.
1820s-1850s	Skilled workers such as carpenters and printers form citywide craft unions. Some local unions form nationwide associations. Because of poor economic conditions, many unions disappear in the late 1830s, but reappear in the 1840s and 1850s as the economy improves. African Americans and women are not included in these craft unions.
1866	National Labor Union (NLU) becomes first nationwide federation of craft unions, but disbands in 1872 after it fails to improve conditions.
1869	National Colored Labor Union formed to avoid hostility of white members of NLU. Knights of Labor set up by group of Philadelphia clothing workers as an industrial union. Members include skilled and unskilled workers as well as farmers and merchants—black and white.
1877	Baltimore & Ohio Railroad Workers strike after wages are cut during economic depression. Federal troops break up strike after rails are torn up, stations burned, and freight cars smashed.
mid-1880s	Knights of Labor claim 700,000 members. Series of violent strikes results in decline in membership and end of group by early 1900s.
1886	American Federation of Labor (AFL) is formed to bring independent craft unions together into a national federation. Membership is limited to white male skilled workers. Haymarket Riots in Chicago protest police action against strikers at a local factory. Seven police are killed. Eight labor leaders are sentenced to death and four are hanged although no evidence is found.
1892	Amalgamated Association of Iron, Steel and Tin Workers strikes the Homestead plant of Carnegie Steel after management demands a wage cut and a 70-hour work week. Armed guards are called in and several strikers as well as guards are killed. The state militia breaks up the strike.
1894	Pullman factory workers and American Railway Unions strike the Pullman Company after a wage cut, and after a union leader is fired. The strike halts rail traffic in and out of Chicago and interrupts rail service in many states. Federal troops and local militia are called. Some strikers and several other people are killed.
early 1900s	AFL concentrates on improving wages and working conditions and claims over 2 million members by 1914 and over 4 million by 1920.
1911	Triangle Shirtwaist Factory fire claims 143 lives, mostly young women clothing workers, trapped on the top floors of a tenement factory.

Figure 13.8 Time Line of American Unionism

1920s	Opposition by business, unfavorable court rulings, and rising anti-labor and anti-immigration feelings cause decline in union membership.
1929	The Great Depression begins. Sympathy grows among the general public for concerns of organized labor.
1932	Congress passes Norris-LaGuardia Act, the first major pro-labor legislation. Act limits power of the courts to stop picketing and boycotts and makes yellow-dog contracts illegal. This is the practice whereby employers require that employees pledge not to join a union.
1935	National Labor Relations Act (Wagner Act) guarantees labor's right to organize and bargain collectively. Act sets up National Labor Relations Board (NLRB) to oversee the establishment and operation of unions.
1938	To organize unskilled workers in such industries as automobiles and steel, some leaders of the AFL form the Congress of Industrial Organizations (CIO). CIO encourages membership of African Americans and women.
1945-47	Wave of strikes to improve wages and working conditions follows end of World War II and contributes to growing anti-union feelings.
1947	Congress passes Labor-Management Act (Taft-Hartley Act) over strong objections of labor. Act outlaws certain strike tactics, permits states to pass laws making union shops illegal, and allows the President to delay a strike if it will threaten the nation's health and safety.
1955	AFL and CIO unite into a single union, AFL-CIO.
1959	Congress passes Labor Management Reporting and Disclosure Act (Landrum-Griffin Act). Act increases government control over unions and guarantees union members certain rights, such as freedom of speech in union activities and control over union dues.
1962	President Kennedy signs into law an order giving federal employees the right to organize into unions, but not to strike. Union membership among government workers grows during the 1960s and 1970s.
mid-1960s-1970s	Union membership among African Americans, women, Hispanics, and agricultural workers increases.
1981	President Reagan fires 11,400 air traffic controllers for striking illegally. AFL-CIO warns of growing anti-union feelings as economy worsens. Some large unions such as the United Auto Workers negotiate contracts that give back some of their earlier gains.
1982-1994	Union membership decreases to about 15 percent of wage and salary workers.

Figure 13.9 ▶
The AFL-CIO
Representing its member unions, the AFL-CIO lobbies for pro-labor legislation at the state and federal levels. It also offers training and advice to the leadership of member unions and promotes the causes of organized labor.

Those unions that also have members in Canada or Mexico are often called international unions.

To help in negotiating a contract between a local and a particular company, plant, or group of businesses, the nationals make available lawyers, professional negotiators, and other staff members. In certain industries such as steel and mining, the national union negotiates the contract for the entire industry.

Once the majority of union members accepts the contract, all the locals within the industry must work under the contract. National unions also send

in organizers to help employees organize campaigns to set up locals.

Some of the largest unions are the International Brotherhood of Teamsters; United Automobile Workers (UAW); United Steelworkers of America (USW); and the American Federation of State, County and Municipal Employees (AFSCME).

At the federation level is the AFL-CIO, which is made up of national and international unions. More than 85 unions with about 14 million members are associated with the AFL-CIO. See **Figure 13.9**.

SECTION 2 REVIEW

Understanding Vocabulary

Define labor union, strike, craft union, industrial union, local union, closed shop, union shop, agency shop, right-to-work laws.

Reviewing Objectives

❶ What obstacles did labor unions face when they began to organize in the 1800s?

❷ How do closed shops, union shops, and agency shops differ?

Thomas Sowell on Discrimination

- 1930–
- doctorate in economics from the University of Chicago
- senior fellow at the Hoover Institution of War, Revolution and Peace
- taught at leading universities in the United States, Singapore, Israel, Switzerland, and Germany
- published books include *Black Education: Myths and Tragedies* (1972) and *The Economics and Politics of Race* (1983)

In the following excerpt from *The Economics and Politics of Race,* Thomas Sowell discusses racism and discrimination. He is concerned that those who debate these issues understand the meanings of the terms they use.

The question is not about the "right" or "best" definition of the word "racism." Words are servants, not masters. The real problem is to avoid shifting definitions that play havoc with reasoning. . . .

One of the most common concepts encountered in discussions of race and ethnicity is discrimination. Yet it is seldom defined. Various overlapping, and sometimes contradictory, meanings of discrimination are used, sometimes in the same analysis. . . .

The first four definitions can be combined into a single definition of discrimination as the offering of different transaction terms— including no terms at all—to groups who do not differ in the relevant criteria (skill, credit-rating, experience, test scores, etc.). . . .

To explain its substandard economic position by discrimination is to show that the group as a whole was underpaid or overcharged. . . .

According to Sowell, political discrimination makes economic discrimination more difficult to measure. If the government provides different qualities of schooling to different groups, economic inequalities will develop. People, however, may link such inequalities to a variety of causes other than discrimination.

While discrimination is usually conceived of in economic terms as discrimination against workers, consumers, tenants or credit seekers, there is also political discrimination against all these groups and also against school children, defendants in court, and others who have contact with governmental institutions. Indeed, political discrimination may make it more difficult to measure economic discrimination. . . .

Much direct political discrimination is disguised by phrasing it as a "preference" for one group rather than discrimination against another.

Checking for Understanding

❶ What is the problem to avoid in discussing racism?

❷ How would Sowell define discrimination?

❸ Who may be victims of political discrimination?

SECTION 3 FOCUS

Terms to Know collective bargaining, mediation, cost-of-living adjustment (COLA), arbitration, picketing, boycott, lockout, injunction

Objectives *After reading this section, you should be able to:*

1. List the six major issues that are involved in **labor-management negotiations**.
2. Describe two workers' actions that can accompany a strike and two **management responses to a strike**.
3. Explain the modern trend in **collective bargaining** in the United States.

A Strike May Occur if Negotiations Break Down

Collective bargaining is the process by which unions and employers negotiate the conditions of employment. At the center of the collective bargaining process is compromise. The company wants to keep wages and benefits low to hold its labor costs down and remain competitive in the market. The union wants to increase wages and benefits for its members as much as possible. Obviously, both sides must be prepared to give and take a little.

**Figure 13.10
Labor/Management
Negotiations**

In most cases negotiations are friendly and result in an agreement that satisfies all parties. In the case of a deadlock, however, the two sides may agree to try mediation. ▼

Negotiations

Negotiations take place when labor and management meet to discuss in detail a wide range of contract issues. See **Figure 13.10**. **Figure 13.11** lists a number of the most important issues that labor and management may negotiate. If necessary, labor and management may try mediation. **Mediation** (MEED-ee-AY-shuhn) occurs when a neutral, or disinterested, person steps in and tries to get both sides to reach an agreement. The mediator suggests possible solutions and works to keep the two sides talking with each other.

The federal government, through

Figure 13.11 Union Contract Issues

Issue	Description
Wages	Most contracts provide for wage increases of a certain percentage for each worker during each year of the contract. Some contracts also provide for an additional increase each year if the general level of prices in the economy rises beyond a certain amount. This provision is known as a **cost-of-living adjustment (COLA).**
Working hours	The contract establishes the number of hours a day that employees must work. Employees who work longer hours must usually be paid extra wages, called overtime pay.
Fringe benefits	Fringe benefits are payments other than wages made to employees. These can include health and life insurance, a retirement plan, and time off for vacations and holidays.
Working conditions	Contracts often provide for a joint union and management committee to ensure that safe and pleasant working conditions exist. Working conditions are a particularly important issue to employees in industries that deal with poisonous substances or dangerous machinery.
Job security	At issue under job security is protection against layoffs because of technological change or a slowdown in business. Most contracts do not forbid layoffs, but rather set up rules that the employer must follow in laying off workers. For example, those with the least seniority—amount of time spent with the company—are usually laid off first.
Grievance procedures	Grievance procedures are a set of formal rules used to resolve a dispute between union members and management. A grievance, or complaint, may be filed if one side feels that the other is not living up to the terms of the contract. If the union and the company cannot settle the grievance, a third party will often be asked to judge the matter objectively.

the Federal Mediation and Conciliation Service (FMCS), provides a mediator free of charge upon request of either union or management. In a typical year, FMCS mediators are involved in thousands of negotiations. In April 1992, for example, FMCS stepped in to help resolve a strike by the United Automobile Workers against Caterpillar, the world's largest builder of earth-moving equipment. A number of state and private mediators also help resolve disputes.

If mediation fails, the negotiation process may go one step further to arbitration. In **arbitration** (AHR-buh-TRAY-shuhn), the two sides submit the issues they cannot agree on to a third party for a final decision. Both sides agree in advance to accept the arbitrator's decision, though one or both sides may not be completely happy with the outcome. The FMCS often helps in these cases by providing labor and management with a list of private arbitrators in their area.

U.S. Labor Strikes, 1975-1992

Number of strikes

250

0

1975   1980   1985   1992

Years

Source: United States Department of Labor, Bureau of Labor Statistics

Figure 13.12 ▲
Striking

Compare the trend in strikes with what is happening in union membership. See **Figure 13.14**. How do you think the two are related?

Figure 13.13
Picketing

Often, members of other unions will not cross a picket line. This may further handicap the business being struck. ▼

Strikes and Management Responses

Most contracts are settled at the bargaining table. Sometimes, though, negotiations break down and a strike results. The number of strikes in the United States has declined sharply since 1975. See **Figure 13.12**.

Strikers usually walk up and down in front of the company carrying picket signs that state their disagreement with the company. **Picketing** is meant to discourage workers from crossing the picket line to work for the employer. It is also aimed at embarrassing the company and building public support for the strike. See **Figure 13.13**.

Striking unions may use a boycott to exert more economic pressure. In a **boycott**, unions urge the public not to purchase goods or services produced by a company. Unions may also ask politicians to push management for a settlement or to support the union's demands publicly.

Strikes can drag on for months and even years. After a long period of time, strikers sometimes become discouraged. Some may decide to go back to work without gaining what they wanted. In most cases, however, strikes are settled as management and labor return to the negotiating table and work out an agreement.

Lockouts When faced with a strike, management has methods of its own to use against strikers. One is the **lockout,** which occurs when management prevents workers from returning to work until they agree to a new contract. Another tactic is to bring in strikebreakers, called *scabs* by strikers. These are people willing to cross a picket line to work for the terms the company offers.

Injunctions Management sometimes requests a court injunction to limit picketing or to prevent a strike from continuing or even occurring. An **injunction** is a legal order of a court preventing some activity. Under the Taft-Hartley Act of 1947, the President of the United States can obtain a court order to delay or halt a strike for up to 80 days if the strike will endanger the nation's safety or health. During this cooling-off period, the two sides must try to reach a settlement.

Collective Bargaining on the Decline

The establishment of the AFL in 1886 is considered the beginning of the modern union era. Since that time, unions have achieved many of their goals. Union supporters list among union accomplishments better wages and working conditions for all employees—union and nonunion. They point out that many workers now enjoy a sense of security and self-respect that helps to maintain some control over their jobs and lives. Union supporters also note that the collective bargaining process has brought more order and fairness to the workplace. It has made clear the rights and responsibilities of both management and labor.

Because working conditions have improved so dramatically over the years, nonunion workers often see little to gain from joining a union. Moreover, many union members no longer feel the same commitment to organized labor that earlier union members did.

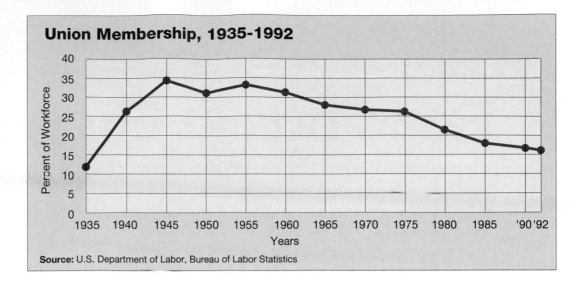

Union Membership, 1935-1992

Percent of Workforce / Years

Source: U.S. Department of Labor, Bureau of Labor Statistics

Critics The labor movement also has its critics. Some opponents charge that unions have grown so large and bureaucratic that they are out of touch with their members' needs. Others claim that increased wages are passed on to consumers in the form of higher prices. Employers often argue that union rules decrease productivity. They point to rules that slow the introduction of new technology or require more employees than necessary to do a job. In addition, corruption among some labor leaders has damaged the reputation of organized labor with the public.

Current Challenges The labor movement today faces many problems. As **Figure 13.14** shows, the percentage of union members among the labor force reached a high in the mid-1940s and

has been declining since. Today union members in the United States represent only a fraction of the civilian labor force.

One reason for this decline is the changing nature of the economy. More jobs are opening in the white-collar and service sectors, while blue-collar jobs are decreasing due to automation. Many service workers and white-collar employees see themselves as working on their own. They often do not identify with groups of their fellow employees in the same way as an assembly-line worker might. With technology comes the potential loss of manufacturing jobs that may result in a further decline in union membership and a weakening of the role of unions in the future—unless unions find ways to meet these challenges.

Figure 13.14 ▲
Union Membership, 1935-1992
What has happened to union membership during the second half of the twentieth century? What factors are responsible for this trend?

SECTION 3 REVIEW

Understanding Vocabulary
Define collective bargaining, mediation, cost-of-living adjustment (COLA), arbitration, picketing, boycott, lockout, injunction.

Reviewing Objectives
① What are the major issues over which union contracts are negotiated?

② What workers' actions and management responses may accompany a strike?

③ How has collective bargaining in the United States changed in recent years?

Readings in Economics

CONGRESSIONAL QUARTERLY   **APRIL 12, 1993**

THE PLAGUE OF DOWNWARD JOB MOBILITY

by Kenneth Jost

James Drone had heard all the stories about corporate downsizing, but the 46-year-old lawyer was unprepared when he became a victim of the trend earlier this year.

Drone was general counsel for a tug and barge business in Houston. The company's fortunes dipped, and Drone, who had worked there for four and a half years, was asked to leave in February. . . .

"I lost quite a bit of sleep, waking up at 3 o'clock in the morning, figuring out what I had done or didn't do," Drone said. "It was strictly economics." Drone, who is married and has four school-age children, is better off than most people who have been sliding down the economic ladder. He got a six-months' severance package and is earning some money practicing law while scouting for another business opportunity.

But even when money is not an issue, the psychological shock of what economists call "downward mobility" can be devastating. "It's an emotional roller-coaster, to say the least," Drone said.

Across the country, the specter of downward mobility has weakened Americans' traditional optimism. A poll taken last year found that more Americans than at any time in the past 20 years felt their personal financial situation was getting worse, not better. And nearly half of those responding to a 1993 poll said they did not think their children would surpass them financially. . . .

Downward mobility poses an array of challenges for workers, employers, and the government—many . . . still only dimly recognized and incompletely understood.

Economic Growth

OPPORTUNITY JOB CENTER

• THINK ABOUT IT •

1. What is downward mobility?

2. What do economists forecast for the future?

Highlights

Americans at Work

Key Terms
civilian labor force (p. 306)
blue-collar (p. 306)
professionals (p. 307)
white-collar (p. 307)
service workers (p. 307)

unskilled workers (p. 307)
semiskilled workers (p. 307)
skilled worker (p. 307)
minimum wage law (p. 309)

Summary

Workers can be divided into categories depending on the type of work. Workers can also be divided into unskilled, semiskilled, skilled, and professional occupations. In the labor market, suppliers are the workers who offer their services, while the demand comes from employers who need workers. Three factors underlie how supply and demand affect wages: skill, type of job, and location.

Organized Labor

Key Terms
labor union (p. 311)
strike (p. 312)
craft union (p. 312)
industrial union (p. 312)
local union (p. 313)

closed shop (p. 313)
union shop (p. 313)
agency shop (p. 313)
right-to-work laws (p. 313)

Summary

In the nineteenth century, unions appealed to working people because they seemed to offer a way to force employers to improve working conditions. Unionism, however, met strong resistance for much of the nineteenth century and early twentieth century. Unions succeeded in the twentieth century in establishing closed, union, and agency shops.

Collective Bargaining

Key Terms
collective bargaining
(p. 318)
mediation (p. 318)
cost-of-living adjustment
(COLA) (p. 319)

arbitration (p. 319)
picketing (p. 320)
boycott (p. 320)
lockout (p. 320)
injunction (p. 320)

Summary

The major issues in collective bargaining usually are wages, working hours, fringe benefits, working conditions, job security, and grievance procedures. When collective bargaining, arbitration, or mediation break down, a strike may ensue in which workers picket the struck company. They may organize a boycott to urge the public not to purchase the goods or services produced by the struck company. Management may respond by locking out workers or having a court issue an injunction.

13 Review

Identifying Key Terms

Write the letter of the definition in Column B below that correctly defines each term in Column A.

Column A
1. unskilled workers (p. 307)
2. agency shop (p. 313)
3. arbitration (p. 319)
4. injunction (p. 320)
5. right-to-work law (p. 313)
6. closed shop (p. 313)
7. boycott (p. 320)

Column B
a. employees are not required to join a union but must pay union dues
b. refusal to purchase the goods and services of a company
c. court order preventing some activity, often a strike
d. no special training in job-related skills
e. undecided issues between labor and management are given to a third party for a final decision
f. company in which only union members can be hired
g. forbids contracts that require employees to join a union

Use terms from the following list to fill in the blanks in the paragraph below.

minimum wage law (p. 309)
labor union (p. 311)
professional (p. 307)
strike (p. 312)
lockout (p. 320)

semiskilled worker (p. 307)
collective bargaining (p. 318)
skilled worker (p. 307)
picketing (p. 320)

Even though teenagers usually do unskilled work when they are young, most of them eventually become a (8), (9), or (10), particularly if they obtain higher education. In most circumstances, no one can be paid less than the wage rate specified by the (11). Sometimes wages are determined by a (12) through its (13) activities. If union-management negotiations fail, a (14) may ensue and the workers may start (15) the work site. Management may respond by putting a (16) into effect.

Recalling Facts and Ideas

Section 1
1. What is the category of the type of worker who has a higher-education degree and additional training?
2. What is the difference between blue-collar and white-collar workers?
3. What are some factors that determine how much a person is paid for his or her work?

Section 2
4. What are the major kinds of labor unions?
5. In 1955 what two union federations merged?
6. How do right-to-work laws affect workers who do not belong to unions?

Section 3
7. Wages are one of the most important major issues in collective bargaining negotiations. What are other important issues?
8. If management and labor have reached a bargaining deadlock, they may try to engage in mediation. If mediation fails, what is the possible next "friendly" step?
9. What do union workers do when they go on strike?
10. What has been the most recent trend in the importance of labor unions in America?

Critical Thinking

Section 1

Determining Cause and Effect Explain why workers with more education and training generally get paid higher wages.

Section 2

Making Generalizations From the time line in **Figure 13.8**, write five major achievements of labor unions between 1900 and 1962.

Section 3

Predicting Consequences What are the factors that may cause a decline in union membership in the future?

Applying Economic Concepts

Economic Costs and Benefits There are costs and benefits of every activity. Strikes are no exception. Workers clearly believe that the benefits exceed the costs or they would not go on strike. Make a list of the benefits to workers of going on strike. Next to it make a list of the costs of going on strike.

Chapter Projects

1. **Individual Project** Strikes were not always a part of the American labor landscape. Some of the first ones were organized in Lowell, Massachusetts, by female textile workers. Research and write a short report on the conditions that led to the Lowell Female Labor Reform Association.
2. **Cooperative Learning Project** This project uses information from the Career Handbook on pages 560–567 in the reference section of this text. Work in groups based on the following categories: unskilled workers, semiskilled workers, skilled workers, and professional workers.

Each member of every group should select a particular job from one of the Career Handbook tables. Group members should compile basic information from the tables about salaries, training, job outlook, and working conditions. Each person should research additional information about the job he or she has selected. Then discuss the relationship between education or training and wages. Also discuss other considerations besides wages that may be important in selecting a job or a career.

Reviewing Skills

Determining Averages: Mean and Median

1. **Determining the Mean** Below are data for the number of unemployed persons over a five-year period. Compute the mean number of unemployed.

1988	6,701,000	1991	8,426,000
1989	6,528,000	1992	9,384,000
1990	6,874,000		

2. **Computing the Median** Compute the median unemployment rate for the seven years listed below.

1986	6.9	1990	5.4
1987	6.1	1991	6.6
1988	5.4	1992	7.3
1989	5.2		

Writing About Economics

Persuasive Writing Write a paragraph on the long-term benefits of staying in school and then going on to college or technical school. Indicate the benefits other than higher salaries. Use what you learned about the different types of jobs that you wrote about in Your Economics Journal to strengthen your argument.

Measuring Productivity

From the classroom of Jamie G. Daily, Holmes High School, San Antonio, Texas

In Unit 4 you read about financing and producing goods. In this experiment, you will learn about productivity and the law of diminishing returns. (You may want to reread the material on pages 271–275 of the text.)

Productivity is the ability to produce better goods and services faster. In part, it is a measure of the amount of output per worker. An assembly line improves worker productivity up to the point where the law of diminishing returns sets in. In this lab, you will develop an assembly-line process and add workers to the team to determine at what point the law of diminishing returns affects productivity.

Tools

1. Supply of simple pictures to be colored
2. 6-8 boxes of eight crayons
3. Several prototypes of finished product (picture colored with four different colors)
4. A pocket calculator

Procedures

Step A Organize into production teams, with seven students per team. One student on each team will serve as the quality control manager for the team, and the others will be production workers. Arrange desks so that each team is an assembly line. Begin with three production workers on Day 1, expanding as instructed later. Each team needs a box of crayons, a supply of uncolored pictures, and a prototype. Each group must color as many pictures to match the prototype as possible within four minutes. Pictures that do not meet quality standards should be discarded. Record these results for Day 1 on a chart like the following:

Example

Group Name	Total Pictures Colored			
	Day 1	Day 2	Day 3	Day 4

Step B From the students on your team who are not yet working, add one member to the assembly line for Day 2. Work for another four minutes. Record the amount of work produced with teams of four students under Day 2 on your chart.

Step C Repeat this process, adding one student to the assembly line each day, coloring and recording the results until you have six members working on the assembly line (Day 4).

You may not alter the technology (break the crayons) when the fifth and sixth workers are added.

Step D Prepare a line graph that shows the total number of pictures that were colored each day. Use the graph below as a sample.

Example:

Then construct a graph that shows productivity per worker during the four days of production. This is accomplished by dividing the total number of pictures colored each day by the total number of assembly line workers. Results should be tabulated on a graph similar to the following "Productivity" graph.

Example:

Lab Report

Step E Use the productivity graphs and your assembly-line experience to answer the questions below.

1. How did your team's productivity compare to that of other teams? What might have accounted for the difference?
2. What were some of the problems in organizing the assembly line?
3. Would a change in technology (more crayons) have helped productivity?

Step F Use the following questions for class discussion

1. Even with additional technology, why would an assembly line eventually reach a point of diminishing returns?
2. Did individual factors, such as personality, influence the team to any extent? How can businesses deal with this type of problem?

U N I T

MACROECONOMICS: MANAGING THE NATION'S ECONOMY

Did You Know

- Nothing "backs" the $1, $5, and other bills that you carry around in your wallet or purse.
- The average American works until about the first week in May to pay for all local, state, and federal taxes.
- Prices rise much less rapidly in the United States than in many countries of the world.
- During national business slowdowns, unemployment among teenagers increases more rapidly than among older people.

In this unit you will be looking at the interrelationships of all sectors of the economy—consumers, businesses, and government. This overall picture is the study of macro-economics, or the economy as a whole.

14 MEASURING THE ECONOMY'S PERFORMANCE

How does the free enterprise system depend on scenes such as these?

What motivates businesses to operate here?

Who provides the money these people might spend here?

What are these people doing?

What choices do these people have as they shop?

Your Economics Journal

For one week, keep track of references in the media to the following: unemployment, consumer spending, manufacturing trends, recession, and prices. After each entry, indicate whether the information was, in your view, positive or negative to the overall economy.

A Healthy GDP Equals a Healthy Economy

People can measure how successful they are economically by the size of their incomes and by their overall standard of living, including how much their spendable income will buy. **Figure 14.1** shows one example.

The well-being of the overall economy is measured in a similar way. Economists constantly measure and record such factors as the amount of goods and services produced yearly by the nation and the amount of income individuals have to spend.

The measurement of the national economy's performance is called **national income accounting.** This area of economics deals with the overall economy's income and output. It also measures the interaction of consumers, businesses, and governments. The major measurements used for the nation's income and production are gross domestic product, net domestic product, national income, personal income, and disposable personal income. **Figure 14.2** shows gross domestic product and its components in descending order of value.

Measuring Gross Domestic Product

The broadest measure of the economy's health is **gross domestic product (GDP).** This is the total dollar value of all *final* goods and services produced in the nation during a single

Figure 14.1 ▶
Vacations
People who can afford luxuries such as cruises have a relatively high standard of living.

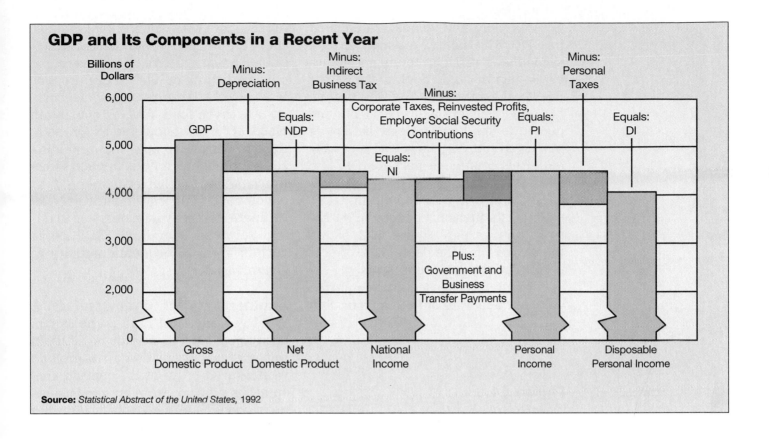

GDP and Its Components in a Recent Year

Billions of Dollars

Minus: Depreciation

Minus: Indirect Business Tax

Minus: Corporate Taxes, Reinvested Profits, Employer Social Security Contributions

Minus: Personal Taxes

GDP

Equals: NDP

Equals: NI

Equals: PI

Equals: DI

6,000

5,000

4,000

3,000

Plus: Government and Business Transfer Payments

2,000

0

Gross Domestic Product

Net Domestic Product

National Income

Personal Income

Disposable Personal Income

Source: *Statistical Abstract of the United States, 1992*

year. This figure tells how much American workers have produced in that year that is available for people to purchase. GDP is one way to measure the nation's material standard of living. It also provides a way of comparing what has been produced in one year with what was produced in another year.

Note the word *value* in the definition. Simply adding up the *quantities* of millions of different items produced, such as shoes and cars, would not mean much. How can we measure the strength of the economy, for example, if we know that 3 billion safety pins and 2 space shuttles were produced? What needs to be totaled is the value of the items, using some common measure. Economists use the dollar as this common measure of value. As a result, GDP is always expressed in dollar terms. For example, in 1993, GDP totalled about $6.5 trillion.

The word *final* is also important. To measure the economy's performance accurately, economists add up only the value of final goods and services to avoid *double counting*. To add the price of memory chips to the price of a computer is not realistic. The final price to the buyer already includes the price of the memory chips.

Figure 14.2 ▲
GDP and Its Components
What is the difference in dollars between gross domestic product and disposable personal income?

Also, only new goods are counted in GDP. The sale of a used car or a secondhand refrigerator is not counted as part of GDP. Such a sale is not due to the production of the nation, but only transfers a product from one person to another. If a new battery is put in an old car, however, that new battery is counted as part of GDP.

GDP Categories In computing GDP, economists measure economic activity in four areas. **Figure 14.3** shows these areas and the percentage of economic activity each represents.

The statistics used in computing GDP are accurate only to a point. Statistics about easily quantifiable things, such as government purchases, are reliable. Some statistics, however, can only be estimated and, therefore, are less reliable. For example, some workers are given food, fuel, or housing in place of or as supplements or additions to wages. An apartment building superintendent, for example, sometimes gets his or her apartment at reduced rent. GDP can include only an estimate of the value of such goods and services. Moreover, GDP omits certain areas of economic activity as **Figure 14.4** shows.

Another Way of Estimating GDP
What you have just read is the expenditure approach to measuring GDP. In this method, gross domestic product is measured by what is spent on consumer goods, government goods, business goods, and net exports. Another way to measure GDP is to measure income earned. When gross domestic product is measured this way, four categories of income are measured. **Figure 14.5** shows the income approach.

Net Domestic Product The loss of value because of wear and tear to consumer durables, such as cars, is called **depreciation.** The same concept

Figure 14.3
Economic Activity as Percentage of GDP

In calculating GDP, economists include:

1. consumer goods—goods and services bought by consumers for their direct use;
2. business, or producer, goods—business purchases of tools, machines, buildings, and so on, used to produce other goods; this figure also includes money spent on business inventories;
3. government goods—the goods and services, ranging from paper clips to jet planes, that are bought by federal, state, and local governments;
4. **net exports**—the difference between what the nation sells to other countries (exports) and what it buys from other countries (imports). This figure may be a plus or minus depending on whether the nation sells or buys more. ▶

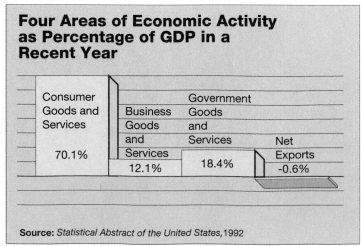

Four Areas of Economic Activity as Percentage of GDP in a Recent Year

Consumer Goods and Services 70.1%

Business Goods and Services 12.1%

Government Goods and Services 18.4%

Net Exports -0.6%

Source: *Statistical Abstract of the United States,* 1992

Figure 14.4
Non-GDP Work
Unpaid work done by individuals for themselves or their families is not counted as part of GDP, even though it adds to the nation's output. This category includes maintenance work on a home, baby-sitting, lawn mowing, and so on. The government cannot estimate the value of this work ◄ accurately.

applies to producer goods—machines and equipment. GDP disregards this factor. It does not take into account that some output is used merely to keep machines and equipment in working order and to replace them when they wear out.

Net domestic product (NDP) accounts for this loss of value. It measures GDP minus the total loss in value of producer goods through depreciation. In recent years, the amount used by economists to account for depreciation has been a little more than 10 percent of GDP. In 1993, for example, GDP was about $6.5 trillion. Subtracting about $650 billion for depreciation, the NDP was about $5.8 trillion. Because NDP accounts for depreciation, it can be a better measure than GDP of the economy's actual productivity.

Measurements of Income

Measuring income is important because it determines how much money is available to be spent by businesses and individuals.

National Income The total income earned by everyone in the economy is called **national income (NI)**. NI includes those who use their own labor to earn an income as well as those who make income through the

Measuring GDP by Income Categories

Wages + Interest + Rents + Profits = GDP

Wages, including all forms of labor income

Interest received by households

Rent that individuals earn for use of their farms, houses, and stores

Profits that corporations, partnerships, and proprietorships earn

Figure 14.5
Measuring GDP by Income
The income approach to GDP gives about the same figure as the expenditure approach. Using this approach: Wages + Interest + Rents + Profits = GDP ◄

ownership of the other factors of production. National income is equal to NDP minus indirect business taxes, including items such as sales and property taxes, and license fees.

As GDP is divided into four areas of economic activity, similarly, NI is divided into five types of income. **Figure 14.6** shows all of these divisions. NI is equal to the sum of all income resulting from these five different areas of the economy.

Personal Income The total income individuals receive before personal taxes are paid is called **personal income (PI)**. PI can be derived from NI through a two-step process. First, corporate income taxes, profits that businesses put back into their businesses to expand, and Social Security contributions employers make are subtracted from NI. These are subtracted because they represent income that is not available for individuals to spend.

Then, transfer payments are added to NI. **Transfer payments** are welfare payments and other supplementary payments, such as unemployment compensation, Social Security, and Medicaid, that a state or the federal government makes to individuals. These transfer payments add to an individual's income even though they are not in exchange for any current productive activity.

Disposable Personal Income The income that people have left after taxes, including Social Security contributions, is called **disposable personal income (DI)**. It is the income available to an individual for the immediate purchase of goods and services and for savings. DI equals PI minus personal taxes. DI is an important indicator of the economy's health because it measures the actual amount of money income people have available to spend.

Figure 14.6
National Income
National Income (NI) is the total of income from all sources shown here. Wages and salaries, however, make up three-fourths of NI.

▼

Elements of National Income

| Wages and salaries paid to employees | Income of self-employed individuals, including farmers and owners of sole proprietorships and partnerships | Rental incomes of property owners | Corporate profits | Interest on savings and investments individuals receive |

S E C T I O N   1   R E V I E W

Understanding Vocabulary

Define national income accounting, gross domestic product (GDP), net exports, depreciation, net domestic product (NDP), national income (NI), personal income (PI), transfer payments, disposable personal income (DI).

Reviewing Objectives

1. What four categories of economic activity are used to measure GDP?
2. What must be subtracted from national income to determine personal income? What must be added?

Using Index Numbers: Price Indexes

Most statistics on prices are expressed in terms of price indexes. Do you know what the concept of a price index is and how to use it?

Measuring Inflation

If last year a light bulb cost 50¢ and this year it costs 75¢, there has been a 50 percent price increase. The price is 1.5 times as high. An index number of this price rise is simply 1.5 multiplied by 100; that is, the index number would be 150.

To compare prices, you must decide the base year. A **base year** is the year to which all other years' prices will be compared.

Computing a Price Index

When we deal with many goods, we must pick a representative sample, called the market basket. We compare the cost of the market basket of goods over time. When we do this, we obtain a price index, which is defined as the cost of a market basket of goods today expressed as a percentage of the cost of the market basket of goods in some base year. In the base year, the price index will always be 100.

Calculating a Price Index

Figure A shows two goods in our market basket—corn and computers. The *quantities* in the basket remain the same between the base year, 1983, and the year 1996. Only the price changes.

Figure A

Market Basket Quantity

Corn	100 bushels
Computers	2

1983 Unit Price

Corn	$4
Computers	$500

1983 Market Basket Cost

Corn	$400
Computers	$1,000
Total	$1,400

1996 Unit Price

Corn	$8
Computers	$450

1996 Market Basket Cost

Corn	$800
Computers	$900
Total	$1,700

$$\text{Index} = \frac{1996 \text{ cost}}{1983 \text{ cost}} \times 100$$

$$\frac{\$1,700}{\$1,400} \times 100 = \$121.43$$

Practicing the Skill

In the example in **Figure A**, assume that the price of computers in 1996 was $400. Recompute the price index.

2 Correcting Statistics for Inflation

When Is a Dollar Not Worth a Dollar?

Rising or falling prices affect the dollar value of GDP. A prolonged rise in the general price level of goods and services is called **inflation.** For example, last year a hamburger may have cost $2.50. This year it may cost $2.75. The physical output—the hamburger—has not changed, only its money value.

Inflation and the Purchasing Power of Money

American–born author Gertrude Stein once said that a rose is a rose is a rose. A dollar, however, is not always a dollar. As **Figure 14.7** shows, the value of a dollar does not stay constant when there is inflation (or deflation). The value of money is usually talked about in terms of its **purchasing power.** A dollar's purchasing power is the real goods and services that it can

Figure 14.7
The Value of Money
As economic conditions change, the purchasing power of money changes. ▼

Increases in price of goods and services = Decreases in purchasing power of money

Consumer Price Index of Selected Categories

	1991	1992	1993
Food	136.8	138.7	141.1
Clothing	128.7	131.9	131.9
Housing	133.6	137.5	141.5
Medical	177.0	190.1	201.1

1993 = June index
Source: Bureau of Labor Statistics

Figure 14.8
Selected Consumer Prices

Price indexes allow you to compare price levels from year to year.

◀

buy. If your money income stays the same, but the price of one good that you are buying goes up, your effective purchasing power falls. Therefore, another way of defining inflation is the decline in the purchasing power of money. The faster the rate of inflation, the greater the drop in the purchasing power of money.

The higher GDP figures that result from inflation do not represent any increase in output. To get a true measure of the nation's output in a given year, inflation must be taken into account. **Deflation**, a prolonged decline in the general price level, also affects the dollar value of GDP, but deflation rarely happens.

Measures of Inflation

If all prices rose at the same rate, only one measure of inflation would be needed. Prices in different sectors of the economy, however, rise at different rates. As a result, the government uses several measures of inflation. The three most commonly used are the consumer price index, the producer price index, and the implicit GDP price deflator.

Consumer Price Index (CPI) The government measures the change in price over time of a specific group of

goods and services the average household uses. This measurement is the **consumer price index (CPI)**. See **Figure 14.8**. The group of items, called a market basket, includes about 400 goods and services in the areas of food, housing, transportation, clothing, entertainment, medical care, and personal care. The CPI is the price index that you are probably most familiar with from the news media. **Figure 14.9** shows the CPI for several years.

The federal Bureau of Labor Statistics compiles the CPI monthly. In compiling the CPI, the base year is set at the average prices for 1982 to 1984

1985	107.6
1986	109.6
1987	113.6
1988	118.3
1989	124.0
1990	130.7
1991	136.2
1992	140.3
1993*	144.4

*June
Source: Bureau of Labor Statistics

Figure 14.9
Consumer Price Index

When the CPI rises, there is inflation. During which two years shown was inflation the greatest?

◀

Figure 14.10 ▶
Calculating
Inflation
At the end of 1991, the CPI was 136.2. At the end of 1992, it was 140.3, which is a difference of 4.1 (140.3 – 136.2 = 4.1). Now if we use 1991 as the base year, we can find out by what percentage consumer prices on average rose from 1991 to 1992. We do this by dividing 4.1 by 136.2, which gives us 0.0301 (4.1 ÷ 136.2 = 3.01 percent when we multiply by 100 to give the result as a percent).

and is given a value of 100. A **base year** is a year used as a point of comparison for other years in a series of statistics. CPI numbers for later years indicate the percentage that the market basket price has risen since the base year. For example, the 1993 CPI of 144 means the cost of living has risen 44 percent since the period 1982 to 1984 (144 – 100 = 44). The CPI also can be used to calculate inflation from year to year as shown in **Figure 14.10.**

Producer Price Index Another important measure of inflation the Bureau of Labor Statistics reports monthly is the **producer price index (PPI).** (It used to be called the wholesale price index.) Actually, a number of producer price indexes exist, including one for finished consumer goods such as processed foods; anoth-

er for intermediate materials, supplies, and components; and yet another for crude materials for further processing. Most of the producer prices included are in mining, manufacturing, and agriculture. The PPIs can be considered general-purpose indexes for non-retail markets.

Although in the long run the various PPIs and the CPI generally show the same rate of inflation, that does not work out in the short run. The PPIs usually increase before the CPI because it takes longer for producer price increases to show up in the prices that consumers actually pay for final products. Often, changes in the PPIs are watched as a hint that inflation is going to increase or decrease.

Implicit GDP Price Deflator Government economists issue another mea-

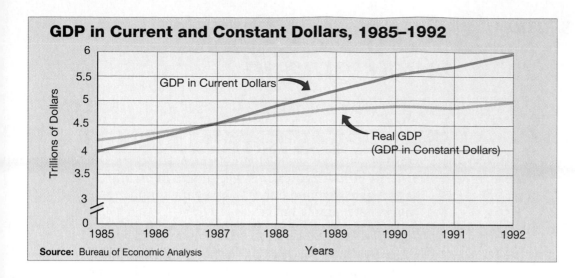

GDP in Current and Constant Dollars, 1985–1992

Source: Bureau of Economic Analysis

**Figure 14.11
GDP in Current
and Constant
Dollars**
Is economic growth in
constant dollars more
or less than growth
measured in current
dollars?

sure of price changes in GDP called the **implicit GDP price deflator.** This index removes the effects of inflation from GDP so that the overall economy in one year can be compared to another year. When the price deflator is applied to GDP in any year, the new figure is called **real GDP.** See **Figure 14.11.** The federal government uses 1987 as its base year to measure real GDP. Each year the price deflator is used to adjust GDP in current, or inflated, dollars to GDP in the base year. For example, GDP in current dollars for 1992 was $5,950.7 billion. To find real GDP for 1992, the government divides 1992 GDP by the 1992 price deflator (120.9) and multiplies the result by 100:

$$\$5,950.7 \div 120.9 \times 100 = \$4,922.0016$$

Real GDP for 1992 was $4,922.0 billion. This figure may now be compared to 1987 GDP of $4,540.0 billion. This is a more meaningful comparison than comparing 1992 GDP in inflated dollars to 1987 GDP. **Figure 14.11** shows both GDP in current dollars and real GDP (in constant dollars) for years 1985 to 1992. Notice that the two curves cross at the year 1987 where GDP in current dollars is equal to real GDP.

SECTION 2 REVIEW

Understanding Vocabulary
Define inflation, purchasing power, deflation, consumer price index (CPI), base year, producer price index (PPI), implicit GDP price deflator, real GDP.

Reviewing Objectives
1. What is the relationship between the purchasing power of money and the rate of inflation?
2. What is the difference between what the consumer price index measures and what the producer price index measures?

SECTION 3 Aggregate Supply and Demand

SECTION 3 FOCUS

Terms to Know aggregates, aggregate demand, aggregate demand curve, aggregate supply, aggregate supply curve

Objectives *After reading this section, you should be able to:*

1. List two reasons why, when the price level goes down, **the aggregate quantity demanded** goes up.
2. Explain why, when the price level goes up and wages do not, producers want to supply more to the marketplace and **aggregate quantity supplied** increases.
3. Explain how the equilibrium price level reflects **aggregate demand and aggregate supply.**

Measuring Supply and Demand in the Whole Economy

The laws of supply and demand can be applied to the economy as a whole, as well as to individual consumer decisions. We would like to know about the demand by all consumers for all goods and services, and the supply by all producers of all goods and services. See **Figure 14.12.** When we look at the economy as a whole in this way, we are looking at **aggregates**—the summation of all the individual parts in the economy. We call these sums aggregate demand and aggregate supply.

The Aggregate Demand Curve

What is the total, or aggregate, quantity of goods and services in the entire economy that all citizens will demand at any one point in time? To answer this question, we have to relate **aggregate demand** to something else. The basic law of demand relates the quantity demanded of an individual product to its price. Now we are talking about all products. We cannot talk about all prices because there are millions. We can, however, talk about the *price level*. The relationship we obtain, therefore, is between the aggregate quantity demanded of all goods and services by all people and the average of all prices, which we measure by a price index. If we use the implicit GDP deflator as our index, our measure of aggregate demand will be based on real domestic output. You can see this relationship in **Figure 14.13**. It is called the **aggregate demand curve.**

Figure 14.12
Producers and Consumers
These people represent the producers of many of the services available to us. The number of jobs in each of these fields depends on several factors, including demand for specific services. These people also represent all consumers of goods and services. ▼

Aggregate Demand Curve

Price Level / Real Domestic Output

Aggregate Demand Curve

AD

Figure 14.13
Aggregate Demand Curve
Although the curve for aggregate demand resembles that for simple demand, it is for the entire economy, not just one good or service.

◀

**Figure 14.14
Export Demand**

Exports add to the total aggregate demand and quantity demanded in the United States. So as our price level goes down, foreigners buy more of our goods, and a larger quantity of real domestic output is demanded each year.

▶

Notice the similarity between the aggregate demand curve labeled *AD* in **Figure 14.13** and the individual demand curve you studied in Chapter 8 (pages 182–189). Both of those curves slope downward—they show an inverse relationship. Here as the price level in the nation's economy goes down, a larger quantity of real domestic output is demanded per year. At least two reasons cause this inverse relationship: one has to do with the real purchasing power of your cash, and the other has to do with the relative price of goods and services sold to other countries.

Consider the first reason. Inflation causes the purchasing power of your cash to go down. Deflation causes your purchasing power to go up. Therefore, when the price level goes down, the purchasing power of any cash that you hold will go up. You and everybody else will feel slightly richer because you are able to buy more goods and services.

Also, when the price level goes down in the United States, our goods become relatively better deals for foreigners who want to buy them. Foreigners then demand more of our goods as exports as **Figure 14.14** shows.

Demand is only one side of the picture. Let us look at aggregate supply and its curve shown in **Figure 14.15**.

Figure 14.15 ▶
Aggregate Supply Curve

Similar to the aggregate demand curve, the aggregate supply curve is a macroeconomic measure.

Aggregate Supply Curve

Price Level

Aggregate Supply Curve

AS

Real Domestic Output

Aggregate Supply and the Aggregate Supply Curve

As the price of a specific product goes up, and if all other prices stay the same, producers of that product find it profitable to produce more. The same is true for all producers in the economy over a short period of time. If the price level goes up and wages do not, overall profits will rise. Producers will want to supply more to the marketplace—they offer more real domestic output as the price level increases. The reverse is true as the price level falls. This is called **aggregate supply.** You can see this positive relationship in **Figure 14.15**—the **aggregate supply curve.**

Putting Aggregate Demand and Aggregate Supply Together

Just as we are able to compare supply and demand for a given product to find an equilibrium price and quantity, we can compare aggregate demand and aggregate supply here. We do this in **Figure 14.16**.

The equilibrium price level in our example is determined where the aggregate demand curve crosses the aggregate supply curve, or at an implicit GDP price deflator of 140. The equi-

librium quantity of real GDP demanded and supplied is $7 trillion. As long as nothing changes in this situation, the economy will produce $7 trillion of real domestic output and the price level will remain at 140—there will be neither inflation nor deflation.

**Figure 14.16
The Equilibrium
Level of National
Output and the
Price Level**
The intersection of aggregate demand and supply gives the equilibrium general price level and national output (real domestic output). ▼

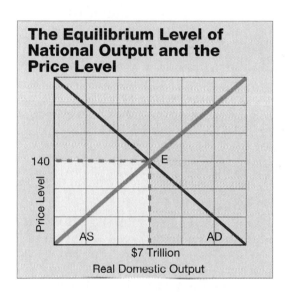

The Equilibrium Level of National Output and the Price Level

140 ·········· E

Price Level

AS ———— AD

$7 Trillion

Real Domestic Output

Understanding Vocabulary

Define aggregates, aggregate demand, aggregate demand curve, aggregate supply, aggregate supply curve.

Reviewing Objectives

1. Why is there an inverse relationship between aggregate quantity demanded and the price level?

2. What causes the aggregate supply curve to slope up (rise, going from left to right)?

3. How do you use aggregate demand and supply analysis to determine the equilibrium price level?

John Maynard Keynes on Equilibrium Employment

- 1883–1946
- born in Cambridge, England, and educated at Cambridge University
- built a fortune in the stock market
- Keynesian economics named after him
- most influential publication was *The General Theory of Employment, Interest, and Money* (1936)

John Maynard Keynes originated the school of economic thought referred to as Keynesian economics. Keynesian economics supports the liberal use of government spending and taxing to help the economy. This is, in part, because Keynes believed that an economy may reach an equilibrium level of employment that is below full employment. In *The General Theory of Employment, Interest, and Money*, he explained that people buy more when their wages increase, but the total additional consumption is not equal to the total increased wages.

When employment increases, aggregate real income is increased. The psychology of the community is that when aggregate real income is increased aggregate consumption is increased, but not so much as income. . . .

Keynes adds that the equilibrium level of employment depends on the level of investment. If the level of investment is low, full employment cannot be achieved.

Thus, to justify any given amount of employment there must be an amount of current investment sufficient to absorb the excess of output over what the community chooses to consume when employment is at a given level. . . . It follows, that . . . the equilibrium level of employment, [that is] the level at which there is no inducement to employers as a whole either to expand or contract employment, will depend on the amount of current investment.

Keynes believed that his theory explained why large pockets of poverty exist in otherwise rich communities or nations.

. . . This analysis supplies us with an explanation of the paradox of poverty in the midst of plenty.
. . . Moreover the richer the community, the wider will tend to be the gap between its actual and its potential production; and therefore the more obvious and outrageous the defects of the economic system.

Checking for Understanding
1. According to Keynes, what is the relationship between employment and current investment?
2. What is the equilibrium level of employment?
3. According to Keynes, what is one of the defects of the economic system?

SECTION 4 FOCUS

Terms to Know business fluctuations, business cycle, peak, boom, contraction, recession, depression, trough, expansion, recovery

Objectives *After reading this section, you should be able to:*
1 List the phases of a **typical business cycle.**
2 Describe three **downturns in the United States economy** since the 1920s.

Peak and Trough, Boom and Bust

Some years unemployment goes up; some years it goes down. Some years inflation is high; other years it is not. We have fluctuations in virtually all aspects of our economy. The ups and downs in an economy are sometimes called **business fluctuations.** Some people associate these ups and downs in business activity with what has been called the **business cycle**—changes in the level of total output measured by real GDP. The term *business cycle* is somewhat misleading, however. *Cycle* usually refers to a regular series of changes. Changes in business activity in the United States show no such regularity, as you will see. (Consequently, many economists no longer use the term *business cycle,* but prefer to talk about *business fluctuations.*)

Model of the Business Cycle

Figure 14.17 shows an idealized business cycle. According to this model, the phases of a business cycle begin with growth leading to an economic **peak** or **boom**—a period of prosperity. New businesses open, factories are producing at full capacity, and everyone who wants work can find a job.

Eventually, however, real GDP levels off and begins to decline. During this part of the cycle, a **contraction** of the economy occurs. Business activity begins to slow down. If the contraction lasts long enough and is deep

**Figure 14.17
A Model of the
Business Cycle**
What does the word *model*
indicate about the business
cycle shown? ▼

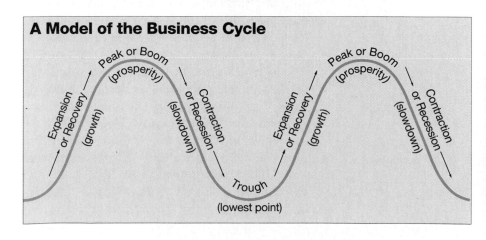

A Model of the Business Cycle

Peak or Boom
(prosperity)

Expansion
or Recovery
(growth)

Contraction
or Recession
(slowdown)

Peak or Boom
(prosperity)

Expansion
or Recovery
(growth)

Contraction
or Recession
(slowdown)

Trough
(lowest point)

Business Activity in the United States, 1915–1975

Percent change in business activity
0 represents the long-term trend

Source: AmeriTrust, Cleveland, Ohio

Years

Figure 14.18 ▲
Business Activity
American business activity declined more than 40 percent in the Depression, yet bounced back as the nation fought World War II.

enough, the economy can continue downward until it slips into a recession. A **recession** is any period of at least two quarters—six months—during which real GDP does not grow. In a recession, business activity starts to fall at a rapid rate. Factories begin cutting back on production and laying off workers. Consumers, with less income, cut back on purchases. With less money income being spent, factories may reduce production further, laying off even more workers. Faced with a worsening economy, fewer new businesses open and many existing ones may fail. If a recession becomes extremely bad, it deepens into a **depression.** Then millions are out of work, many businesses fail, and the economy operates far below capacity.

At some point, the downward spiral of the economy levels off in a trough. A **trough** is the lowest point in the business cycle. It occurs when real GDP stops going down, levels off, and begins slowly increasing. The increase in total economic activity that

follows is called an **expansion** or a **recovery.** Consumer spending picks up, signaling factories to hire workers and increase production to meet demand. As more people are hired, the public has more income to spend, which further encourages growth. New businesses begin to open, and factory production climbs back toward full capacity. The recovery continues until the economy hits another peak, and a new cycle begins.

Ups and Downs of Business in the United States

What you have just read is a description of the business cycle model. In the real world, as you can see from **Figure 14.18**, the cycles are not that regular. However, the peaks and troughs are clear. The largest drop that resulted in a depression immediately followed the stock market crash in October 1929. The preceding years had been a time of widespread prosperity as **Figure 14.19** shows. By September 1929, heavy speculation had driven stock prices to an all-time peak. Then the stock market began to collapse. Stock prices started to fall in early October and continued to fall. Suddenly, on October 28, there was a nationwide stampede to unload stocks. In one day the total value of all stocks fell by $14 billion. The next day the economic crisis was even worse.

Not long after the stock market crash, the United States fell into a serious recession. See **Figure 14.20** (page 350). Factories shut down, laying off millions of workers. Businesses and banks failed by the thousands. Real GDP fell sharply over the next few years, pushing the nation into the depths of the Great Depression. Then began a recovery, with some short slips downward until about 1937, when another downturn occurred. A gradual upward rise climaxed in the boom period of World War II.

After the war and throughout the 1950s, small ups and downs occurred. Recessions were short and mild, however, and the economy was generally prosperous. From 1960 through 1969, there were no recessionary periods. In the 1970s and the 1980s, the American economy suffered recurring recessions. The 1980s started off with a small recession that developed into the most serious economic downturn by some measurements since World War II. This downturn ended in 1982 and was followed by relative prosperity, except for a severe stock market crash in October 1987. The 1990s began with a mild recession, and then the recovery was relatively slow by historic standards.

▼ **Figure 14.19**
Prosperity Before the Crash
The twenties had been a decade in which Americans began buying increasing numbers of radios, stoves, and automobiles. During these years, prices remained stable, and the standard of living rose about 3 percent per year.

▼ **Figure 14.20**
Recession Conditions
The Great Depression of the 1930s forced millions of Americans out of work. Used to the boom era of the 1920s, Americans during the bust era of the Depression often relied on handouts.

SECTION 4 REVIEW

Understanding Vocabulary
Define business fluctuations, business cycle, peak, boom, contraction, recession, depression, trough, expansion, recovery.

Reviewing Objectives
❶ What are the phases of a typical business cycle?
❷ What were the three most severe downturns in the United States economy since the 1920s?

5 *Causes and Indicators of Business Fluctuations*

SECTION 5 FOCUS

Terms to Know innovations, economic indicators, leading indicators, coincident indicators, lagging indicators

Objectives *After reading this section, you should be able to:*

① List the potential **causes of business fluctuations.**

② List the broad categories of **economic indicators** that predict and reflect business fluctuations.

Problems in Predicting Economic Changes

For as long as booms and recessions have existed, economists have tried to explain why business fluctuations occur. If they could understand the causes, government could take actions to smooth out business fluctuations. No one theory, however, seems to explain past cycles or to serve as an adequate measure to predict future ones. The difficulty arises because at any one time, several factors are working together to create business fluctuations.

Causes of Business Fluctuations

For many years economists believed that business fluctuations occurred in regular cycles. No one knew why. A nineteenth-century English economist, W. Stanley Jevons, even blamed the cycles on sunspots. See **Figure 14.21**. Later economists realized that business fluctuations were related to changes in the rate of saving and investing. Today economists link business fluctuations to four main forces: business investment, government activity, external factors, and psychological factors. See **Figure 14.22** (pages 352–353).

Business Investment Some economists believe business decisions are the keys to business

**Figure 14.21
Crops, Sunspots, and Business?**
W. Stanley Jevons believed periodic dark spots that appeared on the surface of the sun about every 11 years caused the weather and crop conditions that affected business.

▼

Figure 14.22
Forces That Affect
Business Fluctuations
Each of the four forces described here has a major impact on business.

B **Government Activity**
Government controls the supply of money.

▲

A **Business Investment**
The computer industry is an example of technology contributing to business growth through innovation.

fluctuations. Suppose a firm believes that prospects for future sales are good. It will most likely increase its capital investment. It will buy new machines, build new factories, expand old ones, and so on. This expansion will create new jobs and more income for consumer spending. After a time, businesses no longer need to expand. When businesses stop purchasing new producer goods, a resulting contraction of the economy may occur.

When businesses anticipate a downturn in the economy, they cut back on their inventories. Producers, in turn, cut back on production to pre-

vent a surplus. Enough inventory cutbacks could lead to a recession. In contrast, if they feel consumer orders are going to rise, businesses will invest in larger inventories. This will stimulate production and increase employment.

Innovations—inventions and new production techniques—can have a similar effect on the economy. When one firm begins to use an innovation, others, to become competitive again, must duplicate the product or production method. All this takes capital. Eventually, however, investment will drop off because no additional capital for the innovation is needed. (This situation is an example of the law of diminishing returns.)

◄ C **External Factors**
War, immigration, crop failures, and changing availability of resources are some external factors that affect business cycles.

Government Activity A number of economists believe that the changing policies of the federal government are a major reason for business cycles. The government affects business activity in two ways: through its policies on taxing and spending and through its control over the supply of money available in the economy.

External Factors Factors outside a nation's economy also influence the business cycle. As you can see from **Figure 14.22**, wars in particular have an important impact. This impact results from the huge increase in government spending during wartime. The end of wartime spending signals an economic slowdown. Discoveries of new sources of raw materials such as oil may have a favorable effect on the economy by lowering operating costs for certain industries. The sudden loss of raw materials and the resulting higher price, however, can have the opposite effect. The huge increase in oil prices in late 1973 by the Organization of Petroleum Exporting Countries (OPEC) was partially responsible for the recession of 1974–1975. The sharp

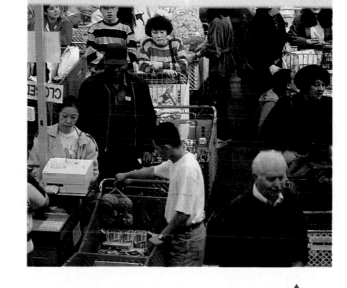

▲

decline in world oil prices helped the return of prosperity in the mid-1980s.

Psychological Factors Finally, it is possible that people's psychological reactions to events also cause changes in business activity. The prospects of peace in a troubled area or the discovery of a new oil field can lead to feelings of confidence and optimism. War or the overthrow of the government of an important trading partner can cause pessimism about the future. These psychological factors sometimes

D **Psychological Factors**
Consumer confidence and increased spending may lead to an expansion.

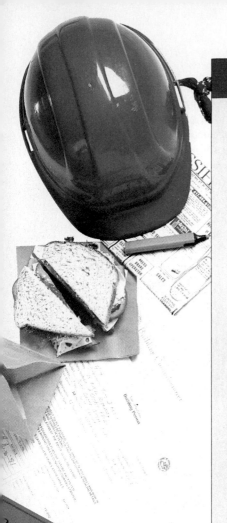

Figure 14.23 Major Economic Indicators

Leading indicators
1. Average workweek for production workers in manufacturing
2. Layoff rate in manufacturing
3. New orders for consumer goods
4. Speed with which companies make deliveries (the busier a company, the longer it will take to fill orders)
5. Number of new businesses formed
6. Number of contracts and orders for plants and equipment
7. Number of building permits issued for private housing units
8. Change in the inventories on hand and on order
9. Change in the PPI for certain nonagricultural raw materials
10. Index compiled from surveys of consumer expectations
11. Stock prices
12. Supply of money in the economy

Coincident indicators
1. Number of nonagricultural workers who are employed
2. Personal income minus transfer payments
3. Rate of industrial production
4. Sales of manufacturers, wholesalers, and retailers

Lagging indicators
1. Average length of unemployment
2. Size of manufacturing and trade inventories
3. Labor cost per unit of output in manufacturing
4. Average interest rate charged by banks to their best business customers
5. Number of commercial and industrial loans to be repaid
6. Ratio of consumer installment debt to personal income
7. Change in Consumer Price Index for services

though these decisions can be based on objective facts, psychological factors such as personal optimism can also influence them.

Economic Indicators

Every day, business and government leaders are faced with the dilemma of trying to predict what will happen to the economy in the coming months and years. Businesspeople base their decisions on such questions as when to build a new plant or what they feel will happen in the future. Government officials also need information about the future in planning taxing and spending policies. To aid these decision makers, government and private economists constantly create and update economic forecasts.

contribute to consumer confidence and increased spending or the lack of confidence and more saving.

Likewise, business executives make decisions based on what they think will happen in the future. Even

These forecasts indicate what is likely to happen in the economy as it moves through the various phases of the business cycle. Although GDP is an important measure of the economy's performance, it is not very helpful in preparing these forecasts. GDP shows what *has* happened in the economy, but it is not a good predictor of what *might* happen. It is also too broad a measure to show detail about activity in the various sectors of the economy.

For these reasons, economists study a number of other economic indicators to learn about the current and possible future state of the economy. See **Figure 14.23**. **Economic indicators** are statistics that measure variables in the economy, such as stock prices or the dollar amount of loans to be repaid. Each month the Department of Commerce publishes statistics for more than 250 economic indicators covering all aspects of the state of the economy.

Those statistics that point to what will happen in the economy are called **leading indicators.** Their activity seems to lead to a change in overall business activity—whether it is an upward or a downward trend. Economists can use leading indicators to predict which phase of the business cycle the economy is moving into. Although the Commerce Department keeps track of dozens of leading indicators, those listed in **Figure 14.23** are the ones that most concern American economists.

Other economic indicators, whose changes in activity seem to happen at the same time as changes in overall business activity, also help economists. When these **coincident indicators** begin a downswing, they indicate that a contraction in the business cycle has begun. If they begin an upswing, they indicate that the economy is picking up and a recovery is underway.

A third set of indicators seems to lag behind changes in overall business activity. For example, it may be six months after the start of a downturn before businesses begin to reduce their borrowing noticeably. The amount of change in these **lagging indicators,** whether up or down, gives economists clues as to the size and timing of all of the phases of the business cycle.

Although economic indicators are essential in making economic forecasts, they are far from perfect predictors. Often, different indicators within each group move in opposite directions. Another problem is the wide variation in lead or lag time between a change in an indicator and a change in the overall economy.

SECTION 5 REVIEW

Understanding Vocabulary
Define innovations, economic indicators, leading indicators, coincident indicators, lagging indicators.

Reviewing Objectives
1. What are some of the potential causes of business fluctuations?
2. What are the three broad categories of economic indicators?

Readings in Economics

KIPLINGER'S PERSONAL FINANCE MAGAZINE   **JANUARY 1993**

McDONALD'S: 95 BILLION BURGERS

by Dan Morea

Just how awesome, how successful, is the restaurant chain that traces its roots to a California eatery started 45 years ago by two brothers named McDonald? Consider this: Sometime in 1993, McDonald's Corp. will have sold enough hamburgers (95 billion—not counting McChickens, Filet-O-Fishes and all the other nonbeef sandwiches) to have fed nearly every human being born since the dawn of time. Or ponder this: In 1993, the hamburgers leaving McDonald's grills (171 per second) would be enough to feed every living person on earth—5.3 billion, give or take a hundred million. Among brand names, only Coke enjoys greater worldwide recognition.

Yes, McDonald's is hugely successful. . . . But scarcely two years ago, the company's juices seemed to have run dry. . . .

So in 1991, McDonald's, a company known for single-minded determination, fired back. In midyear it introduced an "extra-value" menu that knocked 20% off the price of sandwiches and made up the revenue loss with high-markup fries and drinks. For health-conscious eaters, McDonald's replaced its McDLT hamburger with the McLean Deluxe, a burger that is 91% fat-free. . . .

Another ingredient contributes to the recent success of McDonald's: overseas franchises. Truth is, U.S. growth is still nothing to brag about—a few percentage points each year. Right now, the sizzle that McDonald's shareholders hear comes from 4,000 overseas outlets (there are 9,000 in the U.S.). Foreign business now contributes 37% of sales, 40% of profits and most of the growth in franchises.

. . . Those overseas outlets are highly concentrated. Seventy percent are located in just six nations—Australia, Canada, France, Germany, Great Britain and Japan.

Section 1

National Income Accounting

Key Terms

national income accounting (p. 332)
gross domestic product (GDP) (p. 332)
net exports (p. 334)
depreciation (p. 334)

net domestic product (NDP) (p. 335)
national income (NI) (p. 335)
personal income (PI) (p. 336)
transfer payments (p. 336)
disposable personal income (DI) (p. 336)

Summary

Gross domestic product (GDP) is the total dollar value of all *final* consumer goods, producer goods, government goods, net exports, and services produced in the nation during a single year. Personal income is found by subtracting corporate income taxes, profits, and employer Social Security contributions from national income and adding transfer payments.

Section 2

Correcting Statistics for Inflation

Key Terms

inflation (p. 338)
purchasing power (p. 338)
deflation (p. 339)
consumer price index (CPI) (p. 339)

base year (p. 340)
producer price index (PPI) (p. 340)
implicit GDP price deflator (p. 341)
real GDP (p. 341)

Summary

When there is inflation, the purchasing power of money falls. The three ways to measure changes in average prices are by the consumer price index (CPI), producer price index (PPI), and implicit GDP price deflator.

Section 3

Aggregate Supply and Demand

Key Terms

aggregates (p. 342)
aggregate demand (p. 342)

aggregate demand curve (p. 343)
aggregate supply (p. 345)
aggregate supply curve (p. 345)

Summary

Aggregate supply and demand measure the entire economy. The intersection of the aggregate demand and aggregate supply curves determines the equilibrium price level and real GDP (national output).

Section 4

Business Fluctuations

Key Terms

business fluctuations (p. 347)
business cycle (p. 347)

peak (p. 347)
boom (p. 347)
contraction (p. 347)
recession (p. 348)
depression (p. 348)
trough (p. 348)
expansion (p. 348)
recovery (p. 348)

Summary

Business fluctuations are measured from one period of prosperity to another. A typical "cycle" starts with the peak (boom). Then the economy begins to contract, during which a recession (trough) may occur followed by recovery.

Section 5

Causes and Indicators of Business Fluctuations

Key Terms

innovations (p. 352)
economic indicators (p. 355)

leading indicators (p. 355)
coincident indicators (p. 355)
lagging indicators (p. 355)

Summary

Economists study many possible causes of business cycles. Economists use leading, coincident, and lagging indicators to measure the activity of certain variables in the economy.

14 Review

Identifying Key Terms

Write the letter of the definition in Column B below that correctly defines each term in Column A.

Column A
1. base year (p. 340)
2. trough (p. 348)
3. economic indicators (p. 355)
4. expansion (p. 348)
5. real GDP (p. 341)
6. business cycle (p. 347)

Column B
a. economic activity is at its lowest point
b. figures for the nation's total income that have been corrected for inflation
c. measurement of specific aspects of the economy such as stock prices
d. used as a point of comparison for other years in a series of statistics
e. periodic ups and downs in the nation's economic activity
f. business recovery period, when economic activity increases

Recalling Facts and Ideas

Section 1
1. Net exports and government goods are two components of gross domestic product. What are the other two components?
2. Besides profit and rents, what two other categories of income are added in the income approach to estimating GDP?
3. If you were given the statistic on disposable personal income, what other information would you need to derive personal income?

Section 2
4. What are the most commonly used price indexes?
5. What is the difference between inflation and deflation?
6. How would you determine *real* GDP if you knew only GDP?

Section 3
7. Why does the aggregate demand curve slope down?
8. Why does the aggregate supply curve slope up?
9. What is determined at the intersection of the aggregate supply and aggregate demand curves?

Section 4
10. What are the main phases of a business cycle?
11. When the economy enters a recession, what normally happens?
12. When was the most serious downturn in economic activity in the twentieth century in the United States?

Section 5
13. What are two theories of the causes of the ups and downs in overall business activity?
14. How might psychological factors affect the business cycle?
15. What two aspects of government activity affect business cycles?

Critical Thinking

Section 1
Evaluating Information How might knowledge of nationwide economic statistics help you?

Section 2
Determining Cause and Effect "Inflation just keeps getting worse because the purchasing power of money is going down." Why is this statement meaningless?

Section 3
Making Comparisons What is the difference between the aggregate demand curve and the demand curve in Chapter 8 that discussed the demand for individual goods and services?

Section 4
Analyzing Information Why is it probably better to talk about business fluctuations rather than business cycles?

Section 5
Making Inferences Many theories try to explain why business cycles occur. None of them can be considered "the truth." Why not?

Applying Economic Concepts

Understanding the Business Cycle Try to analyze what you think occurs throughout the economy during a recession. Make a list of some of the things that business owners may do to react to a recession, such as reduce employees' overtime hours.

Chapter Projects

1. **Individual Project** Go to the library and find the latest edition of the *Statistical Abstract of the United States*. Locate the tables in the "Prices" section that give price indexes for consumer goods for selected cities and metropolitan areas. Make a line graph showing the rise in the index for "all items" over the last six years. Draw on the same graph a line indicating the "city average" index for "all items" in a city or area near you during the same period of time.
2. **Cooperative Learning Project** Work in three groups. Each group will choose one of the following:

- Lagging indicators
- Coincident indicators
- Leading indicators

Each group will do library research to determine the following:

- For each type of indicator, what are the various subgroups?
- How long has the indicator been reported by the United States government?
- Can you find instances when the indicator was wildly inaccurate? For example, what if the leading indicator was still indicating that times were good when, in fact, the economy was already in a serious recession?

Have a class discussion about how useful any of these indicators might be in accurately predicting changes in overall national economic activity.

Reviewing Skills

Using Index Numbers: Price Indexes
Constructing a Price Index Assume the following data on the price of comparable personal computers: 1990 $1,000; 1991 $800; 1992 $700; 1993 $600; 1994 $500; 1995 $250; 1996 $200. Construct a price index for computers using 1990 as the base year.

Writing About Economics
Persuasive Writing Imagine that you are the President. You need to assure the nation that the economy will do better if you are reelected. Write a two-paragraph speech about how you would improve the economic conditions you recorded in Your Economics Journal this week.

CHAPTER

15 MONEY AND BANKING

Why are these people waiting in line?

How do you operate an automated teller machine (ATM)?

Why do people need cash?

How much money is in circulation?

Why are ATMs so popular?

Your Economics Journal

Keep track of all of the purchases you make during one week. Write down a list of these purchases, the amount of money involved, and how you paid. Indicate after each item whether you purchased it using cash or another form of money.

SECTION 1 The Functions and Characteristics of Money

SECTION 1 FOCUS

Terms to Know money, medium of exchange, barter, double coincidence of wants, unit of accounting, store of value, commodity money, representative money, fiat money, legal tender

Objectives *After reading this section, you should be able to:*
1 List the three **functions of money**.
2 Name six **characteristics that money** should have.

It's Only Money

American businesses produce, market, and distribute goods and services. Money makes it possible for businesses to obtain what they need from suppliers and for consumers to obtain goods. **Money** is defined as anything customarily used as a medium of exchange, a unit of accounting, and a store of value. The basis of the market economy is voluntary exchange. In the American economy, the exchange usually involves money in return for a good or service.

The Functions of Money

Most Americans think of money as bills, coins, and checks. Historically, and in other economies, money might be shells, gold, or even goods such as sheep. Economists identify money by the presence or absence of certain functions. Anything that is used as a medium of exchange, a unit of accounting, and a store of value is considered money. **Figure 15.1** shows a partial list of the things that have been used as money. For example, Native Americans used wampum—beads made from shells. Fijians have used whales' teeth.

Medium of Exchange The three functions of money are shown in **Fig-**

ure 15.2 (page 364). To say that money is a **medium of exchange** simply means that a seller will accept it in exchange for a good or service. Most people are paid for their work in money, which they then can use to buy whatever they need or want. Without money people would have to **barter**—exchange goods and services for other goods and services.

Suppose you worked in a grocery

Feathers

store and were paid in groceries because money did not exist. To get whatever else you needed, such as clothes and housing, you would have to find people who have the goods that you want. In addition, those people

Figure 15.1
Selected Items Used as Money

These items are but a sampling of the items that have been used as money.

Corn

Whale teeth
Porpoise teeth
Boar tusk

Rum
Molasses

Pots
Pitch
Wine

Gold
Silver
Iron
Leather
Copper
Brass

Rice

Crystal salt

Salt

Tobacco

Round stones with centers
Polished beads (wampum)

Goats
Cows

Playing cards
Paper

Tortoise shells

Snail shells

**Figure 15.2 ▲
Three Functions
of Money**
All money serves three
functions. The money
this woman has is serv-
ing as a medium of
exchange; the vendor
will accept it in
exchange for tomatoes.
The money is also a unit
of accounting—the prod-
ucts in the market are all
priced in dollars, so the
woman can compare
values of different items.
Finally, the money serves
as a store of value—the
woman has stored her
purchasing power in the
form of dollars.

would have to want the exact goods—
in this case, groceries—that you have.
Barter requires what economists call
a **double coincidence of wants.** Each
party to a transaction must want exactly what the other person has to
offer. This situation is rare. As a result, people in societies that barter for
goods spend great amounts of time
and effort making trades with one another. Bartering can work only in small
societies with fairly simple economic
systems.

Unit of Accounting Money is the
yardstick that allows people to compare the values of goods and services
in relation to one another. Money that
is a measure of value functions in this
way as a **unit of accounting.** Each nation uses a basic unit to measure the
value of goods, as it uses the foot or
meter to measure distance. In the
United States, this base unit of value is
the dollar. In Japan, it is the yen; in
France, the franc. An item for sale is
marked with a price that indicates its

value in terms of that unit.

Using money as the single unit of
accounting provides a simple and convenient way to compare the values of
various items. By using money prices
as a factor in comparing goods, people
can determine whether one item is a
better bargain than another. A single
unit of accounting also allows people
to keep accurate financial records—
records of debts owed, income saved,
and so on. Businesspeople can better
calculate their profits and losses over
the years by using a single money unit
of accounting.

Store of Value Money also serves as
a **store of value.** You can sell something, such as your labor, and store
the purchasing power that results
from the sale in the form of money for
later use. People usually receive their
money income once a week, once
every two weeks, or once a month.
However, they usually spend their income at different times during a pay
period. To be able to buy things be-

Figure 15.3 Characteristics of Money

Characteristic	Description
Durable	Money must be able to withstand the wear and tear of being passed from person to person. Paper money lasts on the average of only one year, but old bills can be easily replaced. Coins, in contrast, last for years.
Portable	Money can be carried around easily. Though paper money is not very durable, people can easily carry large sums of paper money.
Divisible	Money must be easily divided into small parts so that purchases of any price can be made. Carrying coins and small bills makes it possible to make purchases of any amount.
Stable in value	Money must be stable in value. Its value cannot change rapidly or its usefulness as a store of value will decrease.
Scarce	Whatever is used as money must be scarce. That is what gives it value.
Accepted	Whatever is used as money must be accepted as a medium of exchange in payment for debts. In the United States, acceptance is based on the knowledge that others will continue to accept paper money, coins, and checks in exchange for desired goods and services.

tween paydays, a person can store some of his or her income in cash and some in a checking account. It is important to note that in periods of rapid and unpredictable inflation, money is less able to act as a store of value.

The Types and Characteristics of Money

Anything that people are willing to accept in exchange for goods can serve as money. At various times in history, cattle, salt, animal hides, gems, and tobacco have been used as mediums of exchange. Each of these items has certain characteristics that make it better or worse than others for use as money. Cattle, for example, are difficult to transport, but they are durable. Gems are easy to carry, but they are not easy to split into small pieces to use.

Figure 15.3 lists the major characteristics that to some degree all items used as money must have. Almost any item that meets most of these criteria can be and probably has been used as money. Precious metals, however, particularly gold and silver, are especially well suited as mediums of exchange, and have often been used as such throughout history. It is only in more recent times that paper money has been widely used as a medium of exchange.

Mediums of exchange such as cattle and gems are considered **commodity money.** They have a value as a commodity, or good, aside from their value as money. Cattle are used for food and transportation. Gems are used for jewelry.

Representative money is money backed by—exchangeable for—some commodity, such as gold or silver. It is not in itself valuable for nonmoney uses, but it can be exchanged for some valuable item. Like commodity money, the amount of representative money in circulation, or in use by people, is limited because it is linked to some scarce good, such as gold. At one time, the United States government issued representative money in the form of silver and gold certificates. In addition, private banks accepted deposits of gold or silver and issued paper money, called bank notes. These were a promise to convert the paper money into coin or bullion on demand. These banks were supposed to keep enough gold or silver in reserve—on hand—to redeem their bank notes. Often, they did not.

Today all United States money is **fiat** (FEE-uht) **money.** As **Figure 15.4** shows, its face value occurs through government fiat, or order. It is in this way declared **legal tender.**

Figure 15.4 ▶
Legal Tender
By law these forms of money must be accepted for payment of public and private debts.
In reality, fiat money is accepted because we all have faith that others will accept this money from us when we use it.

SECTION 1 REVIEW

Understanding Vocabulary
Define money, medium of exchange, barter, double coincidence of wants, unit of accounting, store of value, commodity money, representative money, fiat money, legal tender.

Reviewing Objectives
1. Money must serve as a medium of exchange. What are two other functions that money must also serve?
2. What are the six major characteristics of money?

John W. Rogers on Money Management

- 1958 –
- attended Princeton University
- founded Ariel Capital Management, a Chicago-based money management firm, at age 24
- led Ariel growth funds to gains of more than 15 percent annually since 1986
- manages about $1.85 billion in assets

John W. Rogers is one of the country's best managers of small-capitalization stocks. Beginning with money from associates and his parents, Rogers built on a successful investment strategy of finding lesser-known companies that were selling for 10 times their earnings or less. Ariel Capital Management grew on a groundswell of rising interest in African American-owned businesses. The following excerpts are taken from the *Chicago Sun-Times*, January 25, 1993 and *Forbes*, September 2, 1991.

In the early '80s, more and more businesses were thinking in terms of minorities. Harold Washington had just been elected mayor of Chicago, and that helped me see there was an opportunity there. . . . If you trust and have faith in people, they'll trust and have faith in you.

As Ariel Capital Management grew, so much new money began flowing into the firm that Rogers was faced with a dilemma. He could not find enough investment opportunities for all the new money in small company stocks. At first Rogers bought bigger stakes in larger companies. Then, rather than take risks

with more and more capital, he decided to close the larger of two mutual funds to new customers.

We can't take on any more new cash and still preserve our focus. . . . The emphasis has always been on lesser-known companies. We've got only about 6 stocks overall in the portfolio. I can't handle more money and see consistent results. There are only so many good ideas.

. . . From now on, it's going to be a very simple story. Our private clients can judge us by just one thing—growth of assets.

Checking for Understanding

1. What event helped Rogers see a new business opportunity?
2. What problem resulted from Ariel's success?
3. How did Rogers try to maintain the company's focus?

SECTION 2 History of American Money and Banking

Serving the Nation's Financial Needs

During the colonial period, England did not permit the American colonies to print or mint their own money. Bartering was common. Colonists used various goods in place of coins and paper money. In Massachusetts Bay for a time, colonists used Native American wampum as a medium of exchange. In the Virginia Colony, tobacco became commodity money. Though scarce, some European gold and silver coins also circulated in the colonies. The Spanish dolár, later called the *dollar* by colonists, was one of the more common coins.

History of American Banking

The Revolutionary War brought even more confusion to the already haphazard colonial money system. To help pay for the war, the Continental Congress issued bills of credit, called Continentals, that could be used to pay debts. See **Figure 15.5**. So many of these notes were issued that people often refused to accept them. The money became so worthless that the phrase "not worth a Continental" was used to describe something of little value.

After the war, establishing a reliable medium of exchange became a major concern of the new nation. The Constitution, ratified in 1788, gave Congress the sole power to mint coins, although private banks were still allowed to print bank notes representing gold and silver on deposit. Because the history of money in the United States is so closely tied to the development of the banking system, the time line in **Figure 15.6** (pages 370–371) describes both.

Banking Services

Banks and savings institutions today offer a wide variety of services, including checking accounts, interest on checking, automatic deposit and payment, storage of valuables, transfer of money from one person to another, and overdraft checking. **Overdraft checking** allows a customer to write a check for more money than exists in his or her account. The bank "loans" the needed amount and the customer pays the money back, usually at a relatively high rate of interest.

In general, the types of services are the same across the country. The exact conditions of the services, however, vary from state to state according to each state's banking laws.

In choosing a bank or savings institution for a checking account, you should consider the service charges. Service charges on checking accounts vary from bank to bank and with the type of account. You may be charged from $.25 to $.50 for each check you write. Some institutions offer "free checking"—no per check fee or monthly fee—providing the balance in the account remains above a certain minimum. If it drops below this minimum, a service charge of about $4 to $6 is collected. The minimum balance generally ranges from $100 to $500.

Electronic Banking

One of the most important changes in banking began in the late 1970s with the introduction of the computer. With it came **electronic funds transfer (EFT)**, a system of putting onto computers all the various banking functions that in the past had to be handled on paper.

◄

Figure 15.5
Continentals
One of the primary mediums of exchange during the Revolutionary War was the Continental bank note. Continentals, as the notes were called, held little of their original value by the war's end.

Figure 15.6 Time Line of American Money and Banking

1780s	The new nation has no reliable medium of exchange. National leaders disagree about the type of banking system the nation needs. One group, led by Alexander Hamilton, believes a well-organized banking system is necessary for industrial development. The opposition, led by Thomas Jefferson, argues that only states should have the right to charter banks.
1791	Congress establishes the First Bank of the United States and gives it a 20-year charter. The bank is a private business, though the government supplies one-fifth of its starting capital. It serves as a depository for government funds, makes loans to the government and private individuals and businesses, and regulates the activities of banks with state charters. It also issues bank notes backed by gold.
1792	Congress passes Coinage Act that organizes a mint and establishes the dollar as the basic unit of currency for the nation. The act also places the nation on a bimetallic monetary standard. A **monetary standard** is the manner in which a nation assigns value to its money. The value of the dollar is fixed according to specific quantities of both silver and gold.
1811	Congress refuses to renew the charter of the First Bank because of questions about its legality and fears that it is gaining too much power. Without federal controls, the number of private, state-chartered banks triples in five years. Dozens of banks lend money and issue bank notes freely, many of which are not backed by enough gold or silver reserves.
1816	Congress establishes the Second Bank of the United States after the financial confusion caused by the War of 1812. Like the First Bank, it brings some order to the banking system. It pressures state-chartered banks to limit lending and to keep enough gold and silver in reserve to redeem their bank notes. However, opposition to a strong national bank remains. In 1832 President Andrew Jackson vetoes legislation to extend the Second Bank's charter.
1830s–1860s	The end of the Second Bank brings another rapid rise in state-chartered banks. The amount of money in circulation varies widely. At times banks lend freely and at other times they make few loans. Such shifts in the amount of money available result in major changes in business activity and prices. Many banks issue their own bank notes.
Civil War	To help pay for the war, the United States for the first time since the Revolution issues fiat money. These United States notes, called greenbacks, change in value as confidence in the Union army rises or falls. Difficulties in raising money for the war make clear the need for a better monetary and banking system. In 1863 and 1864, Congress passes the National Bank acts. These acts establish a system of federally chartered private banks, called national banks. The government also sets up a safe, uniform currency by requiring that all national bank notes be fully backed by government bonds. The Comptroller of the Currency is created to grant charters for national banks and to oversee their activities.

Figure 15.6 Time Line of American Money and Banking

Late 1860s–early 1900s	The nation shifts to a gold monetary standard in 1879. Federal government begins redeeming early 1860s greenbacks for gold coins. Despite the new banking system, problems remain. There is no simple way to regulate the amount of national bank notes in circulation, so periodic shortages of money occur. Financial panics occur in 1873, 1884, 1893, and 1907. Many banks with low reserves are forced to close.
1913	To control the amount of money in circulation, Congress establishes the Federal Reserve System. It serves as the nation's central bank with power to regulate reserves in national banks, make loans to member banks, and control the growth of the money supply. In 1914 the system begins issuing paper money called Federal Reserve notes. These notes soon become the major form of currency in circulation.
1929	The Great Depression begins. Stocks and other investments owned by banks lose much of their value. Bankrupt businesses and individuals are unable to repay their loans.
1929–1933	A financial panic causes thousands of banks to collapse. When President Franklin Roosevelt takes office, he declares a "bank holiday," closing all banks. Each bank is allowed to reopen only after it proves it is financially sound. Congress passes the Glass-Steagall Banking Act in June, establishing the Federal Deposit Insurance Corporation (FDIC). The new agency helps restore public confidence in banks by insuring funds of individual depositors in case of a bank failure. Nation switches from gold standard to a fiat monetary standard. Government stops converting greenbacks into gold, calls in all gold coins and certificates, and prohibits private ownership of gold.
1930s–1960s	Banking reforms of the 1930s allow banks to enter a period of long-term stability, in which few banks fail.
Late 1960s–1970s	Congress passes a series of laws to protect consumers in dealing with financial institutions. Truth in Lending Act of 1968, Equal Credit Opportunity Act of 1974, and Community Reinvestment Act of 1977 make clear the rights and responsibilities of banks and consumers. Banks begin using computers to transfer money electronically and to handle many banking activities. Congress passes Electronic Fund Transfer Act of 1978 to protect consumers using these new services.
1980s–1990s	As part of the general move toward deregulation of business, Congress passes the Depository Institutions Deregulation and Monetary Control Act in 1980. The savings and loan industry faces many bankruptcies. Congress passes the Financial Institutions Reform, Recovery, and Enforcement Act of 1989. The full cost of bailing out the thrifts is $300 billion, or about $4,000 per United States family in future taxes. The FDIC takes over regulation of the thrift institutions industry. Savings and loans and commercial banks continue to fail, but at a slower rate.

One of the most common features of EFT, shown in **Figure 15.7**, is **automated teller machines (ATMs).** These units let consumers do their banking without the help of a teller.

A few banks have authorized customers with home computers to use them for banking transactions. If problems with security can be resolved, many people may one day bank by computer from home.

Figure 15.7 ATMs

ATMs receive deposits, give out funds from checking or savings accounts, transfer funds from one account to another, verify balances, and accept payments. To use an ATM, the customer inserts an encoded plastic card into the machine and enters a personal identification number (PIN) to access his or her account. ▼

EFT Concerns Although EFT can save time, trouble, and costs in making transactions, it does have some drawbacks. The possibility of tampering and lack of privacy are increased because all records are stored in a computer. A person on a computer terminal could call up and read or even alter the account files of a bank customer in any city, if he or she knew how to get around the safeguards built into the system. Another problem for customers—but a benefit for banking institutions—is the loss of "float," or the time between when you write a check and when the sum of the check is deducted from your account.

In response to these and other concerns, the Electronic Fund Transfer Act of 1978 describes the rights and responsibilities of participants in EFT systems. For example, EFT customers are responsible for only $50 in losses when someone illegally uses their card, if they report the card missing within two days. If they wait more than two days, they could be responsible for as much as $500. Users are also protected against computer foul-ups. If the balance appearing on a person's statement or given out by an automatic or human teller is less than the customer believes it should be, the bank must investigate and straighten out the problem within a certain period of time.

SECTION 2 REVIEW

Understanding Vocabulary
Define overdraft checking, electronic funds transfer (EFT), monetary standard, automated teller machines (ATMs).

Reviewing Objectives
1. What are some of the most important events in the history of American money and banking?

2. Besides checking accounts, what are some of the other services offered by banks and savings institutions?

3. How has electronic banking changed banking services?

Keeping a Checking Account

The largest part of the money supply in the United States consists of checkable accounts. Do you know how to write a check and balance a checkbook?

Writing a Check

Always fill out your checks completely and clearly in ink. See the sample check in **Figure A**.

Balancing Your Checkbook

At the end of each month when you receive your bank statement, balance your checkbook by following these steps:

❶ Sort your checks by number. Check each off in your checkbook.

❷ Check off your deposit slips.

❸ Deduct service charges and bank fees from your checkbook balance.

❹ Add to the bank statement balance any deposits that have not cleared.

❺ Total the amount of checks that have not cleared. Subtract this total from the amount on your bank statement.

Figure A

Bernadette C. Dabney	December 31 19 99
12 Vico Lane	
Haddonfield, NJ 08033	$ 100.00
Pay to _cash_	Dollars
One Hundred & 00/XX	
FIRST NATIONAL BANK	
OF CHICAGO	Bernadette C. Dabney

Figure B

Number	Date	Description	Payment of Debt	Fee	Deposit of Credit	Balance
						$ 827 91
						$ 794 91
132	10/26	Fashion Shop	$ 33 00	$		332 41
133	11/1	Rent	462 50			270 41
134	11/7	Phone	62 00			220 41
135	11/14	Cash	50 00			210 41
136	11/15	J.W. Little	10 00			189 41
137	11/15	N.Y. Times	21 00			193 41
—	11/22	John's check			4 00	694 02
—	11/23	Paycheck			500 61	653 86
138	11/29	Walk-A-Bout	40 16			191 36
139	12/1	Rent	462 50			

FIRST NATIONAL BANK OF CHICAGO

Bernadette C. Dabney
12 Vico Lane
Haddonfield, NJ 08033

123-456-7
ACCOUNT NUMBER
1 DEC 1999
STATEMENT DATE

SUMMARY OF ACCOUNTS

ACCOUNT NUMBER	PREVIOUS BALANCE	TOTAL CREDITS	TOTAL DEBITS	TOTAL CHARGES	CURRENT BALANCE
123-456-7	827.91	504.61	628.50	3.00	701.02

PREVIOUS BALANCE		CURRENT BALANCE		BALANCE
827.91				701.02
		CREDITS		794.91
DEBITS				332.41
NOV 4	132	33.00		270.41
8	133	462.50		220.41
15	134	62.00		199.41
	135	50.00		203.41
21	137	21.00	NOV 22	4.00	704.02
			23	500.61	701.02
SC		3.00		

Practicing the Skill

❶ Why should you draw a line through the unused space on the dollar amount line on a check?

❷ The sample checkbook register in **Figure B** shows that you have a running total of $191.36 in your account. Balance this total against the bank statement in **Figure B** for the month of November.

The Adams National Bank

Why Women's Banks?
During the 1970s, the idea of banks owned by women, run by women, and catering mostly to women customers gained favor in the banking community. Because women (as well as minorities) seemed to have a harder time receiving bank loans and lines of credit, these banks would specialize in the women's market. A dozen women-owned banks were chartered in the 1970s. Many believed that this marketing niche was here to stay. One of the first of these banks was The Women's National Bank in Washington, D.C. It was actually the first women-owned bank to secure a national charter.

Collapsing Market In 1975, however, Congress passed the Equal Credit Opportunity Law. This law banned discrimination against credit applicants on the grounds of sex or marital status. The perception that women's banks were necessary changed as it became easier for women to receive bank credit. Many of the women's banks had been founded with thin capitalization, and then made loans and extended credit lines for idealistic, rather than sound banking, reasons. Also, many of the women bankers associated with these banks wanted to join the banking mainstream. The banking industry also began to consolidate. Smaller banks merged into larger banks, and the original ownership was diluted. Most of the women's banks chartered in the 1970s either collapsed or were bought out by larger banks.

The Name Change

Very few women-owned banks, however, survived. One survivor was The Women's National Bank. In 1987 The Women's National Bank underwent a name change. According to Barbara Blum, the CEO since 1983, the bank's owners elected to change its name "because a lot of men wouldn't bank here." The new name, according to Blum, was to define the ownership of the bank, and not the customer base. The bank wanted to pursue a broad customer base, rather than the women-only market. The Women's National Bank changed its name to the more generic-sounding The Adams National Bank, but named the holding company that owns the bank the Abigail Adams National Bancorp. By naming the bank for one of the nation's first feminists, the owners were able to keep some of the spirit of the original name.

Since the name change, Barbara Blum has managed to convince her earlier clientele (mainly women's groups and environmental organizations) that the new name did not mean that the bank was abandoning them or turning its back on feminism. The Adams National Bank continues to be successful and is now one of only three women-owned banks in the country (the others being First Women's Bank of Rockville, MD, and Women's Bank of Denver). In 1989, Adams had 3 branches and more than $55 million in assets.

One unique difference between The Adams National Bank and other banks is its support of art and artists. The first floor of the main bank building is actually used as an art gallery. Thus The Adams National Bank keeps its image, both as a solid women-owned bank, and as a supporter of important causes.

Free Enterprise in Action

1 What was the original name of The Adams National Bank?

2 Why did the bank change its name?

3 Why did many women's banks chartered in the 1970s go out of business in the 1980s?

SECTION 3 FOCUS

Terms to Know checking account, demand deposits, checkable deposits, thrift institutions, debit card, near moneys, M1, M2

Objectives *After reading this section, you should be able to:*

1. Explain the difference between **money and near moneys**.

2. List the components of the **M2** definition of the **money supply**.

Money Is More Than Cash

When you think of money, you may think only of paper bills and coins. What does it mean to have "money in the bank"?

Money and Near Moneys

Money in use today consists of more than just currency. It also includes deposits in checking and savings accounts in banks and savings institutions, plus certain other investments.

Currency All United States coins in circulation today are token coins. The value of the metal in each coin is less than its exchange value. A quarter, for example, consists of a mixture of copper and nickel. If you melted down a quarter—which is illegal—the value of the resulting metal would be less than 25 cents. The Bureau of the Mint, which is part of the Treasury Department, makes all coins. Of the currency in circulation in the United States today, about 7 percent is in coins.

Most of the nation's currency is in the form of Federal Reserve notes. Federal Reserve banks issue these notes. The Bureau of Engraving and Printing, also part of the Treasury Department, prints all Federal Reserve notes. They are issued in denominations of $1, $5, $10, $20, $50, and $100.

The Treasury Department has also issued United States notes in $100 denominations only. These bills have the words *United States Note* printed across the top and can be distinguished from Federal Reserve notes by a red Treasury seal. United States notes make up less than 1 percent of the paper money in circulation. Both Federal Reserve notes and United States notes are fiat money or legal tender.

Checks A **checking account** is money deposited in a bank that a person can withdraw at any time by writing a check. The bank must pay the amount of the check when it is presented for payment, that is, on demand. Such accounts used to be called **demand deposits.** Today we call these **checkable deposits,** and a variety of financial institutions offer them. Commercial banks used to be the only financial institutions that could offer checkable accounts. Today all **thrift institutions**—mutual savings banks, savings and loan associations (S&Ls), and credit unions—offer checkable deposits.

Credit Cards and Debit Cards Even though many people use their credit cards to purchase goods and services, the credit card itself is not money. It does not act as a unit of accounting nor as a store of value. The use of your credit card is really a loan to you by the issuer of the card, whether it is a bank, retail store, gas company, or American Express. See **Figure 15.8.** Basically, then, credit card "money" represents a future claim on money that you will have later. Credit cards defer rather than complete transactions that ultimately involve the use of money.

As **Figure 15.9** illustrates, the **debit card** automatically withdraws money

Figure 15.9 ▲
Using Debit Cards
If the store in which you are shopping has a direct electronic link to the bank, that transfer may be made instantaneously.

▼

▼ **Figure 15.8**
Credit Card Loans
The proceeds of a credit card loan are paid to the business that sold you something. You must pay back the loan to the issuer of the credit card, either when you get your statement or with interest each month throughout the year if you do not pay off your balance owed.

Figure 15.10 ▲
Types of Money
Money is not limited just to the bills and coins in circulation today.

from a checkable account. When you use your debit card to purchase something, you are in effect giving an instruction to your bank to transfer money directly from your bank account to the store's bank account. The use of a debit card does not create a loan. Debit card "money" is similar to checkable account money.

Near Moneys Numerous other assets are almost, but not exactly, like money. See **Figure 15.10.** These assets are called **near moneys.** Their values are stated in terms of money, and they have high liquidity in comparison to other investments, such as stocks. Near moneys can be turned into currency or into a means of payment, such as a check, relatively easily and without the risk of loss of value.

Figure 15.11 ▲
M1 and M2
M1, the narrowest definition of the money supply, consists of moneys that can be spent immediately and against which checks can be written. It includes currency, traveler's checks, and checkable deposits. A broader definition of the money supply, **M2,** includes all of M1, plus such near moneys as money market mutual fund balances and Eurodollars.

For example, if you have a bank savings account, you cannot write a check on it. You can, however, go to the bank and withdraw some or all of your funds. You can then redeposit it in your checking account or take some or all of it in cash.

Time deposits and savings-account balances are near moneys. Both pay interest, and neither can be withdrawn by check. Time deposits require that a depositor notify the financial institution within a certain period of time, often 10 days, before withdrawing money. Savings accounts do not usually require such notification

The Money Supply

How much money is there in the United States today? That question is not so easy to answer. First, the money supply must be defined and agreed upon. Currently, two basic definitions are used, although others exist. The first is called M1 and the second M2. Both definitions include all the paper bills and coins in circulation. **Figure 15.11** (page 378) expands on both M1 and M2. Measuring M1 or M2 exactly is difficult. **Figure 15.12** shows the growth of M1 and M2 over a 10-year period.

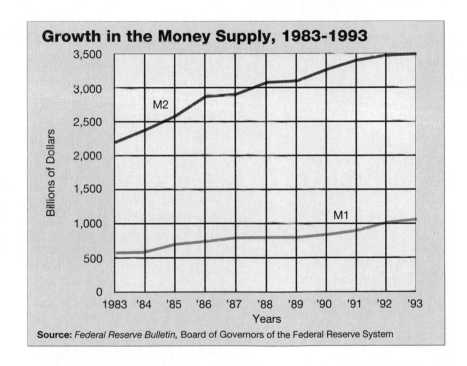

Growth in the Money Supply, 1983-1993

Source: *Federal Reserve Bulletin,* Board of Governors of the Federal Reserve System

◀

Figure 15.12
Growth in the Money Supply, 1983–1993
With the deregulation of banking services in the early 1980s, the definition of the money supply was enlarged to include the new types of accounts.

SECTION 3 REVIEW

Understanding Vocabulary
Define checking account, demand deposits, checkable deposits, thrift institutions, debit card, near moneys, M1, M2.

Reviewing Objectives
① What is the difference between money and near moneys?

② There are two definitions of money, M1 and M2. What does the M2 definition of money include?

News Clip

Readings in Economics

KIPLINGER'S PERSONAL FINANCE MAGAZINE   **JANUARY 1993**

HAD IT WITH YOUR BANK'S FEES?

by Kristin Davis

Some banks offer as many as nine different kinds of accounts, says Anne Moore, president of Synergistics, a banking research firm. The key is finding the account that charges least for your banking pattern.

Review recent account statements. How many checks do you write per month? How many ATM transactions do you make? How widely does your balance fluctuate? If you write fewer than ten or so checks, a "basic" account may be cheapest. Fees are usually minimal, but you pay a per-check charge if you go over the limit. . . . If you *never* use a live teller, an account that offers free ATM use but charges a fee for teller transactions may save you money. Wells Fargo and Bank of America offer such accounts.

Compare minimum balances. With interest rates on money-market accounts below 3%, it costs you relatively little in forgone income to keep a minimum balance in a checking account (even a non-interest-bearing one) to avoid checking fees. Keeping the average minimum balance of $500 in a non-interest-bearing account costs you about $15 a year in lost interest—less than the average fee of around $60 a year. . . .

Beware of "special" fees. Some banks charge for things like copies of checks. If you need services such as money orders, cashier's checks or a safe-deposit box, ask about "packaged" accounts that include those services in your fee. But don't pay more for a bundled account if you don't need the extras.

Ask about fee waivers. If you use direct deposit for your paycheck, some banks give you a break. . . .

Skip the middleman when ordering checks. Direct mailers such as Current . . . or Checks in the Mail . . . sell 200 checks for $5 to $7. Banks typically charge twice that.

• THINK ABOUT IT •

1. **What four things does Moore think people should look for when opening new accounts?**

2. **What is the advantage of ordering checks from direct mailers?**

Section 1

The Functions and Characteristics of Money

Key Terms

money (p. 362)
medium of exchange (p. 362)
barter (p. 362)
double coincidence of wants (p. 364)
unit of accounting (p. 364)

store of value (p. 364)
commodity money (p. 365)
representative money (p. 366)
fiat money (p. 366)
legal tender (p. 366)

Summary

Anything is considered money that is used as a medium of exchange, a unit of accounting, and a store of value. Today all United States money is fiat money. It is portable, divisible, stable in value, and accepted. Paper currency is not very durable, however.

Section 2

History of American Money and Banking

Key Terms

overdraft checking (p. 369)
electronic funds transfer (EFT) (p. 369)

monetary standard (p. 370)
automated teller machines (ATMs) (p. 372)

Summary

The history of the nation's money and banks has been a process of gradually bringing order to a disordered system. Congress took the first step in this direction in 1792 when it established the dollar as the basic unit of currency and set up the first mint. Modern banking services include many services in addition to checking and savings accounts.

Section 3

Types of Money in the United States

Key Terms

checking account (p. 376)
demand deposits (p. 377)
checkable deposits (p. 377)
thrift institutions (p. 377)

debit card (p. 377)
near moneys (p. 378)
M1 (p. 378)
M2 (p. 378)

Summary

United States money today is in the form of currency, checkable deposits, and near moneys. The M1 definition of the money supply includes currency, traveler's checks, and checkable deposits in commercial banks and thrift institutions. The M2 definition of money includes M1 plus certain near moneys.

15 Review

Identifying Key Terms

Write the letter of the definition in Column B below that correctly defines each term in Column A.

Column A
1. fiat money (p. 366)
2. checkable deposits (p. 377)
3. M1 (p. 378)
4. commodity money (p. 365)
5. near moneys (p. 378)
6. legal tender (p. 366)
7. electronic funds transfer (EFT) (p. 369)

Column B
a. money that by law must be accepted for payment of debts
b. currency in circulation, traveler's checks, plus checking-type deposits
c. money in a bank that can be withdrawn at any time
d. money that has value because the government has established it as acceptable payment for debts
e. computerized banking functions that previously were handled on paper
f. assets that can be turned into money fairly easily
g. money that has value aside from its value as money

Use terms from the following list to fill in the blanks in the paragraph below.

store of value (p. 364)
representative money (p. 366)
checking accounts (p. 376)

The United States used to print __(8)__, which consisted of silver and gold certificates. Every money should serve the function of a medium of exchange, a unit of accounting, and a __(9)__. Virtually all banks and thrift institutions offer __(10)__, so that people can withdraw money at any time.

Recalling Facts and Ideas

Section 1
1. What is the alternative to using money?
2. Money should be durable and divisible. What other characteristics should money have?
3. Is the type of money used in the United States commodity, representative, or fiat?

Section 2
4. What type of system did the early colonists use when they bought and sold goods and services?
5. When was the most serious banking panic of the twentieth century?
6. Electronic banking is increasingly common today. What form of this system do most consumers use?

Section 3
7. What are the only denominations of paper currency being issued today by the federal government?
8. Why did checking accounts used to be called demand deposits?
9. What is the distinction between money and near moneys?
10. Why is M1 considered a narrower definition of the money supply than M2?

Critical Thinking

Section 1
Making Comparisons Compare the costs and benefits of engaging in barter to the costs and benefits of using money.

Section 2
Drawing Conclusions Why are pure gold and/or pure silver coins not used as the only money in the United States?

Section 3

Making Generalizations Why are debit cards similar to money, whereas credit cards are not?

Applying Economic Concepts

The Functions of Money The three functions of money are medium of exchange, unit of accounting, and store of value. Keep track of any time you use money, see money used, or see dollar values written out somewhere. Try to determine in each instance what function the money is serving. For example, if you see a headline that says "Microsoft Corporation sales increased to $10 billion," you know that money is being used as a unit of accounting.

Chapter Projects

1. **Individual Project** Do a survey of the ATMs in your area. Some are offered by banks and some are on multiple bank systems. What is the difference? What bank cards, debit cards, and ATM cards can be used in the different machines? What other services do ATMs offer, particularly the ones that are physically connected to a bank?

2. **Cooperative Learning Project** Between 1929 and 1933, the United States underwent a tragic economic depression. The banking system, prices, incomes, and employment changed dramatically during this period. Work in groups to research a history of the following:

   - What happened to incomes and prices?
   - What happened to banks and savings accounts?
   - What happened to the availability of jobs?

   The members of each group should interview at least one person who lived during that period and who was old enough to be aware of what was happening economically. Each person should take notes on the interviews. Each group will summarize the different interview notes to develop an oral history of what actually happened during the Great Depression.

Reviewing Skills

Keeping a Checking Account

Balancing Your Checkbook Write a paragraph explaining the process you used when you were practicing the skill of balancing a checkbook on page 373.

Writing About Economics

Descriptive Writing During the week, you probably recorded several items in Your Economics Journal that you purchased without using fiat money. Imagine a society in the past or in the future that does not depend on fiat money such as the currency used by the United States. Write a description of how an individual in that society obtains necessities such as food, clothing, and shelter.

Point

ISSUE: Can the Economy Be Fine-Tuned Using Fiscal and Monetary Policies?

For years, economists have debated the question of whether the government should enact activist fiscal and monetary policies to fix economic problems. Not only do economists debate whether these policies should be used, but they also debate whether the policies even work. Traditional Keynesian economics tells us that government should spend more and tax less during bad economic times. Some economists argue that this type of fiscal policy is irresponsible, enlarging the deficit while helping the economy very little.

PRO In an article in *The New York Times*, Peter Passell presents the traditional Keynesian view. He refers to the Keynesian economists as "they":

As recently as the early 1970s most economists thought they knew how to take the sting out of recessions. A decline in the inclination of businesses and consumers to spend, they said, could leave a gap between the total demand for goods and the economy's capacity to provide them. And while the gap would eventually close without government intervention, eventually could be a very long time indeed. What was needed to offset swings in private demand, they argued, was some combination of tax

cuts and government spending, plus an increase in funds available for bank loans.

In the early 1980s, economist and Nobel Laureate James Tobin offered his view of activist policies to smooth out business cycles:

. . . I don't believe stable government policies necessarily mean the economy will be stabilized. History doesn't suggest the economy will stay on even keel if the government just keeps its hands off or runs things according to some well understood rules. Shocks of nongovernmental origin—from overseas, and in our technology and the tastes of consumers—have created business fluctuations throughout the history of capitalism. What governments have tried to do since 1945 is to offset these shocks.

Sometimes, it is true, government has been the source of shocks. But if you compare pre-World War II history with the recent era, in which governments . . . have pursued activist economic policies, the results of activism have been very good.

Counterpoint

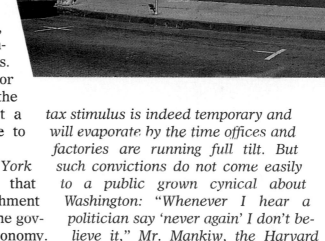

CON Milton Friedman has been one of the major critics of activist fiscal and monetary policies. He writes that, because of time lags involved in fiscal policy, any government action may make the problem even worse. He claims that government intervention policies have intensified business cycles. He also blames the monetary policy of the Federal Reserve for contributing to economic instability, leading to more inflations and contractions than in the pre-Fed years. Friedman has often written in favor of a "monetary rule," whereby the money supply would increase at a fixed rate that does not change to counter business cycles.

In his article in *The New York Times*, Peter Passell writes that today the economics establishment has lost faith in the ability of the government to fine-tune the economy. He quotes economist Gregory Mankiw of Harvard on some of the problems of fiscal policies:

Once the need for fiscal stimulus is recognized, he notes, it may take months to pass the necessary legislation. Hence the full impact may only hit the economy after the recovery is under way and the stimulus is no longer welcome. Even if the stimulus does hit in timely fashion, public fears that it will ignite inflation may push up interest rates and slow business investments.

That should not be a significant problem if the public is convinced that the spending of tax stimulus is indeed temporary and will evaporate by the time offices and factories are running full tilt. But such convictions do not come easily to a public grown cynical about Washington: "Whenever I hear a politician say 'never again' I don't believe it," Mr. Mankiw, the Harvard economist, said.

Exploring the Issue

Reviewing Facts

1 What does Tobin view as the purpose of fiscal policy?

2 According to Milton Friedman why does fiscal policy harm the economy?

Critical Thinking

3 What do you think a "traditional Keynesian" economist would think of Friedman's idea of a monetary rule?

CHAPTER 16

THE FEDERAL RESERVE SYSTEM AND MONETARY POLICY

Who determines how many dollar bills are in circulation?

What happens when dollar bills wear out?

Where will these dollar bills go?

Do you ever receive crisp, new dollar bills?

Where was this money printed?

Your Economics Journal

Study the bills you have in your purse or wallet. The face of each bill identifies the Federal Reserve Bank that issued it. Keep a log to record the bank that issued each bill you see during the week. At the end of the week, your class can tally all the logs to determine how much local currency originated in your district Federal Reserve Bank.

1 Money Supply and the Economy

SECTION 1 FOCUS

Terms to Know the Fed, monetary policy, loose money policy, tight money policy, fractional reserve banking, reserve requirements

Objectives *After reading this section, you should be able to:*

1. Contrast **loose money and tight money policies**.
2. Describe **fractional reserve banking**.
3. Explain **money expansion** in the banking system.

The Federal Reserve and the Money Supply

Congress created the Federal Reserve System in 1913 as the central banking organization in the United States. Its major purpose was to end the periodic financial panics that had occurred during the 1800s and into the early 1900s. Over the years, many other responsibilities have been added to the Federal Reserve System, or **the Fed**, as it is called. See **Figure 16.1**. The jobs of the Fed today range from processing checks to serving as the government's banker. Its most important function, however, involves control over the rate of growth of the money supply.

Figure 16.1
The Fed
The 12 Federal Reserve banks that serve the nation's banks are distributed throughout the country. Trillions of dollars a year pass through the Fed.

Loose and Tight Money Policies

You may have read a news report in which a business executive or public official complained that money is "too tight." You may have run across a story about an economist warning that money is "too loose." In these cases the terms *tight* and *loose* are referring to the monetary policy of the nation's Federal Reserve System. **Monetary policy** involves changing the rate of growth of the supply of money in circulation to affect the amount of credit and, therefore, business activity in the economy.

Credit, like any good or service,

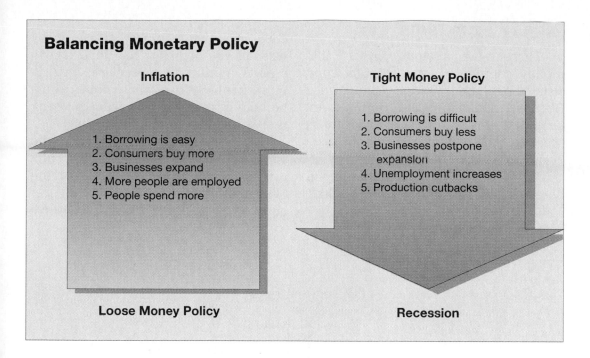

Balancing Monetary Policy

Inflation

1. Borrowing is easy
2. Consumers buy more
3. Businesses expand
4. More people are employed
5. People spend more

Loose Money Policy

Tight Money Policy

1. Borrowing is difficult
2. Consumers buy less
3. Businesses postpone expansion
4. Unemployment increases
5. Production cutbacks

Recession

Figure 16.2 Loose Money Versus Tight Money Look at the chart and determine the differences between loose money policy and tight money policy. Which of these can lead to a recession? Why is this possible?

is subject to the laws of supply and demand. Also, like any good or service, credit has a cost. The cost of credit is the interest that must be paid to obtain it. As the cost of credit increases, the quantity demanded decreases. In contrast, if the cost of borrowing drops, the quantity of credit demanded rises.

Figure 16.2 shows the results of monetary policy decisions. If a country has a **loose money policy,** credit is inexpensive to borrow and abundant. If a country has a **tight money policy,** credit is expensive to borrow and in short supply.

If this is the case, why would any nation want a tight money policy? The answer is to control inflation. See **Figure 16.2.** If money becomes too plentiful too quickly, prices increase and the purchasing power of the dollar decreases dramatically. This situation occurred during the Revolutionary War. The supply of Continental currency grew so rapidly that notes became almost worthless.

The goal of monetary policy is to strike a balance between tight and loose money. It is the Fed's responsi-

bility to ensure that money and credit are plentiful enough to allow expansion of the economy. The Fed cannot, however, let the money supply become so plentiful that rapid inflation results.

Fractional Reserve Banking

Before you are able to understand how the Fed regulates the nation's money supply, you need to understand the basis of the United States banking system and the way money is created. The banking system is based on what is called **fractional reserve banking.**

Since 1913 the Fed has set specific **reserve requirements** for many banks. They must hold a certain percentage of their total deposits either as cash in their own vaults or as deposits in their district Federal Reserve bank. Currently most financial institutions must keep 10 percent of their checkable deposits in reserves with the Federal Reserve. They do not have to keep any reserves on so-called nonpersonal time deposits.

Money Expansion

Currency is a small part of the money supply. A larger portion consists of bank deposits the public owns. Because banks are not required to keep 100 percent of their deposits in reserve, they can use their deposits to create what is, in effect, new money.

Suppose you sell a government bond to the Fed and receive $1,000. This is $1,000 in "new" money be-cause the Fed simply creates it by writing you a check. You deposit it in a bank. With a 10 percent reserve requirement, $100 of that money must be held in reserve. However, the bank is free to lend the remaining $900.

Suppose another customer asks the same bank for a $900 loan. The bank creates $900 simply by transferring $900 to the customer's checking account. The bank must keep in reserve

**Figure 16.3
Expanding the
Money Supply**
The chart shows how
$1,000 expands to
$5,000 by simple loans.
How does this happen?
▼

Multiple Expansion of the Money Supply

Round	Deposited by	Amount of Deposit	Required Reserves (20%)	Excess Reserves (80%)	Loaned to	Paid to
1	Student (you) (Bank A)	$1,000	$200.00	$800.00	John Jones	Jackson's Supply Company
2	Jackson's (Bank B)	800	160.00	640.00	Ms. Wang	Mr. Diaz
3	Mr. Diaz (Bank C)	640	128.00	512.00	Mrs. Fontana	Mrs. Powers
4	Mrs. Powers (Bank D)	512	102.40	409.60	Mr. Gibbs	Mr. Santana
5	Mr. F. Santana (Bank E)	409.60	81.92	327.68		
6						
Eventual Totals		$5,000	$1,000			

10 percent of this new deposit—$90, but now it can lend the remaining $810. This $810 is in turn treated as a new deposit. Ninety percent of it—$729—can again be lent. The original $1,000 has become $3,439. So it goes; each new deposit gives the bank new funds to continue lending.

Of course, a bank is not likely to continue lending and receiving back the same money. Its customers will most likely withdraw money and spend it or deposit it in another bank; however, this does not stop the creation of money. As the money finds its way into a second and third bank, and so on, each bank can use the nonrequired reserve portion of the money to make more loans.

How the Money Supply Increases

Money expansion may seem confusing. Let's examine step by step the example shown in **Figure 16.3**. **Round 1:** Suppose you have $1,000 that you take to your bank (Bank A) and deposit in your checking account. Assume that the Fed requires your bank to keep 20 percent of its total deposits on reserve. Your bank must hold $200 of your deposit on reserve. This leaves the bank with $800 of excess reserves, which is not earning interest.

Round 2: Bank A decides to loan out $800 to earn interest. John Jones applies to the bank for an $800 loan. Bank A finds him creditworthy and credits his account with $800. Mr. Jones borrowed the money to buy a machine for his business from Jackson's Supply Company. He writes a check to Jackson's, and the company deposits it at Bank B, which credits $800 to Jackson's account balance. Bank B's reserves increase by $800. Of this amount, $160 (20 percent of $800) are required reserves, and the remaining $640 are excess reserves.

Round 3: To earn profits, Bank B loans its excess reserves to Ms. Wang, who wants to borrow $640. She, in turn, buys something from Mr. Diaz, who does his banking at Bank C. He deposits the money from Ms. Wang. Bank C now has $640 in new deposits, of which $128 are required reserves. Bank C now loans $512 of excess reserves to Mrs. Fontana, who buys something from Mrs. Powers, and so on. The result is that a deposit of $1,000 in new money that was outside of the banking system has caused the money supply to increase to $5,000. This process is called the multiple expansion of the money supply.

SECTION 1 REVIEW

Understanding Vocabulary

Define the Fed, monetary policy, loose money policy, tight money policy, fractional reserve banking, reserve requirements.

Reviewing Objectives

1 What is the difference between loose money and tight money policies?

2 What is the purpose of fractional reserve banking?

3 If there is a 10 percent reserve requirement, how much does the money supply expand if the Fed injects $100 of new money?

Personal Perspective

Milton Friedman on the Federal Reserve

Profile

- 1912–
- won Nobel Prize for Economics in 1976
- leading supporter of monetarism
- among his many publications are *The Monetary History of the U.S. 1867–1960* with Anna J. Schwartz (1963), *Capitalism and Freedom* (1962), and *Free to Choose* with Rose Friedman (1980)

Milton Friedman has written extensively on the monetary history of the United States. He is often critical of the actions of the Federal Reserve System. In the following excerpt from *Capitalism and Freedom*, Friedman explains why he does not approve of the Federal Reserve and gives a possible replacement solution to regulating the money supply.

The establishment of the Federal Reserve System . . . established a separate official body charged with explicit responsibility for monetary conditions, and supposedly clothed with adequate power to achieve monetary stability or, at least, to prevent pronounced instability. It is therefore instructive to compare experience as a whole before and after its establishment— say, from just after the Civil War to 1914 and from 1914 to date.

. . . The stock of money, prices, and output was decidedly more unstable after the establishment of the Reserve System than before. . . .

The Great Depression in the United States, far from being a sign of the inherent instability of the private enterprise system, is a testament to how much harm can be done by mistakes on the part of a few men when they wield vast power over the monetary system of a country.

. . . Any system which gives so much power and so much discretion to a few men that mistakes—excusable or not—can have such far-reaching effects is a bad system. It is a bad system to believers in freedom just because it gives a few men such power without any effective check by the body politic—this is the key political argument against an "independent" central bank.

. . . My choice at the moment would be . . . instructing the monetary authority to achieve a specified rate of growth in the stock of money. . . . I would specify that the Reserve System shall see to it that the total stock of money so defined rises . . . at an annual rate of X per cent, where X is a number between 3 and 5.

Checking for Understanding

1. What does Friedman's study reveal about the stability of monetary conditions in the United States after the establishment of the Fed?
2. What is Friedman's argument against an "independent" central bank?
3. What rule does Friedman propose to govern decisions of the Federal Reserve System?

SECTION 2 Organization and Functions of the Federal Reserve System

The Federal Reserve Serves Many Functions

The organization of the Federal Reserve System is shown in **Figure 16.5** on page 394. As its name states, the Fed is a system, or network, of banks. Power is not concentrated in a single central bank but is shared by a governing board and 12 district banks.

Organization of the Federal Reserve System

The Federal Reserve System is made up of the Board of Governors assisted by the Federal Advisory Council, the Federal Open Market Committee, 12 Federal Reserve banks, and about 5,000 member banks. This system is responsible for monetary policy in the free enterprise system of the United States.

Board of Governors The Board of Governors directs the operations of the Fed. It establishes policies regarding such things as reserve requirements and discount rates. The board also supervises the 12 district Federal Reserve banks and regulates certain activities of member banks and all other depository institutions.

The seven full-time members of the Board of Governors are appointed by the President of the United States with the approval of the Senate. See **Figure 16.4**. The President chooses one member as a chairperson. Each member of the board serves for 14 years.

**Figure 16.4
The Board**
The Board of Governors can raise or lower the discount rate in relation to prevailing market rates. ◀

The terms are arranged so that an opening occurs every two years. Members cannot be reappointed, and their decisions are not subject to the approval of the President or Congress. Their length of term, manner of selection, and independence in working frees members from political pressures. Members do not have to fear that their sometimes-unpopular decisions will cause them to lose their jobs at election time.

The Board of Governors is assisted by the Federal Advisory Council (FAC). It is made up of 12 members elected by the directors of each Federal Reserve bank. The Federal Advisory Council meets at least 4 times each year and reports to the Board of Governors on general business conditions in the nation.

Federal Open Market Committee
The **Federal Open Market Committee (FOMC)** meets approximately eight times a year to decide the course of action that the Fed should take to control the money supply.

Federal Reserve Banks Each of the 12 Federal Reserve district banks is set up as a corporation owned by its member banks. A 9-person board of directors made up of bankers and businesspeople supervises each Federal Reserve district bank. The system includes 25 Federal Reserve branch banks as shown on the map in **Figure 16.6**. These smaller banks act as branch offices and aid the district banks in carrying out their duties.

Member Banks All national banks—those chartered by the federal government—are required to become members of the Federal Reserve System. Banks chartered by the states may join if they choose to do so. Currently, the 5,000 member banks include all of the national banks and some of the state banks. To become a member bank, a national or state bank buys stock in its district's Federal Reserve bank.

Figure 16.5
Organization of the Federal Reserve System
Since the change in banking regulations in the early 1980s, nonmember banks are also subject to some control by the Federal Reserve System.

▼

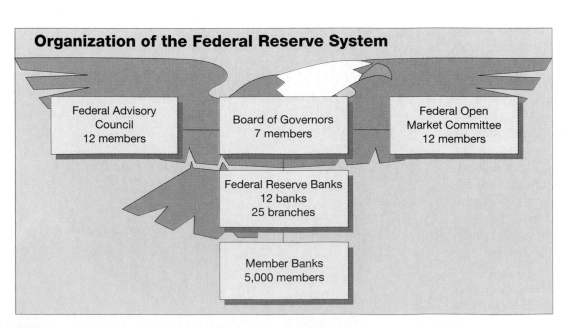

Organization of the Federal Reserve System

Federal Advisory Council
12 members

Board of Governors
7 members

Federal Open Market Committee
12 members

Federal Reserve Banks
12 banks
25 branches

Member Banks
5,000 members

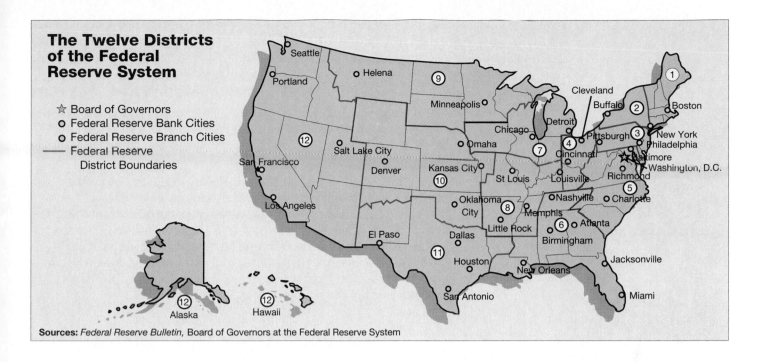

The Twelve Districts of the Federal Reserve System

☆ Board of Governors
○ Federal Reserve Bank Cities
○ Federal Reserve Branch Cities
— Federal Reserve District Boundaries

Seattle
Portland
Helena
⑨
Minneapolis
Cleveland
Buffalo
②
Boston
①
Detroit
Chicago
Pittsburgh
③
New York
Philadelphia
④
Cincinnati
⑦
Omaha
Salt Lake City
⑫
San Francisco
Denver
Kansas City
⑩
St Louis
Louisville
Richmond
Baltimore
Washington, D.C.
⑤
Los Angeles
Oklahoma City
⑧
Nashville
Charlotte
Memphis
Little Rock
Atlanta
⑥
El Paso
Dallas
Birmingham
⑪
Houston
New Orleans
Jacksonville
San Antonio
Miami
Alaska ⑫
Hawaii ⑫

Sources: *Federal Reserve Bulletin,* Board of Governors at the Federal Reserve System

In the past, only member banks were required to meet regulations, such as those setting specific reserve requirements. Now all institutions that accept deposits must keep reserves in their district Federal Reserve bank. Federal Reserve services are also available to all depository institutions—member or nonmember—for a fee.

Figure 16.6 ▲
The Federal Reserve System
Look at the map of the Federal Reserve System above. Note that the Fed is headquartered in Washington, D.C. The United States Treasury appears on the back of the $10 Federal Reserve Note. Find and list the 12 Federal Reserve district bank cities.
▼

IN GOD WE TRUST

Figure 16.7 Functions of the Federal Reserve

Responsibility	Description
Clearing checks	**Check clearing** is the method by which a check that has been deposited in one depository institution is transferred to the depository institution on which it was written. Figure 16.9 (page 398) explains this process.
Acting as the federal government's fiscal agent	The federal government collects large sums of money through taxation and spends and distributes even more. It deposits some of this money in the Federal Reserve and distributes the rest among thousands of commercial banks. As the federal government's fiscal, or financial, agent the Fed keeps track of these deposits and holds a checking account for the United States Treasury. Checks for such payments as Social Security, tax refunds, and veterans' benefits are drawn on this account. The Fed also acts as a financial adviser to the federal government.
Supervising member banks	The Fed along with the Comptroller of the Currency and the Federal Deposit Insurance Corporation (FDIC) supervises and regulates member commercial banks. Nonmember commercial and savings banks as well as savings and loan associations and credit unions are regulated by other agencies. Because the comptroller supervises national banks, the Fed oversees state-chartered member banks. Among the Fed's duties are setting limits for loans and investments by member banks, approving bank mergers, and examining the books of member banks.
Holding and setting reserve requirements	All depository institutions are required by law to keep a certain percentage of their deposits in reserve. Each of the 12 Federal Reserve banks holds the reserve requirements of member and nonmember depository institutions in its district. By raising or lowering the percentage required, within the limits set by Congress, the Fed can change the amount of money in circulation.
Supplying paper currency	Since 1914 the Federal Reserve System has been responsible for printing and maintaining much of the nation's paper money. All Federal Reserve notes are printed in Washington, D.C., at the Bureau of Printing and Engraving. Each note, however, has a code number indicating which of the 12 Federal Reserve banks issued it. The money is shipped from the bureau to the appropriate bank to be put into circulation. Much of this money simply replaces old bills; however, each Federal Reserve bank must have on hand a sufficient amount of cash to meet the demands for paper currency during different times of the year. For example, during the Christmas season, commercial banks find that their depositors withdraw large amounts of cash. The banks then must turn to the Federal Reserve banks to replace it. After Christmas, depositors redeposit their money. The banks can then return what they borrowed to their district Federal Reserve bank.
Regulating the money supply	The primary responsibility of the Federal Reserve is determining the amount of money in circulation, which, in turn, affects the amount of credit and business activity in the economy.

Figure 16.8 ▶
Federal Reserve Banks
All Federal Reserve banks, like the one in San Francisco, help formulate monetary policy, including regulating the money supply. Before the Fed was established in 1913, the United States had not had a central bank since the Second Bank of the United States in the mid-1800s, and individual banks often printed money.

Today the major advantage of membership is that member banks, as stockholders in their district bank, are able to vote for six of its nine board members. Member banks also receive dividends on their stock in the district bank.

The Functions of the Federal Reserve System

The Federal Reserve has a number of functions as shown in **Figure 16.7**. Among them are check clearing, acting as the federal government's fiscal agent, supervising member banks, holding and setting reserve requirements, supplying paper currency, and regulating the money supply. The most important function of the Fed is regulating the money supply. See **Figure 16.8**. Check clearing is also an important and complex function. See **Figure 16.9** (page 398).

Consumer Protection The Federal Reserve also sets standards for certain types of consumer legislation, mainly truth-in-lending legislation. By law, sellers of goods and services must make some kinds of information available to people who buy on credit. This information includes the amount of interest and size of the monthly payment to be paid. The Federal Reserve System decides what type of credit information must be supplied to consumers.

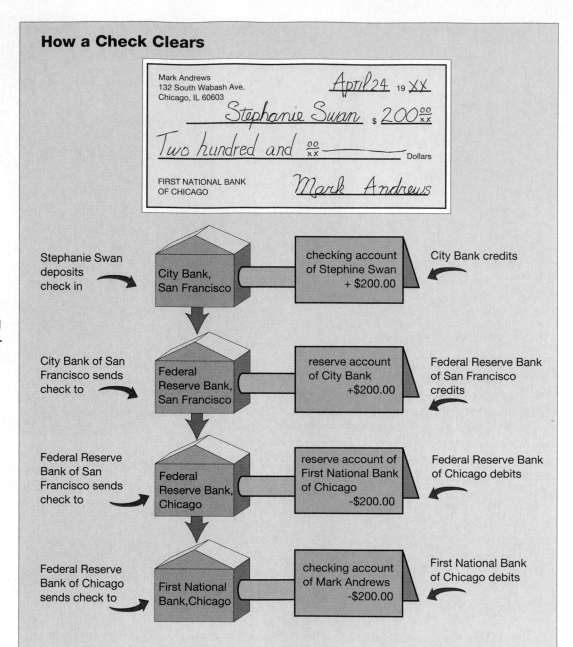

How a Check Clears

Mark Andrews
132 South Wabash Ave.
Chicago, IL 60603

April 24 19 XX

Stephanie Swan $ *200.00/xx*

Two hundred and 00/xx _____ Dollars

FIRST NATIONAL BANK
OF CHICAGO

Mark Andrews

Stephanie Swan deposits check in → City Bank, San Francisco — checking account of Stephine Swan + $200.00 — City Bank credits ←

City Bank of San Francisco sends check to → Federal Reserve Bank, San Francisco — reserve account of City Bank +$200.00 — Federal Reserve Bank of San Francisco credits ←

Federal Reserve Bank of San Francisco sends check to → Federal Reserve Bank, Chicago — reserve account of First National Bank of Chicago -$200.00 — Federal Reserve Bank of Chicago debits ←

Federal Reserve Bank of Chicago sends check to → First National Bank, Chicago — checking account of Mark Andrews -$200.00 — First National Bank of Chicago debits ←

Figure 16.9 ▶
Check Clearing
All depository institutions may use the Federal Reserve's check-clearing system. *Reserve account* refers to a bank's account in its Federal Reserve district bank.

SECTION 2 REVIEW

Understanding Vocabulary

Define Federal Open Market Committee (FOMC), check clearing.

Reviewing Objectives

❶ How is the Federal Reserve System in the United States organized?

❷ The Federal Reserve clears checks and acts as the government's fiscal agent. What are three other functions of the Federal Reserve?

Understanding Real and Nominal Values

Inflation has been a problem since World War II. This means that to make comparisons between the prices of things in the past and those of today, you have to make the distinction between *nominal*, or current, and *real*, or constant, values.

The Price of Houses

If a couple told you that they bought their house for $50,000 10 years ago and sold it for $100,000 today, would they have made a "profit" of $50,000? The answer is no, because of inflation. If, for example, the consumer price index (CPI) was 100 when they bought the house and had risen to 200 when they sold their house, the *real* price of their house would not have changed at all, as **Figure A** shows.

Determining What Happens to Your Income

Sometimes much of the raise a worker receives is eaten away by inflation. To determine the real value of a raise, subtract the rate of inflation. For example, assume you are making $10 an hour (after taxes) this year and next year your boss gives you a 5 percent raise. Are you 5 percent better off? The answer depends on the rate of inflation during that year. If the increase in the CPI was 3 percent, your real salary increase was only 2 percent as **Figure B** shows.

The government uses an implicit price deflator to compare GDP year by year. See **Figure C**.

Figure A
Determine Percentage Increase in Nominal Price

Divide amount of increase by original price. Multiply result by 100 to get percent.

$$\frac{50,000}{50,000} = 1 \times 100 = 100\%$$

Determine Percentage Increase in Consumer Price Index

Divide amount of increase in CPI by original index. Multiply result by 100 to get percent.

$$\frac{100}{100} = 1 \times 100 = 100\%$$

Determine Percentage Increase in Real Price

Subtract percentage increase in CPI from percentage increase in nominal price.

100%	increase in nominal price
−100%	increase in CPI
0%	increase in real price

Figure B

Real salary increase equals increase in nominal salary minus rate of inflation.

5%	nominal raise
− 3%	inflation rate
2%	real raise

Figure C

The real GDP is found by dividing the nominal GDP by the implicit price deflator and multiplying the result by 100.

$$\frac{\text{nominal GDP}}{\text{implicit price deflator}} \times 100 = \text{real GDP}$$

Practicing the Skill

Real GDP in 1987 was $4,539.9 billion. In 1992, nominal GDP was $5,950.7 billion. The implicit GDP price deflator was 120.9. What was real GDP in 1992 expressed in 1987 dollars?

Figure 16.10
The Economy
When a nation's economy is running smoothly with low inflation, people are more inclined to spend income on nonessentials or luxuries. Restaurants enjoy more business during economic booms.

▶

The Fed's Difficult Job

The Federal Reserve has as its goal maintaining enough money to keep the money supply growing steadily and the economy running smoothly without inflation. See Figure 16.10. To accomplish this, it has three major tools: reserve requirements, the discount rate, and open-market operations.

Changing Reserve Requirements

The Federal Reserve can choose to control the money supply by changing the reserve requirements of financial institutions. The lower the percentage of deposits that must be kept in reserve, the more dollars are available to loan. The reverse is also true. **Figure 16.11** explains how changes in the reserve requirement affect the nation's money supply.

As **Figure 16.11C** shows, the Fed may raise reserve requirements. To build up its reserves to meet the new requirement, a bank has several possibilities. It can call in some loans, sell off securities or other investments, or borrow from another bank or the Fed-

Raising and Lowering Reserve Requirements

Bank A deposits = $1,000,000
Reserve requirements 10% x $1,000,000 = $100,000
Bank may loan $900,000
Suppose a bank has $1 million in deposits and the reserve requirement is 10 percent. The bank must keep at least $100,000 in reserves.

Bank B deposits = $1,000,000
Fed lowers reserve requirement to 5% x $1,000,000 = $50,000
Bank may loan $950,000
If the Fed wanted to increase the money supply, it could lower the reserve requirerment to 5 percent, for example. The bank would then need to keep only $50,000 in reserve. It could lend out the other $950,000. This additional $50,000 would expand the money supply many times over as it was lent and redeposited. This could help pull the economy out of a recession.

Bank C deposits = $1,000,000
Fed raises reserve requirement to 15% x $1,000,000 = $150,000
Bank may loan $850,000
Suppose instead that the Fed wanted to decrease the money supply, or at least slow down its rate of growth. It could do this by increasing the reserve requirement from 10 to 15 percent. The bank in the example above would then need to keep $150,000 on reserve – $50,000 more than before with a 10% reserve requirement.

▲
Figure 16.11
Reserve Requirements
Look at the chart above to see how depository institutions are affected if the Federal Reserve decides to raise or lower the reserve requirement.

cral Reserve. Obviously, because all banks would have to increase their reserves, this action would greatly decrease the amount of money in the economy. This could be used to help slow down the economy if it were expanding too rapidly.

Even small changes in the reserve requirement can have major effects on the money supply. As a result, some believe that this tool is not precise enough to make frequent small adjustments to the money supply. In recent years, changing the reserve requirement has not been used often to regulate the money supply.

Changing the Discount Rate

Sometimes a depository institution will find itself without enough reserves to meet its reserve requirement. This situation may occur if customers unexpectedly borrow a great deal of money or if depositors suddenly withdraw large amounts.

The bank must then borrow to meet its reserve requirement, at least temporarily. One of the ways it can do this is to ask its district Federal Reserve bank for a loan. The district bank, like any other bank, will charge interest. The rate of interest the Fed charges is called the **discount rate.**

A bank, like a consumer, follows the law of demand. At higher discount rates, a bank may decide to borrow fewer reserves from the Fed or none at all. It could meet its reserve requirement by borrowing from another bank. This money would then be taken out of circulation and would not be available for lending to individuals or businesses.

If a bank does decide to borrow at a high discount rate, it will need to pass its increased costs on to customers in the form of higher interest rates on loans. For example, it might raise its **prime rate**—the rate it charges its best business customers. High discount rates, by discouraging borrowing, will also keep down the growth of the money supply. In contrast, if the discount rate is low, even a bank with sufficient reserves might borrow money. The loan will raise the bank's reserves and increase its ability to make loans. Thus, a reduction in the discount rate increases the total money supply.

Open-Market Operations

Buying and selling United States securities, called **open-market operations,** is the tool the Fed most often uses. Open-market operations affect the money supply by changing depository institution reserves, thereby putting money into or taking it out of circulation in the economy.

The term *open market* is used because these securities are traded in the open market through regular securities dealers. An open market is one that is open to private businesses and one that the government does not own or control. When the government buys securities such as Treasury bills, it pumps new reserves into the economy. When the government sells Treasury bills, it takes reserves out of circulation. **Figure 16.12** examines this process.

Of course, individuals using cash do not carry out most open-market transactions. Financial institutions and large investors such as mutual

Figure 16.12
Buying and Selling
Treasury Bills
Look at this diagram that examines the process of buying and selling Treasury bills. Explain how the government is able to affect the money supply through this process. ▼

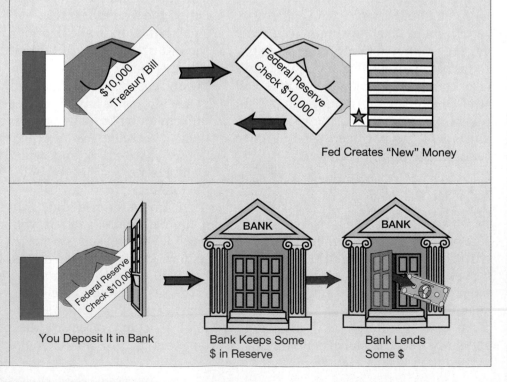

A. Suppose you sell a $10,000 Treasury bill to the Federal Reserve and receive that amount of money in the form of a Federal Reserve check. This is "new" money because the Fed created it simply by writing the check on itself. When you deposit the $10,000 in a bank, that bank will keep part in reserve and lend the rest. *The process of money creation has begun.*

Fed Creates "New" Money

You Deposit It in Bank

Bank Keeps Some $ in Reserve

Bank Lends Some $

funds make most transactions. If a bank purchases Treasury securities from the Fed, the purchase amount will be deducted from the bank's reserve account. The bank then has less money to lend, and the money supply eventually will be smaller. If a bank sells its government securities, the Fed will credit the money to the bank's reserve account. The bank can then make additional loans, and the money supply will grow. In each case, however, the Fed must decide which course is best for the economy in the long-run.

Monetary Policy Decision Making

The Federal Open Market Committee (FOMC) meets periodically to decide how best to control the money supply through open-market operations. At the beginning of each meeting, staff economists present data about what has happened to the money supply in the past, what current credit conditions are like, and what is likely to happen to the economy in the future. Statistics on unemployment, retail sales, gross domestic product, and so on, are presented. The information is discussed, and at the end of the meeting the committee votes on a course of action. The FOMC's decision summarizes current economic conditions and outlines the Fed's long-term goals for its monetary policy. To help meet these goals, the FOMC also sets objectives for the rate of growth of the money supply or the cost of credit for the next month or so.

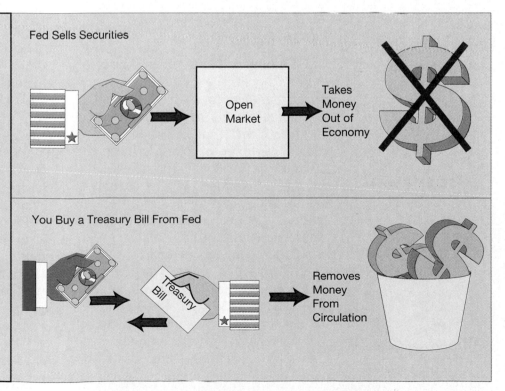

B. When the Fed wants to decrease the money supply, it sells securities on the open market. The sales take money out of the economy. Suppose you decide to buy a Treasury bill and use cash for the transaction. Turning the cash over to the Fed removes the money from circulation.

Fed Sells Securities

Open Market

Takes Money Out of Economy

You Buy a Treasury Bill From Fed

Treasury Bill

Removes Money From Circulation

Figure 16.13 ▶
Changing the Money Supply
The brake/accelerator model is one way to remember how the Fed can regulate the money supply. Explain how the model works.

Changing the Money Supply

To increase the money supply: accelerate

1. Reduce reserve requirements
2. Reduce discount rate for borrowing reserves
3. Buy government securities in the open market

To decrease the money supply: brake

1. Increase reserve requirements
2. Raise discount rate for borrowing reserves
3. Sell government securities in the open market

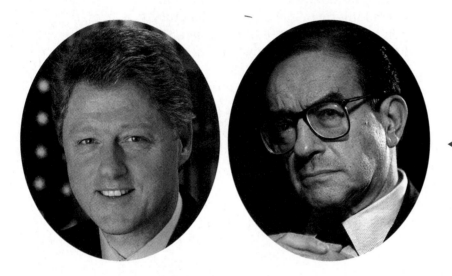

Figure 16.14
Independence of the Fed
The Fed is free of executive branch control. For example, when President Clinton, a Democrat, took office, Alan Greenspan, whom President Reagan, a Republican, had appointed to chair the Fed, continued his term.

The Difficulties of Monetary Policy

Economists sometimes describe the Fed's control over the money supply as similar to a driver's control over a car. Like a driver, the Fed can accelerate or brake, depending on what phase of the business cycle the economy is in. See **Figure 16.13**. Remember, though, that this is only a model and, therefore, simplified. In reality, the Fed cannot control the money supply as quickly and as surely as a driver can control a car.

One problem is the difficulty in gathering and evaluating information about M1 and M2. As you know, the money supply is measured in terms of M1—currency, traveler's checks, and checkable accounts—and M2—M1 plus certain near moneys. In recent years, new savings and investment opportunities have appeared. Keeping track of the growth of M1 and M2 becomes more difficult as money is shifted from savings accounts into interest-paying checkable accounts or from checkable accounts into money market deposit accounts (MMDAs). The increased use of credit cards and electronic funds transfer has also changed the way money circulates through the economy.

Throughout its history, the Federal Reserve's monetary policies have been criticized. In instances of rising inflation, the Federal Reserve increased the amount of money in circulation, thereby worsening inflation. During other periods when the economy was slowing down and going into recession, the Federal Reserve decreased the money supply. This action made the recession worse. To prevent such misjudgments, some critics of the Federal Reserve have requested that the money supply simply be increased at the same rate every year. They recommend that the Fed *not* engage in monetary policy.

The Fed's Board of Governors is protected from direct political pressure. See **Figure 16.14**. It nonetheless still receives conflicting advice from many directions as shown in **Figure 16.15**. The President could suggest one course of action—lower interest rates, for example—while members of Congress may be urging a different course. Private business may call for one policy, while organized labor asks for the opposite. Finally, the Fed is not the only force working to affect the economy. The spending and taxing policies of the federal government are also at work. The Federal Reserve's task is to consider all these factors as it plots a course for the growth of the economy.

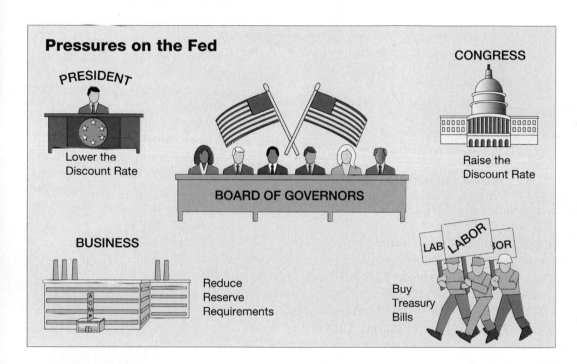

Pressures on the Fed

PRESIDENT
Lower the Discount Rate

BOARD OF GOVERNORS

CONGRESS
Raise the Discount Rate

BUSINESS
Reduce Reserve Requirements

LABOR
Buy Treasury Bills

Figure 16.15
Pressures
Examine the chart and explain how the Federal Reserve could be influenced by outside pressures.

SECTION 3 REVIEW

Understanding Vocabulary
Define discount rate, prime rate, open-market operations.

Reviewing Objectives
1. How can the Federal Reserve System use reserve requirements to alter the money supply?
2. How does the discount rate affect the money supply?
3. How does the Fed use open-market operations?
4. What are some of the difficulties of carrying out monetary policy?

Readings in Economics

THE NEW YORK TIMES   **AUGUST 23, 1993**

CENTRAL BANK GRIPES ABOUT A NEW WORLD

by Steven Greenhouse

To most people the analogy would be farfetched, but at a conference of central bankers . . . , the bankers often compared themselves to generals waging war.

The reason offered is that those who forge monetary policy, like those who wage war, have to grapple with an unending torrent of chance and change. . . .

Benjamin M. Friedman, a Harvard University economist, said, "It may be true that war is the human activity most vitally subject to chance and happenstance, but monetary policy runs a close second. . . ."

As a result of the rapid changes in capital markets, many central banks have discovered that their tried-and-true rules for carrying out monetary policy have become as useless as buggy whips. Without neat rules to lean back on, central bankers often feel exposed. Many are increasingly turning to seat-of-the-pants discretion to guide policy—a development that caused heated debate here. . . .

Probably the strongest lament among the central bankers was that the tool they used most to guide monetary policy—growth in the money supply— had become unreliable.

For most of the 1970's and 1980's, the Federal Reserve and many other countries' central banks sought to create a certain level of growth in the money supply. Those targets would more or less steer their economies toward a desired level of inflation and economic growth. Briefly put, X amount of monetary growth produced Y amount of economic growth.

That relationship has broken down because of financial deregulation and major changes in the way that individuals invest their savings. The Federal Reserve has concluded that it can now produce a certain amount of growth with less growth in one of its major money-supply indexes, the M-2, a measure of money that includes cash, savings and checking accounts, and small certificates of deposit.

• THINK ABOUT IT •

1. What is the chief role of central banks?

2. Why has the relationship between monetary growth and economic growth broken down?

Money Supply and the Economy

Key Terms
the Fed (p. 388)
monetary policy (p. 388)
loose money policy
(p. 389)
tight money policy
(p. 389)

fractional reserve
banking (p. 389)
reserve requirements
(p. 389)

Summary
A loose money policy means that the growth of the money supply is increased and money is abundant and inexpensive to borrow. With a tight money policy, the opposite occurs. With the system of fractional reserve banking, only a fraction of the deposits in a bank are kept on hand. The rest are lent to borrowers or otherwise invested. Because of the fractional reserve banking system, for any given change in new money in circulation, a multiple change will occur in the money supply.

Organization and Functions of the Federal Reserve System

Key Terms
Federal Open Market
Committee (FOMC)
(p. 394)
check clearing (p. 396)

Summary
The Board of Governors of the Federal Reserve System directs the operations of the Federal Reserve System and establishes policies regarding such things as reserve requirements and discount rates. The Federal Reserve System serves many functions in addition to clearing checks for banks and regulating the money supply.

Regulating the Money Supply

Key Terms
discount rate (p. 401)
prime rate (p. 401)
open-market operations
(p. 402)

Summary
To regulate the money supply, the Fed uses changes in reserve requirements, the discount rate, and open-market operations. Monetary policy is sometimes difficult because the government may not always have accurate information on M1 and M2. Also, the Fed is not the only force working to affect the economy.

16 Review

Identifying Key Terms

Write the letter of the definition in Column B below that correctly defines each term in Column A.

Column A	Column B
1. the Fed (p. 388)	a. the central banking system in the United States
2. prime rate (p. 401)	
3. tight money policy (p. 389)	b. means of changing the growth rate of supply of money in the economy
4. reserve requirements (p. 389)	c. purchases and sales of United States securities by the Federal Reserve System
5. monetary policy (p. 388)	d. situation in which credit is expensive to borrow and in short supply
6. open-market operations (p. 402)	e. interest rate that the Federal Reserve charges banks for loans
	f. require banks to keep a certain percentage of their deposits as cash on account with the Federal Reserve

Use terms from the following list to fill in the blanks in the paragraph below.

fractional reserve banking (p. 389)
discount rate (p. 401)
loose money policy (p. 389)
check clearing (p. 396)

When credit is inexpensive to borrow, we can be pretty sure that the Fed has engaged in (7). Because banks do not have to keep 100 percent of their deposits on reserve, we have a (8) system. One of the functions in the Federal Reserve is to handle (9), which is the method by which a check deposited in one bank is transferred to another bank. Sometimes banks need to borrow from a Federal Reserve district bank. The rate that they pay is called the (10).

Recalling Facts and Ideas

Section 1

1. What are the two basic types of monetary policies?
2. In a fractional reserve banking system, what happens to the money supply when the Fed injects $100 of new money into the American economy?
3. Why do banks have to keep money in reserve accounts?

Section 2

4. What does the Board of Governors do within the Federal Reserve System?
5. How many Federal Reserve banks and branches are there?
6. Which agency of the federal government supplies paper currency to the economy?

Section 3

7. The Fed can change the money supply in circulation by changing reserve requirements. What are two other methods that it can use to do this?
8. If the Fed wants to decrease the money supply, what can it do?
9. Why is it difficult for the Fed to gather and evaluate information about M1 and M2?
10. Why do some of the Fed's critics think the Fed should not engage in monetary policy?

Critical Thinking

Section 1
Expressing Problems Clearly Draw a flowchart to show how a bank creates money.

Section 2
Making Comparisons What is the advantage to Federal Reserve membership today? How does this differ from the past?

Section 3
Analyzing Information How do you think the Fed would operate differently if it were under the control of the executive branch?

Applying Economic Concepts

Monetary Policy Imagine that you are a member of the Federal Open Market Committee. Eight times a year, you meet with the other members of the FOMC. The research staff presents information on the state of the economy. Write a list of the different types of information you think the members of the FOMC receive during their meetings.

Chapter Projects

1. **Individual Project** In a library, check the most recent issue of the *Federal Reserve Bulletin* for the current reserve requirements and discount rate. Check the same month's issue for the last four years to see how often they have changed and how much. Track these data on a chart.
2. **Cooperative Learning Project** Work in three groups. Each group will study one potential tool of monetary policy:

   - changing reserve requirements
   - changing the discount rate
   - changing the money supply via open-market operations

   The task of each group is to develop a con-vincing argument in favor of its monetary tool over the use of the other two monetary tools. Members of each group can contribute separate arguments. Appoint one member to summarize the arguments and present that summary in a short speech to the class using an outline.

Reviewing Skills

Understanding Real and Nominal Values
The Real Cost of College Below are some hypothetical numbers that show a price index each year and the nominal dollar price of attending one academic year in a private university.

Private University

Year	Price Index	Tuition
1980	68.4	$10,040
1985	96.0	$12,343
1990	104.0	$16,420
1995	119.0	$21,200

What was the real cost for each academic year in a private university?

Writing About Economics

Informative Writing Write a letter to someone who has never seen American money. Include a paragraph about the currency you have seen this week and a summary from Your Economics Journal record that tracked where the money was issued.

17 GOVERNMENT SPENDS, COLLECTS, AND OWES

Who decides what paintings and sculptures to put in museums?

Who usually owns big museums?

Why are there not more museums?

How expensive is it to operate a museum?

Why do people go to museums?

Your Economics Journal

Keep track of what you do during a one-day period. List each activity. Indicate what role the government might have in that activity. For example, when you drive, it is usually on a government-provided public road.

1 Growth in the Size of Government

SECTION 1 FOCUS

Terms to Know public-works projects, Medicare

Objectives *After reading this section, you should be able to:*
1 Describe two measurements of **government growth**.
2 Explain **why government has grown** rapidly.

Is More Government Better Government?

In the United States, the forces of supply and demand operating in the marketplace affect many of the decisions that answer the basic economic questions you learned about in Chapter 2. The United States is not a pure market economy, however. In addition to market forces, other forces affect the distribution of resources throughout the economy. One of the most important of these forces is government on all levels—local, state, and federal. Government at every level is involved in almost every aspect of the United States economy.

Government Growth

Government has grown considerably in the last 50 or so years. In 1929, just before the Great Depression began, government at all levels employed slightly more than 3 million civilian workers. During the Depression, however, there was a need for more government services, as **Figure 17.1** illustrates. Today slightly fewer than 3 million people work for the federal government alone. If you add local and state employees, government employs about 18.7 million civilian workers. This figure represents more than a sixfold increase during a period in which the population only doubled.

As the functions of government have grown, so has government spending. **Figure 17.2** shows one way of looking at government activities.

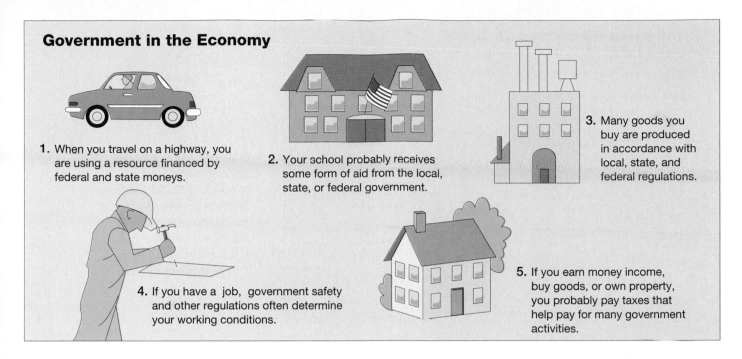

Government in the Economy

1. When you travel on a highway, you are using a resource financed by federal and state moneys.

2. Your school probably receives some form of aid from the local, state, or federal government.

3. Many goods you buy are produced in accordance with local, state, and federal regulations.

4. If you have a job, government safety and other regulations often determine your working conditions.

5. If you earn money income, buy goods, or own property, you probably pay taxes that help pay for many government activities.

Figure 17.1
Government Growth

As more people lost their jobs during the Great Depression, local government services, such as soup kitchens, proved inadequate. New government services and a larger government labor force resulted.

▼

Figure 17.3 (page 414) shows another.

As you can see from **Figure 17.3,** the different levels of government have grown at different rates. During the early 1960s, state and local governments spent less than the federal government. The federal government paid for national defense, **public-works projects,** and the salaries of members of Congress, federal judges, and the employees of executive departments such as the State Department. This situation continued until the mid-1960s. Then, state and local government spending for such items as sewers, roads, and schools increased rapidly.

Why Has Government Grown?

Economists have often tried to explain the huge growth in government spending since the Great Depression. One theory is that as the nation became richer, especially in the late 1960s and early 1970s, people demanded more government services to even out certain income inequities. This goal relates to the economic

Figure 17.2 ▲
Government in the Economy

Government plays a major role in most aspects of our lives. Some individuals argue that government should be even larger. Others believe that government has grown too large and that the private sector should provide goods and services without government intervention.

Government Purchases of Goods and Services, 1959–1994

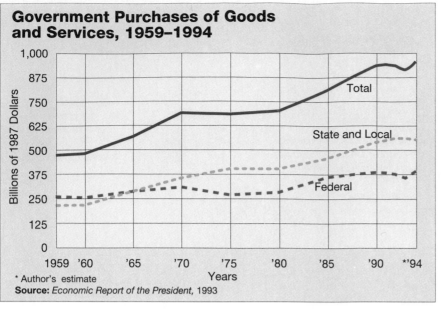

Billions of 1987 Dollars

Total

State and Local

Federal

1959 '60 '65 '70 '75 '80 '85 '90 *'94

Years

* Author's estimate

Source: *Economic Report of the President*, 1993

◀ **Figure 17.3
Government
Purchases of
Goods and
Services,
1959–1994**
Government purchases
of goods and services
(excluding Social Security
and other welfare
payments and interest)
corrected for inflation
show an increase in all
levels of government.

▼ **Figure 17.4
Government
Spending as a
Percentage of
Gross Domestic
Product, 1959–1993**
Total government
expenditures, including
Social Security and other
welfare payments, as well
as interest payments,
expressed as a percentage
of GDP have grown from
1959 to the present.

question of who should share in what
is produced.

In the late 1970s and early 1980s,
however, the economy suffered a series of recessions. Americans began
to feel that maintaining all the programs they wanted was too costly. At
some point, Americans—voters and
politicians alike—had lost sight of the
economic principle of scarcity. To
remedy the situation, politicians
began to think of ways to cut government spending. In doing so, they had
to decide on the trade-offs Americans

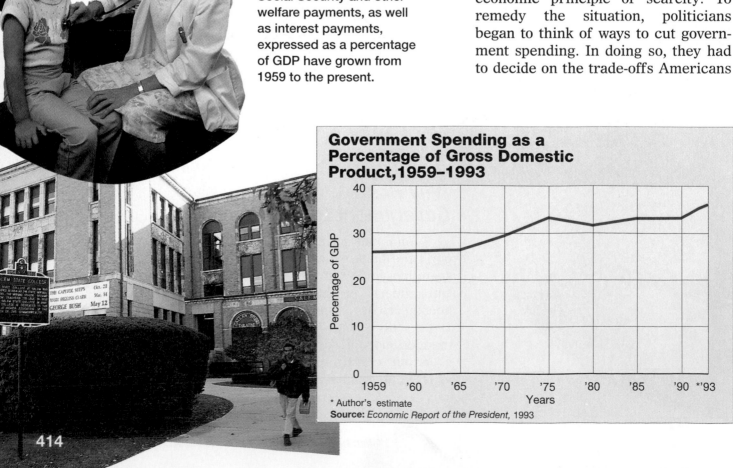

Government Spending as a Percentage of Gross Domestic Product, 1959–1993

Percentage of GDP

40

30

20

10

0

1959 '60 '65 '70 '75 '80 '85 '90 *'93

Years

* Author's estimate

Source: *Economic Report of the President*, 1993

would be willing to accept: fewer services and less money for research, education, public assistance, and health care, for example.

Today total government *purchases* represent about 20 percent of GDP. This figure, however, does not include such items as interest payments on the national debt and transfer payments such as welfare programs. Total government *outlays* exceed one-third of GDP. See **Figure 17.4**. Moreover, the size of government cannot be measured only by the cost of government spending. Any discussion of government's size must include where government spends this money.

The True Size of Government
When the government taxes you to provide you with a particular service, such as **Medicare** (health care for the aged), this cost of government is included in government spending. What if the government legislates a requirement that your employer provide that same service? Is there any difference? State governments are doing just that. In Massachusetts, for example, employers with five or more em-

ployees must provide medical insurance for each employee. On one hand, government taxes employees to pay for government-provided health insurance and, on the other hand, it requires that employers provide health insurance directly. The true size of government may be even greater than government estimates show.

Can We Say That the Growth of Government Is Good or Bad?
Everyone knows that government in the United States has grown in the 1900s—particularly during the Depression and during the 1960s and 1970s. See **Figure 17.5**. Can we say whether this is good or bad for society?

Is there an answer to such a debate? Not really, because the side that one takes depends on one's values. No right or wrong answer exists when values are at stake.

Figure 17.5 ▶
1960s and 1970s Government Growth
More aid was demanded for education, medical care, welfare, and so on. The economy was booming, and many believed that taxpayers could afford higher government spending.

SECTION 1 REVIEW

Understanding Vocabulary
Define public-works projects, Medicare.

Reviewing Objectives
1. How rapidly has government grown since 1929?
2. What do some economists believe caused the rapid growth of government?

SECTION 2 The Functions of Government

Terms to Know public goods, merit good, Social Security, workers' compensation, Supplemental Security Income, Aid to Families With Dependent Children, Medicaid, demerit goods, income redistribution, social insurance programs, public-assistance programs, welfare

Objectives *After reading this section, you should be able to:*
1. List four examples of **public goods**.
2. Describe the two main areas through which government **redistributes income**.
3. List four ways government **regulates economic activity**.
4. Name two ways government **promotes economic stability**.

What Government Does for You

Government in the United States serves four important functions: (1) providing public goods, (2) redistributing income and providing for the public well-being, (3) regulating economic activity, and (4) ensuring economic stability. Federal, state, and local governments share responsibilities for the first three functions. The fourth responsibility, ensuring economic stability, is handled almost entirely by the federal government.

Providing Public Goods

Public goods are goods or services that government sometimes supplies to its citizens. Many individuals can use these goods at the same time, without reducing the benefit each person receives. Public goods include national defense and certain types of health care.

National defense is one of the few public goods only the federal government provides. Usually different levels of government share responsibilities. For example, the legal system, which is a type of public good, involves all three levels. Federal, state, and local governments maintain separate systems of courts, correctional institutions, and law-enforcement agencies.

Merit Goods In any society, certain goods and services are considered to have special merit. A **merit good** is defined as any good that the government has deemed socially desirable. Examples of merit goods in our society are museums, ballets, and virtually

Social Insurance and Public-Assistance Programs

Social Insurance Programs

Social Security	Workers' Compensation	Medicare

Social Security, a federal program, provides monthly payments to people who are retired or unable to work.

Workers' Compensation, a state program, extends payments for medical care to workers injured on the job. Also, people who have lost jobs can receive payments through unemployment insurance.

Medicare, a federal program, provides low-cost health care for the aged and disabled.

Both programs also pay benefits to dependents of workers who have died.

Public–Assistance Programs

Supplemental Security Income	Aid to Families With Dependent Children	Medicaid

Supplemental Security Income covers federal programs including food stamps, veterans' benefits, and payments to the aged, blind, and disabled.

Aid to Families With Dependent Children is a state-run program that provides money to needy single parents raising young children.

Medicaid, a state and federal program, provides free health care for low-income and disabled persons.

all plays and classical music concerts. The government provides these merit goods to the people in society who would not otherwise purchase them at a full market price. Governments, therefore, often subsidize classical music concerts, ballets, museums, and plays.

Demerit Goods At the opposite end of the socially desirable spectrum are **demerit goods,** goods that the government has deemed socially undesirable. Gambling and injurious drugs such as heroin are examples. The government exercises its role in the area of demerit goods by taxing, regulating, or prohibiting the manufacture, sale, and use of such goods. For example, governments justify very high taxes on alcohol and tobacco products by declaring them demerit goods. The government prohibits many other drugs and strictly regulates prescription medicines.

Redistributing Income

Another function of government is to provide for the public well-being by assisting specific groups such as the aged, the ill, and the poor. Through their elected representatives, Americans have chosen to see that almost everyone in the nation is provided with a certain minimum level of income. See **Figure 17.6**. This task is accomplished primarily through **income redistribution,** using tax receipts to help citizens in need.

Figure 17.6 ▲
Social Insurance and Public Assistance
Government programs that redistribute income taken from some people through taxation and given to others fall into two areas: social insurance and public assistance.

Figure 17.7 Major Functions of Government Regulations

1	Protecting Consumers
2	Promoting Competition
3	Supervising Labor and Management Relations
4	Regulating Negative By-products of the Production Process

Figure 17.7 ▶ Government Regulations
Government under the American free enterprise system regulates certain aspects of the economy. For example, industrial processes, such as the spray painting process shown on page 419, are regulated.

Social insurance programs pay benefits to retired and disabled workers, their families, and the unemployed. Benefits are financed by taxes that workers and employers have paid into the programs. **Public-assistance programs,** often called **welfare,** make payments based on need, regardless of whether an individual or his or her employer has paid taxes.

Regulating Economic Activity

Figure 17.7 illustrates the four major ways in which the government regulates economic activity. One of the most important regulatory functions concerns the production process and emitting pollutants into the atmosphere as **Figure 17.8** shows. When a steel mill produces steel, for example, the resulting pollution from the smokestacks may cause health problems in the surrounding area. The steel mill does not have to correct these negative by-products in the absence of a law. Therefore, the federal government has often stepped in to require plants to install equipment that will reduce pollution. Local and state governments also have pollution laws. These include everything from city laws against littering to state laws regulating the dumping of toxic wastes in rivers.

Promoting Economic Stability

Encouraging and promoting economic stability means smoothing the ups and downs in the nation's overall business activity. Such intervention helps shield citizens from the effects of business fluctuations.

This function is the responsibility of only the federal government. The high unemployment rates during the Great Depression of the 1930s, and new theories about possible ways in which government could reduce unemployment, led to a landmark piece of legislation at the end of World War II. The Employment Act of 1946 specifies clearly the federal government's responsibility for economy-wide stabilization:

The Congress hereby declares that it is the continuing policy and responsibility of the Federal Government to use all practicable means consistent with its needs and obligations and other essential considerations of national policy, with assistance and cooperation of industry, agriculture, labor and State and local governments, to coordinate and utilize all its plans, functions, and resources for the purpose of creating and maintaining, in a manner calculated to foster and promote free

◄
Figure 17.8
Protecting Citizens
Government, through the Environmental Protection Agency, regulates industrial emissions of pollutants. For example, industrial processes, such as high-pressure spray painting, must comply with emissions regulations.

competitive enterprise and the general welfare, conditions under which there will be afforded useful employment opportunities, including self-employment, for those able, willing, and seeking to work and to promote maximum employment, production, and purchasing power.

One way that the federal government attempts to stabilize the overall national economy is through monetary policy. The federal government also can use fiscal policy, which is the government's set of financial policies on taxation and spending, to even out the business cycle.

SECTION 2 REVIEW

Understanding Vocabulary
Define public goods, merit good, Social Security, workers' compensation, Supplemental Security Income, Aid to Families With Dependent Children, Medicaid, demerit goods, income redistribution, social insurance programs, public-assistance programs, welfare.

Reviewing Objectives
1. What are public goods?
2. How does government redistribute income?
3. How does government regulate economic activity?
4. What two tools does the government use to promote economic stability?

Robert Reich on Government

Profile

- 1946–
- lawyer and political economist
- head of the Department of Labor under President Clinton
- previously a lecturer at Harvard University's Kennedy School of Government
- authored a number of books including *Minding America's Business* with Ira C. Magaziner (1982) and *Tales of a New America* (1987)

In the following excerpts from *Tales of a New America*, Robert Reich talks about the social program known as "workfare," and then goes on to talk about the problem of cutting all social programs as a way of decreasing consumption and increasing investment.

Programs [workfare] that simply require able-bodied recipients to take any job offered or assigned to them, regardless of the skills it conveys or the salary it pays, are not so much a screen to sort the willing from the shiftless as they are a simple penalty on requiring aid. The purpose of such programs . . . is to deter misrepresentation by making welfare less attractive to all recipients. To the extent that beneficiaries are capable of work but aspire to a life of leisure, such requirements might indeed enforce responsibility. But they do nothing to increase people's capacity to take active responsibility for their fate.

Reich discusses the need for "workfare" to help people on a long-term basis.

Assistance is conditioned upon the recipients taking steps to improve their prospects by, for example, finishing high school or obtaining vocational training. Along the way they might be counseled in how to find a job and perform reliably in it, and assisted with day care for their small children and with transportation to and from work. Regardless of the specific features of the program, the basic logic is to impose requirements that improve recipients' odds for a more self-sufficient future. . . .

Consider the implications of redefining investment to include not just bricks, mortar, and machines, but also spending on the health and education (both technical and moral) of our nation's children. First, cutting taxes solely to increase the pool of savings available for investment is a dubious strategy in a world of global capital markets. . . . Second, reducing government spending on the capacity of the next generation to produce wealth means cutting a crucial investment. . . . Far from constituting luxuries to be traded off against growth and productivity, investments in human capital ought to be viewed as a central means of achieving prosperity.

Checking for Understanding

1. What is "workfare"?
2. How can "workfare" be more productive?
3. Why should the government be careful in cutting social programs in order to devote more resources to investment?

The Federal Budget and the National Debt

S E C T I O N   3   F O C U S

Terms to Know fiscal year, deficit financing, national debt, balanced-budget amendment

Objectives *After reading this section, you should be able to:*

1. List the steps in the federal **budget-making process.**
2. Explain how **deficit spending increases the nation's public debt.**
3. Discuss various **attempts at deficit reduction.**

Budget Deficits Add to the National Debt

To carry out all of its functions, government must spend large sums of money. As a result, the federal budget is huge and has numerous categories. Figure 17.9 shows the major areas of spending.

Considerable debate and compromise are necessary in preparing an annual budget. Because all resources are scarce, an increase in spending in one area will cause a decrease in spending in some other area. Every spending action by the government has its own opportunity cost, and trade-offs between types of spending, even for the government, always exist. This fact was overlooked in some years when the economy was booming and government was collecting large revenues. In the 1990s all levels of government became more aware of the dangers of overspending because of the massive federal debt.

The Budget-Making Process

A complicated budget-making process goes on throughout every year, not only in Washington, D.C., but in every state and local government unit.

Figure 17.9
Federal Spending
The federal budget is based on a fiscal, rather than a calendar, year. Spending is calculated from the beginning of the budget year on October 1 of one year to September 30 of the next year, which is the federal government's **fiscal year.** ▼

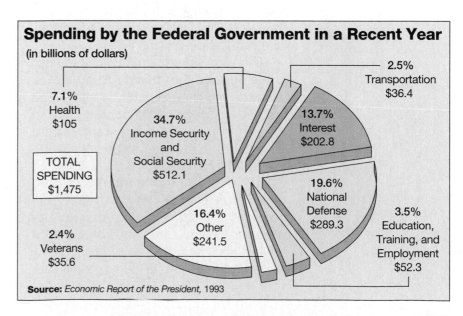

Spending by the Federal Government in a Recent Year
(in billions of dollars)

7.1% Health $105

34.7% Income Security and Social Security $512.1

2.5% Transportation $36.4

13.7% Interest $202.8

TOTAL SPENDING $1,475

19.6% National Defense $289.3

3.5% Education, Training, and Employment $52.3

2.4% Veterans $35.6

16.4% Other $241.5

Source: *Economic Report of the President, 1993*

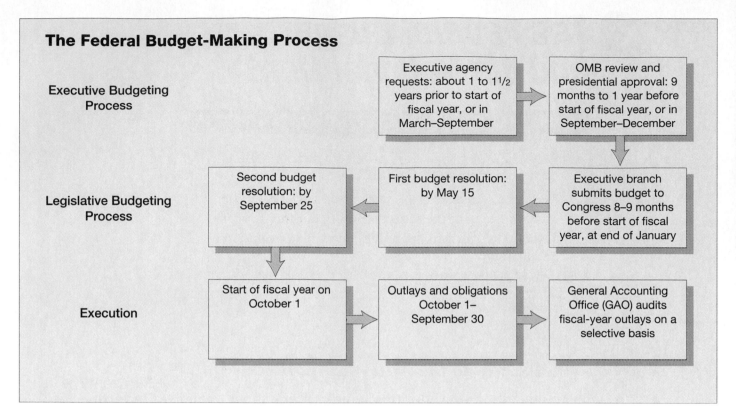

The Federal Budget-Making Process

| Executive Budgeting Process | Executive agency requests: about 1 to 1½ years prior to start of fiscal year, or in March–September | OMB review and presidential approval: 9 months to 1 year before start of fiscal year, or in September–December |

| Legislative Budgeting Process | Second budget resolution: by September 25 | First budget resolution: by May 15 | Executive branch submits budget to Congress 8–9 months before start of fiscal year, at end of January |

| Execution | Start of fiscal year on October 1 | Outlays and obligations October 1–September 30 | General Accounting Office (GAO) audits fiscal-year outlays on a selective basis |

Figure 17.10 ▲
The Federal Budget-Making Process

The Office of Management and Budget (OMB) starts the budget process, with the advice of the Council of Economic Advisers (CEA) and the Treasury Department.

The Federal Budget About eighteen months before the fiscal year begins on October 1, the executive branch of the government begins to prepare a budget as **Figure 17.10** shows. Working with the President, the Office of Management and Budget (OMB) makes an outline of a tentative budget for the next fiscal year. The various departments and agencies receive this outline and usually start bargaining with the OMB for a larger allocation of federal funds. See **Figure 17.11**.

The President reviews and approves the budget plan. The budget is printed, and the President submits the budget to Congress by January. Then its committees and subcommittees examine the budget's proposals, while the Congressional Budget Office (CBO) advises the committees and subcommittees about different aspects of the budget. Throughout the summer each subcommittee then holds a series of discussions.

Congress is supposed to pass a sec-ond budget resolution setting binding limits on spending and taxes for the upcoming fiscal year. In practice, however, the required budget resolutions often do not get passed on time. Moreover, when they are passed, the resolutions are not always treated as binding. As a result, the fiscal year sometimes starts without a budget, and the agencies must operate on the basis of a continuing congressional resolution. They can continue spending as they spent the year before until the new resolution is passed.

State and Local Budgets **Figure 17.12** shows how state and local governments spend the revenues they collect. By far the largest single category in state and local expenditures is education because state and local funds provide most elementary and secondary education, as well as a considerable portion of higher education. Other large expenses are for public assistance (welfare), hospitals, health

Figure 17.11
The Budget Challenge
Point B represents the final budget. How does the cartoonist capture the complexity of the budget-making process?

maintenance, and highways. The "other" general expenditure also is large. It includes expenditures for state parks. See **Figure 17.13** (page 424).

Deficit Spending and the Nation's Public Debt

In spite of the budget process outlined above, federal government revenues have not been equal to government expenditures. For years, the federal government has spent more than it has received. When government spends more than it collects through taxation, it must raise the extra money through borrowing. This borrowing is similar to an individual overspending his or her income and using credit. The government's spending more money than it takes in is called **deficit financing.** From 1940 through 1995, the federal government

Figure 17.12
Government Spending
State and local government expenditures increased in recent years, as these governments shouldered the rising costs of social welfare programs. ▶

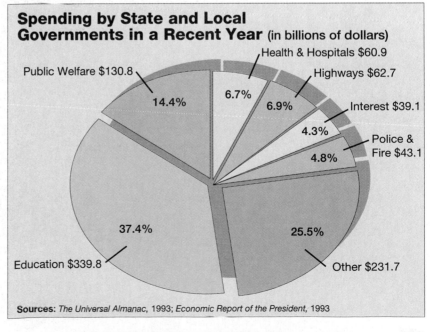

Spending by State and Local Governments in a Recent Year (in billions of dollars)

Public Welfare $130.8 — 14.4%
Health & Hospitals $60.9 — 6.7%
Highways $62.7 — 6.9%
Interest $39.1 — 4.3%
Police & Fire $43.1 — 4.8%
Education $339.8 — 37.4%
Other $231.7 — 25.5%

Sources: *The Universal Almanac,* 1993; *Economic Report of the President,* 1993

had a deficit in 49 out of the 56 years. Federal government spending averaged 23 percent of GDP through the early 1990s. Federal government revenues, however, were roughly 19 percent of GDP. The difference had to be made up by borrowing.

Government Borrowing Government borrows by selling securities to individuals and businesses. Federal securities include Treasury bonds, notes, and bills. When you buy United States savings bonds, you are also lending money to the federal government. In

Figure 17.13
State Preservation
Sometimes states need local pressure to preserve landmarks. In 1903, for example, Adina Emilia De Zavala was one of the first Texans to try to preserve sites important in Texas history. She barricaded herself inside the Alamo to prevent it from being torn down. Today the Alamo is a state park and the state's number one tourist attraction.

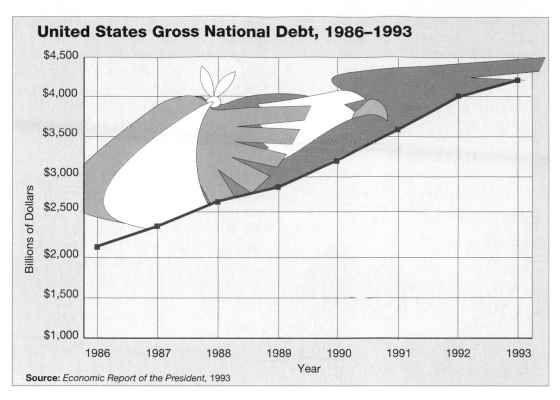

United States Gross National Debt, 1986–1993

Billions of Dollars

$4,500	
$4,000	
$3,500	
$3,000	
$2,500	
$2,000	
$1,500	
$1,000	

1986 1987 1988 1989 1990 1991 1992 1993

Year

Source: *Economic Report of the President,* 1993

Figure 17.14 ▲
Gross National Debt
The national debt of the United States more than doubled between 1986 and 1993. Many feared that such a rise would mortgage young Americans' futures.

addition, individual agencies of the federal government, such as the Tennessee Valley Authority, are authorized to sell bonds. State and local governments can borrow by selling municipal bonds to finance some of their activities.

Each year the federal government creates new debt by issuing new securities. At the same time, it retires old debt by paying off bonds, notes, and bills as they come due. The total amount of debt outstanding for the federal government is called the **national debt** or public debt. As you can see from **Figure 17.14**, in recent years the dollar amount of the national debt has been growing at a steep rate. This increase concerns many public officials and private citizens who think the government is living too far beyond its means. Others, however, have pointed out that the national debt expressed as a percentage of GDP has actually decreased steadily

**Figure 17.15
Cutting
Government
Programs
to Reduce
the Deficit**

The Budget Reconciliation Act of 1993 proposed spending cuts in many programs. Among the programs slated for reduced funding were student loans. The act proposed cutting student loans by $3.6 billion by 1998.

▶

since World War II until the last few years. They believe that federal borrowing, if controlled, is not necessarily a reason for alarm.

Attempts at Deficit Reduction

Some argue that congressional legislation should limit the deficit. See Figure 17.15. Others think the only

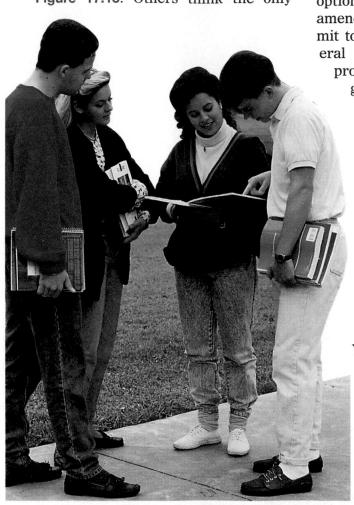

way to reduce federal government budget deficits is by a **balanced-budget amendment** to the Constitution. Two-thirds of the state legislatures can petition Congress for a constitutional convention to address this issue. To date, the required number of legislative petitions has not been filed.

As an alternative, Congress has the option of passing such a constitutional amendment, which it would then submit to the states for ratification. Several amendment bills have been proposed. As of 1994, however, Congress had passed no such amendment. Congress did pass the Gramm-Rudman-Hollings Act, also known as the Balanced Budget Act, in December 1985. Its goal was to reach a balanced budget by fiscal year 1991. After Congress failed for two years to comply with the act's target deficit reductions, Congress revised it. Congress again failed to meet the required deficit reductions for the first four years of the revised act. Yet another revision was passed in 1990, only to be virtually eliminated by the Budget Enforcement Act of 1990.

SECTION 3 REVIEW

Understanding Vocabulary
Define fiscal year, deficit financing, national debt, balanced-budget amendment.

Reviewing Objectives
1 What are the steps in the federal budget-making process?

2 In what type of activity does the federal government engage when it spends more than it receives?

3 What attempts have been made to reduce the federal deficit?

LEARNING ECONOMIC SKILLS

Understanding Federal Income Tax Withholding

Each year employers withhold a portion of the federal income tax so that employees do not have to make one large payment at the end of the year. Have you ever filled out a Form W-4 for withholding?

The Personal Allowances Worksheet

How much should your employer withhold? Your employer provides Form W-4, which includes a Personal Allowances Worksheet to help determine your "allowances." The more "allowances" you claim, the less the employer will withhold for income tax purposes. See **Figure A**.

Employee's Withholding Allowance Certificate

Attached to the worksheet is a certificate that the employee files with his or her employer. The employer may then determine how much tax to withhold each pay period. The certificate asks for the employee's name, address, Social Security number, and marital status. Then it provides a box for the employee to fill in his or her allowances from line G. Employees may have an additional amount withheld, or they may claim an exemption from withholding, providing they can show that they had no tax liability in the last tax year and will have none for the coming tax year.

Practicing the Skill

❶ Assume that you are a working single parent and a head of household. You have one child and child care expenses of $2,300 per year. How many allowances should you claim?

❷ Under what conditions would an employee file for an exemption from withholding?

Figure A

Personal Allowances Worksheet.

A. Enter "1" for **yourself** if no one else can claim you as a dependent. ____

B. Enter "1" if
You are single and have only one job;

You are married, have only one job,

and your spouse does not work; or

Your wages from a second job or your spouse's wages (or the total of both) are $1,000 or less. ____

C. Enter "1" for your **spouse**. ____

D. Enter the number of dependents whom you will claim. ____

E. Enter "1" if you will file as **head of household** on your tax return. ____

F. Enter "1" if you have at least $1,500 of **child or dependent care expenses** for which you plan to claim a credit. ____

G. Add lines A through F and enter the total . ____

SECTION 4 FOCUS

Terms to Know benefits-received principle, ability-to-pay principle, progressive tax, regressive tax, proportional tax

Objectives *After reading this section, you should be able to:*

1. Give an example of a tax levied according to each of the two **principles of taxation**.
2. List the three **forms of taxation** according to their effect on taxpayers.
3. Explain how **taxes are used to direct economic activity**.

Taxes Distribute the Cost of Government Among Taxpayers

You, the American taxpayer, are the source of most of the money the government spends. About 85 percent of federal, state, and local government revenue comes from taxation. **Figure 17.16** lists the major taxes that the various levels of government use to raise revenue.

Principles of Taxation

Taxes can be justified according to one of two major principles. Under the **benefits-received principle,** those who use a particular government service support it with taxes in proportion to the benefit they receive. Those who do not use a service do not pay taxes for it. For example, a gasoline tax to pay for highway construction and repair is based on the benefits-received principle. Those who use the highways often buy more gasoline and, therefore, pay more in gasoline taxes.

A tax based on the benefits-received principle is useful in raising money to pay for a service only certain individuals use. Many government services, however—national defense, for example—benefit everyone equally. Also, those who most need services, such as the aged and poor, are the individuals least able to pay taxes.

Under the **ability-to-pay principle,** those with higher incomes pay more taxes than those with lower incomes, regardless of the number of government services they use. For example, in most cities all property owners, even those without school-aged children, must pay property taxes to support the local school system.

Forms of Taxation

Actual taxes are classified according to the effect they have on those who are taxed as shown in **Figure 17.17** (page 430). In the United States today, these classifications include progressive taxes, regressive taxes, and proportional taxes. Congress

Figure 17.16 Major Taxes

Tax	Description	Type
Personal income	Tax is a percentage of income and a major source of federal revenue; many states and local governments also levy	Progressive at the federal level, but is sometimes proportional at the state level
Social insurance	Taxes covered by the Federal Insurance Contributions Act (FICA); second largest source of federal revenue	Proportional up to $60,600 in 1994, regressive above that
Corporate income	Federal tax as a percentage of corporate profits; some states also levy	At the federal level, progressive up to $100,000, proportional above that
Excise	Tax paid by the consumer on the manufacture, use, and consumption of certain goods; major federal taxes are on alcohol, tobacco, and gasoline; some states also levy	Regressive if people with higher incomes spend a lower proportion of income on taxed items
Estate	Federal tax on the property of someone who has died; some states also levy	Progressive; percentage increases with the value of the estate
Inheritance	Tax paid by those who inherit property; state tax only	Varies by state
Gift	Tax paid by the person who gives a gift; federal tax only	Progressive; percentage increases with the value of the gift
Sales	Tax paid on purchases; almost all states as well as many local governments levy; rate varies from state to state and within states; items taxed also vary	Regressive if people with higher incomes spend a lower proportion of income on taxed items
Property	State and local taxation of the value of property; both real property, such as buildings and land, and personal property, such as stocks, bonds, and home furnishings, may be taxed	Proportional; percentage is set by state and local governments
Customs duties	Tax on imports; paid by the importer	Proportional

Taxes Classified by Their Effects

Classification	Description	Example
Progressive Tax	A **progressive tax** has been justified on the basis of the ability-to-pay principle. It takes a larger percentage of higher incomes than lower incomes. As an individual earns more income, a larger percentage of that income is taken for federal taxes. Those who make less than a certain minimum pay no federal tax.	Federal personal income tax
Regressive Tax	A **regressive tax** is one that falls hardest on those with the least amount of income. It takes a larger percentage of lower incomes than of higher incomes. For example, because low-income families spend a larger percentage of their income on food than middle- or high-income families, they also spend a larger portion of their income on taxes on food.	State sales tax on food
Proportional Tax	A **proportional tax** is a tax that takes the same percentage of all incomes. As income rises, the amount of tax paid also rises. The percentage of income represented by that tax, however, remains the same.	Some state income taxes are the same rate for every taxpayer.

Figure 17.17 ▲
Taxes Classified by Their Effects
Do you think that higher taxes for the wealthy are fair? Why or why not?

passed a tax law in 1986 to make the tax code more fair. It eliminated many of the deductions and tax shelters that had seemed to favor the wealthy. The new tax code lowered the top tax rates for individuals gradually from 50 percent to 28 percent. It also shifted some of the tax burden from individuals by raising corporate taxes. Tax legislation in 1993 increased the top tax rates for high-income earning individuals. Corporate taxes were also increased.

Taxes as a Way of Directing Economic Activity

Taxation is more than a way for government to raise money. It is also a way in which government can direct the use of resources by businesses and individuals and a way to regulate economic activity.

Encouraging Business Taxes are commonly used to encourage certain activities by businesses and individuals. Often cities and states will temporarily reduce or exempt taxes for a company as a way of persuading it to locate in a particular area. Governments at all levels encourage investment in their bonds by offering tax-free interest. Taxes are also used to direct resources toward investments that are desirable but costly. See **Figure 17.18**.

Discouraging Activities Taxes can also be used to discourage certain activities. Excise taxes that are supposed to discourage the use of such items as cigarettes and alcohol are sometimes known as sin taxes. Customs duties are supposed to reduce sales of imported goods. Other taxes are used as penalties for certain actions. For example, a person withdrawing money from an Individual Retirement Account (IRA) before age 59½ must pay 10 percent of it as a federal tax penalty.

Controlling Economic Activity
Taxes also can be used to control the nature and growth of economic activity. Government does this by adjusting tax rates and the distribution of taxes—who pays which taxes. Government officials, however, must keep in mind that individuals and businesses may react to these changes. For example, raising taxes for a state or city can actually decrease revenues if businesses and homeowners move away to escape high taxes. A city can also find itself short of funds if it grants too many tax reductions to try to attract business.

Figure 17.18 ▲
Tax Deductions
Many states encourage homeowners to insulate their homes by allowing the cost to be deducted from their income before computing their state income taxes.

Readings in Economics

SUMMER FESTIVALS: THE HIGH PRICE OF HAVING FUN

by Charles Mahtesian

In 1990, after six years of existence, Washington, D.C.'s annual Riverfest celebration drowned in a current of red ink. No one questioned its popularity—in fact, local residents complained that it attracted too many spectators—but city officials deemed it too expensive to operate.

... By pulling the plug on Riverfest, Washington joined a growing number of cash-strapped cities that have been reconsidering the pros and cons of the summer festival, one of the showcase economic development and promotion schemes for local government in the 1980s. In recent years there has been a major change in urban festival psychology.

... It is no longer possible for cities to ignore the fact that any large-scale festival requires significant police overtime and sanitation services. And in the case of smaller charity events, more than a few cities have calculated that it would be cheaper to cancel the event and make a direct charitable contribution from the treasury than to assign city cops and garbage collectors. So what most cities are now doing is telling the festivals if they want city services, it will cost them.

The truth, however, is that only a handful of special events draw huge crowds and make big money. There is a misguided perception, says Carolyn Pendergast, vice president of the International Festivals Association, that festivals are cash cows. "A lot of times festivals are perceived as large events that draw large numbers of people," she says, "but in reality, most festivals are at around the break-even point."

• THINK ABOUT IT •

1. Why are many cities across the United States canceling summer festivals?

2. What necessary city services contribute to the large costs of holding a festival?

Growth in the Size of Government

Key Terms

public-works projects (p. 413)

Medicare (p. 415)

Summary

Government in the United States has grown from about 3 million employees in 1929 to about 19 million today. Several factors are responsible for this spurt in government growth.

The Functions of Government

Key Terms

public goods (p. 416)
merit good (p. 416)
Social Security (p. 417)
workers' compensation (p. 417)
Supplemental Security Income (p. 417)
Aid to Families With Dependent Children (p. 417)
Medicaid (p. 417)

demerit goods (p. 417)
income redistribution (p. 417)
social insurance programs (p. 418)
public-assistance programs (p. 418)
welfare (p. 418)

Summary

Four important functions of government are: (1) providing public goods, (2) redistributing income and providing for the public well-being, (3) regulating economic activity, and (4) ensuring economic stability. The government provides public goods to all citizens. Government uses social insurance programs and public assistance programs to redistribute income. At the same time, government works to promote economic stability.

The Federal Budget and the National Debt

Key Terms

fiscal year (p. 421)
deficit financing (p. 423)
national debt (p. 425)

balanced-budget amendment (p. 426)

Summary

The federal budget-making process includes several steps involving the executive and legislative branches. Even with safeguards and attempts at deficit reduction, the national debt is growing at a rapid rate.

Taxation

Key Terms

benefits-received principle (p. 428)
ability-to-pay principle (p. 428)

progressive tax (p. 430)
regressive tax (p. 430)
proportional tax (p. 430)

Summary

Two principles of taxation are the benefits-received principle and the ability-to-pay principle. Taxes are classified according to how they spread the tax burden among taxpayers, while some taxes are levied to affect economic activity.

17 *Review*

Identifying Key Terms

Write the letter of the definition in Column B below that correctly defines each term in Column A.

Column A
1. benefits-received principle (p. 428)
2. public goods (p. 416)
3. ability-to-pay principle (p. 428)
4. income redistribution (p. 417)
5. national debt (p. 425)

Column B
a. the taking of money from some to give to others
b. system by which those with higher incomes pay higher taxes
c. payment for a particular government service by those who use the services
d. goods and services whose use by one person does not reduce use by another
e. amount of money the government owes

Use terms from the following list to fill in the blanks in the paragraph below.

Medicare (p. 415)
Supplemental Security Income (p. 417)
workers' compensation (p. 417)
Social Security (p. 417)
Medicaid (p. 417)
welfare (p. 418)

   Major income redistribution programs are in place in the United States. Social insurance programs pay benefits to people in the form of (6), (7), and (8). Many public assistance programs are often called (9). They include Aid to Families With Dependent Children as well as (10) and (11).

Recalling Facts and Ideas

Section 1
1. In what ways has the government grown since the Great Depression?
2. What percent of GDP is accounted for by total government purchases of goods and services?

Section 2
3. What are the main functions of government?
4. Give some examples of public goods (but do not confuse them with all government-provided goods).
5. If the government designates a particular good or service as a merit good, what does the government normally do?

Section 3
6. What are the main steps in the federal government budget-making process?
7. How frequently has the federal government used deficit financing since World War II?
8. What causes the nation's public debt?

Section 4
9. What are the principal taxes that exist in the United States today?
10. If all income were taxed at exactly the same rate, what type of tax would be in existence?
11. Besides raising revenue, what other uses does government have for taxes?

Critical Thinking

Section 1
Synthesizing Information Look at **Figure 17.3** on page 414. When were the two periods of rapid growth in government purchases? Why?

Section 2

Making Comparisons What is the difference between Medicare and Medicaid?

Section 3

Determining Cause and Effect Why is it impossible for the government to spend more than it receives without increasing the national debt?

Section 4

Drawing Conclusions What is the process by which taxes can direct economic activity?

Applying Economic Concepts

Theories of Taxation You learned about two theories of taxation, one of which was the benefits-received theory. Assume that you want to use this theory to justify a progressive income tax system. Write a list of the reasons explaining why, as a person's income goes up, that person receives more benefits from the government and therefore should be taxed progressively.

Chapter Projects

1. **Individual Project** A number of states have laws that require a balanced state budget. Check your state constitution to see if your state has such a requirement. Research and write a brief report explaining why and when the amendment was passed, and whether it makes the budget process more difficult.
2. **Cooperative Learning Project** Work in groups representing each of at least three regions of the United States. Each member of each group should pick one or more states to research. The information needed will be:

   ■ Highest tax rate applied to personal income
   ■ Highest tax rate applied to corporate income
   ■ Sales tax rate

   Each group should determine which states have the highest tax rate.

Reviewing Skills

Understanding Federal Income Tax Withholding

1. **Determining Allowances** How many allowances should you claim on Form W-4 if you are a single person with only one job and your parents claim you as a dependent on their federal income tax return? Use the worksheet below as your guide.

   Personal Allowances Worksheet

   A. Enter "1" for **yourself** if no one else can claim you as a dependent. ____

   B. Enter "1" if
   You are single and have only one job;
   You are married, have only one job, and your spouse does not work; or
   Your wages from a second job or your spouse's wages (or the total of both) are $1,000 or less. ____

   C. Enter "1" for your **spouse**. ____

   D. Enter the number of dependents whom you will claim. ____

   E. Enter "1" if you will file as **head of household** on your tax return. ____

   F. Enter "1" if you have at least $1,500 of **child or dependent care expenses** for which you plan to claim a credit. ____

   G. Add lines A through F and enter the total. ____

2. **Understanding Withholding** Why do employers withhold taxes from each paycheck?

Writing About Economics

Informative Writing Imagine you are writing an introduction to a high school government text. Your topic is "How government affects every citizen." Write a paragraph using examples from Your Economics Journal.

CHAPTER

18

CONTROLLING UNEMPLOYMENT AND INFLATION

How might this project benefit the economy?

Who will benefit from this project?

If these people were not working on this project, what might they be doing?

Who pays for federally funded projects?

How does federal spending affect employment?

Your Economics Journal

Keep track of the number of times that you read about or hear about the topics of unemployment and inflation. Write down the source from which you heard or read this information. After each entry, indicate whether the economic news was good.

SECTION 1 FOCUS

Terms to Know stabilization policies, unemployment rate, full employment, underground economy, demand-pull inflation, stagflation, cost-push inflation

Objectives *After reading this section, you should be able to:*

① List two problems that economists face in **measuring unemployment.**

② Distinguish between the causes of demand-pull inflation and cost-push **inflation**.

Figure 18.1
Trying to Track the Economy
In the 1830s President Jackson and his successor had little insight into economic problems. Today, knowledgeable economists advise Presidents, but they often disagree about the causes and cures of the economic problems that periodically face the nation. ▼

Two Problems That Destabilize the Economy

The American economy experiences ups and downs in its overall business activity—booms, recessions, and even depressions. To keep the economy healthy and to make the future more predictable for planning, saving, and investing, the federal government uses monetary and fiscal policies. Together these are called **stabilization** (STAY-buh-luh-ZAY-shuhn) **policies**. Unfortunately, neither policy is always successful in solving the complex problems of the economy, as **Figure 18.1** explains. Two of the biggest threats to the nation's economic stability are high unemployment and too much inflation.

Measuring Unemployment

The **unemployment rate** is the percentage of the civilian labor force that is without jobs but that is actively looking for work. High unemployment is usually a sign that all is not well with the economy. Moreover, the waste of human resources that unemployment causes is an extremely serious problem. Unemployment can reduce living standards, disrupt families, and take from an individual his or her feeling of self-respect. As a result, maintaining a low unemployment rate is one of the major goals in stabilizing the economy.

Figure 18.2 Types of Unemployment

Type	Definition	Characteristics
Cyclical	Unemployment associated with fluctuations up or down in the business cycle	Rises during recessions and depressions; falls during recoveries and booms
Structural	Unemployment caused by changes in the economy such as technological advances or discoveries of natural resources	Can result when workers are replaced by computers or other machines or when cheaper natural resources are found elsewhere; often affects less skilled workers
Seasonal	Unemployment caused by changes in the seasons or weather	Affects construction workers, particularly in the Northeast and Midwest; also affects farm workers who are needed in certain areas only during certain months of the growing season
Frictional	Temporary unemployment between jobs because of firings, layoffs, voluntary searches for new jobs, or retraining	Always exists to some degree because of the time needed between jobs to find new work and the imperfect match between openings and applicants

Types of Unemployment Many types of unemployment exist. **Figure 18.2** describes these kinds of unemployment. Some people work in seasonal jobs or jobs that are sensitive to technological advances or changes in the marketplace. As a result, not all unemployment can be eliminated. Moreover, economists disagree over what the level of full employment should be.

In the 1960s, some economists thought the unemployment rate should not exceed 4 percent. This figure was raised to 5 to 6 percent in the 1970s. After much careful study, economists now generally have come to consider the economy at **full employment** when the unemployment rate is less than 6.5 percent. It is important to remember that the unemployment rate is only an estimate. The unemployment rate does not include people who are out of work and have stopped looking for work. Nor does it include people who work in family businesses without receiving pay.

Economists classify unemployment into four broad categories: cyclical, structural, seasonal, and frictional. Most of the people who are in these unemployment categories are out of work because of forces beyond their control.

Unemployment is difficult to measure accurately because government statisticians cannot possibly interview every person in and out of the labor force. Survey results are also imperfect because of the existence of the underground economy. The **underground economy** consists of people who do not follow federal and state laws with respect to reporting earnings as **Figure 18.3** (page 440) shows.

The Underground Economy

Illegal Activities

1. Tax Avoiders These people work for cash payments without reporting their earnings to the Internal Revenue Service.	**2. Gamblers and Drug Traffickers** These people may be working, but will deny they are when interviewed by government officials.	**3. People Working "Off The Books"** These people are officialy unemployed and are receiving unemployment benefits, but are really working.

Figure 18.3 ▲
The Underground Economy
How do illegal activities make measuring the true unemployment rate difficult?

Figure 18.4
Higher Inflation, Lower Living Standards
If you earn $300 per week and inflation averaged 5 percent this year, how much per week would you have to earn next year to maintain your purchasing power?

Inflation

A second major problem that faces the nation is inflation. The economy can usually adapt to gradually rising prices. Unpredictable inflation, however, has a destabilizing effect on the economy. Consumers and businesses act differently than they would if the economy were growing at a stable rate. For example, during periods of unanticipated high inflation, consumers may borrow and spend more. They realize that the dollars they use to make loan payments will be worth less and less as inflation rises. As a result, creditors eventually raise interest rates to maintain the level of profit they had before inflation began to rise rapidly. This, in turn, tends to have a slowing effect on the economy's growth. In the long run in a time of anticipated high inflation, consumers and businesses often borrow less because of the high interest rates.

Inflation may also affect con-sumers' living standards. Suppose you receive a 5 percent raise in a year in which inflation has risen 8 percent. As **Figure 18.4** shows, you have actually lost purchasing power. Inflation is a particularly serious problem for people who live on *fixed* incomes, such as those who are retired. Each year a little of the purchasing power of that income is eaten away.

Unfortunately, no single answer explains why inflation occurs. Two competing ideas have developed, however: the demand-pull theory and the cost-push theory.

Demand-Pull Theory of Inflation According to the theory of **demand-pull inflation,** prices rise as the result of excessive business and consumer demand. If demand increases faster than total supply, the resulting shortage will lead to the bidding up of prices.

Demand-pull inflation can occur for several reasons. Inflation can occur if the Federal Reserve causes the money supply to grow too rapidly. Individuals, in their attempt to spend the additional dollars, will compete for the limited supply of goods and services. This increased demand will cause prices to rise. Increases in government spending and in business investments for expansion can also increase overall demand. It can also increase if taxes are reduced or consumers begin saving less. Either results in more money income being spent.

Higher Inflation, Lower Living Standards

Your Raise	Inflation Rate	Purchasing Power
5%	1%	4%
5%	8%	−3%

Cost-Push Theory of Inflation The demand-pull theory indicates that inflation usually happens only when there is full employment in the economy. Before full employment is reached, increased demand will increase output and reduce unemployment. Experience, however, has shown that rising prices and unemployment can occur at the same time. This combination of inflation and low economic activity is sometimes called **stagflation.** The United States experienced this type of inflation for the first time during the 1969-1970 recession. It remained a problem through much of the 1970s; it appeared again in 1982; and, to a lesser extent, it was evident in 1990-1991.

According to some economists, stagflation is a result of cost-push inflation at work in the economy. The theory of **cost-push inflation** states that the wage demands of labor unions and the excessive profit motive of large corporations push up prices as shown in **Figure 18.5**.

According to this theory, large unions have the power to demand and receive wage increases that are not necessarily justified by the productivity of workers. When businesses have to pay higher wages, their costs increase. To maintain their profit level, businesses must raise prices. Each time this happens, it causes the cost of living to go up. Workers then demand higher wages to balance the decline in their purchasing power.

During periods of cost-push inflation, unemployment can remain high. Prices are being adjusted for higher wages and profits and not because of increased aggregate demand—total demand for goods and services. Without additional aggregate demand, producers have no reason to increase output by hiring new workers. As a result, unemployment continues.

Figure 18.5 Cost-Push Inflation

Cost-push inflation may also result from increasing costs of natural resources. Where on the circle would you place the costs of resources?

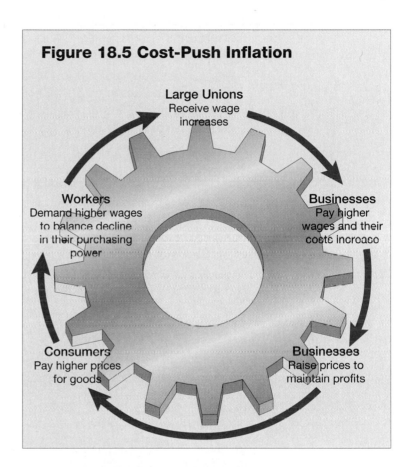

Figure 18.5 Cost-Push Inflation

Large Unions
Receive wage increases

Businesses
Pay higher wages and their costs increase

Businesses
Raise prices to maintain profits

Consumers
Pay higher prices for goods

Workers
Demand higher wages to balance decline in their purchasing power

---

SECTION 1 REVIEW

Understanding Vocabulary

Define stabilization policies, unemployment rate, full employment, underground economy, demand-pull inflation, stagflation, cost-push inflation.

Reviewing Objectives

1 What are two problems the government faces in measuring unemployment?

2 If prices are going up because too many consumer dollars are competing for goods and services, what type of inflation is occurring?

Paul Samuelson on Unemployment and Inflation

Profile

- 1915 –
- graduate school at Harvard University
- taught at the Massachusetts Institute of Technology
- publications include *Full Employment, Guideposts and Economic Stability* with Arthur F. Burns (1967) and numerous editions of *Principles of Economics*

Paul Samuelson participated in a series of Rational Debate Seminars in the 1966–67 academic year. The following excerpt is taken from *Full Employment, Guideposts and Economic Stability*, a publication from these seminars. Samuelson addresses the problem of maintaining full employment without causing rapid inflation. He says we have moved beyond "simple Keynesianism."

During the great slump of the 1930s economists learned that expansionary fiscal and monetary policies could bring a depressed economic system toward full employment. You might call these the days of happy and simple Keynesianism.

However, by the end of World War II when full employment had long been a reality, the honeymoon was over.

... Perhaps even with government intervention, we cannot long enjoy both high employment and reasonable price stability. That is the basic issue we face....

Samuelson believed that government could produce steady growth by establishing wage-price guideposts along with fiscal and monetary policies.

I cannot stress too strongly that wage-price guideposts are not substitutes for proper macroeconomic fiscal and monetary policies. Economists have always known that excessively easy monetary policy and/or enlarged expenditures coupled with small tax receipts can produce demand-pull inflation. The only cure for that situation is tighter money and/or more restrictive fiscal policy.

Samuelson concludes that some unemployment might be necessary in order to keep price increases under control.

... Experience suggests that in the short run there is a trade-off between the intensity of unemployment of men [and women] and capital and the intensity of price increase.

Checking for Understanding

❶ What basic issue did economists face after World War II?

❷ What did Samuelson believe to be the cure for demand-pull inflation?

❸ What trade-off seemed to be likely?

2 The Fiscal Policy Approach to Stabilization

SECTION 2 FOCUS

Terms to Know fiscal policy, circular flow of income

Objectives *After reading this section, you should be able to:*

① Explain a simple model of **how income flows** between businesses and consumers.

② Explain how Keynesian economists believe **fiscal policy** should have been used at the beginning of the Great Depression.

③ Indicate how **fiscal policy** might reduce **inflation**

Government Policies of Taxing and Spending

Most economists fall into one of two groups on the question of economic stabilization. Both groups share some ideas, but they take different approaches toward controlling unemployment and inflation. One group emphasizes the role of monetary policy and of the Federal Reserve in stabilizing the economy. The other group concentrates more on the use of fiscal policy. **Fiscal policy** is the federal government's use of taxation and spending policies to affect overall business activity. John Maynard Keynes, shown in **Figure 18.6**, developed fiscal policy theories during the Great Depression. Keynes believed that the forces of supply and demand operated too slowly in a serious recession and that government should step in to stimulate aggregate demand.

The Circular Flow of Income

Many economists use what is known as the **circular flow of income** in explaining their theories. This model pictures income as flowing continually between businesses and consumers. Income flows from businesses to households as wages, rent, interest, and profits. These are payments for the use of the factors of production households control—their

**Figure 18.6
John Maynard Keynes**
Keynes and his followers believed that fiscal policy could help reduce unemployment.
◄

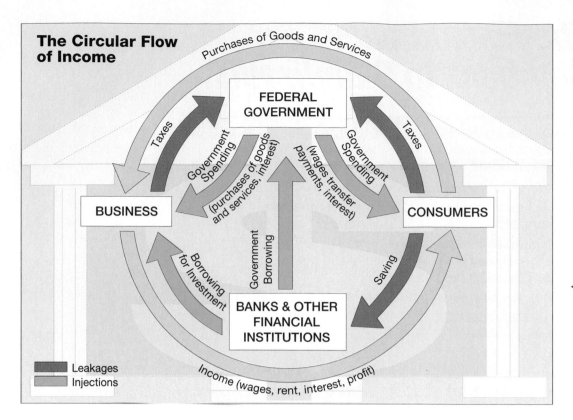

The Circular Flow of Income

Purchases of Goods and Services

FEDERAL GOVERNMENT

Taxes

Government Spending (purchases of goods and services, interest)

Government Spending (wages transfer payments, interest)

Taxes

BUSINESS

CONSUMERS

Borrowing for Investment

Government Borrowing

Saving

BANKS & OTHER FINANCIAL INSTITUTIONS

Income (wages, rent, interest, profit)

Leakages
Injections

Figure 18.7
The Circular Flow of Income
Government occupies a central position in the circular flow of income. By using fiscal policy, the federal government partially controls the levels of leakages and injections. This, in turn, may control the overall level of economic activity.

labor, land, capital, and entrepreneurship. Income flows from households to businesses as payments for consumer goods and services.

Not all income, however, follows this circular flow. Some of it is removed from the economy through consumer saving and government taxation. Economists use the term *leakage* to refer to this removal of money income. **Figure 18.7** shows these leakages.

Offsetting these leakages are injections of income into the economy. Injections occur through business investment and government spending. The term *investment*, in this sense, means the purchase of new plants and equipment and increases in inventories. Much of the income for investment comes from saving—a part of the leakage from circular flow. Government spending benefits both businesses and consumers. Businesses sell goods and services to government agencies, while consumers receive wages and transfer payments. Interest payments on government borrowing flow to both sectors.

In Keynesian theory, both leakages and injections of income have an effect on aggregate demand, as **Figure 18.7** shows. Leakages reduce aggregate demand by removing income from the economy. This is income that households could have used to purchase goods and services or that businesses could have used. Injections increase aggregate demand by placing more dollars in the hands of households and businesses. Ideally, leakages and injections balance each other. In this state of equilibrium, the income that households save is reinjected through business investment. Income taken out through taxes is returned through government spending.

What happens if leakages of income are greater than injections? If saving and taxes are greater than business investment and government spending, economic activity will decrease. Aggregate demand will drop, and because businesses will not be able to sell all of their goods, they will lay off workers. Unemployment will increase.

In contrast, if more income is injected than leaked, the economy may eventually expand too rapidly and cause inflation. This view supports the demand-pull theory of inflation. If business invests heavily and/or government spends large amounts of money, more income will be injected into the economy. The same will happen if households reduce saving or the government cuts taxes. In all these cases, aggregate demand increases.

Fiscal Policy and Unemployment

Keynesian economists believe the Great Depression resulted from a serious imbalance in leakages and injections. They point out that during the 1920s, the public engaged in a higher level of saving than usual. As long as businesses continued to invest, injections balanced leakages. In the months following the stock market crash of 1929, however, the desire and ability of businesses to invest also collapsed. Capital investment fell steeply, reducing output and causing a high rate of unemployment. As you can see from **Figure 18.8**, unemployment eventually reached about 25 percent.

According to Keynesian theory, at the beginning of the Depression, government should have filled the gap created when businesses began limiting their investments. The government could have increased injections of government spending or cut taxes to reduce its own leakages. Either would have given businesses and consumers more spendable income. Either would have brought leakages and injections back into equilibrium.

During the 1930s, the federal government did create a number of jobs programs to hire unemployed workers. See **Figure 18.9** (page 446). These new jobs reduced some unemployment and injected more wages into the economy. These were not enough, though, to make up for the large drop in consumer demand. It was not until World War II that the nation moved

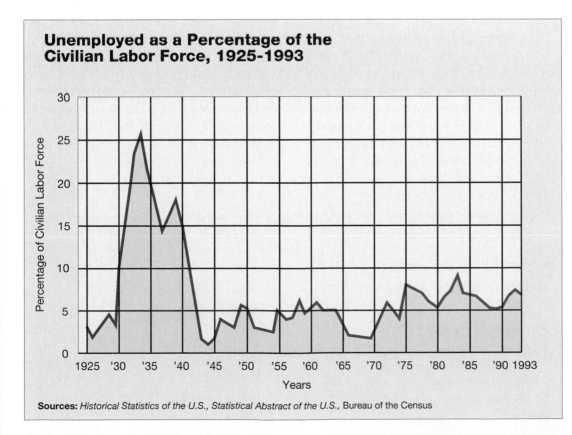

Unemployed as a Percentage of the Civilian Labor Force, 1925-1993

x-axis: Years (1925, '30, '35, '40, '45, '50, '55, '60, '65, '70, '75, '80, '85, '90, 1993)

y-axis: Percentage of Civilian Labor Force (0–30)

Sources: *Historical Statistics of the U.S., Statistical Abstract of the U.S.,* Bureau of the Census

Figure 18.8
Unemployed as a Percentage of the Civilian Labor Force, 1925-1993
During which year after the Great Depression did unemployment peak?

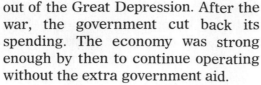

Figure 18.9
Jobs Programs, 1930s

Posters such as this one announced employment opportunities created by the government during the Great Depression.

▼

out of the Great Depression. After the war, the government cut back its spending. The economy was strong enough by then to continue operating without the extra government aid.

Since the Great Depression, many public officials and labor leaders have suggested starting jobs programs to reduce unemployment and stimulate the economy. Several suggestions for forming new government-sponsored jobs programs to bring down unemployment rates were made in the early 1980s and again in 1992 and 1993.

Cuts in federal taxes are another way in which fiscal policy has been used in an attempt to speed up economic activity and fight unemployment. For example, when President John F. Kennedy took office in 1961, the nation was slowly pulling itself out of a recession that had started in 1958. To help the recovery, Kennedy convinced Congress to pass a law giving businesses tax credits on investments. Businesses could deduct from their taxes some of the costs of new capital equipment. The goal was to encourage businesses to expand production and hire more workers. In 1964 President Lyndon

Johnson signed into law a tax cut of about $11 billion. Keynesian economists believe that as a result, unemployment fell from 5.2 percent in 1964 to 4.5 percent in 1965. This stimulated investment and consumer spending.

Fiscal Policy and Inflation

Fiscal-policy supporters also believe that inflation can be reduced by increasing taxes and/or reducing government spending. They argue that such actions will reduce the aggregate demand for goods and services.

Tax Increase Because people are paying higher taxes, they are taking home less spendable income. They will, therefore, have to cut back on their purchases. As purchases decline, businesses will cut back on production. This reduction in demand will cause businesses to reconsider raising prices. Often, as inflation falls, unemployment rises slightly because of less business activity.

When Policy Failed Fiscal policy as a means of reducing inflation has not been used frequently. One example of its application, however, occurred in 1968. Government spending was increasing rapidly to finance both the Vietnam War and new social programs. President Johnson persuaded Congress to pass a tax increase to slow inflation. However, the increase did not have the desired effect.

SECTION 2 REVIEW

Understanding Vocabulary
 Define fiscal policy, circular flow of income.

Reviewing Objectives
① In the circular flow of income, what types of income flow from businesses to consumers?

② What is the Keynesian economists' explanation of the Great Depression?

③ How can the federal government use fiscal policy to combat inflation?

Using the Consumer Price Index

The most often reported price index in America is the consumer price index, or CPI. Changes in the CPI show changes in the cost of a market basket of goods based on quantities in the base year. Do you know how to interpret the CPI?

The Monthly Survey

Every month the Bureau of Labor Statistics samples stores and other retail outlets. It obtains more than 600,000 food prices per year, 350,000 other prices, and 700,000 estimates of rent charges. Every month the *Monthly Labor Review* lists the consumer price indexes for many goods and services.

Consumer Price Indexes for Selected Consumer Groups

Every month the consumer price index for groups of consumer expenditures is compiled. At the end of each year, the yearly change in the prices is reflected in a summary of statistics. **Figure A** shows the consumer price indexes for selected consumer groups for a 10-year period (base years 1982-84 = 100).

Inflation is the percent change in prices from year to year. To determine the inflation rate for an item, divide the CPI increase by the previous price and multiply by 100. As **Figure B** shows, the CPI for clothes increased 4.8 from 1987 to 1988. The rate of inflation for clothes was 4.3%.

Figure A

| | | | Medical |
Year	Food	Clothes	Care
1983	99.4	100.2	100.6
1984	103.2	102.1	106.8
1985	105.6	105.0	113.5
1986	109.0	105.9	122.0
1987	113.5	110.6	130.1
1988	118.2	115.4	138.6
1989	125.1	118.6	149.3
1990	132.4	124.1	162.8
1991	136.3	128.7	177.0
1992	137.9	131.9	190.1

CPI for Selected Consumer Groups*

*1982-84 =100

Figure B

CPI for Clothes

1988	115.4
1987	−110.6
CPI increase =	4.8

$$\frac{4.8}{110.6} = .043 \times 100 = 4.3\% \text{ rate of inflation}$$

Practicing the Skill

1. What was the rate of inflation for food between 1990 and 1991?
2. For which group listed did the consumer price index go up the most between 1991 and 1992?

SECTION 3 Monetarism and the Economy

SECTION 3 FOCUS

Terms to Know monetarism, monetarists, monetary rule, time lags

Objectives *After reading this section, you should be able to:*

1. Explain the **monetarists' view of the Fed's role in the Great Depression**.
2. Describe how monetarist theory influenced **government policy in the 1980s**.
3. Explain the **monetarists' criticism of fiscal policy**.

Figure 18.10 Money Supply and Aggregate Demand

Monetarists believe that an increase in the rate of growth of the money supply increases aggregate demand for goods and services. If the economy is operating below capacity, this extra demand will lead to a rise in output. To produce more, businesses will have to hire more workers, and unemployment will decrease. If there is already full employment, this increased demand will lead to a rise in prices—inflation.

The Theory of Monetarism

Monetarism is the theory that deals with the relation between the amount of money the Federal Reserve places in circulation and the level of activity in the economy. The supporters of this theory are called **monetarists**. Monetarism is often linked with Milton Friedman. Operating under the monetarist theory, the Fed can use reserve requirements, the discount rate, and open-market operations to change the growth of the money supply. Friedman and his supporters believe that when the amount of money in circulation expands, people spend more. See **Figure 18.10**.

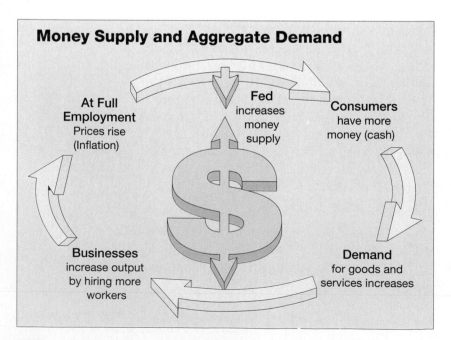

Money Supply and Aggregate Demand

At Full Employment
Prices rise (Inflation)

Fed increases money supply

Consumers have more money (cash)

Businesses increase output by hiring more workers

Demand for goods and services increases

Monetarist View of the Great Depression

Friedman views much of what happened during the Great Depression differently from the supporters of Keynes. Monetarists do not deny the importance of decisions made by businesses about investments in the early 1930s. Friedman, however, places more emphasis on the drop in the amount of money in circulation as a cause for the drop in aggregate demand. See **Figure 18.11**. This, in turn, caused businesses to reduce their investment. Despite the Fed's stated goal of stimulating the economy, the

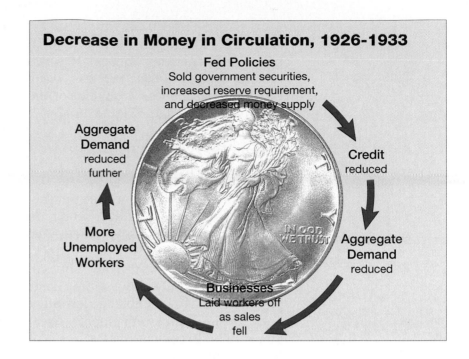

**Figure 18.11
Decrease in Money
in Circulation,
1929-1933**

To monetarists, the reduction in the amount of money in circulation could mean only one thing—a reduction in aggregate demand. With less demand, fewer workers were needed and unemployment increased. ▶

Decrease in Money in Circulation, 1926-1933

Fed Policies
Sold government securities, increased reserve requirement, and decreased money supply

Credit
reduced

Aggregate Demand
reduced

Businesses
Laid workers off as sales fell

More Unemployed Workers

Aggregate Demand
reduced further

money supply decreased by one-third from the start of the recession in 1929 to the depths of the Great Depression in 1933 and 1934.

The monetarists claim that what would have been just another recession became the Great Depression because of the Fed's actions. During the period, the Fed claimed it wanted banks to loosen their credit. At the same time, the Fed continued to sell government securities. This reduced the money supply. The monetarists believe that the Fed should have increased greatly the amount of money in circulation. As a result, people would have started spending more, and businesses would have been able to invest more.

Government Policy According to Monetarists

Friedman and his monetarist followers believe the economy is so complex and so little understood that government does more harm than good in trying to second-guess businesspeople and consumers. As a result, monetarists generally oppose

using fiscal policy to stimulate or slow the economy. For example, they do not believe the government should operate with budget deficits each year in an attempt to stimulate the economy. Instead, monetarists believe that the government should balance the federal budget. This action would keep government from competing with private business to borrow money in the credit market. It would also reduce the amount of interest that the government must pay each year.

The Fed, according to monetarists, should also stop trying to smooth the ups and downs in the economy. Rather, the Fed should allow the money supply to grow at a rate of perhaps 3 to 5 percent per year. This policy is called a **monetary rule.**

Monetarists believe that a steady growth in the money supply within strict guidelines (or targets, as they are called) is the best way to provide businesses and consumers with more certainty about the future. According to monetarism, this policy would result in a controlled expansion of the economy without rapid inflation or high unemployment.

Monetarist Theory and the Federal Reserve Monetarist theory had a major influence on Federal Reserve policies in the 1980s. You can trace the changing monetary policies of the Fed from the 1970s in **Figure 18.12**.

Monetarists' Criticism of Fiscal Policy

Monetarists point out that the theory of fiscal policy never ends up being the reality of fiscal policy. Two reasons account for this discrepancy. One has to do with the political process of fiscal policy. Monetarists point out that no single government body designs and implements fiscal policy. The President, with the aid of the director of the Office of Management and Budget (OMB), the secretary of the Treasury, and the Council of Economic Advisers, designs, but only *recommends*, the desired mix of taxes and government expenditures. Congress, with the aid of many committees (the House Ways and Means Committee, the Senate Finance Committee, and the Senate Budget Committee, to name a few), actually enacts fiscal policy. One built-in organizational problem is that the power to enact fiscal policy does not rest with one government institution. Disagreement as to the proper fiscal policy emerges among members of Congress and between Congress and the President.

Monetarists also point out that even if fiscal policy could be enacted when the President wanted, there are various **time lags** between when it is enacted and when it becomes effective. It takes many months if not years

**Figure 18.12
Changing Fed
Policies**
What happened to the unemployment rate when Fed policies began to lower inflation in 1980-1982?

▼

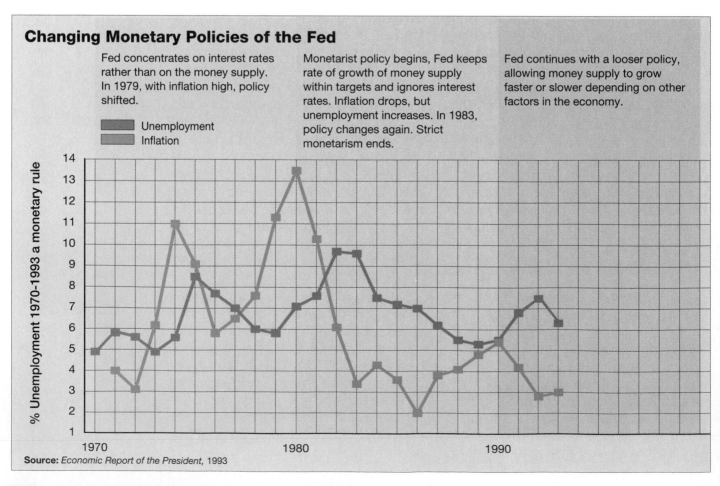

Changing Monetary Policies of the Fed

Fed concentrates on interest rates rather than on the money supply. In 1979, with inflation high, policy shifted.

Monetarist policy begins, Fed keeps rate of growth of money supply within targets and ignores interest rates. Inflation drops, but unemployment increases. In 1983, policy changes again. Strict monetarism ends.

Fed continues with a looser policy, allowing money supply to grow faster or slower depending on other factors in the economy.

■ Unemployment
■ Inflation

% Unemployment 1970-1993 a monetary rule

Source: *Economic Report of the President, 1993*

for fiscal policy stimulus to cause employment to rise in the economy. Consequently, a fiscal policy designed to combat a recession might not produce results until the economy is already experiencing inflation. In this event, the fiscal policy worsens the situation.

Monetarists also point out that many fiscal policy actions have been enacted after the end of the recessions, as shown in **Figure 18.13**.

Just because the monetarists point out the failures of fiscal policy does not mean that they favor stabilizing the economy through monetary policy. Remember from our previous discussion that they favor a monetary rule, which means, in effect, no monetary policy either.

Figure 18.13
Faulty Timing
If you were a member of Congress, how would your knowledge of time lags affect your decisions on economic issues? ◀

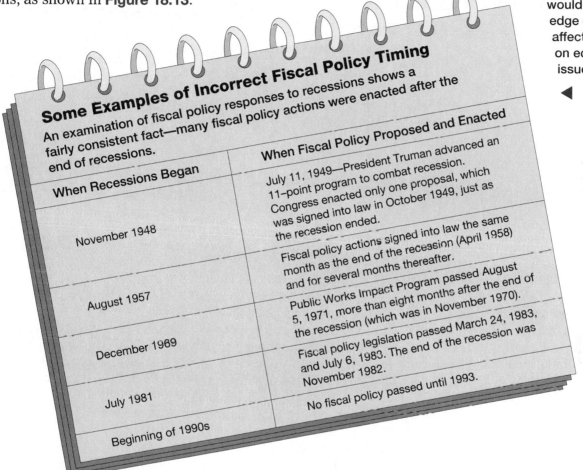

Some Examples of Incorrect Fiscal Policy Timing

An examination of fiscal policy responses to recessions shows a fairly consistent fact—many fiscal policy actions were enacted after the end of recessions.

When Recessions Began	When Fiscal Policy Proposed and Enacted
November 1948	July 11, 1949—President Truman advanced an 11-point program to combat recession. Congress enacted only one proposal, which was signed into law in October 1949, just as the recession ended.
August 1957	Fiscal policy actions signed into law the same month as the end of the recession (April 1958) and for several months thereafter.
December 1969	Public Works Impact Program passed August 5, 1971, more than eight months after the end of the recession (which was in November 1970).
July 1981	Fiscal policy legislation passed March 24, 1983, and July 6, 1983. The end of the recession was November 1982.
Beginning of 1990s	No fiscal policy passed until 1993.

SECTION 3 REVIEW

Understanding Vocabulary
Define monetarism, monetarists, monetary rule, time lags.

Reviewing Objectives
❶ How would a monetarist explain the effect of the Fed's role in the Great Depression?

❷ What type of monetary policy would monetarists prefer that the Federal Reserve System follow?

❸ Why do monetarists criticize fiscal policy?

Readings in Economics

BOSTON SUNDAY GLOBE   **AUGUST 15, 1993**

TEENAGERS' CASH
by Joanne Ball Artis

Armed with her first paycheck last month from her camp counseling job—$180 a week after deductions—Katie Burns, 13, headed straight for the mall.

Once at South Shore Plaza in Braintree [Massachusetts], Burns began supplementing her summer wardrobe: shorts and Jordache jeans from Cummings, totaling $48; a $10.50 shirt from The Gap; another shirt from JW for $20; an outfit from Jordan Marsh for "$40 something. . . ."

Burns, of Dorchester, counts herself part of a fast-growing, money-ed class of consumers: teenagers.

Their economic clout is unequaled by any previous generation of teenagers and so is the advertising directed at them. US teenagers had an income of nearly $70 billion last year—more than $90 billion by some estimates. According to national surveys, teen-agers also influence the spending of more than $140 billion of their parents' money. . . .

Merchants who once saw trouble in teenagers congregating in front of their stores now see dollar signs, as teen-agers have emerged as an economic force behind everything from fash-ion to entertainment equipment to hair care. . . .

Today's teenagers are markedly different from their predecessors, said Joanna Jacobson, senior vice president of marketing at Converse, head- quartered in North Reading. "These kids start-ed making their own buying de-cisions earlier than other generations. At 4 years old they're picking out footwear. These are decisions that be-fore were solely held by mom. By the time they're teenagers they're incredibly sophisticated consumers."

18 *Highlights*

Section 1

Unemployment and Inflation

Key Terms
stabilization policies
(p. 438)
unemployment rate
(p. 438)
full employment (p. 439)
underground economy
(p. 439)
demand-pull inflation
(p. 440)
stagflation (p. 441)
cost-push inflation
(p. 441)

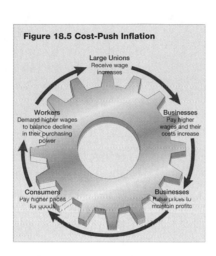

Figure 18.5 Cost-Push Inflation

Large Unions
Receive wage
increases

Businesses
Pay higher
wages and their
costs increase

Businesses
Raise prices to
maintain profits

Consumers
Pay higher prices
for goods

Workers
Demand higher wages
to balance decline
in their purchasing
power

Summary
Defining full employment is difficult because economists do not agree about what the level of full employment should be. The underground economy makes surveys of unemployment inaccurate. Demand-pull inflation generally happens during times of full employment. Cost-push inflation most often occurs when inflation and unemployment are both high.

Section 2

The Fiscal Policy Approach to Stabilization

Key Terms
fiscal policy (p. 443)
circular flow of income
(p. 443)

Summary
Economists use a model to explain the circular flow of income. Keynesian economists believe that fiscal policy—government taxation and spending—should be used to regulate the overall level of economic activity. They want the government to use fiscal policy to reduce inflation.

Section 3

Monetarism and the Economy

Key Terms
monetarism (p. 448)
monetarists (p. 448)
monetary rule (p. 449)
time lags (p. 450)

Summary
Monetarists believe that the Federal Reserve System made errors that deepened the Great Depression. Their theories influenced government policies beginning in the 1980s. Monetarists are critical of the ability of fiscal policy to address the problems of inflation and unemployment.

18 Review

Identifying Key Terms

Write a one-sentence explanation of the following terms.

unemployment rate (p. 438)

full employment (p. 439)

underground economy (p. 439)

demand-pull inflation (p. 440)

stagflation (p. 441)

cost-push inflation (p. 441)

Use terms from the following list to fill in the blanks in the paragraph below.

monetarism (p. 448)   time lags (p. 450)
monetary rule (p. 449)

Keynesian economists believe that the Great Depression was caused by reduced capital investment in the economy. Those who believe in (1) disagree. They think that the Great Depression was caused by a significant reduction by the Federal Reserve System in the money supply. Monetarists argue in favor of a (2). They also think that (3) are so severe that fiscal policy never can be effective.

Recalling Facts and Ideas

Section 1
1. Many individuals are not included in the government statisticians' monthly estimates of those who are working. In which part of the economy are these unreported workers?
2. What causes demand-pull inflation?
3. What causes cost-push inflation?

Section 2
4. What are the leakages out of the circular flow of income?

5. What are the injections of income into the circular flow of income?
6. What do Keynesian economists think the government should have done during the Great Depression?

Section 3
7. Who is the economist most often linked to monetarism?
8. What one factor do monetarists associate with having caused the Great Depression?
9. What do monetarists believe the Fed should do in terms of monetary policy?
10. What are some examples of incorrect fiscal policy timing?

Critical Thinking

Section 1
Analyzing Information Why can full employment never be defined as zero unemployment?

Section 2
Understanding Cause and Effect Why might the unemployment rate rise if fiscal policy were used to combat inflation?

Section 3
Identifying Alternatives According to the monetarists, what is the alternative to using fiscal policy to combat unemployment or inflation?

Applying Economic Concepts

Unanticipated Versus Anticipated Inflation Unanticipated inflation may affect you in many ways. For example, when inflation is high, banks charge higher interest rates to compensate for inflation. If you borrowed money at the high interest rates and then the rate of inflation fell, you would be worse off. You would be paying too much interest on that borrowed money. Make a list of other problems that you might encounter if there were a change in the rate of inflation that you did not anticipate.

Chapter Projects

1. **Individual Project** Numerous government publications give the unemployment rates for various groups of workers according to the following:
    - age
    - occupation
    - race
    - gender

    Two of these publications are *The Statistical Abstract of the United States* and *The Economic Report of the President.* Using either of these sources, draw a graph that shows the unemployment rates for the past five years for various groups of workers according to the classifications given above.

2. **Cooperative Learning Project** Organize into four groups. The first three groups will each track one of the following: government fiscal policies, monetary policies, and major economic indicators. The last group will create visuals from the information that is collected.

    Using the front page of at least 10 consecutive issues of the *Wall Street Journal,* 3 groups will record a summary of news in each of their categories. Fiscal policy includes taxes and government spending. Monetary policy includes central bank interest rates, money supply, open-market operations, and reserve requirements. Economic indicators include such measurements as the CPI, industrial production, producer prices, sales, stocks and bonds, and unemployment. Each item should include the category, the date of the news, and a brief summary of the news.

As the information is being gathered, the last group should begin creating headlines that place the events in chronological order on a bulletin board. Discuss the state of the economy as reflected in the headlines to conclude the project.

Reviewing Skills

Using the Consumer Price Index

1. **Calculating the Consumer Price Index** The figures below show the percent change per year of the consumer price index for several years. Assume that the base year for this price index is 1982–84. If the price index is 137.9 at the end of 1991, what is the index at the end of 1992?

    1988—4.4%   1989—4.6%   1990—6.1%
    1991—3.1%   1992—2.9%

2. **Specific Price Indexes** Look at the data below showing renters' versus homeowners' costs of shelter. **(a)** Which price index increased more from 1983 to 1988? **(b)** Which price index increased more during the entire time span? **(c)** By how much more did the faster-rising price index increase than the slower-rising price index?

Years	Renters	Homeowners
1983	103.0	102.5
1988	133.6	131.1
1992	160.9	155.3

Writing About Economics

Expository Writing Using information gathered in Your Economics Journal, write a letter to the editor about unemployment or inflation. Explain how the government should deal with the problem, either through fiscal or monetary policy.

Filing a Tax Return
From the classroom of Phil Peters, Gahanna Lincoln High School, Gahanna, Ohio

In Unit 5 you studied the federal government's role in the nation's economy. In this experiment, you will learn more about the federal income tax and your responsibilities as a taxpayer. (You may want to reread the material on pages 428–431 of the text.)

Regardless of whether you file income tax form 1040, 1040A, or 1040EZ, the Internal Revenue Service has divided your reporting into five main steps. The simplest federal income tax form is 1040EZ for single and married filers with no dependents. The steps below relate to this form.

Tools

1. Calculator
2. Tax table (sample provided)

Procedures

Step A In part, the amount of your income tax depends on your filing status. Whether you were single or married on December 31 determines your status for the entire year. Copy the table below and fill in your status.

Example

1		
Filing Status	☐ Single	☐ Married filing joint return (even if only had one income)

Step B In this step you add together all the sources of your income. It includes wages, salaries, tips, interest, and other earnings. For example, assume you had a part-time job. Your employer reports on your withholding statement (W-2 form) that you earned $8,500 last year. In addition, the bank reports that it paid you $38 in interest on your passbook savings account last year. Finally, you earned $560 in tips as a waiter at a local restaurant. Calculate your total income on a table like this one.

Example

2	Total wages, salaries, and tips. This should be shown in box 1 of your W-2 form(s). Attach your W-2 form(s).	_____
3	Taxable interest income of $400 or less. If the total is over $400, you cannot use Form 1040EZ.	_____
4	Add lines 2 and 3. This is your **adjusted gross income**.	_____

Step C Your status and exemption(s) help determine how much of your adjusted gross income is taxable. If you are single, and no one else may claim you as a dependent on another tax return, you may deduct $6,050.

Determine your taxable income on a table like this one.

Example

4	Adjusted gross income	_____
5	Minus	$6,050.00
6	**Taxable income**	_____

Step D Your employer withheld part of your wages and paid it to the Internal Revenue Service (IRS). Your employer reports this to you in Box 9 of your W-2 form. *Assume that your employer reports withholding $390.*

Now you can determine the tax you owe by using the tax table that is in your tax booklet. Find your tax from this segment of the table:

Example

If Form 1040EZ, line 6, is—		And you are—	
At least	But less than	Single	Married filing jointly
		Your tax is—	
3,000			
3,000	3,050	454	454
3,050	3,100	461	461
3,100	3,150	469	469
3,150	3,200	476	476
3,200	3,250	484	484
3,250	3,300	491	491
3,300	3,350	499	499
3,350	3,400	506	506

Step E Next, determine whether enough taxes have been withheld from your income or whether you owe the government an additional amount. If more was withheld than you owe, the government will refund part of your money. If less was withheld

than you owe, you must pay the IRS the balance by check or money order.

Example

7	Enter your Federal income tax withheld from box 2 of your W-2 form(s).	_____
8	**Tax** (from tax tables)	_____
9	If line 7 is larger than line 8, subtract line 8 from line 7. This is your **refund**.	_____
10	If line 8 is larger than line 7, subtract line 7 from line 8. This is the **amount you owe**.	_____

Lab Report

Step F Use what you have learned about filing an income tax return to answer the following questions.

1. Did you owe additional taxes to the IRS? If so, how much? If not, how much was your refund?
2. Why might an employer have failed to withhold enough taxes?
3. What is one advantage and one disadvantage of having more taxes withheld than what you owe?
4. What was the percentage in taxes you paid on your adjusted gross income?
5. What was the percentage in taxes you paid on your taxable income?

457

THE INTERNATIONAL SCENE

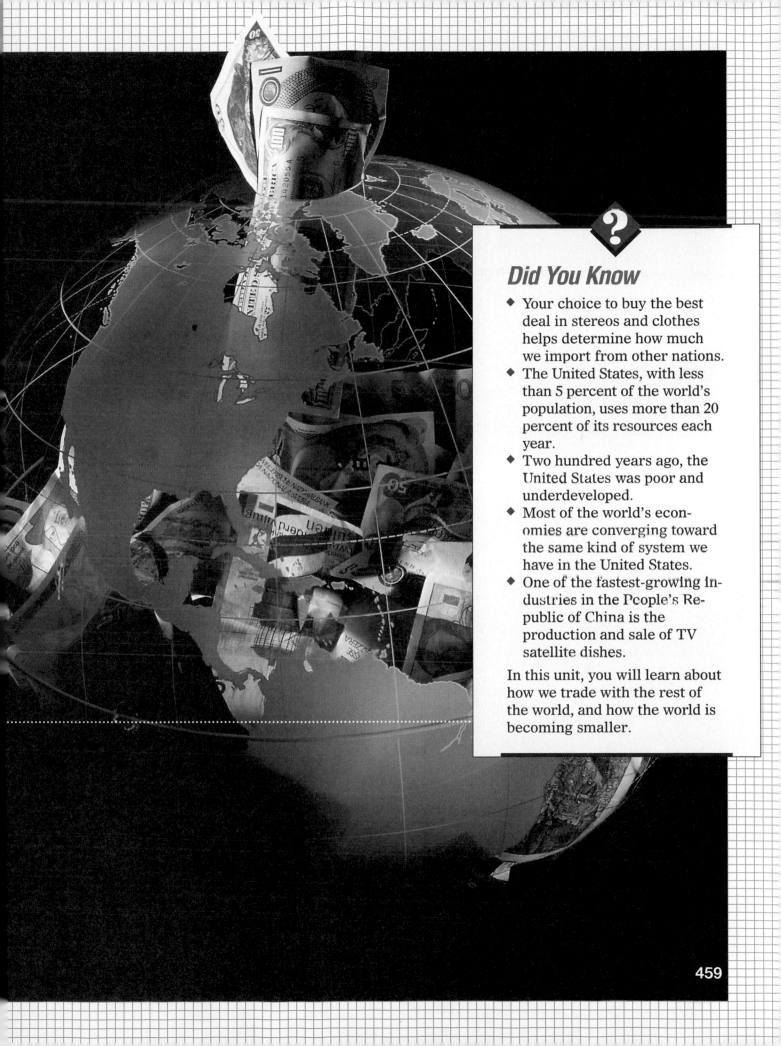

Did You Know

- Your choice to buy the best deal in stereos and clothes helps determine how much we import from other nations.
- The United States, with less than 5 percent of the world's population, uses more than 20 percent of its resources each year.
- Two hundred years ago, the United States was poor and underdeveloped.
- Most of the world's economies are converging toward the same kind of system we have in the United States.
- One of the fastest-growing industries in the People's Republic of China is the production and sale of TV satellite dishes.

In this unit, you will learn about how we trade with the rest of the world, and how the world is becoming smaller.

459

19 TRADING WITH OTHER NATIONS

How many Americans will travel abroad this year?

What happens to the dollars they spend outside the United States?

How much will they spend in other countries?

What percent of goods in American stores are foreign-made?

Do any government restrictions affect what Americans can buy from abroad?

Your Economics Journal

Keep track of what you wear during one week. Examine the clothing labels to find out where each was produced and put this information next to the name of each product. If it was not produced in the United States, write why you think you or your family bought this imported item.

1 *The Benefits of World Trade*

Exports Pay for Imports

What would happen if the United States could no longer buy goods from other countries or sell goods in return? Before you answer, you should be aware that the value of **imports**—goods bought from other countries for domestic use—is about 10 percent of GDP in the United States. That figure seems small. Many inconveniences would result, however, without imports. For example, we would have no coffee, chocolate, or pepper. Consider also that more than 60 percent of the radios, television sets, and motorcycles sold in the United States are imported. Many raw materials also come from foreign sources. More than 90 percent of the bauxite, from which aluminum is made, is imported.

Benefits of Trade

Imports tell only half the story. Many American workers are employed in industries that export their products overseas. **Exports** are goods sold to other countries. For example, more than 11 percent of the nation's trucks and buses and 40 percent of its engineering and scientific instruments are sold overseas. In addition, about one-fifth of the corn, one-tenth of the cotton, and almost two-thirds of the wheat produced in the United States are shipped abroad.

Made in the U.S.A.? Sometimes it is hard to distinguish between goods made in America and those purchased abroad. Consider the Boeing 777.

This new plane is hardly "made in America." International suppliers provide rudders, elevators, outboard flaps, wing-tip assemblies, engines, nose-landing gears, nose-landing gear doors, and main-landing gears. Japanese suppliers, in particular, provide cargo doors, fuselage panels, and passenger doors. The complicated Boeing 777 jet aircraft is a jigsaw puzzle in which the pieces come from all over the world. The same is true for both American and foreign cars, as shown in **Figure 19.1**.

If you buy an American-made IBM computer, many of its parts are made abroad. If you drink American-brand orange juice, such as Minute Maid or Tropicana, you will find in tiny print on the label that it is made from concentrate from not only the United States but from Mexico and Brazil as well. In short, international trade affects you whether you like it or not. We have truly entered an age of a global economy, so learning about international trade is simply learning about everyday life.

Why does trade occur among nations? A voluntary exchange is a transaction that benefits both parties.

Differences Among Nations Nations benefit through world trade because each differs in the type and amount of the factors of production it has available for use. The availability of natural resources is considered one of the most important of these differences. See **Figure 19.2** (page 464).

The type and amount of labor and capital available to a nation are equally important. For example, much of the economy of the United States is based on high-technology production. A highly skilled labor force and large amounts of capital—in the form of advanced equipment and machinery—make this possible. Another nation having the same natural resources but without the same labor and capital resources as the United States could have a very different economy.

Absolute and Comparative Advantage

The amount of importing and exporting a nation does is affected by the specific combination of all its resources. Depending on this combination, a nation has either an absolute or a comparative advantage in production.

Figure 19.1
Who Made the Parts?
The Ford Crown Victoria has shock absorbers from Japan, front-end spindles from England, electronic engine controls from Spain, electronic anti-lock brake system controls from Germany, and seats, windshields, instrument panels, and fuel tanks from Mexico.

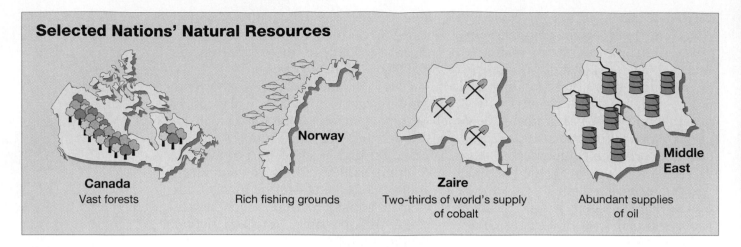

Selected Nations' Natural Resources

Canada
Vast forests

Norway
Rich fishing grounds

Zaire
Two-thirds of world's supply of cobalt

Middle East
Abundant supplies of oil

Figure 19.2 ▲
**Selected Nations'
Natural Resources**
The chart shows how certain nations have abundant supplies of one natural resource. In the Middle East, for example, oil is not only the most important resource, it is one of the few. In Canada, in contrast, vast forests are one of many resources.

Absolute Advantage The particular distribution of resources in a nation often gives it an absolute advantage over another nation in the production of one or more products. Brazil's tropical climate and inexpensive labor make it ideally suited for growing bananas. Even using the same amount of land, labor, capital, and entrepreneurship, a country with a moderate climate, such as France, would produce far fewer bananas. Brazil, therefore, has an absolute advantage in banana production over France. **Absolute advantage** is the ability of one country, using the same amount of resources as another country, to produce a particular product at less cost.

A nation often finds it profitable to produce and export a limited assortment of goods for which it is particularly suited. This concept is usually known as **specialization** (SPESH-uh-luh-ZAY-shuhn). Specialization helps determine the goods the United States imports and exports, as shown in **Figure 19.3**. For example, it is because of specialization that many people associate Japan with consumer electronics.

Comparative Advantage A nation may not need to have an absolute advantage in the production of a certain good to find it profitable to specialize

and then to trade with other countries. For example, consider two imaginary nations, Country X and Country Y. Assume that each country produces only soybeans and corn.

When producing only soybeans, Country X produces 10 million bushels, while Country Y produces only 8 million. The next year, suppose the two countries decide to grow only corn. Country X produces 50 million bushels, while Country Y produces 25 million. According to this example, Country X has an absolute advantage in the production of both soybeans and corn. That is, with the same amount of inputs, Country X can produce more of either crop than Country Y.

Does this mean that Country X will produce both crops and, therefore, have no reason to trade with Country Y? No. Country X can produce slightly more soybeans than Country Y, however, it can produce a great deal more corn. It would make little sense for Country X to take land, labor, and capital resources away from the efficient production of corn and use them for the less efficient production of soybeans. Country X's opportunity cost—what it gives up to get something else—would be less if it invested all its resources in the production of corn. It could export its surplus corn and use the money it receives to import soybeans from Country Y.

Country X has a comparative advantage in corn production. **Comparative advantage** is the ability of a country to produce a product at a *lower opportunity cost* than another country. Country Y has a comparative advantage in soybean production. Country Y can produce about the same amount of soybeans as Country X, but only half as much corn. By using its resources to grow soybeans only, Country Y is only giving up the relatively inefficient production of corn. Country Y, then, has a lower opportunity cost for soybean production than does Country X. Country Y should produce the maximum amount of soybeans, export soybeans to Country X, and import corn. Both countries benefit when each country concentrates on that production for which it is relatively most efficient.

The Relationship Between Imports and Exports You should consider international trade as an economic activity just like any other. It is subject to the same economic principles. International trade can be looked at as a kind of production process that transforms exports into imports. For you and everyone else in the United States, the purpose of international trade is to obtain imports, not to export. What we gain as a country from international trade is the ability to import the things that we want. We have to export other things in order to pay for those imports. A fun-

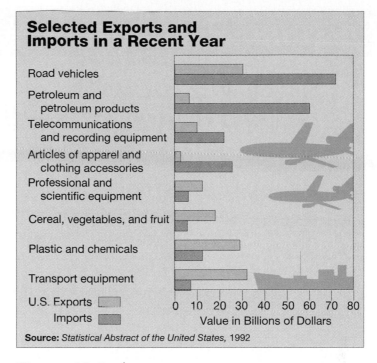

Selected Exports and Imports in a Recent Year

U.S. Exports
Imports
Value in Billions of Dollars

Source: *Statistical Abstract of the United States*, 1992

Figure 19.3 ▲
Exports and Imports of the U.S.
Look at the graph above to see what products the United States imports and exports. Name the products that the United States exports more than it imports.

damental proposition in international trade is:

In the long run, exports pay for imports.

The reason that exports ultimately pay for imports is that people in other countries want something in exchange for goods that are shipped to the United States. For the most part, they want goods made in the United States.

S E C T I O N 1 R E V I E W

Understanding Vocabulary

Define imports, exports, absolute advantage, specialization, comparative advantage.

Reviewing Objectives

1. How important is international trade to the total United States economy?
2. What is the difference between absolute advantage and comparative advantage?

David Ricardo on Trading With Other Nations

- 1772–1823
- made a fortune as a stockbroker in London
- member of House of Commons for five years
- introduced the principle of comparative advantage to international trade
- published the *Principles of Political Economy and Taxation* in 1817

In the following excerpt from the *Principles of Political Economy and Taxation*, David Ricardo stresses the importance of trade and the gains that can be had from international trade.

No extension of foreign trade will immediately increase the amount of value in a country, although it will very powerfully contribute to increase the mass of commodities, and therefore the sum of enjoyments. . . .

It is quite as important to the happiness of mankind that our enjoyments should be increased by the better distribution of labour, by each country producing those commodities for which by its situation, its climate, and its other natural or artificial advantages it is adapted, and by their exchanging them for the commodities of other countries as that they should be augmented by a rise in the rate of profit.

Foreign trade, then, [is] highly beneficial to a country as it increases the amount and variety of the objects on which revenue may be expended, and affords, by the abundance and cheapness of commodities, incentives to saving, and to its accumulation of capital. . . .

Under a system of perfectly free commerce, each country naturally devotes its capital and labour to such employments as are most beneficial to each. This pursuit of individual advantage is admirably connected with the universal good of the whole. By stimulating industry, by rewarding ingenuity, and by using most efficaciously [effectively] the peculiar powers bestowed by nature, it distributes labour most effectively and most economically: while, by increasing the general mass of productions, it diffuses general benefit, and binds together, by one common tie of interest and intercourse, the universal society of nations throughout the civilised world. It is this principle which determines that wine shall be made in France and Portugal, that corn shall be grown in America and Poland, and that hardware and other goods shall be manufactured in England.

Checking for Understanding

❶ How does trade help increase the "sum of enjoyments" in a specific country?

❷ Why is trade good for a country?

❸ Why is trade good for the world?

Trading Currencies in Foreign Exchange Markets

The United States uses the dollar as its medium of exchange; France uses francs; Great Britain, pounds; and Japan, yen. **Figure 19.4** shows some of the variety of world currencies. To engage in world trade, countries must have a way of exchanging one type of currency for another. A Japanese videodisc player manufacturer who exports players to the United States probably does not want American dollars in payment. The firm needs Japanese currency to pay its workers and suppliers. Fortunately, international trade is organized so that individuals and businesses can easily and quickly convert one currency to another. **Foreign exchange markets** allow for these conversions. Foreign exchange markets deal in buying and selling foreign currency for businesses that want to import goods from other countries. Some of the currency trading takes place through banks.

Fixed Exchange Rates

From 1944 to the early 1970s, the foreign exchange market operated with a **fixed rate of exchange.** Under this system, a national government sets the value of its currency in relation to a single standard. Then, a government can establish equivalents between its currency and that of other countries. The **International Monetary Fund (IMF)** monitored a fixed exchange rate system. Member

Figure 19.4
World Currencies
Some national currencies have the same name. Canada, Australia, and the United States, for example, all call their currencies dollars. Other countries, such as Portugal with its escudos, have currencies with unique names. Most can be exchanged for other currencies, thus making international trade easier.
▼

governments of the International Monetary Fund (including the United States, of course) were obligated to keep their foreign exchange rates more or less fixed.

A fixed rate of exchange had some advantages for world trade. Importers and exporters knew exactly how much of a foreign currency they could purchase with their own nation's money. Also, the system allowed central banks to affect the level of exports and imports in their country by devaluing the currency. **Devaluation** means lowering a currency's value in relation to other currencies by government order.

Take a Japanese VCR as an example. **Figure 19.5** shows how the cost of a Japanese VCR would decrease after Japan devalues its yen by one-half.

This system of fixed exchange rates eventually proved impractical. The basic problem was the difficulty of fixing exchange rates in an international economic climate that was constantly changing. Suppose one nation such as the United States suffered from high inflation and a trading partner such as Japan did not. Then American goods would become very costly for the Japanese to buy. Because the price of Japanese goods would not be rising, Americans could use their inflated, or "cheaper," dollars to buy more Japanese products. The United States would be importing huge quantities of goods but exporting little to Japan.

Flexible Exchange Rates

Most of the world's nations arrived at the solution of the **flexible exchange rates.** Under this arrangement, the forces of supply and demand are allowed to set the price of various currencies. With flexible exchange rates, a currency's price may change, or float, up or down a little each day. For example, Japanese currency might be trading at 112.6 yen to the dollar on one day and 117.8 yen to the dollar on the next. On August 15, 1971, President Richard Nixon officially announced what would become the end of fixed American exchange rates. The International Monetary Fund slowly lost its importance in the world as fewer and fewer countries attempted to fix their exchange rates.

The forces actually determining exchange rates are the supply and demand of goods and services that can

Figure 19.5
Effect of Devaluation
These charts show how devaluation of the Japanese yen affects consumers in the United States. Do you think an American consumer would prefer to buy a VCR before or after devaluation? Why?

▶ **Effects of Official Devaluation of Japanese Yen**

Before Devaluation
Japanese VCR costs 20,000 yen
Exchange Rate: 100 yen = $1 U.S.
$VCR = \dfrac{20,000 \text{ yen}}{100 \text{ yen per \$}} = \$200.00$
An American would have to pay $200 for the Japanese VCR

After Devaluation
Japanese VCR costs 20,000 yen
Exchange Rate: 200 yen = $1 U.S.
$VCR = \dfrac{20,000 \text{ yen}}{200 \text{ yen per \$}} = \$100.00$
An American would have to pay $100 for the Japanese VCR

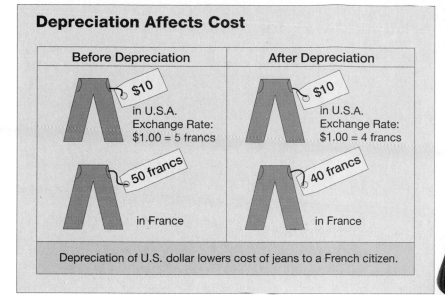

Depreciation Affects Cost

Before Depreciation	After Depreciation
$10 in U.S.A. Exchange Rate: $1.00 = 5 francs	$10 in U.S.A. Exchange Rate: $1.00 = 4 francs
50 francs in France	40 francs in France

Depreciation of U.S. dollar lowers cost of jeans to a French citizen.

◀ **Figure 19.6**
Depreciation Affects Cost
In the example of depreciation given in the chart, how does the French consumer benefit? How does the American manufacturer of jeans benefit? Do you think the American consumer ever benefits from depreciation? ▼

SALE

be bought with a particular currency. For example, suppose the amount of dollars wanted by Japanese exporters is greater than the quantity of dollars supplied by Americans who want to buy Japanese goods. Because the quantity demanded exceeds that supplied, the American dollar will become more expensive in relation to the yen. It will take more yen to equal $1. If the quantity of dollars American importers supplied is more than the quantity demanded by Japanese exporters, the price of a dollar will become cheaper in relation to the yen. Fewer yen will equal $1.

When the price of a currency falls through the action of supply and demand, it is termed **depreciation**. As with devaluation, depreciation of a country's currency improves its competitive edge in trade. **Figure 19.6** uses the price of jeans as an example of the effect of depreciation.

Besides import-export transactions, political or economic instability within a country may encourage people to exchange their currency for a more stable currency, often the United States dollar. In that case, the value of the dollar would rise in relation to the other nation's currency. A country that is experiencing rapid inflation will find its

currency falling in value in relation to other currencies. Such depreciation happened to Brazil's and Mexico's money during the 1980s.

Exchange Rates and the Balance of Trade

The rate at which a currency is being exchanged can have an important effect on a nation's balance of trade. The **balance of trade** is the difference between the value of a nation's exports and its imports. If a nation's currency depreciates, the nation will likely export more goods because its products will become cheaper to other nations. If a nation's currency increases in value, or price, the amount of its exports will drop.

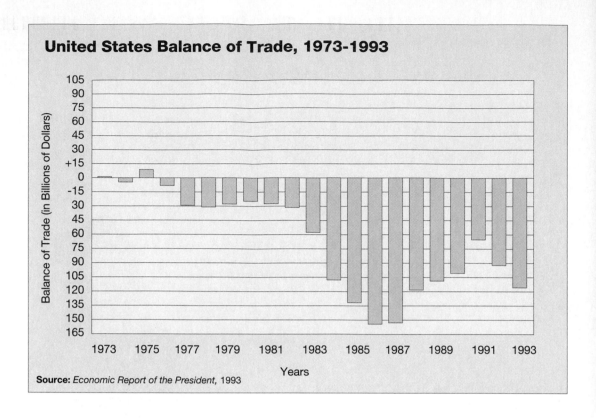

United States Balance of Trade, 1973-1993

Balance of Trade (in Billions of Dollars)

105
90
75
60
45
30
+15
0
-15
30
45
60
75
90
105
120
135
150
165

1973 1975 1977 1979 1981 1983 1985 1987 1989 1991 1993

Years

Source: *Economic Report of the President,* 1993

Figure 19.7 ▲
Balance of Trade
This graph shows how the United States has basically had a negative balance of trade since the early 1970s.
Since 1977, in what year was the United States balance of trade most unfavorable? Least unfavorable?

When the value of goods leaving a nation exceeds the value of those coming in, a positive balance of trade is said to exist. In this case, the nation is bringing in more money as payments for goods than it is paying out. A negative balance of trade exists when the value of goods coming into a country is greater than the value of those going out. This situation is called a trade deficit. As you can see from **Figure 19.7**, the United States has had a negative balance of trade for many years beginning in the 1970s.

SECTION 2 REVIEW

Understanding Vocabulary
Define foreign exchange markets, fixed rate of exchange, International Monetary Fund (IMF), devaluation, flexible exchange rates, depreciation, balance of trade.

Reviewing Objectives
❶ Why do nations need a system of currency exchange rates?
❷ How do the forces of supply and demand determine flexible exchange rates?
❸ What has been the normal state of America's balance of trade in recent years?

Exchanging Foreign Currency

Many Americans at one time or another will travel to another country where they will have to exchange United States money for the local currency. Do you know how to exchange foreign currency?

The Dollar Value of Foreign Currency

Prices of foreign currencies are posted at places where you can buy foreign money, such as foreign-exchange counters in airports and banks throughout the world. Prices are also listed in major newspapers.

When you exchange your dollars for another currency, you will be "paid" the exchange rate as shown in **Figure A**.

If you were in France on this particular day, exchanging $1, you would get back approximately 5.8 francs. If you exchange $1,000, you would get back 5,773 francs.

Units of Currency Per Dollar

Exchange rates can all be expressed in their mirror image. If, for example, one United States dollar buys 100 Japanese yen, then one Japanese yen is equal to one cent. **Figure B** expresses units of other currencies per dollar.

Suppose you want to buy a piece of crystal in France. It costs 4,827 francs. To find out how much it is in American dollars, you multiply that number times the dollar value of one franc, or $4,827 \times .1732 = \$836.03$.

Practicing the Skill

Study **Figure B**. Someone offers you 10,000 Belgian francs for a valuable painting. How much less would you be paid in Belgian francs than in Swiss francs in terms of dollars?

Figure A

National Currencies	Unit of Other Currencies per Dollar
Belgian franc	34.935
British pound	.6636
Hong Kong dollar	7.7565
French franc	5.7733
German mark	1.7112
Japanese yen	108.10
Swiss franc	1.507
Thai baht	25.24

Figure B

National Currencies	Dollars per Unit of Foreign Currencies
Belgian franc	.0286
British pound	1.507
Hong Kong dollar	.1289
French franc	.1732
German mark	.5844
Japanese yen	.0093
Swiss franc	.6636
Thai baht	.0396

SECTION **3** *Restrictions on World Trade*

SECTION 3 FOCUS

Terms to Know tariff, revenue tariff, protective tariff, import quota, embargo, protectionists, General Agreement on Tariffs and Trade (GATT), U.S.-Canadian Free Trade Agreement, North American Free Trade Agreement (NAFTA)

Objectives *After reading this section, you should be able to:*

① List three ways that **imports can be restricted**.

② Explain the main **arguments for and against free trade**.

③ List one worldwide trade agreement and three regional **trade agreements**.

To Trade or Not to Trade?

The difficulties different currencies cause are only one problem of world trade. There are also natural barriers, which include the differences in languages and cultures between various trading partners. In addition, nations may set restrictions to discourage or limit trade. Three major barriers to world trade are tariffs, quotas, and embargoes.

Three Ways to Restrict Imports

The most commonly used barrier to free trade is the **tariff,** a tax on imports. A **revenue tariff** is one used primarily to raise income without restricting imports. Although tariffs today account for less than 2 percent of the federal government's income, they were the major source of federal funding until the early 1900s.

A **protective tariff** is one designed to raise the cost of imported goods and thereby protect domestic producers, as **Figure 19.8** shows. As **Figure 19.9** shows, tariff rates have been as high as 62 percent of the value of the imported goods. Tariffs are much lower today but are still used to pro-

Figure 19.8
Domestic Goods

As you learned from the law of demand, the quantity demanded of an item falls as the price rises. Higher prices for foreign goods because of tariffs mean that Americans will buy more domestic goods and fewer goods from abroad. ▼

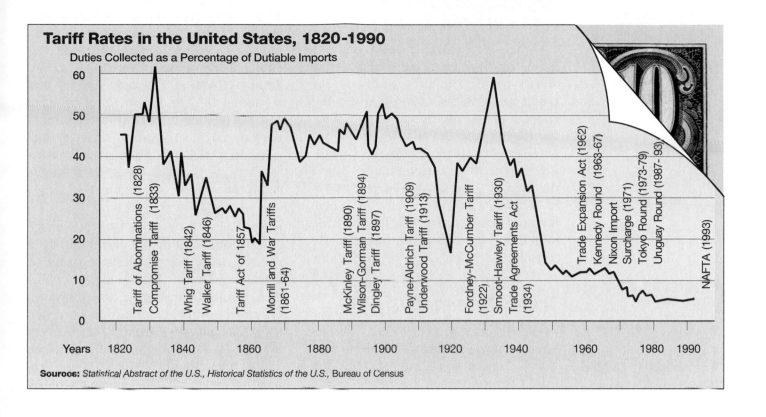

Tariff Rates in the United States, 1820-1990

Duties Collected as a Percentage of Dutiable Imports

- Tariff of Abominations (1828)
- Compromise Tariff (1833)
- Whig Tariff (1842)
- Walker Tariff (1846)
- Tariff Act of 1857
- Morrill and War Tariffs (1861–64)
- McKinley Tariff (1890)
- Wilson-Gorman Tariff (1894)
- Dingley Tariff (1897)
- Payne-Aldrich Tariff (1909)
- Underwood Tariff (1913)
- Fordney-McCumber Tariff (1922)
- Smoot-Hawley Tariff (1930)
- Trade Agreements Act (1934)
- Trade Expansion Act (1962)
- Kennedy Round (1963-67)
- Nixon Import Surcharge (1971)
- Tokyo Round (1973-79)
- Uruguay Round (1987-93)
- NAFTA (1993)

Sources: *Statistical Abstract of the U.S., Historical Statistics of the U.S.,* Bureau of Census

tect such industries as textiles from foreign competition.

An alternative method for restricting imports is the quota system. An **import quota** is a restriction imposed on the value of or the number of units of a particular good that can be brought into the country. The United States has placed quotas on imports of sugar, shoes, shirts, and cloth.

An **embargo** is a complete restriction on the import or export of a particular good. Often embargoes are enacted for political reasons. For example, in 1980 President Jimmy Carter ordered a halt of all grain sales to the Soviet Union. This was in response to Soviet intervention in Afghanistan. President Ronald Reagan lifted the grain embargo in 1981, however, he placed new restrictions on the sale to the Soviets of certain high-technology equipment such as computers. The United States has also ordered embargoes on goods from certain countries. In 1986, Congress passed an embargo on trade with South Africa. It ended in 1993.

Figure 19.9 ▲
Tariff Rates

As you can see on the graph, United States tariff rates have fluctuated greatly over the last 180 years. What seems to be the trend in tariff rates now? Why do you think this is the case?

Arguments For and Against Free Trade

Since World War II, the trend has been toward relaxing barriers to world trade. The pros and cons of trade restrictions are still often the subject of intense public debate. **Protectionists** are those who argue for trade restrictions. **Figure 19.10** outlines three main arguments for trade protection.

Those who favor free or unrestricted trade usually point to three benefits. **Figure 19.11** examines these arguments.

Trade Agreements

For much of the 1900s, nations have worked to lower trade restrictions. Recent agreements have followed this pattern.

The General Agreement on Tariffs and Trade (GATT) After World War II, numerous bilateral trade agreements were brought together in the **General Agreement on Tariffs and Trade (GATT).** The agreement was signed in 1947 and took effect January 1, 1948. Under GATT, countries meet periodically to negotiate tariff reductions that are mutually advantageous to all members. The latest GATT tariff reductions were reached in 1993.

Regional Trade Agreements Three of the most important agreements to reduce tariff barriers are the unified European Union (EU), which was formerly called the European Community and the European common market, the **U.S.-Canadian Free Trade Agreement,** and the **North American Free Trade Agreement (NAFTA).** The European Union currently consists of 12

Figure 19.10
Arguments Against Free Trade

Protectionists object to free trade based on the three areas shown below.

A **Job security is threatened.** Opponents of relaxing trade restrictions argue that many domestic workers will be unemployed if foreign competitors sell goods at lower prices than American firms. In the 1980s, American steel mills laid off many workers due to foreign competition. ▼

B **Protection of the nation's economic security is needed.** Certain industries, such as oil, should be protected against foreign competition. Protectionists argue that these industries are crucial to the economy of the United States. ▼

C **Protection of infant industries is needed.** Tariffs and quotas are needed as temporary protection for new, infant industries. If foreign competition is restricted for a time, a young industry such as video camera manufacturing may become strong enough to compete in the world market. ▼

Figure 19.11
Arguments For Free Trade

People who want free trade base their support on the three areas shown below.

A Competition means improved products. Foreign competition encourages United States firms to improve technology and production methods.

B Trade restrictions damage export industries, putting Americans out of work. The fewer goods the United States imports, the less American money there is available outside the United States to buy American exports.

member nations—France, Germany, Britain, Denmark, Italy, Spain, Greece, Portugal, Luxembourg, Belgium, Holland, and Ireland. Starting on January 1, 1993, the EU eliminated most of its restrictions on trade among its member states. Also, both labor and capital are supposed to be freely mobile within those 12 nations.

On January 1, 1989, a historic free trade agreement (FTA) between the United States and Canada took effect. The goal is to eliminate high tariffs on furniture, textiles, appliances, petrochemicals, plastics, metal, paper, and fish products. The U.S.-Canadian FTA guarantees that both countries have access to each other's petroleum, gas, coal, and electricity at prices paid by nationals under comparable commercial circumstances.

The North American Free Trade Agreement (NAFTA) is designed to extend the U.S.-Canadian FTA to include Mexico. The United States Congress approved NAFTA in 1993. NAFTA will likely benefit some industries and hurt others. Mexico will probably import more industrial machinery and grain from the United States. It will also import more United States banking services. Industries in the United States that will be hardest hit by increased competition from Mexico will be footwear, steel, and clothes. Citrus growers, too, particularly in California and Florida, may face increased competition from lower-priced Mexican fruit growers.

C Specialization and comparative advantage lowers prices. The consumer benefits because comparative advantage in production brings more goods at lower prices.

SECTION 3 REVIEW

Understanding Vocabulary

Define tariff, revenue tariff, protective tariff, import quota, embargo, protectionists, General Agreement on Tariffs and Trade (GATT), U.S.-Canadian Free Trade Agreement, North American Free Trade Agreement (NAFTA).

Reviewing Objectives

1. How can a nation restrict imports?
2. What are three arguments for and three arguments against free trade?
3. What are one international and three regional trade agreements?

Readings in Economics

USA TODAY **SEPTEMBER 15, 1993**

TAKING SIDES

by Juan J. Walte

Raul and Roberto Quinones run a thriving business from four stores here [Ciudad Juarez, Mexico], selling Mexican-made ceramic tiles to Americans who cross the Rio Grande to buy at low prices.

But the brothers spend much of their free time debating the merits of the North American Free Trade Agreement. . . .

The Quinones brothers' debate is taking place on both sides of the border, with both Mexicans and Americans arguing both sides of the issue. . . .

But the debate is especially intense here and in El Paso across the border, where people say their whole future is meshed with the fate of the proposed NAFTA agreement. . . .

"Look around you and you'll see we are already very much under the influence of the 'American way of life'."

True, Mexicans cross the international bridges to spend their money at El Paso malls and dozens of stores near the border.

Even on the Mexican side of the border they can shop at Wal-Mart and K Mart and eat at McDonald's, Burger King and Church's Chicken.

Many of the Mexicans visiting those U.S. franchises earn their money at U.S.-owned businesses that set up in free-trade zones along the border.

About 2,100 such plants—called *maquiladoras* (Spanish for "twin plants"— referring to the connections within a plant in the USA) — have opened here, employing 500,000, primarily in low-skill, low-paying jobs. . . .

Most are assembly plants where workers piece together parts made in the USA or Japan. The final product is exported; it cannot be sold here.

The fate of these businesses remains open to question.

• THINK ABOUT IT •

1. What is the subject being debated?

2. What are *maquiladoras*?

19 *Highlights*

The Benefits of World Trade

Key Terms
imports (p. 462)
exports (p. 462)
absolute advantage
  (p. 464)
specialization (p. 464)
comparative advantage
  (p. 465)

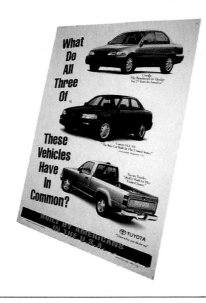

Summary
Nations benefit from world trade because each nation differs in the type and amount of the factors of production it has available for use. Absolute advantage is the ability of a country, using the same amount of resources as another country, to produce more of a particular good than the other country. If a country has a comparative advantage in at least one product, it will be advantageous for that country to specialize in the production of that good. The country can then trade with other countries to obtain other goods it desires.

Financing World Trade

Key Terms
foreign exchange markets
  (p. 467)
fixed rate of exchange
  (p. 467)
International Monetary
  Fund (IMF) (p. 467)

devaluation (p. 468)
flexible exchange rates
  (p. 468)
depreciation (p. 469)
balance of trade (p. 469)

Summary
With a fixed rate of exchange, national governments set the value of their currencies in relation to a single standard. With flexible exchange rates, the forces of supply and demand set the prices of currencies. When the value of our exports exceeds the value of our imports, we are running a surplus in our balance of trade.

Restrictions on World Trade

Key Terms
tariff (p. 472)
revenue tariff (p. 472)
protective tariff (p. 472)
import quota (p. 473)
embargo (p. 473)
protectionists (p. 474)

General Agreement on
  Tariffs and Trade
  (GATT) (p. 474)
U.S.-Canadian Free Trade
  Agreement (p. 474)
North American Free
  Trade Agreement
  (NAFTA) (p. 474)

Summary
Legal restrictions on world trade are attempts to protect a nation's industries and workers. The pros and cons of trade restrictions are often intensely debated. GATT and several regional trade agreements govern most of the world's trade.

19 *Review*

Identifying Key Terms

Write the letter of the definition in Column B below that correctly defines each term in Column A.

Column A
1. absolute advantage (p. 464)
2. devaluation (p. 468)
3. depreciation (p. 469)
4. embargo (p. 473)
5. protectionists (p. 474)
6. balance of trade (p. 469)
7. comparative advantage (p. 465)

Column B
a. lowering of currency's value in relation to other currencies
b. complete restriction on the import or export of a particular good
c. difference between the value of a nation's exports and its imports
d. ability of a nation to produce a product at a lower opportunity cost
e. drop of the price of a currency in response to supply and demand
f. ability of a country to use the same amount of resources as another to produce a product at less cost
g. those who oppose the relaxation of trade restrictions

Write a paragraph on tariffs and international and regional agreements to reduce tariffs using the following words:

revenue tariff (p. 472)
protective tariff (p. 472)
import quota (p. 473)
General Agreement on Tariffs and Trade (GATT) (p. 474)
U.S.-Canadian Free Trade Agreement (p. 474).
North American Free Trade Agreement (NAFTA) (p. 474)

Recalling Facts and Ideas

Section 1
1. How does a country determine whether it has a comparative advantage in the production of certain goods?
2. What does the United States gain as a country from international trade?
3. "America can produce more compact discs per labor hour than can any other country in the world." Is this an example of an absolute or a comparative advantage?

Section 2
4. What international organization monitored the world's fixed exchange rate system?
5. Why is it difficult to maintain a system of fixed rates of exchange?

Section 3
6. What is the difference between a revenue tariff and a protective tariff?
7. What are three arguments against free trade?
8. What is also affected when restrictions are put on imports?
9. What are the 12 member nations of the European Union (EU)?

Critical Thinking

Section 1
Drawing Conclusions Some people worry that highly competitive nations will end up producing everything. How do absolute and comparative advantage relate to this conclusion?

Section 2
Making Predictions If the value of the dollar fell in relation to other currencies, what would you expect to happen to American exports?

Section 3

Determining Cause and Effect How does protection of infant industries allow them to grow?

Applying Economic Concepts

The Benefits of International Trade Even though international trade accounts for only about 10 percent of the American economy, it affects all Americans. To understand how international trade affects you, try to describe what your world would be like if international trade were outlawed. You can do this by writing a list of all the products you would *not* be able to purchase or whose price would go up dramatically without international trade. Some examples that quickly come to mind are rice and coffee. What are some others?

Chapter Projects

1. **Individual Project** There are virtually no restrictions on trade within the 50 states, mainly because the Constitution forbids it. First find the section or sections in the Constitution that prohibit at least one restriction on international trade and write them down. Next write out a list of the problems that might arise if the Constitution had been silent on trade among the several states.

2. **Cooperative Learning Project** Working in groups of four, concentrate on one or more countries taken from the following list:
   - Mexico
   - Canada
   - Japan
   - Zaire
   - Morocco

   Each member of the group will research one of the following items:
   - The size of the international sector within each country (i.e., the percentage of GDP accounted for by imports or exports)
   - The natural resource base of the nation
   - The top three items that are exported
   - The top three items that are imported

Each group will decide what the relationship is between the natural resource base and what is exported and what is imported. Each group will try to determine whether any relationship exists between what is imported and what is exported. Finally, each group will write a summary of how life in each country would be different if international trade were prohibited.

Reviewing Skills

Exchanging Foreign Currency

Using the Right Currency Look at the set of exchange rates with the U.S. dollar below.

Currency	Units per Dollar
Argentine peso	0.9901
Australian dollar	1.4995
Irish pound	0.6971
New Zealand dollar	1.846
Philippine peso	27.33
Singapore dollar	1.6245
Taiwan dollar	26.34

You are selling a valuable ring to a foreigner who offers you 1,000 pesos. You think she is referring to Argentinean pesos, but in fact she is referring to Philippine pesos. What is the difference in the dollar price?

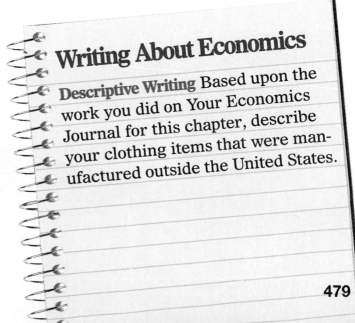

Writing About Economics

Descriptive Writing Based upon the work you did on Your Economics Journal for this chapter, describe your clothing items that were manufactured outside the United States.

20 CONVERGING ECONOMIC SYSTEMS

Are there any restrictions on who may buy and sell real estate in the United States?

Why are these properties being sold?

Who determines the prices for each property?

Who owns these houses?

Who has put these houses up for sale?

Who is permitted to buy these houses?

Your Economics Journal

Keep track of the products and services you buy during the week. For each, try to find out whether the price was determined by supply and demand or by an agency of government. For example, cable TV rates are regulated by the federal government.

SECTION **1** *Comparing Capitalism and Socialism*

SECTION 1 FOCUS

Terms to Know three *P*'s, private property rights, price system, communism, proletariat, democratic socialism, authoritarian socialism

Objectives *After reading this section, you should be able to:*
1. List five characteristics of **pure market capitalism**.
2. List six characteristics of **pure socialism**.
3. Describe **the development of socialism**.
4. Compare **planning under socialism and under capitalism**.
5. Explain the benefits of **capitalism**.

Figure 20.1
Characteristics of Pure Capitalism
Market capitalism operates on the basis of the **three *P*'s:**
- Prices
- Profits
- Private property
Under pure capitalism government is limited to providing such public goods as defense and police protection. ▼

Who Should Control Pricing and Production?

When you buy a sweater, change jobs, or invest in a savings bond, you are affecting the nation's economy. Some government intervention occurs in the American economy, but it is largely the marketplace that answers the four basic economic questions. See Chapter 2. In command economies, government, not the market, answers these four basic questions.

In this chapter you will study different economic systems. You must remember, though, that all principles of economics apply to all economic systems. No matter what the system, the fundamental economic problem of scarcity must be solved.

The system that we know best in the United States is market capitalism. At the other extreme is pure command socialism.

Pure Market Capitalism

In its purest theoretical form, market capitalism, or pure capitalism, has distinct characteristics and components. **Figures 20.1** and **20.2** show these.

Characteristics of Pure Capitalism

1. **Private property rights** exist, are legal, and are enforced by the government.

2. Pure capitalism is a **price system**. Prices are allowed to seek their own level as determined by the forces of supply and demand.

3. Resources, including labor, are free to move in and out of industries in competing geographic locations. The movement of resources follows the lure of profits — higher expected profits create an incentive for more resources to go where those profits are expected to occur.

4. Those who take risks may be rewarded by higher profits. When those risks turn out to be bad business decisions, the risk takers lose money.

5. The four basic economic questions are all decided in a decentralized way by individuals. What and how much should be produced, who should produce what, how it should be produced, and for whom it should be produced are all left to the market.

Pure Socialism

Pure socialism is an economic system in which there is virtually no private property and the state owns virtually all the factors of production. **Figure 20.3** lists the characteristics of pure socialism.

A Price System ▲

B Decentralization ▶

Figure 20.2
The Components of Pure Capitalism
Pure capitalism has five characteristics, as shown in this illustration.

C
Resources ▼

D
Private Property ▼

PRIVATE PROPERTY NO TRESPASSING

Figure 20.3 ▲
Characteristics of Pure Socialism
Few examples of pure command socialism exist today. Perhaps the most extensively centralized controlled command social system is in North Korea. There has also been a command system in Cuba under dictator Fidel Castro.

E Profit/Loss ▼

SUN-MAID CALIFORNIA SUN-DRIED RAISINS
100% NATURAL
NO FAT · NO CHOLESTEROL
RESEALABLE 15 OZ. BAG
$1.89 sale $1.39
NET WT. 15 OZ. (425 g)

The Change From Capitalism to Socialism According to Marx

Step 1	Step 2
Capitaism would suffer extreme recessions and depressions that would harm workers. A few rich capitalists would have all industrial power.	The wide gap between the rich and the poor would cause workers to unite and overthrow capitalism.

Step 3	Step 4
The victorious workers would establish a new socialist system. Workers, through the state, would own and control the means of production.	The system would evolve into pure **communism**—an ideal system with no need for a government. Workers would contribute to society to their full abilities and, in return, take only what they needed.

Figure 20.4 ▲
The End of Capitalism
Clearly Marx did not accurately predict what would happen in capitalist nations.

The Development of Socialism

Socialism as a modern economic system grew out of protests against the problems caused by the Industrial Revolution of the 1800s.

The Marxian View of Socialism
Karl Marx viewed history as a continual struggle between various groups, or classes, in society. He saw this struggle in his own day as going on between capitalists—owners of the land, machines, and factories—and the **proletariat** (PROH-luh-TER-ee-uht), or workers. Marx believed capitalists exploited the proletariat, or used them unfairly. According to Marx, the value of goods depends only on how much labor is used in producing them. When capitalists sold a good and kept the profit, they were taking money that rightly belonged to the proletariat.

Despite capitalism's dominance in the nineteenth century, Marx believed it was doomed to fail. Marx outlined the collapse of capitalism and predicted the evolution of socialism into communism as **Figure 20.4** shows.

Socialism Since Marx In the twentieth century, socialism has split into two major trends: democratic socialism and authoritarian socialism. **Democratic socialism** is a type of socialist system that works within the constitutional framework of a nation to elect socialists to office. In democratic socialist nations, government usually controls only some areas of the economy.

Authoritarian socialism, in contrast, follows the lead of Marx. Its supporters advocate revolution as the means to overthrow capitalism and bring about socialist goals. In authori-

Figure 20.5 ▶
Planning in Market and Command Economies
Planning is unavoidable, no matter what the economic system. The United States has a highly planned economy. The difference between economic planning in the United States and in command economies is who does the planning.

Planning in Market and Command Economies

The Market System: Decentralized	The Command System: Centralized
In the United States market system, planning is undertaken by private firms, individuals, and elected government representatives. In the private sector in the United States, all plans are built around relative prices. It is changing relative prices in our market economy that communicates scarcity and priorities. The market system coordinates "the plan."	In pure socialist systems, central planners undertake the planning on behalf of everyone. The signals given to central planners in socialist economies have proved to be weak, inaccurate, or nonexistent, however. The result generally has been low rates of growth and low standards of living in centrally planned socialist economies.

tarian socialist nations, a central government controls the entire economy. *Communism,* the term Marx applied to his ideal society, has come to mean any authoritarian socialist system.

Planning Under Capitalism and Socialism

It is often said that pure socialism requires centralized economic planning, and pure capitalism does not. The reality is that all economies are planned in one way or another. See **Figure 20.5.**

The Benefits of Capitalism

Many economists like to compare the advantages and disadvantages of capitalism and socialism. Often such comparisons are based on individual values. Those who place a high value on personal freedom, initiative, and individuality prefer capitalism. Such critics of socialism point out that socialism brings with it immense government intervention in all parts of the economy and, by necessity, in people's personal lives. By definition, a socialist system is one in which government controls numerous production and pricing decisions throughout the nation.

The supporters of capitalism point out that capitalism allows for more efficiency in the marketplace and for greater rates of economic growth. Moreover, considerable evidence shows that unregulated economic systems—those that are closer to pure capitalism—have higher rates of economic growth.

Of course, capitalism as it exists in the world has some problems. Critics point out that income is unequally distributed throughout the economy. They also say that although capitalist nations have enough government-provided goods such as highways, they do not have enough schools and museums for the general public. Such critics clearly value the political goals of socialism. They overlook the fact that despite their shortcomings, capitalist countries are economically healthier. Comparison of historical economic statistics—such as GDP, food consumption, and ownership of goods such as automobiles, for example—tells us that capitalist nations have had higher living standards, more economic freedom, and higher rates of growth. In addition, a look at emigration figures and patterns tells us that more people have moved from socialist nations to live in capitalist nations than the reverse.

SECTION 1 REVIEW

Understanding Vocabulary
Define three P's, private property rights, price system, communism, proletariat, democratic socialism, authoritarian socialism.

Reviewing Objectives
1. What are the key characteristics of pure market capitalism?
2. What are the key characteristics of pure socialism?
3. What were the major steps in the development of socialism?
4. How does planning under socialism differ from planning under capitalism?
5. What are the benefits of capitalism?

Newspapers and magazines are good sources of economic news. Understanding economic news requires the ability to interpret information. You can do this if you know the background of the news and look for the five *W*'s and one *H* of news articles.

Figure A

China: The Next Great Economy?

If current trends continue, China may be the world's next great economy. This is the conclusion of a new report from the International Institute for Management Development.

China's economic growth leaped ahead in the 1980s, when some parts of the country became the fastest-growing regions of the world.

Figure B

Soviet '88 Economic Report Gloomy

Sweden to Allow More Foreign Investment

Soviets to Receive U.S.-Subsidized Wheat

Communists Lose 19 of 23 Cabinet Posts in Poland

Hungarian Communist Party Renounces Marxism

Berlin Wall Opens

Poland Announces Privatization Plans

Knowing the Background or Context of Economic News

Economic news can be better understood when the reader knows some of the background to the news. Sometimes the news article gives the reader this background. Other times the writer assumes that the reader knows the context. Look at the news article in **Figure A**. Knowing something about China's changing economy would help you understand the article.

Note that there are two types of economic news articles: strictly news and editorials. While a news story should be factual or descriptive and simply inform, an editorial is meant to persuade the reader about a point of view.

The Five *W*'s and One *H* of News Articles

The most important information in a news article is usually at the beginning. Look for the who, what, where, and when in the opening paragraphs. The rest of the article often describes the why and how.

Practicing the Skill

Study the headlines from 1989 in **Figure B**. What background should the reader know to best understand the news articles that would accompany these headlines?

Changing Authoritarian Socialism—The Case of China

SECTION 2 FOCUS

Terms to Know five-year plans, special economic zones

Objectives *After reading this section, you should be able to:*

1. Explain how the **Chinese economic system** developed following World War II.
2. Describe the benefits of **special economic zones** in the People's Republic of China.

Economic Change in the People's Republic

The People's Republic of China remains the largest nation that has some form of command socialism. A growing geographic area of modern-day China, however, has an economic system that is much closer to that of the United States. See **Figure 20.6**.

Development of China's Economic System

The communists won China's civil war following World War II. The new government started an economic system based on so-called **five-year plans.** The first such five-year plan, implemented in 1953, failed to fully meet expectations. Starting in the mid-1950s, the Chinese began to alter their strict centralized planning. In 1958 they reformed their system to allow decision-making powers for local governments rather than only from the central government. The national planning system was transformed into a regional planning system. The 1958 reforms did not transform the Chinese economy, however, because it was still not governed by capitalism's three *P*'s—prices, profits, and private property. Economic conditions worsened after 1958.

Figure 20.6
The Shift to a Free Market
China—after the failure of command economies throughout the world— began to allow limited free enterprise. ▼

China: Guangdong Province

China

Guangdong Province

Hong Kong

income and benefits for their workers. After all, their workers are politically important. Now, the government is shedding itself of many firms. In the early 1980s, state-run companies accounted for 70 percent of industrial production. Today it is less than 50 percent and is declining steadily.

Special Economic Zones

Beginning in 1979, the Chinese party designated certain geographic areas in the People's Republic of China as **special economic zones.** One of them is Guangdong Province, which you can see on the map in **Figure 20.7**.

Figure 20.7 ▲
The Return of Capitalism
Guangdong Province in southern China was the site of the rebirth of free enterprise in the nation. In 1997 the capitalist enclave of Hong Kong will rejoin the nation of China.

In 1978 Chinese leaders designed a reform to motivate individuals to work harder. Private individuals were permitted to rent land for up to 15 years. Each peasant household became responsible for its own plot of land. Whatever it produced in excess of a minimum amount the state required remained the property of the household. The results were impressive. Between 1979 and 1984, overall farm productivity increased dramatically.

Another set of reforms and a restructuring of the economy occurred in the mid-1980s. These reforms are continuing today. Managers in state-owned businesses are allowed much more decision-making power than before. They can set production according to market demand after they fulfill state production requirements. They also are allowed to sell part of their output to whomever they choose at market prices.

The problem with state-run factories is that managers have little incentive to make them run efficiently. Rather, these managers maximize the

Figure 20.8
Capitalist Investors
Signs of free enterprise abound in today's China. ▼

◄

**Figure 20.9
Rising Living
Standard**

A On a per-person
basis, China's living
standard is relatively
low compared to that
in the United States
and Japan. None-
theless, it is much
higher than it was
before China started
on its road to capital-
ism in 1979.

Move Toward Capitalism For the last decade and a half, this formerly command socialist region of the country has been moving toward unrestricted decentralized capitalism. Not surprisingly, the economy of the region has grown faster every year than any other place in the world.

A foreigner dropping into the city of Shenzhen, which is not far from Hong Kong, would have difficulty knowing he or she was in the People's Republic of China. There are McDonald's restaurants, business executives with portable phones and pagers, advertisements for Levi's, Seven UP, Heinz, and Head & Shoulders shampoo everywhere. See **Figure 20.8**.

There is a stock market and an active property market. The population of Shenzhen has grown from 50,000 in 1980 to more than 200,000 today. All these changes have affected the Chinese people. See **Figure 20.9**.

Spread of Capitalism Outside Guangdong Province, China is moving more slowly toward a market economy. In the summer of 1992, for example, the government announced that it would no longer use state-controlled pricing of raw materials. At the beginning of the 1990s, the government had already started phasing out its below-market prices for electricity, coal, iron, steel, oil, and telecommunications. Further, the government has continued to sell parts of its state-owned firms to private individuals.

Since 1979 when special economic zones were started, China's annual rate of economic growth—the increase in total national output per year—has averaged between 9 and 10 percent each year as shown in **Figure 20.10** (page 490).

B Workers at a modern plant earn much higher wages than they did a few years ago. ▼

Figure 20.10
Growth of People's Republic of China's Economy, 1979–1992
Since opening special economic zones in 1979, China's economic growth rate has generally been impressive. ▶

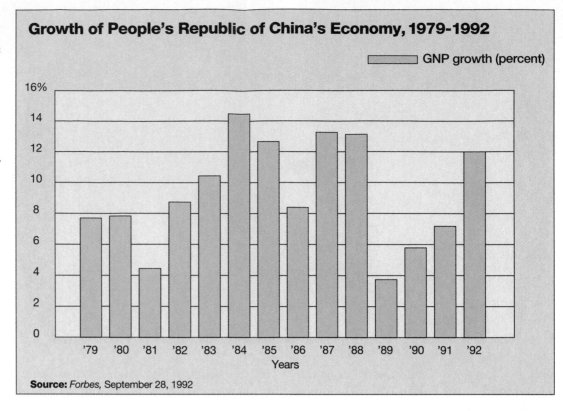

Growth of People's Republic of China's Economy, 1979-1992

GNP growth (percent)

Years

Source: *Forbes*, September 28, 1992

Prospects for the Future Not surprisingly, most of China's economic growth has been in the non-state sector, which includes private enterprises and foreign-invested businesses. Government leaders now believe that the state-run sector of manufacturing will account for only 25 percent of business volume in the year 2000—down from its current 50 percent today. The future in China looks much brighter than it does in other former socialist countries, such as Russia and countries of eastern Europe.

SECTION 2 REVIEW

Understanding Vocabulary
Define five-year plans, special economic zones.

Reviewing Objectives
1. The communist Chinese based their economic system on what concepts immediately following World War II?

2. What has been the economic growth rate in special economic zones in the People's Republic of China?

Personal Perspective

Karl Marx on Communism

Profile

- 1818 –1883
- born in Germany and educated in Bonn and Berlin
- deeply influenced by philosopher George Hegel
- published *The Communist Manifesto* with Friedrich Engels (1848) and *Das Kapital* (1867)

In the following excerpt from *The Communist Manifesto*, Karl Marx answers some questions most frequently asked of Communists: "Who are the Communists and what is their basic theory?"

The Communists do not form a separate party opposed to other working-class parties.

They have no interests separate and apart from those of the proletariat as a whole.

They do not set up any sectarian principles of their own, by which to shape and mold the proletarian movement.

... The immediate aim of the Communists is the same as that of all the other proletarian parties: formation of the proletariat into a class, overthrow of the bourgeois supremacy, conquest of political power by the proletariat.

... In this sense, the theory of the Communists may be summed up in the single phrase: Abolition of private property....

Property, in its present form, is based on the antagonism of capital and wage labor.

... It has been objected that upon the abolition of private property all work will cease, and universal laziness will overtake us.

According to this, bourgeois society ought long ago to have gone to the dogs through sheer idleness; for those of its members who work, acquire nothing, and those who acquire anything, do not work. *The whole of this objection is but another expression of the tautology [needless repetition of an idea]: that there can no longer be any wage labor when there is no longer any capital.*

... The workingmen have no country. We cannot take from them what they have not got. Since the proletariat must first of all acquire political supremacy, must rise to be the leading class of the nation, must constitute itself the nation, it is, so far, itself national, though not in the bourgeois sense of the word.

National differences and antagonisms between peoples are daily vanishing, owing to the development of the bourgeoisie, to freedom of commerce, to the world market, to uniformity in the mode of production and in the conditions of life corresponding thereto.

The supremacy of the proletariat will cause them to vanish still faster.

Checking for Understanding

1. What single phrase sums up communist theory?
2. Why was incentive to work an issue Marx had to address?
3. What did Marx mean when he wrote "The workingmen have no country"?

SECTION **3** *Nations Move Toward the Market System*

**Figure 20.11
Russian
Economic
Changes**
Russia and the other republics within formerly centrally planned economies are now all moving at different rates toward market capitalism. One of the ways they are moving toward market capitalism is by privatizing former state industries. ▼

Recipe for Economic Growth—a Little More Market

Economics textbooks written 10 or 15 years ago included sections on the Soviet Union and its satellite countries in Eastern Europe. The centralized command economy lasted for 74 years in the Soviet Union, and more than 40 years in Eastern Europe. In the Soviet Union, from the revolution in 1917 until the economic and political system collapsed on Christmas Day in 1991, it consisted of five-year plans, central-planning commissions, and hundreds of other types of commissions. Today all of that is fading history, as **Figure 20.11** shows.

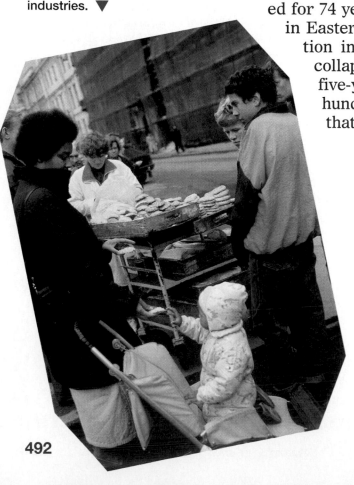

Privatization in Russia

Privatization simply means the change from state ownership of business, land, and buildings to private ownership. The private owners can be partnerships, domestic or foreign corporations, or individuals. Sometimes workers even buy the companies in which they are working, and foreign companies have purchased formerly state-owned companies in Russia and elsewhere. Volkswagen of Germany, for example, bought the state-owned autoworks in Czechoslovakia before that nation split in two in 1993.

Resistance to Privatization When a state enterprise is sold to a private interest, disruptions can occur. In particular, workers may find themselves out of a job. One of the problems with state-owned firms is that they are inefficiently run. When private owners take over, they often modernize the equipment and streamline the production processes. Consequently they sometimes require fewer workers. Because of the possibility of increased unemployment, many sectors of the population have resisted privatization.

Some workers even demanded that old-style centralized planning be brought back to Russia. They held demonstrations against the market-capitalist reforms that Russian President Boris Yeltsin had supported. Frustrations with continued economic problems contributed to the coup, or revolt, that attempted to oust Yeltsin in the fall of 1993.

Privatization by Voucher By 1993 the Russian government had started to make good on its promise of mass privatization. At the end of 1992, each Russian citizen had received a privatization voucher with a face value of 10,000 rubles (worth about $25 then, but probably less than $10 at exchange rates in the fall of 1993). Voucher owners could either sell them for cash to other investors, the way securities are sold in a **secondary market,** or they could use them to buy shares in the privatization of 6,000 companies scheduled to occur in 1993.

Value of Vouchers What would these vouchers buy you in terms of factories and capital? *The Economist,* a British publication, calculated that if you purchased every voucher on the secondary market in May 1993, you would have to pay $730 million. In principle, this was the price tag for obtaining ownership of roughly half of Russia's manufacturing industry!

For $730 million the most you could buy in the United States was one company like Cray Research, which builds super computers, or in Great Britain, the engineering company, Vickers. So, it would seem that for the same price, buying half of Russia's manufacturing industry would be a good deal.

Not everyone was convinced, however. Tremendous problems remain in this former Soviet republic. See **Figure 20.12.**

Certainly a change in the incentive structure can alter factory managers' behavior, but these changes will not necessarily happen overnight. In addition, even if a factory manages to

Figure 20.12 ▲
Challenges Facing Russian Manufacturing
In many factories, production lines work only three to four days a week. Many factories have plenty of physical capital, but it is so outdated and poorly maintained that its market value is effectively zero. In addition, a cadre of managers who have never been forced to look at "the bottom line" (profits) still run many factories.

Figure 20.13 ▶
Tax Levels in Sweden and the United States, 1960–1990

Tax levels in Sweden in 1960 were about equal to those in the United States, but rose to more than 20 percentage points higher. Despite these high taxes, the Swedes enjoyed a high standard of living. ▼

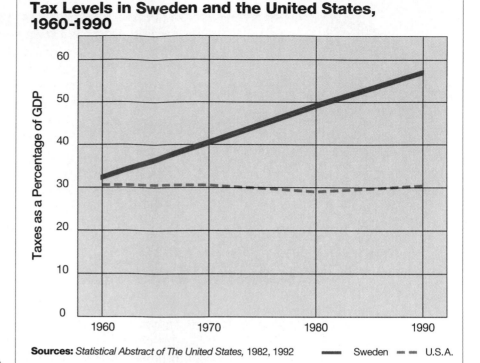

Tax Levels in Sweden and the United States, 1960-1990

Taxes as a Percentage of GDP (y-axis: 0, 10, 20, 30, 40, 50, 60)
(x-axis: 1960, 1970, 1980, 1990)

Sources: *Statistical Abstract of The United States,* 1982, 1992 — Sweden - - - U.S.A.

produce a marketable product, sometimes the distribution system in Russia is so poor that the product cannot get to the right geographical location in the market in order to be sold. Finally, there continues to be a deep-seated suspicion of for-profit activities. Privatization will probably not lead to immediate increases in Russian output.

Changes in Sweden

Sweden has been labeled a **welfare state**—a blend of capitalism and socialism. It combines private ownership of the means of production and competitive allocation of resources with the goal of social equality for its citizens. The so-called Swedish model helped transform what was an underdeveloped country in 1870 into a modern nation with one of the highest per-capita incomes in the world a century later.

Government Expenditures and Taxes Currently government expen-ditures (and taxes) account for almost 60 percent of Sweden's annual economic activity. As recently as 1960, this figure was little more than 30 percent. See **Figure 20.13**.

Swedish Welfare The Swedish government passed an employment security bill in the 1970s that almost guarantees lifelong employment. It also passed a law requiring labor union participation in company decision making. Full employment has existed for a number of years because the government took over many large industries and firms, such as steelworks. The government sector's share of employment was 20 percent in 1970, but today it is close to 35 percent.

Move Toward Free Enterprise Now Sweden has initiated changes in the model of combining capitalism with welfare socialism. In the 1990s, the government started to cut taxes and eliminate some public jobs. It also eased business regulation and approved foreign ownership of certain companies. The government ended the monopoly in both taxicabs and airlines and has plans to move further toward a market system in the future.

Changes in Latin America

Many nations in Latin America—especially Mexico, Venezuela, Chile, Brazil, and Argentina—have experienced high rates of growth since the mid-1980s. Though virtually all Latin American countries have economic systems that operate under market capitalism, most have had large government sectors. Since 1985, however, many government enterprises have been privatized.

Mexico is a good example as **Figure 20.14** shows. Other countries in Latin America are trying to follow the Mexican model, but because of multiparty infighting, they are not having an easy time. (One party has dominated Mexico for many years.) Nonetheless, Chile has privatized its airlines, phones, utilities, and pension funds. The Argentinean government has sold state-run oil fields, waterworks, petrochemical plants, and even army housing.

Converging Economic Systems

Many of the consequences of the changes in economic systems throughout the world can be analyzed by using the method of economic analysis that you have already learned in this text. The supply and demand model helps to predict what will happen when property is privatized, markets are freed, and the lure of profits becomes legal. Remember that the differences across countries are less related to cultures, religions, creeds, and ethnic characteristics and more related to how the structure and use of incentives are changing. The model that you can use most successfully always asks the question, How will people react to changed incentives?

**Figure 20.14
Privatizing in Mexico**
In 1989 Mexico made a wholesale move to free markets. The government started to sell off its vast holdings of companies and at the same time reduced the size of the government bureaucracy. Private companies in Mexico are building toll roads and phone systems.

▼

SECTION 3 REVIEW

Understanding Vocabulary
Define privatization, secondary market, welfare state.

Reviewing Objectives
1. What has been happening to state-owned property in Russia and in eastern Europe?
2. How has the Swedish economy been changing?
3. How have Latin American economies been changing in recent years?
4. What economic model helps predict what will happen as economies shift from command to market systems?

Readings in Economics

NEWSWEEK   **APRIL 12, 1993**

WHY CHINA DOES IT BETTER

by Joe Klein

As Russia unravels, China booms....

What have the Chinese done right that the Russians have done wrong?

... It might be argued that there have been three major factors in China's economic surge, two of which the Russians can't replicate. Obviously, Deng Xiaoping's [Chinese leader's] transition model was more sophisticated than anything the Russians have tried. Deng gradually liberated the economy, and prices—first encouraging farmers to grow for profit, then inviting foreign investment in rudimentary light industries (toys, shoes, clothing), which created the explosive growth in provinces like Guangdong that is now spreading inland....

But even if Boris Yeltsin [Russian leader] had followed Deng's model, there are two other factors that he couldn't have matched. For one thing, the Chinese seem to have an entrepreneurial edge. Their farmers welcomed the chance to make a profit. Their emerging middle class rushed to buy stocks when the Shenzhen exchange opened (they even rioted last year trying to gain access). Most Russians, by contrast, have reacted to liberalization with their distinctive mixture of skepticism and pessimism....

In much of Southeast Asia, ethnic Chinese already run the show—and that is the third, and perhaps most significant, factor at work here: the power and pride of the Chinese diaspora [people scattered outside their homelands]. There are an estimated 55 million Chinese living outside the People's Republic. They include a disproportionate number of successful businessmen who have now decided that it's safe to invest on the mainland.... The diasporans are ... returning home to sweep their ancestors' graves. They are the entrepreneurial heart of a Greater China that seems destined to become an economic, cultural—and perhaps military—superpower in the next century.

• THINK ABOUT IT •

1. What two economies, moving toward market systems, are contrasted in this article?

2. What three factors account for China's relative success in beginning to develop a market system?

20 *Highlights*

Comparing Capitalism and Socialism

Key Terms
three *P*'s (p. 482)
private property rights
  (p. 482)
price system (p. 482)
communism (p. 484)
proletariat (p. 484)
democratic socialism
  (p. 484)
authoritarian socialism
  (p. 484)

Summary
Pure market capitalism can be described on the basis of the three *P*'s—prices, profits, and private property. Private property rights exist and are legal; prices are allowed to seek their own level as determined by supply and demand; resources move to where the highest profits are made. In pure socialism, most prices are set by the state, the major factors of production are owned by the state, economic decisions are made by the state through central-planning agencies, and the movement of resources is strictly controlled. Planning under capitalism is decentralized. Capitalism offers personal freedom and rewards individual initiative.

Changing Authoritarian Socialism—The Case of China

Key Terms
five-year plans (p. 487)
special economic zones
  (p. 488)

Summary
After World War II, the Chinese instituted a series of five-year plans, none of which worked very well. Starting in 1979, special economic zones were designated. The rates of economic growth in these special economic zones have been extremely high.

Nations Move Toward the Market System

Key Terms
privatization (p. 492)
secondary market (p. 493)
welfare state (p. 494)

Summary
The trend in Russia, in the other former Soviet republics, and in eastern Europe, is toward increased privatization. Sweden, a welfare state for many years, has also moved recently toward privatization and less welfare. Led by Mexico's changes in the mid-1980s, an increasingly large number of countries in Latin America are privatizing government-owned companies.

20 *Review*

Identifying Key Terms

Use terms from the following list to fill in the blanks in the paragraph below.

private property
  rights (p. 482)
price system (p. 482)

five-year plans (p. 487)
privatization (p. 492)
secondary market (p. 493)

    In pure market capitalism, __(1)__ are guaranteed by the government. Pure market capitalism can be described as a __(2)__ because supply and demand determine prices. After World War II, the Chinese government instituted several __(3)__. In the former Soviet Union and in eastern Europe (as well as in parts of China), __(4)__ is occurring at a rapid pace. There is even a __(5)__ for the buying and selling of shares of newly privatized companies.

Write a paragraph on different types of socialism using the following words:

communism (p. 484)
proletariat (p. 484)
democratic socialism (p. 484)
authoritarian socialism (p. 484)
welfare state (p. 494)

Recalling Facts and Ideas

Section 1
1. What is the role of supply and demand in pure market capitalism?
2. Why do we call pure capitalism a price system?
3. Can individuals take business risks under pure socialism? Explain.
4. What term did Karl Marx apply to his ideal society?

Section 2
5. How have special economic zones changed parts of the People's Republic of China?
6. In what way can you tell that capitalism has benefited the People's Republic of China?

Section 3
7. Describe the main economic change that is occurring in the former Soviet Union and in eastern Europe.
8. Why has Sweden been labeled a welfare state?
9. In what way have the world's economic systems converged?

Critical Thinking

Section 1
Making Comparisons Compare the type of planning used in a decentralized capitalist system with the type of planning used in a centralized command socialist system.

Section 2
Determining Cause and Effect Why do you think Guangdong Province has had such a high economic rate of growth compared to the rest of the People's Republic of China?

Section 3
Making Inferences What is the relationship between privatization and decentralization of an economy?

Applying Economic Concepts

The Importance of Profits In many economies through the years, profits have been given "bad press." Specifically, journalists and politicians as well as laypersons have often decried profits as "evil." Yet economic theory tells us that profits are necessary as a type of signal in our economic system. Make a list of what profits signal in our economy and the results of those signals. Then list some of the things that might happen if profits were outlawed, or at least restricted severely.

Chapter Projects

1. **Individual Project** Today the United States is not a pure market capitalist economy. There are many elements of government planning and control. Write down as complete a list as you can of those parts of our American economic system that do *not* follow the five key attributes of pure market capitalism listed on page 482. For example, in the United States not just anyone could start a new electric utility company and offer electricity for sale. The government regulates who can offer electricity and, indeed, maintains a monopoly for the one electric utility company in each area.

2. **Cooperative Learning Project** In much of the world, government is selling off government-owned businesses and property. The speed of privatization in each country is different, though. Working in groups of four, look at privatization in different parts of the world. These areas should include:
   - Russia
   - The other republics of the former Soviet Union
   - Eastern Europe
   - The European Community (Union)
   - Latin America
   - People's Republic of China

   The members of each group should look for magazine and newspaper articles on privatization in their designated area of the world. Each person should attempt to find out at least the following:
   - How much of the country's government-owned businesses and property is being privatized

- How fast it is being privatized
- The benefits of privatization
- The problems associated with privatization

Your group should present a conclusion about privatization in its part of the world. Are the problems of privatization more than outweighed by the benefits?

Reviewing Skills

Understanding Economic News
The Five *W*'s and one *H* Look at the following economic news article. List four of the five *W*'s.

> *President Clinton signed his hard-won budget-reconciliation bill ... into law at a White House ceremony Aug. 10, just four days after it squeaked through the Senate with the tiebreaking vote of Vice President Al Gore. But back on Capitol Hill, members were already girding for another round of budget fights, and there was talk of undoing some of what Clinton had just signed.*
>
> —*Congressional Quarterly*, August 14, 1993

Writing About Economics

Comparative Writing Write a letter to a pen pal in Sweden. Using information about prices from Your Economics Journal, explain how the economic system in the United States is primarily a free-market system, but not entirely so.

Point

Issue: Does Free Trade Help or Hurt Americans?

Although most economists favor free trade, the popular wisdom today is that free trade steals American jobs and helps other countries at the expense of the United States. In particular, many people feel that we import too much from Japan, while Japan restricts American imports. They feel that only through protectionism (more tariffs and quotas) or managed trade (asking that a minimum percentage of Japans's industrial needs will be purchased from American suppliers) can the United States lower its trade deficit and Japanese trade surplus. Those in favor of free trade feel just as firmly that more protectionism or managed trade will hurt the United States as much as any other country.

PRO → Marc Levinson writes in *Newsweek* that, even though some jobs disappear as a result of free trade, this is simply a result of economic change. More new jobs will be created to replace the old ones, and imports from free trade lead to greater efficiency and actually keep down the inflation rate. He says industries sheltered from foreign competition have the greatest price rises.

Economist Alan Binder agrees that protectionism only leads to "job swapping" — protecting jobs in some industries while destroying jobs in others. He argues that the cost of saving jobs is extremely high and that it is doubtful that any jobs are actually saved in the long run. Finally, Martin B. Zuckerman writes in *U.S. News and World Report* that protecting American jobs is actually putting the United States last, not first:

America-first protectionists never work through to the logical end of their policies; if they did, America would come last. Yes, some jobs may be saved by keeping out a cheaper foreign product. But it does not end there. Take steel. Some 17,000 jobs have been saved through restrictions on imports. But stop cheering. According to the Center for the Study of American Business, the more expensive domestic steel has cost an extra $150,000 for every single job saved. That higher cost has been paid by steel users not simply in cash but also in work lost. In fact, 54,200 jobs were lost in other industries to save the 17,000 in steel. Another example is textiles and apparel. Tariffs are adding about $20 billion annually to consumer bills, leaving less to spend on the output of other workers.

Counterpoint

CON A poll by *Newsweek* magazine showed that nearly 4 out of 5 respondents felt that imports are at least partly to blame for slow economic growth. Business executives, farmers, and labor unions want the United States to enact more import restrictions. They believe imports and foreign competition have wiped out American jobs in some sectors of the economy.

A 1992 survey by the *Los Angeles Times* found that 70 percent of respondents would support protectionist measures against Japan, and 41 percent selected "tightening restrictions on trade with Japan" as the best way to stimulate the U.S. economy. In presenting the results of this poll, staff writer Karl Schoenberger presents a typical view of those against free trade:

Another respondent . . . said it's not the fault of the Japanese that they have prospered while America's economy declined. The blame, he said, should be placed on the U.S. Government, which "is responsible for the trade agreements we make with foreign governments and should make sure we get treated fairly.

"I don't believe we have a fair deal in our trade with Japan, because we're open to their products and they're closed to ours." . . . "I believe in an eye for an eye, and it's not Japan's fault that the American government doesn't protect our interests."

Katherine Newman writes in *Newsweek* about the future and places the blame on United States trade policies:

The international economy is less an opportunity than a threat. It's not just that imports have put their jobs at risk. Their unhappiness is broader . . . and the blame is pinned squarely on what is perceived to be America's diminished position in the world economy.

. . . Here, voices rise in criticism of our international competitors, and our politicians. . . . International competition means endless worries about future living standards.

Exploring the Issue

Reviewing Facts
❶ Why does it seem that economists and non-economists disagree over the free trade issue?

Critical Thinking
Analyzing Information
❷ If free trade means that some jobs are lost, while others are created, why should anyone be unhappy?

21

ECONOMIC GROWTH IN DEVELOPING NATIONS

What will be the benefits of building this dam in Brazil?

How much does a project like this cost?

Who is paying for this construction project?

Should the United States increase foreign aid for projects like this?

Who is employed on this project?

Your Economics Journal

Keep track of all the foreign countries that you read about or hear mentioned on the radio or on TV. Collect clippings and make a list of these countries. After the name of each country, indicate whether you think it is a developing country.

SECTION 1 *Characteristics of Developing Nations*

How the Other Three-Fourths of the World Lives

Many Americans may not realize it, but even the poorest families in the United States usually have an income far above the average income in much of the rest of the world. More than one-half of the world's population lives at or close to subsistence, with just enough to survive.

Developed and Developing Nations

Of the more than 175 nations in the world, only about 30 are considered **developed nations**. See **Figure 21.1**. These nations include the United States, Canada, most European countries, plus Japan, Australia, and New Zealand.

The remaining three-fourths of the world's population live in **developing nations.** These are nations with less industrial development and a relatively low standard of living. Within this general definition, however, nations differ in many ways. **Figure 21.2** compares two developing nations, Madagascar and Mexico. The average income per person in Mexico is only one-fifth that of the United States. In contrast, Mexico is much more developed and prosperous than almost all other devel-

Figure 21.1
Life in Developed Nations
Many people in developed nations with industrial economies live comfortably. These nations with about 25 percent of the world's population account for almost 80 percent of world GDP. ▼

oping nations. In Madagascar, average per capita income is very much less than average per capita income in Mexico.

Besides differences in the standard of living among developing nations, great differences often exist within a nation. For example, about 26 percent of India's population lives and works in urban areas, many of which are like those in developed nations. In rural India, however, the majority of the population may not have enough to eat. The average family lives three to a room, often in mud houses. Only a fraction of these homes have running water and electricity.

Economic Characteristics

Economists often use per-person GDP as a rough measure of a nation's prosperity. While source estimates of world economic data vary, the United States and other developed nations have per capita GDP that ranges between $12,000 per year and about $27,000 per year.

Low GDP Per capita GDP in developing nations, in contrast, is considerably less, and in the world's poorest nations it is extremely low. Look at **Figure 21.3** (page 506), which shows per capita GDP for a number of developing countries and for a number of developed countries. While developing nations may have many natural and human resources, they lack the equipment, financing, and knowledge necessary to put those resources to use.

An Agricultural Economy Agriculture is central to developing nations' economies. Much of the population exists through **subsistence agriculture.**

Figure 21.2 ▶
Two Developing Nations
Among developing nations there is a wide variance in standards of living. How does the per capita GDP of Madagascar compare to that of Mexico?

▼

Two Developing Nations*

	Madagascar	Mexico
Percent employed in agriculture	90	40
Average per capita GDP	$219	$2,212
Telephones per 100 population	0.4	9.6
Life expectancy at birth	52.6 years	72.2 years

*Figures representative of period 1986–1990.

Sources: *Statistical Abstract of The United States*, 1992: *World Tables*, 1993

Per Capita GDP Around the World

Developed Countries

Japan $25,659

Germany $22,175

United States $21,790

Italy $16,940

Great Britain $16,137

Developing Countries

Brazil $2,797

Mexico $2,212

Indonesia $587

China $370

India $367

0 2 4 6 8 10 12 14 16 18 20 22 24 26

Source: *World Tables*, 1993, The World Bank

Figure 21.3
Measuring GDP
What do you think the huge difference in per capita GDP between developing and developed countries means in terms of everyday life?

See **Figure 21.4**. Each family grows just enough to take care of its own needs. This means that no crops are available for export or to feed an industrial work force.

Figure 21.4
Agriculture in Developing Nations
People in developing nations may not have modern farming technology or animals or new types of seed.

Poor Health Conditions Poor health conditions are also common in many developing nations. Many people die from malnutrition or illness due to lack of food. Developing nations may also suffer from a shortage of modern doctors, hospitals, and medicines. The result is often a high **infant mortality** (infants who die during the first year of life) rate and a low life expectancy among adults.

Low Literacy Rate A fourth characteristic of developing nations is a low adult literacy rate—the percentage of people who are able to read and write. Governments have few resources to build and maintain schools. Many children miss school to help their families with farming. The lack of a large pool of educated workers makes it difficult to train the population for needed technical and engineering jobs.

Rapid Population Growth A fifth characteristic of developing nations—rapid population growth—is often the source of many other problems in developing nations, such as lack of food and housing. For example, the population in the United States grows at less than 1 percent a year. The growth rate in many developing nations in Africa and Southwest Asia is three and sometimes four times this rate. This means a nation such as Ghana, with a growth rate of 3.2 percent, will double its population in 22 years.

Figure 21.5 lists several economic and social statistics for a number of nations. As you can see, the differences between developing and developed nations are often large. In Afghanistan, the infant mortality rate is more than 17 times higher than in the United States.

Figure 21.5 ▶ Comparing Nations

What relationship between literacy rates and infant mortality rates is apparent from the chart?

Economic and Social Statistics for Selected Nations in a Recent Year

Life Expectancy at Birth	Infant Mortality: Deaths Per 1,000 Live Births	Country	Literacy (%)	Per Capita Daily Caloric Supply Available
76	10	United States	97*	3,702
80	4	Japan	99	2,700
77	8	Australia	99	3,810
78	9	Israel	92	3,140
78	8	Italy	98	3,004
71	33	China	70	2,620
73	29	Mexico	90	2,580
57	105	Pakistan	35	2,220
58	81	India	48	2,121
48	134	Mozambique	14	1,642
54	112	Bangladesh	47	1,840
44	164	Afghanistan	29	1,690

* True functional literacy is much lower in the United States.
Source: United Nations, *World Development Report*, 1993; *The World Almanac*, 1994

The Four Tigers

Developing countries vary greatly in their ability to experience economic growth. One group has achieved annual economic growth rates that are two to three times that of the United States. Three newly industrialized countries—Singapore, Taiwan, and South Korea—and the British crown colony (until 1997) of Hong Kong are the so-called Four Tigers. From 1960 to 1990, per capita GDP in these countries grew more than fivefold.

In contrast during the same period, some sub-Saharan African nations saw a fall in per capita GDP. For many parts of the world, the income gap between nations has increased rather than decreased recently.

SECTION 1 REVIEW

Understanding Vocabulary

Define developed nations, developing nations, subsistence agriculture, infant mortality.

Reviewing Objectives

1. About how many nations in the world are considered developed?

2. What are five economic characteristics of developing nations?

3. What are the Four Tigers?

Focus on Free Enterprise

The Chicago Pizza Pie Factory

Missing Chicago-Style Pizza The Chicago Pizza Pie Factory is a very successful chain of pizza restaurants in Europe. They are even recommended in Frommer's travel guides for both London and the United Kingdom. The idea behind the Chicago Pizza Pie Factory is for Americans and Europeans alike to discover a little piece of Chicago in Europe.

The Factory was founded by an American, Robert Payton, and still operates under his ownership. Payton, a former Chicago advertising executive, was transferred to London in the early 1970s. Although he liked London, he missed certain amenities from home. One of the main things he missed was the pizza—in particular, deep-dish Chicago-style pizza.

Payton felt that in London there was a market for pizza ready to be tapped. He quit his advertising job, sold other investors on his idea, and formed a company called My Kinda Town, Ltd. Payton invested all his savings into the company's first venture—a pizza restaurant in the heart of London.

The European-Style Chicago Pizza One of Payton's start-up problems was trying to make authentic, Chicago-style pizza using European ingredients. He used wedding cake pans to get the right deep-dish look and texture, and he found a Danish cheese that resembled the cheese used in Chicago. Unable to find the "right" cooking oil, he obtained the recipe from a Chicago oil supplier and began to make his own oil.

Bears, Bulls, and Cubs The theme of The Chicago Pizza Pie Factory is centered around the city of Chicago, not just its pizza. Chicago street signs and memorabilia, as well as Chicago Bears, Bulls, and Cubs posters and banners, decorate the walls. The television replays videos of Chicago's teams. A Chicago radio station also sends tapes each week to provide background music and Chicago news and weather.

Expanding Through Europe The taste of Chicago-style pizza served in a Chicago-like atmosphere proved to be so popular among London natives and visiting Americans that Payton's company moved to expand. A Chicago Pizza Pie Factory opened up in Barcelona and another in Paris. My Kinda Town, Ltd. also started up different restaurants following the same winning formula. The Chicago Rib Shack, Chicago Meatpackers, Tacos, The Criterion, Salsa!, and Henry J Bean's But His Friends All Call Him Hank Bar and Grill all proved to be quite successful. Currently, there are more than 20 restaurants across Europe that are modeled after the first Chicago Pizza Pie Factory. These restaurants are located in Germany, Spain, France, Belgium, and Ireland. A Chicago Pizza Pie Factory has even

opened up in Israel. Some of the restaurants are owned directly by Payton, while others are franchises. Overall, the Chicago Pizza Pie Factory has proved to be a successful idea that has continued to grow throughout Europe. It is now possible to travel around Europe without ever being too far from the tastes and sounds of Chicago or Chicago-style pizza.

Free Enterprise in Action

1 Why did Robert Payton choose to start a pizza business in London?

2 Why was it difficult to find the tools and ingredients for Chicago-style pizza?

3 How was a Chicago atmosphere created in the European restaurants?

SECTION 2 The Process of Economic Development

SECTION 2 FOCUS

Terms to Know foreign aid, economic assistance, technical assistance, military assistance

Objectives *After reading this section, you should be able to:*

1. Describe two major outside sources for **financing economic development.**
2. Identify five nations that supply **foreign aid** and two international agencies through which aid is given.
3. List four **reasons for giving foreign aid.**

Most nations pass through three stages of economic development. The first is the agricultural stage, when most of the population has jobs in farming. The second is the manufacturing stage, when much of the population has jobs in industry. In the third stage, many workers shift into the service sector—sales, food service, repair work, and so on. In its economic development, the United States has followed these stages. It began as an agricultural nation in the late eighteenth century and passed into an industrial economy in the late nineteenth century. The mid-twentieth century saw the beginning of rapid growth of the service sector.

Figure 21.6
The Agricultural Stage
What are two basic needs of nations in the agricultural stage?

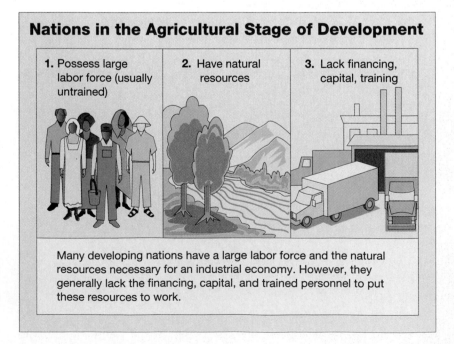

Nations in the Agricultural Stage of Development

1. Possess large labor force (usually untrained)

2. Have natural resources

3. Lack financing, capital, training

Many developing nations have a large labor force and the natural resources necessary for an industrial economy. However, they generally lack the financing, capital, and trained personnel to put these resources to work.

Financing Economic Development

Most developing nations are still in the agricultural stage. As **Figure 21.6** shows, three factors are evident in this stage. A basic problem for many developing nations is how to finance the equipment and training necessary to improve their standard of living.

One source of money capital is domestic savings. Many people believe that people in developing nations cannot save because they are barely subsisting. In fact, even very poor people do save something for their future. However, it may not be in a form that

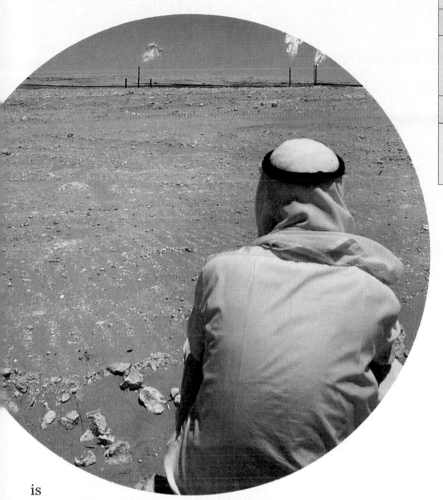

Attractions and Risks to Foreign Investors		
Attractions:		
1. Low wage rates 2. Few regulations 3. Abundant raw materials		
Risks:		
1. Political instability - uncertainty 2. Threat of losing investment if government takes over private firms		

◀ **Figure 21.7** ▲
Attractions and Risks to Foreign Investors
Why would it be in a developing nation's best interest to discourage terrorism within its borders?

is useful for capital investment. For example, in a traditional economy, saving may involve storing grain that can later be traded for other goods. While this is saving, it does not provide a pool of money capital from which businesses can borrow for investment. Although they have some money capital available from domestic savings, many developing nations must look to outside sources for investment capital.

Foreign Investment: Attractions and Problems The two major outside sources of capital are investment by foreign businesses and foreign aid from developed nations. Developing nations often have attractions for investors and also some problems, as shown in **Figure 21.7**. Investment may include a corporation's setting up branch offices, fully owned companies, or buying into companies in developing nations.

Developing Nations: Problems With Foreign Investment Problems exist from the developing nation's viewpoint as well. In nations with heavy foreign investment, citizens often resent the economic control these foreign companies have over their resources. For example, the Gulf and Western Corporation (now Paramount) has been accused of operating a "state within a state" in the Dominican Republic. During the late 1970s, Gulf and Western owned 264,000 acres, or 8 percent, of the nation's arable land. It produced one-third of the nation's sugar and had investments in livestock, tobacco, and fruit and vegetable production as well. The

Figure 21.8 ▲
Corporate Control
Over Foreign Resources
Local and international groups accused Gulf and Western of, among other things, contributing to a food shortage in the Dominican Republic. Supposedly the corporation did this by converting farmland from growing food for local consumption to the more profitable production of sugar cane. In its defense, Gulf and Western maintained that its investments had improved the nation's standard of living. The company increased fruit and vegetable production and sold some land to its employees.

company owned resort hotels, shipping facilities, part of the nation's railway system, and more than 80 other businesses. **Figure 21.8** explains some of the problems that arose.

Assistance From Other Nations Foreign aid is a second type of financing available to nations. It has played an increasingly important role in economic development.

Foreign aid is the money, goods, and services given by governments and private organizations to help other nations and their citizens. There are several kinds of foreign aid as shown in **Figure 21.9**.

Emergency shipments of food, clothing, and medical supplies to victims of drought, earthquakes, floods, and so on, are also considered foreign aid. Governments, many private organizations, and several agencies of the United Nations provide such assistance. This type of foreign aid, however, is not directed toward economic development.

Who Supplies Foreign Aid?

Many of the developed nations of the world offer some type of foreign aid to developing nations. Although the dollar amount of American foreign aid has been increasing in recent years, the amount of aid after correcting for inflation has actually fallen. Expressed in constant dollars—dollars adjusted for inflation—the United States gives only about one-fourth of what it gave in the years immediately following World War II. At that time, the United States devoted most of its foreign assistance to help rebuild

What Does Foreign Aid Provide?

1. Economic Assistance	2. Technical Assistance
Producer goods	3. Military Assistance

Figure 21.9 ▶
Kinds of Foreign Aid
Foreign aid may be in the form of economic, technical, or military assistance.

1 **Economic assistance** consists of loans and outright grants of money or equipment to other nations. One use of such aid is to help build transportation and communications systems. Roads, bridges, and airports, for example, must be built to link isolated regions to the overall economy. A second use for economic assistance is to purchase basic producer goods. These include machinery that will increase a nation's productivity.

2 **Technical assistance** includes providing professionals such as engineers, teachers, technicians, and so on, to teach skills. Such training is designed to strengthen a nation's human resources in the same way economic assistance increases a nation's capital resources.

3 **Military assistance** involves giving either economic or technical assistance to a nation's armed forces. For example, a country may lend a developing nation the money to purchase airplanes or tanks, or it might make a gift of such goods.

Europe's war-torn economy through the Marshall Plan.

A New Focus In the 1950s, after European nations had regained much of their economic strength, the United States shifted the focus of its foreign-aid program to developing nations. Today most American foreign aid is sent to developing nations in the Middle East and Southeast Asia. Nations in Africa receive about 11 percent, in Latin America, 14 percent, and in East Asia and the Pacific, 5 percent. **Figure 21.10** shows one example of American foreign aid.

Comparing Aid Many other major industrial nations also give foreign aid. France and Great Britain, for example, have concentrated most of their aid programs on their former colonies in Africa and Asia. Germany and

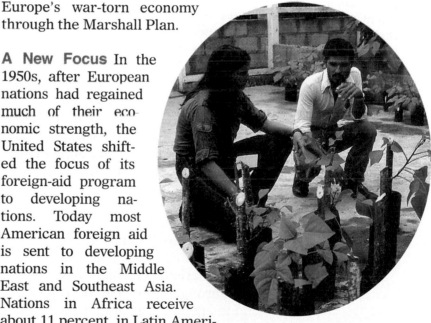

Figure 21.10 ▲
American Foreign Aid
The goal of technical assistance is to make people self-sufficient.

Chapter 21 Economic Growth in Developing Nations **513**

Figure 21.11
Why Give Foreign Aid?

Support for government-sponsored foreign aid is based on four major factors: humanitarianism, economics, politics, and national security.

B Economics ▲
American foreign aid often widens the markets for American exports and provides new opportunities for private investment. This is, in part, because nations are often required to spend American foreign aid on American-made goods and services.

▲

A Humanitarianism
Many rich nations, including the United States, have decided that they have a responsibility to help end world hunger and disease.

Japan both began giving aid to developing nations after their economies had recovered from World War II. Today several nations devote a greater percentage of their GDP to foreign aid than does the United States. Norway's foreign aid, for example, is about 0.8 percent of that nation's GDP. By comparison, foreign aid given by the United States is less than 0.2 percent of its GDP.

Channels of Aid The United States channels much of its foreign aid to other nations through the Agency for International Development (AID). Some nations channel their foreign aid through a number of United Nations agencies, including the International Bank for Reconstruction and Development—usually called the World Bank. The World Bank was set up in 1945 to make loans to developing nations at low interest rates. Two affiliates of the bank are the International Development Association (IDA) and the International Finance Corporation (IFC). The IDA lends money to nations that are the least able to obtain

financing from other sources. The IFC encourages private investment in developing nations. In the 1980s, foreign aid agencies grew increasingly alarmed as many developing nations found themselves unable to repay their foreign debts. The World Bank, for example, had to reschedule payments for several nations. Growing foreign debt has been the focus of several international meetings.

Reasons for Giving Foreign Aid

Humanitarianism is the basis of some foreign aid. The relief of human suffering is a major goal in particular of many private aid organizations.

At least three other reasons can be given for providing support for government-sponsored foreign aid. See **Figure 21.11**. The first involves economics. It is usually in the best interests of developed nations to encourage international trade.

Politics is also a reason for giving foreign aid. During the cold war, an important objective of American for-

C Politics
Foreign aid has been given to make developing nations more prosperous and stable and enhance the appeal of democracy. The United States also has used foreign aid to build political friends that will support it in such international bodies as the United Nations.

◀

▲ **D National Security**
Through alliances, or partnerships with other nations, the United States has gained overseas military bases and observation posts that it can use to gather information about other nations.

eign aid and that of other major capitalist nations was to prevent Communists from coming to power.

A fourth reason for giving foreign aid is to help protect a nation's own security. Economic aid is often, in effect, a down payment on a military alliance with a developing nation. However, this type of plan can backfire if a friendly government loses power. In such a situation, the military equipment given that nation would fall into the hands of the new government, one that may be hostile to the nation that supplied the military equipment.

SECTION 2 REVIEW

Understanding Vocabulary
Define foreign aid, economic assistance, technical assistance, military assistance.

Reviewing Objectives
❶ From where do developing countries obtain outside sources of financing for economic development?

❷ What agencies channel aid from major industrial nations to developing nations?

❸ Why do nations give foreign aid?

To predict what will happen in the future, you have to recognize trends and what has happened in the past. Can you recognize a trend?

What is a Trend?

A trend is the general movement of change over a period of time. Businesspeople and government officials must often make decisions about the future based on their reading of trends. For example, clearly there is a trend in the labor force in the United States as shown in **Figure A**. The labor force is continually increasing. Trends can be downward also; for example, the percentage of the population in America that smokes cigarettes is going down.

Establishing a trend requires a long enough period of time to be able to recognize a general pattern. Otherwise, what you thought was a trend may only be a temporary change.

Real versus Nominal Trends

Of key importance in recognizing trends in prices, production, or income is to make sure that you correct for inflation (or deflation). **Figure B** shows per capita disposable personal income in uncorrected nominal dollars. It appears that the trend in the average, per capita, disposable personal income is upward. In inflation–corrected, or real, dollars, however, there is no trend at all from 1988 to 1992.

Practicing the Skill

Figure C shows data on the average duration of unemployment expressed in number of weeks. Is there a trend in the average number of weeks of unemployment? Why or why not?

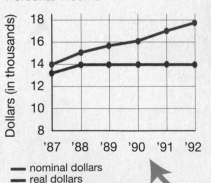

Figure A Labor Force (including resident armed forces, in millions)

1986	119,540
1988	123,379
1990	126,424
1992	128,548

Figure B Per Capita Disposable Personal Income

(graph: Dollars (in thousands) vs. years '87 '88 '89 '90 '91 '92)
— nominal dollars
— real dollars

Figure C

1986	15
1987	14.5
1988	13.5
1989	11.9
1990	12.1
1991	13.8
1992	17.9

SECTION 3 Obstacles to Growth in Developing Nations

SECTION 3 FOCUS

Terms to Know bureaucracies, nationalization

Objectives *After reading this section, you should be able to:*

1. List some of the **obstacles to economic growth** in developing nations.
2. Explain why **Indonesia** failed to experience rapid economic growth.

The successful rebuilding of the European economy following World War II convinced many economists that injections, or additions, of money capital into a nation could achieve rapid economic growth. See **Figure 21.12**. As a result, billions of dollars flowed into developing nations during the 1950s and 1960s. However, aid to many of these nations failed to produce the same growth as it did in Europe.

Critics of foreign aid pointed out that Europe's rapid recovery following the war was a special case. In 1945 Europe already had skilled labor forces, advanced organizations such as corporations and trade groups, and experienced government **bureaucracies,** or offices and agencies. It lacked only the money capital to rebuild the physical machinery of what had been well-functioning economies. Economists today are using much the same arguments to explain the rapid economic growth of Singapore, South Korea, Taiwan, and Hong Kong.

Four Obstacles to Growth

Many developing nations, however, face a number of obstacles to growth that are not immediately solved by injections of money capital. See **Figure 21.13** (page 518). Attitudes and beliefs are usually slow to change. In many developing nations, people live and work much as their ancestors did hundreds of years before. Innovation of any sort is often viewed with suspicion. A high

Figure 21.12
Rebuilding Europe
Through the Marshall Plan, the United States provided billons of dollars to rebuild Europe.

517

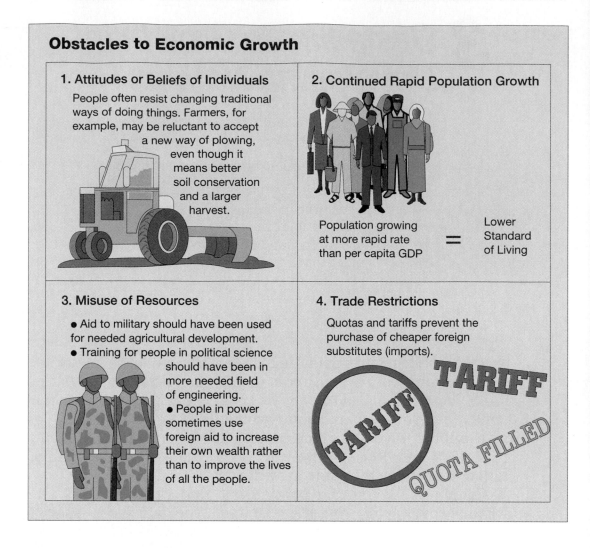

Figure 21.13 ▶
Analyzing the Obstacles
Some of the obstacles to growth are more difficult to remove than others. Rank the obstacles from most to least difficult and give reasons for your ranking.

Obstacles to Economic Growth

1. Attitudes or Beliefs of Individuals

People often resist changing traditional ways of doing things. Farmers, for example, may be reluctant to accept a new way of plowing, even though it means better soil conservation and a larger harvest.

2. Continued Rapid Population Growth

Population growing at more rapid rate than per capita GDP = Lower Standard of Living

3. Misuse of Resources

- Aid to military should have been used for needed agricultural development.
- Training for people in political science should have been in more needed field of engineering.
- People in power sometimes use foreign aid to increase their own wealth rather than to improve the lives of all the people.

4. Trade Restrictions

Quotas and tariffs prevent the purchase of cheaper foreign substitutes (imports).

TARIFF
TARIFF
QUOTA FILLED

---

population growth rate may reduce the rate of growth of a nation's standard of living. Even if a nation's economy is growing, per capita GDP will decrease if its population is growing at a faster rate.

Nations have been held back from more rapid development through the misuse of natural or human resources. For example, defense spending as a percentage of GDP is more than 8 percent in Ethiopia, almost 8 percent in Egypt, and more than 12 percent in Libya. All of these percentages are higher than in the United States—a very developed country.

Trade restrictions on imports are a fourth obstacle to growth. To develop domestic industries, many developing nations have used import restrictions such as quotas and tariffs.

Case Study: Indonesia

When Indonesia won independence from the Netherlands in 1949, it seemed well equipped for economic growth. With a population of about 76 million, it was the world's sixth most populous nation. It was rich in minerals such as nickel, tin, bauxite, and copper, and had vast oil reserves as well as valuable farmland and rain forests. During his regime, President Achmed Sukarno (soo-KAHR-noh) obtained foreign aid totaling more than $2 billion from both capitalist and communist nations. Yet at the end of this time, Indonesia's economy was a disaster.

The reasons behind this failure reveal some of the problems of trying to bring rapid growth to developing

Figure 21.14 Indonesia's Economy under Sukarno and Suharto

President Sukarno's Regime
(1949–1965)

1. Loss of foreign aid from the United States due to strong opposition to capitalism.
2. Foreign aid from former Soviet Union and others was often wasted on projects for the rich such as sports stadiums and department stores. Mineral resources were not developed and decaying roads and rail lines went without repairs.
3. **Nationalization** of businesses placed them under government ownership, discouraging foreign investment.
4. Heavy regulation of business, a huge government bureaucracy, and widespread corruption hurt the economy.
5. Inflation soared out of control. The nation's price index rose from 100 in 1953 to 3,000 only 10 years later. By the mid-1960s, the national debt was $2.5 billion.

General Suharto's Regime
(1965–)

1. Control of the money supply was tightened and confidence in government increased. Corruption was reduced and bureaucracy decreased.
2. Alliances with some Western nations were made.
3. Foreign aid and investment increased and resources were focused on improving agricultural output and oil production.
4. Industry was developed. More money could be spent on industry because less was needed to import food.

nations. One problem involved attitudes. Indonesians lacked a sense of national identity. Indonesia had been formed from several former Dutch colonies, and its people were divided by nationality, religion, and politics. These differences sometimes resulted in violent clashes. The major blame for economic failure, however, can be placed on Sukarno's economic policies. Later improvement in Indonesia's economy is credited to General Suharto (soo-HAR-toh) who replaced Sukarno in 1965. See **Figure 21.14** for a comparison of economic policy under two regimes in Indonesia.

Due chiefly to Suharto's economic policies, Indonesia was one of the fastest-growing economies among developing nations by the end of the 1970s. This was in part due to growth in industry. Mostly, however, it was the result of increases in food output and oil production. Unfortunately, Indonesia, like many developing nations recently, has found that reliance on a few products can be dangerous. In the early 1980s, the world "oil glut" and falling prices for farm products cut deeply into the nation's trade income. Despite Indonesia's promising growth, this change, along with its rapidly growing population, make the future uncertain.

Readings in Economics

TIME   JANUARY 18, 1993

IS SINGAPORE A MODEL FOR THE WEST?

by Jay Branegan

Singapore, long an object of curiosity for its unique blend of open economics, authoritarian politics and social engineering, is attracting attention as a model modern society. . . .

With low pollution, lush tropical greenery, a mix of modern skyscrapers and colonial-era buildings, the city resembles a clean and efficient theme park; even the subway stations are as spotless and shiny as Disney World. . . .

But what makes Singapore work would hardly succeed in the individualist West. There are hefty penalties, vigorously enforced, on human foibles: littering ($625), failing to flush a public toilet ($94) or eating on the subway ($312). The sale of chewing gum was banned last year, and 514 people were convicted of illegally smoking in public. . . .

The industrial policy debate here was settled long ago: the government coldly ushers fading industries like textiles offstage, and targets promising new ones like biotechnology with investment, grants and retraining workers.

Oddly in such a capitalist nirvana, the government owns scores of firms, from the telephone, electricity and airline companies to banks, supermarkets and taxis, but they all run on a competitive, profit-making basis. Says a Western analyst: "Fortune 500 executives love it here because the government runs the country the way AT&T would."

Most citizens would agree with Goh, [a] small businessman: "We have plenty of freedom here, except political freedom."

• THINK ABOUT IT •

1. What laws illustrate the strict political control of Singapore's government?

2. How would you classify Singapore's economic system?

21 Highlights

Characteristics of Developing Nations

Key Terms

developed nations (p. 504)
developing nations
(p. 504)

subsistence agriculture
(p. 505)
infant mortality (p. 506)

Summary

Three of every four people in the world live in developing nations. Economists consider several factors when they measure the development of a nation. Several Asian nations have shown steady and rapid growth in recent years.

The Process of Economic Development

Key Terms

foreign aid (p. 512)
economic assistance
(p. 513)
technical assistance
(p. 513)

military assistance
(p. 513)

Summary

The economic development of a nation may be financed through a combination of domestic savings and foreign investment and aid. Foreign aid consists of economic, technical, and military assistance. Many industrial nations supply foreign aid because of humanitarian goals, economic and political goals, and national security objectives.

Obstacles to Growth in Developing Nations

Key Terms

bureaucracies (p. 517)
nationalization (p. 519)

Summary

Developing nations face several obstacles to growth. Indonesia's lack of economic growth teaches us that simply pouring money into a developing nation will not guarantee economic growth. Foreign aid must be used wisely along with domestic savings, foreign investment, and government policies that ensure economic stability.

Industrialization and the Future

Key Terms

property rights (p. 523)
vicious cycle of poverty
(p. 524)

Summary

Rapid industrialization may not be the answer for developing nations that do not have a comparative advantage in producing some good that they decide to manufacture. The more certain private property rights are, the more investment, both domestic and from abroad, there will be.

21 Review

Write the letter of the definition in Column B below that correctly defines each term in Column A.

Column A
1. foreign aid (p. 512)
2. subsistence agriculture (p. 505)
3. developing nations (p. 504)
4. technical assistance (p. 513)

Column B
a. raising food sufficient for one's own or one's family's needs only
b. nonindustrialized countries
c. money, goods, and services given by one nation to another nation
d. aid in the form of professional expertise from engineers, doctors, teachers, and other specialists

Write a paragraph on different types of development problems, using the following words.

developed nations (p. 504)
bureaucracies (p. 517)
nationalization (p. 519)
property rights (p. 523)
vicious cycle of poverty (p. 524)

Recalling Facts and Ideas

Section 1
1. The per capita income in countries such as the United States, Japan, and Germany is approximately how many thousands of dollars?
2. What characteristics identify most developing nations?

3. What area of the world has seen rapid economic growth in recent years?

Section 2
4. List two affiliates of the World Bank.
5. What is the difference between military assistance and technical assistance?
6. In what stage of development are most developing nations?
7. What are some reasons for giving foreign aid?

Section 3
8. How does defense spending expressed as a percentage of GDP compare in many developing countries with the same variable in the United States?
9. How is rapid population growth an obstacle to economic development?
10. How do international trade restrictions hinder economic growth of developing nations?

Section 4
11. What is true about the early history of every developed country in the world today?
12. Why are property rights a factor in economic development?
13. How can a developing nation's government influence foreign investment?

Critical Thinking

Section 1
Making Inferences Some developed countries in the world today, such as the United States, have large natural resource bases. Does this necessarily mean that many natural resources are required in order for a country to have economic growth and development?

Section 2

Making Comparisons What is the difference between the level of development and education that existed in Europe's war-torn economy at the end of World War II and the level of development and education that exists in today's developing nations? How does your answer impact on the potential use of foreign aid in today's developing nations?

Section 3

Drawing Conclusions Why do restrictions on international trade represent an obstacle to economic growth for a developing nation?

Section 4

Determining Cause and Effect What is the relationship between well-defined and government-enforced private property rights and the incentive structure for investment in a nation?

Applying Economic Concepts

Foreign Aid Many republics of the former Soviet Union are extremely poor. Even the largest and one of the richest republics, Russia, has a per capita income that is a small percentage of that in the United States. The developed countries have been giving foreign aid to Russia during the 1990s. Use the information you have obtained in this chapter about the problems facing developing countries and the difficulty of using foreign aid correctly. Make a list of the obstacles that Russia faces in properly putting to good use the foreign aid that it is receiving.

Chapter Projects

1. **Individual Project** Select a developing nation and write a research report about the economic and social conditions of that nation by collecting facts on housing, food production, transportation, medical care, and the role of the government. The most reliable sources are the International Monetary Fund Reports, United Nations reports, and government statistical bulletins.

2. **Cooperative Learning Project** Organize into at least five groups. Each group will study one part of the world, such as: northern Africa, Central Africa, Southeast Asia, Central America, or western Europe.

   The goal of each group is to determine the percentage of the economy devoted to agriculture and the percentage devoted to industry. Each member of each group will obtain the relevant information for one or more countries in his or her chosen region. Compare the information obtained, selecting one person to prepare summary statistics for your group's region.

Reviewing Skills

Recognizing Trends

Spotting Real Trends Below are the data for the United States government's expenditures on international aid in various years. What can you say about the trend in spending on international aid?

1989	$9.6 billion
1990	$13.8 billion
1991	$15.9 billion
1992	$16.1 billion
1993	$18.7 billion

Writing About Economics

Comparative Writing Choose two of the countries about which you have collected similar information in Your Economics Journal. Write a brief radio news story that compares economic conditions in these two countries. Remember that news answers the who, what, when, where, and sometimes the why and how of events.

22

THE GLOBAL ECONOMY

How does the state of Japan's economy affect our economy?

How would a person in Tokyo find out a day's closing figures on the New York Stock Exchange?

How have improved methods of worldwide communications impacted economic fluctuations?

Does the United States have many investments in foreign markets?

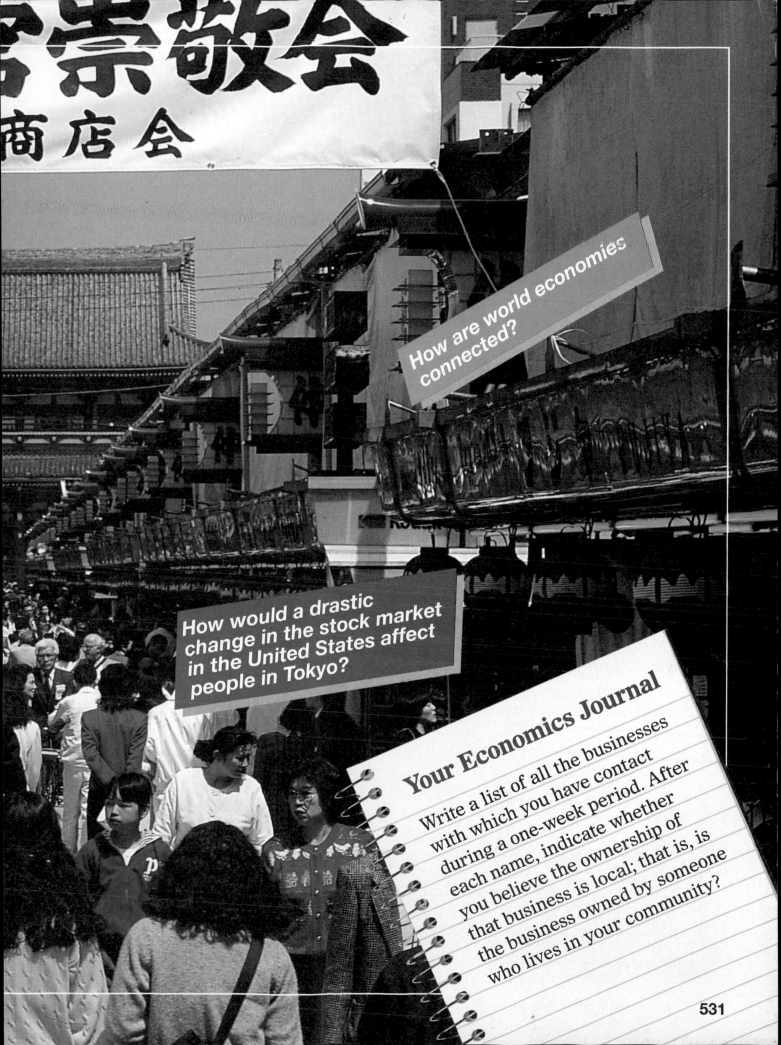

How are world economies connected?

How would a drastic change in the stock market in the United States affect people in Tokyo?

Your Economics Journal

Write a list of all the businesses with which you have contact during a one-week period. After each name, indicate whether you believe the ownership of that business is local; that is, is the business owned by someone who lives in your community?

SECTION **1** *Reasons for and Results of Global Integration*

S E C T I O N 1 F O C U S

Terms to Know global integration, telecommunications

Objectives *After reading this section, you should be able to:*

① Explain how **improved telecommunications** have caused increased global integration.

② Name three kinds of financial instruments now traded in **global markets**.

③ Identify a major **problem with the worldwide stock market**.

Global Trade Affects All of Us

In the United States it would not be unusual to ride on a bus that was made in Germany or in a Japanese-made car. Suppose you eat lunch at a local restaurant. You may not know it, but a Canadian owns the restaurant. Some of the restaurant's food has been imported from Mexico, France, and Spain. While reading the newspaper at lunch, you read about interest rates falling because political upheavals in other countries have caused businesses there to invest their money capital in politically stable America.

We now live not just as Americans, but as part of the global economy. **Global integration** has increased dramatically over the past several decades. Many reasons explain this increase. One has to do with improved **telecommunications,** or long-distance electronic communications.

Improved Telecommunications

The first transatlantic telegraph cable was completed in 1866. Before then it took two weeks to find out the price of the dollar in London. The telegraph cable reduced that time to two minutes. With the invention of the semiconductor—the computer chip—

Figure 22.1
Decreasing Costs

The price per million units of computing power (expressed in millions of instructions per second) from 1978 to 1995 has fallen dramatically. ▼

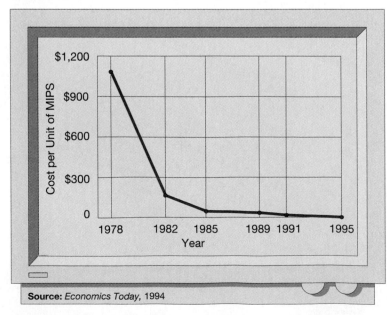

Falling Cost of Computing Power

Source: *Economics Today*, 1994

Figure 22.2
Satellite Communications
Even in the People's Republic of China—where the government has much control—satellite dishes are a growth industry. More Chinese are seeing how the rest of the world looks, thinks, and operates.

◀

telecommunications really took off. Look at how much the price of computing power has fallen just in the last few years in **Figure 22.1**.

Several other inventions and factors have influenced the rapid improvement in worldwide telecommunications. Communications satellites circle the earth day and night. Radio and television waves, beamed up to them, are reflected down to other parts of the earth. On the earth itself, fiber-optic cables are being placed throughout much of North America and already exist in parts of Europe. Cellular telephones are another important aspect of this worldwide communications system.

Consider some of the ways cheap and readily available satellite television has transformed the information received in the Eastern Hemisphere.

Before the 1990s virtually all of the television (and radio) available in the Eastern Hemisphere was state-run and state-controlled. Viewers saw few programs and advertisements from other parts of the world. Today, people in Asia receive sports, music, soap operas, news, and advertisements free of government control via satellite. See **Figure 22.2**.

How does this increase in communications affect the rest of the world, particularly Asia? Viewers in other parts of the world are changing their habits. In India they go so far as to buy copies of outfits worn by popular music television personalities. In addition, because most popular programs are transmitted in English throughout the world, more of the world's people want to learn English as a second language.

Figure 22.3
Global Crash

Examine the graph to see how the stock market crash of 1987 affected certain nations of the world. Which nation shown experienced the greatest change as a result of the 1987 stock market crash? Which nation shown was least affected? ▶

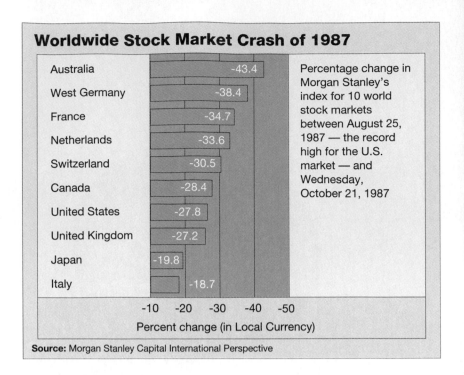

Worldwide Stock Market Crash of 1987

Nation	Percent change
Australia	-43.4
West Germany	-38.4
France	-34.7
Netherlands	-33.6
Switzerland	-30.5
Canada	-28.4
United States	-27.8
United Kingdom	-27.2
Japan	-19.8
Italy	-18.7

Percent change (in Local Currency)

Percentage change in Morgan Stanley's index for 10 world stock markets between August 25, 1987 — the record high for the U.S. market — and Wednesday, October 21, 1987

Source: Morgan Stanley Capital International Perspective

The Globalization of Financial Markets

Because of the speed and power of computers and the affordability of telecommunications, the world has become one financial market. This globalization started in the 1960s and 1970s, when United States banks developed worldwide branch networks for loans and foreign exchange trading. Today money and financial capital markets are truly global, and many instruments are traded on them.

Markets for United States government securities (bonds the United States government sells), foreign exchange, and shares of stocks are now trading continuously, in vast quantities, around the world. For example, trading in United States government securities is the world's fastest growing 24-hour market. Foreign exchange—the buying and selling of foreign currencies—became a 24-hour worldwide market in the 1970s. Worldwide markets exist in commodities such as grains, gold and silver, and stocks. The worldwide stock market, started in about the mid-1970s, however, has some problems.

Problems With the Worldwide Stock Market

When each country's stock market is linked worldwide, problems can arise. One such problem occurred during the biggest one-day stock market crash that the United States has ever faced. Historians emphasize the Great Depression that started when the stock market crashed on October 28, 1929. Another huge stock market crash occurred on October 19, 1987, almost 60 years later. The Dow Jones Industrial Average fell 508 points, the largest one-day loss in United States history. In less than seven hours, more than $500 billion of corporate value disappeared. The stock markets in Sydney, London, and Hong Kong soon followed. Two years later the United States stock market finally regained its previous level, but several other world markets took even longer to recover.

The important lesson of the crash of 1987 was that a globalized financial market, through its electronic information system, now causes everybody everywhere to feel the effects of a financial panic. In **Figure 22.3** you see that many other countries experienced even more severe drops in their stock market index than the United States did in the crash of 1987.

Many managers of investment companies looked worldwide to sell their shares on October 19, 1987. They did not think they could sell their shares in the United States at very attractive prices because of the declining stock market. Investment managers in other countries did the same thing. The United States crash led to stock sales in foreign markets, which caused their stock markets to crash, too. Foreigners sold in the United States market in response. This vicious cycle continued for several days. **Figure 22.4** gives some idea of the worldwide impact.

Figure 22.4 ▲
Impact of the '87 Crash

The collapse of the stock market affects most of the world's people in one way or another. It is, therefore, major news. The newspapers shown here devoted their front pages to the story and news magazines ran feature stories in their next issues.

SECTION 1 REVIEW

Understanding Vocabulary
Define global integration, telecommunications.

Reviewing Objectives
❶ How have improved telecommunications affected global integration?

❷ What kinds of financial instruments are traded in global markets?

❸ What major problem affected the worldwide stock market in 1987?

Making Inferences From Statistics

To infer means to evaluate information and arrive at a conclusion. For example, a person may infer that an item is not selling well because prices for that item are declining. To imply is to express or to suggest something indirectly. Generally, a speaker or writer implies, and a reader infers. Making inferences is an important study skill and a vital economics skill.

Analyzing Statistics

Often a graph or a table contains more information than a reader may see at first glance. For example, **Figure A** shows changes in United States military aid by region between 1985 and 1990. To make inferences from this, follow these steps:

❶ Read the labels on the table to understand exactly what is being reported.

❷ Compare the statistical information to determine trends or changes.

❸ Ask yourself why the changes may have occurred.

❹ Apply related information that you may already know to make inferences from the table.

For example, based on decreased military aid to Africa, you might infer that the region had fewer conflicts in 1990 than it did in 1985.

Figure A

United States Military Aid by Region, 1985 and 1990 (in millions of dollars)

Region	1985	1990
Europe	$ 531	$ 89
Near East and South Asia	4,248	4,241
Africa	279	114
Latin America	269	234

Figure B

Direct Foreign Investment (millions of dollars)

Region	1981	1990
New England	$ 5,686	$ 19,402
Middle Atlantic	20,216	71,136
West South Central	34,651	82,951
Mountain	12,353	33,077
Pacific	34,409	120,164

Practicing the Skill

Study the statistics in **Figure B** about direct foreign investment in various regions of the country. From the data, what can you infer about the relationship between geography and foreign investment? Why does this relationship exist?

SECTION 2 Direct Foreign Investment—Should We Be Worried?

SECTION 2 FOCUS

Terms to Know direct foreign investment (DFI)

Objectives *After reading this section, you should be able to:*

1. Explain the history of **foreign investment** in the United States.
2. Indicate how important **Japanese foreign investment is in the United States**.
3. Describe concerns that nations may have about **direct foreign investment**.

Who Owns Whom?

Nothing seems more American than Burger King or the Pillsbury Dough Boy, right? Not quite, for those companies are now owned by the British. In addition, the Japanese own about 40 percent of the office space in downtown Los Angeles. An Indonesian firm owns Chicken of the Sea Tuna, and a German company owns A&P Supermarkets. A group from East Asia owns the Algonquin Hotel in New York—a famous gathering place of American writers and artists. Mitsubishi, a Japanese company, owns half of Rockefeller Center in the middle of Manhattan. Foreign investment in the United States, however, is not new. See **Figure 22.5**.

Foreign Investment, Then and Now

Direct foreign investment (DFI) in the United States has increased to the point where some Americans want to restrict it. Direct foreign investment is evidence of the global integration of the American economy. In any one year, foreigners purchase billions of dollars of American real estate and businesses. Any time political upheaval strikes any other part of the world, foreign investment in the United

Figure 22.5 Foreign Investment Foreign investment in the United States is not new. In the late 1800s, for example, the British helped finance the expansion of the railroads. ▼

Figure 22.6
Foreign Investment in the United States

Foreigners own much of downtown Los Angeles as well as many formerly American-owned companies. S.A.Q. of Switzerland now owns the Carnation Company. The Japanese company Bridgestone owns Firestone Tire and Rubber. Carnation and Firestone were both formerly American owned.

▶

States increases because we remain a politically stable country.

Foreigners Have Always Invested in the United States The United States has a long history of foreign investment. For example, Great Britain was the biggest foreign investor in American railroads in the late 1800s and early 1900s. At the beginning of World War I, the United States owed more money to foreign lenders than any other country in the world.

Foreign Control of American Companies Many people argue against foreign ownership of American companies because they are worried about foreign control. Is foreign control important? See **Figure 22.6**. Presumably, foreign investors purchase American assets in order to maximize profits. Foreigners' interest in running a corporation would seem to be identical to the interest of any domestic investor who owned the same corporation. The profit-making behavior of a corporation presumably does not depend on the nationality of that corporation. If the British took over a hotel on Miami

Beach, would the service necessarily be any different in the long run? Economists do not think so.

What about the foreign investors' influence over the United States government? Foreigners own about 18 percent of all United States government securities that now exist. Can they use this to control United States foreign policy? Probably not. Foreigners purchase United States government securities when they think the rate of return is higher than they can get elsewhere. Remember that whenever foreigners buy United States government securities or private corporate securities, they free up United States financial capital for other productive uses.

It is actually the United States government that has more control over foreigners. Because they own about 18 percent of the United States public debt, as you can see in **Figure 22.7**, foreign investors are subject to United States government policy. For example, the federal government could, through its Federal Reserve System, create tremendous inflation. In so doing, it would wipe out the real value of the United States government debt that foreigners own.

Finally, in a larger sense, because foreign corporations do invest in the United States, they may indirectly influence our government. Our government cannot make the business climate in America too difficult for these corporations or they will take their investments elsewhere.

Japanese Investment

In recent years the Japanese have invested heavily in the United States, as **Figure 22.8** (page 540) shows. Some social, political, and economic commentators have raised the question of whether they are "buying up America." A few years ago an American historian, Theodore White, wrote, "The Japanese are on the move again in one of history's most brilliant commercial offenses as they go about dismantling American industry." Mr. White suggested that the Japanese economic invasion of the United States during the 1980s was equivalent to its military attack on Pearl Harbor in 1941. Is this true?

Europe's Share of the United States Today, western European investors own about 50 percent of all foreign-owned assets in the United States.

Japan's share of total foreign holdings in the United States is less than 15 percent. Japan owns a little more than 1 percent of an estimated $16 trillion in American capital. Compared to western European ownership of American assets, Japan's does not look so imposing.

Why does Japanese investment in the United States seem like such a threat today? The answer probably lies with the more visible direct investments that Japan has made. Conspicuous Japanese investment in the United States also reminds Americans of the special relationship that exists between Japan and the United States: Japan relies almost exclusively on the United States for its national defense. In effect, the American taxpayer provides Japan's national defense system. This special relationship has allowed Japan to concentrate on economic growth while the United States has presumably borne a disproportionate share of defense costs.

Direct Foreign Investment

Despite the concern some have about foreigners owning the United States, the total share of foreign ownership of American industries is about 6 percent.

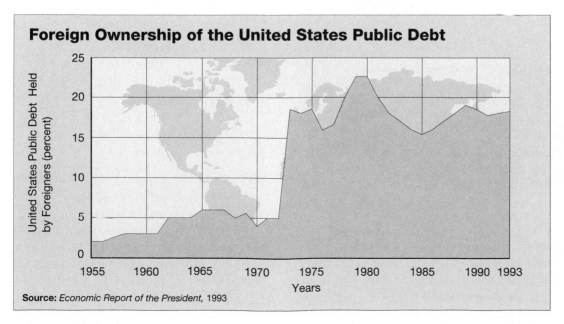

Foreign Ownership of the United States Public Debt

United States Public Debt Held by Foreigners (percent)

25
20
15
10
5
0

1955 1960 1965 1970 1975 1980 1985 1990 1993

Years

Source: *Economic Report of the President,* 1993

**Figure 22.7
Foreign Ownership**
Examine this graph carefully to see how foreign ownership of the United States public debt has changed. When did foreigners own their largest percentage? What has been the most recent trend? How do you explain this?

◀

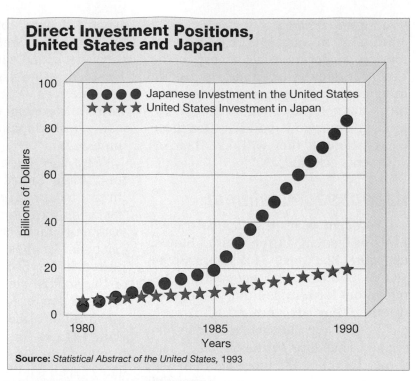

Direct Investment Positions, United States and Japan

Billions of Dollars

● ● ● ● Japanese Investment in the United States
★ ★ ★ ★ United States Investment in Japan

Source: *Statistical Abstract of the United States,* 1993

Figure 22.8 ▶
Direct Investment Positions, United States and Japan
Clearly, Japan has invested much more heavily in the United States than this country has in Japan. When the Japanese purchased 51 percent of an American landmark—Rockefeller Center in New York City —it generated a great deal of publicity. ▼

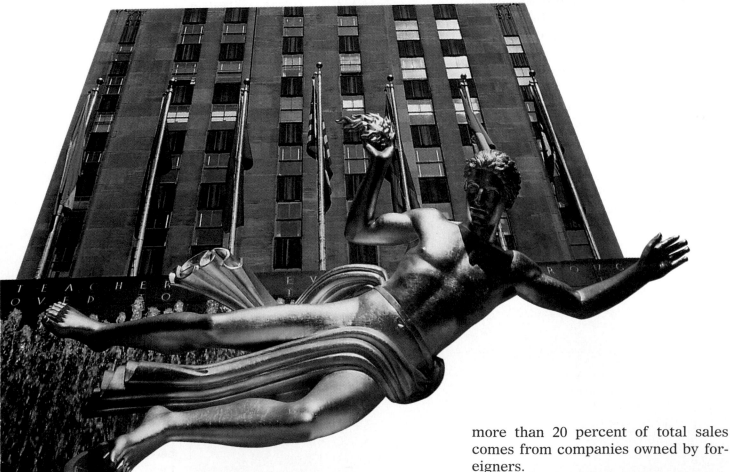

The Final Analysis Although foreign investment here is readily visible, as **Figure 22.9** shows, it is relatively low when compared to that of other nations. In Great Britain, for example, more than 20 percent of total sales comes from companies owned by foreigners.

How much investing do American companies carry out abroad? The United States' share of worldwide direct investment is more than 40 percent. In the 1970s, for example, there were cries

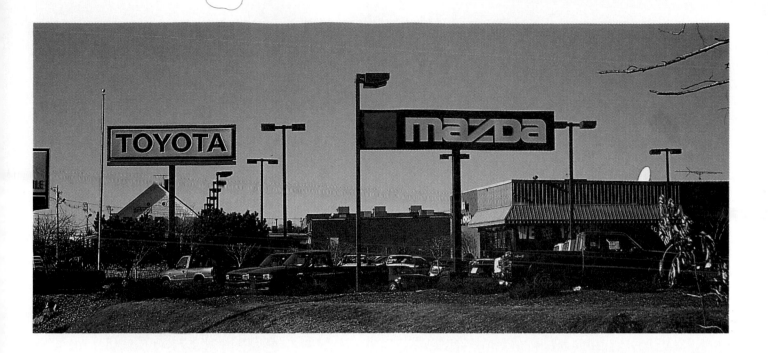

in Europe, especially France, that the United States was going to dominate its society. Indeed, throughout the world many people fear that United States culture has taken over everybody else's culture. Some people have called this *economic imperialism*.

Here is another way to view investment: If a Texas company purchases a business in Omaha, Nebraska, not many people worry. Nebraska will not likely try to pass legislation to prevent Texans—or other Americans, for that matter—from owning any kinds of businesses there. No one doubts that the reason the Texas firm purchased the Nebraska firm was to make a profit.

Most purchasers of goods and services anywhere in the world have little knowledge about who ultimately owns the company that provided the good or service—and they do not really care.

Some even argue that we should *encourage* direct investment and debt purchases by foreigners. Why? Foreigners then would have an increased incentive for the American economy to remain strong, for real estate prices *not* to collapse, for the legal structure to stay on a stable course, and for United States businesses to compete effectively by providing goods and services that consumers want.

Figure 22.9 ▲
Visible Foreign Investment
Unlike Burger King or Firestone or some other companies that are not obviously owned by foreigners, there are some companies that are clearly visible as being foreign-owned. Mazda and Toyota are only two of these.

Laura Tyson on the Global Economy

In this article from *Fortune* magazine, Laura Tyson talks about free trade in the real world. She believes free trade may not be a real choice for policy-makers in a world where protectionist policies create unfair advantages for foreign competitors.

Trade isn't always free. And the choice of policy-makers is often not between free trade and protectionism. It is somewhere in the middle, between one kind of manipulated trade and another.

In an ideal world, our competitive industries would not be meeting subsidized or protected industries abroad. But that is not the world we face. . . . Do we want to be in the business of influencing market outcomes? It's a very hard call, and it is not one that I think any of us take lightly. We would much rather start with an effort to try to reduce the subsidy or protectionist activity abroad.

. . . There is no social or global justification for certain types of subsidies. Production subsidies. . . are simply market grabbing. But research and development subsidies may have the defense of at least possibly creating innovations.

Laura Tyson describes how the United States can improve its trade balance with Japan. She hints that the United States might limit imports through "quantitative market-share indicators."

The trade imbalance between the U.S. and Japan is primarily a macroeconomic phenomenon, the result of big U.S. budget deficits and big Japanese surpluses. The U.S. is now on an appropriate course, and it's time for the Japanese to get on one as well, by stimulating their economy.

When you have negotiated and been unable to address the problem of structural barriers, and there is evidence that competitive opportunities in an industry are not being accorded to competitive producers, then moving to a set of quantitative market-share indicators for foreign imports may be defensible. This should be a last step.

Checking for Understanding

1. What is the choice that policy-makers often face?
2. What measures would be the United States' first effort to make trade fair?
3. What would be the United States' last resort?

SECTION 3 Multinationals and Economic Competition

SECTION 3 FOCUS

Terms to Know multinationals, allegiances, foreign affiliates, alliances, tolerance

Objectives *After reading this section, you should be able to:*

1. Indicate the **number of multinationals** in the world today.
2. Identify important **cross-border investments**.
3. Describe the advantages of **corporate alliances**.
4. Explain why **South Korea** has lost foreign investment dollars.
5. Discuss how recent immigration patterns have increased the need for **tolerance** in the United States.

Cross-Border Investing by Multinationals

For the last few years, international investing has grown faster than world output and faster than world trade. Much cross-border investing is undertaken by **multinationals.** See **Figure 22.10**. In the past, critics argued that because these firms are so large, they may dominate the world economy. Such firms were seen as ruthless companies that would exploit the poor and manipulate governments. Few people agree with such sentiments today. Multinationals bring modern technology and management skills to developing countries.

The Size and Number of Multinationals

In the 1970s, many people predicted that a few hundred multinationals would control 80 percent of the world's production by the mid-1980s. By the mid-1990s, there were an estimated 35,000 multinationals with 170,000 **foreign affiliates,** or branches of their firms. The largest 100 multinationals (excluding those in banking and finance) account for more than $3 trillion of worldwide assets. **Figure 22.11** (page 544) lists the top 25 multinationals.

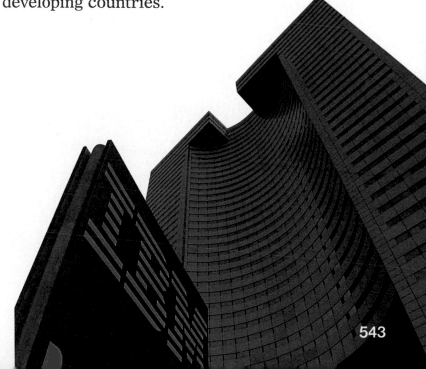

Figure 22.10 Multinationals
A multinational firm is simply one that does business in many countries and has offices and factories in many countries around the world. In a sense, a multinational firm has many national **allegiances,** or loyalties, not necessarily just to the country in which it has its main or principal office. ▼

Figure 22.11 The Largest Multinationals in the World

Largest Nonfinancial Multinationals, 1990, Ranked by Foreign Assets

Rank		Industry	Country	Foreign assets $bn	Total assets $bn	Foreign sales $bn	% of total sales
1	Royal Dutch/Shell	Oil	Britain/Holland	n.a.	106.3	56.0	49
2	Ford Motor Co.	Cars and trucks	United States	55.2	173.7	47.3	48
3	General Motors	Cars and trucks	United States	52.6	180.2	37.3	31
4	Exxon	Oil	United States	51.6	87.7	90.5	86
5	IBM	Computers	United States	45.7	87.6	41.9	61
6	British Petroleum	Oil	Britain	39.7	59.3	46.6	79
7	Nestlé	Food	Switzerland	n.a.	27.9	33.0	98
8	Unilever	Food	Britain/Holland	n.a.	24.8	16.7	42
9	Asea Brown Boveri	Electrical	Switzerland/Sweden	n.a.	30.2	22.7	85
10	Philips Electronics	Electronics	Holland	n.a.	30.6	28.6	93
11	Alcatel Alsthom	Telecoms	France	n.a.	38.2	17.7	67
12	Mobil	Oil	United States	22.3	41.7	44.3	77
13	Fiat	Cars and trucks	Italy	19.5	66.3	15.8	33
14	Siemens	Electrical	Germany	n.a.	50.1	15.1	40
15	Hanson	Diversified	Britain	n.a.	27.7	5.6	46
16	Volkswagen	Cars and trucks	Germany	n.a.	41.9	27.5	65
17	Elf Aquitaine	Oil	France	17.0	42.6	12.2	38
18	Mitsubishi	Trading	Japan	16.7	73.8	41.2	32
19	General Electric	Diversified	United States	16.5	153.9	8.3	14
20	Mitsui	Trading	Japan	15.0	60.8	43.6	32
21	Matsushita Electric Industrial	Electronics	Japan	n.a.	59.1	16.6	40
22	News Corp.	Publishing	Australia	14.6	20.7	5.3	78
23	Ferruzzi/Montedison	Diversified	Italy	13.5	30.8	9.1	59
24	Bayer	Chemicals	Germany	n.a.	25.4	21.8	84
25	Roche Holding	Drugs	Switzerland	n.a.	17.9	6.8	96

Sources: United Nations and *The Economist*, March 27, 1993

Figure 22.11 ▲
The Largest Multinationals in the World
Examine the chart above. Notice that certain nations and certain industries appear several times on the list of the world's largest multinationals. Why do you think this is the case?

Worldwide Ownership The top 100 multinationals are very important, accounting for probably about 45 percent of all cross-border assets. This means nothing, however, without comparing these assets to the worldwide total. No one knows the value of the world's assets today, but a best guess is about $20 to $25 trillion. If this is true, the top 100 multinationals account for only about 15 percent of the world's productive assets—hardly a dominant share.

It is also true today that the United States and Great Britain no longer dominate multinationals. In 1970, for example, of the 7,000 multinationals identified by the United Nations, the Americans and the British owned more than 50 percent. Today, Americans, Japanese, Germans, and the Swiss own about half of the 35,000 multinationals. Numerous multinationals are based in the industrializing Asian countries such as Taiwan and South Korea.

The Regional Flavor of Cross-Border Investments

While it may be true that many of the biggest multinationals invest everywhere in the world, most do not. Most invest in regions that are closest to home. For example, the European Union (EU) plus Scandinavia and Switzerland engage in more foreign direct investment in western Europe itself than anywhere else.

In a world in which borders matter less, the line separating sales at home and those abroad becomes less important. The most appropriate way to look at patterns of direct investment is to include direct domestic sales as a part of regional sales. European firms principally invest in western Europe. American firms principally invest in the United States, Canada, Mexico, and South America. Japanese firms principally invest in Japan, South Korea, Greater China, and Southeast Asia. **Figure 22.12**, for example, shows Japanese investment in Tokyo. Some obvious exceptions to this rule of regional investing by multinationals do exist. For historical reasons, the British as part of the EU invest heavily in India, once a colony of Great Britain.

Beyond Multinationals— Alliances

In addition to multinational direct investments in other countries, firms in different countries are forming **alliances.** These may be joint ventures. Indeed, many foreign governments have insisted that multinationals enter their markets through joint ventures with local firms in the hope that locals will capture some of the profits. Companies also make licensing deals. For example, an American jogging shoe company licensed its design to a company in South Korea.

Most alliances have been between firms from industrialized countries. Alliances are even popular within nations like the United States. For example, International Business Machines (IBM) developed its personal computer in alliance with Microsoft (for the software), Intel (for the central processing unit), and Lotus. In the late 1980s, IBM entered into an alliance with Siemens of Germany to work on memory chips. In the 1990s, IBM

**Figure 22.12
Japan's Major Investment**
Japan, like most countries, invests most heavily in its own nation. Downtown Tokyo shows evidence of how heavily Japanese companies dominate the nation's capital. ▼

**Figure 22.13
Investing in
South Korea**
Many multinationals
pulled out of South
Korea in the early 1990s.
How might this affect
other potential foreign
investors' decisions? ▶

entered into an alliance with Apple Computers, once its archrival.

Alliances can be seen as each firm's acceptance of its own limitations, whether they be financial, technological, or geographical. Alliances can be used to help a firm leapfrog its competitors or catch up with them. Such a strategy is particularly effective in an industry that has seen rapid changes such as computer memory chips and software.

A Case Study in South Korea

Multinationals, by their very nature, can move money capital from one part of the world to another. One reason they move money capital is if they think they can make a higher long-run average rate of return on their investment elsewhere. When one country starts offering better "deals" to multinational firms, they will take them. When one country makes life difficult for multinationals or foreign investors in general, money capital will flow out of that country.

This capital flow is exactly what has happened to South Korea. See **Figure 22.13**. In the early 1990s, foreign investors withdrew large amounts of money capital from South Korea. As reasons they cited complex govern-ment regulations and a lack of incentive to remain in the country. In 1992 new foreign investment dropped more than 35 percent from the previous year. The value of the joint ventures South Korea lost in 1992 was more than five times the value of the previous year's losses. In the early 1990s, General Motors Corporation, Goodyear Tire and Rubber Company, and DuPont Company abandoned their plans to build sophisticated production facilities in South Korea.

ALCOA Consider one specific example. The Aluminum Company of America (ALCOA) created a joint venture with South Korea's Samsun Industrial Company. The American company wanted skilled labor to manufacture aircraft parts for export to Asia. The South Korean company wanted technology that it did not yet have. The plan was for ALCOA to take over and retool one of Samsun's aluminum plants. The total investment by both companies was to be about $40 million, but the deal went sour. ALCOA wanted to build defense-related component parts as well as commercial ones. South Korea's military establishment was worried. The government therefore issued guidelines to give other companies a better chance at obtaining defense industry business. ALCOA pulled out.

Other companies have found that it takes years before their request to build factories is approved. Cargill Corporation had to wait four years after its application to build a $21 million soybean processing plant.

Investing in the People's Republic

Where are many foreign investors taking their money? Amazingly, many of them are going to the People's Republic of China. See **Figure 22.14.** Much of the money being invested in China is being taken out of South Korea. In a world of mobile financial capital, governments cannot treat foreign businesses poorly and expect them to continue investing.

The Global Village and Tolerance

One of the results of the globalization of our world is increased immigration. America has become a truly multicultural society because of such immigration. In many cities the combined numbers of African Americans, Hispanics, Asians, and other minorities now constitute a majority of the population. In the 1980s, for example, the Asian population in America increased more than 100 percent and the Hispanic population more than 50 percent. Public schools are more diverse than ever. This diversity means that the need for

tolerance and open-mindedness is more important today than it ever has been. **Tolerance** can be defined as a fair, objective, and permissive attitude toward the opinions, practices, religions, races, and nationalities of others that differ from one's own. It also includes an interest in and concern for the ideas, opinions, and practices that are foreign to one's own. For Americans this includes learning one or more foreign languages and maintaining friendships with those of different ethnic/cultural/national/religious backgrounds.

Nothing in our Constitution or in our laws requires us to be open-minded and tolerant. These qualities are part of our heritage. Those who acquire and use them will benefit, as will the nation as a whole.

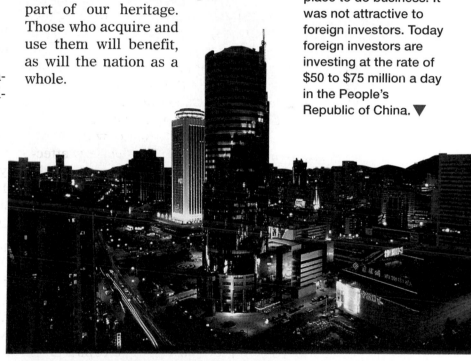

Figure 22.14
The China Business Boom
China used to be known as an impossible place to do business. It was not attractive to foreign investors. Today foreign investors are investing at the rate of $50 to $75 million a day in the People's Republic of China. ▼

SECTION 3 REVIEW

Understanding Vocabulary
Define multinationals, allegiances, foreign affiliates, alliances, tolerance.

Reviewing Objectives
1. Approximately how many multinationals are there in the world today?
2. Give an example of a cross-border investment.
3. What are the advantages of corporate alliances?
4. What caused many foreign investors to reduce their investments in South Korea?
5. How have recent patterns of immigration to the United States increased the need for tolerance?

THE INVASION OF THE AMERICAN WAY

by Maarten Huygen

The American way of life is on its way—via videocassettes, movies, and shopping habits—toward overrunning the world. And American culture, computers, and the English language are not content to conquer a single continent; they are on their way toward making the "American Era" a planetary phenomenon.

The fruits of the harvest are sweet. If a "European" culture ever emerges, it will be an adaptation to or a copy of American culture, the only one powerful enough to overpower every other culture. Every Euro-citizen can now watch Oprah Win-

frey on his own national channel, dubbed or subtitled in his own language. There are no local equivalents, in spite of the limits that Europe imposed in 1991 on the import of American programs. . . .

The most popular band in Vietnam sings Bruce Springsteen numbers. In Eastern Europe, since the Berlin Wall fell, the thin strains of Voice of America, and the few films and tapes that circulated officially and unofficially, have been replaced by a deluge of American images, sounds, and words.

For many Eu-

ropeans, when we made our first trip to the United States, we found everything familiar, since we had seen it all on TV. . . .

But it is not just the powerful communications apparatus that makes American culture so prominent. There is also the very openness of America itself. Many new developments come out of the American subcultures. It was only in an American form that African rhythms reached a world audience, first through jazz and the blues and now through rap. Country music, the favorite of the now-graying baby boomers, began among the fiddle-playing Scottish immigrants in the Ozark mountains of Arkansas. Only America can cultivate so many diverse elements in every last corner of its continent.

• THINK ABOUT IT •

1. What has made the spread of American culture possible?

2. How have subcultures played a role in the spread of American culture?

22 *Highlights*

Section 1

Reasons for and Results of Global Integration

Key Terms
global integration (p. 532)
telecommunications (p. 532)

Summary
One of the most important reasons for increased global integration has been improved telecommunications due to the dramatically reduced cost of computer chips. Today many financial instruments are traded on world markets. Events in one national market impact other markets around the world.

Section 2

Direct Foreign Investment— Should We Be Worried?

Key Terms
direct foreign investment (DFI) (p. 537)

Summary
Foreigners have always invested in the United States and continue to do so today. Foreign direct investment is a relatively small part of our total economy, however. The ultimate reason for direct foreign investment on the part of nations like Japan is to maximize profits.

Section 3

Multinationals and Economic Competition

Key Terms
multinationals (p. 543)
allegiances (p. 543)
foreign affiliates (p. 543)
alliances (p. 545)
tolerance (p. 547)

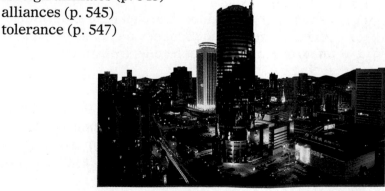

Summary
Cross-border investing is undertaken by 35,000 multinationals throughout the world. Most multinationals invest in regions that are close to home; for example, United States companies invest primarily in the United States, Canada, Mexico, and South America. Corporations may form alliances with former competitors for many reasons. World competition for foreign investment funds means that when government bureaucratic hassles and high taxes become a problem in one country, foreigners take their investments to other countries where the climate is more favorable for business investment.

22 *Review*

Identifying Key Terms

Use terms from the following list to fill in the blanks in the paragraph below.

global integration (p. 532)
telecommunications (p. 532)
direct foreign investment (p. 537)
foreign affiliates (p. 543)
multinationals (p. 543)
allegiances (p. 543)
tolerance (p. 547)

__(1)__ has increased over the past several decades, in part due to the rapid spread of cheap __(2)__. There has been __(3)__ in the United States and elsewhere for hundreds of years. Much of this has been undertaken by __(4)__, which are companies that do business and have offices and factories in many countries. Such large businesses apparently do not have any single national __(5)__. They do have almost 200,000 __(6)__. When dealing with other people with different cultures, the watchword is __(7)__.

Recalling Facts and Ideas

Section 1

1. Why have improved telecommunications led to increased global integration?
2. What happened elsewhere when the stock market crashed in the United States in 1987?
3. What language is the leading second language in the world and why?

Section 2

4. What foreign nation's investors own half of the office space in downtown Los Angeles?
5. Why do foreigners purchase United States government securities?

6. Has Japan had to spend very much money on its national defense since World War II? Explain your answer.
7. What is the United States share of worldwide direct investment?

Section 3

8. How can multinationals help developing countries throughout the world?
9. What four countries own about half of the 35,000 multinationals that exist today?
10. In geographic terms, where do most companies invest?
11. Why do firms in different countries form alliances with one another?

Critical Thinking

Section 1

Making Generalizations While cheap telecommunications are widespread in the United States, they are not so widespread in Africa, Asia, and South America. What will happen to global integration as the rest of the world catches up with the United States?

Section 2

Drawing Conclusions The Japanese government does not spend much money on defense. Explain how this would affect foreign investment.

Section 3

Evaluating Information "Because multinational firms have no allegiance to any one country's government, they are dangerous to every country's stability." What is your opinion of this statement?

Applying Economic Concepts

Investment Incentives While the popular press may refer to "foreigners" as if they were different types of people when they invest in the United States, just about everybody makes each investment for one reason—to earn the highest rate of return possible on that investment. Consequently, Americans should not be afraid of the British, the French, the Germans, the Japanese, the Dutch, or anybody else owning "too much" of America. Make a list of the reasons that people sometimes give for why they are afraid of direct foreign investment in this country. For each reason, present a one-sentence counter argument.

Chapter Projects

1. **Individual Project** Choose a country other than the United States and investigate how much direct foreign investment occurs there each year. Try to establish the dollar volume of such direct foreign investment, what percentage of total investment this represents, and the major foreign countries that do the investing. Write a summary of your results. (United Nations and World Bank publications are useful sources.)
2. **Cooperative Learning Project** Working in groups of four, study the following innovations:
   - the fax machine
   - overnight delivery service (e.g., Federal Express and Airborne)
   - plain-paper copy machines
   - high-speed computer modems
   - satellite television
   - portable cellular phones
   - microcomputers

   Each team member will be responsible for one or more of the following:
   - Explaining what the innovation involves
   - Information on when it was first used and how much it cost then
   - How the innovation changed the way business is done
   - The future of the innovation

Reviewing Skills

Making Inferences
1. **Understanding Symbols** What can you infer from the content of the cartoon?
2. **Recognizing Point of View** Examine the cartoon and determine the cartoonist's point of view.

3. **Analyzing Information** In Jamaica about 3,500 people work in offices connected to the United States by satellite signals. They make airline reservations, process tickets, and handle credit card applications for Americans. Skilled workers in Jamaica earn far less than their counterparts in the United States. Based on this, what inference can you draw about the global workforce?

Writing About Economics

Descriptive Writing Choose a local business from Your Economics Journal. Could it become a multinational? Write a business plan describing the steps this business could take to reach global markets and develop foreign branches.

Economic News Report

From the classroom of Cliff Booth, Tuscaloosa County High School, Northport, Alabama

In Unit 6 you read about international economics. In this experiment, you will learn how economic events in distant parts of the world affect you. (You may want to reread the material on pages 532–547 of the text.)

Today Americans have nearly instant access to international economic events that affect governments and consumers. To become more responsible citizens and wiser consumers, students must associate what is taught in the classroom with what is going on in the real world. In this lab, you will research international economic news, design a news presentation, and simulate a broadcast called Economic News Report (ENR).

Tools

1. Copies of newspapers and magazines
2. Radio and television news reports
3. Cassette tape recorder or videotape camera; tapes
4. Props for a television set

Procedures

Step A The class will form teams of 7 to 10 members. Each group will be responsible for a segment of news broadcast time. Each group will select a news director, two news anchors, one analyst, and several reporters. The news director organizes the order of the news and the format of the broadcast. The anchors share responsibilities for the main news stories. The analyst prepares an editorial comment on one or more events. The reporters prepare additional news stories.

Step B Reporters and anchors should scan magazines, newspapers, and television and radio news reports, collecting a wide variety of international economic news stories. Clippings and notes should be brought to class where the news team, led by the director, will choose the stories that will make up the newscast. The analyst should read all the news stories and begin to prepare an editorial comment. The following table will help the team organize the newscast. Stories should be no longer than one minute and should be placed in a logical order with smooth transitions from one to another.

Example

Title of event and summary	Reporter or anchor	Time in seconds	Order

Step C After reporters, anchors, and the analyst have rewritten and edited their stories for length, the director should prepare a preliminary newscast format.

Example

Story	Read by	Length in sec.	Program time
Economic News Report Format **Date:**			
Eurodollar	J. Wright anchor	40	:40
European markets	B. Engle reporter	35	1:15
Wall Street affected	R. Sanchez anchor	45	2:00
China's GDP	S. Smalz reporter	30	2:30
China's growth	J. Wright anchor	60	3:30
Commercial break		60	4:30
Developing nations' debt	R. Sanchez anchor	60	5:30
Bad weather in Brazil	V. Paine reporter	40	6:10
Brazil (wrap to commentary)	J. Wright anchor	20	6:30
Growth, slow or fast	T. Soong analyst	60	7:30
Tomorrow's feature	R. Sanchez anchor	20	7:50
Close	Sanchez and Wright	10	8:00

If the teams plan to videotape the news, the class should create a set with charts, pictures, or other props. After the set is ready, news teams should rehearse.

For example, anchors will introduce stories by reporters. For videotape, reporters may tape at remote locations, and the tape may be edited to insert these reports. For audiotaping to simulate a radio report, teams should rehearse using a recorder. After all the technical issues have been resolved, each team's director should prepare a final news format for the team. Each team should present the newscast to the class live or by tape.

Lab Report

Step D Use your experience preparing a news program to answer the questions below.

1. What criteria did your group use to determine which news stories to report?
2. How do you think the national and local news media determine which stories to cover?
3. How did the time or length requirements affect your coverage of each story?
4. Was any important story not reported because it did not fit the flow of your news format? Justify your group's decision or explain why it might be unfair to the listener.

Step E Use the following questions for class discussion.

1. Do you think the news media may be biased in its coverage of economic news? Explain your answer.
2. Is economic news as important as political or social news? Why or why not?

553

554

APPENDIX

ATLAS KEY

SYMBOL KEY

⊛ National capital	—— International boundary	▢ Non-subject
★ State/province capital	------ Disputed boundary	⊢⊢⊢ Canal/waterway
● Major cities	·········· Undefined boundary	⅄ Waterfalls
○ Other cities	—— State/province/republic boundary	▲ Peaks

THE WORLD

- • World's most populous cities
- International boundary
- Republic boundary
- Disputed boundary
- Undefined boundary

0   1000   2000 Miles

0   1000   2000 Kilometers

Projection: Robinson

CENTRAL AMERICA AND WEST INDIES

Projection: Bipolar Oblique Conic Conformal

0   250   500 Miles

0   250   500 Kilometers

558

CANADA

Lake of the Woods
Red Lake
Duluth

MINNESOTA
Minneapolis ★ St. Paul
Rochester
x City
IOWA
Des Moines
Council Bluffs

Lake Superior

WISCONSIN
Green Bay
Appleton
Madison ★
Milwaukee
Racine
Dubuque
Cedar Rapids
Davenport
Rockford
Aurora
Peoria
Joliet

MICHIGAN
Lake Michigan
Lake Huron

Grand Rapids
Flint
Lansing
Detroit
Ann Arbor
South Bend
Gary
Hammond
Fort Wayne

Lake Ontario
Niagara Falls
Buffalo
Rochester
Syracuse
Utica
Albany
Lake Erie
Erie

ADIRONDACK MTNS.
Lake Champlain
Montpelier ★
Concord
Manchester
Boston
Worcester
Springfield
Hartford
New Haven
Providence

MAINE
Moosehead Lake
Bangor
Augusta ★
Lewiston
Portland

VT.
N.H.
MASS.
Cape Cod
R.I.
CONN.

Mt. Washington 6,288 ft. (1,905 m.)

St. Lawrence River

NEW YORK
Binghamton

Susquehanna River
Newark
Allentown
Yonkers
New York
N.J.
Trenton

ILLINOIS
Chicago
Peoria
Springfield ★
Decatur

CENTRAL LOWLAND

INDIANA
Muncie
Indianapolis ★
Dayton
Parkersburg
Cincinnati
Columbus

OHIO
Akron
Canton
Youngstown
Cleveland
Toledo

PENNSYLVANIA
Pittsburgh
Wheeling
Harrisburg
Philadelphia
Camden
Wilmington
Dover
DEL.
DELAWARE BAY

ATLANTIC OCEAN

WEST VIRGINIA
Charleston
Huntington

MD.
Baltimore
Arlington
Washington D.C.
Annapolis

Kansas City
Topeka
Independence
Jefferson City ★
ence
as City

Harry S. Truman Res.

MISSOURI
Springfield

Evansville
Louisville
Frankfort
Lexington

KENTUCKY
Owensboro

Wabash R.
Ohio River
Cumberland River

East St. Louis
St. Louis

VIRGINIA
Roanoke
Richmond
Newport News
Norfolk

CHESAPEAKE BAY
Roanoke River

OZARK PLATEAU
lsa
R.S. Kerr Res.

ARKANSAS
Fort Smith
Little Rock
North Little Rock
Hot Springs
Pine Bluff

Lake Eufaula

TENNESSEE
Nashville ★
Chattanooga
Knoxville
Memphis
Huntsville
Tennessee River

APPALACHIAN MOUNTAINS
PLATEAU
Mt. Mitchell 6,684 ft. (2,037 m.)

Winston-Salem
Greensboro
Durham
Raleigh
Charlotte

NORTH CAROLINA

Greenville
Spartanburg
Columbia

Cape Hatteras

SOUTH CAROLINA

Greenville

Birmingham
Tuscaloosa

ALABAMA
Meridian
Jackson
Montgomery ★

CUMBERLAND

Atlanta ★
Augusta
Macon

GEORGIA
Columbus
Albany

Charleston

Savannah

COASTAL PLAIN

Shreveport
Toledo Bend Res.

LOUISIANA
Baton Rouge ★
Lafayette
Lake Pontchartrain
New Orleans

MISSISSIPPI
Hattiesburg
Biloxi
Mobile
Pensacola

Sam Rayburn Reservoir
Houston
Lake Charles

Chattahoochee R.
Alabama R.

Tallahassee ★

Jacksonville

FLORIDA
Orlando
Cape Canaveral
Tampa
St. Petersburg
Lake Okeechobee
Palm Beach
Miami
Miami Beach

Cape Sable
Key West
Strait of Florida

GULF OF MEXICO

THE BAHAMAS

CUBA

UNITED STATES

- ⊛ National capital
- ★ State capital
- ● Major city
- ○ Other city
- ▬ International boundary
- — State boundary

0   100   200 Miles
0 100 200 Kilometers

Projection: Albers Equal Area

General Outlook

Trends in the Labor Force The American civilian labor force is expected to surpass 140 million in the year 2000, increasing a little more than one percent per year. This figure represents a slower rate of growth than in the recent past, mainly because the rate of population growth has slowed.

Labor is an increasingly diverse group as the United States approaches the twenty-first century. Women and minority group members make up a growing share of workers. African Americans, Hispanics, Asians, and other groups will soon account for about one-third of labor force entrants. By 2000, it is estimated 4 out of 5 women between the ages of 25 and 54 will be in the labor force, and women will account for nearly one-half of the total workers.

Trends in Occupations The new jobs that will be added to the United States economy by 2000 will not be evenly distributed across occupations. The shift from goods-producing to service-producing jobs will continue. By 2000 nearly 4 out of 5 new jobs, however, will be in industries that provide services. Job creation will be fastest in such fields as health care, business services, and retail trade. Education, government, transportation, and communications industries will also account for significant job growth. Among goods-producing industries, only construction employment is expected to increase significantly. Manufacturing, mining, and agricultural jobs will either remain steady or decline slightly.

Occupational Profiles How do various occupations compare in earnings, job requirements, opportunities, and working conditions? The following tables and profiles provide a sampling of information about a broad range of careers. In the tables, most salaries represent approximate yearly averages for beginning and top levels, unless designated otherwise. In some cases, only the median range is available. The "Training" column uses symbols for levels and kinds of training normally required:

HS = high school, **Tr** = some specialized training, **TS** = technical school, **AD** = 2-year associate degree, **CD** = 4-year college degree, **ACD** = advanced college degree, **L** = license (usually by testing), **Exam** = examination.

"Job Outlook" and "Working Conditions" categories give very brief descriptions of general conditions. You should seek out more specific information about job opportunities and the nature of the work before making a career decision. The *Occupational Outlook Handbook*, a Department of Labor publication, provides details about hundreds of careers.

Executive, Administrative, and Managerial

Occupation	Salaries	Training	Job Outlook	Working Conditions
Certified Public Accountant	$25,000-$45,000	ACD,L	favorable	office, some travel
College Registrar	$46,000 median	ACD	average	office, some travel
Financial Manager	$18,300-$68,000	CD or ACD	favorable	office, regular hours
Hospital Administrator (CEO)	$70,000-$203,000	ACD	very favorable	long hours, some travel
Hotel Manager	$25,000-$80,000	TS or CD	favorable	some stress, weekends
Industrial Production Manager	$68,000 median	CD and Tr	average	long, irregular hours
Insurance Underwriter	$24,000-$54,000	CD	favorable	office, 30-40 hour week
Marketing Manager	$20,000-$79,000	CD or ACD	favorable	long hours, travel
Personnel Manager	$19,000-$65,000	TS or CD	favorable	office, some travel
Property, Real Estate Manager	$10,300-$47,300	CD	favorable	travel, long hours
Purchasing Agent	$16,100-$45,300	CD	average	35-40 hour week
Restaurant Manager	$18,200-$48,000	AD, CD, or Tr	favorable	evenings, stress
Underwriter	$23,900-$54,100	CD	average	office, some travel
Wholesale Buyer	$13,500-$46,700	CD and Tr	average	long hours, travel

Career Handbook

Professional Specialty

Occupation	Salaries	Training	Job Outlook	Working Conditions
Architect	$18,000-$66,000	ACD, L	favorable	office, deadlines
Actuary	$28,300-$62,000	CD, L	favorable	office, some travel
Biological Scientist	$13,000-$55,600	CD, ACD	favorable	laboratory, vary
Chemical Engineer	$32,000-$94,000	CD, L	favorable	40 hour week, some stress
Computer Systems Analyst	$23,000-$63,000	CD or TS	very favorable	40+ hour week, office
Economist	$19,000-$68,000	CD, ACD	average	deadlines, some travel
Lawyer	$25,000-$120,000	ACD, L	favorable	long hours, some travel
Meteorologist	$17,0000-$45,000	CD	favorable	irregular hours
Psychologist	$25,000-$67,000	ACD, L	very favorable	vary with type of practice
Social Worker	$23,000-$36,000	CD, L	favorable	some stress
Statistician	$38,600-$54,700	CD, ACD	favorable	office, regular hours
Surveyor	$17,400-$43,700	CD or Tr, L	average	office and field work
Teacher, Secondary School	$33,700 average	CD, ACD	favorable	long hours, some stress
Technical Writer	$20,000-$45,000	CD	favorable	deadlines

Medical Professional

Occupation	Salaries	Training	Job Outlook	Working Conditions
Chiropractor	$24,000-$180,000	ACD, L	favorable	average workweek
Dentist	$85,000 average	ACD, L	average	vary, some weekends
Optometrist	$75,000 average	ACD, L	average	office
Physician Assistant	$40,000 average	CD, L	very favorable	vary greatly
Recreational Therapist	$15,000-$30,000	CD	favorable	physically demanding
Veterinarian	$27,000-$100,000	ACD, L	favorable	vary, long hours

Medical Technical

Occupation	Salaries	Training	Job Outlook	Working Conditions
Dental Hygienist	$15-$20 per hour	CD or TS, L	favorable	some part time
Dispensing Optician	$18,000-$35,000	Tr or AD	favorable	standing
Emergency Medical Technician	$30,000 average	Tr, L	average	physically demanding
Licensed Practical Nurse	$10-$15 per hour	Tr, L	very favorable	irregular hours, stress
Medical Records Technician	$23,000 average	Ad, L	very favorable	office, some stress
Radiologic Technologist	$12 to $20 per hour	Tr, AD	very favorable	emotional stress

Career Handbook

Technical

Occupation	Salaries	Training	Job Outlook	Working Conditions
Broadcast Technician	$13,000-$48,000	CD	below average	irregular schedule
Computer Programmer	$19,000-$52,000	Tr or CD	favorable	long hours at times
Drafter	$15,000-$42,000	AD	below average	some eyestrain
Engineering Technician	$20,000-$39,000	Tr or AD	favorable	40 hour week
Paralegal	$20,000-$28,000	AD	favorable	some overtime
Pilot, airline	$40,000-$165,000	Flight Tr, L	favorable	irregular schedule

Marketing and Sales

Occupation	Salaries	Training	Job Outlook	Working Conditions
Advertising Sales	$27,000 median	HS or CD	very favorable	competitive, stress
Insurance Agent	$15,000-$59,000	HS or CD, L	average	long hours, travel
Manufacturing Sales Representative	$16,000-$60,000	Tr or CD	average	travel
Real Estate Agent	$19,000 median (varies widely)	Tr, L	average	long hours, travel
Securities Agent	$28,000-$79,000	CD, L	favorable	vary
Travel Agent	$12,000-$22,000	Tr	favorable	office

Clerical and Administrative Support

Occupation	Salaries	Training	Job Outlook	Working Conditions
Bank Teller	$10,000-$21,500	HS	below average	some part time
Computer Operator	$13,000-$34,000	Tr or CD	below average	hours vary
Dispatcher	$10,000-$34,000	HS	below average	stress, sitting long hours
Insurance Claims Examiner	$30,000 median	CD or Tr	average	office, some travel
Mail Carrier	$24,000-$30,000	HS, exam	below average	early hours
Word Processor	$20,000 median	HS, Tr	below average	stress, some part time

Services

Occupation	Salaries	Training	Job Outlook	Working Conditions
Barber	$7-$14 per hour	Tr, L	average	standing, long hours
Chef	$12,000-$40,000	HS, Tr	favorable	vary
Flight Attendant	$13,000-$35,000	HS, Tr	very favorable	nights, weekends
Groundskeeper	$7.50 per hour median	HS	favorable	weather, some part time
Nurse's Aide	$10,000-$22,000	Tr	favorable	hours vary
Police Officer	$19,000-$37,000	HS, Tr, Exam	average	hazardous, irregular hours
Security Guard	$5-$12 per hour	Tr	favorable	night and irregular hours

Construction Trades, Repair, Mechanic

Occupation	Salaries	Training	Job Outlook	Working Conditions
Automotive Body Repairer	$6-$19 per hour	Tr	average	strenuous
Carpenter	$240-$740 per week	3-4 yr. Tr	average	outdoors
Diesel Mechanic	$15 per hour	Tr/AD	average	physically demanding
Electrician	$300-$840 per week	4-5 yr. Tr	favorable	strenuous, dangerous
Heating, Air Conditioning Technician	$270-$780 per week	Tr/AD	average	vary, some outdoors
Plumber	$290-$680 per week	4-5 yr. Tr	average	strenuous
Roustabout	$12 per hour average	Tr/AD	below average	strenuous, outdoors

Agriculture, Forestry, Transportation

Occupation	Salaries	Training	Job Outlook	Working Conditions
Bus Driver	$200-$600 per week	Tr, L	favorable	stress, varying hours
Farm Manager	$15,000-$32,000`	Tr/CD	below average	vary from long hours to part time
Ship captain, Mate	$280-$1000 per week	Tr, L	below average	irregular hours, travel
Timber Cutter, Logger	$16,000 average	Tr	below average	dangerous
Truck Driver	$8-$14 per hour	Tr, L	average	long hours, stress

ability-to-pay principle: principle of taxation in which those with higher incomes pay more taxes than those with lower incomes, regardless of the number of government services they use (p. 428).

absolute advantage: ability of one country, using the same quantity of resources as another country, to produce a particular product at less cost (p. 464).

accounts receivable: money owed to a business by its customers (p. 266).

agency shop: company in which employees are not required to join the union, but must pay union dues (p. 313).

aggregate (A-grih-guht) demand: total quantity of goods and services in the entire economy that all citizens will demand at any one time (p. 342).

aggregate demand curve: a graphed line showing the relationship between the aggregate quantity demanded of all goods and services by all people and the average of all prices, measured by the implicit GDP deflator (p. 343).

aggregates: summation of all the individual parts in the economy (p. 342).

aggregate supply: real domestic output of producers based on the rise and fall of prices (p. 345).

aggregate supply curve: a graphed line showing the macroeconomic measure of aggregate supply based on real domestic output using the implicit GDP deflator as the price index (p. 345).

Aid to Families with Dependent Children: state-run public-assistance program that provides money to needy parents raising young children (p. 417).

allegiances: loyalties to countries, people, or causes (p. 543).

alliances: joint ventures formed by firms in different countries; often between firms from industrialized countries (p. 545).

annual percentage rate (APR): cost of credit expressed as a yearly percentage (p. 93).

antitrust legislation: laws passed by federal and state governments to prevent new monopolies from forming and to break up those that already exist (p. 244).

arbitration (AHR-buh-TRAY-shuhn): stage of negotiation process in which union and management submit the issues they cannot agree on to a third party for a final decision. Both sides agree in advance to accept the arbitrator's decision (p. 319).

articles of incorporation: document filed with the state establishing a corporation within a state; these articles include basic information about the corporation, the board of directors, and the stock being issued (p. 221).

assembly line: production system in which the good being produced moves on a conveyor belt past workers who perform individual tasks in assembling it (p. 275).

assets: items of value such as houses, cars, jewelry, and so on (p. 214).

authoritarian socialism: system that supports revolution as the means to overthrow capitalism and bring about socialist goals; the entire economy is controlled by a central government; also called communism (p. 484).

automated teller machines (ATMs): units that allow consumers to do their banking without the help of a teller (p. 372).

automation: production process in which machines do the work and people oversee them (p. 275).

bait and switch: deceptive advertising practice in which a store attracts consumers with an ad offering a product at a low price, then tries to sell a similar product but at a higher price (p. 65).

balanced-budget amendment: proposal to reduce the federal government budget deficits by amending the Constitution (p. 426).

balance of trade: difference between the value of a nation's exports and its imports (p. 469).

bankruptcy: the inability to pay debts based on the income received; a condition in which debtors give up most of what they own for distribution to creditors (p. 100).

barriers to entry: obstacles to competition that prevent others from entering a market (p. 238).

barter: exchange of goods and services for other goods and services (p. 362).

base year: year used as a point of comparison for other years in a series of statistics (p. 340).

benefits-received principle: system of taxation in which those who use a particular government service support it with taxes in proportion to the benefit they receive; those who do not use a service do not pay taxes for it (p. 428).

blue-collar: category of workers employed in crafts, manufacturing, and nonfarm labor (p. 306).

bond: certificate issued by a company or the government in exchange for borrowed money; a bond promises to pay a stated rate of interest over a stated period of time and to repay the borrowed amount in full at the end of that time (p. 155).

boom: period of prosperity in a business cycle in which economic activity is at its highest point; also called peak (p. 347).

boycott: economic pressure exerted by unions urging the public not to purchase the goods or services produced by a company (p. 320).

brand name: word, picture, or logo on a product that helps consumers distinguish it from similar products (p. 66).

broker: person who acts as a go-between for buyers and sellers of stocks and bonds (p. 157).

bureaucracies: offices and agencies of the government that deal with a specific area (p. 517).

business cycle: irregular changes in the level of total output measured by real GDP (p. 347).

business fluctuations: ups and downs in an economy (p. 347).

capital: all property—machines, buildings, tools, and money—used in the production of other goods and services (p. 10).

capital gain: increase in value of an asset from the time it was bought to the time it was sold (p. 157).

capitalism: economic system in which private individuals own the factors of production and decide how to use them within the limits of the law (p. 37); also called market economic system (p. 33), free enterprise system (p. 38).

capital loss: decrease in value of an asset or bond from the time it was bought to the time it was sold (p. 158).

cartel: arrangement among groups of industrial businesses, often in different countries, to reduce international competition by controlling the price, production, and distribution of goods; international form of monopoly (p. 239).

certificates of deposit (CDs): time deposits that state the amount of the deposit, maturity, and rate of interest being paid; CDs earn more interest than savings accounts, but there is a penalty for early withdrawal; also called savings certificates (p. 148).

channels of distribution: routes by which goods are moved from producers to consumers (p. 293).

charge account: credit extended to a consumer allowing the consumer to buy goods or services from a particular company and to pay for them later (p. 89). *See also* installment charge account; regular charge account; revolving charge account.

checkable deposits: money deposited in a bank that can be withdrawn at any time by presenting a check; formerly called demand deposits (p. 377).

check clearing: method by which a check that has been deposited in one depository institution is transferred to the depository institution on which it was written (p. 396).

checking account: account in which deposited money can be withdrawn at any time by writing a check (p. 376).

circular flow of income: economic model that pictures income as flowing continuously between businesses and consumers; income flows from businesses to households as wages, rent, interest, and profits; income flows from households to businesses as payments for consumer goods and services (p. 443).

civilian labor force: total number of people 16 years or older who are either employed or actively seeking work (p. 306).

closed shop: company in which only union members may be hired; outlawed in 1947 (p. 313).

closing costs: fees involved in arranging for a mortgage or in transferring ownership of property; can include fees for title search, legal costs, loan application, credit report, house inspections, and taxes (p. 129).

coincident indicators: economic indicators whose changes in activity seem to happen at the same time as changes in overall business activity (p. 355)

collateral (kuh-LA-tuh-ruhl): something of value that a borrower lets the lender claim if a loan is not repaid (p. 95).

collective bargaining: process by which unions and employers negotiate the conditions of employment (p. 318).

command economic system: system in which the government controls the factors of production and makes all decisions about their use; also called controlled economy (p. 33).

commercial bank: bank offering wide range of services; main functions are to accept deposits, lend money, and transfer funds among banks, individuals, and businesses (p. 86).

commodity money: mediums of exchange such as cattle and gems that have value as a commodity, or a good, aside from their value as money (p. 365).

communism: term used by Karl Marx for his ideal society in which no government is necessary; has come to mean any authoritarian socialist system that supports revolution as a means to overthrow capitalism and bring about socialist goals; a central government controls the entire economy (p. 484).

comparative advantage: ability of a country to produce a product at a lower opportunity cost than another country (p. 465).

comparison shopping: getting information on the types and prices of products available from different stores and companies (p. 66).

competition: rivalry among producers or sellers of similar goods to win more business by offering the lowest prices or better quality (p. 39).

competitive advertising: advertising that attempts to persuade consumers that a product is different from and superior to any other (p. 64).

complementary good: one product often used with another product; as the price of the second product decreases, the demand for the first product will increase; as the price of the second product increases, the demand for the first product will decrease (p. 188).

condominium: separately owned single unit in an apartment building or a series of townhouses; common areas such as hallways and the land on which the building is built are owned in common (p. 126).

conglomerate merger: buying out of unrelated businesses (p. 245).

conglomerates: large corporations made up of smaller corporations dealing in unrelated activities (p. 245).

consumer: any person or group that buys or uses goods and services to satisfy personal needs and wants (p. 58).

consumer durables: manufactured items that people use for long periods of time before replacement (p. 80).

consumer finance company: company that makes loans directly to consumers at high rates of interest (p. 88).

consumer goods: goods produced for individuals and sold directly to the public to be used as they are (p. 271).

consumerism: movement to educate buyers about the purchases they make and to demand better and safer products from manufacturers (p. 68).

consumer price index (CPI): government measure of the change in price over time of a specific group of goods and services used by the average household (p. 339).

contraction: part of the business cycle during which economic activity is slowing down; leading to a trough (p. 347).

convenience stores: stores open from 16 to 24 hours a day, carrying a limited selection of items generally at higher prices than supermarkets or warehouse stores (p. 109).

cooperative (co-op): apartment whose owner owns equal shares in the company that owns the building and the land on which the building stands; the owner does not own his or her own apartment but rather holds a lease on it (p. 126).

corporate charter: license to operate granted to a corporation by the state where it is established (p. 221).

corporation: organization owned by many people but treated by the law as though it were a person; it can own property, pay taxes, make contracts, and sue and be sued (p. 219).

cosigner: person who signs a loan contract along with the borrower and promises to repay the loan if the borrower does not (p. 96).

cost-benefit analysis: a financial process in which a business estimates the cost of action and compares it with the benefits of that action (p. 258).

cost-of-living adjustment (COLA): union contract or other provision providing for an additional wage increase each year if the general level of prices in the economy rises beyond a certain level (p. 319).

cost-push inflation: theory that the wage demands of labor unions and the excessive profit motive of large corporations push up prices resulting in stagflation (p. 441).

craft union: union made up of skilled workers in a specific trade or industry (p. 312).

credit: receipt of money either directly or indirectly to buy goods and services in the present with the promise to pay for them in the future (p. 80).

credit bureau: private business that investigates a person's income, current debts, personal life, and past history of borrowing and repaying debts to determine the risk involved in lending money to that person (p. 94).

credit card: credit device that allows a person to make purchases at many kinds of stores, restaurants, hotels, and other businesses without paying cash (p. 90).

credit check: investigation of a person's income, current debts, personal life, and past history of borrowing and repaying debts (p. 94).

credit limit: maximum amount of goods or services a person or business can buy on the promise to pay in the future (p. 89).

credit rating: rating of the risk involved in lending money to a specific person or business (p. 94).

credit union: depository institution owned and operated by its members to provide savings accounts and low-interest loans to its members only (p. 87).

debit card: credit device used to make cashless purchases of goods and services; money is electronically withdrawn from the consumer's checkable account and transferred directly to the store's bank account (pp. 91, 377).

debt financing: raising money for a business through borrowing (p. 265). *See also* intermediate-term financing; long-term financing; short-term financing.

deficit financing: spending by the government that exceeds the money it takes in through taxation (p. 423).

deflation: prolonged decline in the general price level (p. 339).

demand curve: line plotted on a graph showing the quantity demanded of a good or service at each possible price (p. 183).

demand deposits: money deposited in a bank that can be withdrawn at any time; now called checkable deposits (p. 377).

demand-pull inflation: theory that prices rise as the result of excessive business and consumer demand; demand increases faster than total supply resulting in shortages leading to higher prices (p. 440).

demerit goods: goods such as gambling and injurious drugs that the government has deemed socially undesirable; use is discouraged through taxation, regulation, or prohibition of the manufacture, sale, and use of such goods (p. 417).

democratic socialism: system that works within the constitutional framework of a nation to elect socialists to office; the government usually controls only some areas of the economy (p. 484).

depreciate (di-PREE-shee-AYT): decline in value over time; occurs as an item wears out or becomes outdated (p. 126).

depreciation (goods): loss of value because of wear and tear to consumer durables, such as cars: also applies to producer goods—machines and equipment (p. 334).

depreciation (monetary): fall in price of a currency through the action of supply and demand; often improves a country's competitive edge in trade (p. 469).

depression: major slowdown of economic activity during which millions are out of work, many businesses fail, and the economy operates at far below capacity (p. 348).

deregulation: gradual reduction of government regulation and control over business activity (p. 246).

devaluation: lowering a currency's value in relation to other currencies by government order (p. 468).

developed nations: nations with relatively high standards of living and economies based more on industry than on agriculture (p. 504).

developing nations: nations with little industrial development and low standards of living (p. 504).

direct foreign investment (DFI): purchase by foreigners of real estate and businesses in another country (p. 537).

direct-mail advertising: type of promotion using a mailer that usually includes a letter describing the product or service and an order blank or application form (p. 291).

discount rate: interest rate the Fed charges on loans to banks (p. 401).

discretionary (dis-KREH-shuh-NEHR-ee) income: money income a person has left to spend on extras after necessities have been bought (p. 58).

disposable income: income remaining for people to spend or save after all taxes have been paid (p. 58).

disposable personal income (DI): income remaining for people to spend or save after all taxes have been paid (p. 336). *See* disposable income.

distribution of income: money payment for work, the amount of health care, education, food, and so on, that each person receives; distribution of goods and services among all members of an economic system (p. 31).

diversification: spreading of investments in several different types of accounts to lower overall risk (p. 164).

dividends: money return a stockholder receives on the amount he or she originally invested in the company by purchasing stock (p. 155).

division of labor: breaking down of a job into small tasks; each task may be performed by a different worker (p. 275).

double coincidence of wants: situation resulting when each party to a transaction wants exactly what the other person has to offer, allowing a direct exchange of goods; this is a requirement for bartering (p. 364).

durability: ability of an item to last a long time (p. 115).

E

economic assistance: loans and outright grants of money or equipment to other nations to add to their capital resources (p. 513).

economic efficiency: wise use of available resources so that people will be confortable given the amount and their need of available resources (p. 45).

economic growth: expansion of the economy to produce more goods, jobs, and wealth (p. 45).

economic indicators: statistics that measure variables in the economy (p. 355).

economic model: simplified representation of the real world which shows people's reactions to changes in the economy; theory (p. 18).

economics: study of how individuals and nations make choices about ways to use scarce resources to fulfill their needs and wants (p. 8).

economic system: way in which a nation uses its resources to satisfy its people's needs and wants (p. 30).

economy: all activity in a nation that affects the production, distribution, and use of goods and services (p. 18).

elastic demand: situation in which the rise or fall in price of a product greatly affects the amount of that product which people are willing to buy; if the prices of certain products rise, consumers will buy cheaper substitutes (p. 185).

elasticity: economic concept dealing with consumers' responsiveness to an increase or decrease in prices; price responsiveness (p. 185).

electronic funds transfer (EFT): system of putting onto computers all the various banking functions that in the past were handled on paper (p. 369).

embargo: complete restriction on the import or export of a particular good (p. 473).

entrepreneur: person who starts a business to gain profits and is willing to take the risks involved (p. 208).

entrepreneurship (AHN-truh-pruh-NUHR-ship): ability to start new businesses, to introduce new products and techniques, and to improve management techniques (p. 11).

equilibrium price: price of a product or service at which the amount producers are willing to supply is equal to the amount consumers are willing to buy. On a graph, the equilibrium price is where the supply curve and the demand curve intersect (p. 197).

equity (E-kwuh-tee): amount of money invested in a property minus the debt, such as the mortgage payments that are still owed (p. 130).

equity (value): that which is fair and just (p. 45).

equity financing: raising money for a company by selling stock in the company (p. 267).

ethical behavior: acting in accordance with moral and ethical convictions about right and wrong (p. 71).

excise (EK-syz) tax: tax on the manufacture, sale, or use within the country of specific products, such as liquor, gasoline, and automobiles (p. 136).

expansion: portion of the business cycle in which economic activity slowly increases; also called a recovery (p. 348).

exports: goods sold to other countries (p. 462).

F

factors of production: resources of land, labor, capital, and entrepreneurship used to produce goods and services (p. 11).

Fed, the: Federal Reserve System created by Congress in

1913 as the nation's central banking organization; functions include processing checks, serving as the government's banker, and controlling the rate of growth of the money supply (p. 388).

Federal Open Market Committee (FOMC): 12-member committee in the Federal Reserve System which meets approximately eight times a year to decide the course of action that the Fed should take to control the money supply (p. 394).

fiat (FEE-uht) money: money that has value because a government fiat, or order, has established it as acceptable for payment of debts (p. 366).

finance charge: cost of credit expressed in dollars and cents (p. 91).

finance company: company that takes over contracts for installment debts from stores and adds a fee for collecting the debt; also make loans directly to consumers (p. 87).

fiscal policy: federal government's use of taxation and spending policies to affect overall business activity (p. 443).

fiscal year: year by which accounts are kept; for the federal government, October 1 to September 30 of the next year (p. 421).

five-year plans: centralized planning system that was the basis for China's economic system; eventually was transformed to a regional planning system leading to limited free enterprise (p. 487).

fixed rate of exchange: system under which a national government sets the value of its currency in relation to a single standard then it establishes equivalents between its currency and that of other countries (p. 467).

flexible exchange rates: arrangement in which the forces of supply and demand are allowed to set the price of various currencies (p. 468).

foreign affiliates: branches of multinational firms (p. 543).

foreign aid: money, goods, and services given by governments and private organizations to help other nations and their citizens (p. 512).

foreign exchange markets: markets dealing in buying and selling foreign currency for businesses that want to import goods from other countries; some currency trading takes place through banks (p. 467).

form utility: the conversion of raw materials to finished goods to satisfy consumer wants (p. 284).

fractional reserve banking: system in which only a fraction of the deposits in a bank is kept on hand, or in reserve; the remainder is available to lend to borrowers or is otherwise invested (p. 389).

franchise: contract in which one business (the franchiser) sells to another business (the franchisee) the right to use the franchiser's name and sell its products (p. 222).

free enterprise system: system in which individuals own the factors of production and decide how to use them within legal limits. Also called capitalism (p. 38).

full employment: condition of the economy when the un-employment rate is lower than a certain number established by economists' studies (p. 439).

General Agreement on Tariffs and Trade (GATT): trade agreement under which countries meet periodically to negotiate tariff reductions that are mutually advantageous to all members; in effect since January 1, 1948 (p. 474).

generalization (JEN-ruh-luh-ZAY-shuhn): statement that pulls together common ideas among facts and is true in most cases (p. 21).

generic (juh-NER-ihk) brands: general name for a product rather than a specific brand name given by the manufacturer (p. 66).

geographic monopolies: market situations occurring when an individual seller has control over a market because of the location (p. 239).

global integration: interdependency among the countries of the world, especially within financial markets and telecommunications (p. 532).

goods and services: end results of factors of production; goods are the things people buy; services are the activities done for others for a fee (p. 11).

government monopolies: market situations created by the government and protected by legal barriers to entry; activity exclusive to government (p. 239).

gross domestic product (GDP): total dollar value of all *final* goods and services produced in the nation in a single year (p. 332).

horizontal merger: buy-out of a company by one in the same business (p. 245).

hypotheses: educated guesses or predictions, used as starting points for investigations (p. 19).

imperfect competition: market situation in which individual or group buys or sells a good or service in amounts large enough to affect price; includes monopoly, oligopoly, and monopolistic competition (p. 237).

implicit GDP price deflator: price index that removes the effect of inflation from GDP so that the overall economy in one year can be compared to another year (p. 341).

import quota: restriction imposed on the value of or on the number of units of a particular good that can be brought into the country (p. 473).

imports: goods bought from other countries for domestic use (p. 462).

income redistribution: government activity that takes income from some people through taxation and uses it to help citizens in need (p. 417).

Individual Retirement Account (IRA): private retirement plan that allows individuals or married couples to save a certain amount of their earnings per year, dependent on total income; also depending on income, the contribution is not taxed and the interest is tax deferred (p. 162).

industrial union: union made up of all the workers in an industry regardless of job or skill level (p. 312).

inelastic demand: situation in which a price change of a product has little impact on the quantity demanded by consumers (p. 186).

infant mortality: death rate of infants who die during first year of life (p. 506).

inflation: prolonged rise in the general price level of goods and services (p. 338).

informative advertising: advertising that benefits consumers by giving information about a product (p. 64).

injunction: court order preventing some activity (p. 320).

innovations: inventions and new production techniques (p. 352).

inside information: information available to a broker that no one else has; it is illegal for a broker to give out this information and illegal for a client to profit from it (p. 159).

installment charge account: credit extended to a consumer allowing the consumer to buy major items such as furniture, televisions, and refrigerators from a particular store and to pay for them in equal payments, or installments, spread over a period of time (p. 90).

installment debt: type of loan repaid with equal payments, or installments, over a specific period of time (p. 80).

interest: amount of money the borrower must pay for the use of someone else's money (p. 80). Payment people receive when they lend money, allowing someone to use their money (p. 146).

interlocking directorate: situation occurring when the majority of members of the boards of directors of competing corporations are the same; in effect, having one group of people manage both companies (p. 244).

intermediate-term financing: borrowing money by a business for 1 to 10 years (p. 265).

International Monetary Fund (IMF): agency whose member governments are obligated to keep their foreign exchange rates more or less fixed (p. 467).

inventory: supply of whatever items are used in a business, such as raw materials or goods for sale (p. 210).

invisible hand: term used by Adam Smith to describe the effect of competition in guiding individuals toward working for their own self-interest, thereby achieving the maximum good for society (p. 37).

joint venture: temporary partnership set up between individuals or companies for a specific purpose and for a short period of time (p. 217).

Keogh (KEE-oh) Plan: retirement plan that allows self-employed individuals to save a maximum of 15 percent of their income up to a specified amount each year and to deduct that amount from their yearly taxable income (p. 161).

labor: work people do; often called a human resource (p. 10).

labor union: association of workers organized to improve wages and working conditions for its members (p. 311).

lagging indicators: indicators that seem to lag behind changes in overall business activity (p. 355)

land: in economics, term used to refer to natural resources and surface land; all things found in nature, on or in the water and earth. Economically, the most important are surface land and mineral deposits (p. 10).

law of demand: economic rule which states that the quantity demanded and price move in opposite directions; as price goes up, quantity demanded goes down; as price goes down, quantity demanded goes up. There is an inverse, or opposite, relationship between demand and price (p. 177).

law of diminishing marginal utility: economic rule stating that the additional satisfaction a consumer gets from purchasing one more unit of a product will lessen with each additional unit purchased (p. 177).

law of diminishing returns: economic rule stating that after some point, adding units of a factor of production (such as labor) to all the other factors of production (such as equipment) increases total output for a time; after a certain point, the extra output for each additional unit will begin to decrease (p. 192).

law of supply: economic rule stating that as the price rises for a good, the quantity supplied rises. As the price falls, the quantity supplied also falls (p. 191).

leading indicators: statistics that point to what will happen in the economy (p. 355)

lease: long-term agreement describing the terms under which property is rented (p. 126).

leasing: renting rather than buying such items as equipment, housing, and cars (p. 266).

legal tender: money that must by law be accepted for payment of public and private debts (p. 366).

liability insurance: insurance that pays for bodily injury and property damage; required by many states before licensing an automobile (p. 139).

limited liability: situation in which an owner's responsibility for a company's debts is limited to the size of the owner's investment in the firm (p. 220).

limited partnership: special form of partnership in which the partners are not equal; the general partner(s) assumes responsibility for all management duties and debts; the other partner(s) contributes money or property and has no voice in management (p. 217).

line of credit: maximum amount of money a company can borrow from a bank during a period of time, usually one year, without having to reapply for a loan (p. 266).

local union: members of a union in a particular factory, company, or geographic area; the local deals with a company by negotiating a contract and making sure contract terms are kept (p. 313).

lockout: situation which occurs when management prevents workers from returning to work until they agree to a new contract (p. 320).

long-term financing: money borrowed by a business for a period of more than 10 years (p. 265).

loose money policy: monetary policy that makes credit inexpensive and abundant, possibly leading to inflation (p. 389).

M1: narrowest definition of the money supply; consists of moneys that can be spent immediately and against which checks can be written; includes all the paper bills and coins in circulation including currency, travelers checks, and checkable deposits (p. 378).

M2: broader definition of the money supply; includes all of M1, plus such near moneys as money market mutual fund balances and Eurodollars; includes all paper bills and coins in circulation (p. 378).

market: freely chosen activity between buyers and sellers of goods and services in which business is done with those who best satisfy the needs and wants of those involved (p. 33).

market economic system: system in which individuals own the factors of production and make economic decisions through free interaction while looking out for their own best interests; the government does not intervene; capitalism (p. 33).

marketing: all the activities needed to move goods and services from the producer to the consumer; includes market research, advertising and promotion, and distribution (p. 282).

market research: gathering, recording, and analyzing data about the types of goods and services that people want (p. 284).

market survey: survey in which researchers gather information about possible users of a product based on such characteristics as age, sex, income, education, and location; written questionnaires and personal interviews are often used (p. 284).

maturity: period of time at which time deposits will pay a stated rate of interest (p. 148).

mechanization: combined labor of people and machines; originally, machines were combined with unskilled workers to replace skilled handwork (p. 274).

mediation (MEE-dee-AY-shuhn): stage in contract negotiations between union and management, in which a neutral person steps in and tries to get both sides to reach an agreement (p. 318).

Medicaid: state and federal public-assistance program that provides free health care for low-income and disabled persons (p. 417).

Medicare: government program that provides health care for the aged (p. 415).

medium of exchange: use of money in exchange for goods or services (p. 362).

merger: situation occurring when one corporation buys more than half the stock of another corporation (p. 244). *See also* conglomerate merger; horizontal merger; vertical merger.

merit good: any good or service that the government has deemed socially desirable such as museums, ballets, and classical music concerts; often subsidized by government so that all people may enjoy it (p. 416).

military assistance: either economic or technical assistance to a nation's armed forces (p. 513).

minimum wage law: federal, state, or city law which sets the lowest legal hourly wage rate that may be paid to certain types of workers (p. 309).

mixed economy: system combining characteristics of more than one type of economy with others so that the mix varies and the economic system created leans more toward one pure type than another (p. 34).

monetarism (MAH-nuh-te-RIH-zuhm): theory that deals with the relationship between the amount of money the Federal Reserve places in circulation and the level of activity in the economy (p. 448).

monetarists: supporters of the theory of monetarism, often linked with Milton Friedman (p. 448).

monetary policy: policy that involves changing the rate of growth of the supply of money in circulation to affect the amount of credit and, therefore, business activity in the economy (p. 388).

monetary rule: monetarists' policy that the Fed should allow the money supply to grow at a specified rate (perhaps 3 to 5 percent) per year and not use monetary policy to stimulate or slow the economy (p. 449).

monetary standard: manner in which a nation assigns value to its money (p. 370).

money: anything customarily used as a medium of exchange, a unit of accounting, and a store of value (p. 362).

money market deposit account (MMDA): account that pays relatively high rates of interest, requires a minimum balance, and allows immediate access to money (p. 148).

money market fund: type of mutual fund that uses investors' money to make short-term loans to businesses and banks; most allow investors to write checks against their investments in the fund (p. 158).

monopolistic competition: market situation in which a large number of sellers offer similar but slightly different products and each has some control over price (p. 240).

mortgage: installment debt owed on real property—houses, buildings, or land (p. 81).

multinationals: firms that do business and have offices or factories in many countries (p. 543).

mutual fund: investment company that pools the money of many individuals to buy stocks, bonds, or other investments (p. 158).

N

national debt: total amount of debt outstanding for the federal government; public debt (p. 425).

national income (NI): total income earned by everyone in the economy (p. 335).

national income accounting: measurement of the national economy's performance, dealing with the overall economy's income and output as well as the interaction of consumers, businesses, and governments (p. 332).

nationalization: placement of railroads, businesses, and so on, under government ownership (p. 519).

natural monopolies: market situations resulting when one company forces its competitors out of business by producing goods or services at the lowest cost; usually found in industries that need large investments to get started and when it is more efficient to have one company rather than several (p. 239).

near moneys: assets, such as savings accounts, that can be turned into money or into a means of payment relatively easily and without the risk of loss of value (p. 378).

net domestic product (NDP): value of nation's total output (GDP) minus total value lost through wear and tear on machines and equipment (p. 335).

net exports: difference between what the nation sells to other countries (exports) and what it buys from other countries (imports). (p. 334).

North American Free Trade Agreement (NAFTA): trade agreement designed to reduce tariff barriers among Mexico, Canada, and the United States; approved in 1993 (p. 474). *See also* U.S.-Canadian Free Trade Agreement.

O

oligopoly (AH-luh-GAH-puh-lee): industry dominated by a few suppliers that exercise some control over price (p. 240).

open-market operations: buying and selling of United States securities by the Fed to affect the money supply by changing depository institution reserves or by putting money into or taking it out of circulation in the economy (p. 402).

opportunity cost: value of the next best alternative given up for the alternative that was chosen (p. 14).

over-the-counter market: purchase and sale of stocks and bonds, often of smaller, lesser-known companies, which takes place outside the organized stock exchanges; most over-the-counter stocks are quoted in the National Association of Securities Dealers Automated Quotations (NASDAQ) listings (p. 157).

overdraft checking: checking account that allows a customer to write a check for more money than exists in his or her account (p. 369).

ownership utility: utility created by assuring orderly transfer of ownership of desired goods (p. 284).

P

partnership: business that two or more individuals own and operate (p. 217).

passbook savings account: account for which a depositor receives a booklet in which deposits, withdrawals, and interest are recorded; also called a regular savings account (p. 147).

past-due notices: reminders sent by businesses and lending institutions that debt payments are overdue (p. 96).

patent: right granted by the government to exclusively manufacture an invention for a specified number of years (p. 239).

peak: period of prosperity in a business cycle in which economic activity is at its highest point; also called a boom (p. 347).

penetration pricing: selling a new product at a low price to attract customers away from an established product (p. 290).

pension plans: company plans that provide for retirement income (p. 161).

perfect competition: market situation in which there are numerous buyers and sellers, and no one buyer or seller can affect price (p. 232).

personal income (PI): total income individuals receive before personal taxes are paid (p. 336).

picketing: activity in which striking workers walk up and down in front of a workplace carrying signs that state their disagreement with the company (p. 320).

place utility: utility created by having a good available where a consumer wants to buy it (p. 284).

points: fee paid to a lender and computed as percentage points of a loan (p. 129).

price elasticity of demand: economic concept that deals with how much demand varies according to changes in price (p. 185).

price leadership: practice of setting prices close to those charged by other companies selling similar products; found especially in oligopolies (p. 289).

price system: system of pure capitalism that allows prices to seek their own level as determined by the forces of supply and demand (p. 482).

prime rate: rate of interest banks charge on loans to their best business customers (p. 401).

principal: amount of money originally borrowed in a loan (p. 80).

private-labeled products: store-brand products carried by some supermarket chains and club wholesale chains as a lower cost alternative to national brands (p. 110).

private property: whatever is owned by individuals or groups rather than the federal, state, or local governments (p. 38).

private property rights: rights of individuals or groups to own goods; these rights are enforced by the government (p. 482).

privatization: change from state ownership of business, land, and buildings to private ownership (p. 492).

producer goods: goods produced for businesses to use in making other goods (p. 271).

producer price index (PPI): measure of the change in price over time of a specific group of goods used by businesses; formerly wholesale price index (p. 340).

product differentiation: manufacturers' use of minor differences in quality and features to try to differentiate between similar goods and services (p. 240).

production: process of changing resources into goods that satisfy the needs and wants of individuals and businesses (p. 271).

production possibilities: all the combinations of goods and services that can be produced from a fixed amount of resources in a given period of time (p. 15).

productivity: ability to produce greater quantities of goods and services in better and faster ways (p. 10).

product life cycle: series of stages that a product goes through from first introduction to complete withdrawal from the market; a cycle has no fixed number of months or years (p. 291).

professionals: highly educated individuals with college degrees and usually additional education or training (p. 307).

profit: money left after all the costs of production—wages, rent, interest, and taxes have been paid (p. 39).

profit incentive: desire to make money that motivates people to produce and sell goods and services that others want to buy (p. 39).

progressive tax: tax that takes a larger percentage of higher incomes than lower incomes; justified on the basis of the ability-to-pay principle (p. 430).

proletariat (PROH-luh-TER-ee-uht): term used by Karl Marx to mean workers (p. 484).

promissory (prah-muh-SOHR-ee) **note:** written agreement to repay a loan by a specified time and with a specified rate of interest (p. 266).

promotion: use of advertising and other methods to inform consumers that a new or improved product or service is available and to persuade them to purchase it (p. 290).

property rights: protection of private property; the government may not legally take private property without paying fair market value (p. 523).

proportional tax: tax that takes the same percentage of all incomes; as income rises, the amount of tax paid also rises (p. 430).

proprietor: owner of a business; from the Latin word *proprietas*, meaning "property" (p. 213).

protectionists: people who argue for trade restrictions (p. 474).

protective tariff: tax on imports used to raise the cost of imported goods and thereby protect domestic producers (p. 472).

public-assistance programs: government programs that make payments based on need; also called welfare (p. 418).

public goods: goods or services that government sometimes supplies to its citizens; can be used by many individuals at the same time without reducing the benefit each person receives (p. 416).

public-works projects: publicly-used facilities such as schools and highways, built by federal, state, or local governments with public money (p. 413).

purchasing power: the real goods and services that money can buy; determines the value of the money (p. 338).

pure monopoly: most extreme market form of imperfect competition in which a single seller controls the supply of a good or service and thus has control over price (p. 237). *See also* geographic monopolies; government monopolies; natural monopolies; technological monopoly.

rational choice: involves choosing the alternative that has the greatest value from among comparable quality products (p. 61).

real estate taxes: taxes paid on land and buildings (p. 125).

real GDP: figure resulting when the GDP is adjusted for inflation by applying the price deflator (p. 341).

real income effect: economic rule stating that individuals cannot keep buying the same quantity of a product if its price rises while their income stays the same; this works in reverse direction also—if the price of a product decreases and income remains the same, purchasing power is increased and the amount of product purchased will likely be increased (p. 179).

recession: portion of the business cycle in which the nation's output, the real GDP, does not grow for at least two quarters (six months) (p. 348).

recovery: portion of the business cycle in which economic activity increases; also called an expansion (p. 348).

registration fee: licensing fee, usually annual, paid to a state for the right to use a car (p. 137).

regressive tax: tax that takes a larger percentage of lower incomes than higher incomes (p. 430).

regular charge account: credit extended to a consumer

allowing the consumer to buy goods or services from a particular store and to pay for them later. Interest is charged on that part of the account not paid within a certain period of time. Also known as a 30-day charge (p. 89).

representative money: money not valuable in itself for nonmoney uses which can be exchanged for some valuable commodity such as gold or silver (p. 366).

reregulation: federal government regulation and control over business activity of formerly heavily-regulated industries (p. 246).

reserve requirements: regulations set by the Fed, requiring banks to keep a certain percentage of their deposits as cash in their own vaults or as deposits in their district Federal Reserve Bank (p. 389).

resource: anything that people can use to make or obtain what they need or want (p. 8).

retailers: businesses that sell consumer goods directly to the public (p. 294).

revenue tariff: tax on imports used primarily to raise income without restricting imports (p. 472).

revolving charge account: credit extended to a consumer allowing the consumer to buy goods or services from a particular store and to pay for them later. Usually a certain portion of the balance must be paid each month; interest is charged on the amount not paid (p. 89).

right-to-work laws: state laws forbidding union shops and closed shops; workers are allowed to continue working in a particular job without joining a union (p. 313).

robotics: sophisticated computer-controlled machinery that operates an assembly line (p. 275).

S

saving: nonuse of income for a period of time so that it can be used later (p. 146).

savings and loan association (S&L): depository institution that, like a commercial bank, accepts deposits and lends money. Originally established to lend money for home building, federal laws in the 1980s permitted S&Ls to provide some of the same services as banks (p. 86).

savings banks: depository institutions originally set up to serve small savers overlooked by commercial banks; most of their business comes from savings accounts and home loans (p. 86).

savings bonds: bonds issued by the federal government as a way of borrowing money; bonds are purchased at half the face value and then increase in value every six months until full face value is reached (p. 155).

scarcity: state in which people do not and cannot have enough income, time, or other resources to satisfy their every desire (p. 9).

secondary market: process through which owners of securities sell the securities to other investors for cash (p. 493)

secured loan: loan that is backed up by collateral (p. 95).

security deposit: money a renter lets an owner hold; if the rent is not paid or an apartment is damaged, the owners may keep all or part of the deposit (p. 130).

semiskilled workers: people whose jobs require some training, in job-related skills, often using modern technology (p. 307).

service flow: amount of use a person gets from an item over time and the value a person places on this use (p. 115).

service workers: people who provide services directly to individuals (p. 307).

shortages: situations occurring when, at the going price, the quantity demanded is greater than the quantity supplied (p. 198).

short-term financing: money borrowed by a business for any period of time less than a year (p. 265).

skilled worker: person who has learned a trade or craft either through a vocational school or as an apprentice to an experienced worker (p. 307).

small business incubator: a business that helps small businesses develop by providing such forms of assistance as a low-rent building, management advice, and computers; often operated with state and federal funds (p. 215).

social insurance programs: government programs that pay benefits to retired and disabled workers, their families, and the unemployed; financed by taxes paid into programs by workers and employers (p. 418).

Social Security: federal program that provides monthly payments to people who are retired or unable to work (p. 417).

sole proprietorship: business owned by one person; most basic type of business organization (p. 213).

special economic zones: designated geographic areas in the People's Republic of China which, since 1979, have been moving toward restricted decentralized capitalism (p. 488).

specialization (spe-shuh-luh-ZAY-shuhn): concept that it is profitable for a nation to produce and export a limited assortment of goods for which it is particularly suited (p. 464).

stabilization (stay-buh-lih-ZAY-shuhn) policies: attempt by the federal government to keep the economy healthy and to make the future more predictable for planning, saving, and investing; includes monetary and fiscal policies (p. 438).

stagflation: combination of inflation and low economic activity (p. 441).

standard of living: material well-being of an individual, group, or nation measured by the average value of goods and services used by the average citizen during a given period of time (p. 45).

startups: newly-established businesses; business advice and assistance are available from the federal and state governments, colleges, and universities (p. 214)

statement savings account: account similar to a passbook savings account except that instead of a passbook, the depositor receives a monthly statement showing all transactions (p. 147).

stock: share of ownership in the corporation issuing the stock; entitles the buyer to a certain part of the future profits and assets of the corporation (p. 154).

stockholders: people who have invested in a corporation and own stock; stockholders hold a claim against a certain part of the profits (p. 155).

store of value: use of money to store purchasing power for later use (p. 364).

strike: deliberate work stoppage by workers to force an employer to give in to their demands (p. 312).

subsistence agriculture: raising of just enough food by a family to take care of its own needs; no crops are available for export or to feed an industrial work force (p. 505).

substitution effect: economic principle stating that if two items satisfy the same need and the price of one rises, people will buy the other (p. 179).

Supplemental Security Income: federal programs that include food stamps, veterans' benefits, and payments to the aged, blind, and disabled (p. 417).

supply curve: line plotted on a graph that shows the quantities supplied of a good or service at each possible price (p. 194).

surplus: situation occurring when supply is greater than demand (p. 198).

tariff: tax on imports; most commonly used barrier to free trade (p. 472). *See also* protective tariff; revenue tariff

tax-exempt bonds: bonds sold by local and state governments; interest paid on the bond is not taxed by the federal government (p. 155).

technical assistance: aid, in the form of professionals such as engineers, teachers, and technicians, supplied by nations to teach skills to individuals in other nations; strengthens a nation's human resources (p. 513).

technological monopoly: market situation resulting when a seller develops a product or production process for which it obtains a patent; company holds exclusive rights to the new invention for a specified number of years (p. 239).

technology: any use of land, labor, and capital that produces goods and services more efficiently. Today, generally means the use of science to develop new products and new methods for producing and distributing goods and services (pp. 11, 197).

telecommunications: long-distance communications, usually electronic, using communications satellites, and fiber-optic cables (p. 532).

test marketing: offering a product for sale in a small area for a limited period of time to see how well it sells before offering it nationally (p. 285).

three *P*'s: prices, profits, and private property—the basis

of market capitalism (p. 482).

thrift institutions: mutual savings banks, savings and loan associations (S&Ls), and credit unions that offer many of the same services as commercial banks (p. 377).

tight money policy: monetary policy which makes credit expensive and in short supply in an effort to slow the economy (p. 389).

time deposits: savings plans that require savers to leave their money on deposit for certain periods of time (p. 148).

time lags: periods between the time fiscal policy is enacted and the time it becomes effective (p. 450).

time utility: utility created by having a good available when a consumer wants to buy it (p. 284).

tolerance: fair, objective, and permissive attitude toward the opinions, and practices of other religions, races, and nationalities (p. 547).

trade-off: exchanging one thing for the use of another; often making unavoidable choices because of the problem of scarcity (p. 13).

trade credit: credit extended by a seller to a business buying goods; allows a buyer to take immediate possession of goods to pay for them at some future date (p. 266).

traditional economic system: system in which economic decisions are based on customs, beliefs, and ways of doing things that have been handed down from generation to generation (p. 32).

transfer payments: welfare and other supplementary payments, such as unemployment compensation, Social Security, and Medicaid, that a state or the federal government makes to individuals, adding to an individual's income even though the payments are not in exchange for any current productive activity (p. 336).

Treasury bills: certificates issued by the U.S. Treasury in exchange for borrowed money in minimum amounts of $10,000 and maturing during a period ranging from three months to one year (p. 156).

Treasury bonds: certificates issued by the U.S. Treasury in exchange for borrowed money in minimum amounts of $1,000 or $5,000 and maturing in 10 or more years (p. 156).

Treasury notes: certificates issued by the U.S. Treasury in exchange for borrowed money with minimum amounts of $1,000 or $5,000 and maturing in 2 to 10 years (p. 156).

trough: lowest portion of the business cycle in which the downward spiral of the economy levels off (p. 348).

underground economy: transactions by people who do not follow federal and state laws with respect to reporting earnings; includes tax avoiders, gamblers and drug traffickers, and those illegally receiving unemployment benefits (p. 439).

unemployment rate: percentage of the civilian labor force that is without jobs but that is actively looking for work (p. 438).

union shop: company that requires that new company employees to join a union after a specific period of time, usually three months (p. 313).

unit of accounting: use of money as a yardstick for comparing the values of goods and services in relation to one another (p. 364).

unlimited liability: requirement that an owner is personally and fully responsible for all losses and debts of a business (p. 214).

unsecured loan: loan guaranteed only by a promise to repay it (p. 95).

unskilled workers: people whose jobs require no specialized training (p. 307).

U.S.-Canadian Free Trade Agreement: trade agreement between the United States and Canada designed to eliminate high tariffs on such things as furniture, textiles, and paper; guarantees that both countries have access to each others' petroleum, gas, coal, and electricity at prices paid by nationals under comparable commercial circumstances (p. 474).

usury law: law restricting the amount of interest that can be charged for credit (p. 99).

utility: ability of any good or service to satisfy consumer wants (pp. 177, 282). *See also* form utility; ownership utility; place utility; time utility.

values: beliefs or characteristics that an individual or group considers important, such as religious freedom, and equal opportunity (p. 20).

vertical merger: a merger in which a business that is buying from or selling to another business merges with that business (p. 245).

vicious cycle of poverty: trap in which a less-developed country with low per-capital incomes cannot save and invest enough to achieve acceptable rates of economic growth (p. 524).

voluntary exchange: principle that is the basis of activity in a market economy; a buyer and a seller exercise their economic freedoms by working out their own terms of exchange (p. 176).

wants: economists' term for everything people desire beyond basic goods and services that meet their needs (p. 9).

warehouse food store: store that carries a limited number of brands and items; less expensive than supermarkets; goods are often available only in large quantities (p. 109).

warranty: promise made by a manufacturer or a seller to repair or replace a product within a certain period of time if it is found to be faulty (p. 60).

welfare: public-assistance programs that make payments based on need; includes Supplemental Security Income, Aid to Families with Dependent Children, and Medicaid (p. 418).

welfare state: country that is a blend of capitalism and socialism, combining private ownership of the means of production and competitive allocation of resources with the goal of social equality for its citizens (p. 494).

white-collar: category of workers employed in offices, sales, or professional positions (p. 307).

wholesalers: businesses that purchase large quantities of goods from producers for resale to other businesses (p. 293).

Workers' Compensation: government program that extends payments for medical care to workers injured on the job; people who have lost jobs can receive payments through unemployment insurance (p. 417).

ability-to-pay principle/principio de capacidad de pago principio de tributación el cual prescribe que aquellos que tengan ingresos más altos paguen más impuestos que aquellos que tengan ingresos más bajos, irrespectivamente del número de servicios gubernamentales que usen (p. 428).

absolute advantage/ventaja absoluta capacidad de un país, que usa la misma cantidad de recursos que otro, para producir un determinado producto a menos costo. (p. 464).

accounts receivable/cuentas por cobrar dineros que le deben los clientes a un negocio (p. 266).

agency shop/empresa con cotización sindical obligatoria compañía en la cual no se les exige a los empleados pertenecer al sindicato, pero deben pagarle cuotas a éste (p. 313).

aggregate demand/demanda total cantidad total de bienes y servicios en la totalidad de la economía que todos los ciudadanos demandan en un momento dado (p. 342).

aggregate demand curve/curva de demanda total línea gráfica que demuestra la relación entre la cantidad total que demandan todos los ciudadanos y el promedio de todos los precios, medidos mediante el índice implícito de deflación del PNB (p. 343).

aggregates/agregados suma de todas las partes que individualmente componen la economía (p. 342).

aggregate supply/oferta total producción nacional real basada en la subida y caída de los precios (p. 345).

aggregate supply curve/oferta total, curva de línea gráfica que demuestra la relación entre la demanda total cuando ésta se mide basándola en la producción nacional real y usando el índice implícito de deflación del PNB como índice de precios (p. 345).

Aid to Families with Dependent Children/Ayuda a Familias con Hijos Dependientes programa de asistencia pública en los Estados Unidos que administran los estados, el cual proporciona dinero a padres necesitados de hijos pequeños (p. 417).

allegiances/lealtades fidelidad a causas, países y personas (p.543).

alliances/alianzas negocios en conjunto formados por firmas en distintos países; a menudo entre firmas de países industrializados (p. 545).

annual percentage rate (APR)/índice de porcentaje anual costo del crédito expresado en términos de porcentaje anual (p. 93).

antitrust legislation/leyes antimonopolistas leyes promulgadas por el gobierno federal y estatal para impedir la formación de nuevos monopolios y para romper los que ya existan (p. 244).

arbitration/arbitraje etapa en un proceso de negociación en la cual el sindicato y la gerencia plantean a un tercero los asuntos sobre los cuales no se pueden poner de acuerdo para que éste dé una decisión final. Ambas partes aceptan por adelantado la decisión del árbitro (p. 319).

articles of incorporation/escritura de constitución documento que establece en un estado una sociedad; dicho documento abarca cierta información básica sobre la sociedad, la junta directiva y las acciones que se emiten (p. 221).

assembly line/cadena de montaje sistema de producción en la cual al artículo que se fabrica lo lleva una banda transportadora a los trabajadores que a su vez lo ensamblan (p. 275).

authoritarian socialism/socialismo autoritario sistema que respalda la revolución como medio para derribar al capitalismo y lograr metas socialistas; un gobierno central controla toda la economía; también llamado comunismo (p. 484).

automated teller machines/cajeros automáticos unidades que les permiten a los clientes realizar sus transacciones bancarias sin la ayuda de un cajero (p. 372).

automation/automatización proceso de producción en el cual las máquinas realizan el trabajo y el personal humano lo fiscaliza (p. 275).

bait and switch/publicidad con cebo práctica publicitaria engañosa mediante la cual una tienda atrae a los consumidores con un anuncio de un producto a bajo precio, y entonces trata de venderles un producto similar a precio superior (p. 65).

balanced budget amendment/enmienda del presupuesto equilibrado propuesta para reducir los déficits del gobierno federal mediante enmiendas a la Constitución (p. 426).

balance of trade/balanza comercial diferencia entre el valor de las exportaciones y las importaciones de una nación (p. 469).

bankruptcy/bancarrota incapacidad de pagar deudas con los ingresos percibidos; condición en la cual los deudores renuncian a la mayor parte de sus propiedades para distribuir éstas a sus acreedores (p. 100).

barriers to entry/barreras para entrar en un mercado obstáculos a la competencia para impedir que otros tengan acceso al mercado (p. 238).

barter/trueque intercambio de bienes y servicios por otros bienes y servicios (p. 362).

base year/año base año utilizado como punto de comparación para los demás años en una serie estadística (p. 340).

benefits-received principle/principio de beneficios recibidos sistema tributario en el cual los que hacen uso de un cierto servicio que preste el gobierno mantienen al mismo con impuestos en proporción a los beneficios que reciban; los que no usen dicho servicio no pagan impuestos por el mismo (p. 428).

blue-collar/obreros categoría de trabajadores que se desempeñan en artesanías, fábricas y trabajo no agrícola (p. 306).

bond/bono certificado emitido por una compañía o el gobierno a cambio de un préstamo de dinero; el bono promete pagar un cierto tipo de interés durante un cierto plazo de tiempo y devolver la suma prestada en su totalidad al final de dicho plazo (p. 155).

boom/período de auge período de prosperidad en un ciclo comercial en el cual la actividad económica está en su más elevado punto; llamado también máximo o cumbre (p. 347).

boycott/boicot presión económica ejercida por los sindicatos que le urgen al público que no adquieran los bienes y servicios que produzca una compañía (p. 320).

brand name/marca de fábrica palabra, imagen o logotipo en un producto que ayuda a los consumidores a distinguirlo de otros productos similares (p. 66).

broker/corredor persona que actúa como intermediario entre los compradores y vendedores de bonos y acciones (p. 157).

bureaucracies/burocracias oficinas y agencias del gobierno que se desempeñan en su propio y específico campo en la administración del gobierno (p.517).

business cycle/ciclo económico cambios irregulares en el nivel de la producción total medida por el PNB real (p. 347).

business fluctuations/fluctuaciones económicas sube-y-bajas en la economía (p. 347).

capital/capital todas las propiedades: máquinas, edificios, herramientas y dinero—que se usen en la producción de otros bienes y servicios (p. 10).

capital gains/ganacias de capital aumento en el valor bienes desde el momento en que se compran hasta el momento en que se vendan (p. 157).

capitalism/capitalismo sistema económico en el cual personas particulares son dueñas de los factores de producción y deciden cómo utilizarlos dentro del margen de la ley; también llamado sistema de mercado; sistema de libre empresa (p. 37).

capital loss/pérdidas de capital disminución en el valor bienes desde el momento en que se compran hasta el momento en que se vendan (p. 158).

cartel/cartel convenio entre grupos de negocios industriales, a menudo en distintos países, de reducir la competencia internacional controlando el precio, producción y distribución de bienes; una forma internacional de monopolio (p. 239).

certificates of deposit/certificados de depósito depósitos a plazo que declaran la cantidad del depósito, el vencimiento y el tipo de interés que paga; los CD ganan más interés que las cuentas de ahorro, pero tienen penalidad por retirar fondos antes de tiempo; se les llama también certificados de ahorro (p. 148).

channels of distribution/canales de distribución rutas mediante las cuales se distribuyen los bienes de los productores a los consumidores (p. 293).

charge account/cuenta de crédito crédito extendido a un consumidor que le permite a éste comprarle bienes y servicios a cierta compañía y pagarlos luego. (p. 89). *Vea también* cuenta de crédito a plazos (installment charge account); cuenta de crédito regular (regular charge account); cuenta de crédito rotativa (revolving charge account).

checkable deposits/depósitos verificables dinero depositado en un banco que se puede extraer en cualquier momento presentando un cheque; anteriormente llamados *demand deposits* (depósitos disponibles o extraíbles a la vista) (p. 377).

check clearing/compensación de cheques bancarios método mediante el cual un cheque que ha sido depositado en una institución depositaria se transfiere a la institución depositaria en la que fue hecho (p. 396).

checking account/cuenta corriente bancaria cuenta en la cual el dinero depositado se puede extraer en cualquier momento haciendo un cheque (p. 376).

circular flow of income/flujo circular de ingresos modelo económico que representa a los ingresos como si fluyeran contínuamente entre los negocios y los consumidores; los ingresos fluyen de los negocios a los domicilios como sueldos, alquileres, intereses y ganancias; los ingresos fluyen de los domicilios a los negocios como pagos por los bienes y los servicios de consumo (p. 443).

civilian labor force/fuerza laboral civil número total de personas de 16 años o más que estén bien empleadas o procurando activamente trabajo (p. 306).

closed shop/empresa con sindicación obligatoria compañía en la cual sólo pueden trabajar los que pertenezcan al sindicato; prohibido en 1947 (p. 313).

closing costs/costos de cierre costos en que se incurre al tramitar una hipoteca o transferir el título de una propiedad; puede incluir gastos por concepto de investigación del título, costos jurídicos, solicitud del préstamo, informe de crédito, inspecciones de la casa e impuestos (p. 129).

collateral/garantía algo de valor que el prestatario permite que el prestamista reclame para sí si no se devuelve el préstamo (p. 95).

collective bargaining/convenio colectivo proceso mediante el cual los sindicatos y los empleadores o patronos negocian las condiciones de empleo (p. 318).

command economic system/sistema de economía dirigida sistema en el cual el gobierno controla los factores de producción y toma todas las decisiones con respecto a su uso; también llamado de economía controlada (p. 33).

commercial bank/banco comercial banco que ofrece una amplia gama de servicios; sus principales funciones son aceptar depósitos, prestar dinero y transferir fondos entre bancos, individuos y negocios (p. 86).

commodity money/dinero mercancía medios de intercambio tales como ganado o joyas que tienen valor como artículo o bien comerciable, fuera de su valor como dinero (p. 365).

communism/comunismo término usado por Carlos Marx para describir su sociedad ideal en la cual no hace falta gobierno; ha venido a significar cualquier tipo de sistema socialista autoritario que respalda la revolución como medio para derrocar al capitalismo y lograr metas socialistas; un gobierno central controla toda la economía (p. 484).

comparative advantage/ventaja comparativa capacidad de un país de producir un producto a un costo de oportunidad menor que otro país (p. 465).

comparison shopping/comparación de las condiciones de venta obtener información sobre los tipos y precios de los productos que hay en distintos comercios y compañías (p. 66).

competition/competencia rivalidad entre los productores o vendedores de artículos similares para conseguirse más negocio ofreciendo los precios más bajos o de mejor calidad (p. 39).

competitive advertising/publicidad competidora publicidad que intenta persuadir a los consumidores de que un producto es distinto y superior a cualquier otro (p. 64).

complementary good/bien complementano producto que a menudo se utiliza con otro; al disminuir el precio del segundo producto, la demanda por el primero aumenta; al aumentar el precio del segundo producto, la demanda por el primero disminuye (p. 188).

condominium/condominio unidades, cada cual con su dueño por separado, en un edificio de apartamentos o en una serie de *townhouses;* las áreas comunes tales como los pasillos y el terreno en el cual está construído el edificio son propiedad en común de todos (p. 126).

conglomerate merger/fusión de conglomerados adquisición de negocios que no están relacionados entre sí (p. 245).

conglomerates/conglomerados grandes compañías compuestas de compañías más pequeñas que se desempeñan en actividades que no están relacionadas entre sí (p. 245).

consumer/consumidor cualquier persona o grupo que compre o utilice bienes y servicios para satisfacer necesidades o deseos personales (p. 58).

consumer durables/bienes duraderos de consumo artículos fabricados que usan las personas durante largo tiempo antes de reemplazarlos (p. 80).

consumer finance company/compañía financiera para el consumidor compañía que le hace préstamos directamente al consumidor a altas tasas de interés (p. 88).

consumer goods/bienes de consumo bienes producidos para personas y vendidos directamente al público para que los usen tal como están (p. 271).

consumerism/consumo movimiento para educar a los compradores acerca de la compras que hacen y demandar productos mejores y más seguros a los fabricantes (p. 68).

consumer price index/índice de precios al consumidor medida usada por el gobierno del cambio en precios durante cierto tiempo de un grupo específico de bienes y servicios que utiliza el domicilio promedio (p. 339).

contraction/contracción parte del ciclo comercial durante el cual la actividad económica está más lenta; llamada también punto bajo ("trough") (p. 347).

convenience stores/tiendas de artículos de consumo frequente tiendas que abren de 16 a 24 horas al día, y que tienen una selección limitada de artículos, por lo general a un precio más elevado que los supermercados o las tiendas almacenes (p. 109).

cooperative/cooperativas apartamento cuyo dueño tiene intereses por partes iguales en la compañía que es propietaria del edificio y del terreno sobre el cual está éste; el dueño no es propietario exclusivo del apartamento en sí sino que más tiene un arrendamiento por el mismo (p. 126).

corporate charter/escritura de constitución licencia para funcionar que le concede a la sociedad el estado en el cual se ha establecido ésta (p. 221).

corporation/corporación organización propiedad de muchas personas la cual, sin embargo, la ley la trata como si fuera una persona; puede tener propiedad, pagar impuestos, hacer contratos y demandar y ser demandada (p. 219).

cosigner/cosignatario persona que firma un contrato de préstamo junto con el prestatario y promete devolver el préstamo si este último no lo hace (p. 96).

cost-benefit analysis/análisis de costo-beneficio proceso financiero mediante el cual un negocio calcula el costo de una acción y la compara con los beneficios de ésta (p. 258).

cost-of-living adjustment (COLA)/ajuste por costo de vida contrato sindical o disposición de algún otro tipo que prescribe un aumento adicional en los salarios si el nivel general de los precios en la economía sube más allá de cierto nivel (p. 319).

cost-push inflation/inflación con estancamiento teoría que las demandas salariales de los sindicatos laborales y el excesivo afán de lucro de las grandes compañías empujan hacia arriba los precios, lo cual resulta en "estanca-inflación" (p. 441).

craft union/gremio sindicato compuesto por obreros calificados en un oficio o industria específico (p. 312).

credit/crédito lo que permite a una persona recibir dinero directamente o indirectamente para comprar bienes y servicios en el presente con la promesa de pagarlos en el futuro (p. 80).

credit bureau/agencia de informes de crédito negocio particular que investiga los ingresos, deudas actuales, vida personal e historial de préstamos y pago de deudas de una persona para determinar el riesgo en prestarle dinero a dicha persona (p. 94).

credit card/tarjeta de crédito dispositivo de crédito que le permita a una persona hacer compras en muchos tipos de tiendas, restaurantes, hoteles y demás negocios sin pagar en efectivo (p. 90).

credit check/investigación de crédito investigación de los ingresos, deudas actuales, vida personal e historial de préstamos y pago de deudas de una persona (p. 94).

credit limit/límite del crédito máxima cantidad de bienes y servicios que una persona o negocio puede adquirir bajo promesa de pagarlos en el futuro (p. 89).

credit rating/evaluación de crédito evaluación del riesgo en prestarle dinero a un cierto negocio o persona (p. 94).

credit union/unión de crédito institución depositaria que es propiedad de y está administrada por sus miembros para proporcionarles exclusivamente a éstos cuentas de ahorro y préstamos de bajos intereses (p. 87).

debit card/tarjeta de débito dispositivo de crédito que se utiliza para hacer compra de bienes y servicios sin usar efectivo; el dinero se extrae electrónicamente de la cuenta corriente del consumidor y se transfiere directamente a la cuenta bancaria de la tienda (pp. 91, 377).

debt financing/financiamiento mediante créditos a la emisión de obligaciones recaudación de dinero para un negocio con préstamos (p. 265). *Vea también* financiamiento a mediano plazo; a largo plazo; y a corto plazo.

deficit financing/financiamiento del déficit gastos del gobierno que exceden lo que éste recauda a través de impuestos (p. 423).

deflation/deflación declinación prolongada en el nivel general de precios (p. 339).

demand curve/curva de demanda línea gráfica que demuestra la cantidad que se demanda de un bien o servicio a cada precio posible (p. 183).

demand deposits/depósitos a la vista dinero depositado en un banco y que se puede extraer en cualquier momento; llamados ahora depósitos extraíbles por cheque (checkable deposits) (p. 377).

demand-pull inflation/inflación de demanda teoría que dice que los precios suben como resultado de demanda excesiva por parte de los negocios y el consumidor; la demanda aumenta más rápido que la oferta total lo cual resulta en insuficiencias de oferta que causan precios más elevados (p. 440).

demerit goods/bienes de demerito bienes tales como juegos al azar y drogas peligrosas que el gobierno considera son socialmente indeseables; se desalienta su uso mediante impuestos, regulaciones o prohibición de la fabricación, venta y uso de dichos bienes (p. 417).

democratic socialism/socialismo democrático sistema que funciona dentro del contexto constitucional de una nación para elegir socialistas a cargos públicos; el gobierno usualmente controla solamente algunas áreas de la economía (p. 484).

depreciate/depreciar declinar en valor con el pasar del tiempo; ocurre al irse gastando un artículo o al quedarse obsoleto (p. 126).

depreciation (goods)/sobregiro pérdida de valor a causa de desgaste y deterioro de bienes duraderos de consumo, tales como automóviles; también se aplica a los bienes de producción, tales como maquinaria y equipos (p. 369).

depreciation (monetary)/depreciación (monetaria) caída del precio de una divisa a causa de la acción de la oferta y la demanda (p. 469).

depression/depresión declinación de importancia en la actividad económica durante la cual millones de personas se quedan sin trabajo, fracasan numerosos negocios y la economía funciona muy por debajo de su capacidad (p. 348).

deregulation/desregulación reducción gradual en la regulación y control gubernamentales de las actividades comerciales (p. 246).

devaluation/devaluación baja del valor de una moneda en relación con otras por orden del gobierno (p. 468).

developed nations/naciones desarrolladas naciones con niveles relativamente altos de vida basados más en la industria que en la agricultura (p. 504).

developing nations/naciones en vías de desarrollo naciones de poco desarrollo industrial y bajos niveles de vida (p. 504).

direct foreign investment (DFI)/inversión extranjera directa compra por parte de extranjeros de cosas tales como bienes raíces y negocios en otro país (p. 537).

direct-mail advertising/publicidad directa por correo tipo de promoción que utiliza un anuncio postal, el cual por lo general contiene una carta que describe el producto o servicio y un pedido o solicitud en blanco (p. 291).

discount rate/tasa de descuento tasa de interés que la Reserva Federal carga sobre los préstamos a los bancos (p. 401).

discretionary income/ingreso discrecional ingreso monetario que queda para gastarlo en cosas adicionales después de haber adquirido lo necesario (p. 58).

disposable income/ingreso disponible ingreso que queda para gastarlo o ahorrarlo después de haber pagado todos los impuestos (p. 58).

disposable personal income/ingreso disponible personal ingreso personal que queda para gastarlo o ahorrarlo después de haber pagado todos los impuestos (p. 336).

distribution of income/distribución de ingresos pago monetario por el trabajo, para cuidados a la salud, para la educación, para alimentos, etc., que cada persona recibe; distribución de bienes y servicios a través de todos los miembros de una economía (p. 31).

diversification/diversificación distribución de las inversiones a varios diferentes tipos de cuentas para reducir el riesgo general (p. 164).

dividends/dividendos créditos monetarios que el accionista recibe sobre la suma que invirtiera en la compañía al comprar las acciones (p. 155).

division of labor/división de trabajo reparto de una labor en varias tareas más pequeñas; cada una la puede realizar un obrero distinto (p. 275).

double coincidence of wants/doble coincidencia de necesidades situación que resulta cuando cada participante en una transacción desea exactamente lo que la otra parte tiene que ofrecer, permitiendo así un intercambio directo de bienes; es un requisito para los trueques (p. 364).

durability/durabilidad capacidad de un artículo de durar largo tiempo (p. 115).

economic assistance/asistencia económica préstamos y francas donaciones de dinero o equipos a otras naciones para aumentar sus recursos de capital (p. 513).

economic efficiency/eficiencia económica uso sabio de los recursos disponibles para que el pueblo salga bien económicamente (p. 45).

economic growth/crecimiento económico expansión de la economía para producir más bienes, empleos y riqueza (p. 45).

economic model/modelo económico representación simplificada del mundo real que demuestra las reacciones de las personas a cambios en la economía; teoría (p. 18).

economics/economía (disciplina) estudio de cómo los individuos y las naciones toman decisiones en cuanto a las maneras de utilizar los escasos recursos para satisfacer sus deseos y necesidades (p. 8).

economic system/sistema económico manera en la cual una nación utiliza sus recursos para satisfacer los deseos y necesidades de su pueblo (p. 30).

economy/economía la suma de las actividades de una nación que afectan la producción, distribución y uso de los bienes y servicios (p. 18).

elastic demand/demanda elástica situación en la cual la subida o caída en el precio de un producto afecta grandemente la cantidad de ese producto que el público está dispuesto a comprar; si los precios de ciertos productos aumentan, los consumidores compran sustitutos más baratos (p. 185).

elasticity/elasticidad concepto económico que tiene que ver con la respuesta del consumidor a los aumentos o disminuciones en precios; sensibilidad a los precios (p. 185).

electronic funds transfer (EFT)/transferencia electrónica de fondos sistema para realizar en computadoras todas las diversas funciones bancarias que en el pasado se hacían con papel (p. 369).

embargo/embargo restricción total sobre la exportación o importación de determinado artículo (p. 473).

entrepreneur/empresario persona que comienza un negocio para obtener ganancias y está dispuesto a afrontar los riesgos que esto implica (p. 208).

entrepreneurship/espíritu empresarial la facultad de empezar nuevos negocios, introducir nuevos productos y técnicas y mejorar las técnicas de administración (p. 11).

equilibrium price/precio de equilibrio precio de un producto o servicio al cual la cantidad del mismo que los productores están dispuestos a suministrar es igual a la cantidad que los consumidores están dispuestos a adquirir. En una gráfica, el precio de equilibrio queda donde la curva de la oferta y la de la demanda se intersectan (p. 197).

equity (financial)/equidad cantidad de dinero que se invierte en una propiedad menos las deudas, tales como pagos de hipoteca, que se deban (p. 130).

equity (value)/equidad lo que es equitativo y justo (p. 45).

equity financing/financiamiento por venta de participación recaudación de dinero para una compañía vendiendo acciones de ésta (p. 267).

ethical behavior/comportamiento ético conducta de acuerdo con convicciones éticas y morales acerca del bien y del mal (p. 71).

excise tax/impuesto interno sobre el consumo impuesto sobre la fabricación, venta o uso dentro del país de determinados productos, tales como licores, gasolina y automóviles (p. 136).

expansion/expansión porción del ciclo comercial durante el cual la actividad económica lentamente aumenta; se le llama también recuperación (p. 348).

exports/exportaciones artículos que se venden a otros países (p. 462).

factors of production/factores de producción recursos de tierras, mano de obra, capital y capacidad emprendedora para producir bienes y servicios (p. 11).

"Fed, the"/El "Fed" sistema creado por el Congreso en 1913 como la organización central bancaria de la nación; entre sus funciones se encuentran el procesamiento de cheques, servir como banquero del gobierno, y control de la tasa de crecimiento del suministro de dinero (p. 388).

Federal Open Market Committee (FOMC)/Comisión Federal de Mercado Abierto comité de doce miembros del Sistema de la Reserva Federal que se reúne aproximadamente ocho veces al año para decidir el curso de acción que la Reserva debe seguir para controlar el suministro del dinero en circulación (p. 394).

fiat money/moneda de curso legal dinero que tiene valor a causa de orden o decreto del gobierno que establece que es aceptable para el pago de deudas. También *moneda fiduciaria* (p. 366).

finance charge/gasto financiero costo del crédito expresado en dólares y centavos (p. 91).

finance company/compañía financiera compañía que asume los contratos de las ventas a plazos de las tiendas y les añade un honorario por cobrar la deuda; también hace préstamos directamente a los consumidores (p. 87).

fiscal policy/política fiscal uso de los impuestos y de las políticas de gastos por parte del gobierno federal para afectar la actividad general del comercio (p. 443).

fiscal year/año fiscal año durante el cual se llevan las cuentas; para el gobierno federal, desde el 1 de octubre al 30 de septiembre del año entrante (p. 421).

five-year plans/planes quinquenales sistema de planificación central que formó la base para el sistema económico chino; finalmente terminó por transformarse en un sistema de planificación regional que condujo a un sistema limitado de libre empresa (p. 487).

fixed rate of exchange/tipo de cambio fijo sistema bajo elcual un gobierno nacional fija el valor de su moneda en relación a una norma exclusiva; el gobierno establece los equivalentes entre su moneda y las de otros países (p. 467).

flexible exchange rates/tipos de cambio flexibles situación en la cual se permite que las fuerzas de la oferta y la demanda impongan los precios de las distintas monedas (p. 468).

foreign affiliates/filiales extranjeras sucursales de firmas multinacionales (p. 543).

foreign aid/ayuda exterior dinero, bienes y servicios que dan los gobiernos e instituciones particulares para ayudar a otras naciones y los ciudadanos de éstas (p. 512).

foreign exchange markets/los mercados de divisas bolsas que negocian con la compra y venta de divisas extranjeras para los negocios que quieran importar productos de otros países; algún cambio de monedas tiene lugar a través de los bancos (p. 467).

form utility/utilidad de forma la conversión de materia prima en productos terminados para satisfacer los deseos de los consumidores (p. 284).

fractional reserve banking/reserva parcial bancaria sistema en el cual sólo una fracción de los depósitos de un banco se mantiene a mano, o en reserva; el resto está disponible para prestárselo a los prestatarios o para invertirlo en otra cosa (p. 389).

franchise/franquicia contrato en el cual un negocio (el otorgante) le vende a otro negocio (el concesionario) el derecho a usar el nombre del otorgante y vender sus productos (p. 222).

free enterprise system/sistema de libre empresa sistema en el cual los particulares son dueños de los factores de producción y deciden cómo usarlos dentro de los márgenes de la ley; llamado también capitalismo (p. 38).

full employment/pleno empleo condición de la economía cuando la tasa de desempleo está por debajo de cierto número establecidos por estudios de los economistas (p. 439).

General Agreement on Tariffs and Trade (GATT)/Acuerdo General sobre Aranceles Aduaneros y Comercio acuerdo de comercio con el cual los distintos países se reúnen periódicamente para negociar reducciones arancelarias que convienen mutuamente a todos los miembros; en efecto desde el 1 de enero de 1948 (p. 474).

generalization/generalización frase que unifica ideas comunes entre los distintos datos y que es acertada en la mayoría de los casos (p. 21).

generic brands/nombres genéricos nombres generales para productos en vez de para nombres específicos de marca dado por los fabricantes (p. 66).

geographic monopolies/monopolios geográficos situaciones de mercado que ocurren cuando un vendedor controla individualmente un mercado a causa de la ubicación del vendedor (p. 239).

global integration/integración mundial interdependencia entre los países del mundo, especialmente en los mercados financieros y las telecomunicaciones (p. 532).

goods and services/productos y servicios resultados finales de los factores de producción; los bienes son lo que el público compra; los servicios son las actividades que se hacen por los demás a cambio de honorarios (p. 11).

government monopolies/monopolios estatales situaciones de mercado creadas por el gobierno y protegidas por barreras legales al acceso; actividad exclusiva al gobierno (p. 239).

gross domestic product (GDP)/producto nacional bruto (PNB) valor total en dólares de todos los productos y servicios finales en la nación durante un solo año (p. 332).

horizontal merger/fusión horizontal compra total de una compañía por otra en el mismo giro (p. 245).

hypotheses/hipótesis opiniones o predicciones basadas en información, que se utilizan como puntos de partida para iniciar investigaciones (p. 19).

imperfect competition/competencia imperfecta situación de mercado en la cual un particular o grupo compra o vende un bien o un servicio en cantidades lo suficientemente grandes como para afectar el precio; abarca monopolio, oligopolio y la competencia monopolística (p. 237).

implicit GDP price deflator/índice implícito de deflación precios del PNB índice de precios que le quita el efecto de la inflación al PNB para que la economía general de un año se pueda comparar con la de otro (p. 341).

import quota/cuota de importación restricción impuesta al valor o al número de unidades de un artículo en particular que se pueda traer al país (p. 473).

imports/importaciones artículos que se traen de otros países para uso nacional (p. 462).

income redistribution/redistribución del ingreso actividad gubernamental que toman los ingresos de ciertas personas mediante los impuestos y los usan para ayudar a los ciudadanos necesitados (p. 417).

Individual Retirement Account (IRA)/Cuenta de Retiro Individual (IRA) plan privado de retiro que les permite a individuos o a parejas casadas ahorrar cierta cantidad de sus ingresos al año, dependiendo del total de los ingresos; dependiendo también de los ingresos, no se le gravan impuestos a esta cantidad y se difiere el impuesto sobre los intereses (p. 162).

industrial union/sindicato industrial sindicato compuesto por todos los trabajadores en una industria irrespectivamente del puesto o del nivel de capacitación (p. 312).

inelastic demand/demanda inelástica situación en la cual la subida o caída de precios de un producto tiene poco impacto en la cantidad que demandan los consumidores (p. 186).

infant mortality/mortalidad infantil índice de mortalidad de lactantes que mueren durante el primer año de vida (p. 506).

inflation/inflación aumento prolongado en el nivel general de precios de los bienes y servicios (p. 338).

informative advertising/publicidad de información publicidad que beneficia a los consumidores al darles información sobre un producto (p. 64).

injunction/interdicción laboral orden judicial que prohíbe cierta actividad (p. 320).

inside information/información interior de un empresa información disponible a un corredor de bolsa pero que no posee nadie más; es ilegal que un corredor dé esta información a alguien de afuera y que un cliente se beneficie de ésta (p. 159).

installment charge account/cuenta de crédito a plazos crédito que se extiende al consumidor permitiéndole a éste comprar artículos de cierto valor, tales como sofás, televisores y refrigeradores a una tienda y pagarlos en pagos, o plazos, iguales que se distribuyen a lo largo de cierto período de tiempo (p. 90).

installment debt/préstamo a plazos tipo de préstamo que se devuelve con pagos iguales, o plazos, que se distribuyen a lo largo de cierto período de tiempo (p. 80).

interest/interés cantidad de dinero que el prestatario debe pagar por el uso del dinero ajeno (p. 80). Pago que se percibe cuando se presta dinero, permitiendo a otra persona hacer uso de éste (p. 146).

interlocking directorate/consejo de administración coincidente situación que ocurre cuando la mayoría de los miembros de juntas directivas de compañías competidoras son los mismos en efecto haciendo que un solo grupo de personas administre ambas compañías (p. 244).

intermediate-term financing/financiamiento a medio plazo préstamo a un negocio durante de uno a diez años (p. 265).

International Monetary Fund (IMF)/Fondo Monetario Internacional (FMI) agencia cuyos gobiernos miembros están obligados a mantener sus tasas de cambio más o menos fijas (p. 467).

inventory/inventario suministro de cualquier tipo de artículos que se usan en un negocio, tales como materias primas o mercancías a la venta (p. 210).

invisible hand/mano invisible término usado por Adam Smith para describir el efecto de la competencia en guiar a los individuos a trabajar para su propio interés, y por ese medio lograr el máximo bien de la sociedad (p. 37).

joint venture/sociedad de personas asociación temporal que se establece entre individuos o compañías con un fin específico y durante un breve período de tiempo (p. 217).

Keogh Plan/Plan Keogh plan de retiro que le permite al que trabaja por su cuenta ahorrar cada año un máximo del 15 por ciento de sus ingresos hasta llegar a cierta cantidad específica y descontarle esa cantidad a sus ingresos anuales gravables (p. 161).

labor/trabajo tareas que la gente realiza; a menudo llamado un recurso humano. También llamado *mano de obra* (p. 10).

labor union/sindicato asociación de trabajadores que se organizan para mejorar los sueldos y condiciones de trabajo para sus miembros (p. 311).

land/tierra en economía, término que se usa para referirse a los recursos naturales y los terrenos superficiales; todas las cosas que se encuentran en la naturaleza, en las aguas y en la tierra. Económicamente, lo más importante son los terrenos de la superficie y los depósitos minerales (p. 10).

law of demand/ley de la demanda regla económica que declara que la cantidad que se demanda y el precio se mueven en direcciones opuestas; al subir el precio, la cantidad demandada baja; al bajar el precio, la cantidad demandada sube. Existe una relación inversa, u opuesta, entre el precio y la demanda (p. 177).

law of diminishing marginal utility/ley de la utilidad marginal decreciente regla económica que declara que la satisfacción adicional que deriva un consumidor de comprar una unidad más de un producto irá disminuyendo con cada unidad adicional que éste adquiera (p. 177).

law of diminishing returns/ley de rendimientos decrecientes regla económica que declara que después de cierto punto, el añadir una unidad de un factor de producción (tal como la mano de obra) a todos los demás factores de producción (tales como equipos) aumenta el rendimiento total por cierto tiempo; después de cierto punto, el rendimiento adicional por cada unidad añadida empieza a decrecer (p. 192).

law of supply/ley de la oferta regla económica que declara que al subir el precio de un producto, la cantidad que se ofrece del mismo aumenta; al caer el precio, la oferta del producto también disminuye (p. 191).

lease/arrendamiento contrato a largo plazo que describe los términos y condiciones bajo los cuales una propiedad se arrienda (p. 126).

leasing/arrendar alquilar en vez de comprar ciertos artículos como equipos, viviendas y automóviles (p. 266).

legal tender/moneda de curso legal moneda que por ley se tiene que aceptar como pago de deudas públicas y privadas (p. 366).

liability insurance/seguro de responsabilidad civil seguro que paga lesiones corporales y daños a la propiedad; lo exigen muchos estados antes de otorgar la matrícula para automóviles (p. 139).

limited partnership/sociedad de personas con responsabilidad limitada forma especial de sociedad en la cual no todos los socios son iguales; los socios generales asumen responsabilidad de todas las deudas y tareas administrativas; los demás socios contribuyen dinero o propiedades y no tienen voz en la gerencia (p. 217).

line of credit/línea de crédito máxima cantidad de dinero que una compañía puede pedirle prestado a un banco durante un período de tiempo, por lo general un año, sin tener que solicitar de nuevo un préstamo (p. 266).

local union/sindicato local miembros de un sindicato en una cierta fábrica, compañía o zona geográfica; el sindicato local tiene tratos con la compañía para negociar contratos y asegurarse de que los términos y condiciones de éste se cumplan (p. 313).

lockout/cierre patronal situación que ocurre cuando la gerencia les impide a los trabajadores volver a su trabajo sino hasta que éstos hayan aceptado un nuevo contrato (p. 320).

long-term financing/financiamiento a largo plazo dinero que se le presta a un negocio durante un período de más de diez años (p. 265).

loose money policy/política de dinero disponible política monetaria que da crédito abundante y barato, y que posiblemente conduce a la inflación (p. 389).

M1: definición más estricta del suministro de dinero; consisten en dineros que se pueden gastar inmediatamente y contra los cuales se pueden hacer cheques; abarca todas las demás letras o documentos en papel y monedas en circulación incluyendo moneda, cheques de viajero y depósitos extraíbles por cheque (p. 378).

M2: definición más amplia del suministro de dinero; abarca a toda la M1, más aquellos bienes convertibles en dinero tales como los mercados monetarios, saldos de fondos mutualistas y Eurodólares; abarca todas las letras y documentos en papel y monedas en circulación (p. 378).

market/mercado actividad libremente escogida entre compradores y vendedores de bienes y servicios en la cual se hacen negocios con aquéllos que puedan satisfacer mejor las necesidades y deseos de los participantes (p. 33).

market economic system/sistema de economía de mercado sistema en el cual los particulares son dueños de los factores de producción y toman las decisiones económicas a través de la libre interacción mientras que al mismo tiempo protegen sus propios intereses; el gobierno no interviene; capitalismo (p. 33).

marketing/mercadeo todas las actividades necesarias para trasladar bienes y servicios del productor al consumidor; abarca la investigación de mercados, publicidad y promoción, y la distribución (p. 282).

market research/investigación de mercado recolección, registro y análisis de datos acerca de los tipos de bienes y servicios que desea el público (p. 284).

market survey/encuesta de mercado encuesta en la cual los investigadores reúnen datos acerca de posibles usuarios de un producto basado en tales características como la edad, el sexo, ingresos, educación y ubicación; a menudo se usan cuestionarios escritos y entrevistas personales (p. 284).

maturity/vencimiento período de tiempo durante el cual los depósitos pagan una determinada tasa de interés (p. 148).

mechanization/mecanización trabajo combinado de personas y máquinas; originalmente, se combinan las máquinas con obreros no calificados para reemplazar a los calificados (p. 274).

mediation/mediación etapa en las negociaciones de contratos entre el sindicato y la gerencia en la cual una persona neutral intercede y trata que las dos partes lleguen a un acuerdo (p. 318).

Medicaid/Medicaid programa de asistencia pública estatal y federal que les proporciona a personas incapacitadas o de bajos ingresos cuidados gratis a la salud (p. 417).

Medicare/Medicare programa gubernamental que proporciona cuidados a la salud a personas de edad avanzada (p. 415).

medium of exchange/medios de cambio uso del dinero a cambio de bienes o servicios (p. 362).

merger/fusión situación que ocurre cuando una sociedad compra más de la mitad de las acciones de otra (p. 244). *Vea también* fusión de conglomerados (conglomerate merger), fusión horizontal (horizontal merger), fusión vertical (vertical merger).

merit good/bien preferente cualquier bien o servicio que el gobierno haya socialmente deseable, tal como os museos, el ballet y conciertos de música clásica; a menudo subvencionados por el gobierno para que el público general pueda disfrutarlos (p. 416).

military assistance/asistencia militar asistencia económica o técnica a las fuerzas armadas de una nación (p. 513).

minimum wage law/ley de salario mínimo ley federal, estatal o municipal que fija el salario legal más bajo por hora que se le puede pagar a ciertos tipos de trabajadores (p. 309).

mixed economy/economía mixta sistema que combina las características de más de un tipo de economía variando la mezcla para que el sistema se incline más hacia un tipo puro que al otro (p. 34).

monetarism/monetarismo teoría que trata la relación entre la cantidad de dinero que la Reserva Federal pone en circulación y el nivel de actividad en la economía (p. 448).

monetarists/los monetaristas personas que apoyan la teoría del monetarismo, a menudo vinculados con Milton Friedman (p. 448).

monetary policy/política monetaria política que trata de cambiar la tasa de crecimiento del dinero en circulación para afectar la cantidad de crédito y, por lo tanto, la actividad comercial en la economía (p. 388).

monetary rule/principio monetario política monetarista que insiste que la Reserva Federal debe permitir el suministro del dinero en circulación crecer a una tasa especificada (quizá del 3 al 5 por ciento) al año y no usar la política monetario para estimular ni desacelerar la economía (p. 449).

monetary standard/patrón monetario manera en que una nación asigna valor a su moneda (p. 370).

money/dinero toda cosa de uso general como medio de intercambio, unidad contable y acopio de valor (p. 362).

money market deposit account (MMDA)/cuenta de depósito en el mercado monetario cuenta que paga tasas relativamente altas de interés, requiere un saldo mínimo y permite extraer fondos en persona en cualquier momento (p. 148).

money market fund/fondos mutuos tipo de fondo mutualista que usa el dinero de los inversionistas para hacer préstamos a corto plazo a negocios y bancos; la mayor parte les permite a los inversionistas hacer cheques contra sus inversiones en el fondo (p. 158).

monopolistic competition/competencia monopolista situación de mercado en la cual un gran número de vendedores ofrecen productos similares pero ligeramente diferentes y cada uno tiene cierto control sobre los precios (p. 240).

mortgage/hipoteca préstamo a plazos que se debe sobre bienes raíces: casas, edificios o terreno (p. 81).

multinationals/empresas transnacionales firmas que hacen negocios y tienen oficinas o fábricas en muchos países (p. 543).

mutual fund/fondo mutuo compañía inversionista que reúne los dineros de muchos individuos para comprar acciones, bonos u otras inversiones (p. 158).

national debt/deuda pública cantidad total de la deuda pendiente del gobierno federal; deuda pública (p. 425).

national income/renta nacional total de rentas o ingresos que ganará todo el mundo en la economía (p. 335).

national income accounting/contabilidad de la renta nacional medición del rendimiento de la economía nacional, que trata sobre los ingresos y producción de la economía en general así como la interacción entre los consumidores, los negocios y los gobiernos (p. 332).

nationalization/nacionalización colocación de los ferrocarriles, los negocios, etc., bajo propiedad del estado (p. 519).

natural monopolies/monopolios naturales situaciones de mercado que resultan cuando una compañía lleva a sus competidores a la quiebra produciendo bienes y servicios en costo más bajo; por lo general se encuentra en industrias que necesitan grandes inversiones para empezar, y cuando es más eficiente tener una sola compañía que varias (p. 239).

near moneys/cuasidinero activo, tal como cuentas de ahorro, que se puede convertir en dinero o medio de pago con relativa facilidad y sin el riesgo de perder valor (p. 378).

net domestic product (NDP)/producto neto nacional (PNN) valor total del producto nacional (PNB) menos el valor total perdido a causa de desgaste y deterioro de la maquinaria y equipos (p. 335).

net exports/exportaciones netas diferencia entre lo que la nación le vende a otros países (exportaciones) y lo que le compra a éstos (importaciones) (p. 334).

North American Free Trade Agreement (NAFTA)/Tratado de Libre Comercio para América del Norte acuerdo comercial diseñado para reducir las barreras arancelarias entre México, Canadá y los Estados Unidos; aprobado en 1993 (p. 474). *Vea también* Acuerdo de Libre Comercio E.E.U.U.-Canadá (U.S.-Canada Free Trade Agreement).

oligopoly/oligopolio industria dominada por unos pocos suministradores que ejercen cierto control sobre los precios (p. 240).

open-market operations/operaciones de mercado abierto compra y venta por parte de la Reserva Federal de obligaciones del gobierno de los Estados Unidos para afectar el suministro de dinero cambiando las reservas institucionales de depósito o colocando o sacando dinero de la circulación en la economía (p. 402).

opportunity cost/costo de oportunidad valor de la segunda mejor alternativa después de haber renunciado a la que se escogiera (p. 14).

over-the-counter market/mercado de valores no oficial compra y venta de acciones y bonos, con frecuencia de compañías más pequeñas y menos conocidas, que tiene lugar fuera de las bolsas de valores organizadas; la mayor parte de los valores "no vendidos en la Bolsa" se cotizan en los listados de la National Association of Securities Dealers Automated Quotations (NASDAQ) (p. 157).

overdraft checking/sobregiro cuenta corriente que permite a un cliente hacer un cheque por más dinero de lo que existe en ésta (p. 369).

ownership utility/utilidad de la transferibilidad del título utilidad creada al asegurar la transferencia ordenada del título de los bienes deseados (p. 284).

partnership/sociedad de personas con responsabilidad limitada negocio propiedad de dos o más individuos que lo hacen funcionar (p. 217).

passbook savings account/cuenta de ahorro con libreta cuenta para la cual el depositante recibe una libreta en la cual se llevan los depósitos, extracciones e intereses; también llamada cuenta de ahorro regular (p. 147).

past-due notices/notificaciones de vencimiento recordatorios que envían los negocios e instituciones de préstamo que los pagos están ya sobrevencidos y morosos (p. 96).

patent/patente derecho otorgado por el gobierno para fabricar con exclusividad un invento durante un número específico de años (p. 239).

peak/cumbre período de prosperidad en un ciclo comercial en el cual la actividad económica está en su más elevado punto; llamado también de auge (boom) (p.347).

penetration pricing/precios de penetración vender un nuevo producto a un precio bajo para sustraerle clientes a un producto establecido (p. 290).

pension plans/planes de pensiones planes de compañía que hacen provisiones para tener ingresos en la jubilación o retiro (p. 161).

perfect competition/competencia perfecta situación de mercado en la que existen numerosos compradores y vendedores, y ningún comprador ni vendedor puede afectar el precio (p. 232).

personal income (PI)/renta personal total de rentas o ingresos que reciben los individuos antes de pagar sus impuestos personales (p. 336).

picketing/piquetes laborales actividad en la cual los huelguistas marchan de un lado a otro en frente al centro de trabajo portando letreros que declaran su desacuerdo con la compañía (p. 320).

place utility/utilidad de lugar utilidad creada al hacer que un artículo esté disponible donde el consumidor desea adquirirlo (p. 284).

points/puntos porcentuales honorario que se paga a un prestamista y se computa como puntos de porcentaje de un préstamo (p. 129).

price elasticity of demand/elasticidad de precios de la demanda concepto económico que versa sobre cuánto varía la demanda dependiendo de los cambios en el precio (p. 185).

price leadership/liderazgo en precios práctica de fijar precios muy cercanos a los de las demás compañías que vendan productos similares; se encuentra especialmente en los oligopolios (p. 289).

price system/sistema de precios sistema de capitalismo puro que permite que los precios encuentren su propio nivel, tal como lo determinen las fuerzas de la oferta y la demanda (p. 482).

prime rate/tasa mínima de interés tipo o tasa de interés que los bancos cobran sobre los préstamos a sus mejores clientes comerciales (p. 401).

principal/principal suma de dinero que se pidiera prestado originalmente en un préstamo (p. 80).

private-labeled products/productos con etiquetas de la casa productos con la marca de la tienda que tienen algunas cadenas de supermercados y de asociaciones de mayoristas como alternativas de bajo costo a las marcas nacionales (p. 110).

private property/propiedad privada bienes de los que son propietarios individuos o grupos en vez de los gobiernos federales, estatales o locales (p. 38).

private property rights/derechos de propiedad privada los derechos de individuos o grupos a ser propietarios de bienes; el gobierno pone en vigor y hace valer estos derechos (p. 482).

privatization/privatización cambio de la propiedad estatal de los negocios, terrenos y edificios a la propiedad privada (p. 492).

producer goods/bienes de producción bienes producidos para que los negocios los usen en producir otros artículos (p. 271).

producer price index (PPI)/índice de precio de producción medida del cambio en precio al pasar el tiempo de un grupo específico de productos utilizados por negocios; anteriormente llamado índice de precios mayoristas (p. 340).

product differentiation/diferenciación de productos uso por parte del fabricante de pequeñas diferencias en características y calidad para intentar diferenciar entre bienes y servicios que son similares (p. 240).

production/producción proceso de convertir los recursos en bienes que satisfagan los deseos y necesidades de comercios e individuos (p. 271).

production possibilities/posibilidades de producción todas las combinaciones de bienes y servicios que se puedan producir con una cierta cantidad fija de recursos en un determinado período de tiempo (p. 15).

productivity/productividad capacidad de producir mayores cantidades de bienes y servicios mejor y más rápidamente (p. 10).

product life cycle/ciclo de vida de un producto serie de etapas por las que atraviesa un producto desde su primera introducción hasta su completo retiro del mercado; el ciclo no tiene un número fijo de meses ni años (p. 291).

professionals/profesionales individuos altamente educados con títulos universitarios y usualmente educación o capacitación adicional (p. 307).

profit/utilidades dinero que queda después que se hayan pagado todos los costos de producción: salarios, alquiler, intereses e impuestos (p. 39). También llamado *ganacia* y *lucro*.

profit incentive/incentivos para obtener utilidades deseo de hacer dinero que motiva a las personas a producir y vender bienes y servicios que los demás quieran comprar (p. 39).

progressive tax/impuesto progresivo impuesto que grava un porcentaje superior de los ingresos más altos en comparación con los más bajos; se le justifica en base al principio de la capacidad económica (p. 430).

proletariat/el proletariado término usado por Carlos Marx para denominar a los trabajadores (p. 484).

promissory note/pagaré convenio escrito para la devolución de un préstamo en determinado momento y a una tasa específica de interés (p. 266).

promotion/promoción uso de la publicidad y demás métodos para informar a los consumidores que un nuevo o mejorado producto o servicio está a su disposición y persuadirlos a que lo compren (p. 290).

property rights/derechos de propiedad privada protección de la propiedad privada; el gobierno no puede legalmente tomar propiedad privada sin pagar por ella el justo valor en el mercado (p. 523).

proportional tax/impuesto proporcional impuesto que toma el mismo porcentaje de todos los ingresos; al aumentar los ingresos, la cantidad de impuesto que se paga también aumenta (p. 430).

proprietor/propietario dueño de un negocio; de la palabra en latín proprietas, que significa "propiedad" (p. 213).

protectionists/proteccionistas aquellos que abogan a favor de restricciones comerciales (p. 474).

protective tariff/arancel proteccionista impuesto sobre las importaciones que se utiliza para aumentar los costos de los bienes importados y de esa manera proteger los productores nacionales (p. 472).

public assistance programs/programas de asistencia pública programas gubernamentales que hacen pagos basados en la necesidad; llamados también de bienestar social (p. 418).

public goods/bienes públicos bienes y servicios que el gobierno a veces suministra a sus ciudadanos; los pueden utilizar muchos individuos al mismo tiempo sin reducir el beneficio que recibe cada cual (p. 416).

public works projects/proyectos de obras públicas instalaciones de uso público tales como escuelas y carreteras, construídas por los gobiernos federales, estatales o locales con dineros públicos (p. 413).

purchasing power/poder adquisitivo los bienes y servicios que el dinero puede realmente comprar; determina el valor que tiene el dinero (p. 338).

pure monopoly/monopolio puro la forma más extrema de competencia imperfecta en la cual un solo vendedor controla la oferta de un bien o servicio y de esa manera controla el precio (p. 237). *Vea también* monopolios geográficos; monopolios gubernamentales; monopolios naturales; monopolio tecnológico.

rational choice/selección racional la selección de la alternativa que tenga el mayor valor de entre productos que tienen una calidad comparable (p. 61).

real estate taxes/impuestos sobre bienes inmuebles impuestos que se pagan por concepto de terrenos y edificios (p. 125).

real GDP/PNB real cifra que resulta cuando se compensa la inflación en el Producto Nacional Bruto aplicando el índice de deflación de precios (p. 341).

real income effect/efecto de ingreso real regla económica que declara que el público no puede seguir comprando la misma cantidad de un producto si el precio de éste sube mientras que sus ingresos se mantienen igual; esto tiene efecto en la dirección opuesta también: si el precio de un producto disminuye y los ingresos permanecen igual, el poder adquisitivo aumenta y la cantidad del producto que se compra probablemente aumentará también (p. 179).

recession/recesión porción del ciclo comercial en la cual la producción nacional, el PNB real, no crece durante al menos dos trimestres (seis meses) (p. 348).

recovery/recuperación porción del ciclo comercial en la cual la actividad económica aumenta; llamada también expansión (p. 348).

registration fee/derecho de registro derecho o cargo de matriculación que cobra el estado, por lo general anualmente, por el derecho de usar un auto (p. 137).

regressive tax/impuesto regresivo impuesto que toma un porcentaje mayor de los ingresos más bajos que de los más altos (p. 430).

regular charge account/cuenta de crédito regular crédito que se le extiende a un consumidor y que le permite comprar bienes y servicios a cierta tienda y pagarlos luego. El interés se cobra por la porción de la cuenta que quede sin pagar en el plazo de cierto período de tiempo. Conocido también como el cargo de 30 días (p. 89).

representative money/dinero en cuenta dinero sin valor de por sí para usos no monetarios que se puede intercambiar por algún artículo comerciable valioso tal como el oro o la plata (p. 366).

reregulation/nueva regulación regulación y control del gobierno federal sobre la actividad comercial de las industrias que antiguamente eran fuertemente reguladas (p. 246).

reserve requirements/reserva obligatoria regulaciones impuestas por la Reserva Federal, que exigen a los bancos que mantengan en efectivo en sus cajas fuertes un cierto porcentaje de sus depósitos o que lo depositen en el Banco de la Reserva Federal de su distrito (p. 389).

resource/recurso cualquier cosa que las personas puedan usar para hacer u obtener lo que deseen o necesiten (p. 8).

retailers/detallistas negocios que le venden bienes de consumo directamente al público (p. 294).

revenue tariff/arancel financiero impuesto sobre las importaciones usado principalmente para recaudar rentas sin restringir las importaciones (p. 472).

revolving charge account/cuenta de crédito rotativa crédito que se le extiende a un consumidor y que le permite comprar bienes y servicios a cierta tienda y pagarlos luego. Por lo general cierta porción del saldo se tiene que pagar cada mes; el interés se cobra sobre la cantidad no pagada (p. 89).

right-to-work laws/ley sobre libertad laboral leyes estatales que prohíben los talleres donde los obreros tienen que pertenecer al sindicato y los talleres cerrados; a los trabajadores se les permite seguir trabajando en cierto puesto sin tener que hacerse miembros del sindicato (p. 313).

robotics/robótica maquinaria con control por computadora altamente sofisticado que funciona en las líneas de montaje (p. 275).

saving/ahorro el no usar los ingresos durante cierto tiempo para poder usarlos después (p. 146).

savings and loan association (S&L)/asociación de ahorro y préstamo institución depositaria que, como un banco comercial, acepta depósitos y presta dinero. Originalmente se establecieron para hacer préstamos para construir casas, pero las leyes federales de la década de 1980 les permitieron prestar algunos de los mismos servicios que los bancos (p. 86).

savings banks/bancos de ahorro instituciones depositarias originalmente establecidas para servir a los pequeños ahorradores dejados al margen por los bancos comerciales; la mayor parte del negocio de estas instituciones proviene de cuentas de ahorro y préstamos para casas (p. 86).

savings bonds/bonos de ahorro bonos emitidos por el gobierno federal a manera de pedir dinero prestado; los bonos se compran a mitad de su valor nominal y aumentan entonces de valor cada seis meses hasta llegar a su pleno valor nominal (p. 155).

scarcity/escasez condición en la cual el público no tiene ni puede tener suficientes ingresos, tiempo y demás recursos para satisfacer todas sus necesidades (p. 9).

secondary market/mercado secundario proceso a través del cual los dueños de valores las venden a otros inversionistas a cambio de efectivo (p. 493).

secured loan/préstamo garantizado préstamo que está respaldado por una garantía (collateral) (p. 95).

security deposit/depósito de garantía dinero que el inquilino que alquila deposita con el dueño; si el alquiler no se paga o el apartamento queda dañado, el dueño puede quedarse con todo o parte del depósito (p. 130).

semiskilled workers/obreros semicualificados personas cuyos trabajos requieren algún entrenamiento en técnicas relacionadas con el trabajo, a menudo utilizando tecnología moderna (p. 307).

service flow/flujo de servicio cantidad de uso que una persona le saca a un artículo durante cierto tiempo y el valor que dicha persona le da a ese uso (p. 115).

service workers/trabajadores en el área de servicios personas que le proporcionan servicios directamente a los demás (p. 307).

shortages/falta situaciones que ocurren cuando, al precio existente, la cantidad que se demanda es mayor que la oferta disponible (p. 198).

short-term financing/financiamiento a corto plazo dinero que pide prestado un negocio por cualquier período de tiempo que sea menos de un año (p. 265).

skilled worker/profesionales persona que ha aprendido una ocupación u oficio bien a través de una escuela de capacitación o como aprendiz de un obrero con experiencia (p. 307).

small business incubator/incubador de pequeños negocios negocio que ayuda a negocios pequeños a desarrollarse proporcionándoles tales formas de ayuda como edificios de bajo alquiler, asesoría administrativa y computadoras; frecuentemente funcionan con fondos estatales y federales (p. 215).

social insurance programs/programas de seguro social programas gubernamentales que pagan beneficios a los trabajadores retirados e incapacitados, a sus familias y los desempleados; financiados con impuestos que pagan a estos programas los trabajadores y los patronos (p. 418).

Social Security/Seguro Social programa federal que proporciona pagos mensuales a personas que están retiradas o que no pueden trabajar (p. 417).

sole proprietorship/propietario único de empresada negocio propiedad de una sola persona; el tipo más básico de organización de negocios (p. 213).

special economic zones/zonas económicas especiales zonas geográficas designadas en la República Popular China las cuales, a partir de 1979, se han estado moviendo hacia un capitalismo descentralizado restringido (p. 488).

specialization/especialización concepto según el cual le es beneficioso a una nación producir y exportar un surtido limitado de bienes para los cuales está particularmente bien dotada (p. 464).

stabilization policies/políticas de estabilización intento por parte del gobierno federal de mantener la economía saludable y hacer que el futuro sea más predecible para la planificación, el ahorro y las inversiones; abarca las políticas monetarias y fiscales (p. 438).

stagflation/inflación con estancamiento combinación de inflación y estancamiento económico (p. 441).

standard of living/nivel de vida bienestar material de un individuo, grupo o nación medido por el valor promedio de los bienes y servicios que usa el ciudadano promedio durante un cierto período de tiempo (p. 45).

startups/negocios recién establecidos nuevos negocios; hay asesoría y ayuda disponibles de parte de los gobiernos estatales y federal, así como de las universidades y facultades (p. 214).

statement savings account/cuenta de ahorros con estado de cuenta cuenta similar a la cuenta de ahorro de libreta, excepto que en vez de la libreta, el depositante recibe un estado de cuenta mensual donde se ven todas las transacciones (p. 147).

stock/acciones participación propietaria en la sociedad que emite las acciones; éstas le dan el derecho al comprador a cierta parte de las futuras ganancias y bienes de la sociedad (p. 154).

stockholders/accionistas personas que han invertido en una sociedad y poseen acciones; los accionistas pueden reclamar cierta parte de las ganancias (p. 155).

store of value/reserva de valor uso del dinero para guardarlo y así hacer acopio de poder adquisitivo para usarlo más adelante (p. 364).

strike/huelga paro deliberado de los trabajadores para forzar a un patrono a ceder a sus demandas (p. 312).

subsistence agriculture /agricultura de subsistencia cultivar para una familia sólo suficiente comida para satisfacer sus propias necesidades; no hay cultivos para la exportación ni para alimentar a una fuerza laboral industrial (p. 506).

substitution effect/efecto de sustitución principio económico que dice que si dos artículos satisfacen la misma necesidad y el precio de uno aumenta, el público comprará el otro (p. 179).

Supplemental Security Income/Ingreso de Seguridad Suplementario programas federales que abarcan los cupones de alimentos, los beneficios a los veteranos y los pagos a las personas ciegas, de edad o incapacitadas (p. 417).

supply curve/curva de oferta línea trazada en una gráfica que demuestra las cantidades ofrecidas de un bien o un servicio a cada precio posible (p. 194).

surplus/superávit situación que ocurre cuando la oferta es mayor que la demanda (p. 198). También llamado *excedente*.

tariff/arancel impuesto sobre las importaciones; la barrera más comúnmente usada para liberar el comercio (p. 472). *Vea también* arancel protector; arancel para rentas

tax-exempt bonds/bonos exentos de impuesto bonos vendidos por gobiernos locales y estatales; el gobierno federal no grava el interés que pagan los bonos (p. 155).

technical assistance/asistencia técnica ayuda, en la forma de profesionales tales como ingenieros, maestros y técnicos que suministran naciones para enseñar conocimientos y técnicas a individuos en otras naciones; fortalece los recursos humanos de una nación (p. 513).

technological monopoly/monopolio tecnológico situación de mercado que resulta cuando un vendedor desarrolla un producto o proceso de producción para el cual obtiene una patente; la compañía posee los derechos exclusivos a la nueva invención por un cierto número de años (p. 239).

technology/tecnología todo uso de terrenos, mano de obra o capital que produzca bienes y servicios con más eficiencia. Hoy, por lo general, significa el uso de la ciencia para desarrollar nuevos productos y métodos para producir y distribuir bienes y servicios (pp. 11, 197).

telecommunications/telecomunicaciones comunicaciones a larga distancia, por lo general electrónicas, que usan satélites de comunicación y cable de fibra óptica (p. 532).

test marketing/mercadeo de prueba ofrecer un producto a la venta en una zona pequeña por un período limitado de tiempo para ver qué tal se vende antes de ofrecerlo nacionalmente (p. 285).

three P's/las tres "P's" del inglés "prices, profits and private property", o sea, precios, ganancias o lucro y propiedad privada, las tres bases del capitalismo de mercado (p. 482).

thrift institutions/instituciones de ahorro bancos de ahorro mutualistas, asociaciones de ahorro y préstamo ("S&L's") y uniones de crédito que ofrecen muchos de los mismos servicios que ofrecen los bancos comerciales (p. 377).

tight money policy/política de dinero escaso política monetaria que hace que haya poco suministro de crédito y que éste sea caro en un esfuerzo por desacelerar la economía (p. 389).

time deposits/depósitos a plazo planes de ahorros que requieren que los ahorradores dejen sus dineros en depósito por cierto tiempo (p. 148).

time lags/desface cronológico períodos entre el momento que la política fiscal se promulga y el momento en que entra en efecto (p. 450).

time utility/utilidad de tiempo utilidad creada al poner un artículo a la disposición del consumidor cuando éste quiere adquirirlo (p. 284).

tolerance/tolerancia actitud justa, objetiva y permisiva con las opiniones y prácticas de otras religiones, razas y nacionalidades (p. 547).

trade-off/compensación de factores alternativos cambiar una cosa por el uso de otra, a menudo tomando decisiones inevitables y difíciles a causa del problema de la escasez (p. 13).

trade credit/crédito comercial crédito que extiende un vendedor a un negocio que le compra artículos; le permite al comprador tomar posesión inmediata de éstos y pagarlos en algún momento en el futuro (p. 266).

traditional economic system/sistema económico tradicional sistema en el cual las decisiones económicas se basan en las costumbres, creencias y maneras de hacer las cosas que se han pasado de generación en generación (p. 32).

transfer payments/pagos de transferencia pagos de bienestar social y demás pagos suplementarios, tales como compensación por desempleo, *Social Security* y *Medicaid*, que el gobierno federal o estatal les hacen a individuos, lo cual aumenta el ingreso del individuo aunque los pagos no se hagan a cambio de ninguna actividad productiva actualmente (p. 336).

Treasury bills/pagarés del Tesoro certificados emitidos por la Tesorería Federal de los Estados Unidos en cantidades mínimas de $10,000 a cambio de dinero prestado y que vencen durante un período que abarca desde tres meses hasta un año (p. 156).

Treasury bonds/bonos del Tesoro a largo plazo certificados emitidos por la Tesorería Federal de los Estados Unidos en cantidades mínimas de $1,000 ó $5,000 a cambio de dinero prestado y que vencen en diez o más años (p. 156).

Treasury notes/bonos del Tesoro a corto plazo certificados emitidos por la Tesorería Federal de los Estados Unidos en cantidades mínimas de $1,000 o $5,000 a cambio de dinero prestado y que vencen en el plazo de dos a diez años (p. 156).

trough/punto bajo porción más baja del ciclo comercial en el cual la caída en espiral de la economía empieza a nivelarse (p. 348).

underground economy/economía sumergida transacciones que hace la gente que no obedecen las leyes federales y estatales con respecto a declarar sus ingresos; abarca a los que evitan pagar impuestos, los jugadores y los narcotraficantes y aquéllos que ilegalmente reciben beneficios de desempleo (p. 439).

unemployment rate/índice de desempleo porcentaje de la fuerza laboral civil que está sin trabajo pero que está activamente buscando empleo (p. 438).

union shop/empresa con sindicación eventual obligatoria compañía en la que se exige que los nuevos empleados se hagan miembros del sindicato después de cierto tiempo, por lo general tres meses (p. 313).

unit of accounting/unidad de contabilidad uso del dinero como punto de comparación de los valores que tienen los bienes y servicios entre sí (p. 364).

unsecured loan/préstamo no garantizado préstamo garantizado solamente por la promesa de devolverlo (p. 95).

unskilled workers/obreros no cualificados personas cuyos empleos no exigen capacitación especializada (p. 307).

U.S.-Canadian Free Trade Agreement/Acuerdo de Libre Comercio entre los E.E.U.U. y Canadá convenio comercial entre los Estados Unidos y Canadá para eliminar ciertos aranceles altos sobre cosas tales como muebles, textiles y papel; garantiza que cada país tendrá acceso al petróleo, gas, carbón piedra y electricidad del otro, a precios que pagan los ciudadanos de la otra nación en circunstancias comerciales comparables (p. 474).

usury law/ley antiusura ley que restringe la cantidad de interés que se le puede cargar al crédito (p. 99).

utility/utilidad capacidad de cualquier bien o servicio de satisfacer los deseos del consumidor (pp. 177, 282). *Vea también* utilidad de la forma (form utility); utilidad de la transferibilidad de título (ownership utility); utilidad de lugar (place utility); utilidad de tiempo (time utility).

values/valores (morales) creencias o características que un individuo o grupo considera importante, tales como la libertad religiosa y la oportunidad igualitaria (p. 20).

vertical merger/fusión vertical fusión en la que un negocio que le compra o vende a otro negocio se fusiona con éste (p. 245).

vicious cycle of poverty/ciclo vicioso de la pobreza trampa en la que cae un país menos desarrollado con bajos ingresos *per cápita* y que no puede ahorrar e invertir lo suficiente como para lograr tasas aceptables de crecimiento económico (p. 524).

voluntary exchange/intercambio voluntario principio que forma la base de la actividad en una economía de mercado; el comprador y el vendedor ejercen sus libertades económicas resolviendo sus propios términos y condiciones de intercambio (p. 176).

wants/necesidades término de los economistas para todo lo que el público desea que va más allá de los bienes y servicios básicos que satisfacen sus necesidades (p. 9).

warehouse food store/almacén para compra de alimentos tienda que dispone de un número limitado de marcas y artículos; menos cara que los supermercados; los artículos frecuentemente están disponibles sólo en grandes cantidades (p. 109).

warranty/garantía promesa que hace un fabricante o vendedor que reparará o reemplazará un producto dentro de un cierto período de tiempo si se determina que tiene fallas (p. 60).

welfare/bienestar social programas de asistencia pública que hacen pagos basados en la necesidad; abarca el *Ingreso Suplementario de Seguridad* (Supplemental Security Income), *Ayuda a Familias con Hijos Dependientes* (Aid to Families with Dependent Children), y *Medicaid* (p. 418).

welfare state/estado de bienestar país que es una mezcla de capitalismo y socialismo, que combina la propiedad privada de los medios de producción y la asignación competitiva de los recursos con la meta de lograr la igualdad social de sus ciudadanos (p. 494).

white-collar/empleados de oficina categoría de empleados que trabajan en oficinas, ventas o cargos profesionales (p. 307).

wholesalers/mayoristas negocios que compran grandes cantidades de artículos a los productores para revenderlos a otros negocios (p. 293).

workers' compensation/indemnización por accidente de trabajo programa gubernamental que hace pagos para el cuidado médico de obreros lesionados en el trabajo; las personas que han perdido sus empleos pueden recibir pagos a través del seguro contra desempleo (p. 417).

1 Puntos destacados

Sección 1

Los problemas básicos en Economía

Términos claves:

economía (p. 8)
recursos (p. 8)
escasez (p. 9)
necesidades (p. 9)
tierra (p. 10)
trabajo (p. 10)
capital (p. 10)
productividad (p. 10)

espíritu empresarial (p. 11)
factores de producción
  (p. 11)
productos y servicios (p. 11)
tecnología (p. 11)

Resumen

La escasez es el problema básico en economía. La economía es el estudio de cómo los individuos y las naciones deciden utilizar los recursos escasos para satisfacer sus necesidades. La tierra, el trabajo, el capital y la iniciativa son factores de producción. Algunos economistas incluyen la tecnología.

Sección 2

Compensación de factores alternativos ("Trade-Offs")

Términos claves

compensación de factores
  alternativos (p. 13)
costo de oportunidad (p. 14)
posibilidades de producción
  (p. 15)

Resumen

Cuando un bien o actividad debe ser abandonado para ser sustituido por otro, ha ocurrido una compensación de factores alternativos. Lo que debe ser sustituido es el costo de oportunidad (o de sustitución) de una acción. Una curva de posibilidades de producción muestra la máxima cantidad de bienes que pueden ser producidos con los recursos de la nación en un período determinado. Cuando una nación opera de acuerdo con la curva de posibilidades de producción, está produciendo de una manera eficiente.

Sección 3

¿Qué hacen los economistas?

Términos claves

economía (p. 18)
modelo económico (p. 18)
hipótesis (p. 19)
valores (p. 20)
generalización (p. 21)

Resumen

Los economistas observan la información proveniente del mundo real para probar los modelos económicos que ellos han formulado sobre el comportamiento de los individuos y las empresas. Los modelos económicos son representaciones de la realidad que sólo toman en consideración los factores más importantes que pueden influir en un problema. Los modelos económicos y los economistas no dicen si determinadas políticas son buenas o malas, debido a que tales juicios dependen de los valores de cada individuo.

---

2 *Puntos destacados*

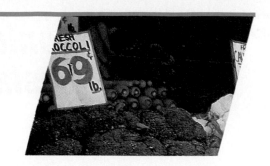

Sistemas económicos

Términos claves

sistema económico (p. 30)
distribución de ingresos
(p. 31)
sistema económico
tradicional (p. 32)
sistema de economía
dirigida (p. 33)

sistema de economía de
mercado (p. 33)
mercado (p. 33)
economía mixta (p. 34)

Resumen

Todos los sistemas económicos responden a cuatro preguntas básicas que determinan el uso de los recursos. En un sistema tradicional las decisiones económicas son dictadas por lo que se hizo en el pasado. El gobierno controla los factores de producción en un sistema de economía dirigida. En un sistema de mercado, los individuos de acuerdo con sus propios intereses deciden las respuestas a las cuatro preguntas básicas. Una economía dirigida contiene elementos de los sistemas de economía dirigida y de mercado.

Características de la Economía de los Estados Unidos

Términos claves

mano invisible (p. 37)
capitalismo (p. 37)
sistema de libre empresa
(p. 38)
propiedad privada (p. 38)

utilidades (p. 39)
incentivos para obtener
utilidades (p. 39)
competencia (p. 39)

Resumen

La decisión de los consumidores es la clave del uso de los recursos en un sistema de libre empresa. Libre empresa significa que los individuos privados son dueños de las empresas, compiten en mercados libres y obtienen utilidades. El papel del estado en una economía de mercado es objeto de debates públicos.

Los objetivos de la nación

Términos claves

eficiencia económica (p. 45)
crecimiento económico
(p. 45)
equidad (p. 45)
nivel de vida (p. 45)

Resumen

Una nación fija sus objetivos económicos en base a su sistema de valores. Algunos objetivos del sistema económico de los Estados Unidos son la eficiencia, el crecimiento, la seguridad, la equidad, la estabilidad y la libertad individual. La libertad personal, la diversidad en los estilos de vida y un alto nivel de vida son beneficios de un sistema de libre empresa.

---

3 Puntos destacados

Consumo, ingreso y la toma de decisiones

Términos claves
consumidor (p. 58)
ingreso disponible (p. 58)
ingreso discrecional (p. 58)
garantía (p. 60)
selección racional (p. 61)

Resumen

Parte del ingreso disponible es discrecional y no tiene que ser gastado en necesidades básicas. Un consumidor inteligente considera varios factores antes de hacer una compra.

Principios de compra o estrategias

Términos claves
publicidad competitiva (p. 64)
publicidad de información (p. 64)
publicidad con cebo ("bait and switch") (p. 65)

comparación de las condiciones de venta (p. 66)
nombres genéricos (p. 66)
marcas de fábrica (p. 66)

Resumen

El valor del tiempo y los esfuerzos de un consumidor para obtener información no deben exceder el valor obtenido al haber hecho la mejor decisión con respecto a un producto. Cierta publicidad tiene fines de información, otra es esencialmente competitiva. Antes de comprar los consumidores deben comparar las condiciones de venta de un producto.

Consumismo

Términos claves
consumismo (p. 68)
comportamiento ético (p. 71)

Resumen

Los consumidores tienen importantes derechos y fuentes de ayuda. Agencias privadas y estatales ofrecen información y ayuda al consumidor. Los consumidores tienen también varias responsabilidades incluyendo la responsabilidad de comportarse con ética.

4 Puntos destacados

Los estadounidenses y el crédito

Términos claves

crédito (p. 80)

capital de un préstamo (p. 80)

interés (p. 80)

deuda a plazos (p. 80)

bienes de consumo duraderos (p. 80)

hipoteca (p. 81)

Resumen

El pago de una deuda a largo plazo brinda algunas ventajas al prestatario. Las personas compran al crédito por varias razones. No obstante, los consumidores deben siempre decidir con cuidado si han de tomar dinero a préstamo y el monto del mismo.

Fuentes de préstamos y créditos

Términos claves

banco comercial (p. 86)

institución de ahorro y préstamo (p. 86)

banco de ahorro (p. 86)

cooperativa de crédito (p. 87)

compañía financiera (p. 87)

compañía de créditos personales (p. 88)

cuenta de crédito (p. 89)

cuenta crédito regular (p. 89)

límite de crédito (p. 89)

cuenta corriente rotativa (p. 89)

cuenta corriente a plazo (p. 90)

tarjeta de crédito (p. 90)

tarjeta de débito (p. 91)

cargo de financiamiento (p. 91)

tasa de porcentaje anual (p. 93)

Resumen

Los consumidores que desean tomar dinero a préstamo pueden escoger entre seis tipos de instituciones financieras. Los consumidores que quieren abrir una cuenta corriente pueden seleccionar entre una cuenta regular, una cuenta rotativa o una cuenta a plazo. En todos los casos, los consumidores deben tener en cuenta que la tasa de porcentaje anual no es igual al cargo de financiamiento convenido.

Solicitud de crédito

Términos claves

agencia de crédito (p. 94)

cheque de crédito (p. 94)

clasificación crediticia (p. 94)

garantía (colateral) (p. 95)

préstamo con garantía (p. 95)

préstamo sin garantía (p. 95)

cosignatario (p. 96)

notificaciones de vencimiento (p. 96)

Resumen

Varios factores se toman en cuenta cuando las instituciones financieras evalúan la solvencia de una persona. Una vez que a una persona se le otorga un crédito, tiene la responsabilidad de usarlo con inteligencia.

Regulación del crédito por el gobierno

Términos claves

leyes sobre usura (p. 99)

quiebra (p. 100)

Resumen

La Ley de Iguales Oportunidades de Crédito ("Equal Credit Opportunity Act") prohíbe la discriminación en el otorgamiento de préstamos en base a varios factores. Muchos estados tienen leyes sobre la usura que también protegen a los prestatarios. Los prestatarios que agotan su capacidad de crédito pueden declararse en quiebra.

Comprando alimentos

Términos claves

almacén para compra de
alimentos (p. 109)
tiendas de artículos de
consumo frecuente (p. 109)
productos con etiquetas de
la casa (p. 110)

Resumen

Los consumidores deben conocer las muchas sugerencias útiles que se obtienen comparando las condiciones de venta de un bien o producto antes de hacer una compra. Existen tres clases importantes de tiendas de comestibles; cada una ofrece sus ventajas.

Selección de ropa

Términos claves

durabilidad (p. 115)
flujo de servicio (p. 115)

Resumen

Los valores de cada persona influyen en su elección de ropa. El valor de la ropa es determinado por el estilo, la durabilidad y el costo de mantenimiento. Reconocer el momento oportuno es un factor importante en la venta de ropa.

CAPÍTULO 6 Puntos destacados

Sección 1

Necesidades y preferencias de vivienda

Términos claves
impuestos sobre bienes inmuebles (p. 125)
condominios (p. 126)
cooperativas (p. 126)
arrendamiento (p. 126)
depreciar (p. 126)

Resumen
Existen cinco tipos diferentes de viviendas disponibles a los consumidores. Los arrendatarios deben tomar en cuenta los pros y los contras de compartir un apartamiento o una casa antes de firmar un contrato de arrendamiento.

Sección 2

Arrendar o comprar

Términos claves
costos de cierre (p. 129)
puntos porcentuales (p. 129)
equidad (p. 130)
depósito de garantía (p. 130)

Resumen
Al tomar una decisión sobre su vivienda, se debe considerar las ventajas y desventajas de arrendar y comprar una casa. Existen normas que determinan cuánto se debe gastar en una casa. Tanto el arrendatario como el arrendador tienen derechos y responsabilidades.

Sección 3

Compra y manejo de un automóvil

Términos claves
impuesto interno sobre el consumo (p. 136)
derecho de registro (p. 137)
seguro de responsabilidad civil (p. 139)

Resumen
La compra de un automóvil implica varios gastos. El dueño de un auto debe también hacer gastos relacionados con el manejo y el mantenimiento del mismo.

7 Puntos destacados

¿Para qué ahorrar?

Términos claves

ahorro (p. 146)
interés (p. 146)
cuenta de ahorro con libreta
(p. 147)
cuenta de ahorro con estado
de cuenta (p. 147)
cuenta de depósito en el
mercado monetario
(p. 148)

depósito a plazo (p. 148)
vencimiento (p. 148)
certificados de depósito
(p. 148)

Resumen

Toda persona debe decidir el momento más oportuno para ahorrar e invertir. Los inversionistas principiantes deben comparar las cuentas de ahorro con libreta, con estado de cuenta y en el mercado monetario. Las cuentas de depósito a plazo brindan asimismo algunas ventajas.

Las inversiones: corriendo riesgos con sus ahorros

Términos claves

acciones (p. 154)
accionistas (p. 155)
dividendos (p. 155)
bonos (p. 155)
bonos exentos de impuesto
(p. 155)
bonos de ahorro (p. 155)
bonos del Tesoro a corto
plazo (p. 156)
pagarés del Tesoro (p. 156)
bonos del Tesoro a largo
plazo (p. 156)

mercado de valores no
oficial (p. 157)
ganancias de capital
(plusvalía) (p. 157)
corredor (p. 157)
pérdidas de capital
(minusvalía) (p. 158)
fondos mutuos (p. 158)
fondo de inversión a corto
plazo en el mercado
de dinero (p. 158)
información interior de una
empresa (p. 159)

Resumen

Las acciones y los bonos ofrecen al inversionista opciones con ventajas distintas. Algunos fondos de inversión disponibles en los mercados de acciones y bonos implican menos riesgos que las acciones y los bonos individuales. Los consejos especulativos no ayudan a los inversionistas a hacerse ricos de la noche a la mañana en el mercado de valores.

Planes especiales de ahorro y objetivos

Términos claves

planes de pensiones (p. 161)
Plan Keogh (p. 161)
Cuenta de Retiro Individual
o IRA (p. 162)
diversificación (p. 164)

Resumen

Los planes de pensiones patrocinados por individuos o empresas ayudan a las personas a ahorrar para el momento de su jubilación. Los intereses y el riesgo deben tomarse en cuenta antes de decidir la cantidad que se debe ahorrar e invertir.

8 Puntos destacados

Sección 1

La demanda

Términos claves

intercambio voluntario
(p. 176)
ley de la demanda (p. 177)
utilidad (p. 177)
ley de la utilidad marginal
decreciente (p. 177)

efecto de ingreso real
(p. 179)
efecto de sustitución (p. 179)

Resumen

En una economía de mercado, el principio de intercambio voluntario ayuda a determinar el precio que los consumidores están dispuestos a pagar por un producto o servicio determinado. La ley de la demanda, según es afectada por la utilidad marginal decreciente, el efecto de ingreso real y el efecto de sustitución, explica cómo reaccionan los consumidores ante las variaciones de precios.

Sección 2

Curva de demanda y elasticidad de la demanda

Términos claves

curva de demanda (p. 183)
elasticidad (p. 185)
elasticidad de precios de la
demanda (p. 185)

demanda elástica (p. 185)
demanda inelástica (p. 186)
bienes complementarios
(p. 188)

Resumen

Los economistas con frecuencia dibujan la curva de demanda para entender mejor la dinámica de los precios. La elasticidad de precios de la demanda influye en las variaciones del precio de un producto. Además de esta elasticidad, otros factores determinan la demanda en una economía de mercado.

Sección 3

La ley de la oferta y la curva de oferta

Términos claves

ley de la oferta (p. 191)
ley de los rendimientos
decrecientes (p. 192)

curva de oferta (p. 194)

Resumen

En el sistema de mercado libre, el incentivo de obtener mayores ganancias afecta la cantidad de productos que los fabricantes están dispuestos y en capacidad de ofrecer. Igual que la curva de demanda, la curva de oferta muestra la relación entre el nivel de la oferta y los precios.

Sección 4

Equilibrio de la oferta y la demanda

Términos claves

precio de equilibrio (p. 191)
tecnología (p. 197)
falta (p. 198)
superávit (p. 198)

Resumen

Cuatro factores determinan la oferta en una economía de mercado. Un cambio en la oferta puede, con frecuencia, producir cambios significativos en los precios. Tanto la falta como el superávit afectan el precio en una economía de mercado. Algunas veces este cambio adopta la forma de un cambio en el precio de equilibrio. Aunque la oferta y la demanda influyen conjuntamente en los precios, las fuerzas que se ocultan detrás de la oferta y la demanda pueden asimismo alterar el precio de un producto o servicio.

9 Puntos destacados

Iniciando un negocio

Términos claves
empresario (p. 208)
inventario (p. 210)

Resumen
Poner en marcha un negocio requiere dos etapas. Una vez que las etapas esten completadas, los empresarios deben considerar detenidamente los cuatro elementos claves de todo negocio.

Empresa de propietario único y sociedades de personas

Términos claves
empresa de propietario
  único (p. 213)
propietario (p. 213)
responsabilidad sin límite
  (p. 214)
bienes (p. 214)
inicio de operaciones (p. 214)

desarrollo de la pequeña
  empresa (p. 214)
sociedad de personas
  (p. 217)
sociedad de personas con
  responsabilidad limitada
  (p. 217)
empresa conjunta (p. 217)

Resumen
La forma de organización empresarial más común en los Estados Unidos es la de propietario único, que tiene sus ventajas y desventajas. Las sociedades de dos o más personas tienen también sus ventajas y desventajas. Las sociedades de personas con responsabilidad limitada tienen que seguir directrices específicas.

El mundo empresarial y las franquicias

Términos claves
corporación (p. 219)
responsabilidad limitada
  (p. 220)
escritura de constitución
  (p. 221)
autorización de constitución
  en sociedad anónima
  (p. 221)

Resumen
Muchas personas comparten la propiedad de las corporaciones, lo que tiene ventajas y desventajas diferentes de las de otras formas de organización empresarial. Las franquicias, por medio de las cuales el franquiciador vende a otro negocio el derecho de usar su nombre y vender sus productos, son comunes en algunas industrias.

10 Puntos destacados

Competencia perfecta

Término clave
competencia perfecta
(p. 232)

Resumen
La competencia perfecta tiene cuatro condiciones que conducen a que las empresas no tengan control de los precios. En los Estados Unidos la agricultura es la rama que se acerca más a cumplir con estas condiciones. Aunque ideal de sí, la competencia perfecta casi no existe en el mundo real.

Monopolio, oligopolio y la competencia monopolista

Términos claves
competencia imperfecta
(p. 237)
monopolio puro (p. 237)
barreras para entrar en un
mercado (p. 238)
monopolios naturales
(p. 239)
monopolios geográficos
(p. 239)
monopolio tecnológico
(p. 239)

patente (p. 239)
monopolios estatales (p. 239)
cartel (p. 239)
oligopolio (p. 240)
diferenciación de productos
(p. 240)
competencia monopolista
(p. 240)

Resumen
Tres condiciones conducen a que un negocio llegue a tener control casi total de los precios en el mercado (monopolio puro). Las cuatro condiciones que producen un oligopolio dan a los vendedores control limitado sobre los precios. La competencia monopolista es el tipo de estructura de mercado más común en los Estados Unidos.

Políticas gubernamentales hacia la competencia

Términos claves
leyes antimonopolistas
(p. 244)
consejo de administración
coincidente (p. 244)
fusión (p. 244)
fusión horizontal (p. 245)

fusión vertical (p. 245)
conglomerados (p. 245)
fusión de conglomerados
(p. 245)
desregulación (p. 246)
nueva regulación (p. 246)

Resumen
Las leyes federales prohíben los consejos de administración coincidentes, pero permiten las fusiones de empresas siempre que no signifiquen la formación de un monopolio. Para promover la competencia y proteger a los consumidores el gobierno ha creado muchas agencias federales regulativas. Muchos de los reglamentos emitidos por estas agencias han sido eliminados, pero algunas personas están a favor de una nueva regulación.

11 *Puntos destacados*

La inversión en el sistema de libre empresa

Términos claves
análisis de costo-beneficio
(p. 258)

Resumen
Las personas y las empresas invierten sus ahorros en muchos lugares incluyendo diferentes bancos, fondos mutuos y planes de pensiones. Financiando sus inversiones, las personas esperan ganar interés. Las empresas recurren a estas inversiones para financiar la expansión. Este financiamiento de la expansión es una forma de determinar la asignación de recursos en un sistema de mercado libre.

Tipos de financiamiento de las operaciones comerciales

Términos claves
financiamiento mediante créditos o la emisión de obligaciones (p. 265)
financiamiento a corto plazo (p. 265)
financiamiento a medio plazo (p. 265
financiamiento a largo plazo (p. 265)

crédito comercial (p. 266)
pagaré (p. 266)
cuentas por cobrar (p. 266)
línea de crédito (p. 266)
arrendamiento (p. 266)
financiamiento por venta de participación (p. 267)

Resumen
Cuando las empresas toman dinero prestado, el plazo para pagar la deuda es un factor importante que debe ser tomado en cuenta. Las empresas que toman dinero prestado consideran la tasa de interés, las condiciones del mercado y su capacidad para hacer frente a la carga de la deuda. Algunas veces las empresas consiguen capital financiero vendiendo acciones o bonos.

El proceso de producción

Términos claves
producción (p. 271)
bienes de consumo (p. 271)
bienes de producción (p. 271)
mecanización (p. 274)

cadena de montaje (p. 275)
división del trabajo (p. 275)
automatización (p. 275)
robótica (p. 275)

Resumen
El proceso de producción implica diseño del producto, planificación, compra, control de calidad y control de existencias. La tecnología ha aumentado la productividad. La mecanización, la cadena de montaje, la división del trabajo, la automatización y la robótica se han combinado para hacer más eficiente la producción.

12 Puntos destacados

Sección 1

El papel cambiante de la mercadotecnia ("marketing")

Términos claves
mercadotecnia (p. 282)
utilidad (p. 282)
utilidad por la forma (p. 284)
utilidad de tiempo (p. 284)
utilidad de emplazamiento (p. 284)
utilidad de la posesión (p. 284)

investigación de mercado (p. 284)
informe de mercado (p. 284)
comercialización de prueba (p. 285)

Resumen

El desarrollo de la mercadotecnia en los Estados Unidos ha tenido cuatro etapas, que han conducido a la soberanía del consumidor. Mediante una serie de preguntas elaboradas de antemano, los estudios de mercados tratan de descubrir la calidad, las características y los estilos que los consumidores desean en un producto, el tipo de embalaje que atraerá a los consumidores y el precio que los moverá a comprar.

Sección 2

Los componentes básicos de la mercadotecnia

Términos claves
liderazgo en la fijación de precios (p. 289)
fijación de precios de penetración (p. 290)
publicidad (p. 290)

publicidad directa por correo (p. 291)
ciclo de vida del producto (p. 291)

Resumen

Los cuatro componentes básicos de mercadotecnia son el producto, el precio, el lugar y la publicidad. Al fijar el precio de un producto, una empresa debe tomar en cuenta los costos de producción, publicidad, venta y distribución, así como las utilidades que desea obtener y el precio que los competidores están cobrando por el mismo producto. El precio es usado también en las estrategias de mercadotecnia. El lugar donde se vende el producto y el tipo de publicidad usada ayudan a determinar el éxito de ese producto.

Sección 3

Canales de distribución

Términos claves
canales de distribución (p. 293)
mayoristas (p. 293)
vendedores al por menor (p. 294)

Resumen

Los mayoristas compran grandes cantidades de productos de los fabricantes para venderlos a otros negocios. Los vendedores al por menor venden bienes de consumo directamente al público. Como parte del proceso de distribución, las mercancías pueden ser almacenadas por el fabricante, el mayorista o el vendedor al por menor para su futura venta. Los aumentos más significativos en la distribución de productos se han logrado por medio de los club-almacenes ("club-warehouses") y la publicidad directa por correo.

13 *Puntos destacados*

La fuerza laboral en los Estados Unidos

Términos claves

fuerza laboral civil (p. 306)
obreros (p. 306)
profesionales (p. 307)
empleados de oficina (p. 307)
trabajadores en el área de servicios (p. 307)

obreros no cualificados (p. 307)
obreros semicualificados (p. 307)
obreros cualificados (p. 307)
ley del salario mínimo (p. 309)

Resumen

Los trabajadores pueden ser clasificados por categorías según el tipo de trabajo. Los trabajadores también pueden ser clasificados como no cualificados, semicualificados, cualificados y profesionales. En el mercado de trabajo, la oferta viene de los trabajadores que ofrecen sus servicios y la demanda de los empleadores que necesitan trabajadores. Tres factores determinan cómo la oferta y la demanda afectan los salarios: la capacidad, el tipo de trabajo y el lugar.

Trabajo organizado

Términos claves

sindicato (p. 311)
huelga (p. 312)
gremio (p. 312)
sindicato industrial (p. 312)
sindicato local (p. 313)
empresa con sindicación obligatoria ("closed shop") (p. 313)

empresa con sindicación eventual obligatoria ("union shop") (p. 313)
empresa con cotización sindical obligatoria ("agency shop") (p. 313)
ley sobre libertad laboral (p. 313)

Resumen

En el siglo XIX, los sindicatos atraían a los trabajadores porque parecían ofrecer un medio para obligar a los empleadores a mejorar las condiciones de trabajo. No obstante, el sindicalismo encontró mucha resistencia durante la mayor parte del siglo XIX y principios del XX. Los sindicatos lograron en el siglo XX establecer empresas donde los trabajadores tienen que estar sindicados, sindicarse transcurrido cierto tiempo o cotizar al sindicato.

Convenio colectivo

Términos claves

convenio colectivo (p. 318)
mediación (p. 318)
ajuste por coste de vida (p. 319)
arbitraje (p. 319)

piquetes laborales (p. 320)
boicot (p. 320)
cierre patronal ("lockout") (p. 320)
interdicción laboral (p. 320)

Resumen

Los asuntos más importantes tratados usualmente en las negociaciones colectivas de trabajo son los salarios, las horas de trabajo, los beneficios complementarios, las condiciones de trabajo, la seguridad en el trabajo y los procedimientos de presentación de agravios. Cuando se rompen las negociaciones colectivas, el arbitraje o la mediación, puede surgir una huelga en la que piquetes de huelguistas pueden hacer guardia alrededor de las instalaciones de la empresa y organizar un boicot exhortando al público a no comprar los productos o servicios fabricados por dicha empresa. La administración puede responder declarando un cierre patronal u obteniendo una interdicción judicial contra los trabajadores.

---

14 *Puntos destacados*

Sección 1

Contabilidad del ingreso nacional

Términos claves
contabilidad del ingreso nacional (p. 332)
producto interior bruto (PIB) (p. 332)
exportaciones netas (p. 334)

depreciación (p. 334)
producto interior neto (PIN) (p. 335)
ingreso nacional (p. 335)
ingreso personal (p. 336)
pagos de transferencia (p. 336)
ingreso personal disponible (p. 336)

Resumen
El producto interior bruto (PIB) es el valor total en dólares de todos los bienes finales de consumo, de producción y estatales, las exportaciones netas y los servicios producidos en la nación durante un año. El ingreso personal se encuentra restando del ingreso nacional los impuestos sobre la renta de las corporaciones, las utilidades y las contribuciones de los empleadores al Seguro Social.

Sección 2

Corrigiendo las estadísticas para la inflación

Términos claves
inflación (p. 338)
poder adquisitivo (p. 338)
deflación (p. 339)
índice de precios de consumo (IPC) (p. 339)

año base (p. 340)
índice de precios al productor (IPP) (p. 340)
deflactor (corrector) de precios del PIB implícito (p. 341)
PIB real (p. 341)

Resumen
Cuando hay inflación, el dinero pierde su poder adquisitivo. Las tres formas de medir los cambios en los precios promedios son el índice de precios al consumidor (IPC), el índice de precios al productor (IPP) y el deflactor de precios del PIB implícito.

Sección 3

Suma total de la oferta y la demanda

Términos claves
suma total (p. 342)
demanda global (p. 342)

curva de demanda global (p. 343)
oferta total (p. 345)
curva de oferta total (p. 345)

Resumen
La suma total de la oferta y la demanda de bienes y servicios representa el total de la economía. La intersección de las curvas de demanda global y de oferta total determina el nivel de precios de equilibrio y el PIB real (producción nacional).

Sección 4

Fluctuaciones económicas

Términos claves
fluctuaciones económicas (p. 347)
ciclos económicos (p. 347)

punto máximo (p. 347)
apogeo ("boom") (p. 347)
contracción (p. 347)
recesión (p. 348)
depresión (p. 348)
punto mínimo (p. 348)
expansión (p. 348)
recuperación (p. 348)

Resumen
Las fluctuaciones económicas se miden de un período de prosperidad a otro. Un "ciclo" típico comienza con el punto máximo (auge); luego la economía comienza a contraerse, período durante el cual puede darse una recesión (punto mínimo) seguida de una recuperación.

Sección 5

Causas e indicadores de las fluctuaciones económicas

Términos claves
innovaciones (p. 352)
indicadores económicos (p. 355)

indicadores anticipados (p. 355)
indicadores coincidentes (p. 355)
indicadores de retardo (p. 355)

Resumen
La economía estudia muchas posibles causas de los ciclos económicos. Los economistas usan indicadores anticipados, coincidentes y de retardo para medir la actividad de algunas variables en la economía.

15 Puntos destacados

Funciones y características del dinero

Términos claves

dinero (p. 362)
medios de cambio (p. 362)
trueque (p. 362)
doble coincidencia de
   necesidades (p. 364)
unidad de contabilidad
   (p. 364)

reserva de valor (p. 364)
dinero mercancía (p. 365)
dinero en cuenta (p. 366)
papel moneda (p. 366)
moneda de curso legal
   (p. 366)

Resumen

Se considera dinero todo lo que es usado como medio de cambio, unidad de contabilidad y reserva de valor. Actualmente, todo el dinero de los Estados Unidos es papel moneda. Es portátil, divisible, de valor estable y aceptado. No obstante, el papel moneda no es muy duradero.

Historia del dinero y la banca en los Estados Unidos

Términos claves

sobregiro (p. 369)
transferencia electrónica de
   fondos (EFT) (p. 369)
patrón monetario (p. 370)
cajeros automáticos (ATMs)
   (p. 372)

Resumen

La historia del dinero y la banca del país ha sido un proceso de ordenamiento gradual de un sistema desordenado. El Congreso dio el primer paso en esta dirección en 1792 cuando estableció el dólar como la unidad básica de cambio y estableció la primera casa de la moneda. Los servicios bancarios modernos incluyen muchos servicios además de las cuentas de cheques y ahorro.

Tipos de dinero en los Estados Unidos

Términos claves

cuenta corriente bancaria
   (p. 376)
depósitos a la vista (p. 377)
depósitos verificables
   (p. 377)
instituciones de ahorro
   (p. 377)

tarjetas de débito (p. 377)
cuasidinero (p. 378)
M1 (p. 378)
M2 (p. 378)

Resumen

Actualmente la oferta monetaria de los Estados Unidos se compone de dinero en circulación, depósitos verificables y cuasidinero. La definición M1 de la oferta monetaria incluye el dinero en circulación, los cheques viajeros y los depósitos verificables en los bancos comerciales y las instituciones de ahorro. La definición de dinero M2 incluye la definición M1 más algunos activos fácilmente convertibles en dinero (cuasidinero).

16 Puntos destacados

La oferta monetaria y la economía

Términos claves

El "Fed" (p. 388)
política monetaria (p. 388)
política de dinero disponible (p. 389)
política de dinero escaso (p. 389)
reserva parcial bancaria (p. 389)
reserva obligatoria (p. 389)

Resumen

Una política de dinero disponible significa que el crecimiento de la oferta monetaria ha aumentado y hay dinero en abundancia y es barato de tomar prestado. Con una política de dinero escaso ocurre lo contrario. Con el sistema de reserva parcial bancario, sólo una fracción de los depósitos en un banco se mantiene disponible. El resto es dado en préstamo o invertido. Debido al sistema de reserva parcial bancario, cualquier cambio en el dinero nuevo en circulación producirá un cambio múltiple en la oferta monetaria.

Organización y funciones del Sistema de la Reserva Federal

Términos claves

Comisión Federal de Mercado Abierto (FOMC) (p. 394)
compensación de cheques bancarios (p. 396)

Resumen

La Junta Directiva del Sistema de la Reserva Federal dirige las operaciones del Sistema de la Reserva Federal y establece políticas con respecto a asuntos como la reserva obligatoria y las tasas de descuento. El Sistema de la Reserva Federal ejerce muchas funciones además de compensar cheques para los bancos y reglamentar la oferta monetaria.

Regulación de la oferta monetaria

Términos claves

tasa de descuento (p. 401)
tasa mínima de interés (p. 401)
operaciones de mercado abierto (p. 402)

Resumen

Para regular la oferta monetaria, el Fed emplea cambios en la reserva obligatoria, la tasa de descuento y las operaciones de mercado abierto. Algunas veces resulta difícil diseñar políticas monetarias porque el gobierno no tiene siempre información correcta sobre las definiciones M1 y M2. Además, el Fed no es la única fuerza que afecta la economía.

17 Puntos destacados

Aumento en las dimensiones del gobierno

Términos claves

proyectos de obras públicas (p. 413)
Medicare (p. 415)

Resumen

El gobierno de los Estados Unidos ha crecido de cerca de 3 millones de empleados en 1929 a cerca de 19 millones actualmente. Varios factores explican este gran crecimiento del aparato estatal.

Las funciones del gobierno

Términos claves

bienes públicos (p. 416)
bienes preferentes (p. 416)
Seguro Social (p. 417)
indemnización por accidente de trabajo (p. 417)
Ingreso de Seguridad Suplementario (p. 417)

Ayuda a Familias con Hijos Dependientes (p. 417)
Medicaid (p. 417)
bienes de demérito (p. 417)
redistribución del ingreso (p. 417)
programas de seguro social (p. 418)
programas de asistencia pública (p. 418)
bienestar social (p. 418)

Resumen

Cuatro funciones importantes del gobierno son: (1) proporcionar bienes públicos, (2) redistribuir el ingreso y asegurar el bienestar público, (3) regular la actividad económica y (4) asegurar la estabilidad económica. El gobierno facilita los bienes públicos a todos los ciudadanos. El gobierno usa los programas de seguro social y los programas de asistencia pública para redistribuir el ingreso. Al mismo tiempo, el gobierno trabaja para promover la estabilidad económica.

El presupuesto nacional y la deuda pública

Términos claves

año fiscal (p. 421)
financiamiento del déficit (p. 423)

deuda pública (p. 425)
enmienda del presupuesto equilibrado (p. 246)

Resumen

El proceso de elaboración del presupuesto federal incluye varios pasos que involucran a los poderes ejecutivo y legislativo. Aun con restricciones para salvaguardar la balanza de pagos e intentos de reducir el déficit, la deuda pública sigue creciendo a un ritmo alarmante.

Impuestos

Términos claves

principio de beneficios recibidos (p. 428)
principio de capacidad de pago (p. 428)

impuesto progresivo (p. 430)
impuesto regresivo (p. 430)
impuesto proporcional (p. 430)

Resumen

Dos principios tributarios son el principio de imputación basado en los beneficios recibidos y el principio de imputación basado en la capacidad de pago. Los impuestos son clasificados de acuerdo con la forma en que distribuyan la carga tributaria entre los contribuyentes, mientras algunos impuestos son gravados para afectar la actividad económica.

18 Puntos destacados

Desempleo e inflación

Términos claves
políticas de estabilización
 (p. 438)
índice de desempleo (p. 438)
pleno empleo (p. 439)
economía sumergida (p. 439)
inflación de demanda
 (p. 440)
inflación con estancamiento
 (p. 441)
inflación de costes (p. 441)

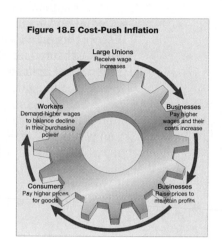

Figure 18.5 Cost-Push Inflation

Large Unions
Receive wage increases

Workers
Demand higher wages to balance decline in their purchasing power

Businesses
Pay higher wages and their costs increase

Consumers
Pay higher prices for goods

Businesses
Raise prices to maintain profits

Resumen

Medir el desempleo es difícil porque los economistas no están de acuerdo sobre el nivel de pleno empleo. Las investigaciones sobre desempleo son inexactas debido a la economía sumergida. La inflación de demanda ocurre generalmente en tiempos de pleno empleo. La inflación de costos ocurre con frecuencia cuando los índices de inflación y desempleo son altos.

Política fiscal y estabilización

Términos claves
política fiscal (p. 443)
flujo circular de ingresos
 (p. 443)

Resumen

Los economistas usan un modelo para explicar el flujo circular de ingresos. Los economistas keynesianos creen que la política fiscal (los impuestos y los gastos del gobierno) debe ser usada para regular el nivel global de la actividad económica. Quieren que el gobierno use la política fiscal para reducir la inflación.

El monetarismo y la economía

Términos claves
monetarismo (p. 448)
los monetaristas (p. 448)
principio monetario (p. 449)
desface cronológico (p. 450)

Resumen

Los monetaristas creen que el Sistema de la Reserva Federal cometió errores que profundizaron la Gran Depresión. Sus teorías influyeron en las políticas gubernamentales a partir de la década de los 1980. Los monetaristas cuestionan la capacidad de la política fiscal para resolver los problemas de la inflación y el desempleo.

CAPÍTULO

19 Puntos destacados

Sección 1

Los beneficios del comercio mundial

Términos claves
importaciones (p. 462)
exportaciones (p. 462)
ventaja absoluta (p. 464)
especialización (p. 464)
ventaja comparativa (p. 465)

Resumen

Las naciones se benefician del comercio mundial porque los factores de producción disponibles en cada nación son diferentes. La ventaja absoluta es la capacidad de un país de producir más cantidad de un producto determinado que otra nación, usando la misma cantidad de recursos. Si un país tiene al menos una ventaja comparativa con respecto a un producto, es ventajoso para ese país especializarse en la producción de dicho producto. Puede entonces establecer relaciones de intercambio con otros países para obtener los productos que desea.

Sección 2

El financiamiento del comercio mundial

Términos claves
los mercados de divisas
  (p. 467)
tipo de cambio fijo (p. 467)
Fondo Monetario
  Internacional
  (FMI) (p. 467)

devaluación (p. 468)
tipos de cambio flexibles
  (p. 468)
depreciación (p. 469)
balanza comercial (p. 469)

Resumen

Con un tipo de cambio fijo, el gobierno nacional fija el valor de su moneda con relación a un solo patrón. Con un tipo de cambio flexible, las fuerzas de la oferta y la demanda de bienes determinan los precios de las monedas. Cuando el valor de nuestras exportaciones excede el valor de nuestras importaciones, tenemos un superávit en nuestra balanza comercial.

Sección 3

Restricciones del comercio mundial

Términos claves
arancel (p. 472)
arancel financiero (p. 472)
arancel proteccionista
  (p. 472)
cuota de importación
  (p. 473)
embargo (p. 473)
proteccionistas (p. 474)

Acuerdo General sobre
  Aranceles Aduaneros y
  Comercio (GATT) (p. 474)
Tratado de Libre Comercio
  entre los E.E.U.U. y
  Canadá (p. 474)
Tratado de Libre Comercio
  para América del Norte
  (NAFTA) (p. 474)

Resumen

Las restricciones legales al comercio mundial tratan de proteger a las industrias y a los trabajadores del país. Los pros y los contras de las restricciones al comercio son con frecuencia objeto de intensos debates. La mayor parte del comercio mundial se rige por el GATT y varios tratados comerciales regionales.

---

20 Puntos destacados

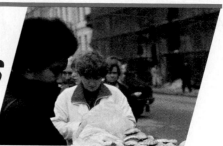

Comparación entre el capitalismo y el socialismo

Términos claves

Las tres "P" (p. 482)
derechos de propiedad privada (p. 482)
sistema de precios (p. 482)
comunismo (p. 484)
el proletariado (p. 484)
socialismo democrático (p. 484)
socialismo autoritario (p. 484)

Resumen

El capitalismo de mercado puro puede ser descrito en base a las llamadas tres "P": precios ("prices"), utilidades ("profits") y propiedad privada ("private property"). Los derechos de propiedad privada existen y son legales; se permite a los precios alcanzar sus propios niveles de acuerdo con la oferta y la demanda; los recursos son dirigidos a las áreas que producen mayores utilidades. En el socialismo puro, el estado fija la mayoría de los precios, el estado es dueño de los principales factores de producción, las decisiones económicas son tomadas por el estado por medio de sus agencias de planificación centralizada y el movimiento de los recursos está estrictamente controlado. La planificación en el capitalismo está descentralizada. El capitalismo ofrece libertad personal y premia la iniciativa individual.

Cambios en el socialismo autoritario: el caso de China

Términos claves

planes quinquenales (p. 487)
zonas económicas especiales (p. 488)

Resumen

Después de la Segunda Guerra mundial, los chinos establecieron una serie de planes quinquenales, ninguno de los cuales dio los resultados esperados. A partir de 1979, se designaron zonas económicas especiales. El índice de crecimiento en estas zonas económicas especiales ha sido muy alto.

Las naciones se dirigen al sistema de mercado

Términos claves

privatización (p. 492)
mercado secundario (p. 493)
estado de bienestar (p. 494)

Resumen

La tendencia en Rusia, en las otras repúblicas de la antigua Unión Soviética y en la Europa oriental es hacia una privatización cada vez mayor. Suecia, que ha sido un estado de bienestar durante muchos años, ha avanzado recientemente hacia la privatización y a una menor participación del estado en la satisfacción de las necesidades básicas del individuo. Empezando con los cambios en México a mediados de la década de los 1980, un número cada vez mayor de países en América Latina están privatizando las compañías pertenecientes al estado.

CAPÍTULO

21 Puntos destacados

Sección 1

Características de las naciones en vías de desarrollo

Términos claves

naciones desarrolladas
  (p. 504)
naciones en vías de desarrollo
  (p. 504)

agricultura de subsistencia
  (p. 505)
mortalidad infantil (p. 506)

Resumen

Tres de cada cuatro personas en el mundo viven en naciones en vías de desarrollo. Cuando los economistas miden el desarrollo de una nación consideran varios factores. Varias naciones asiáticas han demostrado un crecimiento rápido y estable en años recientes.

Sección 2

El proceso de desarrollo económico

Términos claves

ayuda exterior (p. 512)
asistencia económica (p. 513)
asistencia técnica (p. 513)

asistencia militar (p. 513)

Resumen

El desarrollo económico de una nación puede ser financiado por medio de una combinación de ahorros domésticos e inversiones y ayuda exterior. La ayuda exterior se compone de asistencia económica, técnica y militar. Muchas naciones industriales brindan ayuda exterior por razones humanitarias, económicas y políticas y de seguridad nacional.

Sección 3

Obstáculos al crecimiento en las naciones en vías de desarrollo

Términos claves

burocracias (p. 517)
nacionalización (p. 519)

Resumen

Las naciones en vías de desarrollo tienen que hacer frente a varios obstáculos que dificultan su crecimiento. La falta de desarrollo económico de Indonesia nos enseña que el solo hecho de proporcionar dinero a una nación en desarrollo no garantiza el crecimiento económico. La ayuda exterior debe ser usada con sabiduría, junto con los ahorros domésticos, la inversión extranjera y políticas gubernamentales que aseguren la estabilidad económica.

Sección 4

La industrialización y el futuro

Términos claves

derechos de propiedad privada
  (p. 523)

ciclo vicioso de la pobreza
  (p. 524)

Resumen

La rápida industrialización no es necesariamente la solución para las naciones en vías de desarrollo que no tienen una ventaja comparativa en la producción de determinados bienes que deciden fabricar. Mientras más seguridad existe con respecto a los derechos de propiedad privada, mayor será la inversión tanto doméstica como extranjera.

22 Puntos destacados

Causas y resultados de la integración mundial

Términos claves
integración mundial (p. 532)
telecomunicaciones (p. 532)

Resumen

Una de las razones más importantes de la mayor integración mundial ha sido las mejoras en las telecomunicaciones debidas a las reducciones considerables de los costos de los "chips" (plaquetas) de computadoras. En la actualidad, muchos instrumentos financieros se venden en los mercados internacionales. Los acontecimientos en un mercado nacional repercuten en otros mercados por todo el mundo.

¿Debe preocuparnos la inversión extranjera directa?

Términos clave
inversión extranjera directa (p. 537)

Resumen

Los extranjeros han invertido siempre en los Estados Unidos y lo siguen haciendo actualmente. Pero la inversión extranjera directa es una parte relativamente pequeña de nuestra economía considerada en su totalidad. No obstante, el objetivo último do la inversión extranjera directa por parte de naciones como el Japón es aumentar al máximo las utilidades.

Las empresas transnacionales y la competencia económica

Términos claves
empresas transnacionales (p. 543)
lealtades (p. 543)
filiales extranjeras (p. 543)
alianzas (p. 545)
tolerancia (p. 547)

Resumen

La inversión fuera de las fronteras nacionales corre a cargo de 35,000 empresas transnacionales por todo el mundo. La mayoría de las transnacionales invierten en regiones que están cerca de casa. Por ejemplo, las compañías de los Estados Unidos invierten principalmente en los Estados Unidos, Canadá, México y América del Sur. Las corporaciones pueden formar alianzas con antiguos competidores por muchas razones. La competencia internacional por los fondos de inversión extranjera significa que cuando las complicaciones de las burocracias estatales y los altos impuestos se vuelven un problema en un determinado país, los extranjeros invierten en otros países con un clima más favorable para la inversión.

TEXT DESIGN: Martucci Studio
COVER DESIGN: Martucci Studio, PHOTOS (l) Suzanne and Nick Geary/Tony Stone/Worldwide (r) Martucci Studio.
ILLUSTRATION: Martucci Studio/Jerry D. Malone
PHOTO RESEARCH: Susan Van Etten
PHOTO CREDITS: i, (l) Susan and Nick Geary/Tony Stone, Worldwide, (r) Martucci Studio. iv, (b) Pictor/Uniphoto v, ©Martucci Studio vi, ©Martucci Studio (bl) Courtesy, Ramsey & Muspratt Collections vii, (t) Courtesy, Charles B. Wang/Computer Associates (m) The Granger Collection (b) ©Martucci Studio viii, (tl&br) The Granger Collection (tr&bl) ©Martucci Studio ix, (tr) ©Martucci Studio (m) Vince Streano/Tony Stone Images/Chicago Inc. (br) David Austen/Stock Boston (bm) Barrie Rokeach/The Image Bank (bl) ©Susan Van Etten x, (t) David Hiser/Tony Stone Images/Chicago Inc. (m) © Martucci Studio (b) Uniphoto xi, (tl) ©Martucci Studio (l) ©Moore & Associates (m) Wide World (b) ©Martucci Studio 4–5, Jake Rais/The Image Bank 6–7, ©Martucci Studio 8, ©Martucci Studio 9, (t) Arnold J. Kaplan/The Picture Cube (b) Wide World 10, Gary Cralle/The Image Bank 11, (l) Guido Alberto Rossi/The Image Bank (r) Don Carroll/The Image Bank 13, (1) Duggal/The Image Bank (r) Arthur Tilley/FPG 14, D.D. Morrison/The Picture Cube 14–15, Chris Hackett/The Image Bank 16, ©Paul Conklin 17, Courtesy, New School for Social Research 18, Jeff Greenburg/The Picture Cube 19, ©Martucci Studio 20, Jay Freis/The Image Bank 20–21, ©Martucci Studio 22, Courtesy, Hyde Athletic Industries, Inc. 23, (t) Gary Cralle/The Image Bank (ml) D.D. Morrison/The Picture Cube (mr) Chris Hackett/The Image Bank (b) Jay Freis/The Image Bank 24, ©Martucci Studio 26, Bob Daemmrich/Stock Boston 26–27, Jim Karageorge 27, Bob Daemmrich/Stock Boston 28–29, Tom McCarthy/The Picture Cube 31, (tr) Alvis Upitis/The Image Bank (l) Pete Turner/The Image Bank 30–31, Pictor/Uniphoto 32, Irven DeVore/Anthrophoto 33, ©Susan Van Etten 34, ©Martucci Studio 35, (t) Pamela Zully/The Image Bank (b) Owen Franken/Stock Boston 37, ©Martucci Studio 38, (l) Bob Daemmrich/Stock Boston (r) Tony Freeman/Photo Edit 39, (r) ©Susan Van Etten (b) ©Paul Conklin 41, The Granger Collection 42–43, ©Martucci Studio 45, (tr) Larry Lawfer/The Picture Cube (tl) Richard Ustinich/The Image Bank (mr) Fotographia, Inc. Stock Boston (br) Eddie Hironaka/The Image Bank 44–45, Bob Daemmrich/Stock Boston 46, (t) ©Susan Van Etten (m) ©Susan Van Etten (b) Steve Dunwell/The Image Bank 48, (l) ©Martucci Studio (t&m) Courtesy, Southwest Airlines/Pam Francis 49, (t) ©Martucci Studio (b) Richard Ustinich/The Image Bank 50, Tom McCarthy/The Picture Cube 54–55, ©Mark Thayer 56–57, Mike Kagan/Monkmeyer Press Photos 59, ©Susan Van Etten 60, 61, ©Martucci Studio 62, Courtesy, Leadership Memphis 63, ©Susan Van Etten 64, ©Martucci Studio 65, ©Susan Van Etten 66, 68, ©Martucci Studio 69, (r) Michael Newman/Photo Edit (l) ©Martucci Studio 70–71, 72, ©Martucci Studio 73, (t) ©Susan Van Etten (b) ©Martucci Studio 74, Mike Kagan/Monkmeyer Press Photos 76, Steve Dunwell/The Image Bank 76–77, Ross H. Horowitz/Stockphotos 77, ©Susan Van Etten 78–79, ©Martucci Studios 81, Gerard Champlong/The Image Bank 82, (l) ©Susan Van Etten (r) ©Martucci Studio 83, ©Martucci Studio 84, Courtesy, Ronal Homer/Boston Bank of Commerce 86, (l) Rob

Crandall/Stock Boston (b) Karl Gehring/Gamma-Liaison 87, (l) David Young-Wolff/Photo Edit (tr) ©Susan Van Etten 88, ©Benson, Arizona Republic, 8/89, Reprinted by permission of Tribune Media Services. 89, Jeff Smith/The Image Bank 90–91, 92, ©Martucci Studio 94, Tony Freeman/Photo Edit 94–95, ©Susan Van Etten 95, Costa Manos/Magnum 96, David Young-Wolff/Photo Edit 98, Robert V. Eckert, Jr./Stock Boston 99, Vera Kelly/FPG 101, ©Martucci Studio 102, (l) ©Susan Van Etten (c) Jane Art/The Image Bank (b) ©Susan Van Etten 103, Jeff Smith/The Image Bank 104–105, ©Martucci Studio 106–107, Gary Gladstone/The Image Bank 108–109, ©Martucci Studio 108–109, Stephen McBrady/Photo Edit 109, (m) Mark Richards/Photo Edit (r) ©Susan Van Etten 110–111, ©Martucci Studio 112, The Bettmann Archive 114, (l) Kevin Forest/The Image Bank (c) Nancy Brown/The Image Bank (r) Mel DiGiacomo/The Image Bank 115, (l) David Browell/The Image Bank (c) Nancy Brown/The Image Bank (r) Eric Wheater/The Image Bank 116, (t) ©Susan Van Etten (b) ©Martucci Studio 118, (t) Williamson/Edwards Concept/The Image Bank (b) ©Martucci Studio 119, (t) ©Stephen McBrady/Photo Edit (br) Mark Richards/Photo Edit 120, Gary Gladstone/The Image Bank 121, Nancy Brown/The Image Bank 112–123, ©Susan Van Etten 125, (t) Frank Siteman/Monkmeyer Press Photos (b) Marc Romanelli/The Image Bank 126, (t) ©Susan Van Etten (b) Tony Freeman/Photo Edit 127, (r) Amy Etra/Photo Edit (l) ©Susan Van Etten 128, The Bettmann Archive 130–133, ©Martucci Studio 135, Stephen Frisch/Stock Boston 136, ©Martucci Studio 137, Lisa J. Goodman/The Image Bank 138, ©Susan Van Etten 139, ©Martucci Studio 140, (t) Reggie Parker/FPG (b) Elizabeth Zuckerman/Photo Edit 141, (t) ©Martucci Studio (m) Frank Siteman/Monkmeyer Press Photos (b) Stephen Frisch/Stock Boston 142, ©Susan Van Etten 144–145, George Ombremski/The Image Bank 146–147, 148, ©Martucci Studio 148, (b) Murray Alcosser/The Image Bank 151, Wide World 152–153, 154, 155, 156, ©Martucci Studio 157, David Jeffery/The Image Bank 160, ©Susan Van Etten 161, Larry Pierce/The Image Bank 164, ©Martucci Studio 166, (t) Steve Niedorf/The Image Bank (bl) ©Susan Van Etten (r) Brett Fromer/The Image Bank 167, (t) ©Susan Van Etten (l) ©Martucci Studio 169, George Ombremski/The Image Bank 172–173, Jook Leung/FPG 174–175, ©Martucci Studio 176, Michael Newman/Photo Edit 177, Bob Daemmrich/Stock Boston 178, 180–181, 184–185, 186, 188, ©Martucci Studio 190, The Granger Collection 191, ©Martucci Studio 192, Steve Allen/The Image Bank 193, 196, ©Martucci Studio 198–199, Bill Varie/The Image Bank 200, Dorothy Littell/Stock Boston 201, ©Martucci Studio 202, Courtesy, Goody's Department Store 203, (t) Michael Newman/Photo Edit (b) Bill Varie/The Image Bank 204, ©Martucci Studio 206–207, Don Swetzer/Tony Stone Images/Chicago, Inc. 209, Peter M. Miller/The Image Bank 211, Lawrence Migdale/Stock Boston 212, Wide World 213, ©Susan Van Etten 214, 215, 216, ©Martucci Studio 217, Lawrence Migdale/Stock Boston 220, ©Martucci Studio 223, David Young-Wolff/Photo Edit 224, ©Joe Moore & Associates 225, (t) Lawrence Migdale/Stock Boston (b) David Young-Wolff/Photo Edit 226, Don Swetzer/Tony Stone Images/Chicago, Inc. 228, Benn Mitchell/The Image Bank 228–229, Pete Turner/The Image Bank 229,

Spencer Grant/Stock Boston 230–231, George Goodwin/Monkmeyer Press Photos 232–233, ©Susan Van Etten 234, Grafton Smith/The Image Bank 235, (l) Steve Proehl/The Image Bank (r) James Carmichael/The Image Bank 237, ©Susan Van Etten 239, (tr) ©Martucci Studio (lr) Tennessee Valley Authority (tl&bl) ©Susan Van Etten 240, ©Susan Van Etten 242, ©Martucci Studio 243, Courtesy, Ramsey & Muspratt Collection 244, The Granger Collection 246, Michael R. Schneps/The Image Bank 248, (l) Terje Rakke/The Image Bank (r) Romilly Lockyer/The Image Bank 249, Grafton Smith/The Image Bank 250, George Goodwin/Monkmeyer Press Photos 254–255, FPG 256–257, Stacy Pick/Stock Boston 260, David Young-Wolff/Photo Edit 261, ©Susan Van Etten 262, Gabriel Covian/The Image Bank 263, David Hamilton/The Image Bank 265, 266, 267, ©Martucci Studio 269, Greg Pease/Tony Stone Images/Chicago, Inc. 270, Courtesy, Dabney & Resnick 271, Erik Leigh Simmons/The Image Bank 272, (l) Les Wollam (r) Jaime Villaseca/The Image Bank 273, Schneps/The Image Bank 274, (t) Michael Melford/The Image Bank (b) The Bettmann Archive 275, (bl) The Bettmann Archive (tl) Ellis Herwig/The Picture Cube (tr) Steve Dunwell/The Image Bank 276, (bl) ©Susan Van Etten (t) Keith Philpott/The Image Bank (bl) Courtesy, Howard Wright 277, Greg Pease/Tony Stone Images/Chicago, Inc. 278, Stacy Pick/Stock Boston 279, Michael Melford/The Image Bank 280–281, ©Martucci Studio 283, (l) The Granger Collection (r) U. of Louisville Photo Archives, Caufield & Shook Collection/Susan Van Etten Historical Files (ll&lr) The Granger Collection 284, (l) Steve Dunwell/The Image Bank (r) Lincoln Russell/Stock Boston (m) Christopher Johnson/Stock Boston (ll) ©Susan Van Etten 288–289, ©Martucci Studio 292, Courtesy, Charles B. Wang/Computer Associates 293, ©Susan Van Etten 294–295, Mark Richards/Photo Edit 295, (ll) © Martucci Studio (lr) ©Susan Van Etten 296–297, ©Martucci Studio 298, (ll) ©Martucci Studio (l) Marc Solomon/The Image Bank (r) ©Susan Van Etten 299, The Granger Collection 300, ©Martucci Studio 302, Lou Jones/The Image Bank 302–303, Lawrence Fried/The Image Bank 303, Alvis Upitis/The Image Bank 304–305, David Young-Wolff/Photo Edit 309, Larry Keenan Associates/The Image Bank 311, 312–313, The Granger Collection 314–315, ©Martucci Studio 316, (l) Bob Daemmrich/Stock Boston (r) ©Susan Van Etten 317, 318, Wide World 319, ©Martucci Studio 320, Rick Browne/Stock Boston 322, (t) ©Susan Van Etten (b) Rob Crandall/Stock Boston 323, ©Susan Van Etten 324, David Young-Wolff/Photo Edit 328–329, Hunter/Freeman Studio, San Francisco 330–331, Hans Wolf/The Image Bank 332–333, ©Susan Van Etten 335, David Brownell/The Image Bank 340, ©Martucci Studio 342–343, ©Jim Pickerell/FPG 344, Louis Padilla/The Image Bank 346, UPI/The Bettmann Archive 349, The Granger Collection 350, Library of Congress/Susan Van Etten Historical Files 351, Bryan F. Peterson/The Stock Market 352, (l) Alvis Upitis/Stock Boston (r) Steve Gottlieb/FPG 353, (t) ©Susan Van Etten Historical Files (b) Mark Richards/Photo Edit 354, ©Martucci Studio 356, (t) ©Susan Van Etten (l) Donald Dietz/Stock Boston (b) ©Martucci Studio 357, David Brownell/The Image Bank 358, Hans Wolf/The Image Bank 360–361, 362–363, ©Martucci Studio 364, Frank Siteman/Stock Boston 365–366, ©Martucci

ACKNOWLEDGMENTS

Studio 367, Courtesy, Ariel Capital Management 368, The Granger Collection 370–371, ©Martucci Studio 372, R. Rathe/FPG 374, 375, ©Martucci Studio 377, (l) Andy Caulfield/The Image Bank (t) Gerald French/FPG (b) Jay Freis/The Image Bank 378, (r) ©Susan Van Etten (l) ©Martucci Studio 380, (l&r) ©Susan Van Etten (b) ©Martucci Studio 381, ©Susan Van Etten 382, R. Rathe/FPG 383, ©Martucci Studio 384, ©Susan Van Etten 384–385, John Lei/Stock Boston 385, Bernard Roussel/The Image Bank 386–387, Al Satterwhite/The Image Bank 388, ©Susan Van Etten 390, ©Martucci Studio 392, Wide World 393, ©Paul Conklin 395–396, ©Martucci Studio 397, ©Susan Van Etten 400, Richard Pasley/Stock Boston 404, (l) White House Press Office (r) L. Chryslin/The Image Bank 406, (l) Comstock (r) Murray Alcosser/The Image Bank 407, (t) Richard Pasley/Stock Boston (m) ©Paul Conklin (b) L. Chryslin/The Image Bank 408, Al Satterwhite/The Image Bank 410–411, Lawrence Migdale/Stock Boston 412–413, The Granger Collection 414, (t) Bob Daemmrich/Stock Boston (b) David Hamilton/The Image Bank 415, David Young-Wolff/Photo Edit 419, R. Schoen 420, ©Paul Conklin 423, ©McNelly/Reprinted by Permission of Tribune Media Services 424–425, ©Susan Van Etten 426, (l) David Hamilton/The Image Bank (r) Ellis Herwig/Stock Boston 428–429, ©Martucci Studio 432, (l) Bob Daemmrich/Stock Boston (r) J. Ramey/The Image Bank (b) ©Susan Van Etten 433, ©Susan Van Etten 434, Lawrence Migdale/Stock Boston 436–437, ©Susan Van Etten 438, G&V Chapman/The Image Bank 439, ©Martucci Studio 442, Wide World 443, UPI/The Bettmann Archive 446, The Granger Collection 449, 452, ©Martucci Studio 453, G&V Chapman/The Image Bank 454, ©Susan Van Etten 458–459, Uniphoto 460–461, 463, ©Susan Van Etten 466, The Granger Collection 467, 469, ©Martucci Studio 472–473, Barrie Rokeach/The Image Bank 474, (l) Mahaux/The Image Bank (b) Bill Gillette/Stock Boston (r) ©Susan Van Etten 475, (t) ©Susan Van Etten (l) Kim Steele/The Image Bank (br) ©Martucci Studio 476, (t&m) Phil Borden/Photo Edit (b) ©Susan Van Etten 477, ©Martucci Studio 478, ©Susan Van Etten 480–481, Miguel/The Image Bank 483, (t) ©Martucci Studio (m) Gary Gladstone/The Image Bank (bm) Pat Lacroix/The Image Bank (ll) ©Susan Van Etten (lr) Hans Wolf/The Image Bank 487, ©Susan Van Etten 488, Don Klumpp/The Image Bank 491, The Granger Collection 492, Vince Streano/Tony Stone Images/Chicago, Inc. 493, Valdimir Pcholkin/FPG 494, Travelpix/FPG 495, 496, (t) ©Susan Van Etten 496, (b) ©Paul Conklin 497, Vince Streano/Tony Stone Images/Chicago, Inc. 498, Miguel/The Image Bank 500, Steve Dunwell/The Image Bank 502–503, ©Paul Conklin 504, Eastcott/Momatuk/Woodfin Camp & Associates 505, (l) David Hiser/Tony Stone Images/Chicago, Inc. (r) David R. Austen/Stock Boston 506, ©Susan Van Etten 508–509, ©Martucci Studio 511, Xavier Richer/Tony Stone Images/Chicago, Inc. 512, Carol Lee/Tony Stone Images/Chicago, Inc. 513, ©Susan Van Etten 514, (l) Dorothy Littell/Stock Boston (r) John McDermott/Tony Stone Images/Chicago, Inc. 515, (l) Blanche/Gamma-Liaison (r) D. H. Hassell/Stock Boston 517, (t) David M. Doody/FPG (b) FPG 519, Wide World 520, (l) Dallas & John Heaton/Stock Boston (r) David Austen/Stock Boston 521, The Granger Collection 523, (l) ©Susan Van Etten (r) Cary Wolinsky/Stock Boston 524, (t) Jay Freis/The Image Bank (b) Mahaux Photo/The Image Bank (m) Harold Sund/The Image Bank 526, (t) David Ball/The Picture Cube (b) Dave Bartruff/Stock Boston (m) Guido Rossi/The Image Bank 527, Eascott/Momatuk/Woodfin Camp & Associates 528, ©Paul Conklin 530–531, Charles Gupton/Stock Boston 533, Forest Anderson/Gamma-Liaison 535, ©Susan Van Etten 537, Library of Congress/Susan Van Etten Historical Files 538, David Frazier/Tony Stone Images/Chicago, Inc. 540, Telegraph Colour Library/FPG 541, ©Susan Van Etten 542, ©Paul Conklin 543, Thomas Craig/FPG 544, ©Martucci Studio 545, David Ball/The Picture Cube 546, P&G Bowater/The Image Bank 547, Alistair Berg/Gamma-Liaison 548, (t) Jeff Greenberg/Photo Edit (b) Andy Caulfield/The Image Bank (l) Alan Oddie/Photo Edit 549, (t) David Frazier/Tony Stone Images/Chicago, Inc. (b) Alistair Berg/Gamma-Liaison 550, Charles Gupton/Stock Boston 551, ©1993 Ohman/Oregonian 554, (t) ©Martucci Studio, (tl), (ml), (ll), The Granger Collection, (m) Frank Siteman/Stock Boston, (lr) Nancy Brown/Image Bank. 555, (tl) Kevin Forest/Image Bank, (r) ©Martucci Studio. 560, ©Donald Dietz/Stock Boston. 561–567, Martucci Studio.